Routledge Handbook of Political Islam

The *Routledge Handbook of Political Islam* provides a multidisciplinary overview of the phenomenon of political Islam, one of the key political movements of our time. Drawing on the expertise from some of the top scholars in the world, it examines the main issues surrounding political Islam across the world, from aspects of Muslim integration in the West to questions of political legitimacy in the Muslim world.

Bringing together an international team of renowned and respected experts on the topic, the chapters in the book present a critical account of:

- Theoretical foundations of political Islam
- Historical background
- Geographical spread of Islamist movements
- Political strategies adopted by Islamist groups
- Terrorism
- Attitudes towards democracy
- Relations between Muslims and the West in the international sphere
- Challenges of integration
- Gender relations

Presenting readers with the diversity of views on political Islam in a nuanced and dispassionate manner, this handbook is an essential addition to the existing literature on Islam and politics. It will be of interest across a wide range of disciplines, including political science, Islamic studies, sociology and history.

Shahram Akbarzadeh is Research Professor of Middle East and Central Asian Politics and holds the prestigious ARC Future Fellowship. He is Deputy Director (International) at the Alfred Deakin Institute for Citizenship and Globalization, Deakin University, Australia, with an active research interest in the politics of Islam and the Middle East.

Routledge Handbook of Political Islam

Edited by
Shahram Akbarzadeh

LONDON AND NEW YORK

First published in paperback 2018

First published 2011
by Routledge
2 Park Square, Milton Park, Abingdon, Oxon OX14 4RN

and by Routledge
711 Third Avenue, New York, NY 10017

Routledge is an imprint of the Taylor & Francis Group, an informa business

British Library Cataloguing-in-Publication Data
A catalogue record for this book is available from the British Library

Library of Congress Cataloging-in-Publication Data
Routledge handbook of political islam / edited by Shahram Akbarzadeh.
p. cm.
Includes bibliographical references and index.
ISBN 978-0-415-48473-2 (hardback) — ISBN 978-0-203-15414-4 (ebook) 1. Islamic
    countries—Politics and government—21st century. 2. Islamic countries—Politics and
    government—20th century. 3. Islam and politics. 4. Islam and world politics. I. Akbarzadeh,
    Shahram.
DS63.1.R68 2011
320.5'57—dc23
2011025970

ISBN: 978-0-415-48473-2 (hbk)
ISBN: 978-1-138-57782-4 (pbk)
ISBN: 978-0-203-15414-4 (ebk)

Typeset in Bembo
by Apex CoVantage, LLC

For Alexandra, Benedict, Pasha and Nikoo

Advisory group

Prof Anoush Ehteshami (Durham University)
Prof John Esposito (Georgetown University)
Prof James Piscatori (Durham University)
Prof Amin Saikal (Australian National University)

Contents

Contents

Contributors

Tahir Abbas has been Associate Professor of Sociology at Fatih University, Istanbul, Turkey since 2010. His books include: *Islamic Radicalism and Multicultural Politics: The British Experience* (Routledge, 2011) and *The Education of British South Asians: Ethnicity, Capital and Class Structure* (Palgrave Macmillan, 2004); as editor, *Islam and Education* (four volumes, Routledge, 2010), *Islamic Political Radicalism: A European Perspective* (Edinburgh University Press and Columbia University Press, 2007) and *Muslim Britain: Communities Under Pressure* (Zed, 2005); and as co-editor, *Honour, Violence, Women and Islam* (with M.M. Idriss, Routledge, 2010) and *Immigration and Race Relations: Sociological Theory and John Rex* (with F. Reeves, I.B. Tauris, 2007). His current interests are in the areas of young Muslim ethno-religious political identities, ethnicity, diaspora studies, 'Islamism', and historical and political sociology. He sits on the editorial boards of a number of international journals. He is Fellow of the Royal Society of Arts (since 2006) and a Fellow of the Muslim Institute (since 2010).

Shahram Akbarzadeh is Professor of Asian Politics (Middle East and Central Asia) and Deputy Director of the National Centre of Excellence for Islamic Studies at Asia Institute, the University of Melbourne. His research focuses on Islamic radicalism and Muslim identity in the West, Middle East politics and Central Asian affairs. He is published extensively and is a regular contributor to the public debate on Islam and Middle East politics.

Eman Mohammad Alhussein is a PhD candidate at the Institute of Arab and Islamic Studies in the University of Exeter. Her research focuses on analysing Orientalist/neo-Orientalist trends in the rhetoric of war following the 11 September 2001 attacks. She earned an MA with distinction in Gulf Studies from the University of Exeter.

Valérie Amiraux is Professor of Sociology at the department of sociology of the University of Montreal where she holds the Canada Research Chair for the study of religious pluralism and ethnicity. She is on leave from her permanent position at the Centre national de la recherche scientifique (CNRS). Since 2003 she has been a senior expert for the Open Society Institute and is the author of the 2011 Paris report on discrimination against Muslims in Paris-Goutte d'or. Her recent publications include: 'Religious authority, social action and political participation. A case study of the mosquée de la rue de Tanger in Paris', in Martin van Bruinessen and Stefano Allievi (eds), *Production and Dissemination of Islamic Knowledge in Western Europe* (Routledge, 2010); 'From Empire to Republic, the French Muslim Dilemma', in Anna Triandafyllidou (ed.), *Muslims in 21st Century Europe. Structural and cultural perspectives* (Routledge, 2010); 'Crisis and new challenges? French Republicanism featuring multiculturalism', in A. Silj (ed.), *European*

Multiculturalism: What went wrong? (Zed Books, 2010); and 'Breaching the Infernal Circle? Turkey, the European Union and religion', in Aziz el Azmeh and Effie Fokas (eds), *Euro-Islam at the Turn of the Millennium. Present Conditions and Future Perspectives* (Cambridge University Press, 2007).

Raja Bahlul teaches philosophy at the United Arab Emirates University. He has researched and published in Arabic, English and Italian in the areas of metaphysics (identity of indiscernible), Islamic philosophy and theology (Ghazali, Islamic Kalam), democracy, and contemporary Islamic political thought. His recent publications include *Mutual Consultation: Contemporary Islamic Views on Democracy* (The Palestinian Institute for the Study of Democracy, 2007); 'Avicenna and the Problem of Universals', in *Philosophy and Theology* (Vol. 21, No. 1/2, 2009); 'Is Constitutionalism Compatible with Islam?', in Pietro Costa and Danilo Zolo (eds), *Rule of Law: History, Theory, and Criticism* (Springer, 2007); and 'Democracy without Secularism?', in John Bunzl (ed.), *Islam, Judaism, and the Political Role of Religions in the Middle East* (University Press of Florida, 2004).

Rebecca Barlow is a research associate at the National Centre of Excellence for Islamic Studies, University of Melbourne, Australia. Her work focuses on the politics of human rights and gender relations in the Middle East. She is author of *Women's Human Rights and the 'Muslim Question': Iran's Change for Equality Campaign* (Melbourne University Publishing, 2012). In 2007, she was one of only four early career researchers selected globally to attend the Nobel Women's Initiative's first international conference, Women Redefining Peace in the Middle East and Beyond.

Howard V. Brasted is Professor of History in the School of Humanities and Director of the Asia Pacific Centre for Research at the University of New England, Armidale, Australia. A long-time editor of the journal *South Asia* (1984–2001) and coordinator of the postgraduate programme in Islamic Studies at UNE, he has published widely on a range of topics including Indian nationalism, decolonisation in South Asia, labour standards in Asia, international relations and contemporary Islam.

Lara Deeb is Associate Professor of Anthropology at Scripps College. She is the author of *An Enchanted Modern: Gender and Public Piety in Shi'i Lebanon* (Princeton University Press, 2006), and articles on the transformation of Shi'i religious ritual, gender in Islam, Hizbullah in Lebanon, and youth, leisure and piety. Her current book project is titled *Leisurely Islam: Negotiating Social Space and Morality in Shi'ite South Beirut*, co-authored with Mona Harb. She is a member of the editorial committee for *Middle East Report* and the editorial board of the *International Journal of Middle East Studies*.

Shahin Gerami is Director of Women's Studies at San Jose State University in California, USA. She holds a law degree from the University of Tehran and a doctorate in sociology from the University of Oklahoma. Her research on religious fundamentalist movements resulted in the book *Women and Fundamentalism: Islam and Christianity* (Routledge, 1996). She is the author of 'Globalism from Below: Extralegal Transnationalism of Afghani Refugees in Iran', *Journal of Interdisciplinary Feminist Thought* (Fall 2008). In 2005, she delivered a keynote address at the University Centre St Ignatius in Antwerp, Belgium, and in 2007 she was the keynote speaker delivering 'Global Masculinity vs Transnational Brown Men: Discursive Identities at Home and Abroad' at the international conference on *Migration, Islam and Masculinities*, Carl von Ossietzky University, Oldenburg, Germany. She continues her exploration of de-territorialised Islamisms and gender arrangements. Currently, she is working on a study of Facebook and Resistance: Iranian women claim another venue of Agency.

Mohammed M. Hafez, an Associate Professor of national security affairs at the Naval Post-graduate School in Monterey, California, specialises in Islamic social movements, Middle Eastern and North African politics, and transnational jihadism. He is the author of *Suicide Bombers in Iraq: The Strategy and Ideology of Martyrdom* (United States Institute of Peace, 2007); *Manufacturing Human Bombs: The Making of Palestinian Suicide Bombers* (United States Institute of Peace, 2006); and *Why Muslims Rebel: Repression and Resistance in the Islamic World* (Lynne Rienner, 2003). Dr Hafez earned a PhD in international relations from the London School of Economics and Political Science, and is the recipient of major research grants from the United States Institute of Peace and The Harry Frank Guggenheim Foundation.

Robert W. Hefner is Director of the Institute on Culture, Religion and World Affairs (CURA) at Boston University, where he has also directed the programme on Islam and society since 1991. He has authored or edited some 15 books, the most recent of which is volume six of the *New Cambridge History of Islam,* entitled *Muslims and Modernity: Society and Culture since 1800* (2010).

Gareth Jenkins is a writer and analyst based in Istanbul, Turkey, where he has been resident since 1989. Although he writes and speaks on diverse aspects of Turkish politics, economics and social change, his special fields of interest are civil–military relations, terrorism and security issues, and political Islam. His most recent book, *Political Islam in Turkey: Running West, Heading East?*, was published by Palgrave Macmillan in 2008. He is currently a Nonresident Senior Fellow with the Central Asia-Caucasus Institute and Silk Road Studies Program Joint Center.

Adeel Khan teaches Religious and Islamic Studies at the University of New England, Australia. He has authored an internationally acclaimed book, *Politics of Identity: Ethnic Nationalism and the State in Pakistan* (Sage, 2005), and published in various peer-reviewed journals. He has also presented papers on nationalism, fundamentalism and violence against women at numerous national and international conferences. Before his academic career, Dr Khan was political correspondent for the English daily *Dawn*, Karachi, covering Pakistan and Afghanistan politics, especially the Islamist fight against the communist government in Afghanistan. He has also served as the political commentator for BBC Pashto service.

M.A. Muqtedar Khan is Associate Professor in the Department of Political Science and International Relations at the University of Delaware. He founded the Islamic Studies Program at the University of Delaware and was its first Director, 2007–10. Dr Khan is a Fellow with the Institute for Social Policy and Understanding. He was a Senior Nonresident Fellow with the Brookings Institution (2003–08) and a Fellow of the Alwaleed Center at Georgetown University (2006–07). He has been the President, Vice-President and General Secretary of the Association of Muslim Social Scientists. He is the author of *American Muslims: Bridging Faith and Freedom* (Amana, 2002), *Jihad for Jerusalem: Identity and Strategy in International Relations* (Praeger, 2004), *Islamic Democratic Discourse* (Lexington Books, 2006) and *Debating Moderate Islam: The Geopolitics of Islam and the West* (University of Utah Press, 2007). His articles on Islam and American Muslims can be read at www.ijtihad.org.

Benjamin MacQueen is a Senior Lecturer in the School of Political and Social Inquiry and Deputy Director of the Global Terrorism Research Centre at Monash University, Australia. He is the author of *Introduction to Middle East Politics* (Sage, 2012) and *Political Culture and Conflict Resolution in the Arab World: Lebanon and Algeria* (Melbourne University Press, 2009). He researches and teaches Middle Eastern politics, with a focus on conflict institutional reconstruction. He is also a regular media commentator for Australian and international outlets.

Beverley Milton-Edwards is a Professor in the School of Politics, International Studies and Philosophy at Queens University Belfast, Northern Ireland. She is the author of numerous books and articles including *HAMAS: The Islamic Resistance Movement* (Cambridge University Press, 2010); *The Israeli–Palestinian Conflict: A People's War* (Routledge, 2008); and *Islam and Violence in the Modern Era* (Macmillan, 2006).

Ahmad S. Moussalli is Professor of Political Science and Islamic Studies, American University of Beirut, and the author of key publications, including *Wahhabism, Salafism, and Islamism: Who is the Enemy?*; *U.S. Foreign Policy and Islamist Politics*; *Dialectics of Shura and Democracy: Democracy and Human Rights in Islamic Thought*; *Encyclopedia of Islamic Movements in the Arab World, Iran and Turkey*; *Islamic Movements: Impact on Political Stability in the Arab World*; *The West, the United States, and Political Islam*; *The Islamic Quest for Democracy, Pluralism, and Human Rights*; *Moderate and Radical Islamic Fundamentalism: The Quest for Modernity, Legitimacy and the Islamic State*; *Islamic Fundamentalism: Myths and Realities*; and *Radical Islamic Fundamentalism: The Ideological and Political Discourse of Sayyid Qutb*.

Mohamed Nawab Bin Mohamed Osman is a PhD candidate at the Department of Political and Social Change, Australian National University. He is also an Associate Research Fellow at the S. Rajaratnam School of International Studies, Nanyang Technological University, Singapore. He has published widely in international refereed journals and his opinion pieces have been featured in various newspapers in Asia, Europe and the Middle East. His research interests include political Islam in South and South-East Asia, terrorism and Islamic political thought.

Ali M. Pedram is based at the School of Government and International Affairs at Durham University. He runs the Durham Governance Initiative established in February 2009 covering the Middle East and North Africa. This programme delivers short courses and workshops for members of public and private sectors on the Middle East and North Africa region.

Bernard Rougier is Assistant Professor in Political Science (University of Auvergne, Faculty of Law and Political Science and Science Po Paris). He is currently assigned to College de France, History of the Contemporary Arab World Program. He has published a major reference book on the Islamist phenomenon in Palestinian camps in Lebanon: *Everyday Jihad, the Rise of Radical Islam among Palestinians in Lebanon* (Harvard University Press, 2007). He has also edited a book on salafism: *What is Salafism?* (*Qu'est-ce que le salafisme?*, PUF, 2008). His last book, *A fragmented Umma* (*L'oumma en fragments*, PUF, 2011) analyses the current struggle for the control of the Sunni constituency in the Levant.

Marc-André Walther is a General Staff Officer in the German Army, currently assigned to the German Ministry of Defence. Trained as an Officer in the Infantry, he was later selected for the General Staff. He earned a degree (diploma) in educational science at the University of the Armed Forces Germany in Hamburg, and a Masters degree in National Security Affairs at the US Naval Post-Graduate School, Monterey, California.

Samina Yasmeen is Professor of Political Science and International Relations and Director of the Centre for Muslim States and Societies at the University of Western Australia. Her research focuses on Islamization in Pakistan and its implications for citizens and security, and Muslim citizens in Western, liberal societies, particularly Australia. She is a regular contributor to local and international media on discussions on Pakistan, and issues affecting Muslim minorities in the West.

Barbara Zollner is a Lecturer in Islamic Studies at the Department of Politics, Birkbeck College, University of London. She has published several articles and chapters on Islamist movements and is particularly interested in ideological and organisational developments of Egyptian groups. She is the author of *The Muslim Brotherhood: Hasan al-Hudaybi and Ideology* (Routledge, 2008).

1

The paradox of political Islam

Shahram Akbarzadeh

Political Islam is a modern phenomenon that seeks to use religion to shape the political system. Its origins lie in the perceived failure of the secular ideologies of nationalism and socialism to deliver on their promises of anti-imperialist prosperity. The great thinkers of political Islam (Sayyid Qutb, Maulana Maududi, followed by Ayatollah Khomeini) were rebelling against the political system that emerged in the second half of the twentieth century, one that copied the Western-inspired system of nation-states governed by the rational decision-making of the people. In reality, the political establishment in the Muslim world was neither rational nor in the service of the public. Instead it was monopolised by a self-serving political elite. Political Islam provided a conceptual alternative that was purportedly based on the teachings of the faith. Sayyid Qutb's concept of Islam as a revolutionary ideology inspired his followers to see Islam as a recipe for change (Musallam 2005). The cry 'Islam is the solution' captures this mood. Political Islam is focused on remoulding public life in accordance with a specific interpretation of Islamic text and traditions. Accordingly, all state affairs are subject to the yardstick of political Islam, used by its self-declared devotees, dubbed Islamists.

Islamism is best understood as a modern-day ideology. Much like other *-isms*, Islamism imposes a normative framework on society in a blatant attempt to make society fit into its mould. This makes Islamists active agents of change, pursuing the goal of a perfect world, one that is run in accordance with divine will and in line with a specific reading of Islamic history. As Mohammed Ayoob has argued, Islamism is a reinvention of history and a re-imagination of the future, borrowing selectively from Islamic history and reinterpreting meanings to justify the ultimate objective: an Islamic state (Ayoob 2005: 952). This capacity to reinterpret and re-evaluate history makes Islamism an adaptive and flexible force, capable of responding to changed circumstances while retaining its relevance. Unlike the classical Islamic body of knowledge which tends to be rigid and fixed, Islamism has proven flexible, offering its adherents the opportunity to reinterpret history and religious text. This flexibility is an important asset that allows Islamism to be regenerated and respond to new challenges with relative ease.

A key point to bear in mind in the study of Islamism is that it has been a voice of dissent. Islamists have defined themselves in contrast to the status quo, whether responding to socialism, nationalism or the cultural and political hegemony of the United States. Islamism has defined itself as a reaction to a set of perceived failures. These range from the failure of the Muslim world to stand up for its own interests, to protect its religious and cultural values against the encroachment of Western culture, to defend Muslim land from non-Muslim occupation, and to provide the socioeconomic prosperity and justice that is believed to be integral to Islam. As Henry Munson points out, to understand the appeal of Islamism one must look at both nationalistic resentment of foreign domination and the 'dire economic situation in much of the Islamic world' (Munson 2003: 51). In a nutshell, Islamism has been a reaction to everything that is 'wrong' in the Muslim world.

Islamists have targeted two distinct bodies for their political agitation. At the local level, national governments have borne the brunt of the Islamist backlash. Khomeini, Qutb and Maududi were all responding to their governments of the day, in their respective countries. Mohammad Ayoob contends that political Islam gained increasing support as 'governing elites failed to deliver on their promises of economic progress, political participation, and personal dignity to expectant populations emerging from colonial bondage' (Ayoob 2004: 3). The rise of political Islam was first and foremost a direct challenge to the national ruling elite.

This challenge has manifested itself in similar forms. In Iran, Islamists managed to ride the tide of popular discontent in 1978 and 1979 to topple the monarchy. This led to the rise of the Islamic Republic of Iran. In Egypt, the groundswell of Islamist agitation against the ruling regime facilitated the rapid growth of the Muslim Brotherhood which has now managed to anchor itself deeply in the Egyptian political scene. A violent offshoot of the Brotherhood took the message of challenging the political regime to an extreme and carried out the assassination of President Anwar Sadat (1981). This pattern of internal dissent against incumbent national regimes has been played out throughout the Muslim world, making Islamists the number one political and security challenge.

The West has been the second target of Islamists. The close relationship between the United States and contested political regimes as well as its military alliance with Israel has made it the target of Islamist wrath. The spread of anti-Americanism throughout the Middle East is rooted in the belief that the United States acts as the international bastion of political power for unpopular regimes. For that reason national grievances that are firmly grounded in the domestic setting have taken on an international dimension. The challenge posed by Islamism is not confined to national boundaries – it has clear international implications. It must be noted that these implications go beyond threatening US interests by undermining US-friendly states. The Islamist challenge has a potent conceptual component that has proven seductive to its followers, and that involves a fundamental critique of the state system.

The system of nation-states that has become the foundation bloc of the international community was imposed on the Muslim world through the experience of colonisation and neo-colonisation. National boundaries that demarcate the Middle East today were the result of negotiation and back-door dealings between the Great Powers of the twentieth century. Once drawn on the map, the boundaries were expected to represent real national communities, but the history of the Arab world does not support such a compartmentalised approach. Arab unity may be a myth as Arabs have lived under competing dynasties and have had their fair share of internal strife, but this division into manageable 'national' entities was a top-down experiment which continues to alienate segments of the population and provide the intellectual framework for the Islamist challenge. The fundamental message by Sayyid Qutb and other Islamist thinkers is that the imposed system of nation-states is 'man-made' and contravenes the divine mandate of Muslim unity. The Islamist challenge to the nation-state and its institutions is far-reaching and encompasses not only the legitimacy of national borders – which are believed to divide the Muslim *umma* (the translational community of faith) – but the legal and political framework that governs the state. The battle cry 'Islam is the solution' is believed to present a clear alternative to the failures of ruling regimes to provide justice, prosperity and welfare for their population. The incumbent regimes are believed to have failed because they deviated from the path of Islam – instead they allowed themselves to become tools of Western domination. The Islamist solution is presented as a return to Islam because only Islam is believed to provide dignity and justice to Muslims (Munson 2003: 44). Although the language of this return is designed to support the revival of a tradition that is supposed to have existed in the past, in reality the Islamist project is modern and centres around the capture of the state machinery.

Islamism is focused on the capture and the remoulding of the state in accordance with what is believed to be Islamic law. This is a major point of contention, as Islamic law is seen to supersede man-made laws, challenging the legitimacy of the political and legal frameworks that have maintained incumbent regimes in the Muslim world. The critical point in this contestation for power is the question of sovereignty. Where does sovereignty reside? For the Islamist, the answer is straightforward: moral, political and legal authority emanate from God. According to Islamists, sovereignty resides with God, making illegitimate any other political system that removes Him from the centre of the equation. This approach is a direct challenge to human rationality on the pillar of sovereignty – one that is grounded in popular will, not divine wisdom. The Islamist approach is a break with the long-established history of reasoning and pursuit of knowledge through human faculties and advocates the view that human beings should not be allowed to tinker with God's will. Any human being meddling in the divine order that is to govern the ideal Islamic state would inevitably corrupt and distort God's design. The Islamist vision of a perfect society is diametrically opposed to the model of democracy, as the latter rests on the sovereignty of the people as the source of legitimacy (Esposito and Voll 2001: 22–23). This is a fundamental point and explains the extent of antipathy felt by Islamists towards the West. The anti-Western position, which has a familiar anti-colonial starting point, is reinforced by the belief that the West is imposing an alien and corrupting mode of government on Muslim lands.

The obvious irony of the Islamist position is that in their attempt to build this ideal Islamic state, they engage in an unavoidable process of interpretation and intervention. Islamic law is open to interpretation, and making it relevant to the modern state requires human reasoning. Consequently, Islamists are engaged in an elaborate process of reinterpretation of religious knowledge to cleanse it of what they see as misunderstandings and corruptions that have accumulated over time.

Islamists claim to have found or uncovered the ultimate truth, a pure and unadulterated interpretation of Islam. Their understanding of Islam is presented as the only authentic version, dismissing alternative views as inauthentic and illegitimate. This is an exclusive claim to God and divine wisdom: only Islamists can read God's mind. As a result, all criticism directed at them is dismissed as illegitimate and unworthy of attention. Criticism of Islamism is seen as criticism of God. This self-righteous perspective is intellectually debilitating and politically dangerous, especially when Islamism is transformed from a socio-political force into a position of authority.

The second irony that chips at the foundation of political Islam is in its implementation. As noted earlier, Islamism dismisses the existing states as man-made products of imperial design. In principle, state boundaries are rejected as dividing the Muslim community – the *umma*. The ultimate goal of Islamists is to create (or recreate in their view) the glorious transnational entity of Islam to uphold the *umma* politically and militarily. In reality, however, Islamists have confined their activities to state boundaries. All major Islamist movements (for example, the Muslim Brotherhood, Hamas and the Iranian Revolution) have operated as national projects. The rhetorical commitment to the transnational *umma* has not been forgotten but the immediate challenge that has consumed the Islamists has been the capture of political process within the existing boundaries of the state and building an 'Islamic state'.

As noted above, the combination of the exclusive claim on divine truth and the capture of political power presents a dangerous mix. This establishment of the Islamic state in this model lends to popular disenfranchisement because political authority and legitimacy are seen to flow from God. Sovereignty resides with God – and with those who have exclusive access to God. Consequently, opposition to this model of government, to policies pursued by the Islamic state, is not simply a matter of divergence of opinions, it is a matter of rejecting God. The exclusive claim to the truth empowers Islamists to reject all opposing views as blasphemy and take all measures to keep God's system supreme.

In the Islamic Republic of Iran, where the Islamist interpretation of Ayatollah Khomeini managed to gain the upper hand against alternative models, this exclusive claim to the divine knowledge opened the way for the brutal elimination of political opposition. The system of the *velayate faqih* paved the way for suppression of dissent and alternative viewpoints. This system raised the stakes to an extent that any point of difference was interpreted as a challenge to God's authority. Dissidents were condemned as warring against God and his messenger, and spreading corruption on earth (Mayer 2003: 124).

The obvious danger in this exclusive view is political intolerance, which can easily manifest as acts of violence. Although political Islam is not necessarily a violent movement, and many Islamists do not engage in acts of violence, the exclusive claim to the truth and the Manichean views of the world divided between the abode of Islam and the abode of disbelief lends itself to extremist tendencies. For the Islamists, there is no middle ground. One is either committed to the implementation of the word of God, or is working against it. There are no innocent bystanders. There is no room for indifference. There is no distinction between civilians and soldiers. This blinkered view of Islam and society has allowed some Islamists to justify terror and brutality in the name of God. Al Qaeda's 11 September 2001 attacks are the most infamous example of such terror.

However, terror is not confined to attacks on Western soil or against Christians and Jews, although such attacks tend to receive more attention in the Western media than others. Islamist terror also targets Muslims, as noted in the assassination of the Egyptian president and the daily violence meted out to anti-Islamist Muslim citizens and intellectuals such as the Pakistani Governor Salman Taseer in Islamabad, who advocated the abolition of blasphemy laws (Dawn 2011).

The extension of this ideology of intolerance and extremism to the West has led to new challenges. Population movements and the settlement of Muslim communities in the West have made redundant traditional divisions between the Muslim world and the world of Judeo-Christianity. The West may be conceived as a geographical entity but it is no longer the exclusive land of Judeo-Christianity. Muslims now account for 0.7 per cent of the total population of the United States, which equates to well over 2 million people (Central Intelligence Agency 2011). The process of enlightenment and the division of Church and State, followed by Muslim migration, the growth of second- and third-generation Muslims in Europe, Australia and the Americas, coupled with the legal, social and political frameworks that protect civil rights, have facilitated the indigenisation of Islam in the West. Despite challenges that persist due to racist hangovers, Islam is now part of the Western landscape. The binary divide between the abode of Islam and the abode of disbelief is incompatible with the reality of the Muslim experience in the West. The incompatibility of such divisions is made even more obvious in Western societies that actively protect the rights of Muslim communities to practise their faith and regenerate their religious and ethnic bonds. The policy of multiculturalism (when applied to Muslims) and provisions for the construction of mosques are two vivid examples of Western incorporation of Islam.

The above experience of inclusion is dismissed by Islamists as an experience of subordination and cultural alienation whereby Muslims are corrupted in their belief and weakened in their bond with God. Represented by such groups as Hizb ut-Tahrir and Al-Muhajiroun, Islamists reject multiculturalism, democracy and parliamentarianism as man-made systems and institutions that contravene God's divine authority and give the Muslims an illusion of being incorporated in the West. Participation in such Western processes, they argue, does nothing for the supremacy of God's will – instead it pushes God to the periphery and acknowledges the reign of secularism (Ahmed and Stuart 2009; Taji-Farouki 1996). This is simply not acceptable to Islamists. According to the constitution of Hizb ut-Tahrir:

> The Islamic *'Aqeeda* [doctrine] constitutes the foundation of the State. Therefore, nothing is permitted to exist in the State's structure, system, accountability, or any other aspect connected with the State that does not take the Islamic *'Aqeeda* as its source. The Islamic *'Aqeeda* is also the source of the State's constitution and laws. Consequently, nothing related to them is permitted to exist unless it emanates from the Islamic *'Aqeeda*.
>
> *(An-Nabhani 1998: 240)*

It is important to note that despite its uncompromising rhetoric, Hizb ut-Tahrir does not condone violence. The position of Hizb ut-Tahrir in relation to 11 September and Al-Qaeda may be ambiguous, but it has deliberately stayed away from promoting violent actions and terror. This may be partly due to the pragmatic consideration that crossing that threshold would make it subject to anti-terror laws in the United Kingdom (where it is currently operating with a degree of freedom) and the inevitable backlash from the Muslim community. However, there is a larger issue at stake here. Despite the violent tendencies of some Islamists and acts of terror carried out by groups like Hamas, which justify their actions in terms of the ultimate battle between good and evil, terrorism is not a necessary outcome of Islamism. Forces aligned with the ideology of political Islam have demonstrated a long track record of working in the social, cultural and political arena without resorting to violence. This process has helped establish them as important players in the socio-political landscape. The majority of Islamic movements have established modern political movements and social organisations, embracing modern means of technology and functioning 'within civil society as social and political activists' (Esposito 1997: 10). The Muslim Brotherhood is a prime example of such Islamist actors. Primarily an Egyptian organisation, as explored in Chapter 5 by Barbara Zollner, the Muslim Brotherhood was initially focused on raising awareness and education on Islam. Over the years, it has expanded its activities to the welfare and political spheres, running hospitals and fielding candidates for parliamentary elections. The Muslim Brotherhood has rejected terror as a political tool and distanced itself from its splinter group Gama'a Islamiyya. The Muslim Brotherhood has coupled its rejection of violence with participation in the system it vows to dismantle.

The Islamist participation in the established system and institutions of power presents a conceptual challenge. On the one hand, actors affiliated with political Islam seek to establish the sovereignty of God. On the other, they take part in the 'man-made' state apparatus they ultimately wish to depose. This contradictory behaviour is often justified in terms of the need to remain relevant to the needs of society and pushing the boundaries from within. Groups like the Brotherhood claim to harbour no illusions about the capacity of the existing regimes to reform and pave the way for God's will to reign supreme, but by operating within the system they also hope to expand their reach, remain relevant and avoid state repression. In other words, such Islamist actors adopt a pragmatic response to the conceptual challenge. This response does not address the inherent contradiction of engaging with an illegitimate system and potentially lending it a degree of legitimacy. Instead the pragmatic response sidetracks the principled rejection of the man-made system by insisting that a complete withdrawal would ultimately limit the scope of Islamism to advance its agenda. This attitude has led many observers to be suspicious of a 'hidden agenda' that governs the behaviour of Islamists. The claim by veteran US diplomat Edward Djerejian that Islamists will uphold the principle of 'one-man, one-vote' only for 'one-time' reflects this cynicism (Djerejian 1992: 37).

The participation of Islamist forces in the established political system may be grounded in strong pragmatic justifications, but there is every reason to believe that the prolonged process of engagement could potentially make a qualitative impression on Islamists. This may fall way short of a complete reappraisal of the Islamist worldview and epistemology, but the process gives Islamists a stake in the system and builds a degree of dependence on how it works. This process is not guaranteed or universal, but once the ruling regimes demonstrate a degree of flexibility and refrain from pursuing the complete eradication of political Islam, political actors of Islamist hue tend to take advantage of the openings in the public domain and grow roots (Esposito and Voll 2000: 613). In turn, this visibility, however restricted it may be, offers Islamists an incentive to refrain from extremism or a full-frontal confrontation with the system. Instead the political platform of Islamism can shift towards reform, not revolution, making Islamism a status quo actor. This is a rather ironic twist as Islamism completes a 180-degree turn, starting from the complete rejection of the state and ending with an accommodation of the state.

The Egyptian Muslim Brotherhood offers a pertinent example of this evolution. Although the Muslim Brotherhood has never denounced its ultimate goal of establishing an Islamic state, its record under 30 years of Hosni Mubarak's rule demonstrates a remarkable degree of accommodation. The irony of the Muslim Brotherhood's behaviour, not as a force for revolution but as a piece of the jigsaw that made the status quo, was most vividly demonstrated during the 2011 uprising in Egypt that led to the departure of President Mubarak from office. Caught by surprise at the ground swell of public anger at the regime and the ferocity of the desire for justice, the Brotherhood hesitated to take the lead and fell behind the spontaneous surge. The Brotherhood's leadership was slow to grasp the enormity of the Arab revolt and failed to act like a force for revolution seeking the complete overhaul of the system. While the slogan of 'Islam is the solution' had become the staple response to any and all ills, in 2011 the Muslim Brotherhood failed to revive its answer to the Arab revolt.

While the Egyptian Muslim Brotherhood may present a case of evolution of Islamism from a force for change to a component of the 'man-made' status quo, the Turkish case offers a fascinating example of Islamism as the pillar of that status quo. The Justice and Development Party (AKP), which gained parliamentary majority in 2002 and has maintained its lead in Turkish politics, has managed to run the government seamlessly. Despite its roots in the Islamist Virtue Party, the AKP is comfortable with running a 'man-made' state machinery that safeguards popular sovereignty and maintains a distinct separation between Islam and politics. The AKP has been very careful to avoid any reference to Islam in politics, except as a national heritage and a moral compass. For example, the AKP has overseen a reform to allow hijab in the public domain and universities, but has repeatedly stated its commitment to maintaining the legal system as secular and shari'a-free. Some AKP critics, generally affiliated with the Ataturk political camp now in opposition, reject the Turkish government as a wolf in sheep's clothing. They view AKP's moves to reinstate Islam in the public domain as paving the way for an Islamist revolution by stealth. Yet there is no evidence to suggest that AKP seeks to Islamise society. In fact, the AKP record raises a fundamental question about the nature of Islamism. Is there a point beyond which an Islamist actor ceases to be Islamist? Indeed, if Islamist actors are susceptible to external stimuli and are capable of evolution, it is perfectly possible for them to cease being Islamists. However, does the departure of actors from the fold mean the evolution of ideas? Can Islamism as an ideology evolve to accommodate the separation of Islam from politics and the supremacy of popular will?

In the Islamic Republic of Iran (IRP) the above tension between the sovereignty of God and the sovereignty of people continues to cripple the state. Nonetheless, the IRP has been hailed by its supporters within and without as a successful experiment to resolve this tension. This position rests on the assumption that as God's creation, human beings will utilise their sovereignty to uphold God's will. As a result, they argue, popular sovereignty paves the way for the establishment of divine order. Needless to say this perspective has not been borne out by the IRP experience, as the ruling Islamist regime has resorted to violence and intimidation to suppress dissent. While the constitution includes specific references to the people as the foundation of political power which allows for an electoral parliamentary system, it also places all authority with God, represented by the Supreme Leader occupying the office of the *velayate faqih*. This places God above people. The IRP does not resolve the inherent tension of Islamism; at best it camouflages the tension.

Defining political Islam presents researchers with a challenge. While the kernel of the definition is about the commitment of establishing Islam as the governing principle of the state, there are some important deviations within the fold. First, the Islamist vision aspires to the transnational unity of Muslims, yet it is very common for forces of political Islam to resign themselves to the established boundaries of states and trim their political objectives to fit state demarcations. Second, Islamism rejects 'man-made laws' as emasculating Muslims and depriving them of their source of authority and pride. This is a rejection of existing political orders as illegitimate and unworthy of Muslim allegiance. Yet so many Islamists seek to take part in the system and influence it from within. Third, while the principle of divine sovereignty comes into direct conflict with popular sovereignty and most Islamists have rejected democracy as a means of subjugating Islam, a discernible trend in Islamism has looked to utilising democracy. This has been dismissed as a cynical abuse of democracy by forces that have no desire to uphold its principles once they gain power. Yet there are significant cases that give reason for pause. Fourth, the Manichean world view and the exclusive claim to the truth that has allowed some Islamist actors to dismiss all opponents as warring against God and therefore cross the threshold to violence and terror is not an inevitable process. Many Islamists present their ideological position in terms of an existential conflict between 'good and evil', but shy away from actions to physically annihilate what they had termed 'evil'.

Political Islam is best understood as a dynamic social phenomenon – not a static ideology. Its origins are uncontested among observers, but the evolution of political Islam over the last decades along divergent paths suggests that scholarship on Islamism needs to retain conceptual agility and intellectual rigour. This agility is necessary in making sense of the various manifestations of political Islam in the twenty-first century. The present volume aims to contribute to this objective.

References

Ahmed, H. and Stuart, H. (2009) *Hizb ut-Tahrir: Ideology and Strategy*, London, Centre for Social Cohesion.

An-Nabhani, T. (1998) *The Islamic State*, London, Al-Khilafah Publications.

Ayoob, M. (2004) 'Political Islam: Image and Reality', *World Policy Journal* Vol. 21, No. 3: 1–14.

—— (2005) 'The Future of Political Islam: The Importance of External Variables', *International Affairs* Vol. 81, No. 5: 951–61.

Central Intelligence Agency (2011) *The World Fact Book*, available at www.cia.gov/library/publications/the-world-factbook/geos/us.html (accessed 15 June 2011).

Dawn (5 January 2011), available at www.dawn.com/2011/01/05/salman-taseer's-funeral-to-be-held-today.html (accessed 15 June 2011).

Djerejian, E. (1992) 'The U.S. and the Middle East in a Changing World', *The DISAM Journal*, Summer: 32–38.

Esposito, J. (1997) 'Claiming the Center: Political Islam in Transition', *Harvard International Review* Vol. 19, No. 2: 8–61.

Esposito, J.L. and Voll, J.O. (2000) 'Islam and the West: Muslim Voices of Dialogue', *Millennium Journal of International Studies* Vol. 29, No. 3: 613–39.

—— (2001) 'Islam and Democracy', *Humanities* Vol. 22, No. 6: 22–26.

Mayer, A.E. (2003) 'Islamic Law as a cure for political law: The withering of an Islamist illusion', in Roberson, B.A. (ed.), *Shaping the Current Islamic Reformation*, London, Frank Cass, pp. 115–38.

Munson, H. (2003) 'Islam, Nationalism and Resentment of Foreign Domination', *Middle East Policy* Vol. 10, No. 2: 40–53.

Musallam, A.A. (2005) *From secularism to Jihad: Sayyid Qutb and the foundations of radical Islamism*, New York, Praeger Publishers.

Taji-Farouki, S. (1996) *A Fundamental Quest: Hizb al-Tahrir and the Search for the Islamic Caliphate*, London, Grey Seal.

2

Sayyid Qutb

Founder of radical Islamic political ideology

Ahmad S. Moussalli

More than anyone else, Sayyid Qutb's ideology constitutes the core fundamentals of radical Islamism. The in-depth study of Qutb's thought would show us the causes of and justifications for many Islamic groups' indulgence in radicalism, revolution, *takfiri jihadism* and terrorism. Qutb, the founder of Islamic radicalism in the Arab world, would himself become its first victim; he was transformed under 'Abd al-Nasser's regime in Egypt from a moderate Islamist writer to the most radical Islamist thinker in the Arab world. His imprisonment and ferocious torture were reified into a radical political theology of *takfir* (excommunication) and jihadism. This might have been his psychological compensation for the regime's radicalism, repression and brutality.

Qutb's attempt to implement his radical vanguard's revolutionary program ended with his execution by hanging in 1966. Earlier, when Qutb was out of jail in 1964, he started forming a 'party', or the vanguard that adhered to his radical discourse and included the following principles: human societies do not follow Islamic ethics, system and the shari'a and are in need of essential Islamic education. Those individuals who respond positively to this education should undertake a course of study of Islamic movements in history in order to set a course of action so as to fight Zionism and colonialism. Also, no organization was to be established until a highly ideological training was undertaken (Barakat n.d.: 19; Khalidi 1983b: 147–49; Moussalli 1995: ch. 1).

Most of the radical Islamist groups in the Arab world and specifically in Egypt have been influenced both directly and indirectly by this Qutbian radical *takfiri jihadist* discourse and by his notions of the need to establish divine governance (*hakimiyya*) in the world and the need to eliminate paganism (*jahiliyya*) of the 'other' at all levels: personally, socially and politically as well as culturally and philosophically.

This chapter explains the foundations of Sayyid Qutb's ideological and political discourse. It begins with a brief on Qutb's life, then analytically explains his ideology under two main divisions: the first discusses the ideological and religious discourse and its main concepts; the second, the political discourse and its main underpinnings. It ends with an evaluation of Qutb's overall discourse and its impact on contemporary radical Islamic groups.

Life

Upon joining the Muslim Brotherhood, Qutb reached the conclusion that he had been living a *jahili* (paganistic, ignorant) life. Though such a life had educated him in the sciences and modern aspects of living, it had not led to inner satisfaction (Moussalli 1995). Qutb, born in 1906 in Musha in the district of Asyut, received his Bachelor of Arts in Education from Dar al-'Ulum where he became instructor and published his first literary book, *Muhimmat al-Sha'ir fi al-Hayat* (al-Hassan 1981: 4).

Qutb joined the Ministry of Education as a teacher from 1933 until 1939. Influenced intellectually and politically by 'Abbas Mahmud al-'Aqqad, Qutb adopted Westernization, and his articles, which were published in respected journals, focused on the critical analysis of political and literary issues with special criticism directed at the government. In 1947 his editorship of *Al-'Alam al-'Arabi* and *Al-Fikr al-Jadid* expressed his dissatisfaction with Egyptian party politics and he consequently resigned from the Sa'dist party (Khalidi 1983a: 64–66, 94–134; Vatikiotis 1969: ch. X; Hasan 1981: 4; Hilal 1977: 200–8).

In 1948 the Ministry of Education sent Qutb to the United States where he was delegated to study at many institutions, including the University of Northern Colorado, where he obtained a Masters degree in Education. His book, *Al-'Adala al-Ijtima'yya fi al-Islam* (Social Justice in Islam) was first published while he was there. The book became the first of a long list of books espousing Islamism as a political ideology and Islam as a way of life. This new commitment led him, upon his return to Egypt, to write for the first time in the Brethren's *Al-Da'wa* journal and to resign his post as adviser to the Ministry of Education in 1951 (Khalidi 1983b: 125, 137–38).

His first book that adopted Islamism as a way of life along with a political agenda, *Al-'Adala al-Ijtima'yya fi al-Islam* was far removed from radicalism and closer to Hasan al-Banna's discourse. His stay in the United States, 1948–51, made him review his previous attitude and adoption of Westernization. His dislike of materialism, racism and the pro-Zionist feelings of the West that he personally experienced in the United States seems to have been the beginning of his alienation from Western culture and return to the roots of the culture in which he was brought up.

Upon his return to Egypt, that is, after the death of Hasan al-Banna and the First Ordeal of the Brotherhood, he joined the Brotherhood and became very active in its intellectual and publishing activities, writing numerous books on 'Islam as the solution'. However, until that point no radicalism or violence were involved. His priority was to rewrite a modern understanding of Islam and the solutions that Islam provides to the basic political, economic, social and individual problems of Egypt and the Arab and Islamic worlds (Qutb 1982: 11–12; Qutb 1965: 71–90; Qutb 1983a: 77–78, 83–87).

In 1953 Qutb was appointed editor-in-chief of the weekly *Al-Ikhwan al-Muslimun*, which was banned along with the Brotherhood's dissolution in 1954 after the fall-out between the Brethren and the Free Officers' regime. He was put in jail and then released. In fact, the Brotherhood in general and Qutb in particular were instrumental to the Officers in paving the way for the Revolution of 1952. However, the Brotherhood refused to accept the Officers' absolute power and called for a referendum that would show the kind of constitution that the people wanted. Furthermore, it supported General Najib against Colonel 'Abd al-Nasser. After major disagreements between the Brotherhood and 'Abd al-Nasser, the Muslim Brethren were accused of cooperating with the communists to overthrow the government. Their movement was dissolved again in 1954 and many Brethren were jailed, including Qutb. He was released that year and arrested again after the Manshiyya incident where an attempt was made on 'Abd al-Nasser's life, and Qutb and others were accused of being affiliated with the movement's secret military section. In 1955 Qutb, sentenced by then to 15 years in prison, and thousands of the Brethren and their supporters, were subjected to ferocious torture leaving unhealed scars up until this very day. In this context, he shifted to radical Islamism and exclusiveness.

His most important books are the gospels of radicalism: *Fi Zilal al-Qur'an*, *Ma'alim fi al-Tariq*, *Hadha al-Din*, *Al-Mustaqbal li Hadha al-Din* and others were written because of and despite the torture that he and others tolerated year after year. Qutb was released in 1965, then arrested on charges to overthrow the government and executed in 1966. Again, isolated from the outside world, under daily tormenting pressures such as witnessing the slaughtering of tens of the Brethren in a jail hospital, Qutb could not blame others. He blamed those who were free outside the jail but would not defend the unjustly imprisoned and ferociously tortured; the free people became for him accomplices in the crimes of the regime and therefore, like the regime, infidels (Moussalli 1995: 31–39; Mitchell 1969: 103, 187–89; Hasan 1981: 7–13, 30–31; Hussain 1983: 7–11, 91).

In order to tolerate his pain and poor prison conditions, Qutb reified his discourse into a radical discourse so that it was not the state and society that were excluding him, but rather he, as the leader of the believing vanguard, was excommunicating (*takfir*) and excluding (*hijra*) individuals, societies and states from true salvation. The whole world became a target of his condemnation and isolation. The state's vengeful exclusion and repressive intolerance to any sort of popular opposition was counterbalanced by his desperate spiritual, moral, social and political radicalism and intolerance. This is a clear contextual and historical example of how the parameters of radical Islamism developed. From there on and from his cell, he began developing his radicalism.

Qutb's ideological discourse

Qutb does not view Islam simply as a religion in the Western sense but rather as a comprehensive and inclusive way of living in this world and the afterlife. Islam is so inclusive that it is difficult to imagine that it does not cover a substantial issue. It includes both religious and worldly affairs, the spiritual and the physical, the ordinary and the extraordinary (Qutb 1974: 22). All of this, however, is linked to *al-mafhum al-kawni al-Islami* or the universal Islamic concept that Qutb invents to function as the main constituent and backbone of his ideological interpretation of Islam. Thus, this concept acts for Qutb as an all-engulfing foundation for the system that is to provide the essentials for building the Islamic discourse on life, truth, knowledge, man's role in the universe, values and, above all, an interpretation of the meaning of life itself.

While Qutb's discussion of this concept lacks the positive theological substantive elaboration of religious issues, he endows it with seven elastic characteristics that, it is hoped, make it superior and substantive. He defines them as the oneness of God, divinity, constancy, comprehensiveness, balance, positivity and realism. The oneness of God, or *tawhid*, viewed by Qutb as both the core component and the main foundation of the universal Islamic concept, covers all religions, especially the monotheistic (like Christianity and Judaism). Islam, therefore, is no more than complete submission to tawhid, an act requiring the following of the divine path (shari'a) in every aspect of life, the doctrinal, the ritualistic, the political, the economic, the social and others. While it also requires complete submission to God and total revolt against any submission to non-Islamic institutions, states and ideologies, for Qutb the only truly Islamic way of life is implemented when all aspects of life are tied together without differentiation into one unified method and system organized around tawhid. Only in such a way can the basic foundation for any legitimate Islamic politics, economics, ethics and others be built. In addition, all of this should be grounded in the revealed text, and not in the traditions or human schools of thought, theology or jurisprudence or politics. For instance, a Muslim's belief that there is no ruler and legislator but God should mean that He is the ultimate organizer of life and the universe. Qutb's political discourse is obsessed with this idea to the extent that it permeates all personal and public aspects of life as well as the social and the political. In fact, it guarantees to Qutb the coherent Islamic character of the individual, society and state.

Qutb's non-traditional and textually derived tawhid reduces his perception of humankind's ways of living into only a duality: the divinely Islamic and legitimate against the jahili (literally ignorant but actually paganist) non-Islamic and illegitimate. This duality leads to the system of life and therefore its individuals who regulate their lives according to the divine to form God's party or *hizb al-Allah*; conversely, the system whose individuals follow any other category or human philosophies or non-textually derived religious doctrines are opponents of the divine or simply the devil's party or *hizb al-shaytan* (Qutb 1965: 12–14, 212–15). Qutb then identifies the divine system as the textually based system centered on the metaphysical doctrine of tawhid that includes a general religious, political, economic and social order.

While any system of life becomes for Qutb a religion, he identifies religion as a system that produces the method to organize human life, both privately and publicly. For true religion is not composed of abstract notions on theology and law but is rather the regulator of life in general and discipliner of behavior in particular. By this twist, Qutb turns communism, socialism and capitalism into religions (Qutb 1965: 15–17). Thus any system that regulates life is a religion, and consequently the religion of an individual is his behavior. Qutb's conclusion intends to lead his reader to believe that the Muslims who do not commit themselves to Islam as a system of life are not true Muslims. The incomplete following of Islam, in Qutb's view, removes an individual from the realm of Islam, since belief without active commitment is not conducive to good Islamic life. This analysis applies as well to governments, states, societies and political life. Here we can see how the ideological roots for *takfir* (apostasy and excommunication) were developed step by step.

Qutb focuses on activism rather than theory for the deepening and developing of belief; activism equals true belief. Defined in this way, he uses religious ideas for encouraging activism in social and political matters and for rejecting non-Islamically derived systems, philosophies and ways of life. To Qutb, Islam is superior to other religious and non-religious systems, for its discourse is characterized by vital and direct symbols to great truths, themselves incomprehensible by human methods, nonetheless addressing the innermost aspects of humankind. Not only do human philosophies limit, unable to express the truth, but they cannot be properly expressed or comprehended in a simple, clear and meaningful manner.

Even though Qutb finds religions to be composed metaphysically of symbols or allusions to truth, he argues that this is the most credible epistemological and practical source and denies the methodological and substantive legitimacy and the validity of modern, medieval and classical philosophies. He further rejects the legitimacy of any elitist discourse, be it religious or philosophical; the Qur'anic discourse is directed at and should be adhered to by all – the common and the elite. The inaccessibility of ultimate universal principles makes any pretension to superior divine or mundane knowledge worthless and pretentious, and reduces proper interactions with the true symbols and allusions that constitute the bases of credible and possible knowledge, a well-ordered life and the fulfillment of humanity.

Because of the second characteristic, divinity (*al-uluhiyya*), Qutb indicates the unchangeability of the concept itself, though it is open to interpretation. It is unchangeable because God is its author and source, and Prophet Muhammad is the agency of transmission whose mission is essentially to preach the divine message. The Prophet, like other Muslims, is bound by the same divine law, though singled out as a messenger of God. His function is then not to philosophize and invent doctrines and philosophies but to literally adhere to the divine law. Consequently Qutb makes the prophetic discourse a consequence of the Qur'anic discourse and dependent on it. Divine knowledge transmitted through revealed texts surpasses human knowledge, even that of the Prophet, insofar as the divine authority surpasses any human source of knowledge. If this is the case with the Prophet, it is rather easier for Qutb to deny any formative role or even more authentic understanding of religion by theologians and jurists.

The divinity of the universal Islamic concept also means that while it is eternal, its understanding is not, but is subject to the conditions of the interpreter and the tools of interpretation. Qutb makes a distinction here between understanding the text and the text itself. The textually derived Islamic concept is eternally valid; human understanding is potentially fluid. The possibility of understanding the universal Islamic concept is extended throughout space and time and becomes linked to the material, political and economic conditions of the reader and interpreter. Thus the basic text, or the Qur'an, can be read, interpreted and understood differently by diverse generations and individuals. Thus past discourses on the meaning of the Qur'an should not be limited to the possibility of diverse modern and contemporary understanding of the text as well as the past itself. Thus Qutb theoretically accepts different readings and discourses on the text insofar as there is no violation of the text itself. The text cannot be contradicted by a past or present human discourse, but only by the text itself. In this fashion, Qutb aims to establish the need to reread the Qur'anic text in light of the modern age and therefore develop a modern Qur'anic discourse.

Qutb further argues that while the divine concept itself is perfect, human thought is imperfect, lacks permanence and the capacity for transcendence, and falls easily victim to paganism (*jahiliyya*), as is the case in the world today. Not only is human thought strongly influenced by its environment but it is also easily motivated by emotions and desire. Thus, for instance, Western thought is not universal, as it claims, but is no more than the by-product of specific political and economic conditions. Even the religious foundation cannot transcend these conditions. Because of this, Qutb easily dismisses the universality of ancient and modern Western culture and philosophy, and argues for the need to exclude them from developing modern Islamic thought and institutions. Again, medieval Islamic philosophy and theology fall within this description and consequently should be as well excluded since they are Greek and, therefore, to Qutb, un-Islamic. For the paganism or *jahiliyya* of Greek thought for Qutb is the first foundation of Western thought and the main root for its opposition (Mahdi 1969: 13–15, 32–33, 44–48; al-Farabi 1926: 2; al-Ghazali 1963: 4–7; Butterworth 1975: 118–27; Anawati 1974: 350–58).

Thus, unlike human thought, the universal concept is divine and therefore has constancy or *al-thabat*, which is its third characteristic, according to Qutb. For its basis, the Qur'an, along with the divine truths contained within, is constant. Basic ideas on divine oneness, angels, the Day of Judgment and other core religious doctrines are not subject to addition or subtraction or to change and development. Its constancy functions as the regulator of human thought in order to safeguard a proper Islamic way of life and to guarantee stability in individual and social values. Qutb is very much disturbed by the poverty and fickleness of modern human spirituality, social interaction, and political governance or *hakimiyya*. He argues that the way Western concepts developed has removed the shreds of human stability and instead replaced the innermost human feelings with interests in material objectives and therefore deprived humankind from enjoying material progress within a constant environment. Human relationships with God and with fellow humans are reduced to rituals, but Islam's intent is to make these relations based on humans' position in the universe and fate, their relation with this universe, and their relation with the Creator within positive, peaceful constancy (Qutb 1965: 11, 58).

This form of constancy harmonizes the Qur'anic discourse and human life, and functions as protection for Muslims against misconceived and shaky doctrines, concepts and systems. Qutb also believes that it provides Muslims with the basis for a stable society, which in turn permits the freedom of development and fighting aggressions against its doctrines and peoples.

Yet, at another level, Qutb formulates comprehensiveness or *al-shumuliyya*, the fourth characteristic of the universal Islamic concept, as the characteristic that protects against human limitedness and partiality. For a divine, constant tawhid is by definition comprehensive, covering all aspects of life and transcending spatial and temporal particularities. Thus, he puts forward this formula: 'the Islamic concept is comprehensive whereas man's concepts are partial and limited'. Again, while man's knowledge and experience are limited, his weaknesses and desires are limitless. Only the Islamic concept gives humankind an intelligible interpretative discourse about the phenomena of life and the universe. Again, only the revealed religious discourse to Qutb should be the center of all aspects of life due to its ability to provide humankind with a meaningful yet true discourse about the divine and the human, the social and the individual, the public and the private (Qutb 1965: 16–26). In opposition to human systems, Islam neither falsely informs human reason nor misdirects human conducts.

The fifth characteristic of the universal Islamic concept, *al-tawazun* (balance), precludes for Qutb the development of rash and exaggerated attitudes and philosophies similar to those postulated by other religions and systems. For tawhid balances the known with the unknown. Thus, while man surrenders to God and accepts on faith metaphysical issues, like the nature of God's existence or the existence of the Day of Judgment, it frees reason to investigate those practical issues that are within the capability of the human mind. Because of their *fitra* (innate nature or constitution), humans possess a natural inclination to submit to the unknown, and Islam satisfies that need by addressing this consciousness. Humans also possess the counter-inclination to know, and Islam also meets this need by calling on humankind to extend its knowledge in the sciences that are within human reach. However, the human mind should be careful not to confuse the two aspects of life, because the investigation of the first is futile and impossible, while too much emphasis on the latter leads to confusion. Islam balances the two by providing humans with a certain scheme of referential authority.

In addition to this, for Qutb the balance of the Islamic concept draws the right relationship between the absolute divine will and the stable and observed universal laws and rules. The laws of nature are, to Qutb, no more than phenomena of the divine will, for there is no necessary relationship between cause and effects, except what has been divinely ordained. What man can do then is to observe and codify laws and consequently realize their objectives and adjust his life accordingly. The most important benefit of balance to Qutb is that in the constancy of the universal laws and the absoluteness of the divine will the conscience is not without solid grounds and is able therefore to adjust its course from one time to another. More importantly, man is not a slave to nature or afraid of its consequences like death anymore, because he then views all of nature as well as his life as part of a totality designed by the divine will. Thus Qutb argues that part of the balance is due to the fact that Islam is part and parcel of nature and an integral part of the universe. In this sense, Islam offers universal concepts and not narrow and conditioned concepts, like what human philosophies do, which have led for centuries to the loss of a comprehensive thought that integrates all aspects of life and unifies mankind. Human thinking suffers from inventing doctrines that corrupt divine concepts, like rationalism and too much dependence on scientific experimentation and its tentative outcomes as a way of understanding the ultimate. This has resulted in replacing metaphysics with science (Qutb 1980a: 25, 140; Qutb 1980b: 30–33; Qutb 1965: 24, 29).

Al-ijabiyya (positivity), the sixth characteristic of the universal concept, is concerned with the manner in which man interacts with God, the universe and life. Mainly, Qutb argues that the divine origin of Islam necessitates activism, and not mere inactive belief. God is neither an inactive perfection nor restricted to one aspect or another – like the Persians' gods of light and the god of darkness, Plotinus' idea of God, the God of only Israel, or mixing the divine and the human as in Christianity. The oneness of God to Qutb embodies a positive concern about the world and the call for Muslims to establish Islamic communities and to deal practically with the individual as well as with society and the state. Islam should not only survive in the conscience, theory or ideals of the spiritual realm but is rather a design for an active commitment to bring about the practical fruits of the divine oneness. Its proper understanding turns it into an individual, social and political motivating force for the community's advancement and well-being.

The seventh and last characteristic is *al-waqi'iyya* (realism), which means to Qutb that Muslims must deal with the real world. Islam does not abstractly view the world but postulates an overall order for improvement. Realism, however, does not mean for Qutb that he accepts any reality, but that what Islam calls for is feasible and possible and is not beyond human reach. For instance, the quest for an Islamic state is realistic in that sense, and not because it actually exists. Islamic realism is also idealistic in the sense that it attempts to raise humankind to adopting an ideal. Thus idealistic realism means that Muslims interact with the realities of this world to uplift humans to their true nature and the divine design. Thus to Qutb realistic idealism is the other side of the coin. In other words, though Islam does not call for things that are not beyond human capabilities, it still aims at the highest possible human perfection. Its demands on humans, societies and doctrines are realistic (Qutb 1965: 3; Qutb 1974: 16–20).

Qutb's political discourse

From Qutb's perspective, the most fundamental political impact of tawhid, the universal Islamic concept, is its postulation of shari'a the political doctrines of which focus on social justice and revolution. Seeking the establishment of a righteous community through obedience to Islamic law, Islam revolts against controlling humankind by human laws and systems, an act that is considered by Qutb to be unbelief. To Qutb, while the proper law governing humankind should be the shari'a, it is also the method that leads humankind to establish just societies. Establishing such societies is more necessary nowadays because humankind is losing its true nature and its problems are on the increase. Qutb's political ideology or theory is then made up of three underpinnings: divine shari'a versus human law, social justice versus materialism, and revolutionary Muslim societies versus jahili societies (Qutb 1965: 32–33).

Human law versus shari'a

Qutb believes that tawhid acts both as a human liberation instrument from the domination of unjust authorities in order to establish the Islamic state and as a social instrument for the development of an Islamic value system and as a system of law. Shari'a plays the role of harmonizing the different aspects of life, from setting up governments to prohibiting the legislation of normative values and doctrines. Qutb argues that the revealed Islamic shari'a takes away the possibility of any unwarranted human control by exploitative legislations. For shari'a sets both social and political systems on a broader moral order and on universal divine laws, as outlined in the Qur'an. Because divine laws are not woven into the interests and customs of particular groups, they do not function, as do human laws, in an alienating and exploitative manner. However, Muslims can at the same time base their 'legislation' and its development on the general *usul al-fiqh* (fundamentals of jurisprudence). While articulating particular doctrines depends on the conditions of the interpreter, these doctrines stay tentative in comparison to the Islamic law itself. On the other hand, human laws have no true reference but people, whose desires and ambitions dictate the principles to be followed. To Qutb, Islamic law is not a social phenomenon but an eternal manifestation of the divine will, which defines the moral, social and political order. In this sense, humankind should not but follow the order because it represents the meta-historical and universal basis. Any human legislation that goes against the order, therefore, has no positive and legal standing. Human legislation should be then limited to codification and re-codification as required by the different conditions of societies (Qutb 1975: 49, 60).

Furthermore, Qutb argues that moral and political sovereignty is a divine right; humans' duty is therefore to submit to it or else humans fall prey to polytheism or *shirk*. Any human action or thinking is correct insofar as it involves no contradiction to the divine law. Sovereignty in principle and legislation belongs to God, and its significance goes beyond rituals and beliefs to include politics and government. While the objective of the law is salvation in the next life, still that cannot be achieved without earthly proper living. The two lives should be integrated, and the instrument for that is the shari'a. Because it harmonizes the life of man with the divine will, its universal application becomes a duty on all Muslims in order to attain the Islamic order (Qutb 1965: 16–18, 19; Qutb 1980b: 49, 114; Qutb 1979: 34; Qutb 1970: 60–61; Qutb 1980a: 105).

Furthermore, Qutb organically links morality and the shari'a and underscores the need for their obedience by the ruler and the ruled. For non-adherence to the shari'a by any government, whether democratic or autocratic, removes whatever legitimacy it has. Qutb views the legitimate Islamic government as being, first, the government of law, and, second, of the ruled. Rulers are, however, no more than servants of Islamic law. Legitimacy is then of substantive nature and does not stop at the formal level. While the formal aspect of the government's function is to regulate human affairs in accordance with *shura* (consultation) and the individual is obliged to obey the government, obedience cannot be unconditional or absolute. For non-adherence to Islamic law removes any formal legitimacy and creates sufficient grounds for disobedience and revolution.

Legitimacy and law thus become synonyms to Qutb, who argues that even the formal aspect of legitimacy, shura, is part of the law and hence is substantive like any other aspect. This is why functionally legitimacy starts with Muslims' choice, but continues through applying the law. That people should continue to obey the ruler stems from his adherence to shari'a. Qutb further makes a distinction between the ruler's function as the executive of law and the initial source of authority that is based on his merits. The ruler derives initial authority and legitimacy from people in general; their perpetuation is, however, linked to proper application of shari'a. The ruler, as an individual, has no intrinsic religious authority or a divine right to rule that is derived from God, however. He derives authority from Muslims' consent (Qutb 1980a: 107). In an indirect way, Qutb participates in the democratic notion of the legitimacy of representative government or 'the government of *umma*', as he calls it. His understanding of people's will is a compromise between popular sovereignty and absolutism. Therefore, the ruler's legitimate authority stems theoretically from two basic components: people's consent and the application of shari'a.

In this way, Qutb becomes capable of turning down many parts of the formal legitimacy that was advocated in medieval Islamic thought. He does this by a process of de-historicizing and modernizing Islamic political thought on questions of instituting and removing governments and legitimacy. Thus, he drops out many of the accepted medieval notions of government and politics, like hereditary government, rule by seizure and the stipulation that the ruler should be from the Prophet's tribe (Quraysh). As a general guide, Islam does not specify any superior groups, not even the Prophet's; all Muslims are equal regardless of origins (Qutb 1980a: 206–7).

More importantly, Qutb directs his conclusions about the past towards dealing with the issues of modern governments and politics. In denying the legitimacy of historical processes, Qutb wants to condemn changes made now to Islamic principles. Rejecting the use of force to attain power in the past is also directed at contemporary Muslim rulers who seize power and are not popularly chosen. Consequently, contemporary Muslims can legitimately free themselves from imposed governments.

Qutb also rejects any indication that the proper Islamic government is a theocratic one because there is no class that should be properly endowed with religious rule. Furthermore, it is only by applying Islamic law that the Islamic government is ideological and religiously legitimized. Because Islam has created a society that is based on law, Qutb's repudiation of theocracy stems from his opposition to the assumed authority of the clergy. Qutb underscores the distinction between 'men of religion' or clergy and religious power: the first have no power, the second is invested in the people. The clergy's rule should not be taken as an Islamic political ideal, for neither theory nor practice supports it (Qutb 1980b: 58, 63–69, 72).

Instead Qutb looks for the Prophetic rule and, its extension, the rule of only the first two caliphs, as a universal human model because of their religious, moral, social and political achievements. This model provided the basis of exemplary conducts and doctrines that ranged from fulfilling humans' true nature to implementing proper political, social and economic duties and rights. However, Qutb is not calling for the reinstitution of that Islamic system or the return to that Muslim society. To him, the Islamicity of any system relates to its adherence to Islamic principles; its form may thus change and is subject to development of society. Thus, a multitude of forms can be accepted as long as they are grounded in general Islamic principles. For Qutb's priority is not the government's form but the cultivation of Muslims who have strong beliefs and are capable of setting up an Islamic society. Organizational systems are then secondary in a real Islamic life (Qutb 1965: 39–42; Qutb 1975: 66, 72; Qutb 1970: 84; Qutb 1980a: 37, 108).

In fact, Qutb's elaboration on forms of governments makes formal legitimacy dependent on public choice and denies all elitist forms. Representative government becomes, because of its basic principle (shura), the cornerstone in forming any state. In one way or another, Qutb is postulating the need for public participation, and demands the people's right to elect rulers. He does that through also de-historicizing and deconstructing the interpretations of shura. For instance, while Muslim *ulama* (religious scholars) had to nominally approve the ruler's selection, once elected, the ruler had a free hand within the shari'a. Moreover, Qutb's argument that shura is not specifically defined and that its form is an organizational matter depending on the needs of every age has no doctrinal or historical precedent. Shura has been turned into the prerogative of scholars who provided rulers with specific consultations and endorsements rather than viewing it as a principle of government.

Therefore, those societies that do not organize their lives in accordance with the divine law are jahili (ignorant and paganist) societies. For the very definition of a real nation for Qutb involves a group of people who are bound by religion as its nationality. Otherwise, there is no real religious nation because attachment to land, race, language and material interests is not adequate for the creation of the Islamicly desired nation (Qutb 1965: 85). Thus the importance of Islam is its capability of uniting humankind on a religious basis and doing away with racial, linguistic, territorial and cultural differences. Religion should be the Muslims' nationality. Therefore, Muslims must not copy from Christians' theology that separated state politics from church. The European experience differs then from the Islamic, and Islam is different from Christianity, which lacks a political code to organize the state (Qutb 1965: 87; Qutb 1975: 58; Qutb 1980b: 59; Qutb 1983a: 7–9; Qutb 1982: 13). Consequently, the setting of Islamic state is a religious duty that is needed for both the perfection of human society and proper performance of religion.

Materialism versus social justice

Qutb positions Islam at a crossroads with two antagonist ideologies challenging Islam: communism on the one hand, and capitalism on the other. Because of usury, monopoly, exploitation and injustice, Qutb refuses to view capitalism as a model that Muslims should follow because capitalism has been linked closely to nationalism. States like England, France, Italy and Germany gave themselves, in the name of national interest, the right to exploit, invade or occupy other countries in the Middle East, India, Africa or Latin America. On the other hand, socialism and Islam converge on many essential points, such as advocating guarantees of minimum life standards, work, housing and social justice. However, an Islamic economic system should be an integral part of Islam and its state.

On yet another level, Marxism and Islam clash head-on: Islam is founded on belief in God; Marxism, on denying Him through dialectical materialism, the Marxist core idea. Ultimately, the conflict presented in economic terms (capitalist, communist or socialist) is, to Qutb, the conflict between spiritualism and materialism: the former is represented by Islam and religion in general; the latter, by capitalism, socialism and communism.

Because Marxism is the most advanced level of mechanical and intellectual materialism, Qutb argues that the capitalist and the socialist camps disagree and wage wars for material benefits, and their difference is a matter of degree, of organization and of method. Because the materialistic idea of life underlies all of them, Qutb predicts the final victory for Marxism over capitalism when the economies of the West reach stagnation. This is so because communism is nothing but a progressive idea when compared to capitalism. It is progressive because it provides basic material needs for people and addresses the exploited, while capitalism addresses governing authorities and the exploiting class. However, the outcome of both ideologies is unjust because in capitalism individuals and their ambitions rule over the community and in communism the state rules over individuals (Qutb 1975: 25; Qutb 1983a: 6; Qutb 1983b: 33–38, 86–89).

Qutb's alternative is Islam, which has stipulated equal opportunity but has made piety and morality rather than material possession the basic values of society. Although it has set forth the right of individual possession and made it the basis of its economic system, it simultaneously imposes limits. An Islamic economic system is neither capitalist nor socialist. What is essential in any Islamic economic system is social justice, and Qutb provides its two primary principles: the harmonious, balanced and absolute unity between the individual and groups as one principle, and the general mutual responsibility (*takaful*) between the individuals and groups, as the other. The importance of justice stems from being an ethical doctrine as well as one of the Islamic bases of government. Entrusted with authority that originally belongs to God, the ruler must manifest this trust in, first, obedience to the shari'a and, second, social, economic and political justice (Qutb 1980a: 33, 39, 73–77, 82). Qutb identifies complete liberation of conscience, human equality and mutual social responsibility as the three principles that guarantee administering justice.

Furthermore, Qutb considers morality to be the basis of a stable and coherent society. True social justice exists only when supported, first, by an internal feeling of the individual's worthiness and the community's need, and, second, by a creed leading to obeying God and to realizing a sublime human society. Economic liberation is insufficient in itself for realizing a good society or the survival of good individuals in society. Furthermore, liberation cannot be only guaranteed by laws because humans are affected by needs and inclinations. What is equally, if not more important than economic liberation is the liberation of conscience. This is true liberation.

The basic manifestation of liberating the human conscience appears in worshipping only God, which frees humankind from submission to other human beings as well as unjust authorities and state, Qutb explains. To do this, Islam disciplines the conscience by inculcating piety and, then, entrusting it as the guardian of society. Islam makes the human conscience the protector and executor of legislation. This trust is manifested, for instance, in legal decisions which are usually dependent on the conscience of witnesses whose testimony can put someone in prison or to death. Nonetheless, Islam does not leave the conscience for itself but considers God as the monitor and witness of people's behavior. For this reason, piety is essential in Islamic life and politics. For when the conscience is liberated from fear, which lowers self-esteem, the individual can be trusted. What this means ultimately to Qutb is that if the conscience is liberated from enslavement and submission to man and is filled with God's love, the individual will be afraid of no one, nor of losing his livelihood or office. Thus liberation from fear and obedience to none but God is one of the cardinal principles to building a just society and a pious state.

Nonetheless, there is still another level of liberation: liberation from enslavement to social values. Qutb is aware that an individual can be liberated from fears but enslaved to social values. Thus, besides the moral and spiritual aspects, liberation also has political and material implications. Private ownership is, thus, allowed so that the individual is provided with financial independence from the state and, in turn, allows political independence. Ultimately, the individual is capable of challenging the state that disobeys the shari'a (Qutb 1980a: 41–42, 45–46, 82–83; Qutb 1975: 52).

Thus, this liberation of conscience becomes to Qutb all the more essential in order to eliminate injustice and cultivate justice. He believes that administering justice depends on cultivating the conscience, for when the conscience has tasted liberation, it finds legal and practical guarantees to assure this feeling. There will be no need for someone to advocate equality in words, for the conscience has tasted its meaning in its depths and has found it a reality in its life. Because it will not tolerate existing inequality, it will demand its right for equality, struggle to establish this right, preserve it when obtained, and accept nothing but equality (Qutb 1980a: 47, 115–16; Qutb 1975: 34–36, 55).

While Qutb acknowledges humans' inequality both physically and intellectually, humans are theoretically and spiritually equal. Unequal qualities are accepted and this is why the Islamic right to own property, for instance, is stipulated. This right is just because it rewards individual efforts, is suitable to human nature and motivates individuals to do their utmost. Here, there is an acknowledgment that unequal efforts deserve unequal rewards. It is unjust to treat people who are unequal equally. Human faculties are unequal and to assert the opposite is a vanity, according to Qutb. Notwithstanding this acknowledgment, Qutb maintains that every individual should have equal opportunity and freedom of conscience (Qutb 1980a: 55).

While success should only depend on an individual's achievement regardless of race and other characteristics, real equality should start even before actual existence. Qutb argues that the Muslim community as a whole is responsible for the protection of the weak, the poor and the needy. Consequently, the state should, for instance, train people to work so that their primary needs can be satisfied. In the case of those who cannot find work and are unable to meet their needs, the state must step in and help. To Qutb, the state is not a joint-stock company. An individual has the right to be supported with basic needs. Therefore, Qutb views Islamic mutual responsibility (takaful) not merely as charity but also as a system of preparing people to work and guarantee basic necessities to those who cannot work. Mutual responsibility is not only an individual but a public duty as well. He states that Islam considers acquiring education, with which one can earn and deserve his livelihood, a duty on every individual. The community has a responsibility to facilitate its fulfillment. If the community is incapable of realizing this duty, it becomes a state responsibility (Qutb 1975: 47, 84). Qutb stresses the importance of society over the state; the state intervenes only where the voluntary efforts of individuals and society fail. Therefore, at the theoretical level, the state is supplementary to the individual and society, and as long as they can get along without the state, the state has a minimal role.

To demonstrate to Muslims one of the positive aspects of Islam, Qutb argues that Islam's esteem for life is comprehensive, and its stipulations on rights and duties are precise and conclusive. It has considered the nation to be one body and, on this basis, has set up severe *hudud* (deterrents) for social crimes, since cooperation requires the protection of individuals. Every individual is responsible for protecting the community's interests. In order to highlight the universality of Islamic social justice, Qutb generally views social and international problems as the outcome of injustice among nations. To be true and Islamic, justice should, then, be extended to all countries, races and religions. He states that Islam secures complete social justice in Islamic countries, not only for its adherents but also for all its inhabitants regardless of their religion, race and language (Qutb 1980b: 32–35, 76; Qutb 1980a: 73–77, 119). From Qutb's view, this Islamic characteristic is unparalleled in any other ideology. Furthermore, Islam has become universal by attaining a high level of fairness and freedom from tribal, racial, familial and national loyalties (Qutb 1975: 59; Qutb 1980a: 35, 113; Qutb 1980b: 36).

Again, mutual responsibility is also of an economic nature, and Qutb's economic thought is based on his doctrine of social justice. In turn, the latter is part of his political theory that is based on tawhid manifesting in the universal Islamic concept. Since the well-being of any society requires an economic infrastructure, Qutb attempts to provide an alternative to communism and capitalism. He argues that the function of the government is the enforcement of the law of nature (*fitra*). He accepts the doctrine of natural rights, including that of property. The first principle in the Islamic economic theory is the right of individuals to private ownership. However, Islam stipulates that ownership is non-existent except by the authority of the Lawgiver, i.e. God. The logic behind this is that rights are not derived from the essence of things but from the permission of the Lawgiver. His reason is that God is the owner of everything, and the human is His vicegerent (*khalifa*). Man's vicegerency allows him to acquire private property, although the acquisition of private property is dependent on labor, physical or otherwise. Any property that is not based on the Islamic legal prescriptions and labor is a false possession because Islam does not acknowledge or guarantee it. Therefore, developing any financial enterprise should be within the framework of Islamic laws. Thus, the benefits of gambling, cheating, monopoly or excessive gain are illegal and should not be guaranteed in an Islamic state (Qutb 1980a: 59).

Since the individual does not possess the thing itself but rather its usage and benefits, Qutb reasons that ownership belongs to the community in general; private ownership is then a function of dispensation with certain conditions and limits. Some kinds of property that benefit all people in common are public and should not be owned by individuals. Also, parts of public properties can be distributed on specific categories of people, like the poor, in order to help improve the individual and communal living standards (Qutb 1980a: 69–70, 124; Qutb 1975: 40).

Consequently, Islam is not against private ownership, but is, however, against the unusual accumulation of wealth. Qutb argues that the owners of large capital are not free to restrict or spend their capital as they wish without taking others into account. Although spending is an individual act, the individual's freedom has to be exercised within an Islamic framework. There is seldom a personal act that has no relation to other individuals, although this relation may not be direct or obvious. For this reason, Islam has fixed for the poor a share provided from *zakat* (almsgiving) to improve their survival and livelihood (Qutb 1980a: 123, 131, 184; Rodinson 1981).

Furthermore, Qutb views Islamic limits on ownership as the essential means of production that must be owned by the community. Even though Qutb encourages market economy as a means of satisfying the needs of society, he argues that when there is an emergency the state must command the economy. Obviously, Qutb wants neither to abolish private ownership nor market economy, but neither does he want to allow unlimited private ownership of means of production nor a complete command of the economy by the state. As with other issues, the state intervenes when necessary. He states that social mutual responsibility should not lead to any conflict between the rights of individuals and the rights of society. It is incumbent upon the state to protect individuals from selfishness when necessary (Rodinson 1981: 147; Qutb 1974: 32).

Jahili societies versus revolutionary Muslim societies

In order to achieve Qutb's main objective, the creation of a Muslim nation based on shari'a and social justice, he postulates the need for taking prior steps, foremost among which is revolution. As tawhid is the basis of an Islamic government and Muslim society, it is as well the pivot of revolution. According to Qutb, it should be the basis of propagating Islam (*da'wa*) and political movement. Because tawhid is a movement of continuous development, Islam does not accept an evil reality as such because its main mission is to eradicate evil and to improve the quality of life. According to Qutb, tawhid involves emancipation from subordination to any and all but the divine law; it is a revolution against the authority of tyrannical lords as well as the rejection of eliminating human individuality. Subordination to others is a crime because God created man free and forbade it. 'No god but God', declares Qutb, is a revolution against the worldly authority that seizes the first characteristic of divinity and against the situations that are based on this seizure and against the authorities that rule by human and un-Islamic laws (Qutb 1975: 44, 46–47; Qutb 1980a: 157–58).

Qutb views revolution as the main tool in the attainment of a Muslim society that is based on the shari'a and social justice. A revolution is the road to conscious transformation of current existing societies. While it is not meant to convert people to Islam, it still aims at creating the Muslim individual, the Muslim society and the Islamic state. This is so because an Islamic revolution aspires as well to the transformation of man's enslavement to man and to material things. As such, this revolution is not directed at a particular society but essentially at all societies that yield to human laws and orders. It is comprehensive and universal.

More importantly, Qutb strongly argues that a proper Islamic revolution does not compromise with non-Islamic (jahili) doctrines and orders. For the road to change necessitates some creative activism that demands total change and not mere patching up of ways of life and orders and even philosophies and ideologies. Making the construction of a society similar to the construction of a building, Qutb argues that there is a difference between having a plan to construct gradually and patching up a building based on another plan. In the end, this patching up does not establish a new building. A new building requires first tearing down the old building (Qutb 1980b: 26, 101; Qutb 1975: 70; Qutb 1980a: 250).

Moreover, while aiming at a gradual Islamic revolution that could first spread out the message of Islam, Qutb's highest aim is a total revolution that sweeps away the governments of his time as well as establishing new revolutionary Muslim societies instead of the un-Islamic, patched-up jahili societies. Qutb relies on a gradual transformation of institutions and the spread of Islamic ideology to achieve this ideal (Qutb 1980b: 24–25). Still, it should shake and destroy the old society in order to build a new one. Not believing in the viability of mild change for a society erected on false or immoral foundations, Qutb insists on the necessity of revolution as the only proper remedy for decaying societies. For Qutb, all societies are essentially decaying. He uses 'earthquaking' or *zalzala* or, in fact, revolution to describe the first step in the process of building the new society (Qutb 1975: 28). However, this *zalzala*, though strong, is not necessarily violent, at least in theory. Its starting point is education in a two-fold manner: first, expounding true Islam and, second, refuting Western ideological fallacies (Qutb 1980b: 23–24).

Because Qutb sees tawhid not as a negative, philosophical and theoretical declaration but rather as a positive, realistic and active declaration, he invokes confronting other philosophies and ideologies. This confrontation requires that Muslims should acquire knowledge of other philosophies and ideologies. An active Islamic movement should confront the material obstacles, foremost among which are the existing political authorities. This intellectual and material confrontation applies not only to Arab societies but to all societies, because Islam is not for the Arabs alone. Therefore, the ultimate goal of Islamic revolution is to abolish those regimes and governments that are established on the basis of humans' governance (*hakimiyya*) over humans and the enslavement of humans by humans in jahili societies. Then the revolution sets individuals free to choose the creed they want. As is obvious, Qutb's declaration means the comprehensive revolution against all human governance in all its forms, systems and orders, and the complete rebellion against every un-Islamic *jahiliyya* (Qutb 1980b: 68).

For Qutb, the Islamic state is established on that territory where the Islamic law rules regardless of whether all or only a portion of the population is Muslim, but that territory that is not ruled by Islamic law is *dar al-harb* (the abode of war), regardless of people's religion. What is significant here is that a Muslim society is Muslim not because it is composed of Muslims but rather because of the rule of Islamic law. This lends support to Qutb's previous argument that the Islamic government is the government of law. Thus, the application of Islamic law in a society, whether composed of a majority of Muslims or non-Muslims, makes that society Muslim. The Islamic state is neither defined by specific territories nor by specific races, and a Muslim society can be established anywhere. On the other hand, those societies that claim to be Muslim are not so because, in his view, they do not uphold Islamic law. In practical terms, this means that those societies that existed during Qutb's time were not Islamic in his view and, thus, must be eradicated. Moreover, dar al-harb includes any state that fights Islamic religious attitudes (Qutb 1980b: 69–71).

While struggle (jihad) aims at transforming any institution that opposes and does not allow Islam to be freely practiced, jihad is neither suicide nor a campaign of atrocities. Qutb announces that jihad has four basic characteristics. Serious realism, the first characteristic, means that Islam faces with *da'wa* and refutation incorrect conceptions and beliefs and faces with power and jihad those regimes and authorities based on incorrect conceptions (Qutb 1980b: 159).

Qutb cannot accept the argument that Islam launches jihad only for defensive purposes, for Islam is not defensive but an offensive against aggression (Qutb 1980b: 64). To him, those thinkers who argue that jihad is only defensive are defeated spiritually and intellectually and do not distinguish between the Islamic method in rejecting the compulsion to embrace Islam and its method in destroying those material and political forces that stand between man and his God. In fact, those thinkers who see jihad as being only defensive do not understand Islam. It is true that Islam defends the territory on which it exists, but it also struggles to establish the Islamic order wherever possible and to abolish the jahili society (Qutb 1980b: 65, 66, 72, 81–91; Badawi 1967: 114; Qutb 1980b: 75–83).

Active realism is the second characteristic. It means that jihad cannot be fought with speeches and propagation only but requires much more preparation. It does not meet, for instance, a strong military force with an abstract theory. Jihad is a movement that can operate in stages and take time and effort as well as organization. Similarly, the third characteristic is a continuous movement which may take many forms and procedures that do not contradict Islamic principles. It can take the forms of writing, assisting others, teaching, self-discipline or other activities. The fourth characteristic is that the regulation of relations between Muslim societies and non-Muslim ones can be only in two ways. The first is that Islam is the basis of international relations; the second is to give Muslims the right to peacefully propagate Islam without barriers imposed by any political regime or force. Qutb's toleration of non-Muslim societies depends upon the freedom to accept or reject Islam (Qutb 1980b: 64–66; Qutb 1965: 11, 91).

The Qutbian revolution is directed to those jahili societies that are not bound by or contradict the universal Islamic concept. By this definition, Qutb includes all existing societies on Earth as un-Islamic and jahili societies, including Christian, Jewish, socialist and capitalist societies. Even Muslim societies are included in Qutb's revolution, for while they do not believe in the divinity of anyone except God, they accept the human *hakimiyya* (governance) (Qutb 1980b: 162–63; Qutb 1982: 62).

Conclusion

The ultimate source of knowledge to Qutb is God, who is beyond human philosophy and cannot definitely be understood by human thought. However, the validity of human knowledge depends on its conformity to nature, which is, in turn, unknown by reason. Thus a human claim to knowledge should be reduced to facts. The knowledge of God or others can therefore only be known from God's revelation. Still Qutb maintains that what is revealed is no more than allusions to truth that is validated by its conformity to nature. Therefore, Qutb has referred to *fitra*, to be found in revelation, so as to argue for the validity or invalidity of any concept or doctrine. This is Qutb's most important argument for attaining and verifying the truth. Nonetheless, the circularity of this argument denies its components of revelation, nature and *fitra* any possible verification by regular human methods.

The Qutbian perspective restricts reason's function to instrumentality in realizing the characteristics of the Islamic concept and as a judge in matters and values concerned with this concept. It is the interpretative instrument of revelation and the universal Islamic concept. For in the absence of Qur'anic injunctions, Qutb focuses on the practicability of discourses and institutions for discerning their validity or invalidity. Ideas per se are not important; rather, their importance lies in their utility. Even when they seem true they are no more than approximations that might change from time to time. This is why Qutb rejects science as being the basis of religion.

Religion and science cannot replace each other, and Qutb's discourse attempts to bring together the religious discourse and the dominant scientific discourse as the underlying bases of the new Islamic society, but each has its own domain. The eternal, textually based religious discourse provides the foundations of society while the scientific discourse addresses the practical needs of society and state. While the scientific discourse cannot produce moral or metaphysical knowledge, it is still important for daily livelihood.

There is no knowledge without presuppositions, and Qutb argues that all knowledge presupposes a prior understanding of the whole. He criticizes the ideal of objectivity and insists on the historical character of all understanding. Understanding and its discourse are conditioned by time, space, environment and culture. Although Qutb disregards the possibility of human understanding of or discoursing on the ultimate source of knowledge (God), he nonetheless believes in His existence by *fitra*. For our comprehension of the real sources of knowledge is not attainable by observation and accumulation of facts and data, or apprehension and comprehension, due to the inherent limits of human reason. Though the truth of God's existence has to be justified to an extent, it is ultimately above human authorities, discourses, philosophy and religion.

Qutb's discourse should be grounded in the contemporary history of the Islamic world and must be viewed as the product of contemporary political crises. Still one must not over-generalize and view it merely as a reaction; it has gone beyond that. Now, his discourse is the religious, ideological, political bases of rather most new militant political discourses, and many Islamists in the Muslim world derive many of their ideologies and perspectives from his discourse. While the militancy of his revolutionary Islamist discourse can be attributed to the crises of contemporary social and political life, his general ideological and religious discourse constitutes normative statements on God, reason, science, history, politics and economics, the understanding of which requires a closer look at Islamic principles, and not only at transient political events and world politics.

Qutb's discourse impoverishes and is impoverished in terms of theology, philosophy, history and science. While Qutb accepts the Qur'an and the sunna as the bases of normative religious and ideological principles, they are rather overshadowed by politics and subordinated to his political discourse. In fact, besides their political signification of divine governance and human paganism, one cannot fathom Qutb's concept of tawhid. Tawhid is primarily interpreted politically, which is a distinguishing mark of Islamism and today's *takfiri jihadism*.

Qutb's appeal and popularity among Islamists, and especially the radical groups, however, can be traced to many factors. First, he tries to justify social justice and freedom within the framework of an Islamicly developed discourse. Instead of adhering to democracy and socialism, he explains important issues for Muslims in an Islamic discourse. Thus, issues such as representative governments are treated without any reference to foreign ideological discourses, and instead offer religious justifications for his religious principles. The principles of representative government and social justice become then religious and political duties, i.e. the principles of government in Islam. By doing so, Qutb preempted the advocates of both democracy and socialism and was able to show the Muslims that Islam and modernity were compatible. Their compatibility was due not to subjecting Islam to modernity but subjecting modernity to Islam. His discourse absorbs democracy as shura or the choice of people of their governments and argues that the Muslims did not really understand it historically. Again, his discourse absorbs socialist social justice and links it to legal, political and moral issues. Therefore, Qutb's fame is derived from creating a new Islamic political and ideological discourse that encompassed the best in the Western traditions, which had been accepted by the majority of people, without negating or subordinating Islam to the West. His discourse reinforces the Islamic notion of Islam's validity for all ages and its capability of accommodating diverse conditions and changing realities. Hence, Qutb urges the Muslims to not relegate the Qur'anic discourse to only prayers, funerals or the personal domain. Instead, they must keep it as their everlasting constitution.

Moreover, Qutb provides a new revolutionary discourse that is not bound by or subordinate to past discourses and could therefore be used by contemporary Muslims to reshape their governments and their ways of life and reject Islamic traditionalism. This new discourse aims at reviving Islam without dependence on its long history. Qutb dismisses history, which is the basis of Islamic traditionalism and its sciences and disciplines, as only a temporary and relative manifestation, but also a normative final Islamic reading, of the truth.

Qutb's ideology has spread widely within contemporary Islamic groups that obviously adopted his views about their own governments and societies. These groups turned the Qutbian doctrines of paganism of the world, the need to spread divine governance, the revolution against all political powers and jihad against their own governments and the world's government into living realities.

After 11 September 2001 and the invasion of Iraq, some Islamic groups merged together and consequently have created neo-Salafism and *takfiri jihadism*. This complexity thus appears in the *takfiri jihadists* who are composed of both neo-Wahhabis, neo-Salafists and radical Islamists. Again, not all *takfiris* are jihadist, and not all jihadists are *takfiri*. These groups are manipulated by different governmental and non-governmental powers.

The war in Afghanistan against the Soviet Union in 1979 brought together, for the first time, all sorts of Islamic groups under the umbrella of jihad. Radical Islamist groups, especially Qutb's followers from many Islamic countries including Egypt and Algeria, along with Wahhabi and Salafist fighters from diverse Muslim regions including Saudi Arabia and Pakistan, fought along with the Afghan mujahideen. The Arab Afghans blended together the neo-Salafism of Abdallah Azzam, the neo-Wahhabism of Osama Bin Laden and the radical Qutbian Islamism of Ayman al-Zawahiri – and the three activists are greatly affected by Qutb's ideological orientations. Today, the most notorious manifestation of this deadly combination is al-Qaeda along with its ideological and military affiliates that have spread throughout the Muslim world.

These new-Salafist, neo-Wahhabi and radical Islamist ideologies and formations are the *takfiri* jihadists along the line of Qutb's discourse. They are trying to establish a religious state and have managed to turn themselves into an outlet for different parties in the region, and indirectly became involved in a different context. They represent the transformation of rather different contradictory Islamic trends into radical *takfiri jihadism*.

Al-Qaeda can only partially be understood as a production of the failure of moderate Islamism, official Wahhabism and conservative Salafism along with Islamic traditionalism in their established forms today, to bring about serious positive changes in the Muslim world's political systems and ways of life. Furthermore, *takfiri jihadism* has created a new front in the Muslim world's encounters with the West. However, some components of this front still exist within the Muslim world itself, namely the current political regimes, both religious and secular. The intellectual, political, religious and military battle with this front and its affiliates is going to greatly shape the politics of Muslim states, the Muslim world and the non-Muslim world. It is really a global phenomenon and consequently requires a multi-faceted global solution. A mere military confrontation will definitely not resolve the issues of radicalism and terrorism.

References

al-Balihi, I.I.A. (1972) *Sayyid Qutb wa-Turathuhu al-Adabi wa-al-Fikri*, Riyadh.
al-Farabi, R. (1926) *Rasa'il al-Farabi*, Hyderabad, Matba'at Majlis Da'irat al-Ma'arif al-'Uthmaniyya.
—— (n.d.) *The Virtuous City*.
al-Ghazali (1963) *Tahafut al-Falasifa*, Lahore, Pakistan Philosophical Congress.
al-Hassan, B. (1981) *Milestones*, Karachi, International Islamic Publishers.
Anawati, G. (1974) 'Philosophy, Theology, and Mysticism', in Joseph Schacht (ed.), *The Legacy of Islam*, Oxford, Oxford University Press.
Averroes (n.d.) *Tahafut al-Tahafut*.
Badawi, M.A.Z. (1967) *The Reformers of Egypt*, London, Croom Helm.
Barakat, Muhammad T. (n.d.) *Sayyid Qutb: Khulasat Hayatih, Minhajihi fi al-Haraka wa al-Naqd al-Muwajah ilayh*, Beirut, Dar al-Da'wa.
Butterworth, C. (1975) 'Elites', in George Hourani (ed.), *Essays on Islamic Philosophy and Science*, New York, State University of New York.
Hasan, B. (1981) *Milestones*, Karachi, International Islamic Publishers.
Hilal, A.D. (1977) *Al-Siyasa wa-al-Hukm fi Misr: 1923–52*, Cairo, Maktabat Nahdat al-Sharq.

Hussain, A. (1983) *Islamic Movements in Egypt, Pakistan, and Iran*, London, Mansell Publishing.

Khalidi, S.A.F. (1983a) *Nazariyyat al-Taswir al-Fanni 'inda Sayyid Qutb*, Amman, Dar al-Furqan.

—— (1983b) *Sayyid Qutb, al-Shahid al-Hay*, Amman, Dar al-Firqan.

Mahdi, M. (1969) *Al-Farabi's Philosophy of Plato and Aristotle*, Ithaca, NY, Cornell University Press.

Mitchell, R.P. (1969) *The Society of Muslim Brothers*, New York, Oxford University Press.

Moussalli, A. (1995) *Radical Islamic Fundamentalism: The Ideological and Political Discourse of Sayyid Qutb*, Beirut, American University of Beirut.

Qutb, S. (1965) *Al-Mustaqbal li Hadha al-Din*, Cairo, Maktabat Wahba.

—— (1970) *Fiqh al-Da'wa*, Beirut, Mu'assasat al-Risala.

—— (1974) *Fi al-Tarikh: Fikra wa-Minhaj*, Cairo, Dar al-Shuruq.

—— (1975) *Ma'rakat al-Islam wa al-Ra'simaliyya*, Beirut, Dar al-Shuruq.

—— (1979) *In the Shades of the Qur'an*, London, MWH.

—— (1980a) *Al-'Adala al-Ijtima'yya fi al-Islam*, Cairo, Dar al-Shuruq.

—— (1980b) *Ma'alim fi al-Tariq*, Beirut, Dar al-Shuruq.

—— (1982) *Nahwa Mujtama' Islami*, Beirut, Dar al-Shuruq.

—— (1983a) *Al-Islam wa-Mushkilat al-Hadara*, Beirut, Dar al-Shuruq.

—— (1983b) *Nahwa Mujtama' Islami*, Beirut, Dar al-Shuruq.

Rodinson, M. (1981) *Islam and Capitalism*, Austin, University of Texas Press.

Vatikiotis, P.J. (1969) *The Modern History of Egypt*, New York, Praeger Publishers.

Three dimensions of the emerging political philosophy of Islam

M.A. Muqtedar Khan

For nearly a century, Islamic political theorists have been trying to argue that not only is Islam compatible with modernity and democracy, but indeed the advent of Islam was the essential beginning of modern enlightenment. Muslim political theorists are a rare commodity but, nevertheless, a few of them who did exist and wrote have tried to demonstrate the antecedents of modern polities within Islamic experience. However, much of their contribution has remained out of the mainstream of Islamic discourse and Muslim conceptions of Islamic scholarship. The political concepts that pervade Muslim discourses today have mostly been crafted by Islamists like Maulana Maududi and Sayyid Qutb, who were Islamic political theorists in some sense, but their approach was too ideological and polemical (Khan 2001a). Nevertheless, while there are rich sources of Islamic thought on democracy, an Islamic democratic theory has yet to emerge.

As the Muslim world became independent from colonial occupation and began searching for authentic models for their newly independent polities, Muslims were faced with the choice of either imitating the contemporary West, often their former colonizer, or trying to reproduce the political and legal structures that preceded the colonial era. Muslim secularists, most prominently Ataturk in Turkey, opted to adopt Western models of secular democracy and some Arab states chose to reproduce medieval models of kingships based on tribal loyalties (Lapidus 1988). It was only when Pakistan emerged as an independent nation that Muslims at that time chose to invent a model of Muslim democracy that recognized the compatibility of Islam and democracy. The debates that shaped the writing of Pakistan's constitution brought out interesting issues about how Islam would shape politics and political structures in the modern era (Choudhury 1969; Hayes 1984; Esposito and Voll 1996).

The promise of the debate about the authenticity of democracy and the challenge of accommodating religion in a multi-religious modern state of Pakistan was unfortunately never realized. Two mutually reinforcing trends within the Muslim world marginalized the importance of this emerging political theory of democracy in Pakistan. The two trends still dominate the Muslim political landscape and they are political Islam and its highly politicized interpretation of Islam and their call for an 'Islamic State'. The other trend is secular authoritarianism, which emerged from Arab socialism. Muslim discourses and Muslim politics in the last 50-odd years have been a debilitating assertion of either secular authoritarianism with military repression or radical Islamism with frequent frenzies of terror and civil strife. One of the casualties of this civil war in the Muslim world was the emerging democratic theory of an Islamic polity in modern times (Moaddel and Talattof 2000; Moussalli 1999).[1]

The juxtaposition of Islamic state or secular democracy, the Iranian model versus the Turkish model, as the only two alternatives for a Muslim polity not only undermined the development of Islamic democratic discourse but also marginalized liberal Muslims and intellectuals (Taspinar 2003; Esposito 1990).[2] However, recent developments in global politics and the most surprising emergence of President George W. Bush as an advocate of the compatibility of Islam and democracy and his determination to facilitate the establishment of such a polity in Iraq gave vitality and centrality to the incipient theory of Islamic democracy (Khan 2003b).[3] One is now witnessing a plethora of academic journals publishing special issues on Islam and democracy, think tanks conducting debates and symposia on Islam and democracy, and even newspapers are now exploring the nuances of faith and freedom. Recently we have also witnessed a series of books that seek to address the issue from both political as well as theoretical perspectives (Khan 2002; Feldman 2003).

Theologians, jurists and political philosophers

The new interest in Islam and democracy will certainly revive old ideas and generate new interpretations; however, the contemporary momentum is driven by theologians, jurists and activists and not by political theorists. The activists are convinced that democratization is the panacea for all Muslim problems and they are happy to run with the slogan that Islam and democracy are compatible and hence we should hasten the process of democratizing the Muslim world. From a political perspective their zeal and enthusiasm is advantageous but they do not really contribute much to the theoretical content of the claim that there is a strong convergence in Islamic values and democratic principles except for the rhetorical equation of democracy with *Shura*. *Shura* is the Qur'anic term for consultation and Muslim advocates of democracy find a theological vindication for their quest in this Qur'anic injunction to consult: 'And their affairs are conducted through mutual consultation' (Al Qur'an 42:38). However, a democratic theory cannot emerge by itself from part of a verse.

The theologians do approach the issue in a comprehensive and systematic way. They go to Islamic roots and identify and exemplify those elements that correspond to liberal democratic principles. An excellent example is the recent work of Abdulaziz Sachedina who shows, relying essentially on Qur'anic sources and eschewing other socially constructed discourses, how Islam strongly advocates pluralism (Sachedina 2001). Sachedina's work is not a treatise in political theory and he does not intend it as such. He envisages his work as a preventative diplomacy tool for Muslim and non-Muslim politicians seeking to advance the cause of pluralism (Sachedina 2001: 13). One of the most important limitations of *The Islamic Roots of Democratic Pluralism* is its treatment of pluralism and democracy as stable, uncontested ideas enjoying widespread consensus.

The work also focuses on religious pluralism without actually distinguishing between religious and political pluralism. For example, while one can find in it excellent resources to argue for religious tolerance and equality of all from a purely Islamic standpoint, one cannot, however, justify the toleration of competing political ideologies such as capitalism and communism. Will an Islamic state allow political parties to exist and compete for power that are ideologically opposed to state ideology? Can communists share power or even come to power in an Islamic democracy? While people of different faiths enjoy equal rights under Islamic pluralism, does the system also tolerate political pluralism? As a theologian, Sachedina focuses on theological differences and offers a theological solution to religious differences but he does not offer a theological or a political solution to political differences. Can a political theorist treat Sachedina's work as a resource to build an Islamic theory of political pluralism? Possibly. Sachedina's work is not only path-breaking but also points to new paths and underscores the necessity for the full-blown development of Muslim/Islamic democratic theory.

All arguments that advocate Islamic democracies or the compatibility of Islam and democracy take the Qur'an as a revealed document, the text of which is absolute but meanings are open to alternative interpretations. There is even a Qur'anic basis to claim the absoluteness of text and relativity of meanings (Al Qur'an 3:7). The Qur'an acts as the anchor, the absolute point from which Muslim thinkers begin and end their thinking. Therefore, when we talk of pluralism and democracy it is important to clarify which democracy – liberal, radical, socialist, deliberative – and which pluralism – religious, epistemological, cultural or political. While arguing the compatibility of Islam with pluralism, modernity or democracy, the merit of these notions cannot be taken for granted. They must be unpacked and their virtues examined from the moral and ethical perspective of the Qur'an (Mahmood 2003). This is the responsibility of Muslim political theorists (Soroush 2000).[4]

While theologians and their work can become a fundamental resource for Islamic political theorists, the fatwa (religious edict) (Esposito 2003: 85) wielding Islamic jurists, who with one stroke can make democracy *Halal* (permissible in Islam) and political philosophy *Haraam* (forbidden in Islam), remain an important barrier to the development of Islamic political theory. An illustrative example of how even well-meaning Islamic legal scholars unable to escape their juristic outlook can undermine the Islamic roots of democracy while actually advocating Islamic democracy is the recent article on the subject by Khalid Abou El Fadl. In this article El Fadl combines an ethical, philosophical outlook to identify various sources of compassion, tolerance, equality and justice in Islamic sources, and unlike Sachedina he does not limit himself to essentially the Qur'an but explores secondary sources too. In the conclusion of the article, though, he allows the colonial tendency of Islamic legalism to subvert his quest for an Islamic democracy (Abou El Fadl 2003).

Islamic intellectual tradition, which includes Islamic legal thought (*usul al-fiqh* and *fiqh*), theology (*kalam*), mysticism (*tasawwuf*) and philosophy (*falsafa*), is easily one of the most developed and profound traditions of human knowledge. However, for various historical reasons, this intellectual heritage of Islam remains strikingly underdeveloped in the area of political philosophy. One of the reasons for this lacuna in Islamic thought is the colonial tendency of Islamic legal thought. Many Islamic jurists equate Islam with Islamic law and privilege the study and exploration of the shari'a over and above all else, thereby colonizing Islamic thought and marginalizing other fields of inquiry. This dominance of legal studies has allowed only episodic exploration of the idea of a polity in Islam. Today, all over the Muslim world there are hundreds of Islamic schools and universities that produce hundreds of thousands of Islamic legal scholars, but hardly any traditional school produces political theorists or philosophers. Excluding the rare exceptions, this intellectual poverty has reduced Islamic thought to the status of a medieval legal tradition (Rahman 1966).[5]

In spite of the intellectual imperialism of the Islamic jurists, Islamic political theory has managed to survive in some form. In the twentieth century we have witnessed the emergence of two distinct approaches to Islamic political theory (Moussalli 1999; Khan 2004). The Islamists who advocate the establishment of an Islamic state, an authoritarian and ideological entity the central concepts of which are *al-Hakimiyya* (the sovereignty of God) and shari'a (the law of God) (Maududi 1955; Martin 2000; Engineer 1996), and the liberal Muslim political theorists who advocate an Islamic democracy, the central themes of which are shura and *mashaf al Madinah* (constitutionalism *a la* Compact of Medina) (Khan 2001a).

Political Islamists on Islam and democracy

Political Islamists do posit the principle of shura as an important element of their Islamic state, but their concept of shura is limited and essentially pays lip-service to the idea of consultation. For them consultative governance is not necessary for legitimacy, since legitimacy comes from the enforcement of the shari'a regardless of the will of the people. Thus if shura contradicts their notion of what constitutes the shari'a their Islamic state will immediately abandon its consultative status and become a totalitarian ideological entity ready to wage jihad to enforce their view of the law of God, even against the will of the people. It is exactly here that political theorists of the Islamist tendency become as authoritative as the jurist, whose understanding of what is God's will is law and always above the will of the people. Needless to say, for the liberal Muslim theorists, shura is paramount and shari'a too must be arrived at through consultative processes and not taken as given (Kurzman 1998).[6]

There is a marked difference between what individual thinkers in the political Islamist school write about Islam and democracy, and how their followers then interpret these writings and try to realize them in the political arena. In principle, all major thinkers such as Maulana Maududi of Pakistan, who advocated the notion of 'theo-democracy', Sayyid Qutb, Ayatollah Khomeini and even Hassan Turabi are all advocates of procedural democracy. They believe in the democratic method for electing leaders. They accept the idea of a parliament as *Majlis-Ashura,* which will act as a legislative body that interprets the divine shari'a for contemporary times, and they accept the notion of democratic accountability and even constitutionalism. The only democratic notion to which they are opposed is the idea that the divine constitution can be reformed or amended in accordance with the popular will. Thus popular will plays a role only in legitimizing the divinely ordained constitution and in procedural aspects of governance, but the determination of norms and values is solely the prerogative of God and above democratic scrutiny (Maududi 1955; Esposito and Voll 1996; Martin 2000). It is a pity that the Islamists fail to acknowledge that given the vast extant diversity of the interpretation of shari'a, reinterpreting Islamic sources is relatively easier than, say, amending the US constitution, which requires a very high degree of consensus building in a very diverse society.

Jurists and democracy

The extraordinary influence of the idea of 'Islam as shari'a' has made law take precedence over state/polity. Because law comes first and then the political community, the structure and the form of the polity become subservient to the application of law. Polity derives legitimacy from its ability to implement shari'a rather than the very idea of law/shari'a emerging to serve the need of the polity. This philosophical error, which amounts to placing the cart in front of the horse, also underpins El Fadl's otherwise erudite discussion of the compatibility of Islam and democracy. This is particularly striking in his conclusion. One expected his treatise to end with some kind of delineation of an Islamic democracy. On the contrary, he concludes by imposing, *a priori,* shari'a-based limitations on democracy. He clearly states that a case for democracy from within Islam should not substitute popular sovereignty for divine sovereignty and should recognize that democratic lawmaking respects that *a priori* nature of the shari'a. He begins his essay as a political philosopher and ends it as an Ayatollah laying down the edict – you can have democracy but only as long as people are not sovereign and shari'a is not violated.

Professor El Fadl's essay is brilliant in its discussion of the moral and ethical principles within Islam that can help make a case for democracy from within Islam. He nevertheless reinforces traditional barriers rather than deconstructing them. One of the most prominent Islamic theologians, Sheikh Ibn Taymiyyah (1263–1328 AD), who in many ways is a source of great inspiration to conservative Muslims who advocate authoritarianism, argued for an Islamic leviathan that would defend the Islamic world from external military threats and Islamic doctrines from internal heresies (Khan 1982; Khan 2004). He claimed that the object of an Islamic state was to impose the shari'a. El Fadl argues similarly that an Islamic democracy should recognize the centrality of shari'a in Muslim life. It raises several questions. Who gets to articulate what constitutes the shari'a? Islamic jurists? Who determines who is an Islamic jurist? Who determines which schools can provide the education that will produce jurists? Who determines when a specific democratically passed law is in violation of the shari'a? Who determines the issues on which people will have freedom of thought and action and the issues on which the so-called shari'a will be unquestionable? The answer to all of these questions is the same – the Muslim jurist. A close reading of El Fadl's arguments suggests that an Islamic democracy as envisioned by jurists amounts to a dictatorship of the Muslim jurists.

There will be no democracy unless jurists are willing to let go and allow the *democratization of interpretation*. Let every citizen be a jurist and let her interpret Islam and shari'a when she votes. In a democracy the vote/opinion/fatwa of every individual must be considered as equal since ontologically all humans are equals. An essentialization of the shari'a with a concomitant assertion of its uncontested centrality is a recipe for authoritarianism. It is eminently apparent that El Fadl is interpretively more liberal than his traditional colleagues and his vision of what constitutes the shari'a is definitely more inclusive, but until we dismantle the authoritative authority of the jurists and democratize *ijtihad*, there can be no Islamic democracy. The moral quality of this Islamic democracy will depend on the extent of Islamic knowledge of the citizens and their commitment to Islam; we have to accept that and live with it. Any attempts to guarantee 'Islamic outcomes' through any other provisions such as 'the essential shari'a must be applied' will necessarily entail the subversion of democracy. Also the Prophet of Islam, peace and blessing be upon him, reportedly said that 'My *umma* will never unite upon error'.[7] There is no such endorsement available about the infallibility of the opinions of the jurists, which clearly suggests that Islam only privileges the overall will of the people.

The point is simple: even what shari'a is and what Islamic law is should be a democratically negotiated conclusion emerging in a democratic society. In the absence of this free and open negotiation, Islamic democracy will be a procedural sham that uses voting mechanisms selectively in non-crucial matters. Clearly until political philosophers and theorists have developed a cumulative, substantive discourse on democratic theory in Islam, the less the jurists intervene the better it will be. Indeed the quest for democracy in the Muslim world is a twin project: it seeks to free the human conscience from the political tyranny of the dictators and also free the human soul and intellect from the legalist tyranny of the Islamic jurist. Islamic jurists, by monopolizing the right to understand and interpret Islam, are depriving all other Muslims of their basic humanity – the right to exercise their reason and be free Muslims (Khan 2003b).[8]

While the theologian's approach is useful and the jurist's approach is counterproductive, political philosophers produce a rich discourse on democracy and, if allowed to flower and develop, this tradition can advance a progressive, ongoing Islamic democratic theory that can help establish and develop Islamic polities facilitating the causes of both faith and freedom. In this discussion I shall explore the work of the Iranian philosopher Soroush, but before that I will review the work of the greatest Islamic political philosopher Al Farabi, who was also the first Muslim to systematically evaluate the merits and limits of democratic polities.

Al Farabi places democracy in the category of ignorant cities. Ignorant cities are those cities that collectively are unaware of God (The First Cause). They also do not have a singular purpose. He recognizes that since democracies are free societies there will be multiple objectives that the citizens of a democracy will seek. He also suggests interestingly that if people who seek security dominate the polity a democracy can become a national security state (Al Farabi talks in terms of cities of war and peace). However, he also makes a very interesting observation which is perhaps the most important lesson that contemporary Muslim thinkers can take from him. Al Farabi suggests that because democracies are free and non-homogeneous societies, there will be some who will excel in good as well as some who will excel in evil. Since one can find the pursuit of perfection present within a democracy, a democracy has the best chance of all ignorant cities of becoming a virtuous city. This is a cautionary but powerful endorsement of democracy especially at a time when the options available to Muslim societies largely fall in the ignorant category (monarchies, dictatorships etc.) (Mahdi 1987, 2001; Khan 2004).

Soroush's approach to the compatibility of Islam and democracy is very different from Sachedina's and El Fadl's. He neither treats Islam as a stable, unproblematic concept nor does he treat modernity or democracy as settled issues. In true philosophical spirit he considers all concepts and all assertions of values as open to negotiation, reflection and understanding. For El Fadl, Islamic law or shari'a is the ultimate criterion, as is the Qur'an, the indisputable word of God, for Sachedina. For Soroush the only thing that is given is the human capacity to understand what is moral, what is reasonable, what is ethical and what is worthy of upholding as a value. For Soroush the ultimate criterion is his reason and his understanding of even God's will and words are essentially the outcome of the interaction of reason (*aql*) and revelation (*wahi*). Therefore, before there is either Islam or democracy, for Abdul Karim Soroush there is reason.

All Muslim intellectuals start with a stated or unstated assumption that Islamic principles or Islamic laws are absolute truths revealed by God and hence cannot be at fault. If there is any seeming deficiency it must necessarily be in the interpretations and hence we need to reinterpret or revive the tradition of *ijtihad* – independent interpretive thinking. However, Soroush starts his arguments essentially by asserting reason as a defining characteristic of humanity and freedom as a necessary existential condition for that humanity to thrive. For the philosopher what is primary is the human agency as a 'thinking being', whereas for the theologian and the jurists human agency is a 'submissive being'. The theologian asserts: here is the Truth, understand it. The jurist commands: this is the Truth, obey! The philosopher says: you can think and if you are free to think, think and you may know the Truth. Soroush articulates this philosophical position clearly. Thus the fulfillment of humanity depends upon the fruition of reason, and reason cannot thrive, grow or be exercised without freedom. If anything, by linking reason and freedom, Soroush makes this very clear: freedom is necessary for reason and reason leads to faith and truth.[9]

Having established the necessity of freedom for reason to thrive, Soroush then argues that it is incorrect to assume or even consider that reason [*aql*] and revelation [*wahi*] are in some way antithetical to each other. He argues (and this has been the position for a long time in Islamic philosophical tradition) that revelation is essentially accessed through reason. Reason is the instrument that enables the apprehension of revelation. One cannot understand the will of God without possessing the faculty of understanding (Khan 1999). Thus he seeks to subvert the widely touted tensions between faith and freedom and reason and religion. If Islam is compatible with freedom and reason – the constitutive elements of democracy – then Islam should be compatible with democracy. Soroush further argues that democracies are basically means to an end and, as long as Islam is understood as a reasoned justification of God's rights over humanity, a religious society should have no problems in establishing a democracy as means to good and just governance.

Soroush's ideas are highly provocative given the cultural context from which they are emerging; nevertheless, they remain at a very high level of abstraction and need to be translated into political theoretical concepts that can be operationalized. How do we integrate reason into general understanding of religion? How do we operationalize freedom as prior condition to faith and government? How do we deal with the existing corpus of Islamic law that is not easily amenable to criticism that will circumscribe its scope and the power of those who wield it? Democracy is not just freedom from the tyranny of political power but also the tyranny of traditional authority. How do we deconstruct the stifling effect of 'shari'a-obsessive Islam' on reason?

Conclusion

In the discussion thus far, we have reflected on the prospects of an Islamic democratic theory in the context of three genres of discourse – theological, jurisprudential and philosophical. My conclusions are that while theological understanding is necessary but not sufficient, philosophical illumination is the answer but needs much more development, and jurisprudence is a challenge rather than an ally of Islamic democratic theory. In this chapter my goal was to underscore the importance of political philosophy and theory. I am afraid that quick-fix solutions as being attempted in Afghanistan and Iraq will not give birth to an authentic Islamic democracy. Neither will the mere reinterpretation of Islam by emphasizing those elements that facilitate and marginalizing those that subvert democracy produce the necessary result.

The barriers to democracy in the Muslim world are both ideational and material. While political activism and even revolutionary change may become necessary to establish democracy, Islamic democratic theory must precede political change in order to remove ideational barriers first. If an authentic Islamic democracy has to emerge, then it must first become an aspiration in Muslim minds and must dominate their discourse. Then, once the idea exists, the form can follow. This is the challenge for Islamic political theory.

Notes

1 While political theory debates involving the democratic elements of Islam became marginal in the Muslim world as the Islamism–Secularism debate occupied center stage, the debate between radical and moderate Muslims continued over the nature of an Islamic polity.
2 For a long time now the West in general and the US in particular have been advocating the Turkish experience as a desired model for democracy in the Muslim world. Turkey's membership of the North Atlantic Treaty Organization (NATO), its close alliance with Israel and its radical secularism that has often used undemocratic means to marginalize Islam from the public sphere, was the preferred alternative to the Iranian or Pakistani style of Islamic state. For Islamists the Islamic Revolution of Iran was a major inspiration and they hoped that similar revolutions in key Muslim states, such as Saudi Arabia, Pakistan, Egypt and Algeria, would duplicate the Shi'a miracle in the Sunni world.
3 While there are several instances when President Bush asserted the compatibility of Islam and democracy, the most outstanding occasion was at the National Endowment for Democracy on 3 November 2003. He asserted that '[a] religion that demands individual moral accountability, and encourages the encounter of the individual with God, is fully compatible with the rights and responsibilities of self-government'.
4 Abdul Karim Soroush, a contemporary Iranian philosopher and political theorist, attempts to answer some of these questions. See Soroush 2000.
5 I am not alone in making this argument about the dominance of legal thought. Fazlur Rahman (1966: 100–16) anticipates it in his analysis of Islamic legal thought and the development of the shari'a.
6 For a review of the ideas of Islamic liberalism as pertaining to democracy, see Kurzman 1998. See also the special issue of *Journal of Democracy* (2003, vol. 14 no. 2) on the theme of liberal Islam.
7 An authentic (*sahih*) tradition of Prophet Muhammad reported in *al Tirmidhi* (4/2167). Also reported in *Hakim* (1/116).

8 My discussion and criticism of Khaled Abou El Fadl's work relies primarily on my response to his article *Islam and the Challenge of Democracy* (2003).

9 See Soroush 2000: 88–104.

References

Abou El Fadl, K. (2003) *Islam and the challenge of democracy*, The Boston Review: A Political and Literary Forum.

Choudhury, G.W. (1969) *Constitutional development in Pakistan*, Vancouver, University of British Columbia, Publications Center.

Diamond, L., Plattner, M. and Brumberg, D. (eds) (2003) *Islam and democracy in the Middle East*, Washington, DC, National Endowment for Democracy.

Engineer, A.A. (1996) *The Islamic state*, New Delhi, Vikas Publishing House.

Esposito, J.L. (ed.) (1990) *The Iranian revolution and its global impact*, Miami, FL, International University Press.

—— (ed.) (2003) *The Oxford Dictionary of Islam*, New York, Oxford University Press.

Esposito, J.L. and Voll, J.O. (1996) *Islam and democracy*, New York, Oxford University Press.

Feldman, N. (2003) *After jihad: America and the struggle for Islamic democracy*, New York, Straus and Giroux.

Hayes, L.D. (1984) *Politics in Pakistan: the struggle for legitimacy*, Colorado, Westview Press.

Khan, M.M.A. (1999) 'Reason and personal reasoning', *American Journal of Islamic Social Sciences* vol. 16, no. 3: v–xi.

—— (2001a) 'The political philosophy of Islamic resurgence', *Cultural Dynamics* vol. 13, no. 2: 213–31.

—— (2001b) *The compact of Medina: a constitutional theory of the Islamic state*, available at www.Ijtihad.org/compact.htm (accessed 10 March 2011).

—— (2002) *American Muslims: bridging faith and freedom*, Maryland, Amana Publications.

—— (2003a) 'Prospects for democracy in the Muslim world: the role of US policy', *Middle East Policy Journal* vol. 10, no. 3: 79–89.

—— (2003b) *The priority of politics: a response to Islam and the challenge of democracy*, The Boston Review: A Political and Literary Forum.

—— (2004) 'The Islamic states', in *Routledge Encyclopedia of Political Science*, London, Routledge.

Khan, Q. (1982) *The political thought of Ibn Taymiyyah*, Delhi, Adam Publishers.

Kurzman, C. (ed.) (1998) *Liberal Islam: a source book*, New York, Oxford University Press.

Lapidus, I. (1988) *A history of Islamic societies*, New York, Cambridge University Press.

Mahdi, M. (1987) 'Al Farabi', in L. Strauss and J. Cropsey (eds), *History of political philosophy*, University of Chicago Press, Chicago.

—— (2001) *Al Farabi and the foundation of Islamic political philosophy*, Chicago, IL, University of Chicago Press.

Mahmood, S. (2003) *Questioning liberalism, too: a response to 'Islam and the challenge of democracy'*, The Boston Review: A Political and Literary Forum.

Martin, V. (2000) *Creating an Islamic state: Khoemeni and the making of a new Iran*, London, I.B. Taurus.

Martinovich, S. (2003) 'Islam and democracy – not an impossible marriage', *The Christian Science Monitor*, 8 May, available at www.csmonitor.com/2003/0508/p18s01-bogn.html (accessed 10 March 2011).

Maududi, A.A.S. (1955) *Islamic law and constitution*, Lahore, Islamic Publishers.

Moaddel, M. and Talattof, K. (2000) *Contemporary debates in Islam: an anthology of modernist and fundamentalist thought*, New York, St Martin's Press.

Moussalli, A.S. (1999) *Moderate and radical Islamic fundamentalism: the quest for modernity, legitimacy and the Islamic state*, Gainesville, The University Press of Florida.

Rahman, F. (1966) *Islam*, Chicago, IL, University of Chicago Press.

Sachedina, A. (2001) *The Islamic roots of democratic pluralism*, New York, Oxford University Press.

Soroush, A.K. (2000) 'Tolerance and governance: a discourse on religion and democracy', in M. Sadri and S. Sadri (trans. and ed.), *Reason, freedom and democracy in Islam: essential writings of Abdul Karim Soroush*, New York, Oxford University Press.

Taspinar, O. (2003) 'An uneven fit? The "Turkish model" and the Arab world', *Brookings Analysis Paper*, Washington, DC, Brookings Institution.

4

Modernity and Islamic religious consciousness

Raja Bahlul

According to Jürgen Habermas, religious consciousness (in the West) has been undergoing a process of modernization since the Reformation and Enlightenment. This modernization has been taking place in response to challenges which include encounters with a plurality of religions and other worldviews, the emergence of modern science, and the spread of positive law and secular morality. These challenges have motivated efforts to re-conceive the relation between secular and religious knowledge, as well as efforts to relate religion to other worldviews, and to uncover human and universal aspects implicit in religion (Habermas 2006: 13–14).

Given that Arab/Muslim societies have been undergoing modernization for more than a century and half, partly as a result of their colonial experience and subsequent integration in a Western-dominated world economy, and partly as a result of internally driven efforts at reform, the question naturally arises as to whether religious consciousness in these societies has also been undergoing modernization.[1]

This question has been answered many times, even if the answer has not always been the same. Thus fundamentalist movements, with their radical old-fashioned ideas about society, have been called 'anti-modern' (Ayubi 1991: 231), but their forms of mobilization and motivations have sometimes been viewed as 'modern' (Habermas 1996: 271; Azmeh 1993: 85). Modernity has also been attributed to 'modern' Islamic thinkers such as Muhammad Abduh and Jamal al-Din al-Afghani, Qasim Amin and Ali 'Abd al-Raziq at the beginning of the twentieth century. It continues to be attributed to many more thinkers and Islamic modes of thought at present.

Discussions of religion and modernity in the West and in Arab/Muslim countries reveal many differences in the nature, purpose and scope of the discussion. This is only to be expected, for in the West such discussions are framed in the context of a relatively long tradition of secularism, whereas in Islamic countries the issue of secularism is far from resolved. Then there are also differences in religion: Christianity differs from Islam in its history, doctrine and, consequently, the inflections that it was able to take – the role that it eventually came to accept in the political life of modern Western societies.[2] Finally, there is the fact of modernity itself, original in the West but at best a recent export to or a violent imposition on much of the Muslim world.[3]

Yet beneath the layer of admittedly important differences, the questions, options, demands, expectations and tensions that modern (secular) and religious citizens and societies face remain basically the same. In what follows I want to explore some of the issues, focusing on what may be called 'political modernity': that is, modernity in its political aspect.

Modernity, of course, is a multi-faceted historical process which manifests itself not only in politics, but in the economy, science, philosophy, education, social organization, law and culture, and many other areas as well. There is a reason for my choice of focus, however: I accept Rawls' argument that the values of the political domain have supremacy over other values. Political values such as right(s), justice, equality, freedom and others have a large-scale effect in that they govern the basic framework of social life (Rawls 1993: 139). Not only that, but political power (as 'the coercive power of free and equal citizens as a corporate body' (Rawls 1993: 139)) is more far-reaching and final than any other power that can be exercised by society. There is no escape from the power of the state, which, in Weber's famous statement, is 'that human community which (successfully) lays claim to the *monopoly of legitimate physical force*' (Lassman and Speirs 1994: 310). Because the political domain stands to have a determining effect on other domains, and because of the far-reaching consequences of political power, it can be claimed that the political dimension of modernity deserves to frame the discussion of religion in modern times.

A suitable starting point which leads directly to the issues we want to discuss here is provided by a remarkable conceptual affinity, a meeting of minds, if you will, between two well-known political philosophies embedded in Western and in recent Islamic tradition: political liberalism and liberal Islamism. Both may be viewed as instances of modern political thinking, as well as reflection on religion in the context of modernity.

Political liberalism is mainly associated with the name of John Rawls. It is a fairly well-defined doctrine, considering that it has been championed by a major political thinker who has engaged in extended dialogues with many critics and supporters. The same cannot be said for liberal Islamism, which subsumes many Islamic thinkers. Nevertheless, the idea of liberal Islamism has some currency, as evidenced by the titles of two important publications, namely those of Leonard Binder (1988) and Charles Kurzman (1998). The term *has* (or can be given) definite content, as we will do in due course.

Political liberalism and religion

Political liberalism is the answer to an important question that makes sense only in the context of modernity: 'how is it possible for there to exist over time a just and stable society of free and equal citizens, who remain profoundly divided by reasonable religious philosophical, and moral doctrines?' (Rawls 1993: 4). This is a particularly 'modern' question in that it views religion (along with moral and philosophical theories) as a set of beliefs, or 'doctrines' as Rawls says. Religion is not regarded as a 'science', nor is it viewed as a way in which an entire life-world may be structured. It is merely 'religious belief' or 'opinion'. According to Talal Asad, this way of viewing religion first established itself in the seventeenth and eighteenth centuries, when 'religion was forcibly defined as belief' to be viewed as a personal matter of private life (Asad 1993: 205).

Political liberalism is a set of ideas and principles based on the rights and liberties familiar in contemporary constitutional democratic regimes (Rawls 1993: 223).[4] It should be, according to Rawls, an object of consensus among the citizens who make up society, with each 'reasonable' religious, philosophical or moral doctrine endorsing this political conception from its point of view (Rawls 1993: 134). Thus political liberalism is to be seen as a non-sectarian position. In fact, the main point of this view lies in its supposed neutrality:

For rather than confronting religious and non-liberal doctrines with comprehensive liberal philosophical doctrine, the thought is to formulate a liberal political conception that those non-liberal doctrines might be able to endorse.

(Rawls 1993: xlvii)

Given this claim of neutrality, it is interesting to see the manner in which religious citizens are allowed to express themselves in public discussions. According to Rawls, when one engages in public discussions over essential constitutional matters and basic justice in society, one is not permitted to invoke reasons and arguments that have their foundations in one's religious doctrine. There is room for the exchange of reasons only within 'a conception that expresses political values that others as free and equal also might reasonably be expected […] to endorse' (Rawls 1993: l). This, of course, excludes religious reasons which non-religious citizens cannot be expected to endorse.

Other authors, writing in a more or less liberal vein, advocate a harder or softer line than we find in Rawls. Audi, for example, requires that a public (non-religious) reason must have such a motivational power that 'one would act on it even if, other things remaining equal, one's other reasons were eliminated' (Audi 1997: 29). Habermas, on the other hand, believes that the secular state 'has an interest in not reducing the polyphonic complexity of public voices, so as not to cut itself off from key resources for the creation of identity and meaning' (Habermas 1996: 10). Secular citizens have a duty to listen patiently and help in the translation of religious language into a language that is accessible to all. Still, Habermas does not allow non-secular reasons to operate beyond a certain point. Says Habermas, 'Every citizen must know and accept that only secular reasons count beyond the institutional threshold that divides the informal public sphere from parliaments, courts, ministries and administrations' (Habermas 1996: 9).

It is evident that liberal writers assume that religious citizens must be prepared to translate their religiously grounded positions into a secular, public language with which secular citizens can critically engage, but how is this to be accomplished? According to Audi, religious citizens should dwell on the basic ethical-humanistic message of religion, instead of the metaphysical foundations of religious morality. This is not a hard or an unfair demand, because of the 'overlap between religiously and secularly grounded obligations in the Hebraic-Christian tradition' (and the Islamic tradition, too, one should add) (Audi 1997: 13). The idea here (which has been championed by Audi and others) is that the all-knowing and all-good God of the Abrahamic faiths would structure our minds and our world so that we are able to use our reason to arrive at the ideas and principles needed to organize our social-political life in a way that accords with divine will.

Liberal Islamism

Thinkers to be viewed as 'liberal Islamists' here all share attributes that have been used to describe a larger class of Islamic 'modernists' or 'reformists': attributes such as perceiving Islam in terms of 'openness' and 'dynamism' (Stowasser 1993: 3); interpreting Islam creatively (Azmeh 1993: 33); preference of *ijtihad* (independent interpretation) over *taqlid* (tradition-following) (Kurzman 1998: 8); and 'reinterpret[ing] Islamic concepts so as to make them equivalent to the guiding principles of European Thought' (Hourani 1962: 344).

However, such descriptions are with some justice applicable to many thinkers who differ significantly from one another. Not all Islamic modernists are equally modern, nor are they all *very* modern to begin with; in fact, some of them advocate ideas that are fairly close to being fundamentalist. For these reasons it matters much to say precisely who the liberal Islamists are and what distinguishes them from others.

A good way to get to know what liberal Islamists stand for is to dwell on the views of other, somewhat moderate thinkers who cannot without hesitation be called liberal. Take Turabi, Ghannouchi and Khatami, for example. These writers are well known for their advocacy of peaceful Islamic engagement in politics. They can be viewed as 'democrats' in some sense, because to them popular consent is necessary for political legitimacy. According to Khatami:

> popular will [is] a main condition for the establishment and durability of the state [...] I can imagine a state being established contrary to popular will and desire, but I find it difficult to imagine its being a stable and durable state [...] It is not possible for an Islamic state to come to being, nor can an Islamic state last regardless of the people and what they choose [...] Besides, nobody can choose a non-democratic path without having recourse to the use of force. There is simply no third way; those who reject the path of democracy are calling for dictatorship and coercion.
>
> *(Khatami 1998: 86, 99)*

Ghannouchi expresses his belief in democracy by saying that:

> it is possible for the mechanisms of democracy [...] to operate in different cultural milieus [... Democracy] resolves itself into popular sovereignty, equality between citizens, governing bodies which emerge from popular will through free elections, [...] recognition of the majority's right to rule [...] There is nothing in these procedures which is necessarily in conflict with Islamic values.
>
> *(Ghannouchi 1993: 88)*

Finally, Turabi is not far behind with his belief that:

> Islamic jurisprudence has known the essence of democracy, or government by the people, since the day Muslims believed in the One God, [...] knowing that they are equal in worshipping Him, and that they are His vice-regents on earth.
>
> *(Turabi 1987: 42)*

Nevertheless, these thinkers are able to offer justifications for privileging Islam in the matter of lawmaking and methods of governing. Turabi explicitly says that 'popular sovereignty does not mean that people have absolute power. Power is limited by commitment to shari'a' (Turabi 1987: 66). Elsewhere he reassuringly says that the power of *government* is limited by shari'a, only to add that nobody is exempt from the power of shari'a: 'The legislature, the Congress, or Parliament or whatever, is not sovereign at all. The shar'ia governs so much' (Lowrie 1993: 25). Ghannouchi is no less explicit. According to him, 'the legitimate sphere of people's sovereignty cannot go beyond God's law as stated in the Qur'an and the Sunna' (Ghannouchi 1993: 109). Nor does democracy fare much better with Khatami. Pressed (in an interview) to say whether 'religiously different' persons can reach high decision-making positions in an Islamic state, Khatami wavers at length. In the end he says vaguely that in the Islamic state, 'religion defines the conditions and background circumstances', that 'if people modify the constitution by allowing the religiously different to reach supreme decision-making position then this is a different matter' (Khatami 1998: 105ff).[5]

There are also difficulties with regard to positions taken by 'moderate' thinkers on matters of gender equality and equal citizenship. Many of them are unable to acknowledge women's right to assume positions of leadership in society or the idea of political equality regardless of faith.

There are also limits on permissible pluralism: it has to be pluralism within a broadly Islamic framework of ideas, where opinions can diverge between an Islamically defined 'extreme conservatism' and an Islamically defined 'extreme modernism'. The gamut is hardly convincing, to judge from the examples given by Qaradawi: an 'extreme conservative' might advocate the view that non-Muslims should pay *jizyah* (poll tax) even in wartime, whereas an 'extreme modernist' may advocate the view that leaders should be elected by popular vote (Qaradawi 1993: 637–38; other examples can be found in Ghannouchi 1993: 295; Turabi 1987: 67–68).

Because Turabi, Ghannouchi, Khatami and many others like them seek to Islamize democracy, because they advocate peaceful engagement in politics, and because they gradually learned to distance themselves from militant Islamic movements and ideologies – for all these reasons it may be unfair to classify them with the fundamentalists. Still, many analysts continue to have doubts about their intentions and final aim, believing that their advocacy of democracy is purely instrumental (opportunistic), and that no sharp line separates them from the fundamentalists (Azmeh 1994: 127; Brown *et al.* 2006: 4; Denoeux 2002: 72–78).

However, if thinkers such as Khatami, Turabi and Ghannouchi are not to be viewed as 'liberal', who can be? What does one have to believe in to be counted a liberal Islamist? According to Kurzman, a liberal Islamist is 'liberal in some sense of the word (in particular, those who express opposition to Islamic revivalism)', and 'Islamic in some sense of the word (those who believe that Islam has an important role in the contemporary world, as opposed to secularists)' (Kurzman 1998: 18). While it is difficult to disagree with the second part of the characterization, the first part is hardly satisfactory. It is a purely negative definition which many non-liberal Islamists easily satisfy; after all, opposition to Islamic revivalism, especially its militant varieties, is widespread.

In situations of unresolved terminological ambiguity, often the best way to make progress is to introduce an element of stipulation, which simply means saying that by such and such a term one chooses to understand such and such. Stipulation is not the same as arbitrariness or sheer willfulness of usage. One stipulates to delineate boundaries beyond which dispute is, for certain purposes, fruitless or time-wasting.

Taking as our starting point the fact that 'liberal Islamists' tend to be more advanced in their advocacy of democracy, pluralism and the need to draw boundaries between religion and politics than any of the writers mentioned above, we stipulate that a liberal Islamist is someone who accepts the following three ideas. Thus we view liberal Islamism as an 'ideal type' which can be exemplified in varying degrees of clarity and completeness.

First, the idea of *differentiation*. Stepan calls this 'the Twin Tolerations', which means that 'religious institutions should not have constitutionally privileged prerogatives that allow them to mandate public policy to democratically elected governments. At the same time, individuals and religious communities […] must have complete freedom to worship privately' (Stepan 2005: 5).

Second, the idea of *constitutionalism*. The writer must accept a plausible version of human rights, together with recognition that human rights principles prevail over any shari'a laws in cases of conflict.[6]

Last, the idea of *democracy*. This is the idea of equal and inclusive citizenship, so that neither gender nor religion nor ethnicity is politically relevant.

To these we can add two more ideas which may be viewed as direct or indirect consequences of differentiation, constitutionalism and democracy. (1) On the *individual* level, Islam is to be understood in terms of personal religious observance and individual piety and spiritual life. (2) On the social level, Islam is to be understood in terms of universal ethical principles that can give direction to social and government policies, but only through peaceful participation in politics.

The ideas that we take here to be definitive of liberal Islamism are closely related to each other. Democracy, inasmuch as it can be viewed as the institutionalization of the ideas of equality and liberty, is already implicit in the idea of human rights. The idea of human rights, it may be argued, requires a situation of differentiation between the political and the religious. For there may be no way for securing equality and liberty and other human rights values under conditions where religious faith has political consequences.

Still, despite conceptual connections, it need not be the case that all ideas that make up liberal Islamism are equally developed in all the writers who may be claimed for liberal Islam. In view of this, the best way to get a measure of liberal Islamism in the concrete is to dwell on basic liberal ideas advocated by different writers. Only in this way can one appreciate the unqualified acceptance of liberal ideas, something which is missing in many modern but non-liberal writers of greater fame.

The first, and probably best-known, writer who deserves to be mentioned, is Ali 'Abd al-Raziq. To him Islam is a religion – ideas and values, but not a political program, nor a blueprint for building a state.

> Islam is a religious call to God and is a school of thought, among many such schools which seek to reform a certain type of people, guiding them to what will render them closer to God […] and opening up the path to everlasting happiness.
>
> *('Abd al-Raziq 1998: 34)*

To prove this, 'Abd al-Raziq uses different methods, ranging from novel interpretations (or reinterpretations) of Qur'anic texts, to drawing implications from past historical practices, to using purely rational considerations. Regardless of their strength and validity, 'Abd al-Raziq's arguments serve to draw boundaries between religion and politics in a clear and unequivocal way. His proposal to view Islam as one school of thought among others is bound to be congenial for a political liberal like John Rawls, who is anxious to make peace among the different competing 'reasonable doctrines' which (he hopes) will accept political liberalism 'each from its point of view'.

Another writer, Abdullahi an-Naim, in effect calls for the abrogation of the historical shari'a and its replacement by one that is based on the ethical-humanistic message contained in the earlier Qur'anic revelation (prior to the establishment of the first Islamic polity in Medina in 622 AD). This earlier message of Islam, argues an-Naim, is fully compatible with the modern notions of human rights and inclusive, non-discriminative citizenship (an-Naim 1990: 179).

Fazlur Rahman offers a criterion of *Islamicity* which requires a *holistic interpretation* of the Qur'an and the Prophetic Sunna. To him, 'a doctrine or an institution is genuinely Islamic to the extent that it flows from the *total* teaching of the Qur'an and the Sunna' (Rahman 1982: 22, emphasis added). Given that the totality of Islamic teachings aims at the establishment of a 'community of justice and goodness' (Rahman 1982: 13), granting authority only to holistic interpretations has the effect of a license to re-construe all legal enactments that are inconsistent with these aims, including probably all currently controversial shari'a laws. Rahman clearly distinguishes between legal enactments and moral principles. He regards the latter as having a more authoritative status, because, in his view, the Qur'an is not to be conceived of as a law book, but as a religious source of law (Rahman 1980: 47).

Khalid Abou el-Fadl gives traditionally interpreted shari'a its due by saying that its endorsement of the ideas of the rule of law and limited government signifies its acceptance of 'core elements of modern democratic practice', but this is not enough. Abou el-Fadl insists on unqualified acceptance of popular sovereignty:

> Democracy's moral power lies in the idea that the citizens of a nation are sovereign, [...] and they express their sovereign will by electing representatives. In a democracy, the people are the source of the law, and the law in turn ensures the fundamental rights that protect the well-being and interests of the individual members of the sovereignty.
>
> *(Abou el-Fadl 2004: 4)*

To Abou el-Fadl shari'a should not be viewed as particular, historically conditioned legal enactments; rather, it should be understood in terms of divine intentions, and principles of divine mercy and justice. 'It ought to stand in an Islamic polity as a symbolic construct for the divine perfection that is unreachable by human effort' (Abou el-Fadl 2004: 22, 33).

The distinction between divine and non-divine aspects of religion is also made by 'Abdul-Karim Soroush. 'Religion is divine,' writes Soroush, 'but its interpretation is thoroughly human and this-worldly' (Soroush 1998: 246). He reaches this conclusion via a Kantian understanding of knowledge, and a post-positivistic philosophy of science:

> the [religious] text does not stand alone, it does not carry its own meaning on its shoulders, its interpretation is in flux, and presuppositions are actively at work here and elsewhere in the field of understanding[...] These assumptions can be of very different nature, ranging from philosophical, historical, and theological to the more specific assumptions such as linguistic and sociological ones.
>
> *(Soroush 1998: 245)*

Consequently, Soroush (like other liberal Islamists) is led to distinguish between moral principles (and divine intentions) and earthly interpretations that go 'through the reason of the age' (Soroush 1998: 251). This distinction, in liberal Islamist hands, is used to bring Islam into conformity with contemporary liberal ideas about politics and social life.

An indication of how far liberal Islamism is willing to go in the direction of privatizing religion can be obtained from this seemingly naïve and simple admission to be found in Mohammad Talbi. According to this author:

> it is possible for a Muslim to live content in his Islam and to live a full Islamic life in London, for example, where the government is in the hands of Mrs. Thatcher. This government would never prevent the Muslim living an excellent and satisfying Islamic life, while the Muslim in another system which claimed to be an Islamic order, might be suppressed and subjugated.
>
> *(Talbi 1992: 101)*

As a corrective to this, however, it should be emphasized that liberal Islamists do not generally advocate a withdrawal into private life, a closing of the door on public life and political involvement. According to Fazlur Rahman the ultimate goal of the Islamic faith is the establishment of an 'ethically-based socio-economic order' (Rahman 1982: 13), something which can hardly be done without involvement in politics. What makes such Islamic advocacy liberal is the fact that the advocates are willing to accept pluralism and democratic methods of work.

Estimate of liberal Islamism

Liberal Islamism fits Rawls' description of 'the reasonable doctrines [which] endorse the political conception, each from its point of view' (Rawls 1993: 134). This fact invites many questions.

Does liberal Islamism represent religious consciousness in any meaningful sense of the term? Does it represent a modern understanding of Islam, or an Islamic version of modernity? How satisfactory is it? Finally, a question about the questions themselves: can they be answered objectively?

Many writers would say that the modernization of religious consciousness that is represented by liberal Islamism is not genuine intellectual accomplishment, but rather a work of 'epistemological legerdemain', in Azmeh's expressive terms (Azmeh 1993: 33). The reasons by no means constitute a conclusive argument, but it is instructive to look at some of them.

Some critics charge that liberal Islamists willfully ignore texts that contradict their understanding of Islam. Such is the view of Fahmi Jadaane who claims that 'Abd al-Raziq's attempt to present Islam as a spiritual, non-political faith ignores a multitude of Qur'anic texts and Prophetic practices that are all patently political in nature, such as the collection of taxes, the conduct of relations with other nations, the waging of war and the conclusion of peace treaties (Jadaane 1981: 342).

However, while this may occasionally be true, liberal Islamists cannot be accused as a group of being unaware of religious texts that seem to contradict their understanding of Islam. This is precisely why they engage in work of interpretation, their aim being to show that the problematic texts need mean what they seem to mean. This is why texts that seem to accept slavery, discrimination against women or inhumane punishments, in addition to 'political texts', have become standard hermeneutical exercises for liberal and modern Islamists.

This, however, is not the end of the story, for liberal interpretations of Islam – in fact, liberal interpretations of religion in general – have been subjected to many criticisms. Critics claim that modernist interpretations of religion involve taking many liberties with the 'original' meaning of the texts, the way texts were understood and practiced by the founders. Such is the view of Earnest Gellner whose estimate of modernist interpretations of religion in general can be applied to liberal Islamism in particular. In such 'softened modernist re-interpretations' of religion, says Gellner, 'the doctrines and the moral demands of the faith are […] turned into something which, properly interpreted, is in astonishingly little conflict with the secular wisdom of the age, or indeed with anything. This way lies peace – and doctrinal vacuity' (Gellner 1992: 4). Taking Christianity as his example, Gellner has the modernist interpreter saying – quite implausibly, of course – that 'the founder of the dominant Western faith had to use simple language because if he talked modern philosophy they would not have understood him. But he really meant the latest philosophic fashion' (Gellner 1993: 40).

In addition to taking great liberties with the meanings and intention of God and the founders, liberal interpretations of religion are also charged with greatly weakening (if not obliterating) distinctions between religions, between Islam and other religions, in particular. In his critique of fundamentalism 'Adel Dhaher expresses 'the doctrinal essence of Islam' briefly as 'believing in the unity of God, the perfection of morals, the establishment of justice and equality between people' (Dhaher 1993: 331). If this is what Islam reduces to, as Dhaher invites the reader to believe, doesn't this obliterate the distinction between Judaism, Christianity and Islam? For all these faiths have the same or a very similar doctrinal essence.

Finally, some critics question the very philosophical motives that lie behind liberalism in religion, something that must apply to liberal Islamism as well. This type of criticism can be found in Harris, who says that:

> The only reason anyone is 'moderate' in matters of faith these days is that he has assimilated some of the fruits of the last two thousand years of human thought. The doors leading out of scriptural literalism do not open from the *inside*. The moderation we see among

non-fundamentalists is not some sign that faith itself has evolved; it is, rather, the product of many hammer blows of modernism that have exposed certain tenet of faith to doubt.

(Harris 2004: 19)

Above and beyond these particular criticisms one may think that liberal Islamism does not in general represent an Islamic political modernity, but is an outright endorsement of a Western liberal conception of politics. One can see how much liberal Islamism seems to favor liberalism over Islam by looking at the demands that liberalism makes on religion, demands to which liberal Islamism accedes, but which are not reciprocal.

Here we need to recall Habermas' imperative for religious citizens to 'convincingly connect the egalitarian individualism and universalism of modern law and morality with the premises of their comprehensive doctrines' (Habermas 2006: 14), as well as Rawls' ideal of public reason which requires citizens to argue only in ways that other citizens as free and equal can be expected to accept (Rawls 1993: l). In response to such demands, liberal Islamism calls for the privatization of Islam, and the differentiation between the political and the religious in ways that can neither be read off the main Islamic religious texts, nor have been practiced before. The extent of the 'surrender' that liberalized religion makes on this score has been persuasively expressed by Wolterstorff. He speaks for many religious citizens when he criticizes Rawls for thinking that:

> though religious people may not be in the *habit* of dividing their lives into a religious component and a non-religious component, and though some might not be *happy* doing so, nonetheless, their doing so would in no case be in violation of their religion. But [Rawls] is wrong about this. It is when we bring into the picture people for whom it is a matter of religious conviction that they ought to strive for a religiously integrated existence – then especially, though not only then, does the unfairness of the liberal position to religion come to light.

(Wolterstorff 1997: 116)

Having said all of this against liberal Islamism, let us see what can be said in its defense. First, consider the charge of taking great liberties with religious texts, to the extent of making them mean something that they do not really mean. To say that liberal Islamists take liberties with texts presupposes the existence of an original and true meaning that is better, more accurately understood by fundamentalists and other non-liberals. The objection assumes that Islamists cannot speak the language of public reason; that is, revelation is not mirrored by reason, that there is no way to Islamically justify a differentiation between faith and politics. Or, to sum it all up, the objector assumes that one cannot lead a religiously integrated existence without being opposed to modernity.

The disagreement between liberals and fundamentalists can without undue simplification be reduced to disagreement over answers to these basic questions: What does it take for one to be a Muslim? What is it for a society to abide by Islamic teachings? Different answers to these questions can yield different definitions of 'true' meaning and, consequently, different answers to the question about 'taking liberties' with texts.

Liberals (modernists) and fundamentalists approach these questions differently. Emphasis on revelation vs. emphasis on reason, adherence to the letter of the scripture vs. adhering to its spirit, reading revelations in context vs. viewing revelation ahistorically – all these distinctions have been called upon to explain the different approaches used by Islamists to answer major social and political questions. To these we can add a fourth distinction which puts us on a track to answer questions about the meaning of 'Muslim' and 'Islamic'. It is a distinction between *essential* and *non-essential* aspects of the faith.

In saying this, one can hardly escape the suspicion of entertaining an 'essentializing view of Islam', a charge that is usually directed against those who say that Islamic ideas and practices never really change or undergo development. This is not what we have in mind when we talk about essential and non-essential aspects of the faith. The distinction we have in mind is closer to the old philosophical distinction between 'essence' and 'accident', the same distinction we use when we say, for example, that man is 'essentially rational', but only accidentally white or black.[7] It is a distinction between features that really matter for the continued existence and identity of something, as opposed to those with respect to which something can change without loss of existence or identity. Far from presupposing that Muslims and Muslim life cannot change, it is precisely because Muslims and Muslim life can change that it makes sense to speak of what is essential and what is not.

Now instead of viewing texts in terms of what is (in one good use of the word) *fundamental* and what is *not*, fundamentalists and non-liberals tend to view texts as a conglomerate of equally important items. For example, many of them will agree with liberals that the basic message of the Qur'an with respect to women is progressive and liberating. They will cite verses that emphasize equality in the sight of God, how Islam granted women rights that they did not have in pre-Islamic times, and many similar arguments to this effect. When it is pointed out that there are Qur'anic verses that seem to discriminate against women, liberal Islamists find a way to suspend judgments contained in such verses, because they do not view all texts as being equally *fundamental*. Not so for fundamentalists: to them each stone in the Qur'anic edifice is a cornerstone, so that its removal threatens the whole edifice with collapse. This is why they will fight battles over such matters as the prohibition of foods and drinks, or modest dress. This represents a reduction of Islam to equally important elements, equating the general with the particular, the absolute with the conditional, the context-free with the context-dependent.

Of course, viewing matters in terms of what is essential and what is not *does* involve value judgments. At some point or other one must face the question of what is more important: the essential message of justice, goodness and mercy that Islam embodies, or the particular laws revealed and applied at particular times, and in particular situations that no longer obtain? Are they equally important from an Islamic point of view? What does God really care for? Does He care more for our living up to the values of goodness and justice, or is He more concerned about the style of a woman's dress? Are these equally important in the divine scheme of things? Depending on one's answer to these questions, one can take a position over interpreting or reinterpreting texts, how literal one can be, even what it means for something to be truly 'the word of God'.

Of course, it cannot be denied that much of the earlier history of religion is a history of fanaticism, conservatism and opposition to reason and science, but the validity of the liberal understanding of religion, Islam included, is not impugned by this fact. Critics who object to liberal Islamism on the ground of taking liberties with texts seem to assume that earlier generations have an epistemologically privileged understanding of religion because they are temporally closer to the point of origin. As a corollary of this assumption it is then thought that if the earlier generations were inspired to be fanatical, or conservative, or misogynist, then this is what religion really implies, that any softened interpretation of religion must be a willful deviation, or an unwilling concession to modernity.

These assumptions may be justified on a purely *naturalistic* understanding of religion, where one says that religion is a human invention. One could then say: this is what *the inventors* meant, and we have no right to replace their meaning by ours, using their words. On a *religious* view of religion, however, God is not closer to the earlier generations than He is to ours, nor need He favor their interpretation over ours. Hence the fact that their understanding of religion led them to intolerance, the fact that it was only under the hammer blows of modernity that people learned to moderate their views – none of this impugns the validity of a modern understanding of religion. Drawing conclusions about validity of a liberal interpretation on the basis of the illiberal history from which it evolved comes close to committing the genetic fallacy. To impugn the validity of a position on the basis of the morally inadmissible motives that may lie behind it is a more or less straightforward instance of yet another fallacy – *argumentum ad hominem*.

None of this proves that liberal Islamism is true. At most it shows that it is a credible view. More than this is rarely achieved in the realm of philosophical and moral discussions, but it may be possible to provide additional strength by dwelling on questions of viability and desirability, and this we can do by comparing the modernizing moves of liberal Islamists with similar moves that have been underway in other faiths. Comparisons of history and intellectual content may show that Islamic religious consciousness is (or can be) travelling down a well-trodden path, a path that has been taken by others before. They can also reveal lessons to be learned and arguments to be examined. This is bound to make the case for liberal Islamism stronger.

Comparisons

Liberal Islamists are not unique in their belief that religion is not opposed to democracy, human rights or life in the modern world in general. Turabi's statement, to the effect that democracy is underpinned by the Muslim belief in equality of all worshippers before God, corresponds to Siedentop's claim that 'The assumption that society consists of individuals […] is a translation of the Christian premise of the equality of souls in the eye of God' (Siedentop 1989: 308), an idea that may be taken to justify the individualism implicit in much modern liberal thinking. Fradkin refers to the fundamental place of the notion of liberty in the Jewish faith, as exemplified in the celebration of the Exodus from Egypt. He also refers to the egalitarianism contained in the idea of a Covenant between God and the people, since this idea requires the consent of the governed (Fradkin 2005: 97–100).

Nor is the claim of providing a suitable framework for democracy unique to the three monotheistic faiths, Judaism, Christianity and Islam. Hinduism, which neither worships one unique God nor claims one prophet, can be presented as favoring democracy. Mehta speaks of 'the supple, open, plural quality of Hinduism' as doing just that, despite the fact that 'dominant interpretations of Hinduism have favored caste for long' (Mehta 2005: 59).

The puzzle is not how it is that religious traditions with deep roots in the undemocratic past of mankind still manage to contain democratic meanings. Rather, it is why it took so long for these meanings to be discovered and, more interestingly, why it is that in some societies, but not in others, these meanings have been integrated into political practice.

The latter question is a pressing one for Muslim societies, because in the case of the two sister monotheistic faiths as well as distant Hinduism, it can be argued that religion has managed to strike a fairly stable even if not completely satisfactory compromise with democratic politics. Religious parties exist and there are parties with religious allegiances and/or history. They participate in elections, share power, work by peaceful means for advancing their vision of the good society, and they seem to have come to terms with the existing pluralism in society, with all the tolerance and forbearing that this entails.

Some of the democracy-compliant religions (if one is permitted to use such a term) have a long history of opposition to democratic politics. According to the example discussed in detail by Daniel Philpott, Catholic Christianity in the past opposed not only democracy but the very idea of the sovereign territorial state. In 1832 Pope Gregory XVI condemned the idea of free-dom of conscience as 'absurd and erroneous opinion'. The Catholic Church continued to uphold the doctrine that temporal authorities ought to promote Church prerogatives well into the twentieth century. Not until the 1930s did Church intellectuals begin to offer principled argument for the freedom of religion, and to provide foundations for constitutional democracy. By 1963 the Catholic Church had endorsed human rights, and after the end of the Cold War Pope John Paul II defended democracy as 'the form of government most conducive to justice and the mission of the Church' (Philpott 2005: 104).

The Christian democratic parties that have been active in European political life since World War II should provide an interesting subject of study to Islamists who want to see different models of the relation between religion and politics. When the notion of democracy started to circulate among Catholic intellectuals and Church members, this was accompanied by the rea-lization of the political advantages of democracy: it offered the concept of a totality of political subjects with a large Catholic component that could be mobilized into a political power (Pombeni 2000: 295).

In the case of the contemporary Islamist political movement, there can be hardly any doubt that part of their attraction to democracy and electoral politics is to be explained by reference to the realization that a politically free population with an overwhelmingly Muslim majority offers unprecedented political opportunities. This has been amply proved by the many political successes that Islamist movements have achieved in different parts of the Arab/Muslim world.

There is a major ideological difference between Christian democracy and popular mainstream Islamist political movements that really matter. With the passage of time, Christian democratic movements seem to have learned to express themselves in modern political idiom, drawing on the large repertoire of ideas and theories that have evolved in the West since the time when Christianity and Greco-Roman culture began to interact with each other. Thus when Christians express their political philosophy by emphasizing the values of community, respect for human life and personhood, opposition to materialism and economic disparities (with affinities to socialist critiques of liberal capitalism), they see themselves as at once standing on Christian ground, as well as speaking a language that other people, including the non-religious citizens, can understand. Christian democracy could not have attained a position of non-sectarian appeal without opting for what one writer calls a 'sort of minimal and secularized Christianity' (Pombeni 2000: 299). 'Minimal' is to be understood in terms of emphasis on matters of *essence*, and not on theological doctrine and fine distinctions. 'Secularization' can be taken to mean willingness to justify and argue using secular reasons that can be religiously grounded.

The two steps of 'minimalization' and 'secularization' *have* been taken by the liberal Islamists, who tend to view Islam (minimally) as an ethical-social message, and who are willing to use secular reasoning, believing that the use of 'reason' is sanctioned by revelation. The same cannot be said for popular mainstream Islamist movements. This can be seen in their demand for the constitutional privileging of Islam, the Islamization of laws in ways that hark back to distant times, and only serve to bring out Islamic particularism (e.g. Islamic penalties, laws of personal status).

Will the liberal message of liberal Islamism ever become politically popular? It is true that most Islamic successes in electoral politics have been achieved by less-than-liberal parties, but we may in fact be witnessing the first stages of the popularization of the political message of liberal Islam. Examples are provided by the Moroccan Party for Justice and Development, and the Wasat Party in Egypt (an offshoot of the Muslim Brotherhood), which presents itself as 'a civil party with an Islamic reference point'.[8] The more convincing example comes from Turkey, where Islamic political movements evolved under a regime of secularism for a relatively long time. Parties with a religious orientation in Turkey accept the secular regime with its republican modernizing project and democratic political system. Comparing his Islamic party to Christian democracy, Erdogan has been quoted as saying that 'A political party cannot have a religion, only individuals can. Religion is so supreme that it cannot be politically exploited or taken advantage of' (Altunisik 2005: 50).

More than political success will be needed to make the case for liberal Islamism. A genuine, deep and thoroughgoing engagement with modernity and modern ideas has to take place. This cannot be simply accomplished by singing the songs of political liberalism. Liberal Islamism must learn to criticize modernity, and it must dare to differ.[9] Here it is possible to benefit from the example of the Christian critique of modernity.

Criticism of modernity from a Christian point of view has been going on for a long time. Muslims are late-comers to this enterprise, and they cannot claim to have experienced the full impact of modernity first-hand as its originators did. Still, they can learn many lessons from the Christian encounter with modernity. Probably the most important lesson to be learned is that the outcome of criticizing modernity cannot be a call for a historical reversal, a reversion to pre-modern modes of thought. The contemporary philosopher Charles Taylor, in calling for a 'Catholic modernity', still acknowledges the achievement of modern culture:

> modern culture, in breaking with the structures and beliefs of Christendom, also carried certain facets of Christian life further than they ever were taken or could have been taken within Christendom [...] For instance, modern liberal political culture is characterized by an affirmation of universal human rights – to life, freedom, citizenship, self-realization – which are seen as radically unconditional; that is, they are not dependent on such things as gender, cultural belonging, civilizational development, or religious allegiance, which always limited them in the past.
>
> *(Taylor 1999: 14)*

There are many things that Taylor finds at fault in modernity. Among these is something that he refers to as exclusive humanism, a humanism that is 'based exclusively on a notion of human flourishing'. It is a humanism that believes 'that human life is better off without transcendental vision altogether' (Taylor 1999: 16). This is something that liberal Islamists can understand, for they cannot attribute an *Islamic* character to their endorsement of the values of human freedom, dignity, justice and goodness by confining themselves to reasoning in exclusively secular terms. They can argue, as Taylor does, that exclusive humanism, with its purely secular ideology, is not enough to ground morality in a fundamental way. For such humanism can be, and in fact has been, implicated in much violence, destruction and cruelty. Europeans can offer communism and Nazism as examples of secular ideologies that cut loose from religion only to produce horrid examples of human suffering. Liberal Islamism can point to similar, if less dramatic examples in many parts of the Arab/Muslim world where secular ideologies prevailed for a time.

To find their own voice liberal Islamists must fight not only against exclusive humanism, but also against those who seek to answer exclusive humanism by turning to what may be termed exclusive theism. Exclusive theism is the belief, in effect, that only God exists, that human life is just a series of marginal notes on the existence of God. A belief like this can easily get man to turn his back on this world. The result will then be an ascetic, other-worldly ideal that represents a denial of life.

This is the box into which Christianity was painted by secular modernity, according to Taylor. Consequently, when modernity came along with its 'affirmation of ordinary (i.e. this-worldly) life', this was taken as a rejection of Christianity (a 'denial of transcendence') (Taylor 1999: 25). Liberal Islamists should be encouraged by the fact that it is not possible to portray

Islam in this fashion. Islam's whole-hearted embrace of ordinary life was never in doubt, as attested by the well-known Tradition that says 'Work for this world as if you would live forever. Work for the world to come as if you would die tomorrow.' Islam has no difficulty turning its face towards the world. This means that it can go a longer way towards accepting secular humanism without fear of betraying its essential message.

This is all the more reason for opening to the world with all its secular ideas and doctrines, always with an aim of learning from the truth that they may contain, but never losing sight of the fact that they are not enough to live by. At one point Habermas says that religious utterances 'bear a semantic potential that unleashes an inspiring energy for all of society as soon as they release their profane truth content' (Habermas 2006: 17), and so he urges secular society to listen patiently to the religious voices in it. A similar injunction can be made on behalf of secular voices: believers in religion (liberal Islamist or other) should also listen to secular voices because they, too, 'bear a semantic potential that unleashes an inspiring energy for all of society as soon as they release their *religious* truth content'.

Liberal Islamism, more than any other 'Islamism' that exists today, is well positioned to offer a balanced critique of modernity while being itself modern. It is not an easy task, because the temptation to go 'modern' all the way is there all the time, as is the temptation to turn one's back on modernity completely. It is also difficult because this task cannot be accomplished without profound appreciation of both religion and modernity. However, we have no reason to believe that this is impossible.

Notes

1 For a discussion of this process of modernization with special reference to the secularization that accompanied it see Azmeh 1992.
2 See Brown (2000: ch. 3 and 4), for a thoughtful discussion of politically relevant differences between Christianity and Islam.
3 See Ghalyun (1979) for a discussion of the 'growing pains of secularization' consequent upon the imposition of this process from outside.
4 Rawls' formulation can be summarized thus: (1) Each person is entitled to equal basic rights and liberties compatible with similar rights and liberties of others. (2) Social and economic inequalities (if any) are to attach to positions that are open to all, and they must be of the greatest benefit to the least advantaged members of society (Rawls 1993: 6).
5 The notion of 'divine sovereignty', inherited from Mawdudi (Mawdudi 1975: 20–23), comes up frequently in discussions of the limits that many Islamist thinkers impose on 'popular sovereignty'. The notion seems to boil down to 'rule of law' (as opposed to arbitrary 'rule of men') (Bahlul 2000), but the notion of 'rule of law' does not say much until one knows what sort of law is under discussion.
6 For a detailed discussion of the prospects of accommodating constitutionalism within an Islamic framework of ideas, see Bahlul 2007.
7 The distinction between *essence* and *accident* is mainly associated with Aristotelian philosophy. It is interesting to note that, according to Aristotle, the distinction between *male* and *female* does not make for a distinction in the species (Aristotle 1941: 1058b, 1–6). This can be used to argue that the distinction between male and female is 'accidental', something which is bound to be welcomed by liberal feminists.
8 The Party goes as far as admitting injustices in the treatment of Copts in Egypt, and will accept non-Muslim members (Brown *et al.* 2006: 4).
9 According to Brown, much effort has been invested in justifying Islam to modernity. 'The implicit values of modernity [...] were implicitly taken as the standard against which Islam was to be measured' (Brown 2000: 149).

References

'Abd al-Raziq, A. (1998) 'Message, Not Government, Religion, Not State', in C. Kurzman (ed.), *Liberal Islam: A Sourcebook*, Oxford, Oxford University Press.

Abou el-Fadl, K. (2004) *Islam and the Challenge of Democracy*, Princeton, NJ, Princeton University Press.

Altunisik, M.B. (2005) 'The Turkish Model and Democratization in the Middle East', *Arab Studies Quarterly* vol. 27, no. 1 & 2: 45–61.

An-Na'im, A.A. (1990) *Toward an Islamic Reformation: Civil Liberties, Human Rights, and International Law*, Syracuse, Syracuse University Press.

Aristotle (1941) *The Basic Works of Aristotle*, R. McKeon (ed.), New York, Random House.

Asad, T. (1993) 'The Limits of Religious Criticism in the Middle East: Notes on Islamic Public Argument', in *Genealogies of Religion*, Baltimore, MD, and London, Johns Hopkins University Press.

Audi, R. (1997) 'Liberal Democracy and the Place of Religion in Politics', in R. Audi and N. Wolterstorff (eds), *Religion in the Public Square: The Place of Religious Convictions in Political Debate*, Lanham, MD, Rowman & Littlefield Publishers.

Ayubi, N. (1991) *Political Islam: Religion and Politics in the Arab World*, London, Routledge.

Azmeh, A. (1992) *Al-'Ilmaniyya min Manzur Mukhtalif* [Secularism from a Different Perspective], Beirut, Markaz Dirasat al-Wihdah al-'Arabiyya.

—— (1993) *Islams and Modernities*, London, Verso.

—— (1994) 'Populism Contra Democracy: Recent Democratist Discourse in the Arab world', in Ghassan Salame (ed.), *Democracy without Democrats? The Renewal of Politics in the Muslim World*, London, I.B. Tauris.

Bahlul, R. (2000) 'People vs. God: The Logic of "Divine Sovereignty" in Islamic Democratic Discourse', *Muslim-Christian Relations* vol. 11, no. 3: 287–97.

—— (2007) 'Is Constitutionalism Compatible with Islam?', in P. Costa and D. Zolo (eds), *The Rule of Law: History, Theory and Criticism*, Holland, Springer.

Binder, L. (1988) *Islamic Liberalism: A Critique of Development Ideologies*, Chicago, IL, The University of Chicago Press.

Brown, J.N., Hamzawy, A. and Ottaway, M. (2006) *Islamist Movements and the Democratic Process in the Arab World: Exploring the Gray Zones*, Carnegie papers: Middle East Series no. 67, Carnegie Endowment for International Peace, available at www.carnegieendowment.org/files/CP67.Brown.FINAL.pdf (accessed 10 March 2010).

Brown, L.C. (2000) *Religion and State: The Muslim Approach to Politics*, New York, Columbia University Press.

Denoeux, G. (2002) 'The Forgotten Swamp: Navigating Political Islam', *Middle East Policy* vol. 9, no. 2: 56–81.

Dhaher, 'A. (1993) *Al-'Usus al-Falsafiyah lil-'Almaniyah* [Philosophical Foundations of Secularism], Beirut, Dar al-Saqi.

Fradkin, H. (2005) 'Judaism and Political Life', in L. Diamond, M. Plattner and P.J. Costopoulos (eds), *World Religions and Democracy*, Baltimore, MD, and London, Johns Hopkins University Press.

Gellner, E. (1992) *Postmodernism, Reason and Religion*, London and New York, Routledge.

—— (1993) 'Marxism and Islam: Failure and Success', in A. Tamimi (ed.), *Power-Sharing Islam?*, London, Liberty for Muslim World Publications.

Ghalyun, B. (1979) *Al-Mas'ala al-Ta'ifiyya wa Mushkilat al-'Aqaliyyat* [The Sectarian Issue and the Problem of Minorities], Beirut, Dar al-Tali'a.

Ghannouchi, Sheikh Rashid (1993) *Al-Hurriyat al-'Ammah fi al-Dawlah al-Islaymiyyah* [Civil Liberties in the Islamic State], Beirut, Center for Arab Unity Studies.

Habermas, J. (1996) *Between Facts and Norms*, Cambridge, MA, MIT Press.

—— (2006) 'Religion in the Public Sphere', *European Journal of Philosophy* vol. 14, no. 1: 1–25.

Harris, S. (2004) *The End of Faith: Religion, Terror and the Future of Reason*, London, The Free Press.

Hourani, A. (1962) *Arabic Thought in the Liberal Age*, Cambridge, MA, Cambridge University Press.

Jadaane, F. (1981) *'Usus al-Taqaddum 'inda Mufakkri al-Islam fi al-'Alam al-'Arabi al-Hadith* [Foundations of Progress According to Islamic Thinkers in the Modern Arab World], Beirut, al-Mu'assasah al-Arabyya lil-Dirasat wal-Nashr.

Khatami, M. (1998) *Mutala'at fi al-Din wa al-Islam wa al-'Asr* [Readings in Religion, Islam, and the Present Age], Beirut, Dar al-Jadid.

Kurzman, C. (ed.) (1998) *Liberal Islam: A Sourcebook*, Oxford, Oxford University Press.

Lassman, P. and Speirs, R. (1994) *Weber: Political Writings*, Cambridge, Cambridge University Press.

Lowrie, L.A. (1993) *Islam, Democracy, the State, and the West: A Round Table with Dr. Hasan Turabi*, WISE Monograph Series, no. 1, Tampa, FL, The World of Islam Studies Enterprise.

Madi, A.I. (2005) Interview, 20 December, Arab Reform Bulletin, Carnegie Foundation for International Peace, available at www.carnegieendowment.org/files/Madi.pdf (accessed 10 March 2010).

Mawdudi, A. (1975) *Tadwin ad-dustur al-Islami* [The Codification of the Islamic Constitution], n.p., Mu'assat al-Risalah.

Mehta, P.B. (2005) 'Hinduism and Self-Rule', in L. Diamond, M. Plattner and P.J. Costopoulos (eds), *World Religions and Democracy*, Baltimore, MD, and London, Johns Hopkins University Press.

Philpott, D. (2005) 'The Catholic Wave', in L. Diamond, M. Plattner and P.J. Costopoulos (eds), *World Religions and Democracy*, Baltimore, MD, and London, Johns Hopkins University Press.

Pombeni, P. (2000) 'The Ideology of Christian Democracy', *Journal of Political Ideologies* vol. 5, no.3: 289–300.

Qaradawi, Y. (1993) *Min Hady al-Islam* [Islamic Guidance], Mansourah, Dar al-Wafa' lil-Nashr.

Rahman, F. (1980) *Major Themes of the Qur'an*, Chicago, IL, Bibliotheca Islamica.

——(1982) *Islam and Modernity: Transformation of an Intellectual Tradition*, Chicago, IL, University of Chicago Press.

Rawls, J. (1993) *Political Liberalism*, New York, Columbia University Press.

Siedentop, L.A. (1989) 'Liberalism: The Christian Connection', *Times Literary Supplement*, 24–30 March: 308.

Soroush, A. (1998) 'The Evolution and Devolution of Religious Knowledge', in C. Kurzman (ed.), *Liberal Islam: A Sourcebook*, Oxford: Oxford University Press.

Stepan, A. (2005) 'Religion, Democracy, and the "Twin Tolerations"', in L. Diamond, M. Plattner and P. J. Costopoulos (eds), *World Religions and Democracy*, Baltimore, MD, and London, Johns Hopkins University Press.

Stowasser, B.F. (1993) 'Women's Issues in Modern Islamic Thought', in J. Tucker (ed.), *Arab Women: Old Boundaries, New Frontiers*, Bloomington and Indianapolis, Indiana University Press.

Talbi, M. (1992) *'Iyal Allah: Afkar Jadida fi 'Alaqat al-Muslim bi-Nafsihi wa-Alakharin* [God's Family: New Ideas on the Relation of the Muslim to Himself and Others], Tunis, Ceres Publishers.

Taylor, C. (1999) 'A Catholic Modernity?', in J. Heft (ed.), *A Catholic Modernity?* Cary, NC, Oxford University Press.

Turabi, H. (1987) *Qadaya al-Huriyya wa al-Wihda wa al Demoqratiyya* [Questions of Freedom, Unity, Consultation, and Democracy], n.p., al-Dar al-Su'udiyya lil-Nashr.

Wolterstorff, N. (1997) 'The Role of Religion in Decision and Discussion of Political Issues', in R. Audi and N. Wolterstorff, *Religion in the Public Square: The Place of Religious Convictions in Political Debate*, Lanham, MD, Rowman & Littlefield Publishers.

Woodbury, R.D. and Shah, T.S. (2005) 'The Pioneering Protestants', in L. Diamond, M. Plattner and P.J. Costopoulos (eds), *World Religions and Democracy*, Baltimore, MD, and London, Johns Hopkins University Press.

5

The Muslim Brotherhood

Barbara Zollner

The Muslim Brotherhood (MB) is one of largest and most established Islamist organizations. Founded by Hasan al-Banna in 1928 in the Suez Canal city of Isma'iliyya, it remains an influential politico-religious player in Egypt. Internationally, the organization plays a role through branches and sister organizations which, dependent on national contexts, act more or less independently of the Cairo base.

The MB pursues the establishment of an Islamic State. While the movement pursues this goal through the Islamization of society, it has a record of political opposition against Egyptian ruling regimes. As such, its history is marked by periods of violence and persecution, but also of accommodation and political participation. In recent decades, the MB emphasized its commitment to democracy and non-violent activism. Since the group was neither recognized as a political party nor was its legality officially confirmed, the MB played out its influence in political processes through its active engagement in institutions of civil society and social networks. In order to gain seats in parliament and regional representative councils, it circumvented party restraints through alliances with recognized political parties and by registering contenders as independent candidates. With the political changes after January 2011, the politcal fortunes of the MB have changed dramatically.

History of the Muslim Brotherhood

The Muslim Brotherhood (*Jama'a al-Ikhwan al-Muslimin*; short: *al-Ikhwan al-Muslimun*) was founded in 1928 by a group surrounding the secondary schoolteacher Hasan al-Banna. Lia's and Mitchell's works on the early period of the MB draw an accurate picture of the rapid expansion of the organization during the 1930s and 1940s (Lia 1998; Mitchell 1993). Starting in Isma'iliyya, the MB found its fellowship in the lower-middle and growing working class, thus rapidly spreading its influence to major Egyptian cities. The headquarters moved to Cairo in 1932 and shortly afterwards it opened its first branches in capital cities of neighbouring countries.

From the onset, the MB defined itself as a group pursuing Islamic reform. While the group's initial goal was concerned with the reform of religious education, political turbulence during the years of Egypt's constitutional monarchy (1928–52) and the persistent influence of the previous mandate-power Britain over the country's domestic affairs set the framework of Brotherhood's evolution into a political mass-movement (Jansen 1992; Zubaida 1993). In this context the MB stood out for its anti-British agitation and its opposition to Egypt's political parties. It presented itself as a nationalist force independent of party interests and guided purely by religious fervour. When failures of the political system became blatantly obvious during the post-war years, the MB used its popular base to mobilize extra-parliamentary protests which further contributed to destabilizing an already fragile democracy (Marsot 1977).

Similar to other Egyptian movements such as the Wafd and communists, the MB developed paramilitary units which were organized parallel to and independent of its popular outlets (Gershoni and Jankwoski 1995; Mitchell 1993). The so-called *al-Nizam al-Khass* (Special Unit; the paramilitary section of the MB was also sometimes referred to as *al-Tanzim al-Sirri*, i.e. Secret Organization) operated as tightly organized military units with its head directly answerable to Hasan al-Banna. In an environment of increased political violence and anarchy, which marked the last years of Egypt's constitutional monarchy, the Special Unit was responsible for several high-profile acts of terror, amongst them the murder of Sa'adi Prime Minister Muhammad al-Nuqrashi in December 1948. Only weeks later and as an act of retaliation, Hasan al-Banna was then gunned down in January 1949 by members of Egypt's Secret Service.

Following the assassination of al-Nuqrashi, the government declared the dissolution of the MB. The official ban and the death of its charismatic *Murshid* (General Guide), Hasan al-Banna, brought the MB to the brink of collapse (Mitchell 1993). Nevertheless, the organization managed to survive the next two years through a network which connected al-Banna's associates and which included the narrowly spun contacts of the Secret Unit. Only when circumstances allowed did a circle of leaders nominate the well-renowned High Court Judge, Hasan al-Hudaybi, as al-Banna's successor in 1951. Al-Hudaybi's nomination was an expression of compromise (Zollner 2009). The leading circle avoided tackling internal frictions and put off fundamental discussions on the MB's strategic and ideological direction. Because of the Brotherhood's precarious legal position, the leading circle decided to agree on al-Hudaybi, who they hoped could be used as a pawn to repair its damaged public profile while sorting out internal discontent. Setting out under extremely difficult circumstances, al-Hudaybi was a disputed figure from the start. Although he is often portrayed as a rather weak leader, the new *Murshid* led the MB for the next two difficult decades.

July 1952 marked a major change. Egypt's constitutional monarchy was overthrown through a coup d'état instigated by a group of 'Free Officers'. While dealings between the Revolutionary Command Council (RCC) and the MB leadership under al-Hudaybi were initially positive, relations turned sour (Zollner 2009). The MB was debilitated by discontent within the leading ranks over self-definition, future political strategies (particularly its role in government), and the continuance of the clandestine units. Al-Hudaybi's vision of the MB as a supra-governmental network, which aims to influence politics in an implicit manner but which does not commit itself to partaking in government, was not shared by leading members who strongly supported the revolution. Internal rifts made it difficult for the MB to react to the power games of the upstart Gamal 'Abd al-Nasser. Accused of trying to assassinate 'Abd al-Nasser during celebrations of the Anglo-Egyptian treaty in Alexandria, the MB found itself accused of conspiring against the state. October 1954 thus marks the beginning of a period of persecution that lasted almost 20 years and during which thousands of MB members were thrown into prison. 'Abd al-Nasser also used the incident to purge the ranks of the RCC, ascend as President and establish his autocratic populist regime, which he led until his death in 1971.

The MB's prison years were a crucial period for their self-image and development, which is often, not quite correctly, equated to the evolution of Sayyid Qutb's revolutionary ideology. There are a number of scholars who have worked extensively on the evolution of Qutb's ideas, amongst them Kepel and, more recently, Abu Rabi'a, Sayyid Khatab (Kepel 1985; Abu Rabi'

1996; Khatab 2006a). It was during the prison years that Qutb gradually turned to radical Islamist and revolutionary views, which he expressed in some of his most important works. The fundamental question he raised was whether it is theologically legitimate to directly or indirectly support a regime that is deemed to have left the path of Islam. This issue influenced future discussions on the Brotherhood's ideological profile.

Qutb had an immediate bearing on the reorganization of the MB members outside the confines of prison. From around 1958 onwards a group took shape which was later known as 'Organization 1965' (Zollner 2007). Being the spiritual guide and leader of this group, Qutb wrote his most famous work, *Ma'alim fi al-Tariq* (Milestones), as a manual for this clandestine cell. While the *Murshid,* al-Hudaybi, was aware of the regrouping of the MB outside prison and of Qutb's involvement, he did not initially react to the shift in ideological direction.

Only after Qutb was hanged in 1966 did the leadership of the MB under al-Hudaybi respond to a growing ideological radicalization, which used theological explanations formulated by Qutb in his most propagandistic work, *Ma'alim fi al-Tariq*, to justify their rejection of the Egyptian state (Zollner 2007). Internal discussions on the implications of this theological stance were then prompted by the 1967 Six-Day War. The conflict with Israel posed the immediate questions of whether to defend the Egyptian state system although its leaders might be deemed illegitimate according to the view of Qutbists. In response to this challenge, the MB leadership surrounding Hasan al-Hudaybi issued the text *Du'at la Qudat* (Preachers not Judges) to counter extremist ideological trends amongst its members. These theological guidelines supplied the principles for future ideological and strategic descriptions and provided the Guidance Council (*Maktab al-Irshad*) and the *Murshid* with the opportunity to regain control of the organization.

With 'Abd al-Nasser's death in December 1971 and the nomination of Anwar al-Sadat as his successor, state policy changed dramatically (Beattie 2000). Hoping for MB support in order to push for a shift in economic and foreign policy, the new President Anwar al-Sadat declared a general amnesty. The MB publicly renounced clandestine activities and political violence, committing itself to working within the political and legal framework. With the end of persecution, the *Murshid* Hasan al-Hudaybi, and, after his death in 1973, his successor 'Umar al-Tilmisani, began to rebuild the Brotherhood's public and political power.

The MB commitment to peaceful political and social engagement is in stern contrast to the violent activities of Egyptian terrorist groups. Groups such as *al-Takfir wa al-Hijra, al-Jama'a al-Islamiyya* (GI) or *Jama'at al-Jihad* (JJ) were inspired by Qutbian ideas and therefore have their ideological roots in the radical fringes of the MB of the late 1960s. While these extremist Islamist groups carried out a number of high-profile attempts on the lives of politicians, amongst them President Anwar al-Sadat who was shot during the October War commemoration celebration in 1981, the MB spoke out emphatically against these terrorist acts.

The status quo between state and MB did not, at least initially, change when Hosni Mubarak came to power. However, the Brotherhood's aim to gain influence and legitimacy, first through informal networks, then though its successes in social movement organizations (SMO), and finally through its participation in elections, led to increasing resentment and, since the mid-1990s, to outright persecution (Al-Awadi 2004).

The MB's political triumph was not necessarily matched by internal cohesion and unity. The two successors of 'Umar al-Tilmisani, namely Muhammad Hamid Abu Nasr (1986–96) and Mustafa Mashhur (1996–2002), were rather weak and affairs were directed rather through the *Maktab al-Irshad*. The two General Guides were elected because they were the oldest representatives on the Guidance Council and not because of outstanding contributions to the cause of the MB. While the locus of power shifted to the Guidance Council, the influence of

Ma'mun al-Hudaybi, the Official Speaker of the MB and son of the second *Murshid*, became increasingly obvious within the Council. When the latter finally took charge of the MB in 2002 as its *Murshid*, his ascent to the highest position and his style of leadership evoked internal disputes about unresolved issues on democratic reform, political involvement and the translation of MB aims into public policy. While al-Hudabyi's leadership brought these issues to the fore, his sudden death in 2004 did not resolve internal conflicts.

During the leadership of his successor, Mahdi 'Akif, internal conflicts became even more prevalent. While the *Murshid* was by no means as strong a leader as al-Hudaybi and in fact only a compromise candidate of the Guidance Council. Calls for ideological reform, a new strategic direction and more democratic inner-organizational participation did not quieten down. The landslide success of the MB in the 2005 parliamentary elections brought these issues to the fore. The concerns brought forward by a 'reformist' faction usually associated with the younger generation of Brothers and with political pragmatists who see the MB as a political organization rather than a religious movement still remain unresolved. When 'Akif resigned in December 2009, the election of the new *Murshid*, Muhammad Badi'a, has to be seen in these terms. The selection of a *Murshid* who, like all his predecessors since Hasan al-Hudaybi, represents the 'old guard', prompted the outrage of political pragmatists. In the elections of the Guidance Council in January 2010, the majority of seats were allocated to Badi'a's supporters, thus alienating reformists within the organization (Awad 2010).

Ideology

There is an ongoing dispute about the MB's ideological framework and, more particularly, whether the organization commits itself to democratic ideals or whether it endorses political violence and extremism. Disputes within the scholarly community about the 'true' intentions of the MB are intrinsically linked to uncertainties about the Brotherhood's theological basis and ideological interpretation.

There is no doubt that Hasan al-Banna personifies the organization's ideological core and identity. Despite many contradictions and disputes over ideology and strategy, members see themselves unified by al-Banna's ideals which are characterized by active political engagement to bring about national confidence, social justice and economic progress through an emphasis on religion. Because al-Banna emphasized activism over intellectual erudition, there are relatively few sources, mostly speeches and public addresses, a few statements and pamphlets and, finally, his autobiography. These sources portray Islam as a universal system that penetrates all aspects of life. Comparable to other mass organizations of the early twentieth century, al-Banna projected the MB as a movement that fuses the personal, social, political and religious. While Diyab points out the totalizing aspect of al-Banna's world view, numerous scholars such as Abed Kotob, and more recently Stacher, Zollner and Wickham, have noted that al-Banna left only a set of crudely defined aspirations, which seek the Islamization of politics, economics, law, culture, public and private life.

These general political goals also find expression in an elusive strategic framework. While today's Brotherhood without doubt rejoices in unity to its foundational leader, al-Banna has thus been used by diverse factions as a reference point to justify opposing viewpoints (Wickham 2009). His candidacy in the 1944 parliamentary elections has, for example, been called upon by the pro-democratic reformist faction, while certain critical remarks on party politics have been used to demonstrate reservations against a democratic system. Similarly, al-Banna's guidance could be differently interpreted as to his position on political violence, gender equality and the relationship to other religious communities and denominations.

Any analysis of MB ideology needs to engage with a set of ideas which developed in the course of the Brotherhood's most challenging time, the years of persecution between 1954 and 1971. The ideological legacy of this period was not expressed through clear strategic guidelines, but debates on the Brotherhood's calling raged on a more fundamental, theological level. The person most associated with the ideological development of these years is Sayyid Qutb, who was hanged in August 1966 after being charged for conspiring against the state. Qutb's theological explanations are to a large extent associated with radical Islamist positions, which, inspired by his most propagandistic work, *Ma'alim fi al-Tariq*, built the ideological base for extremist groups (Kepel 1985). However, two issues need to be recognized: first, Qutb's legacy as a whole must not be reduced to his impetus on extremist Islamist theology; and second, the MB leadership tried to counterbalance a radicalization in their midst by the end of the 1960s (Zollner 2007).

It is undeniable that Qutb's views in *Ma'alim fi al-Tariq* have been used as ideological guidelines by militant Islamists. These split from the MB around 1967 and subsequently formed terrorist groups in the course of the 1970s. As has variously been pointed out, *Ma'alim fi al-Tariq* uses the concepts of *hukm Allah, jahiliyya* and *jihad* to present a simple dichotomy (Khatab 2006b). Arguing that the world can be categorized into 'true Islam' and its enemies, Qutb's work set the tone for extremist political action and terror in the name of Islam. If Qutb is only measured by his *Ma'alim fi al-Tariq*, then he can indeed be seen as the father of radical Islamist ideology; yet Qutb's overall legacy as a modernist writer – his effect on theological interpretation through his popular Qur'anic commentary and his impact on Islamist ideology including his lasting impact on the Muslim Brotherhood through his political writing – is multi-faceted. Qutb can therefore not be simply reduced to the equation that he represents Islamist militancy (Zollner 2007).

Moreover, the leadership of the Muslim Brotherhood under Hasan al-Hudaybi developed a theological counter-narrative in the second half of the 1960s. An internal document was issued under the title *Du'at la Qudat*. It had the purpose of setting principled theological premises which draw on Islamic law as a mode of discussion (Zollner 2009). The book therefore established a theological base which was neither provided by al-Banna nor further elucidated by Qutb. In fact, this unique theological and juridical approach became the common basic framework of the Brotherhood and constitutes an indirect refutation of a simple theological dichotomy adopted by Qutbists. Nevertheless, because of the *Du'at la Qudat* theological approach, but also because of the historical controversies underlying the authorship of the text, the book remained largely a teaching text for members interested in religious interpretation. Still, concepts explained in *Du'at la Qudat* certainly appear in subsequent policy and strategic publications, although the text itself is not much quoted.

While al-Banna provided the Brotherhood with its identity, Qutb and al-Hudaybi were important contributors who elaborated further the Brotherhood's ideological, theological and juridical foundations. Based on these principal authors, the MB gradually developed its strategic stances in the course of the last decades (Abed-Kotob 1995). At the centre of internal discussions since the early 1970s are issues such as its position with regard to democracy and the Egyptian nation-state; related to these are also questions regarding the Brotherhood's participation in elections and its view on economic liberalization and privatization. On these issues, the Muslim Brotherhood adopted a largely accommodationist attitude, which aims for democratic participation rather than revolutionary objectives.

Nevertheless, the degree of adjustment with the political system in Egypt and, related to it, the question of internal reform is one of much debate amongst members. Internal debates about the Brotherhood's ideological and strategic future weigh heavy on the organization's current situation. Driven by the Brotherhood's success in the 2005 elections and its success in parliament, a faction within the MB calls for more openness, transparency and liberalization, while aiming to push for party recognition even if this means the renegotiation of long-held positions (Stacher 2008; Leiken and Brooke 2007). This grouping within the MB could be best described as the politically pragmatic wing and its members are often referred to as the 'new generation'. This vision conflicts at points with the old-style leadership, which was previously represented by the late Ma'mun al-Hudaybi, but also by his successors, Mahdi 'Akif and Muhammad Badi'a. As indicated above, the attitudes of the 'old guard' are moulded by the experience of persecution. The memories of the near-destruction of the organization feed caution and suspicion about the political system. Rejecting the notion that politics ideates religious interpretation, the 'old guard' is considerably more conservative in its outlook. It resents the idea that beliefs can be submerged in order to pursue political interests. There is therefore a tendency to define itself as a social movement that works above and in constant opposition to the political system, rather than merely as a political party that adjusts its policies to the will of its membership.

Social movements and social engagement

Defining the MB's profile at the fifth General Assembly in 1939, al-Banna declared that one of the main areas was that of a social movement (Mitchell 1993). As indicated above, the MB struggled throughout its history to find a clear answer to the question of whether it should define itself as a social movement with an element of political opposition or as a political opposition with a social agenda. Nevertheless, the political restrictions of the recent decades led the MB to emphasize its social engagement as an outlet of political commitment.

Returning to the political scene in the early 1970s, the Brotherhood used informal networks and personal affiliations to gradually build up its sway within institutions of civil society. Wickham's study illustrates how the MB used its engagement in institutions of civil society to channel its influence in politics since direct participation was restricted (Wickham 2004). Not being able to find recognition as a political party, the MB began to dominate non-governmental organizations (NGOs), student organizations, professional organizations and syndicates in the course of the 1980s. It was through these formal social movement channels that the MB managed to circumvent restrictions, thus gaining enormous influence as a political opposition.

Responding to the fact that the MB built up its influence as an SMO, the government attempted to curb the Brotherhood's steadily growing power through additional legal constraints. However, these legal measures had only limited success. Furthermore, they were and still are highly criticized by observers and activists, secular as well as religious, as evidence that the government lacks commitment to democratic development.

Using this tight organizational structure, the MB thus managed to grow a network of welfare services. As Clarke and Wickham show, the MB's social provisions include social clubs and a wide range of welfare institutions such as kindergartens, schools, libraries and even hospitals (Wickham 2004; Clarke 2004). These areas of social engagement make the Muslim Brotherhood a provider of alternative social services, which, in many cases, are reported to be better managed than those of the state. Critics, however, remark that the Brotherhood uses its social profile as a means to spread its world view, to gain public approval and sympathies, to recruit new members and to extend its structure and influence. Less unfavourable voices such as those of Ismail emphasize that the MB actually provides alternative resources where the state cannot answer demand (Ismail 2006). This then would indicate that the MB does not necessarily use its welfare services for recruitment purposes. This argument recognizes that the

Brotherhood's engagement in welfare is part of its mission and self-definition as a social movement, which is led by ideals such as social justice and care for those in need.

Analogous to formal channels of civil society, the MB also steadily extended its power as an SMO through informal networks. At the heart of these informal networks are close personal relations which are built into the administrative structure of the MB (Mitchell 1993). So-called 'families' organize the membership base and connect it through a tight system to the leadership council. This grid enables the Brotherhood to coordinate its activities efficiently. Informal social networks also connect the Muslim Brotherhood to SMOs with axiomatically different political ideologies, as Abdelrahman shows (Abdelrahman 2009). Their common political opposition to the existing state system and its reluctance to fully introduce democratic participation connects the Brotherhood with movements of the secular left. As such, the shared opposition against the authoritarianism of Husni Mubarak's regime, but also against recent amendments of the constitution and the continuous state of emergency, binds these informal networks of SMOs together. While these SMOs might not agree in all details, they are not, as Abdelrahman observes, necessarily unstable, as least not as long as their common interest holds them together. Looking at the parliamentary election of 2005 or analysing current preparations for the 2010 and 2011 elections, one can see that these informal networks of SMOs have an immense bearing on the political scene (Hamzawy 2010).

Political power

From the beginning of the Muslim Brotherhood, al-Banna was inspired by the idea of Islamic reform. Following the footsteps of Muhammad 'Abduh and Rashid Rida, Hasan al-Banna saw the solution for the perceived decline of the Muslim world in the revival of Islam as a social and political force. Following the end of the Caliphate in 1924, al-Banna aimed to change Egyptian society by working towards the re-establishment of an Islamic State as Egypt's political framework.

As we have seen above, the Brotherhood is built on a universalist ideology which argues that 'Islam' encompasses the individual and the social, and synthesizes the religious with the political. This ideological basis and the influence of modernism led al-Banna to adapt a strategy not dissimilar to other mass movements. As such it addressed the wider public directly and aimed for the mobilization of large segments of society in order to engage in political protest and to encourage popular expression of political opposition. At the same time, al-Banna tried to influence political processes through informal networks and personal relationships, which connected him to leaders of the *Wafd*, to Shuyukh al-Azhar and to upcoming officers of the military.

Al-Banna's strategy to use the power of the Muslim Brotherhood to organize itself as a political protest movement rather than as a political party was particularly successful in the context of Egypt's struggle to define itself as a state independent of British influence and as a nation-state adopting a modern parliamentary system. Al-Banna argued that political parties of Egypt's constitutional monarchy merely followed their own short-sighted interests. Speaking of *hizbiyya* (party-ism), he regarded these as dishonest, corrupt and incompatible with Islamic principles.

While al-Banna rejected the concept of parties as the representatives of public will, he supported the concept of a parliament as a forum for the participation of the nation-state. Evidence for this is that the Muslim Brotherhood actively rallied against the suspension of parliament during and after the war period. Furthermore, al-Banna put his name forward as an independent candidate for parliamentary elections in 1944. Nevertheless, political activities during these years are overshadowed by al-Banna's decision to establish a military wing which eventually engaged in political violence.

It was not al-Banna but his successor, Hasan al-Hudaybi, who had a taste of political power. Al-Hudaybi's early years coincided with the July 1952 coup d'état during which a group of officers took control. The Muslim Brotherhood, which already had friendly relations with leaders of the RCC, such as the first president of the new republic, Muhammad Naguib, but also with the upstart, Gamal 'Abd al-Nasser, and the still young Anwar al-Sadat, was invited to participate in reshaping the government. However, internal conflicts on the movement's future direction and al-Hudaybi's lack of commanding full support made the Brotherhood vulnerable and gradually dampened relations with the RCC. They finally broke completely in October 1954 when the Muslim Brotherhood was accused of instigating an assassination attempt on 'Abd al-Nasser in Alexandria. The event, which marked the beginning of the time of persecution, was the end of any hopes of political participation and initiated 'Abd al-Nasser's populist autocracy.

After 'Abd al-Nasser's death, relations with the regime relaxed. The new president, Anwar al-Sadat, allowed the MB greater freedom to express its ideas in public and engage in civil society. Nevertheless, al-Sadat did not lift the 1954 ban, leaving the organization with an ambiguous legal status which continues to hamper the MB even today. The decision to aim for direct political participation through parliamentary activities soon triggered hostile responses from a regime which did not intend to give up its authoritarian rule. Because the MB was not recognized as a political party, it circumvented electoral restrictions by setting up coalitions and, since the change of the electoral law in 1990, by running its candidates on the list of independents. This tactic proved to be successful, as the 2007 electoral victory evidences.

In 1980 it entered into a temporary symbiosis with the liberal Wafd Party (winning six of 360 seats in the *Majlis al-Sha'b*, or lower house) and in 1987 the MB extended its strategy to initiate a tripartite coalition between MB, liberal Wafd and socialist Labour (winning 36 seats). These remarkable results in elections directly challenged the dominance of the ruling party, the NDP. In response, the government changed the electoral law from a party-based system to one based on individual candidacy for seats in constituencies. The changes resulted in an election boycott by all opposition parties. The following election campaign to the election of the *Majlis al-Sha'b* in 1995 was overshadowed by heavy-handed government harassment and the arrest of a number of MB members. Nevertheless, the MB returned to the ballots but only managed to win a single seat. The elections of 2000 were fought under similar pressures, but the MB increased its influence in parliament, gaining 17 seats. Five years later, in 2005, the MB had a landslide victory, winning 88 seats or 20 per cent of the total, making it the largest opposition bloc in the history of the Egyptian Republic (Shehata and Stacher 2006; Stacher 2008). These two elections, a Carnegie Report found, displayed a strategic dilemma for the MB (Ottaway and Hamzawy 2008). While the MB bloc, like all parties involved in the political process, would, of course, like to extend its seats in parliament, it could not afford to display too much success as this could have evoked drastic responses against them. Hence, the Brotherhood only competed with 19 candidates in the 88-seat *Majlis al-Shura* (upper house of the parliament) and, in a last-minute decision, withdrew from the 2008 municipal elections after the government refused to register the majority of suggested candidates. The November 2010 elections to the *Majlis al-Sha'b* need to be seen in conjunction with the regime's aim to prepare conditions for a handover from President Hosni Mubarak to a successor of his choice, with his son Gamal Mubarak as the favourite option (Al-Anani 2010; Hamzawy 2010). The poll, which was criticized for systematic electoral infringements, vote rigging and violence, ended with heavy losses for the MB, which secured only a single seat.

The protests of January and February 2011, which resulted in the departure of President Hosni Mubarak and which initiated a process of transforming the Egyptian state system, also had decisive effects on the MB's political presence. Shaking off a 56-year official ban, the organization was catapulted into the public arena. Its political party, the Freedom and Justice Party (FJP), is seen as a major political force within an evolving multi-party system. The sudden change in the MB's fortunes brought about questions on the organization's political agenda and its maturity as a political actor. The parliamentary elections and presidential elections, which at the time of writing were scheduled for autumn 2011, will show what role the MB will play in shaping the democratic future of post-revolutionary Egypt and how it fits into its evolving political landscape.

International aspects and diaspora

The Muslim Brotherhood's influence reaches beyond Egypt. In fact, from the movement's very beginning it saw its calling beyond national interests. As such, branches in neighbouring countries were already established in the 1930s.

In the course of the Brotherhood's development and due to the fact that the leadership of the organization was more or less debilitated after Hasan al-Banna's death, the dissolution order of 1949, and even more so by the harsh persecutory measures under 'Abd al-Nasser between 1954 and 1971, MB branches outside Egypt developed into movements that acted more or less independently from the mother organization in Egypt. As the national Muslim Brotherhood movements in countries of the Near and Middle East responded to the context of their own national conflicts and debates, it is wrong to talk about 'branches' in states such as Syria, Jordan, Sudan, Libya, Tunisia, etc. Evidence for this is the fact that national Brotherhood movements outside Egypt established their own recruitment and membership structures as well as independent systems of organizational participation and networks. As such, members of national Brotherhoods outside Egypt have no voting power on either the Guidance Council or the position of the *Murshid* in Egypt and, furthermore, cannot bring forward any candidates.

Nevertheless, consultations and cooperation between Brotherhood movements and the 'mother organization' in Egypt exist. What unites national MB organizations is a common heritage of al-Banna's ideological base and, connected to this aspect, the idea of a universal Muslim bond of brotherhood. Amongst others, the Muslim Brotherhood in Egypt is affiliated with ideologically moderate movements such as the Tunisian *al-Nahda* (Renaissance) or the accommodationist Jordanian Brotherhood with its parliamentary wing, *Jabhat al-'Amal al-Islami* (the Islamic Action Front). Yet it is also linked on a certain level to organizations that are seen to be associated with terrorism, such as the Palestinian Hamas. Depending on the issue and political circumstances, but also on the relative closeness of leading cadres and informal networks, this sense of brotherly identity is either emphasized or downplayed.

The presence of the Muslim Brotherhood in the Middle East needs to be, at least to some degree, distinguished from that in Western countries. While organizational structures, agendas and, to a certain extent, membership can be identified for the various national movements in the Middle East, no such organizational unity exists for members and supporters affiliated to the MB in Europe and the US.

It is therefore more accurate to speak of loose personal networks rather than a formal MB presence. Still, one can identify clusters where members take active part and sometimes even dominate Muslim social movements in Europe and the US. Vidino and various contributors in Meijer's edition trace some MB activities in organizations aiming to represent the Muslim

Barbara Zollner

community such as the European Institute for Fatwa and Research, the Muslim Association, the Muslim Council of Britain, the Muslim American Society, etc. (Meijer 2011; Vidino 2010).

The obvious fact that Muslims constitute a minority in Europe and the US has, of course, an impact on the aims of Muslim Brotherhood activists and supporters. Moreover, most MB supporters in Europe and the US live in exile or, more recently, are a second generation that follows the footsteps of the first generation of activists. This context guides the raison d'être of their engagement to a major extent, which lies in Muslim community affairs on the one hand and, more importantly, a continuous interest in political developments in the Middle East.

References

Abdelrahman, M. (2009) '"With the Islamists? – Sometimes. With the State? – Never!" Co-operation between the left and Islamists in Egypt', *British Journal of Middle Eastern* Studies vol. 36, no.1: 37–54.

Abed-Kotob, S. (1995) 'The Accommodationists Speak: Goals and Strategies of the Muslim Brotherhood of Egypt', *International Journal of Middle East Studies* vol. 27, no. 3: 321–39.

Abu Rabi', I.M. (1996) *Intellectual Origins of Isalmic Resurgence in the Modern Arab World*, New York, State University of New York Press.

Al-Anani, K. (2010) *The Myth of Excluding Moderate Islamists in the Arab World*, Working Paper No. 4, Washington, DC, The Saban Center for Middle East Policy at the Brookings Institute.

Al-Awadi, H. (2004) *In Pursuit of Legitimacy. The Muslim Brothers and Mubarak 1982–2000*, London and New York, Tauris Academic Studies.

Awad, M. (2010) 'Egypt's Muslim Brotherhood Conservatives Win Vote', *Reuters*, 10 February. Available at www.reuters.com/article/idUSTRE5BK3CB20091221?loomia_ow=t0:s0:a49:g43:r1:c1.000000:b30326 924:z0 (accessed 12 June 2010).

Ayubi, N. (1991) *Political Islam. Religion and Politics in the Arab World*, London and New York, Routledge.

Beattie, K.J. (2000) *Egypt During the Sadat Years*, New York and Basingstoke, Palgrave.

Bowen, I. (forthcoming) 'The Brotherhood in the UK', in R. Meijer (ed.), *Transnationalizing Islam: The Muslim Brotherhood in Europe*, London, Hurst.

Carré, O. and Michaud, G. (1983) *Les Frères Musulmans. Egypt et Syrie (1928–82)*, Paris, Gallimard Julliard.

Clarke, J.A. (2004) *Islam, Charity and Activism. Networks and Middle-Class Activism in Egypt, Jordan and Yemen*, Bloomington, Indiana University Press.

El-Gobashy, M. (2005) 'The Metamorphosis of the Egyptian Muslim Brothers', *International Journal of Middle Eastern Studies* vol. 37, no. 3: 373–95.

Gershoni, I. and Jankwoski, J. (1995) *Redefining the Egyptian Nation, 1930–45*, Cambridge, Cambridge University Press.

Gordon, J. (1992) *Nasser's Blessed Movement. Egypt's Free Officers and the July Revolution*, New York and Oxford, Oxford University Press.

Hamzawy, A. (2010) 'Egypt's (Un)Dedemocratic Elections', Q&A, Carnegie Endowment for International Peace, available at www.carnegieendowment.org/publications/index.cfm?fa=view& id=40898 (accessed 5 June 2010).

Heyworth-Dunne, J. (1950) *Religious and Political Trends in Modern Egypt*, Washington, DC, McGregor Werner.

Husaini, I.M. (1952) *The Moslem Brethren: The Greatest of the Modern Islamic Movements*, Beirut, Khayat's College Book Cooperative.

Ismail, S. (2006) *Rethinking Islamist Politics: Culture, the Sate and Islamism*, London, I.B. Tauris.

Jansen, J.G. (1992) 'Hasan al-Banna's Earliest Pamphlet', *Die Welt des Islams* vol. 32, no. 2: 254–58.

Kepel, G. (1985) *Muslim Extremism in Egypt: The Prophet and the Pharaoh*, London, al-Saqi.

Khatab, S. (2006a) *The Political Thought of Sayyid Qutb: The Theory of Jahiliyya*, Abingdon, Routledge.

—— (2006b) *The Power of Sovereignty. The Political and Ideological Philosophy of Sayyid Qutb*, Abingdon, Routledge.

Leiken, R.S. and Brooke, S. (2007) 'The Moderate Muslim Brotherhood', *Foreign Affairs* vol. 86, no. 2: 107–21.

Lia, B. (1998) *The Society of Muslim Brothers in Egypt: The Rise of an Islamic Mass Movement 1928–1942*, Reading, MA, Ithaca.

Marsot, A.A.L. (1977) *Egypt's Liberal Experiment: 1922–36*, Berkeley and London, University of California Press.

Meijer, R. (2011) *Transnationalizing Islam: The Muslim Brotherhood in Europe*, London, Hurst.

Mitchell, R. (1993) *The Society of the Muslim Brothers*, Oxford and New York, Oxford University Press.

Ottaway, M. and Hamzawy, A. (2008) *Islamists in Politics: The Dynamics of Participation*, Carnegie Paper, Washington, Carnegie Endowment for International Peace.

Phelps-Harris, C. (1964) *Nationalism and the Revolution in Egypt: The Role of the Muslim Brotherhood*, The Hague, Mouton.

Rutherford, B.K. (2008) *Egypt after Mubarak: Liberalism, Islam and Democracy in the Arab World*, Princeton, NJ, Princeton University Press.

Shehata, S. and Stacher, J. (2006) 'The Brotherhood Goes to Parliament', *Middle East Report* 240: 32–40.

Stacher, J. (2008) *Brothers in Arms? Engaging the Muslim Brotherhood in Egypt*, London, Institute for Public Policy Research.

Vidino, L. (2010) *The Muslim Brotherhood in the West*, Columbia, Columbia University Press.

Wickham, C.R. (2004) *Mobilizing Isla: Religion, Activism and Political Change*, New York, Columbia University Press.

—— (2009) 'What Would Hassan al-Banna Do?: Modern (Re-)Interpretations of the Brotherhood's Founding Discourse', MESA Conference, Boston, MA.

Zollner, B. (2007) 'Prison Talk: The Muslim Brotherhood's Internal Struggle During Gamal Abdel Nasser's Persecution', *International Journal of Middle East Studies* vol. 39, no. 3: 411–33.

—— (2009) *The Muslim Brotherhood: Hasan al-Hudaybi and Ideology*, Abingdon, Routledge.

Zubaida, S. (1993) *Islam, the People, and the State*, London, I.B. Tauris.

6

Hamas

Between pragmatism and radicalism

Mohammed M. Hafez and Marc-André Walther

On 25 January 2006 Palestinians conducted free and fair legislative elections for the Palestine National Authority (PA). Few expected Hamas to win the landslide victory the world observed on that day. Israel and many Western countries view Hamas as an extremist Islamist organization driven by a radical religious ideology that prefers violence to peace, and suicide bombings to negotiations. The Palestinian electorate, however, gave Hamas 76 of 132 seats in the government, ending Fatah's domination of the PA (Klein 2007: 42). This resounding victory for Hamas created a dilemma for Western states: a legitimate, democratic electoral process brought forth a party that does not recognize the state of Israel and disavows the Oslo Peace Process on which negotiations for a two-state solution is the basis for settling the Palestinian–Israeli conflict. Accepting official and direct negotiations with Hamas is unacceptable to Israel unless Hamas recognizes its right to exist and renounces violence once and for all. Rejecting talks with Hamas amounts to rebuffing the free choice of the Palestinian people and subverting the spirit of democracy. The Middle East Quartet, comprising the United Nations (UN), the European Union (EU), the United States (US) and Russia, formed in 2002 to mediate the Palestinian–Israeli peace process, along with Israel have opted to isolate Hamas in the Gaza Strip and, instead, focus their aid and efforts on revitalizing the Fatah movement, currently led by President Mahmoud Abbas, in the West Bank (Tocci 2007: 139).

In this chapter we seek to address the origins of Hamas, its leadership and organizational structure, and its strategy in the Palestinian nationalist struggle for independence. Hamas is a sophisticated organization that engages in political contestation, social services and charitable works inside the Palestinian territories, but it also employs all forms of violence, including suicide bombers and homemade rockets against Israeli civilians. Hamas rejects the extremism of al-Qaeda and has limited its militancy to fighting Israel within Palestine's historic territory (Israel proper, the West Bank and Gaza), thus avoiding a broader military confrontation with the US and EU. It is an organization that is capable of combining its militant activism and radical ideology with strategic thinking and pragmatism.

Since 2006, the people of Gaza have had to contend with political isolation, sanctions, blockades and border closures. This policy has been counterproductive politically and questionable morally. It amounts to the collective punishment of Palestinians in Gaza and sabotage of their democratic choice. It also undermines the broader Western discourse on democracy promotion in the Middle East because it signals an unwillingness to abide by the free choice of the people when their votes contravene the wishes of Israel and its allies. Gaza's isolation emboldens the hardliners in Hamas' leadership and accelerates the internal political division of the Palestinian camp, which makes an ultimate settlement of the conflict more difficult than it already is. Surveys of Palestinian perceptions toward the humanitarian crisis inflicting Gaza's populations show that the people rarely blame Hamas for their dire situation (Shikaki 2007: 7). The blame, instead, is placed on Israel, the US and all those countries that are aligned with them.

We begin this chapter by asking the question 'what is Hamas?' in order to discuss the competing viewpoints surrounding this movement. We go on to analyze Hamas' decision-making in three critical time periods since 1993, treating each period as a case study of Hamas' strategic decision-making. The first case is Hamas' reaction to the Oslo peace accords between Israel and the Palestine Liberation Organization (PLO). The second is the post-11 September 2001 security environment that gave Israel a golden opportunity to frame its war on Hamas and all violent Palestinian factions as part and parcel of the US global war on terrorism. The third case study is Hamas' decision to participate in the 2006 legislative elections. All these cases reveal the strategic nature of Hamas' decision-making and its potential to act both radically and pragmatically to further its organizational standing in Palestinian politics. We conclude that engagement with Hamas, not isolation, is the key to moving the Palestinian–Israeli peace process forward.

What is Hamas?

Hamas means 'zeal' in Arabic, but it is also the Arabic acronym for the Islamic Resistance Movement (*Harkat al-Muqawama al-Islamiyya*). It was founded in 1987 as a political activist wing of the Palestinian Muslim Brotherhood (MB) during the first Palestinian uprising (*intifada*). The MB movement existed in Palestine from the mid-1940s, prior to the formation of Israel in 1948 (Abu-Amr 1994; Milton-Edwards 1996). It was a quietist civic organization that focused on charitable works and proselytizing (*dawa*) among local populations and (later) refugees. Over time, the work of the MB revolved around three networks: *al-Mujam'a al-Islami* (Islamic Center), *al-Jam'iyah al-Islamiyya* (Islamic Association), and *al-Jami'ah al-Islamiyya* (Islamic University). The first two provided services such as medical care, day care, youth sport activities, *zakat* (alms) collection, and education; the Islamic University was an academic extension of al-Azhar University in Egypt (Mishal and Sela 2000).

During the early 1980s, the MB came under heavy criticism from the Palestinian Islamic Jihad for not participating in the armed struggle or jihad against Israel. When the first Palestinian uprising broke out in December 1987, Sheikh Ahmed Yassin, one of the founders of the Islamic Center and a member of the MB, along with other members felt the need to participate in the popular rebellion that was rapidly spreading to all of the occupied territories. They agreed on the formation of Hamas as a militant political wing of the MB (Hroub 2000).

Robinson (2004: 125) describes the formation of Hamas as a revolt 'of the activist second stratum of the Muslim Brotherhood against the more reform-minded first stratum'. The formation of Hamas may not have been quite a revolt, but the center of gravity in the MB shifted from the older to the younger leadership who were the driving factor in the formation of Hamas and the change of strategy due to new political opportunities (Gunning 2008: 38). The foundation of Hamas was necessary to secure the survival of the MB because public support for the uprising was palpable and the MB's rivals – the Palestinian Islamic Jihad and Fatah – were active participants in the intifada.

Soon after its formation, Hamas published its 1988 Charter. In Article 11, Palestine is declared a 'waqf', an endowment given to the Muslims by God. Defining Palestine as such allows Hamas to legitimize its violence in terms of defensive jihad (striving or struggle). When the secular PLO recognized Israel's right to exist and accepted the framework of the Oslo Peace Process in 1993, Hamas stood in opposition to the Process and the PA dominated by Yasser Arafat's Fatah faction. Armed resistance for the complete liberation of Palestine became its official raison d'être.

Since its emergence, Hamas has deployed a range of violent tactics against Israel, ranging from assassinations and hit-and-run operations, to kidnappings and homemade rockets. Suicide bombings emerged as one of its preferred and most deadly tactics. Hamas repeatedly conducted 'martyrdom operations' against Israel and has convinced the wider Palestinian public of its legitimacy, leading some to argue that a culture of martyrdom has penetrated this conflicted society (Hafez 2006). Suicide attacks have dwindled in the last few years due to Israeli counter-measures, checkpoints and closures, and a security barrier (or 'Wall of Racial Segregation' as many Palestinians call it).

Hamas is a controversial Palestinian faction, and academic scholarship and policy analysis of the movement reflects this controversy. One prevailing viewpoint asserts that Hamas is a terrorist organization whose desire for the elimination of Israel is deeply rooted in an inherently uncompromising religious fundamentalism. Critics of the movement argue that unlike the PLO, which in the past rejected Israel's right to exist in the same way that Hamas refuses to accept Israel's legitimacy today, Hamas can never accept a two-state solution and remain the same organization that it is today. The PLO's conversion was possible because it was (and remains) a secular faction that forms its decisions on worldly cost-benefit analysis and changing circumstances. Hamas, on the other hand, is a religious fundamentalist movement that draws its inspiration from divine dogma that, by definition, is immutable.

According to this school of thought, Hamas uses civic and political strategies to facilitate and legitimize its extremist objective of destroying a neighboring state. Matthew Levitt (2006: 39) argues that Hamas' charitable institutions provide the basis for its core military mission – ideological socialization, recruitment and financing of terrorism. Hamas' complex organization is intended to support its ultimate mission of destroying Israel. The social institutions provide the funding for the organization's terrorist cells, whereas the political organizations grant legitimacy to Hamas as an alternative to its rivals.

Moreover, critics of Hamas assert that it is closely allied with the theocratic regime in Iran, which extends the movement's political and economic support (Bahgat 2007: 174–75). Hamas, like Hezbollah in Lebanon, is a proxy actor for Iran's regional ambitions, which directly conflict with regimes friendly to the United States. Two of these states, Egypt and Jordan, have made peace with Israel. Some go as far as to suggest that Hamas may under certain circumstances 'target the West' in the distant future (Levitt 2007: 925). The policy implication of this viewpoint is that Hamas poses a major hurdle to the resolution of the Arab–Israeli conflict. Its elimination or marginalization is a prerequisite to lasting peace between Palestinians and Israelis (Laqueur 2004; Rubin 2008).

We take a different view and argue, as others have done before us, that Hamas can be given incentives to give up its core maximalist demands and, therefore, it is not an insurmountable obstacle to peace (Hroub 2000; Mishal and Sela 2000; Robinson 2004; Klein 2007; Gunning 2008). Hamas is a complex and heterogeneous social movement with important internal divisions between ideological doctrinaires and strategic pragmatists, or hardliners and moderates for short. It is more accurate to describe Hamas as a nationalist movement that employs religious discourse to differentiate itself from secular competitors rather than as a religious fundamentalist organization driven by immutable absolute principles. The identities of their supporters are much more fluid and intricately bound by internal Palestinian divisions and circumstances under an enduring Israeli occupation (Lybarger 2007). This assessment does not deny the fact that Hamas deploys terrorism against Israeli civilians and even against Palestinians suspected of collaboration with Israel, but the history of nationalist movements in the modern world is replete with anti-civilian violence directed at foreigners and, most often, at indigenous populations from which these movements arise.

Hamas is a movement that brings together social welfare institutions, political organizations, and security and military militias. Since 2006, it formed the Change and Reform Party to contest the legislative elections and, after taking power in Gaza, its members have filled the ranks of the police and security services. In its formative phase, it subsumed the MB's charitable organizations and with them the existing communal networks that combined mosques with schooling, sports clubs and medical care. These structures help to develop organic personal networks between the organization and its popular base. The charitable organizations are a means to combine Hamas' Islamist message and spirit of resistance with the necessities of daily living and existential hardships.

Hamas did not only maintain the institutions of the MB, but also established new ones. During the Oslo period (1993–2000), it founded the Scientific Medical Association and the Association for Science and Culture (Robinson 2004: 127). College students are perhaps the most important segment for Hamas. Fatah patron–client networks dominate the bureaucracies of the PA, leaving Hamas to rely on support among students for political competition.

Hamas' current armed wing is known as *Katib al-Shahid Izzedin al-Qassam* (The Brigades of the Martyr Izzedin al-Qassam). It formed in Gaza in 1991 and officially merged with its West Bank branch in January 1992. It is named after Sheikh Izzedin al-Qassam, a Syrian-born rebel who fought against the French in Syria in the 1920s and the British in Palestine in the 1930s; he was killed in a British manhunt in November 1935. Prior to the formation of the Qassam brigades, Hamas had a militia as early as 1988 known as *al-Mujahidun al-Falastiniun* (The Palestinian Holy Fighters) under the command of Sheikh Salah Shahada (killed by Israel in July 2002 and replaced by Mohammed Deif, the current general commander of the Qassam brigades). The initial organization divided Gaza into eight zones and appointed a commander over each zone, headed by the general commander Walid Hasan Ibrahim Aql. Each zone commander formed a cell made up of four members. Most of their initial operations targeted Palestinians suspected of collaborating with Israel. They also attempted to use roadside bombs against Israeli patrols, but they quickly abandoned that effort because it proved ineffective. In the West Bank, the task of recruiting cells fell to Salah al-Arouri, who divided the West Bank into seven zones, each with its own commander and cell.

From 1992, Hamas' armed operations, carried out by its military wing, became more organized and sophisticated. They included armed infiltrations of settlements, armed attacks on Israeli checkpoints, hostage-taking operations and improvised explosive devices capable of destroying fortified military transport vehicles and some tanks. Their ultimate weapons, however, are homemade rockets and the human bomb.

During the 1990s, in order to survive Israeli countermeasures, the organization was segmented into social, militant and political wings. The leadership is divided into an internal leadership and an external one. Over time this division solidified into a heterogenic structure. Decision-making inside Hamas depends on two types of leadership within the hierarchy. Prior to participation in the 2006 elections, the external leadership, together with the militia leaders, represented the hardline faction, while the internal leadership presented the less hawkish one.

The external leadership is represented by the political bureau, which formed in 1992 and is headed today by Khaled Mishal (currently based in Syria). The political bureau has control not only of the general political orientation of the movement and foreign relations, but also the military wing (Mishal and Sela 2000: 59; International Crisis Group 2008: 16). Furthermore, it controls much of the funding which ensures it considerable influence. The internal leadership has control of the institutions on the ground within Palestine. Members elect leaders internally and decisions are made by consensus in committees at the different levels (Gunning 2008: 100–7), but this consensus is influenced by the stance the particular leadership faction has at that time. Additionally, the personal influence of individual leaders like the late Sheikh Yassin and Mishal is of utmost importance. The division in the leadership does not mean that hardliners always reject political solutions while moderates always reject violence. The complexity of an internal and external leadership inevitably leads to tensions within Hamas, but the heterogeneous structure also shows that it is capable of conducting politics in a multi-faceted way. While the charitable organizations link Hamas with the daily life of the Palestinians, the student organization and the political party allow permanent participation in politics.

As a mass-based nationalist movement, Hamas depends on public support for political survival in a field densely populated with competitors. Throughout the course of its history, Hamas has pursued its goals by numerous means, not just violence. Its decision-making reflects its situational awareness, cost-benefit analysis and strategic opportunism (Mishal and Sela 2000: 129). While it cannot abandon its religious discourse without a price, it has shown the ability to draw on Islamic traditions to justify extended ceasefires and even a peace deal with Israel without recognition of the latter's right to exist in historic Palestine. In other words, Hamas is capable of doing what many other states in the region have done: live alongside Israel without recognizing its legitimate right to exist.

Hamas' decision-making depends on two interrelated factors: the relative power of its leadership factions, and the political, economic and security perceptions of its mass base. Hamas' militant strategies are intimately linked to these two factors. As conditions worsen in the Palestinian territories, the hardline leaders become emboldened in arguing against moderate strategies. As the political, economic and security situation of Palestinians on the ground improves, Hamas' leaders feel pressure to avoid militancy, thus empowering the moderates to take the lead.

The implication of this analysis is that the key to Hamas' moderation is the Palestinian mass public. If the latter views the peace process with Israel as bearing fruit in their lives by producing progress on core issues that divide Palestinians and Israelis – removing closures, facilitating internal travel, increasing economic opportunities, freeing prisoners and reducing Israeli settlement activities – then it will be disinclined to view Hamas' violence favorably. Hamas' terrorism will be seen as counterproductive sabotage of a legitimate peace process. This climate will force Hamas to reconsider its violence. However, if the peace process remains stalled, Hamas' violence will be seen as a reaction to Israeli intransigence and as legitimate resistance against occupation. This climate encourages Hamas to pursue uncompromising policies and strategies to win over public support in its competition with other Palestinian factions.

Hamas and the Oslo Peace Process

The 1993 Oslo peace accords between the PLO and Israel are an example of how Hamas can be constrained by Palestinian public opinion. The accords made it difficult to legitimize jihad for the Palestinian cause because many Palestinians supported the process. Yet Hamas did not wish to accept this process because it benefited its chief rival, the PLO, and implied subordination to the

PA. Hamas decided to follow three strategies. To preserve its support, Hamas officially announced the Oslo accords as illegitimate and tried to increase the public's opposition to them. Due to the broad support for the accords, however, Hamas carefully avoided being blamed for sabotaging the process. Hamas did not reject the principle of peace, but framed the Oslo Peace Process as an inadequate solution to redress the injustices inflicted on Palestinians since the foundation of Israel, nor did it meet the aspirations of Palestinian nationalism. Hamas, thus, positioned itself as the defender of a just peace, not capitulation in the guise of peace (*salaam, la istisslam*).

Hamas did engage sporadically in violence against Israel during the Oslo Peace Process (1993–2000), but it did so only when it could frame its violence as retaliation for Israeli aggression. Such was the case in February 1994, when Baruch Goldstein, a Jewish settler from New York living in the settlement of Kiryat Arba, massacred 29 Muslim worshipers while praying in the Tomb of the Patriarchs or Ibrahimi Mosque in Hebron. Hamas used this occasion to avenge the killings by sending two suicide bombers inside Israel in April of that year, killing approximately 13 and injuring over 70 people.

Another opportunity for Hamas came in January 1996, when Israeli intelligence assassinated Yahya Ayyash, famously known as 'the engineer'. Ayyash was the chief bomb-maker for Hamas responsible for a number of suicide bombings. The daring assassination using a hidden bomb in a mobile phone and involving a betrayal by close aides was a shock to Hamas. Following the assassination, Hamas unleashed four suicide attacks inside Israel, resulting in the killing of approximately 57 and injuring over 130 Israelis.

In both instances, Hamas justified its attacks as defensive and not as direct attempts to sabotage a popular peace process. Hamas hoped to preserve its radical base by affirming its ideological legitimacy and aura of armed resistance while simultaneously avoiding any damage to its mass popularity among the general Palestinian population. By continuing the armed struggle, Hamas was able to preserve its identity and its legitimacy because its definition of the illegitimate peace further allowed defensive resistance. Hamas' retaliatory violence was widely supported because it was perceived as the best means to redress Israeli assassinations (Mishal and Sela 2000).

The third strategy adopted by Hamas during the Oslo Peace Process concerned negotiations with the PA and calibration of positions vis-à-vis Israel. Hamas was fully aware that it could not sabotage the Peace Process indefinitely. Hamas was competing against Fatah and had to cope with the growing popularity of Arafat and the PA. The circumstances favored Hamas' competitors. International support, the popularity of the Peace Process, and Israel's position toward the PA weakened Hamas' position inside the territories. Hamas tried to avoid a direct confrontation with the PA and negotiated with it. Ultimately, Hamas had to back down from violent confrontation with Israel because of the PA's dominant position and its capacity to arrest and detain Hamas leaders and activists. Hamas agreed not to conduct any attacks from PA territory; at the same time it was able to act from Israeli controlled territory, a move calibrated with the PA to strengthen the latter's hand in negotiations with Israel over the size and speed of territorial concessions and redeployments, respectively. This allowed the movement to continue limited attacks against Israel, thus preserving its militant core, while avoiding an all-out confrontation with the PA and its international supporters.

The period of the Oslo Peace Process revealed a pattern that continues to this day: 'Hamas had calculated its strategy on a cost-benefit basis and […] recognized the limits of its power [… J]ihad turned out not to be an ultimate goal but a political instrument wielded by political considerations' (Mishal and Sela 2000: 64). Maintenance of the organization was the main concern in the group's decision-making and a necessary contribution to the protection of the group's center of gravity. Hamas adapted to the circumstances in order to preserve its base and popularity within the broader Palestinian public. Violence was a political means to an end and its use did not exclude political compromise.

On 28 September 2000 Likud Party candidate Ariel Sharon made a controversial and well-publicized visit to Haram al-Sharif or Temple Mount in Jerusalem. Palestinians considered this visit a deliberate provocation and began rioting, thus marking the end of the Oslo Peace Process and the beginning of another chapter in the long history of uprisings against foreign occupation – *al-Aqsa intifada*.

The uprising was also a revolt against the PA's failure to deliver good governance and an end to occupation and settlements in the territories. At the end of the 1990s, public opinion swung against the PA and the Peace Process (Palestinian Center for Policy and Survey Research 2008a). According to Gunning (2008: 48–49), the 'PA had lost much of the popular goodwill it had received upon its arrival'. The PA and Fatah, in the eyes of many Palestinians, proved to be inept, corrupt and autocratic. Israeli settlements increased, further proving to the Palestinians that the PA was unable to constrain Israel despite its concessions to the latter. In short, all the internal Palestinian developments seemed to confirm Hamas' pessimistic narrative of the Peace Process.

The outbreak of the al-Aqsa intifada presented Hamas with a golden opportunity to take a leadership position in Palestine's factional competition. Not only did the Palestinians feel a common grievance with the failure of the Peace Process; after the escalation of the violence they felt a common threat from the excessive force used by the Israelis. In return, this allowed Hamas to legitimize its suicide attacks against Israeli civilians (Hafez 2006).

As polls have shown, the support for suicide attacks increased after the second intifada gained momentum (Hafez 2006: 59; Palestinian Center for Policy and Survey Research 2008b). Hamas now had an incentive to win the public's support by accelerating its suicide bombings. The Israeli counteractions radicalized the Palestinian population even more. Palestinian fatalities created a public opinion in favor of escalating violence. The painful blows delivered by suicide attacks provoked intense Israeli retaliation and contributed further to the spiral of violence.

The failure of the Oslo Peace Process and the tit-for-tat violence of the al-Aqsa intifada strengthened the militants within Hamas' internal and external leaderships, leading to their decision to participate in the al-Aqsa intifada with full force. This policy marked a shift away from the earlier one of limited violence negotiated with the PA. Hamas, ever aware of popular sentiment, sought to position itself as the avenger of Palestinian suffering. By the time the al-Aqsa intifada came to an end, it had created fertile ground for Hamas. Security and civil services in Palestine were weakened or had broken down, and internal public order had further deteriorated (International Crisis Group 2007a). Fatah's position was weakened also due to its close ties to the failing Palestinian government. In contrast, Hamas still maintained its charity organizations and provided public support. Additionally, it had gained support during the second intifada as a viable option to the PA, which by this time was perceived as venal and thoroughly ineffectual.

Hamas and the 'war on terror'

The 11 September 2001 terrorist attacks on the United States created a new security environment that was profoundly threatening to Hamas. The 9/11 attacks brought all radical Islamist movements into the crosshairs of American security and intelligence agencies, regardless of whether they were al-Qaeda partners or not. Hamas is an Islamist nationalist organization with no connections to al-Qaeda, nor any interest in transnational terrorism (or 'global jihad' as it is often labeled). Hamas is a product of the Palestinian–Israeli conflict and it defines its objectives in reference to Palestinian national aspirations and factional struggles.

More importantly, Hamas derives its strength out of its organic linkages to a local nationalist struggle. Even the funding it receives from abroad is not linked to al-Qaeda and, more significantly, could be jeopardized if linked to transnational terrorist networks. Thus, Hamas has every reason to distance itself from al-Qaeda and has been criticized by the latter for not supporting its extremist ideology and strategy (Cragin 2009). As Gunning (2008: 227) explains, and as can be seen from Hamas' Charter and center of gravity, participation in the global jihad would have sidelined 'the Palestinian question', thereby weakening Hamas' position in Palestine and its cause for a Palestinian state. As a matter of fact, Hamas' leadership avoids any connection with al-Qaeda (Gaess 2002).

Despite its ideological and organizational separation from al-Qaeda, 9/11 gave Israel an opportunity to frame Hamas as al-Qaeda's partner in terror. Concomitantly, Israel's fight against Hamas was part and parcel of America's war on terrorism. Hamas attempted to keep a low profile after the attacks of 9/11 and did not offer any support to Osama bin Laden's fight with the US. It went so far as to condemn violence against innocent civilians, making sure to explain that its own attacks on Israeli civilians are distinct because Israel has a citizen-army, among other justifications. Furthermore, it refrained from launching attacks in the immediate aftermath of the 9/11 attacks.

Once more Hamas was attuned to its environment, rationally considering the new threats against the organization. A pragmatic strategy entailed deescalating attacks against Israel in order to deprive its adversaries of the opportunity to paint it with the same brush as al-Qaeda. Palestinian public support for violence after 9/11 was still strong; the majority did not view Palestinian armed struggle against Israel as terrorism (Palestinian Center for Policy and Survey Research 2009a).

2006 legislative elections

After Arafat's death in 2004, the political vacuum created by his absence and the 2006 elections presented new opportunities for Hamas' political participation. From 1996 Hamas' prime rival Fatah dominated the PA. Hamas refused to participate in legislative elections for fear it would legitimize a peace process that it rejected on ideological grounds. Just as importantly, the Peace Process was still relatively popular in the mid-1990s, which meant that Hamas was not likely to do well in such elections. It was, however, fully aware of the power of political legitimacy and had successfully participated in elections below the municipality level (Hroub 2000).

The situation had changed substantially by 2006. The Peace Process was in tatters and Fatah was increasingly fragmented internally and disdained by a general public that saw it as increasingly ineffective and venal. Fatah and President Abbas were unable to improve law and order or the economic situation. Now, the political system opened for Hamas participation with prospects of success. Additionally, gaining political power against Fatah was a common interest of both the hardliner and the moderate leaders. To participate in elections presented an opportunity to maintain the position Hamas had gained in the al-Aqsa intifada and to cope with the decreasing public support for violence (Palestinian Center for Policy and Survey Research 2008c).

Hamas' move toward political participation was further facilitated by a momentum shift from hardliners to moderates. In the course of events in the intifada, the military wing had been weakened by Israeli countermeasures and improved intelligence. Furthermore, Hamas had to compensate for the loss of senior leadership members due to Israeli arrests and assassinations.

The containment of its militant activities decreased the capabilities for armed operations. Syria curtailed its strong support of Hamas and pressured its leaders to roll back their militant activities because it was concerned about possible US actions against it.

The political legitimacy Hamas could gain from elections presented an 'insurance policy' (Klein 2007: 446) against possible repressive actions by PA security figures like Mohammed Dahlan and Jibril Rajoub, both of whom could well have exercised a major crackdown on Hamas had their faction, Fatah, retained complete control of PA. Their task would be much more difficult if Hamas was seen as a legitimate democratic participant of Palestinian legislative politics. Additionally, the Israeli withdrawal from the Gaza Strip in August 2005 allowed a suitable starting point for political participation because Hamas, argues Gunning (2008: 233), was able to take 'credit for having made continued occupation too costly'.

In order to enter into political participation, Hamas founded the Change and Reform Party, which was not part of its original political agenda or Charter. Hamas did not envision nor foresee the landslide victory it achieved in the 2006 elections; success caught its leaders by surprise (Klein 2007; Shikaki 2007). Political participation was valuable because it provided the movement with the official position of a legitimate party. Its political program addressed the core concerns of the Palestinian public: security, rampant corruption, the deteriorating economic situation and increasing anarchy. Its campaign, according to Hroub (2006: 6–12), somewhat vaguely emphasized 'administrative reform and fighting corruption', 'social policy' and 'youth issues', as well as 'transport and border crossing'. Hamas avoided overly religious rhetoric in its campaigning, did not denounce its adversaries as infidels and apostates, but largely stuck to 'bread-and-butter' issues. Its candidates were chosen on the basis of their professional and technocratic abilities, not their clerical credentials (Gunning 2008: 164). Hamas' candidates did benefit from the public's perception of them as 'god-fearing people' who are not prone to corruption and mismanagement.

Public support for reconciliation and a unity government gave Hamas an incentive to cooperate with Fatah in the form of a unity government. In what came to be known as the Mecca Agreement (due to Saudi Arabia's sponsorship of the accord), both sides compromised on a combined government (Palestinian Center for Policy and Survey Research 2009b). The unity government, however, ultimately failed because of missing international acceptance of Hamas and US pressure on President Abbas to break the Mecca accord.

The Quartet's rejection of Hamas' moderates and its imposed isolation shifted the momentum back to the hardliners. The isolation approach forced even the moderate leaders to reject further political participation. In this new situation, Hamas had to cope with different challenges. First, it had to compete against its rival Fatah. Second, Hamas had to continue to govern and to prove its viability in order to maintain public support. Third, it had to cope with complete isolation of the Gaza Strip. Isolation did not turn public opinion against Hamas (International Crisis Group 2007b). On the contrary, it bolstered the hardliners in Hamas and precipitated violent clashes between Hamas and Fatah throughout 2007. The hardliners within Hamas explained this decision as an act of self-defense because Fatah seemed to be cooperating with external forces seeking to undermine Hamas' governance (Rabbani 2008: 74). The takeover of the Gaza Strip was a concerted and well-organized action. It included a crackdown on its opponents and the installation of Hamas' cadres in government administration and public service (International Crisis Group 2008: 1).

In order to govern Gaza, Hamas agreed to a ceasefire with Israel in July 2008. The ceasefire was intended to achieve two objectives. First of all, Hamas needed to improve the economic situation in Gaza in order to govern. Therefore, it needed the truce to let Israel open up the border crossings. Furthermore, the maintenance of the truce, although it was fragile, was necessary for Hamas to maintain law and order in the Gaza Strip. Second, as the government needed to prove its ability to govern it needed to establish connections to the international community. Although this attempt failed due to Western isolation, the truce showed Hamas' willingness to negotiate on the international level.

Hamas' attempt to improve the economic situation in Gaza through a ceasefire agreement with Israel failed. Throughout 2008 it was still able to provide supplies and basic goods by smuggling. The International Crisis Group (2008: 14) estimated that Hamas was in control of about 90 percent of the sanction-busting tunnels. In the long run, however, it was not able to overcome the blockade on the Gaza Strip. The situation became intolerable for Hamas because it challenged its ability to govern and, thus, its base of popular support (International Crisis Group 2009: 10).

The inability to provide for the basic needs of Gaza's population forced Hamas to act. An extension of the truce would have been one option, but it would have to be coupled with an end to the blockade on Gaza. Otherwise, an extension of the ceasefire without con-cessions would have undermined Hamas' popular support due to its inability to deliver good governance. Hamas, according to the International Crisis Group (2009: 10), adopted the stance of 'let us govern, or watch us fight'. As a Hamas leader in the Gaza Strip put it, 'between fighting and opening the crossings, we will choose the latter. But between surrender and fighting, we will fight' (International Crisis Group 2009: 12). Hamas chose to increase the pressure on Israel with renewed rocket attacks. Dealing with a harsh Israeli military operation was preferable for Hamas rather than coping with diminishing public support in the Gaza Strip.

Conclusion

In January 2009 Israel launched Operation Cast Lead in the hopes of crushing Hamas with decisive military force. The long-term damage inflicted on Hamas from this operation is still not known, but Hamas continues to rule the Gaza Strip and maintains a firm grip on law and order (BBC News 2009). Politically, Hamas remains operational too. Its leaders in the Gaza Strip, as well as the leadership abroad, are active and again engaged in negotiations and discussions with local and regional interlocutors (Witte and Finer 2009). Neither Fatah nor President Abbas is in a position to end the conflict with Israel completely due to the presence of Hamas in Gaza.

The analysis of Hamas, its organization and its actions in critical phases shows that it is a complex movement rather than a mere terrorist bomb squad. Hamas will not reject its 'right to resist' through nationalist violence, but it also does not employ violence irrespective of the costs. Hamas' toolbox includes both violent resistance and pragmatic politics. Hamas is keen on ana-lyzing changing circumstances – the opportunities and constraints – in its environment. Violence or pragmatic politics are pursued in line with its cost-benefit analysis and strategic thinking, not blind adherence to dogma. Hamas' objective is to stay on top within Palestinian factional competition. As with other organizations, Hamas derives its power from its popular base and the legitimacy of resistance to Israeli occupation of Palestinian lands. How then should stakeholders approach Hamas?

The complete negation of Hamas as a political interlocutor and the attempt to eliminate it by isolation and military means has proven to be ineffectual and morally questionable. We reject this option because military force against Hamas can only contain the movement, but not neutralize it altogether. Earlier attempts at eliminating the organization have failed, and each time the effort came at a high cost in lives for both Palestinians and Israelis.

Another option would be to engage Hamas in official political dialogues unconditionally as a legitimate representative of the Palestinian people. This option is risky because it would strengthen the position of Hamas hardliners who could credibly argue that they achieved political recognition without having made any concessions to Israel or the international community. Such a move would undermine the status of moderate Palestinian factions that have made the decision to recognize Israel during the Oslo peace process and have yet to make progress on their nationalist aspirations.

We recommend a third option: an indirect approach to influence Hamas away from violence by shaping the conditions on the ground that make it difficult for the organization to sabotage peace without paying a high price in terms of public support. Lifting the blockade on Gaza and allowing Hamas to govern unhindered by international sanctions could entice the movement to seek a durable ceasefire with Israel without appearing to capitulate to Israel's principal demand of recognition. Strategically, it would be attractive for Hamas to abandon militancy under these circumstances because further violence would damage its public standing among the beleaguered people of Gaza. Additionally, the approach allows Hamas to initiate the process to redefine resistance away from violence to non-violent political means by itself, rather than responding to external pressure that threatens its identity.

In the short term, the best we can hope for is an indefinite ceasefire by Hamas based on a negotiated agreement whereby it governs in Gaza without sanctions and blockades in exchange for the complete cessation of armed attacks on Israel. In the long term, Hamas may make the historic compromise that the PLO made in 1988: recognize Israel and pursue a peace process on the basis of a two-state solution. In the meantime, it could coexist with Israel in the same way that other Arab states have come to live alongside the Jewish state without conceding its right to exist. In this enduring nationalist conflict, a less than optimal peace may be the most feasible solution toward which we can work.

References

Abu-Amr, Z. (1994) *Islamic Fundamentalism in the West Bank and Gaza: Muslim Brotherhood and Islamic Jihad*, Bloomington, IN, Indiana University Press.
Bahgat, G. (2007) 'Terrorism in the Middle East', *The Journal of Social, Political, and Economic Studies* vol. 32, no. 2: 163–200.
BBC News (2009) 'Gaza Smugglers Get Back to Work', available at news.bbc.co.uk/2/hi/middle_east/7844497.stm (accessed 30 January 2009).
Cragin, K. (2009) 'Al Qaeda Confronts Hamas: Divisions in the Sunni Jihadist Movement and its Implications for U.S. Policy', *Studies in Conflict and Terrorism* vol. 32, no.7: 576–90.
Gaess, R. (2002) 'Interviews from Gaza: What Hamas Wants', *Middle East Policy* vol. 9, no. 4: 112–21.
Griff, W. and Finer, J. (2009) 'Battered Gaza Still in the Grip of Hamas; Islamist Group Retains Strength Despite War', *The Washington Post*, 24 January.
Gunning, J. (2008) *Hamas in Politics: Democracy, Religion, Violence*, New York, Columbia University Press.
Hafez, M.M. (2006) *Manufacturing Human Bombs: The Making of Palestinian Suicide Bombers*, Washington, DC, United States Institute of Peace.
Hroub, K. (2000) *Hamas: Political Thought and Practice*, Washington, DC, Institute for Palestine Studies.
—— (2006) 'A New Hamas through its New Documents', *Journal of Palestine Studies* vol. 35, no. 4: 6–27.
International Crisis Group (2007a) *Inside Gaza: The Challenge of Clans and Families*, Middle East Report 71, Brussels, International Crisis Group.
—— (2007b) *After Mecca: Engaging Hamas*, Middle East Report 62, Brussels, International Crisis Group.
—— (2008) *Round Two in Gaza*, Middle East Briefing 24, Brussels, International Crisis Group.
—— (2009) *Ending the War in Gaza*, Middle East Briefing 26, Brussels, International Crisis Group.
Khalil, S. (2007) *With Hamas in Power: Impact of Palestinian Domestic Developments on Options for the Peace Process*, Crown Center Working Papers.
Klein, M. (2007) 'Hamas in Power', *The Middle East Journal* vol. 61, no. 3: 442–59.

Laqueur, W. (2004) *Voices of Terror: Manifestos, Writings, and Manuals of Al Qaeda, Hamas, and Other Terrorists from Around the World and Throughout the Ages*, New York, Reed Press.

Levitt, M. (2006) *Hamas: Politics, Charity, and Terrorism in the Service of Jihad*, New Haven, CT, Yale University Press.

—— (2007) 'Could Hamas Target the West?', *Studies in Conflict and Terrorism* vol. 30, no.11: 925–45.

Lybarger, L.D. (2007) *Identity & Religion in Palestine: The Struggle between Islamism & Secularism in the Occupied Territories*, Princeton, NJ, Princeton University Press.

Milton-Edwards, B. (1996) *Islamic Politics in Palestine*, London, I.B. Tauris.

Mishal, S. and Sela, A. (2000) *The Palestinian Hamas: Vision, Violence, and Coexistence*, New York, Columbia University Press.

Palestinian Center for Policy and Survey Research (2008a) *Public Opinion Poll no. 46*, available at www.pcpsr.org/survey/cprspolls/2000/poll46a.html (accessed 15 November 2008).

—— (2008b) *Public Opinion Poll no. 2*, available at www.pcpsr.org/survey/polls/2001/p2a.html (accessed 15 November 2008).

——(2008c) *Public Opinion Poll no. 18*, available at www.pcpsr.org/survey/polls/2005/p18e1.html (accessed 15 November 2008).

—— (2009a) *Public Opinion Poll no. 3*, available at www.pcpsr.org/survey/polls/2001/p3a.html (accessed 25 January 2009).

—— (2009b) *Public Opinion Poll no. 23*, available at www.pcpsr.org/survey/polls/2007/p23e1.html (accessed 25 January 2009).

Rabbani, M. (2008) 'The Making of a Palestinian Islamist Leader: An Interview with Khalid Mishal: PART II', *Journal of Palestine Studies* vol. 37, no. 4: 59–73.

Robinson, G.E. (2004) 'Hamas as Social Movement', in Q. Wiktorowicz (ed.), *Islamic Activism: A Social Movement Theory Approach*, Bloomington, Indiana University Press.

Rubin, B. (2008) 'Setting U.S. Policy Toward Hamas', in D. Pollock (ed.), *Prevent Breakdown, Prepare for Breakthrough: How President Obama can Promote Israeli–Palestinian Peace*, Washington, DC, The Washington Institute for Near East Policy.

Shikaki, K. (2007) 'With Hamas in Power: Impact of Palestinian Domestic Development on Options for the Peace Process', *Crown Center Working Papers* no. 1: 1–18.

Tocci, N. (2007) 'The Impact of Western Policies Towards Hamas and Hezbollah: What Went Wrong?', in M. Emerson and R. Youngs (eds), *Political Islam and European Foreign Policy: Perspectives from Muslim Democrats of the Mediterranean*, Brussels, Centre for European Policy Studies.

Witte, G. and Finer, J. (2009) 'Battered Gaza Still in the Grip of Hamas: Islamist Group Retains Strength Despite War', *The Washington Post*, 24 January: A07.

7

Hizbullah in Lebanon

Lara Deeb

The Lebanese political party Hizbullah has been in the news a great deal over the past several years, even meriting mention in at least one State of the Union address. The group was accused of single-handedly instigating the July 2006 war with Israel and subsequently of attempting to topple the Lebanese government. For those with longer memories, Hizbullah is generally associated with the 1983 bombings of the US embassy, Marine barracks and French MNF headquarters in Beirut, and with the 1985 hijacking of a TWA flight to Beirut. They are also cited by the US State Department in connection with the kidnappings of Westerners in Lebanon and the hostage crisis that led to the Iran-Contra affair. Despite the uncertainty of these allegations (Blanford 2003; Harik 2004: 65), they are the purported reason for the party's listing on the US State Department's list of terrorist organizations, and for the recent characterization of Hizbullah as the 'A-list' of terrorism.[1]

However, as A.R. Norton (1999, 2000) and others have argued, 'Hizballah may not simply be dismissed as an extremist or terrorist group' (Norton 1999: 2), because such a dismissal removes Hizbullah from its political, historical and social context.[2] Since its origins as a resistance militia in the 1980s, Hizbullah has developed into a legitimate Lebanese political party and an umbrella organization for myriad social welfare institutions. Today the party is an inextricable part of the political, economic and social fabric of life for many Lebanese. This chapter provides a contextually grounded history of Hizbullah, including its ideological and social background, and also traces the ways in which the party has transformed over time to become an integral part of the Lebanese polity. It begins by laying out the political and economic conditions that led to Hizbullah's establishment, then follows the trajectory of development for each of the party's three major wings: military, political and social welfare. Finally, the chapter touches upon Hizbullah's constituency and the various complex reasons why different people support the party in Lebanon today.

Lebanon

Shi'a Muslims have resided in areas that are today part of Lebanon since the ninth century, primarily in the south, in a region called Jabal 'Amil, and in the Beqaa Valley, with another small community north of Beirut near Jbeil.[3] In 1920 the French mandate established the existing borders of the Lebanese nation-state by combining the Christian-majority Ottoman province of Mount Lebanon with surrounding areas, including the Beqaa Valley and the south. According to the 1932 census, the last census ever taken in Lebanon, Shi'a Muslims were 17 percent of the population, making them the third largest minority in a nation with no clear majority and 16 recognized religious groups.[4] A decade later, an unwritten National Pact was established among the major communities in Lebanon, especially the Sunni Muslims and Maronite Christians. Among other things, the Pact laid the groundwork for a confessional political system, distributing government positions according to the 1932 census' proportions. As such, Shi'a Muslims received ten seats in the 55-member Parliament.[5] Additionally, the Pact stipulated that the cabinet would be divided equally between Christians and Muslims, with equal numbers of Maronite and Sunni members, a move that ensured Shi'a under-representation. Finally, with independence in 1943, it was understood that the President would always be Maronite, the Prime Minister always Sunni and the relatively powerless speaker of Parliament, Shi'a.

The confessional nature of this system was structurally stagnant. Throughout later decades, it would fail to take into consideration population changes, exacerbating Shi'a under-representation. Furthermore, the institutionalization of sectarianism in Lebanon was accompanied by a more subtle process by which the category of sect became increasingly necessary to the groups themselves. A sectarian political leadership supported the establishment of sectarian social institutions (e.g. schools, hospitals) rather than common ones, so that sect became a means of accessing resources (Joseph 1975). Here, under-representation contributed directly to poverty as government funds were routed into other communities. Aggravating this was the fact that Shi'a seats in Parliament were usually filled by feudal landowners and other elites – men detached from the realities of life in rural Shi'a regions of the country.

Post-independence economic and structural development in Lebanon was concentrated mainly in Beirut. The Maronites and urban Sunni were tied into a network of Western capital inaccessible to the relatively isolated Shi'a, who were by far the most rural of Lebanon's communities.[6] Living conditions in Shi'a villages did not approach the standards of the rest of the nation. For example, at independence the Southern Lebanon district – consisting of 300 mostly Shi'a villages – contained no hospitals and no irrigation schemes. Poverty and illiteracy were the norm among the Shi'a peasantry (Ajami 1986; Cobban 1985; Picard 1997; Norton 1987).

After a brief civil war in 1958, the new President Shihab began a program of nationwide development and modernization – known as Shihabism – seeking to raise the standards of the rural infrastructure to those of Beirut. At that time, transportation routes were built tying villages into the road network and schools were established in rural areas. The new government also began hiring more Shi'a Muslims in military and civil service positions, and introduced 'export-based agro-capitalism' which replaced earlier economic bases with cash crops like tobacco.[7] These new policies and infrastructures prompted a mass migration of rural Shi'a Muslims to Beirut.[8] Many of these migrants settled in a ring of suburbs around the capital, commonly known as the 'misery belt' (Khuri 1975). This was the origin of the growth of the southern suburb of Beirut, *al-dahiya al-junubiyya*.[9]

By this time Beirut had become the undisputed center of the financial network linking the industrial world with the oil-producing nations of the Gulf,[10] but the rapid urbanization that came with incorporation into the capitalist world economy further exacerbated economic, social and regional disparities within Lebanon (Kubursi 1993). Much of the new urban population consisted of young Shi'a men seeking their fortunes in Beirut. Upon arrival in the city, these young men often found themselves trapped in wage-labor at a level substantially below that of their education. Some worked in factories, although many remained unemployed or self-employed as peddlers, because the service sector was saturated by the mid-1960s (Halawi

1992). In addition to producing a discontented youth, the new accessibility of Beirut blatantly exposed the uneven distribution of resources across sectarian groups and created new arenas for inter-sectarian competition.

Unequal modernization and an ever-growing sense of disenfranchisement were factors that would contribute to the eventual political mobilization of the Shi'a. In addition, Beirut was a space of contact for Shi'a Muslims from different regions of Lebanon. Equally important, the road networks facilitated constant movement between village and city. Migrants returned to their villages to marry, visit family and vote. Rather than an urbanized population, what emerged was a connected population.[11]

The initial mobilization of the Shi'a was not along sectarian lines. As the state became tangible in the city, political parties on both ends of the spectrum competed for Shi'a loyalties. In the 1960s and early 1970s Shi'a Muslims made up much of the rank-and-file membership of the Lebanese Communist Party and the Syrian Social Nationalist Party. They also participated in the early days of the Palestinian liberation movement in Lebanon, though that connection did not last long. This environment – combining political awareness and discontent with the desire for modernization – provided the ground for a Shi'a sectarian mobilization.

The man most often credited by scholars with challenging the leftist parties for the loyalty of Shi'a youth and successfully uniting many Lebanese Shi'a Muslims into a separate non-secular political movement of their own is Sayyid Musa al-Sadr (Ajami 1986; Halawi 1992; Norton 1987). He was an Iranian Shi'a cleric with Lebanese family ties who came to Lebanon in 1959 to replace the late clerical leader in the southern Lebanese city of Tyre. A charismatic orator, al-Sadr challenged the leftist parties for the loyalty of Shi'a youth, offering in their stead an infusion of religion into the political world. Halawi puts it thus: '[Sayyid Musa] was ready to defend the faith […] to revitalize Islam and counterpose it to radical ideologies as an appropriate vehicle for change' (Halawi 1992: 114). He was instrumental in establishing the Supreme Islamic Shi'a Council – a body created to articulate Shi'a needs to the state – in 1969. In 1970 he led the first general Shi'a strike in Lebanon, calling on the government to assist those displaced by Israeli attacks in the south.[12] Four years later al-Sadr established *Ḥarakat al-Maḥrūmī n* – the Movement of the Deprived, a political movement dedicated to attaining rights for the deprived, which essentially meant the Shi'a. When war began the next year, a militia branch was founded: Amal.[13] However, at this point the movement was still small and many Shi'a youth fought with secular party militias during the first few years of civil war (1975–76).[14]

Yet despite academic focus on al-Sadr's role, and despite an almost universal acknowledgment of his importance to Shi'a mobilization, one cannot overlook another crucial stream of Shi'a political, social and religious activism that had begun to take shape in Lebanon in the 1960s and 1970s. While al-Sadr's roots were in Iran, many other activist Shi'a religious leaders came from Iraq, and especially the religious schools (*hawza*s) of Najaf. Among them were Sayyid Muhammad Husayn Fadlallah, the most popular Shi'a religious leader or *marja'* in Lebanon today, and Sayyid Hasan Nasrallah, who is the current Secretary-General of Hizbullah. Najaf was the center of *Hizb al-Da'wa al-Islāmiyya* (literally, the Party of the Islamic Call), which had a branch in Lebanon at this time. Hizb al-Da'wa is an Iraqi Shi'a Islamist party established in the late 1950s.

At the beginning of the civil war in 1976, the eastern suburb of Beirut – Nab'a – where many Shi'a Muslims lived and where Fadlallah worked, fell to the Phalangists (a Maronite Christian militia) and the Shi'a population fled to al-Dahiya. With them went Fadlallah, who, in keeping with the ideals of Najaf, began teaching and establishing social institutions in the area. He emerged in the early 1980s as one of the key figures in the community. In contrast to Musa al-Sadr's work to establish Shi'a political institutions in relation to the Lebanese state,

Fadlallah worked at the grassroots level, believing that cultural and educational work was the necessary first step to mobilizing and developing the community.[15] The basic place where these two paths differed was in their approach to politics: one worked from outside the system and the other from within.

Despite these differences, they agreed on the importance of sect-based mobilization in combating Shi'a marginalization. In addition, both drew upon themes from Shi'a Islamic history, especially the martyrdom of Imam Husayn, in their organizational work. Unlike in Sunni Islam, Shi'a Muslims believe that the Prophet Muhammad bequeathed leadership of the Muslim community to his son-in-law Imam Ali, and to his descendants, called the Imams. The third Imam, Imam Husayn, Muhammad's grandson, was martyred by the Caliph's troops at Karbala in 680 CE, and he is believed to have gone knowingly to his death in order to take a stance against oppression. Husayn is frequently drawn upon to provide a model for forms of Shi'a political resistance in different contexts, as an ideal example of the redemption of the oppressed. His martyrdom is commemorated annually during the first ten days of Muharram, known among Arab Shi'a as Ashura (from the root for ten). At different moments in Lebanon, these commemorations and the imagery and meaning carried within their narratives have taken on political significance.

The emergence of Hizbullah as a resistance militia

Between 1978 and 1982 a number of events propelled the nascent Shi'a mobilization forward and further divorced it from the leftist parties. First, when the Lebanese civil war began in 1975, the 'Movement of the Deprived' (along with most Lebanese political groups and movements) formed its militia branch, Amal, which today is another Shi'a political party in Lebanon, alternately Hizbullah's main political competitor or strongest ally.[16] Second, in 1978, while on a visit to Libya, al-Sadr mysteriously disappeared, catapulting him directly into a Shi'a millenarian narrative about the return of the Hidden Twelfth Imam, and initiating a surge in his popularity. Suddenly, al-Sadr's face was on posters all over the south, the Beqaa and parts of Beirut. That same year, Israel invaded south Lebanon, displacing 250,000 people. The initial consequence of these two events was Amal's revitalization, as it grew and entered the fray of war (Norton 1987). Another consequence was Shi'a perceptions that the Lebanese left had failed, both in securing greater rights for the poor and in protecting the south.[17]

The next key event in this chain was the 1979 Islamic Revolution in Iran, with its global reverberations. Those reverberations were particularly loud in Lebanon. By embracing revolution directly and calling on the notion of *velayate faqih*,[18] Khomeini's path differed from those of both Musa al-Sadr and Hizb al-Da'wa, setting a new sort of example for the mobilizing Shi'a Muslims. It also provided an alternative counter-narrative to the West from that espoused by the political left, at precisely the moment when the Lebanese left lost the faith of many of its Shi'a constituents. Not only did the Islamism that emerged from Iran speak to historical redemption and the rise of the oppressed, but it did so *successfully*.

Finally, the last ingredient in this cauldron of events was the second Israeli invasion of Lebanon in June 1982, during which another 450,000 people were displaced. This time Israeli troops marched north and laid West Beirut under siege. Tens of thousands of Lebanese were killed and injured during the invasion and siege, many of them Shi'a Muslims. It was during this time that the Sabra and Shatila massacres took place. Between 16 and 18 September 1982, under the protection of the Israeli military and then Israeli Defense Minister Ariel Sharon, a Lebanese Phalangist militia unit entered the Sabra and Shatila refugee camps in Beirut, and raped, killed and maimed thousands of civilian refugees.[19] Approximately one-quarter of those refugees were Shi'a Lebanese who had fled the violence in the south. The second Israeli invasion was perhaps the most essential catalyst in the eventual formation – from many of the existing strands of Shi'a mobilization – of Hizbullah.

Following the events of 1982, many prominent members of Amal left the party.[20] Many of them, along with Nasrallah, went on to form the leadership of Hizbullah. In addition, the Iranian revolution had contributed to the waning of support for Hizb al-Da'wa and its methods, and many of its members and Fadlallah's followers also went on to become Hizbullah members.[21] At this point, a number of small, armed groups of young men had begun to fight the Israeli troops that were occupying their villages in the south and the Beqaa. Iranian revolutionary guards had arrived in the Beqaa to train some of these fighters. Over time, these groups, which included many of Fadlallah's followers, former Amal members, Islamic Amal (a splinter group), the Lebanese Union of Muslim Students, Hizb al-Da'wa and a group called 'The Committee Supporting the Islamic Revolution' which had existed since 1979, among others, began to coordinate with one another and to coalesce around an Islamic ideology.[22] In 1984 Iran facilitated a meeting that led to the formation of an organization bringing all these groups together, and this was the origin of Hizbullah and its armed wing, *al-muqawama al-islamiyya*, the Islamic Resistance – though they did not formally announce their existence until the following year, in an 'Open Letter' or manifesto, released in 1985.

That same year, Israel withdrew from most of Lebanon, but continued to occupy around 10 percent of the south until 2000, using both Israeli soldiers and a proxy Lebanese militia of collaborators called the Southern Lebanese Army (SLA). Following escalating tensions between Hizbullah and Amal – including all-out warfare in 1988–89 – Hizbullah's presence emerged as the stronger one. The party's Islamic Resistance soon took the lead in fighting the Israeli occupation, along with other resistance contingents, including Amal and some of the leftist parties. Over the years levels of national support for the resistance fluctuated. Israeli attacks on Lebanese civilians and infrastructure – including the destruction of power plants in Beirut in 1996, 1999 and 2000 – generally contributed to increases in national support for the Resistance. This was especially true after Israel bombed a United Nations (UN) bunker where civilians had taken refuge in Qana on 18 April 1996, killing over 100 people.[23]

Since its origins in the mid-1980s, Hizbullah has developed from its roots as a resistance militia into a full-fledged political organization and party which includes military, political and social welfare aspects. This chapter now turns to those elements of today's Hizbullah.

Politics and resistance; resistance politics

The Lebanese wars came to a spluttering and unresolved end in 1990, following the signing of the Ta'if Accords in 1989, an agreement that essentially reasserted a variation of the original sectarian system. The Ta'if Accords also made a formal exception for Hizbullah, and allowed the party to retain its armed wing in order to continue resisting the ongoing Israeli occupation of south Lebanon. It was also at this time that Hizbullah made two moves that mark its transition into Lebanese national politics. First, the party expanded its decision-making apparatus. Two new institutions – an executive council and a politburo – were added to the original religious council (*majlis al-shura*). The second marker of this transition was Hizbullah's decision to participate in the first post-war elections, held in 1992. There was a great deal of debate about this within the party leadership between those who wanted to maintain a revolutionary stance outside the state, and those who thought that working within the state was the preferred route. Nasrallah took the latter view. He had just become Secretary-General of the party after Israel assassinated his predecessor, and it was under his leadership and direction that the party committed itself to working *within* the Lebanese state. Reasons cited for this shift include: the end of the Lebanese wars and the re-establishment of the state, the end of the Cold War and Syria's integration into the international community, the possibility of imagining an end to the Arab–Israeli conflict, and changes underway in Iran (Picard 1997; Norton 2000).

In that first election, Hizbullah won eight seats, giving them the largest single bloc in the 128-member Parliament, and its allies won an additional four seats. During the next decade Hizbullah developed a reputation – among Muslims and Christians alike – for being a reputable political party on both the national and local levels.[24] This reputation is especially important in Lebanon, where governmental corruption is assumed, clientelism is the norm (Hamzeh 2001), political positions are often inherited, and the Parliament is the wealthiest legislative body in the world in terms of its members' personal wealth.

The occupation of south Lebanon was costly for Israel. Israeli Prime Minister Barak made withdrawal a campaign promise, and later announced that it would take place by July 2000. A month and a half before this deadline, in the wake of the collapse of potential talks with Syria and SLA desertions,[25] a chaotic withdrawal from Lebanon ensued, taking many by surprise. At 3.00 a.m. on 24 May 2000 the last Israeli soldier stepped off Lebanese soil and locked the gate at the Fatima border crossing behind him. Many predicted that lawlessness, sectarian violence and chaos would fill the void left by the Israeli occupation forces and the SLA, which rapidly collapsed in Israel's wake. Those predictions proved false, as SLA members either fled or surrendered; most of the latter were given short jail sentences (Norton 2000, 2002).

However, when Israel withdrew from Lebanon, they did not withdraw from a small 15-square-mile border region called the Shebaa' Farms. Lebanon and Syria both assert that the Shebaa' Farms belong to Lebanon, and Israel and the UN have declared it to be part of the Israeli-occupied Golan Heights. Two other major points of difference were over a map of Israeli-planted landmines, and over prisoners, where a number of Lebanese were still detained in Israel. In this continuing low-grade conflict, between May 2000 and July 2006 both Hizbullah and Israel generally operated within a set of what Israeli journalist Daniel Sobelman has called the unstated 'rules of the game'.[26] These rules were based on an agreement not to target civilians that was written after the Qana attack in 1996, which had the effect of generally confining violence to the Shebaa' Farms area and to armed fighters.

At the same time, as documented in the biannual reports of observers with the UN Interim Force in Lebanon, both sides occasionally broke these rules, including by abducting people from across the border. For example, Israeli forces kidnapped a number of Lebanese shepherds and fishermen. Hizbullah kidnapped an Israeli businessman who they claimed was a spy. In January 2004 several years of negotiations brokered by Germany ended in a prisoner exchange during which the kidnapped Israeli and the bodies of three Israeli soldiers killed in Lebanon prior to Israel's 2000 withdrawal were exchanged for Lebanese and Arab detainees in Israel, including a Hizbullah official who had been kidnapped from Lebanon 15 years earlier. However, at the last minute, Israeli officials held on to a few detainees, leading Nasrallah to vow that the party would secure their release through future exchange negotiations.

The July 2006 war

On 12 July 2006 Hizbullah set in motion a plan that the party thought would lead to the keeping of that vow, capturing Israeli soldiers on the border in order to reinitiate exchange negotiations. According to both the precedent set by the 2004 negotiations and the 'rules' that cross-border conflict had been following, Israel's response to the soldiers' capture would have been the selective bombing of a few sites in the south and perhaps one Lebanese power plant, followed by indirect negotiations. This time, though, the rules were broken.

For over a month, Israeli warplanes battered so-called 'Hizbullah strongholds' in Lebanon, unleashing an aerial assault on Lebanon's cities, villages, civilians and infrastructure of a scale unseen since the 1982 Israeli invasion of the country. A naval blockade and ground invasion accompanied the air force attack. By the time a ceasefire went into effect in mid-August, in conjunction with UN Security Council resolution 1701, 1,300 Lebanese were estimated to have been killed, the majority of whom were civilians, mainly children.[27] Thousands were wounded and nearly 1 million were displaced from their homes – one-quarter of the country's population. Entire villages in the south of Lebanon were flattened in this attack, as were whole neighborhoods in the southern suburbs of Beirut. Analyst estimates of infrastructural damage to the country ranged from \$3–8 billion, and included the destruction of runways and fuel tanks at Beirut International Airport, roads, ports, power plants, bridges, gas stations, TV transmitters, cell phone towers, a dairy and other factories, wheat silos and grocery stores. Humanitarian and environmental crises loomed, not least due to unexploded 'bomblets' remaining from Israeli-dropped (US-manufactured) cluster munitions.[28]

The magnitude of this Israeli strike was especially glaring because between 2000 and July 2006 there had been no deliberate Hizbullah attacks against Israeli civilian targets, the Islamic Resistance only had an active contingent of around 500 fighters and Hizbullah was in talks with the Lebanese government about disarmament. While the goal of the attack was supposedly to obtain the release of two captured Israeli POWs, this military response was so antithetical to the 'rules of the game' that it cast immediate doubt on the relationship of the attack to those captured soldiers. Indeed, Israel's original rhetoric gave way to two new stated goals: the disarmament or at least 'degrading' of Hizbullah's militia and the 'removal' of Hizbullah from Lebanon.[29] Despite the devastation wrought, that goal was not met and, in fact, at the end of the war Nasrallah declared victory. This chapter now turns to the internal political ramifications of this war, and that declaration, for Hizbullah.

Lebanese political machinations

Hizbullah's popularity among its constituents, and more broadly in the Middle East, soared after the July war, and many party supporters (as well as the party itself) cast the war as a victory. Nasrallah became one of the most popular leaders among people across the Middle East and beyond, his image appearing in taxicabs and store windows as far as Senegal. However, soon after, this notion of the war as a victory became one of the rhetorical weapons thrown around in an ongoing standoff between the government and the opposition.

This political bifurcation had begun to consolidate after Prime Minister Rafiq Hariri was assassinated on 14 February 2005. Calls quickly emerged for the withdrawal of Syrian troops from Lebanon. On 8 March of that year Hizbullah and its allies held a rally thanking the Syrian troops, while on 14 March Hariri's Future Movement Party, now led by his son Saad, and its allies held a demonstration against Syria. To this day, the Hizbullah-led coalition is known as the 'March 8' group and the Future-led coalition as the 'March 14' group. When elections were held a few months later, Hizbullah won 14 parliamentary seats in a voting bloc with other parties that took 35. For the first time, the party also chose to participate in the cabinet, and was allotted the Ministry of Energy. The 2005 elections demonstrated Hizbullah's willingness to play the political game in Lebanon, where candidates run as multi-confessional district slates rather than as individuals, allying (however temporarily) with politicians who do not back its program. Ironically, the Sunni Muslim on Hizbullah's slate in Sidon was Bahiyya al-Hariri, sister of the assassinated premier and a 14 March stalwart.

In another twist, since the 2005 elections, former General Michel Aoun (and his party, the Free Patriotic Movement), once the quintessentially 'anti-Syrian' figure in Lebanese politics, has joined Hizbullah and Amal in the opposition and is now a key leader of the 8 March alliance. When Hizbullah represented the July 2006 war as a victory, the 14 March politicians quickly responded with accusations that the resistance had caused the war. A few months later, in October, the 8 March alliance called for a national unity government giving them one-third plus one of the cabinet seats, enough to hold a de facto veto. Prime Minister Siniora refused this demand and rhetoric on both sides continued to escalate until all six Shi'a Muslim ministers resigned, leaving the executive branch of the government without representation from the largest confessional group in the country. This was followed by an opposition sit-in in downtown Beirut, beginning on 1 December 2006 and fizzling out over a year later.

Perhaps the only success of the sit-in was to highlight the class dimensions of this conflict. The area of downtown where the sit-in took place is the area on which the rebuilding of Beirut under Rafiq Hariri had focused, replete with prohibitively expensive apartments and office space, designer stores and clubs. In contrast, those maintaining the sit-in on a daily basis included many who were displaced or were unemployed because of the July war. Despite having little in the way of an economic platform, the opposition also supported labor unions' stances against Siniora's proposal for a neoliberal economic reform plan to accompany requests for foreign government donations to alleviate Lebanon's over $40 billion in debt – mostly accumulated during the post-civil war reconstruction of that elite downtown Beirut. As rhetoric continued to polarize, both class biases and anti-Shi'a sentiment emerged explicitly.

As the stalemate continued, Lebanon saw general strikes that included small outbursts of violence, several rounds of talks that led nowhere, and a period where the country was literally without a President. Tensions culminated in May 2008, when in response to government majority calls to shut down its secure telecommunications networks, Hizbullah fighters led the opposition in a brief military incursion into several West Beirut neighborhoods, and for the first time since Ta'if, used their military strength internally. Eleven people were killed during the May battles, and more wounded. After quickly gaining the upper hand and taking control of these neighborhoods from Future Movement militiamen, Hizbullah and its opposition allies handed them over to the Lebanese Army, which promptly reversed the telecommunications decision. Talks were then held that ended the political stalemate for the time being.

One recent arena for this bipolar conflict was the 2009 Lebanese elections, which eclipsed all other news in the country for much of the first half of the year. In those elections, Hizbullah held on to its 14 parliamentary seats, although the opposition as a whole did not emerge with a majority in Parliament, much to General Aoun's disappointment. With the formation of a new government in 2009, an uneasy and short-lived rapprochement was achieved. But by summer 2010, conflict re-emerged, sparked by rumblings that the report of the UN Special Tribunal for Lebanon investigating Hariri's assassination would point fingers at Hizbullah members. In January 2011, the 8 March coalition resigned en masse from the cabinet, causing the government's collapse by constitutional means. It took the new Prime Minister, Najib Miqati, months to form a government, which eventually received the necessary vote of confidence from Parliament in July 2011. For the first time, Hizbullah is, as this goes to press, part of the government majority coalition.

In general in politics, although Hizbullah is often accused of being a puppet of either Iran or Syria, the group's decisions and actions have focused on maintaining its position and the support of its constituents within the Lebanese polity.[30] Hizbullah does officially follow Ayatollah Khomeini as the party's *marja' al-taqlid*, or source of emulation in religious matters,[31] consults with Iranian leaders, and receives an indeterminate amount of economic aid from Iran. This relationship does not, however, mean that Iran dictates Hizbullah's policies or decision-making, or can necessarily control the actions of the party. Meanwhile, Iranian efforts to infuse the Lebanese Shi'a with a pan-Shi'a identity centered on Iran have run up against the Arab identity and increasing Lebanese nationalism of Hizbullah itself. Similarly, while the party keeps good relations with the Syrian government, Syria does not control or dictate Hizbullah's decisions or actions. Party decisions are made in accordance with Hizbullah's view of Lebanon's interests and the party's own interests within Lebanese politics.

There is no doubt that Hizbullah is a nationalist party. Its view of nationalism differs from that of many Lebanese, especially from the nationalism based on the Phoenician origins myth espoused by Lebanon's Christian right, and from the neoliberal US-backed nationalism of Hariri's party. Hizbullah instead offers a nationalism that views Lebanon as an Arab state that cannot distance itself from Arab causes like that of Palestine. Its political ideology maintains an Islamic outlook, and the 1985 Open Letter that is often read as the party's initial 'manifesto' notes the desire to establish an Islamic state, but only through the will of the people, stating 'We don't want Islam to reign in Lebanon by force' (Hizbullah 1985). The party's decision to participate in elections in 1992 underscored its commitment to working through the existing (sectarian) structure of the Lebanese state, and also shifted the party's focus from a pan-Islamic resistance to Israel toward internal Lebanese issues. Furthermore, since 1992 Hizbullah leaders have frequently acknowledged the contingencies of Lebanon's multi-confessional society and the importance of sectarian coexistence and pluralism within the country. It should also be noted that many of Hizbullah's constituents do not want to live in an Islamic state; rather, they want the party to represent their interests within a pluralist Lebanon.

In 2009 Hizbullah articulated many of these positions and policies in their new *wathiqa siyasiyya* – which the party itself is calling its Manifesto in English (although 'political document' would be a more accurate translation). This document represents the first formal statement by the party of its principles and positions since the 1985 Open Letter. The manifesto includes leftist and economically oriented language in its diagnoses of the state of the region and country, but does not provide concrete economic solutions; it emphasizes Hizbullah's commitment to the Lebanese state as well as its continued commitment to Resistance against Israeli threat; it abstractly calls for the disestablishment of sectarianism in Lebanon; and it calls for greater rights for Palestinians in Lebanon and continued relationships with Arab and Islamic states in the region. As detailed above, none of this is particularly new, yet the document grants a formalized quality to the ideas and practices espoused by the party since the 1990s.

What sets Hizbullah apart from other Lebanese organizations is the professional level of organization that exists within the party and its institutions. This is the Lebanese political party that best responds to its constituencies' needs and desires in the country, politically and economically. In contrast to many of the stereotypes about Shi'a Muslims held in Lebanon or stereotypes about religious Muslims held in the West, this is related to the party's explicit embrace and promotion of a particular conception of modernity that is integrative of material and spiritual goals of progress in such a way that the two come to depend upon one another (Deeb 2006). In this vision, Islam and development go hand in hand, and in fact promote one another. It is the adherence to this particular vision of development and progress that appeals to many of Hizbullah's supporters. This chapter now turns to one manifestation of that vision: the party's social welfare networks.

Social welfare in the southern suburbs, the south and beyond

Like politics, most social welfare organizations, or *jam'iyyas*, in Lebanon are sectarian in orientation. Among the consequences of the civil war and Israel invasions were economic stagnancy, government corruption and a widening gap between the ever-shrinking middle class and the ever-expanding poor.[32] Shi'a areas of Beirut also had to cope with massive displacements from the south and the Beqaa. In this economic climate, sectarian clientelism became a necessary survival tool. 'Lebanon may have its charms, but the government has no social conscience and provides no safety net for the poor. One turns to the family and a variety of sectarian charities for assistance' (Norton 2002: 44).

One of the consequences of historic Shi'a marginalization in Lebanon was a lack of resources being funneled into Shi'a areas. Before the 1960s there were only a few scattered Shi'a organizations, including the 'Charity and Benevolence Society' established in the south by Musa al-Sadr's father-in-law in 1948.[33] Beginning in 1963, al-Sadr added to this organization, building institutions in Beirut as well as in Tyre, including the Imam al-Khu'i orphanage in Beirut. Following al-Sadr's disappearance, his *irth*, or inheritance, was divided among the major players in the Shi'a Islamic movement. In that division, the Imam al-Khu'i orphanage came to Fadlallah. From that starting point, he established al-Mabarrat Charitable Association (*jam'iyyat al-mabarrāt al-khayriyya*, henceforth, al-Mabarrat). Today, al-Mabarrat has grown into one of the best-respected charitable associations in Lebanon, with over 20 schools, six orphanages, hospitals, cultural centers, and institutions for the blind, deaf and physically disabled spanning the country.[34]

The other major group of large-scale Shi'a Islamic *jam'iyyas* in the area are those affiliated with Hizbullah. Staffed mainly by highly trained volunteers, these institutions assess the needs of their constituents and work to meet those needs, whether by providing monthly support, or supplemental nutritional, educational, housing or health assistance. The institutions are located around Lebanon and serve the local people regardless of sect, though they are concentrated in the mainly Shi'a Muslim areas of the country.[35] Examples include the Islamic Charity Emdad Committee (ICEC), the Martyr's Association, *Jihād al-Binā'* Development Organization, the Hizbullah Women's Committee, the Association for the Wounded, and the Islamic Health Committee. Some of these organizations, such as the ICEC and the Martyr's Association, were founded by young Lebanese volunteers assisted by representatives from sister organizations in Iran. By 2000 the ICEC was running several schools and institutions and supporting over 4,000 orphans by helping their mothers or extended families raise them at home with monthly support and supplemental nutritional, educational, housing and health assistance. The association's budget comes mainly from donations, religious tithes, Ramadan fundraisers, almost 3,000 full orphan sponsorships, and the ubiquitous collection boxes that are scattered all over Lebanon.

All of these social welfare organizations are heavily dependent on volunteer labor. For example, the ICEC in 2000 had only around 90 employees, but over 350 volunteers. Like the resistance fighters who were with the initial mobilization that eventually became Hizbullah, many women volunteers began their work during the mid-1980s, before there was an institutional structure to facilitate it. Just as resistance fighters found inspiration in Shi'a religious history, and especially the martyrdom of Imam Husayn, Shi'a women volunteers found inspiration in the active leadership of Husayn's sister, Sayyida Zaynab, and look to her as a model. Not only was Sayyida Zaynab at the Battle where Husayn was killed, she was also the leader of the Shi'a community for a time after his death and is credited with holding the community together during a time of crisis.

Hizbullah actively promotes this activist model for pious Shi'a women and promotes women's public participation. The party has provided many of the venues where pious women are able to find employment, for example, not only at their social welfare institutions but also at media outlets like their television station and at their hospitals and clinics. The party also has a Women's Committee that holds educational seminars on everything from health issues to interpreting religious texts to combating sexism within their community. They have also devoted time to convincing the party to run women as candidates on election slates, thus far successfully running women on municipality slates and having the first woman elected to the party's politburo.

Hizbullah's social welfare network is one aspect of the party's activities that sometimes leads to accusations that Hizbullah is a state within a state, but this type of welfare network actually fits quite well into the way that Lebanon has worked as a sectarian system. Hizbullah is filling gaps left by the state when it comes to welfare issues, by providing resources for a sectarian community in precisely the ways that other religious organizations in Lebanon do.

It is in part the efficiency and efficacy of the party's social welfare networks on the ground that contributed to the maintenance and increase in Hizbullah's popularity among many Lebanese following the July 2006 war. In a televised address marking the end of the war, Nasrallah devoted one-third of his airtime to discussing plans to rebuild homes and house the displaced. The very next day party volunteers with clipboards were out assessing damage, prioritizing repairs, providing rent money and basic needs for displaced families and school supplies for students, and beginning the work of reconstruction.[36] Yet the social welfare networks do not fully or adequately explain why so many Lebanese support Hizbullah. As this chapter concludes, it turns to an exploration of the party's civilian constituencies.

Civilian constituencies: What does it mean to be a Hizbullah supporter?

Hizbullah is of Lebanon, but does not have a metonymic relationship to Lebanon. It does not represent all Lebanese, nor does it represent all Shi'a Muslim Lebanese, despite recent sectarian political polarizations in Lebanon. Similarly, not all Hizbullah supporters are Shi'a Muslim. The religion into which one is born, the religion one may or may not practice, does not determine one's political affiliations or preferences.

Nor does one's socioeconomic status. The view that Hizbullah is using its social organizations to 'buy' support betrays a simplistic view of the party. Hizbullah's constituents are not only the poor, but increasingly come from the middle classes and include many upwardly mobile, highly educated Lebanese. In fact, much of the financial backing of the party's institutions comes from its supporters, including many expatriate Lebanese. The idea that Hizbullah's work of rebuilding will be funded entirely by Iran ignores that millions of dollars are donated to the party annually by Shi'a Muslims around the world, in the form of religious taxes, individual contributions and orphan sponsorships. Pious Shi'a Muslims pay an annual tithe called the *khums*, one-fifth of the income they do not need for their own family's upkeep. Half of this tithe is give to the care of a *marja al-taqlid* of their choice – a religious leader who is emulated and consulted on religious matters. Since 1995, when Ayatollah Khomeini appointed Nasrallah and another Hizbullah leader as his religious deputies in Lebanon,[37] the *khums* revenues of Lebanese Shi'a who follow Khomeini have gone directly into Hizbullah's coffers. These Shi'a also give their *zakat*, the alms required of all Muslims able to pay, to Hizbullah's vast network of social welfare institutions. Other Lebanese Shi'a instead pay this tithe to the care of Sayyid Fadlallah, and many of the independent social welfare organizations in the southern suburbs have been delegated acceptable 'surrogates' for these donations as well.

Hizbullah's popularity among Lebanese is multi-faceted, based on a combination of its resistance (and crucially, successful resistance) to Israeli occupation and attacks, Islamic ideology, political platforms and record in Lebanon, and an approach to political-economic development that includes an efficient welfare-provision network. Different Lebanese find different aspects of the party appealing for different reasons. As with political affiliation and allegiance anywhere, these are not simple equations. For some, Hizbullah is viewed as providing a viable alternative to a US-supported government (it is part of the opposition in the current government) and its neoliberal economic project in Lebanon and as an active opposition to the role of the US in the Middle East more broadly. For others, Hizbullah is seen as the only viable possibility for protecting their villages, homes and livelihoods from Israeli attack. For some, the ability to send their children to schools that teach Islamic values along with the Lebanese state curriculum, or to visit single-sex beaches or restaurants that do not serve alcohol is appealing. For others, the financial support provided by the party's organizations was invaluable in helping them rebuild their lives after the civil war. Various of these views may coexist, and there are also people who vehemently oppose the party's Islamic outlook, while supporting Hizbullah's resistance militia's activities and their right to defend the south.

'Hizbullah supporter' itself is a vague phrase. Among many others, there are official members of the party; there are fighters with the Resistance; there are volunteers in party-affiliated social welfare organizations; there are recipients of aid from those organizations; there are those who voted for the party in the last election; there are those who support the Resistance in the current conflict without supporting other aspects of the party's political platform. The best way to think of the relationship among these various ideologies, positions and activities, and the Lebanese who support or align themselves with them, is to think of imperfectly overlapping circles and ideas that are constantly shifting. Individuals traverse this terrain of institutions and ideologies in complex ways, as they do in any society. Indeed, there are indications that support for the party from people outside its immediate constituencies is decreasing as a direct result of Nasrallah's stance in support of the Asad regime in Syria, a stance that has highlighted for many Lebanese the party's hypocrasy when it comes to the so-called 'Arab Spring', as it has supported uprisings across the region with the significant exception of that in Syria.

Hizbullah is much more than an armed militia. As we have seen, in addition to its resistance militia, it is a political party and a social welfare network. It has to do with economic interests as well as religious ideologies, local politics and anti-imperialist stances. The party's future depends on a number of factors, including, *inter alia*, continuing political negotiations and machinations with regard to Lebanon's Parliament and cabinet; future military conflicts with Israel; US politics in the Middle East; the ever-changing Saudi Arabia–Syria–Iran dance; the Arab Spring; and the Palestinian–Israeli conflict. Despite all these contingencies, however, it is likely that Hizbullah's role within the Lebanese polity and its importance among its constituents will continue to grow for three main reasons. First, because the party's popularity is also rooted in the desire to have a voice and a stake within the sectarian political system, and because many of its constituents grew up in a Lebanon where Hizbullah has been the only group that has made much progress in giving them that voice and stake. Second, it is crucial not to underestimate the appeal that a particular sort of religious lifestyle supported by Hizbullah has for many Lebanese, as evidenced by the plethora of recently opened restaurants and cafés that facilitate a particular moral lifestyle (Deeb and Harb 2008). Finally, because until people in Lebanon, and especially in the south and in the southern suburbs, trust that they will be protected from Israeli attack, many of them will support the existence of the party's Islamic Resistance.

Notes

1 Aside from the US, only Israel and Canada list Hizbullah as a 'terrorist organization'; Canada's listing came under legal pressure from pro-Israel groups in 2002.
2 The label 'terrorist' itself is problematic, as it has become a catch-all term used to justify US and allied rhetoric and violence. Only applied to non-state actors, it leaves 'terror' committed by Israeli (or US military forces) as 'legitimate'. See also Harb and Leenders 2005.
3 Following the Arabic terms, I use 'Shi'i' as the adjective form, 'Shi'a' as the collective noun and 'Shi'a Muslims' as the plural.

4 Today there are 18 recognized groups.

5 The ratio of Christians to Muslims in Parliament was 6:5. Christian seats were primarily allocated to Maronites. Sunni Muslims received 11 of the 25 Muslim seats and the Druze received four.

6 Picard (1997) notes that in 1948 Shi'a made up 70–85 percent of the population of the rural south and Beqaa, and only 3.5 percent of the population of Beirut.

7 See Picard (1997) and Halawi (1992) on these economic shifts.

8 By 1973 only 40 percent of Shi'a Muslims remained rural, and Shi'a Muslims constituted 29 percent of Beirut's population (Picard 1997).

9 Despite CNN's insistence on describing this area as 'the Hizbullah stronghold', it is today a vibrant and densely populated part of Beirut's urban fabric that is far more diverse than that media misnomer suggests. See Harb 2000.

10 Lebanon's location, geography, pro-business government policies and banking secrecy laws facilitated this, along with the closures of Haifa and the Suez Canal due to the Arab–Israeli conflicts.

11 In addition, by the mid-1950s many Shi'a Muslims had emigrated to West Africa, including Senegal, the Ivory Coast, Sierra Leone, Liberia and Ghana. They maintained ties to Lebanon and had a high rate of return, contributing to the connectedness of the population.

12 Many Shi'a Muslims initially supported Fatah, the military wing of what became the Palestine Liberation Organization (PLO), but in the 1970s, when Israeli retaliations began to affect Shi'a villages, many turned against the Palestinians. The first Shi'a militia, Amal, was initially trained by Fatah (Norton 1987), but this relationship disintegrated into violence during the 1980s 'Camp Wars'.

13 'Amal' means 'hope' in Arabic and is also an acronym for *Afwāj al-Muqāwama al-Lubnāniyya* (the Lebanese Resistance Brigades).

14 Musa al-Sadr's success in uniting the Shi'a under a sectarian banner has been variously evaluated, with some (Ajami 1986) attributing him greater success than others (Norton 1987).

15 AbuKhalil (1991) observes that Fadlallah and al-Sadr were working from different perspectives as early as the 1960s.

16 Before it ended in 1990, the civil war involved over 20 militias and several state armies, including those of Syria and Israel. It is crucial in the contemporary climate to note that this was not a religious war or a sectarian war, but rather a war rooted in political issues that rarely overlaid sectarian divisions. In fact, some of the most devastating fighting took place within sectarian communities.

17 Other contributing factors to this distancing from the left include a general mistrust of atheism and the end of the Nasser era. For more on the failures of the Lebanese left, see AbuKhalil 1988.

18 Meaning 'guidance of the jurisprudent', this is the basis of the Islamic state in Iran: spiritual and political authority reside in the same institution, headed by a cleric who is the Hidden Imam's representative on Earth.

19 There is some debate as to whether it was a Phalangist or Lebanese Forces militia. Casualty figures range from 800 to 3,500, and are most likely in the vicinity of 2,000. Several hundred people also 'disappeared'. The 1983 Israeli Kahan Commission attributed 'personal responsibility' for the massacres to Sharon (Harik 2004). For reports and documentation of these massacres, see Fisk (1990), Kapeliouk (1983), Siegel (2001), the reports of the Kahan Commission (1983) (available from www.mfa.gov.il) and the MacBride Commission (MacBride *et al.* 1983). See also Harik (2004: 35–36, 64–65).

20 This was related to a shift in Amal's leadership after al-Sadr disappeared; since 1980 it has been led by Nabih Berri, who angered many by participating in US-brokered negotiations in 1982. Today, Amal remains one of the two major Shi'a political parties in Lebanon, with strength in parts of the south and a few al-Dahiya neighborhoods – and Berri is Speaker of the Lebanese Parliament.

21 Fadlallah is frequently inaccurately characterized as 'the spiritual leader' of Hizbullah. He has always held that Islamic work should occur through multiple institutions and has always denied having any official role in the party. Yet as one of the most prominent figures in the Lebanese Shi'a community, Fadlallah's teachings and sermons have influenced many Hizbullah members.

22 There is a plethora of literature detailing Hizbullah's origins, history, relations with Iran and Syria, and military and political activities. See especially AbuKhalil (1991), Hamzeh (2000), Harik (2004), Norton (2007), and Saad-Ghorayeb (2002).

23 See the UN Report on this incident, dated 1 May 1996. It states that, contrary to Israeli claims, 'it is unlikely that the shelling of the United Nations compound was the result of gross technical and/or procedural errors'.

24 For more on Hizbullah parliamentary politics from 1992–96, see el-Bizri (1999). For more on the 1998 municipal elections, see Hamzeh (2000) and Harik (2004: 95–110).

25 Norton notes that 'unilateral withdrawal was a *default strategy*' for Israel, which would have preferred withdrawal to take place in conjunction with an Israeli-Syrian agreement (Norton 2000: 31).

26 Daniel Sobelman (2004) 'Still playing by the rules', *Bitterlemons International* 36, no. 2, available at www.bitterlemons-international.org.

27 During this time Hizbullah killed 118 Israeli soldiers and 41 civilians. Israel claimed to have killed over 300 Hizbullah fighters, but Hizbullah denied that number and publicly mourned its dead at much lower numbers. The ratio of Lebanese to Israeli civilian casualties was 30:1.

28 See Human Rights Watch (2006) and Zaatari (2006).

29 For an excellent analysis of this particular Israeli attack on Lebanon and its relationship to the US 'war on terror', see Kalman (2006) and Hersh (2006), as well as the writings and interviews of political anthropologist Augustus Richard Norton in various media sources, posted on his blog at www.bostonuniversity.com, the commentary of political scientist As'ad AbuKhalil at www.angryarab.blogspot.com, and collected analyses at www.electroniclebanon.net.

30 While she overstates the control Iran has today over the party, Shaery-Eisenlohr (2009) provides a good discussion of the historical complexity of the relationship of Hizbullah and the Lebanese Shi'a community more broadly to Iran, pre- and post-revolution, especially with regard to changing Iranian perspectives on that relationship. She also shows the historical complexity and roots of accusations of being 'Iranian' in Lebanon, relevant to contemporary political machinations in the country.

31 Party members, however, are free to follow any *marja' al-taqlid* they choose, and many follow Sayyid Muhammad Husayn Fadlallah instead.

32 See Norton (2002) and Kubursi (1993) on the post-war economy. Per capita income went from $1,800 in 1974 to less than $250 in 1989 (Kubursi 1993). Severe inflation sent the value of a US dollar in Lebanese lira rocketing from the single digits to 2,000 in the span of a few years. Today the lira is fixed at 1,507 to one US dollar, and both currencies are used interchangeably.

33 El Khazen (2000) lists social service associations by sect in 1965 and 1977–78. In 1965 there were 13 Shi'a organizations, as compared to 28 Maronite, 42 Greek Orthodox and 26 Sunni. In 1977–78 there were 38 Shi'a organizations, as compared to 70 Maronite, 44 Greek Orthodox and 66 Sunni (El Khazen 2000: 67). These differences are magnified by differential populations (e.g. there were many more Orthodox institutions per capita).

34 Much of the money for this expansion has come from wealthy Shi'a Muslims who followed Khu'i and/or follow Fadlallah as their *marji'*, especially in the Gulf States. For example, the Bahman Hospital in al-Dahiyya was built from a donation of $60 million by its Kuwaiti namesake.

35 For more on this social welfare network, see Deeb 2006.

36 Personal communication from several of the displaced. See also Agence France Presse 2006.

37 This is not a political appointment, but rather an appointment as Khamenei's deputies in his (contested) capacity as *marji' al-taqlid*. The importance of this appointment is that it allows for the collection of *khums* on his behalf.

References

AbuKhalil, A. (1988) 'The Palestinian-Shiite war in Lebanon: An examination of its origins', *Third World Affairs* vol. 10, no. 1: 77–89.

—— (1991) 'Ideology and practice of Hizballah in Lebanon: Islamization of Leninist organizational principles', *Middle Eastern Studies* vol. 27, no. 3: 390–403.

Agence France Presse (2006) 'Hizbullah's efficiency leaves Lebanese government behind', *Daily Star*, available at www.dailystar.com.lb/article.asp?edition_id=1&categ_id=3&article_id=75062 (accessed 28 February 2011).

Ajami, F. (1986) *The vanished Imam: Musa al-Sadr and the Shi'a of Lebanon*, Ithaca, NY, Cornell University Press.

Blanford, N. (2003) 'Hizballah in the firing line', *Middle East Report Online*, available at www.merip.org (accessed 2 March 2011).

Cobban, H. (1985) *The Making of Modern Lebanon*, London, Hutchinson.

Deeb, L. (2006) *An Enchanted Modern: Gender and Public Piety in Shi'a Lebanon*, Princeton, NJ, Princeton University Press.

Deeb, L. and Harb, M. (2008) 'Sanctioned Pleasures: Youth, Piety and Leisure in Lebanon', *Middle East Report* vol. 245: 12–19.

El-Bizri, D. (1999) '*Islamistes, parlementaires et Libanais: Les interventions a l'Assemblee des elus de la Jama'a Islamiyya et du Hizb Allah (1992–1996)*', Centre d'etudes et de recherches sur le Moyen-Orient contemporain.

El Khazen, F. (2000) *The breakdown of the state in Lebanon: 1967–1976*, Cambridge, MA, Harvard University Press.

Fisk, R. (1990) *Pity the nation: The abduction of Lebanon*, New York, Simon and Schuster.

Halawi, M. (1992) *A Lebanon defied: Musa al-Sadr and the Shi'a community*, Boulder, CO, Westview Press.

Hamzeh, N. (2000) 'Lebanon's Islamists and local politics: a new reality', *Third World Quarterly* vol. 21, no. 5: 739–59.

—— (2001) 'Clientalism, Lebanon: Roots and trends', *Middle Eastern Studies* vol. 37, no. 3: 167–78.

Harb, M. (2000) 'Post-war Beirut: Resources, negotiations, and contestations in the Elyssar Project', *The Arab World Geographer* vol. 3: 272–89.

Harb, M. and Leenders, R. (2005) 'Know thy enemy: Hizbullah, "terrorism" and the politics of perception', *Third World Quarterly* vol. 26, no. 1: 173–97.

Harik, J. (2004) *Hezbollah: The Changing Face of Terrorism*, London, I.B.Tauris.

Hersh, S. (2006) 'Watching Lebanon: Washington's interests in Israel's war', *The New Yorker*, 21 August, available at www.newyorker.com/archive/2006/08/21/060821fa_fact (accessed 1 March 2011).

Hizbullah (1985) 'Nass al-Risala al-Maftuha allati wajahaha Hizballah ila-l-Mustad'afin fi Lubnan wa-l-Alam', al-Safir, Beirut.

Human Rights Watch (2006) 'Israeli Cluster Munitions Hit Civilians in Lebanon', 24 July, available at www.hrw.org/de/news/2006/07/24/israeli-cluster-munitions-hit-civilians-lebanon (accessed 1 March 2011).

Joseph, S. (1975) *The politicization of religious sects in Borj Hammoud, Lebanon*, PhD dissertation, New York, Columbia University.

Kalman, M. (2006) 'Israel set war plan more than a year ago', *San Francisco Chronicle*, 21 July, available at www.sfgate.com/cgi-bin/article.cgi?f=/c/a/2006/07/21/MIDEAST.TMP (accessed 1 March 2011).

Kapeliouk, A. (1983) *Sabra and Shatila: Inquiry into a massacre*, Belmont, Association of Arab-American University Graduates Press.

Khuri, F. (1975) *From village to suburb: Order and change in Greater Beirut*, Chicago, University of Illinois Press.

Kubursi, A. (1993) 'Reconstructing and/or Reconstituting the Post-War Lebanese Economy: The Role of Infrastructural Development', in S. Khalaf and P. Khoury (eds), *Recovering Beirut: Urban Design and Post-War Reconstruction*, New York, Leiden.

MacBride, S., Asmal, A.K., Bercusson, B., Falk, R.A., Pradelle, G. de la and Wild, S. (1983) *Israel in Lebanon: The Report of International Commission to enquire into reported violations of International Law by Israel during its invasion of the Lebanon*, London, Ithaca Press.

Norton, A. (1987) *Amal and the Shi'a: Struggle for the soul of Lebanon*, Austin: University of Texas Press.

—— (1999) *Hizballah of Lebanon: Extremist ideals vs. mundane politics*, New York, Council on Foreign Relations.

—— (2000) 'Hizballah and the Israeli withdrawal from southern Lebanon', *Journal of Palestine Studies* vol. 30: 22–35.

—— (2002) 'Lebanon's malaise', *Survival* vol. 42: 35–50.

—— (2007) *Hezbollah: A Short History*, Princeton, NJ, Princeton University Press.

Picard, E. (1997) 'The Lebanese Shi'a and political violence in Lebanon', in D. Apter (ed.), *The legitimization of violence*, New York, New York University Press.

Saad-Ghorayeb, A. (2002) *Hizb'ullah: Politics and religion*, London, Pluto Press.

Shaery-Eisenlohr, R. (2009) 'Territorializing Piety: Genealogy, Transnationalism, and Shi'ite Politics in Modern Lebanon', *Comparative Studies in Society and History* vol. 51, no. 3: 533–62.

Siegel, E. (2001) 'After nineteen years: Sabra and Shatila remembered', *Middle East Policy* vol. 8, no. 4: 86–100.

Zaatari, M. (2006) 'Scientists suspect Israeli arms used in South contain radioactive matter', *Daily Star*, 21 August, available at www.dailystar.com.lb/article.asp?article_ID=74891&categ_ID=1&edition_id=1# (accessed 1 March 2011).

8

Hizb ut-Tahrir

Mohamed Nawab Bin Mohamed Osman

> They are the selected elite of the *umma*, the beautiful mole that no eye can miss, the lamps of light
> boast in their mouths, their tongues speak of the evidences of the Book (Qur'an), they are the
> selected elite.
>
> *(Awdallah 2006)*

Since its inception, Hizb ut-Tahrir (HT) members have seen themselves as the chosen Muslim
elites who will save the Muslim world and bring it back to its glory days. It is this belief that has
drawn hundreds of thousands of its activists around the world to work towards its final goal of re-
establishing the Islamic Caliphate. HT is indeed an interesting and unique organization in many
senses. First, HT is one of the few Muslim organizations that remains truly transnational, with
party chapters spanning North America to Australia controlled by a central leadership based in the
Middle East. Second, the movement has remained non-violent despite the intense physical
repression it has encountered in some Muslim countries. Third, the movement seems to be
growing in strength surprisingly at the expense of Islamic political parties operating in several
Muslim countries. Immediate examples that come to mind are the HT movements in Palestine
and Bangladesh. Thus, HT merits a more in-depth study, which this chapter seeks to fulfill. There
will be three parts to this chapter. The first part will provide some brief details about HT's history.
The second will provide an analysis of its aims, beliefs, ideology and methodology, examining how
it sets out to propagate and implement them. The final part will attempt to highlight the nature of
HT's activism following the terrorist attacks of 11 September 2001. Specifically, we will see how
HT has modified its strategy of engagement following the events of 9/11.

Hizb ut-Tahrir: a brief history

The HT movement was founded in 1952 by Sheikh Taqiuddin An-Nabhani (1909–77) in the
city of Hebron, Palestine, together with several of his colleagues: Abdul Qadeem Zalloum (later
to become the second leader of HT), Sheikh As'ad Rajab Bayyud al-Tamimi, Khaled Hassan
and Sheikh Ahmad Daour. Born in 1909 in the village of Ijzim (part of the city of Hebron in
today's Israel), in the then Ottoman Syria, An-Nabhani hailed from a family of leading religious
intellectuals. His maternal grandfather, Sheikh Yusuf An-Nabhani (1849–1932), was an official

working at the Ottoman judiciary and was a major influence for the younger An-Nabhani. Naturally, the young An-Nabhani received his education in various prestigious Islamic institutions, including the Al-Azhar University. Upon completion of his studies, An-Nabhani worked as a religious teacher and subsequently as a judge (*qadi*) in Hebron, Palestine. Two major developments that shifted his life's perspective were the collapse of the Ottoman Caliphate in 1914 and the outbreak of the Arab–Israeli War that led to the defeat of the Arabs. These events left a major imprint on his mind and the need to revive the Islamic Caliphate became a hallmark of his political program.

The defeat of the Arabs in the Arab–Israeli war affected An-Nabhani deeply as he felt that the defeat could be attributed to their lack of belief in Islam (Taji-Farouki 1996: 2). He began engaging other Islamic scholars and thinkers of his time to formulate ways to return the Arab empire to its former glory. Amongst those he met and learned from were luminaries such as Hassan Al-Banna, leader of the *Ikhwan al-Muslimun* (Muslim Brotherhood – MB), Sheikh Al-Akhtar Hussein and Sayyid Qutb (another leader of the MB) (An-Nabhani 1950). It is perhaps important at this point to highlight An-Nabhani's relationship with the MB. Many authors of the HT movement are of the belief that An-Nabhani was a member of the MB. However, several factors seem to indicate otherwise. First, a prominent HT member who subsequently left the party for MB, Abdul Aziz Al-Khayyat, has noted in his biography that this was not the case. Second, it is also known that An-Nabhani stood firm on his decision of refusing to allow the *Jamiyyat Al-Ihtisam*, an Islamic society that he had formed in 1941 with several of his associates, to be absorbed by the MB (Commins 1991). Last, An-Nabhani, convinced that none of these thinkers had a clear solution to the Muslim problem, devised a new approach to the understanding of Islam by fusing a modernist Islamic political ideology with traditional Islamic teachings. To implement the ideas he had envisaged, An-Nabhani formed the HT party. The name of the party attested to its key aim of liberating Muslim countries from what it deemed un-Islamic political systems, and reviving the medieval Islamic Caliphate.

The HT emerged from its humble beginnings in Palestine and spread to other parts of the Arab world due to An-Nabhani and his HT colleagues' tireless efforts to introduce his ideas to as many Muslims as possible. He traveled extensively around the Middle East including places such as Syria, Lebanon, Iraq, Egypt and Turkey (Al-Wahwah 2010). An-Nabhani himself shifted the central command of HT from Jerusalem, Amman, Damascus and Beirut. He was personally involved in HT's coup attempts in Jordan and Iraq. In 1976 he was arrested and tortured by the Iraqis, resulting in his hands becoming paralyzed. He was then deported to Syria from where he later went to Lebanon. Here, his health deteriorated and he died on 20 June 1977. Some figures within HT, including his son, believe that the Lebanese authorities poisoned him (Al-Wahwah 2010). However, there is no conclusive evidence by which this could be ascertained. By the time of his death in 1977, HT had established chapters in virtually all Middle Eastern and North African countries. Following his death, An-Nabhani was succeeded by his long-time follower Abdul Qadeem Zalloum (1924–2003).

HT expanded further under the leadership of Sheikh Abdul Qadeem Zalloum, its second leader. Zalloum, a former member of the MB, faced many problems in his attempts to transform the movement, so that it remained relevant and viable. This was because the movement faced persecution in many Arab countries, following its history of initiating several coup attempts in Egypt and Jordan.[1] The intensity of the persecution it faced resulted in the party's leadership going underground. With the exception of its key leaders, HT members did not even know the whereabouts of Zalloum (Haniff 2007). The 1990s spelt a new era for HT. As mentioned earlier, HT members in the Middle East began seeking refuge in Western countries to escape persecution that they were facing from their respective governments. Paradoxically, it is the Western countries that were often criticized for an anti-Islamic agenda that provided HT with the space and freedom to expand its agenda. By the late 1990s, HT had a presence in the United States, Australia and most Western European countries. While it is not the aim of HT to revive the Caliphate in non-Muslim countries, it sees its role in Europe as preparing the Muslim ground for the eventual revival of the Caliphate. It was in Europe that the party began capturing the attention of the world's media. The party's vociferous campaign against Salman Rushdie after the publication of *The Satanic Verses* and its criticism of the Serbian act of genocide against Bosnian Muslims made the party extremely popular amongst Muslims in Europe. During this period, some cracks were starting to show in the movement. Splits within the party's leadership that saw the departure of key HT leaders such as Ismail Al-Wahwah (Australia), Abdul Rahman Al-Baghdadi (Indonesia), Iyad Hilal (United States) and Dr Tawfiq Mustafa (Germany) led to the weakening of the party. This conflict is generally attributed to the increasingly dictatorial nature of HT's leadership under Zalloum. Many HT leaders also felt that Zalloum was becoming overly paranoid with regard to his personal safety.[2] These HT detractors formed a group called the Reformers of HT. Owing to these internal conflicts, HT activities became stagnant. HT leaders were busy trying to sort out differences within the movement rather than focusing on the activities of the party. It was at this time that HT in Britain began playing a more important role within the party. Zalloum instructed leaders of HT in Britain (who remained loyal to his faction) to send HT members to Pakistan, India and Bangladesh to start new chapters of HT. HT members from Britain such as Maajid Nawaz were sent to Pakistan while Abu Ismail and Moien Ibrahim were sent to India (Nawaz 2007; Ismail 2007; Ibrahim 2007). This decision was prompted by Pakistan's testing of nuclear bombs, which brought the state into the league of nuclear states. The rationale of this move was that the security of the first Caliphate state would be better secured if the state possessed nuclear weapons. HT's expansion occurred rapidly until the death of Zalloum in April 2003. Sheikh Abdul Khalil Ata Abu Rashta, the former spokesman for HT in Jordan, succeeded him.

Abu Rashta began his leadership of HT by consolidating support from the different chapters of the party. Although he failed to bring HT's splinter groups back into the fold, he managed to weaken them by bringing back some leaders, such as Ismail Al-Wahwah, to HT. Abu Rashta also began taking important steps to respond to the new dynamics of world politics after the events of 9/11. HT was late in responding to this development due to internal problems within the party and the ailing health of Zalloum. HT became even more visible in many parts of the world such as in East Africa and North America where new chapters of the party emerged. In the Middle East and South-East Asia, the party's chapters in Palestine, Malaysia and Indonesia have positioned themselves as the true bearers of Islam after Islamist political parties in these countries were forced to adopt more moderate stances in facing the realities of governance. In Pakistan and Bangladesh, HT had become a menace enough for these governments to ban the party despite their long-standing tolerance of Islamist groups. In essence, HT under Abu Rashta is experiencing growth in many parts of the world as a whole. The coordination of the party's activities in other parts of the world, by making efforts to engage the public in a more suave public relations campaign, is helping to attract more adherents. Some of these themes will be discussed in the last section of this chapter. Prior to this, it is perhaps useful for a brief discussion to be accorded to HT's organizational structure, ideology, beliefs and political methodology.

HT's organizational structure

HT's organizational structure is reflective of the long history of repression that the party encountered in the Middle East. Repressive political conditions often result in an exclusive organizational structure of social movements. HT found its chapters immobilized (such as in Iraq and Syria) when the government in these countries started clamping down on the group. HT is an interesting example of a social movement that fused the model of exclusive and inclusive organizational structures (Al-Wahwah 2010). Nevertheless, HT leaders are aware that political repressions in some parts of the Muslim world such as Malaysia and Indonesia are less severe. As such, the party will benefit from utilizing open public spaces to recruit and draw resources. To ensure that the party is not immobilized in case of a clamp-down, HT maintains an exclusive internal structure in virtually all its chapters in the Middle East, North Africa and Central Asia with the exception of Lebanon, the United Arab Emirates, Kuwait and Iraq. In more democratic settings such as Indonesia and Europe, the party maintains an open external structure.

At the top of the HT organizational structure is the *Ameer* or leader of HT. A committee made up of HT leaders assists the Ameer (Taji-Farouki 1996: 115–16).[3] The exact number of members within this committee as well as their specific tasks is unknown. However, at least one member of this committee, Abu Mahmud, is assigned by the Ameer to travel to different parts of the world to oversee activities of HT chapters around the world, or at least in South-East Asia. Similar to the structure of HT's envisioned Islamic Caliphate, the party divides the Muslim world into provinces (*wilayah*). Interestingly, despite its rejection of the concept of nation-states, the borders of these wilayah mirror closely those of the current nation-states. For instance, the countries of Sudan, Pakistan, Malaysia and Indonesia are all considered separate wilayah. At the helm of the wilayah leadership is the *Mu'tamad*. Members of HT in a particular country appoint the Mu'tamad through a system of nomination. The Ameer of HT must approve the decision. While there have not been any known instances of the Ameer rejecting the decision of HT members in a particular wilayah, the Mu'tamad in some countries have been sacked by the Ameer for misconduct or infringing party rules. A committee of HT leaders in the wilayah assists the Mu'tamad. The exact composition of the wilayah and the manner in which this committee operates vary. For instance, in Indonesia the identities of the HT leaders are known. In fact, these leaders also identify themselves according to their portfolio within the HT provincial committee. In countries where HT is banned, such as Uzbekistan and Kazakhstan, little is known about the party's leadership (Karagiannis 2010).

Within each province there are several layers of leadership beyond the Mu'tamad and his committee. The first layer is the *Ma'sul* who takes charge of a particular province within a country. The second layer is the *naqib* who is in charge of several *halaqah* assigned to a particular locality. The third layer is the *mushrif* who is in charge of a halaqah. A naqib reports directly to the Ma'sul (Mohamed Osman 2009). Each halaqah will have between five to eight members known as *daris* (students). Each halaqah is led by a member of HT's local committee (*mushrif*). There is also a strong culture of secrecy within HT. At each level of membership, members will report directly to their immediate superior. In theory, each naqib will not know the identity of the other naqib and members of their other halaqah. However, in practice, HT members from different halaqah do discuss issues related to the party.[4] The Mu'tamad and his committee members often make direct contacts with members of HT in their respective countries by attending (and conducting) the different halaqah. Similarly, the Ameer of HT will send his representative to each of the wilayah to meet both leaders and members of HT every three months or as frequently as necessary (Al-Khaththath 2010). This representative will communicate with as many HT members as possible to ensure that HT central leadership gets to hear of any unhappiness amongst members, especially about the leadership. It is this organizational structure that has allowed the party's leadership to remain largely unaffected by the sacking of some of its key leaders.

HT's religious-political ideology

An-Nabhani advocated strongly that Muslims must subscribe to Islamic teachings and view themselves as a single cohesive community. It is thus obligatory for Muslims to strive for the establishment of this community by working towards the revival of the Islamic Caliphate. An-Nabhani's approach to Islam is indeed unique and interesting. This is especially in the realm of religious thought. Unlike most Muslim thinkers such as Sayyid Qutb and Maulana Abu A'la Maududi who reject Islamic traditions as espoused by classical Muslim scholars, An-Nabhani offers an interesting fusion of the modernist Islamic political ideology and traditional Islamic teachings. This traditional influence came mainly from his grandfather, Yusuf An-Nabhani, who was critical of Muslim modernist thinkers such as Muhammad Abduh, Rashid Rida and Jamal al-Din al-Afghani (An-Nabhani 2001b). Yusuf An-Nabhani was also known for his strong affiliation to Sufism. It is thus of little surprise that while many Muslim reformers reject Islamic traditions and Sufism as archaic and un-Islamic, An-Nabhani is a strong advocate of Islamic tradition and is highly tolerant of Sufism. It is this tolerant attitude towards Sufism that has gained HT strong support in Muslim countries where Sufi Islam is dominant, such as Indonesia and Uzbekistan. An-Nabhani also accepts *Ijma' Al-Sahabah* (Interpretations of the Prophet's Companions) and *qiyas* (reasoning) as legal resources that could be used in determining a ruling on a particular jurisprudence issue (An-Nabhani 1998: 242). This could be contrasted with the views of Salafi and Wahhabi scholars who generally reject Ijma' and qiyas as sources that could be used to derive Islamic laws (Olivetti 2002: 22–29). An-Nabhani's fusion of traditional and modernist ideas is expressed in his espousal of the restoration of the Islamic Caliphate. However, An-Nabhani rejects the Western conception of the nation-state and seeks to revive the medieval Caliphate with its traditional accompanying institutions and functionaries (Taji-Farouki 1996: 65–66).

Upon setting up HT, An-Nabhani outlined the party's objectives, which included the revival of the Muslim world from its perceived current decline, the liberation of Muslims from the thoughts, systems and laws of unbelievers, and the restoration of the Islamic Caliphate (An-Nabhani 1973). For An-Nabhani, Islam is an ideology (*mabda'a*), which comprises an idea (*fikrah*) and method (*tareeqah*) (An-Nabhani 2002: 52). This notion, for An-Nabhani, encapsulates the basic doctrine of Islam as well as the solutions and regulations that emanate from it. In his diagnosis of the failure of Islamic movements, An-Nabhani argued that there are several weaknesses in these movements. He notes that the movements are established based on a generally undefined idea (fikrah), which was vague, unclear, lacked focus, purity and clarity. Second, the movements did not define a method (tareeqah) to implement their idea; rather, they proceeded through arbitrary and twisted means. Third, the movements relied upon individuals who lacked awareness and determination. Last, the individuals carrying the responsibility of these movements did not have a correct bond amongst them and were merely bound by their membership, actions and titles (An-Nabhani 2001b: 11). To resolve these problems, An-Nabhani proposed that individuals must undergo a culturing process in which they are taught an ideologically correct culture. Taking them through this culturing process requires that each one of them assumes the role of a beginner (student), whose mind is reshaped anew. After generating harmony in the individual, the next task would be to generate harmony between the individual and the society (An-Nabhani 2001b: 12).

Democracy, capitalism and nation-states as un-Islamic concepts

As in the case of many jihadist groups (and diametrically opposed to MB), HT staunchly rejects many concepts related to modernity such as democracy, capitalism and the nation-state, deeming these concepts as un-Islamic. For An-Nabhani the concept of democracy is contrary to the teachings of Islam due to the fact that the final power within the state rests in the hands of human beings so that all individuals, regardless of religion, have equal rights with regard to establishing the state, appointing rulers and making laws as well as anything else that is related to governance and the state (Zalloum 1995: 7). An-Nabhani's main argument against democracy is the fact that its laws are man-made, as opposed to the divine rules in the shari'a, which are ordained by God for all humans. For HT, the act of legislating new laws when the shari'a was already ordained for humans is not Islamic, thus making the act of electing for the legislators equally unacceptable. Another aspect of democracy that HT had vehemently opposed is the concept of freedom of expression. HT leaders noted that Islam could never accept complete freedom for human beings. Freedom is allowed only as long as it does not contravene Islamic laws. The leader for HT in the Scandinavian region, Chadi Freigeh, noted:

> Islam does not accept that in the name of freedom of expression that the Holy Prophet can be denigrated in cartoons as this obliterate the sanctity of the Prophet. If freedom of expression is an important tenet of democracy, surely democracy is an un-Islamic concept.
>
> *(Freigeh 2010)*

He added further that:

> In reality there is no real freedom in the West. Freedom is used as a tool of the West to destroy Islam. Our brother Fadi Abdel Latif was arrested and jailed for distributing alleged anti-Semite literature but yet in the name of freedom, Danish politicians and journalists insulted Muslims by drawing the cartoons of the Prophet. Where is the freedom in democracy?
>
> *(Freigeh 2010)*

HT thus sees democracy as a dangerous concept and seeks to undermine it. A manifestation of this anti-democracy position is the campaigns undertaken by HT in various countries to boycott elections stating that participation in elections is prohibited in Islam. Interestingly, despite this intense opposition to democracy, the party has adopted some features of democracy within its organizational structure such as giving members power to elect the leaders of the party at the provincial level. The party also stated that there should be complete freedom in the future Caliphate for any Muslim to correct the Caliph if he makes any mistake.

In a similar vein to its criticism of democracy, HT has described capitalism as an un-Islamic concept. HT's rejection of capitalism stems from its belief that capitalist systems tend to benefit a small number of elites at the expense of the masses who will remain impoverished (An-Nabhani 1997: 14), while Islam believes strongly in the fair distribution of wealth. An-Nabhani also believed that interest (*riba'*), which is prohibited in Islam, forms an important element of capitalism, making the economic system un-Islamic. He also noted that the capitalist system encourages people to be individualistic, leading them to indulge in anything – even illicit activities – in pursuit of money and other worldly gains. HT leaders also believe that capitalism involves large corporations controlling the world at the expense of the masses. HT believes that there are 'public goods' such as water and oil which cannot be sold as commodities and must be distributed without charge. HT also rejects all forms of taxes except those ordained by Islam. In HT Pakistan's Manifesto (2009), the HT leadership explained its position on taxes:

Under the capitalist system, citizens face a great burden of taxation. Income tax eats into the people's salaries, general sales tax makes buying essential food and medicine a burden whilst taxation on fuel and energy chokes industrial and agricultural production. Islam is free of cruel taxes like GST and income tax. Rasulullah said in a hadith, 'The collector of taxes will not enter heaven' (Ahmad). Instead, Islam has its own unique system of revenue collection, including revenue from public properties, such as gas, and agricultural production, such as kharaj, and industrial manufacture through Zakah on goods.

(Hizb ut-Tahrir Pakistan 2009: 12)

While HT members try to internalize its rejection for capitalism in their own lives, many continue to pay taxes as a necessary evil to live in the current capitalist system. However, members of HT try to internalize the 'Islamic economic system' in other ways, including avoiding the purchase of goods such as cars and houses on credit. As such, HT members often live in rented homes or homes inherited from their families. HT also sees the need for the current 'exploits' of the capitalist system to be exposed. In Indonesia, the party started a journal and website, *The Journal of Economic Ideology*, to highlight problems with the Indonesian economy and solutions offered by Islam to these problems. One of HT's key proposals to resolve the current economic problems is gold as a replacement for the dollar as the currency of trade among nations. This proposal was promulgated with the view that gold has real value attached to it while the dollar is flat money with no real value. However, HT has done little to explain how these proposals would be implemented.

HT also does not recognize the borders within the Muslim world because it believes strongly that these borders are colonial constructs designed to weaken Muslims (Hizb ut-Tahrir 1997: 25). Many of the Muslim countries created through the process of redrawing of borders are artificial creations of the West. They believe that nationalism was spread within the Muslim world to weaken the Muslims and trace the collapse of the Caliphate to the creation of Arab nationalism aimed at undermining the Islamic Caliphate led by the Turks (Yusanto 2007). In several countries where the state ideology is nationalism, HT has been the most fervent critic of this concept. An example is the case of HT in Malaysia. HT Malaysia has explicitly rejected one of the key policies that defines the Malaysian state, the *bumiputra* policy. This policy is an affirmative policy aimed at improving the economic standing of the 'indigenous' Malaysians (comprising mainly Muslim Malays). Describing this policy as un-Islamic, the leader of HT Malaysia argued that Islam does not recognize such racist ideals and sought to unite people regardless of race or color (Osman 2010). Osman also argued that:

This disease of nationalism is an artificial bond whereas Islam has made it clear that the only bond between Muslims must be the bond of their belief in Islam. The Prophet himself said that He who calls for, strives for or dies for Assabiyah is not one of us. This is the problem with the bumiputra ideology.

(Osman 2010)

It must be noted that despite this strong condemnation of nationalism, HT acknowledges that it is difficult to eradicate this sense of nationalism, especially amongst the Arabs. To eradicate such feelings, HT has held several major international gatherings where its members from all around the world can gather and interact with one another. The first such event was the 2007 International Khilafah Conference in Jakarta, Indonesia, where approximately 80,000 people gathered in one of the largest venues in the city. The choice of Indonesia for this gathering has to do with the fact that most HT members know very little about the Far East. The mammoth gathering changed many long-held prejudices and misconceptions that some HT members (especially those of Middle Eastern background) held about Indonesia and Indonesians. The fact that the gathering was the largest HT had ever held impressed upon at least one participant from the Middle East that 'Islam is alive and kicking in Indonesia' (HT member from Lebanon, 2007).

As far as HT is concerned, the concepts of nationalism as well as democracy and capitalism must be eradicated from the minds of its members and the larger Muslim community. This would then allow them to be more open in accepting the Islamic systems and concepts proposed by HT.

HT's conception of the Islamic state

HT's conception of the Islamic state is a rejection of all other models of this concept. For HT's leaders the current models are too gradualist and thus un-Islamic. For a land to be considered an Islamic state, the country's constitution, rule and law, must emanate from the shari'a (An-Nabhani 1998: 240). This uncompromising attitude can be observed in HT's denunciation of Sudan, Iran and Saudi Arabia (these countries claim to implement Islamic laws). HT's leaders observe that a monarchical system such as that practiced by the Saudi government has no place in Islam (Waheed 2007). Similarly, some HT leaders have dismissed Iran as a colonial creation after Ayatollah Ruhollah Khomeini, the late leader of the Iranian Revolution and the subsequent spiritual leader, rejected HT's demand for the Ayatollah to implement its Constitution (Haniff 2007). Other HT leaders have rejected the Iranian model for its strong affiliation to Iranian nationalism and its political structures that are derived from un-Islamic political systems (Al-Wahwah 2010). In particular, the Iranian state's conduct of elections is condemned as a derivation from democracy, which is a concept forbidden in Islam. For HT leaders, Iran's adherence to capitalism, another system deemed un-Islamic, is a further manifestation of the state's un-Islamic system. HT also believes in the immediate implementation of Islamic laws in Muslim countries, rejecting any gradualist approach to the Islamic state. HT leaders have also vehemently rejected the claim that its criticism of Iran is due to the state's strong affiliation to Shiite Islam, highlighting that the leadership of its chapters in Lebanon and Iraq are largely Shiite (Bakash 2010). In this regard, HT leaders are critical of the gradualist approach proposed by MB-affiliated political parties around the world. In Indonesia, the decision of the MB-affiliated Prosperity Justice Party (Partai Keadilan Sejahtera, PKS) to be part of the governing coalition was criticized by HT Indonesia as PKS' betrayal of the Islamic cause (Abdurrahman 2007).

HT does not simply reject the current models of the Islamic state. It is perhaps one of the few Islamic movements that have undertaken the task of producing a draft constitution of its proposed Islamic state. An-Nabhani has also written extensively on the Islamic state proposing alternatives to current political, economic and social systems. Powers in the Islamic state that HT has proposed lie in the hands of the Caliph and *Majlis al-Umma* (Assembly of the People) (An-Nabhani 1998: 240–45). The people will elect members of this assembly and in turn the assembly will elect the Caliph. All laws in the country must conform to Islamic laws. While its constitution proposes the composition and responsibilities of the judiciary, it also outlines the policies in spheres such as the economy, education, foreign relations and defense (An-Nabhani 1998: 245–60). It has proposed a system whereby different 'public resources' such as oil and water could be provided to its citizens for free (Hizb ut-Tahrir 2009: 77). In its economic system, the constitution proposes that the only currency of the state should be gold and silver. The most interesting dimension of its proposed Islamic state is in the realm of foreign relations. The constitution forbids the Islamic state from establishing relations with Western 'colonial' powers such as Britain and the United States due to their hostile stance towards the Muslim world (An-Nabhani 1998: 270). The Islamic state is also expected to declare war on Israel to free Jerusalem from Jewish rule. The state is also forbidden from joining international organizations such as the United Nations and the World Bank (An-Nabhani 1998: 276). All in all, the constitution proposed by HT contains many populist policies aimed at attracting the Muslim masses to its cause. These policies are especially attractive to many Muslims in countries where basic necessities are lacking, such as in the Middle East and Central Asia.

Political methodology

An-Nabhani claims that HT deferred to Prophet Muhammad's method of setting up the state of Medina in its effort to revive the Caliphate. In doing so, the party divided its method of action into three stages. In the first stage, known as the stage of culturing (*tatsqif*), it aimed to produce people who believed in the ideas and the methods of the party, so that they form the party's core group. These individuals are initiated into its ideology of reviving the Caliphate, and anti-democracy, anti-communism, anti-secularism and anti-capitalism stances. An-Nabhani set up his first core group of HT members who were ingrained with the party's ideology within a study group called a *halaqah* (study cell). New recruits to the party underwent a process of indoctrination where they were required to read key books of HT guided by a more senior member. These texts have evolved over time. Currently, many of the books that are in the compulsory reading list include titles authored by An-Nabhani and other HT ideologues. These books are constantly updated and revised by HT's central leadership. Members can also subscribe to a number of other books which students and members of HT are encouraged to read. Subscriptions of non-compulsory books are open to members according to their needs as perceived by HT's leadership. For instance, in around 2001 the HT leadership added *The Reliance of the Travellers* by Nu Hamim Keller, a prominent Sufi scholar, to the reading list. This was essentially due to criticism within the party that members lacked spirituality (Khan 2006; Al-Khaththath 2009). Upon 'graduation', these individuals are then given more important tasks within the party. Individuals who are not deemed suitable for membership are retained as supporters. Often these individuals are viewed as not being serious about assisting the party and are given a nominal role within the party structure. This process of membership can be a long, drawn-out process, which may take several years.

At the second stage, known as the stage of interaction (*tafa'ul*) with the Muslim community, the party seeks the support of the Muslim masses for the establishment of the Caliphate. At this stage of interaction, HT members will explain the key ideas of the party to the public. Members of the Muslim community who are interested in its ideas are encouraged to participate in its interaction process.

At the third stage, known as the stage of accepting power and ruling (*istilamu al-hukmi*), the party works towards establishing a government, implementing Islam comprehensively, and carrying it as a message to the world (Hizb ut-Tahrir Britain 2000: 81–110). An-Nabhani suggested that to accelerate the third stage, leaders could seek *nusrah* (assistance to gain power) from important members of the country such as military leaders, judges and politicians (Khan 2003). The end game is then the establishment of the first Caliphate state. This Caliphate state will then call on other Muslim states to join this new state in forming a new Caliphate. The Caliphate state will be allowed to wage war against any Muslim states that refuse to do so.

HT and the use of violence

Any discussion of HT's political methodology strategy must address the question of HT's attitude towards violence. Some terrorism analysts and political commentators studying HT in Europe and Central Asia have suggested that HT's ideology condones and even supports the use of violence. The term 'conveyor belt for terrorism' has been used in several academic works to describe HT (Cohen 2003; Baran 2004). HT has also come under scrutiny for its alleged support for terrorism. Such views emerged due to HT's position on various terrorist attacks. HT has advocated that 9/11, the 7 July 2005 (7/7) London bombings and other major terrorist acts were perpetrated by the Central Intelligence Agency (CIA) as part of America's plan to undermine the Muslim world (Yusanto 2007). While HT could be described as a radical group due to its anti-Semitic ideology, there is little evidence that HT has resorted to violence to further its cause. HT leaders point out that the struggle to revive the Islamic Caliphate is an intellectual struggle as it is about convincing people of the importance of the Caliphate. They note that a violent revolution could lead to a new Islamic government but this government could never survive, as the society is not sufficiently Islamic to support the new government (Yusanto 2007).

One of the leading scholars on HT, Suha Taji-Farouki, has noted that while HT members have advocated jihad, only the Caliph can call for offensive jihad (Taji Farouki 2000: 29).[5] Since there is no real Islamic state in the world, this form of jihad cannot be upheld. HT has also stated its position on terrorism clearly. It has categorically condemned all acts of terrorism such as the 9/11 and 7/7 attacks as un-Islamic while maintaining that US and British presence in Iraq and Afghanistan are also acts of terrorism (Hardwood 2007). One of the best examples of HT's condemnation of terrorism is an article analyzing the Madrid bombings. The writer had argued that even in conditions where jihad is valid, the killing of civilians is prohibited and as such terrorist acts like the Madrid bombings are un-Islamic (Ansari 2004: 8–11). Interestingly, HT in Indonesia has proven its ability to be a reverse conveyor belt for terrorism. There have been a large number of Muslim activists, formerly associated with violent Muslim organizations, such as the Laskar Jihad, Majlis Mujahideen Indonesia and the Islamic Defenders Front, who have denounced violence and joined HT.[6] These HT members noted that through interaction with other members, they have understood that the struggle for Islam is a comprehensive struggle that is about winning the hearts and minds of people (Mohamed Osman 2010). HT has also convinced leaders of violent organizations such as Abu Bakar Ba'asyir (often cited to be the spiritual head of Jemaah Islamiyah, the South-East Asian arm of Al-Qaeda) to denounce violence. In recent times, Ba'asyir has stated explicitly that it is more important for Muslims to work towards the re-establishment of the Islamic Caliphate than perpetrating acts of violence (Mohamed Osman 2010). It is quite evident from here that HT is in fact drawing Indonesian Muslims away from violence.

HT's general non-violent position does not mean that the party is avowedly non-violent at all times. The party considers it an obligation of Muslims to fight when their lands are occupied. As such, HT members are instructed to fight against 'foreign occupiers' in Iraq and Palestine. A prominent HT leader noted that the party had sacked members who failed to engage in armed struggle against occupying forces in southern Lebanon during the Israeli–Hizbollah conflict in 2007, and in Iraq when the Americans entered the country in 2005 (Al-Wahwah 2010). HT has also stated that it is the obligation of the Caliphate state to wage wars against any Muslim countries that refuse to come under the sovereignty of this state. As such, the party approves of the use of violence once the Caliphate state is born, and is willing to use any amount of violence to ensure that all Muslim lands are united under one Caliphate.

Funding the party's operations

Funds are extremely important for social movements like the HT. These funds are necessary for the group to pay for printing costs of publications, renting venues for events and paying salaries of full-time members of the group (Al-Khaththath 2010). Officially, HT claims that the party funds itself. Members are known to contribute a percentage of their income to the party. This percentage varies according to a member's financial condition. Members also make special contributions to the party (*infaq*) before a major event is organized.[7] Unlike other Islamic organizations that receive funds from members' zakat contributions, HT has avoided receiving these funds. This is because they feel that political parties like themselves do not qualify as recipients ordained by the laws governing zakat. Although HT leaders have vehemently denied receiving funding from the central leadership of HT, a former leader of HT Indonesia confirmed that the party's chapters receive funding from the party's leadership (Al-Khaththath 2010). These funds are accrued by the party's central leadership through contributions from wealthy members living in the Gulf Arab States (especially Kuwait and the United Arab Emirates) and Europe. These funds are subsequently reallocated to party chapters in the Middle East, Asia and Africa. Apparently, the amount a party chapter receives is dependent on the importance of the chapter in HT's larger scheme. Chapters in the Levant Arab states, Egypt and Pakistan receive the largest amount of funds, given that these countries are still viewed as primary target areas by HT. This has led to some criticism by former members of HT in countries like Indonesia, who have noted that the party's leadership is too Arab-centric (Al-Baghdadi 2009; Nawaz 2007; Al-Khaththath 2010).

HT in the post-9/11 world

There is no doubt that the 9/11 attacks provided both a challenge and an opportunity for HT. HT's ambiguous statements on the issue of terrorism have led to the group being labeled as the next al-Qaeda and a conveyor belt for terrorism. The radical positions that HT took on many issues have also resulted in a backlash against the organization in several European countries. In particular, the tough stance it has taken against the state of Israel and its open loathing for Jews have resulted in tough actions taken against the party in Germany and Denmark. In January 2003 the German government nearly banned the party for promoting anti-Semitism and inciting the use of violence (Lambroschini 2004). Claims have also been made that the group has worked closely with neo-Nazi groups. The German Interior Minister Otto Schily has stated that HT in Germany had sought contact with the far Right and that prominent neo-Nazis had attended an HT meeting held by the group at the Technical University in Berlin in October 2002 (Finn 2003). Nevertheless, HT leaders claim that the group is prohibited only from organizing public activities but membership of the party is not illegal (Hardwood 2007). The party is contesting the ban at the European Court. In Denmark the party's spokesman, Fadi Abdel Latif, was jailed for distributing pamphlets that indirectly called for the killing of Jews.[8] In the United Kingdom and Australia there have been calls for the group to be proscribed. Yet the authorities have found no evidence to ban the group. Nevertheless, the increasing limelight that has been shed on HT has made its leaders more cautious of the organization's public image. Convinced that the 'war on terror' is in fact a war on Islam, HT leaders have formulated strategies to confront this new challenge.

Toning down radicalism

One of the first tasks undertaken by Abu Rashta upon assuming the leadership of HT is a re-branding of the image of the party. Under Zalloum, the image of HT was that of an underground clandestine organization with young, firebrand and extremist members. The HT leadership under Abu Rashta began a process of softening the image of the organization. This process involved several strategies. First, the party started operating in an environment that promoted openness. Even in places where the party was banned, official spokesmen of the party were publicly featured in order that they were well recognized. While Abu Rashta avoids being identified publicly (his photos are nowhere to be found and his whereabouts is unknown), he has started a personal website where his views and speeches are featured. Second, the party leaders of the various chapters have been adept at promoting the party and underplaying its views on jihad while emphasizing its non-violent methodology and focus on an intellectual struggle.[9] Michael Whine has pointed out that HT has exercised considerable restraint against the Danish cartoon caricature issue. He noted that:

> The group's response to the Danish cartoons issue is instructive. Both in its online and printed material, the party called for peaceful demonstrations and diplomatic and educational initiatives, while condemning the more violent manifestations that incited violence.
>
> *(Whine 2006: 2)*

The party's website also avoids issuing statements or articles that seem supportive of acts of violence. It must be added that HT has often utilized the wars in Iraq and Afghanistan to deflect the issue of violence.

Re-branding HT's image

The party has also tried to revamp its image by utilizing professional-looking publications and organizing more professional events. HT's publications often use high-quality glossy paper.[10] Often these publications bear catchy phrases meant to attract the attention of readers. In some cases, these publications do not bear the name of HT. One such publication is the *Female Reader*, a publication of HT in Indonesia. This magazine, which has an English title, features a good-looking Muslim female model, wearing the Muslim headscarf and clothing, on its front cover. Articles in the magazine are focused on women's issues such as health and fashion. However, the centerfold of this magazine often features articles relating to women's responsibility in reviving the Islamic Caliphate. The efforts are essentially directed at giving the HT a chic and fashionable image. In addition, the party is also beginning to form media teams in countries where it is allowed to operate legally. These media teams organize talk shows and conduct interviews in a style similar to that of international media bureaus such as CNN and the BBC. All this is in line with creating an image of HT as a professional organization that is well run and coordinated.

HT leaders have also begun courting the media to publicize their cause. Press conferences are now organized in all countries where HT is allowed to operate legally. These press conferences are often held after a major HT event or to simply explain HT's position on several issues. At the same time, the media (especially in Western countries) have sought interviews with HT leaders to ascertain the level of their radicalism. These media engagements have given the party an outlet to clear misconceptions about the group while allowing the party to air their views to the public (Doureihi 2009). In 2009, after HT America held its first conference, an American journalist commented that it is American democracy and freedom that made it possible for HT to organize a conference in the United States. The journalist added that HT would be arrested and prosecuted in Muslim countries like Iran and Syria if the party attempted to hold a conference. HT's representative Mohamed Al-Mawalki agreed with the journalist, arguing that the lack of freedom in the Muslim world is exactly what HT sought to change. Al-Mawalki added that under the system that the HT sought to establish, political parties do not even need to be registered officially, alluding that there would be even more freedom under the system that HT envisaged.[11] Such a positioning is undeniably an attempt by HT to quell fears about the group's radical ideology. Nevertheless, such media engagements have certainly an important role to play in allaying its negative image.

Coordinating efforts of different party chapters

Taking into account the global expansion of HT, the party's leadership has streamlined the activities of its organization worldwide. In view of this, since 2007 the party has been organizing coordinated conferences in various parts of the world. The conferences are organized each year in the Islamic month of Rajab, on the day the Islamic Caliphate was dismantled by the regime of Mustafa Kemal Ataturk, the founding father of the modern Turkish state (Zalloum 2000). They are coordinated and organized concurrently in order to commemorate the fall of the Ottoman Caliphate. It was almost certain that the decision to organize these conferences was made by the central leadership of HT. The organization of these coordinated conferences by the HT is an attempt to showcase its strength to the outside world. It is also noteworthy that different HT chapters also utilize the same format in organizing these conferences. For instance, both the HT chapters in Lebanon and Indonesia organized conferences that focused on Islamic religious scholars (*ulama*) in 2009. Excerpts from these events were then compiled into a video, which was posted on various websites.[12] Videos such as these are obvious tools that HT can utilize to recruit potential members. HT also has a compilation of a list of its activities pertaining to the various chapters of the party. All of the different chapters' websites also compile their own articles relating to HT activities. This is a means by which members are kept informed about the developments in other party chapters while showcasing to potential members the strength and massive presence of the party.

HT has also been identifying suitable countries within the Muslim world as the hub of its activism for different regions. While HT Britain has played this role for it in Europe, newer countries have been identified for this role. The level of freedom that HT enjoys in a country would decide which country is selected. These hub centers are to form important centers for transmission of HT's activities in any particular area. In the Levant area of the Middle East, Lebanon has been identified as the new hub center. Sudan is playing this role in Africa, Bangladesh in South Asia, Yemen in the Arabian Peninsula, Uzbekistan in Central Asia (and Caucasus) and Indonesia in the Asia Pacific. Of late, Indonesia, in particular, has been playing an especially important role in spearheading HT's activities. Besides organizing the largest ever HT event, held in 2007, the Indonesian chapter has been an important anchor for transmitting HT's ideology to other parts of the Asia Pacific region (Mohamed Osman 2010).

Conclusion

HT has proven to be a remarkably robust group. Since its formation in 1953, the party has endured violent prosecutions, proscription and internal splits. Yet the party remains intact and continues to grow in different parts of the world, and has started new chapters in Asia, Africa and the Americas. HT's radical ideology, political methodology and uncompromising stance towards the West seem to be its key strengths. It is likely that HT will continue to grow at the expense of Islamic political parties around the Muslim world, which have begun maintaining a more moderate path to attain power. This is already occurring in Malaysia and Indonesia, where more radical members of mainstream Islamist parties have left their respective parties for HT. Another trend that is likely to fuel the growth of HT is the lethargy that is beginning to set in amongst violent Islamic groups. The increasing realization that violence does little more than cause destruction could also mean that members of these groups would turn to HT, which is equally radical (in some cases more radical) in its ideology, but maintains a non-violent political methodology.

Notes

1 For more details of the Iraqi coup attempt, see Tripp 2002: 167–93. For the Jordanian coup attempt, see Awdallah 2006: 23.
2 Al-Baghdadi, the former Indonesian Mu'tamad, related an incident that exemplifies this paranoia. Leaders of the Jamaat-e-Islami in Pakistan had initiated a meeting with HT in 1999 and wanted to meet Zalloum. Zalloum had instructed Al-Baghdadi and another HT leader to attend the meeting. Al-Baghdadi refused to go as he felt that it was important for the leader of HT to attend such a meeting. Al-Baghdadi felt that the paranoia was too extreme in this case.
3 Taji-Farouki noted that these committees have had different names including the general party leadership (*qiyadat al-hizb al-'amma*), the supreme leadership (*al-qiyada al-'ulya*) and the central committee (*al-lajna al-markaziya*). See Taji Farouki 1996: 115–16.
4 Personal observation of author at HT events in Malaysia, Indonesia and Australia.
5 Another article that has conclusively rejected the notion that HT is a terrorist organization or a conveyor belt for terrorism is by Swiss scholar Jean Francois-Meyer (2004).
6 Author's interviews with former members of MMI, FPI and Laskar Jihad who are now members of HTI. Due to their former links to violent organizations, these activists preferred not to be identified. These interviews were conducted in March 2009.
7 The author observed this infaq contribution in the office of Hizbut Tahrir Indonesia in the province of Aceh on 15 July 2009.
8 'Muslim Group Spokesman Gets Suspended Jail Sentence for Posting Flyers Urging Jews Killed', *Associated Press*, 14 March 2003. Imran Waheed, the spokesman for HT Britain, claimed that the accusation was falsified in an interview in November 2008.
9 See various interviews with HT leaders in Australia, Pakistan, Bangladesh and Lebanon. Interview with Naveed Butt, spokesman for HT Pakistan, at www.youtube.com/watch?v=5EpNdXPxinw (accessed 20 September 2009). Interview with Moinuddin Ahmed, spokesman for HT Bangladesh, at www.youtube.com/watch?v=YlU31qq8rQo& feature=PlayList&p=6BCF26FD698339A0&index=8 (accessed 20 September 2009). Interview with Ahmed Al-Qasas, spokesman for HT Lebanon, at www.youtube.com/watch?v=_ulau9EYEyA&feature=PlayList&p=6BCF26FD698339A0&index=6 (accessed 20 September 2009). Interview with Waseem Doureihi, Media Representative of HT Australia, at www.youtube.com/watch?v=Op60dpPKo88&feature=PlayList&p=6BCF26FD698339A0&index=7 (accessed 20 September 2009).
10 An example of this publication is the *New Civilization* magazine published by HT Britain. It was first published in Autumn 2004. An online version of the magazine can be found at www.newcivilisation.com/index.php/main/newciv/back_issues.
11 For details of this interview, see HT America's official website at www.khilafahconference2009.com.
12 See videos titled 'Call of the Hour (Global Wrap-Up 2007)' and 'Call of the Hour (Global Wrap-Up 2008)' at www.youtube.com/results?search_query=call+for+khilafah&search_type=&aq=f (accessed 21 September 2009).

References

Abdurrahman, H. (2007) Interview by author, August, Jakarta, Indonesia.
Ahmed, M., Interview, spokesman HT Bangladesh, available at www.youtube.com/watch?v=YlU31qq8rQo&feature=PlayList&p=6BCF26FD698339A0&index=8 (accessed 20 September 2009).
Al-Baghdadi, A.R. (2009) Interview by author, October, Bogor, Indonesia.
Al-Khaththath, M. (2009) Interview by author, August, Jakarta, Indonesia.
—— (2010) Interview by author, May, Jakarta, Indonesia.
Al-Qasas, A., Interview, spokesman for HT Lebanon, available at www.youtube.com/watch?v=_ulau9EYEyA&feature=PlayList&p=6BCF26FD698339A0&index=6 (accessed 20 September 2009).
Al-Wahwah, I. (2010) Interview by author, March, Sydney, Australia.

An-Nabhani, T. (1950) *Ingadh Filasinn*, Damascus, Ibn Zaydun Press.
—— (1973) *Thinking*, London, Khilafah Publishers.
—— (1997) *Economic System of Islam*, London, Khilafah Publications.
—— (1998) *The Islamic State*, London, Khilafah Publications.
—— (2001a) *The Structuring of a Party*, London, Khilfah Publications.
—— (2002) *The Concepts of Hizb ut-Tahrir*, London, Khilfah Publications.
An-Nabhani, Y. (2001b) *Al-Qasidat Al-Raiyya Al Sughrafi Dhamm Al-Bidati Wa-Ahliha Wa-Madhi Al-Sunnati Al Gharra* [The Minor Rhyming Poem on the Blame of Innovation and the Praise of the Radiant Sunna], Beirut, Dar al-Kutub al-Ilmiyah.
Ansari, J. (2004) 'Madrid Bombings and the Attempts to Demonise Islam', *Khilafah Magazine* vol. 17, no. 4: 8–11.
Awdallah, S.T. (2006) *Beloved by Allah: Emergence of Light from Al-Aqsa Mosque Launch of Hizb ut-Tahrir March*, London, Khilafah Publications.
Bakash, O. (2010) Interview by author, July, Beirut.
Baran, Z. (2004) *Hizb ut-Tahrir: Islam's Political Insurgency*, Washington, DC, Nixon Centre.
Cohen, A. (2003) 'Hizb ut-Tahrir: An Emerging Threat to U.S. Interests in Central Asia', *Heritage Foundation Backgrounder*, 1 May.
Commins, D. (1991) 'Taqi Al-Din An-Nabhani and Islamic Liberation Party', *The Muslim World* vol. 31, no.3: 194–211.
Doureihi, W. (2009) Interview, media representative of HT Australia, available at www.youtube.com/watch?v=Op60dpPKo88&feature=PlayList&p=6BCF26FD698339A0&index=7 (accessed 20 September 2009).
Finn, P. (2003) 'Germany Bans Islamic Group', *Washington Post*, 10 January.
Francois-Meyer, J. (2004) *Hizb ut-Tahrir – The Next Al-Qaida, Really?* Geneva, PSIO.
Freigeh, C. (2010) Interview by author, July, Beirut.
Haniff, B. (2007) Interview by author, June, London.
Hardwood, J. (2007) Interview by author, June, London.
Hizb ut-Tahrir (1997) *Dangerous Concepts to Attack Islam and Consolidate Western Culture*, London, Khilafah Publications.
—— (1999) *Dangerous Concepts to Attack Islam and Consolidate Western Culture*, London, Khilafah Publications.
—— (2007) 'Call of the Hour', available at www.youtube.com/results?search_query=call+for+khilafah&search_type=&aq=f (accessed 21 September 2009).
—— (2009) *Safe World under the Shade of the Islamic Economic System*, London, Khilafah Publications.
Hizb ut-Tahrir America, official website available at www.khilafahconference2009.com (accessed 11 September 2009).
Hizb ut-Tahrir Britain (2000) *The Method to Re-Establish the Khilafah and Resume the Islamic Way of Life*, London, Khilafah Publications.
Hizb ut-Tahrir Pakistan (2009) *Manifesto of Hizb ut-Tahrir for Pakistan: Pakistan, Khilafah and the Reunification of the Muslim World*, n.p.
Husain, E. (2008) *The Islamists*, London, Penguin.
Ibrahim, M. (2007) Interview by author, June, London.
Ibrahim, S. (2010) Interview by author, February, Johor Bahru, Malaysia.
Ismail, A. (2007) Interview by author, August, Singapore.
Karagiannis, E. (2010) *Political Islam in Central Asia: The Challenge of Hizb ut-Tahrir*, London, Routledge.
Khan, A. (2003) 'The Search for the Nusrah', *Khilafah Magazine* vol. 16, no. 1: 18–21.
Khan, J. (2006) Interview by author, June, Singapore.
—— (2007) Interview by author, November, Singapore.
Lambroschini, S. (2004) 'Germany: Court Appeal By Hizb Ut-Tahrir Highlights Balancing Act Between Actions, Intentions', *Radio Free Europe*, 26 October, available at www.rferl.org/content/article/1055527.html (accessed 8 August 2011).
Lateline (2009) Interview with Wassim Doureihi, Spokesman of HT Australia, available at www.youtube.com/watch?v=ZHFZy0pU9YQ (accessed 30 August 2009).
Mohamed Osman, M.N. (2009) 'Reviving the Caliphate in Malaysia', *Studies in Conflict and Terrorism* vol. 32, no. 7 (July): 646–63.
—— (2010) 'The Transnational Network of Hizbut Tahrir Indonesia', *South East Asia Research* vol. 18, no. 4 (December): 735–55.
Nawaz, M. (2007) Interview by author, October, London.

Olivetti, V. (2002) *Terror's Source: The Ideology of Wahhabi-Salafism and its Consequences*, Birmingham, Amadeus Books.

Osman, H. (2010) Interview by author, August, Kuala Lumpur.

Osman, M. and Nawab, M. (2009) 'Reviving the Caliphate in the Nusantara', *Studies in Conflict and Terrorism* vol. 32, no.7: 646–63.

—— (2011) 'Transnational Activism of Hizbut Tahrir Indonesia', *Southeast Asia Research* (forthcoming).

Taji-Farouki, S. (1996) *The Fundamental Quest: Hizb al-Tahrir and the Search for the Islamic Caliphate*, London, Grey Seal.

—— (2000) 'Islamists and the threat of *Jihad*: Hizb al-Tahrir and al-Muhajiroun on Israel and the Jews', *Middle Eastern Studies* vol. 36, no. 4: 21–46.

Tripp, C. (2002) *History of Iraq*, Cambridge, Cambridge University Press.

Waheed, I. (2007) Interview by author, October, London.

Whine, M. (2006) *Is Hizb ur-Tahrir Changing Strategy or Tactics*, Washington, DC, Center for Eurasian Policy.

Yusanto, I. (2007) Interview by author, August, Jakarta.

Zalloum, A.Q. (1995) *Democracy is a System of Kufr*, London, Khilafah Publications.

—— (2000) *How Khilafah Was Destroyed*, London, Khilafah Publications.

9
Islamic radicalism in a democratizing Indonesia

Robert W. Hefner

After the fall of President Muhammad Suharto's 'New Order' regime in May 1998, Indonesia began an uncertain but hopeful transition from authoritarian rule. During its first five years, the transition was torn by two contrary currents. On one hand, the country made steady progress toward the consolidation of democratic institutions, including free and fair elections; freedom of the press, assembly and labor; the strengthening of a balance of powers between the executive and the legislature; and the withdrawal of the armed forces from Parliament. On the other hand, the early years of the post-New Order transition witnessed outbreaks of ethnoreligious violence, the spread of hardline Islamist paramilitaries, and several spectacular terrorist attacks, including the infamous Bali bombings of October 2002 in which more than 200 people (most of them Western tourists) perished.

For some observers, these latter developments seemed to raise questions as to the democratic commitments of Indonesia's Muslim citizens. Nonetheless, the 1999, 2004 and 2009 parliamentary elections provided a resounding confirmation of the democratic moderation of the Muslim electorate. Voters steered clear of both radical Islamism and conservative secular nationalism. Although most political parties and most voters signaled their comfort with Islam playing a greater role in public life, some 80 per cent of the electorate cast their vote for parties committed to the multi-confessional ideals of Indonesia's state ideology, the *Pancasila* (Five Principles). Among the remaining parties of Islamist hue, those that attracted the most support did so by highlighting their commitment to clean government, not the establishment of an Islamic state.

Despite the achievements of the post-New Order transition, radical varieties of Islamism remain active on the political margins. Although they pose little threat to the overall course of the transition, the most powerful of the radical Islamists have formed large militias (*laskar*) with tens of thousands of followers organized into quasi-military hierarchies. Although more restrained than in the early years of the post-Suharto transition, the militias continue to operate in cities and towns across Indonesia. The militias have also been active in campaigns for the implementation of shari'a-influenced bylaws, and have mounted fierce attacks on Islamic liberals and Muslims deemed heterodox.

In this chapter, I trace the genealogy and political impact of radical Islamism in post-New Order Indonesia. By 'Islamism', I refer to a variety of Muslim politics and social reform based on three principles: first, that Islam is a 'total' system (*al-nizam al-Islami*) and, as such, requires a comprehensive transformation of state and society; second, that the transformation must take place in accordance with Islamic shari'a understood in a formalistic rather than ethicalized way (Roy 2004: 58; Bayat 2007: 6–9); and, third, that government legislation must be subject to some measure of authorization by scholars of the law. In Indonesia as in much of the Muslim world, one can in turn distinguish two types of Islamists: mainline Islamists, willing to work for social change peacefully and within established structures, and radical Islamists, who so reject the existing political order that they use militancy and even violence to advance their cause. It is the latter variety of Islamism with which I am concerned here in Indonesia.

In the early years of the post-New Order transition, many policy analysts, particularly in the West, were convinced that the radicals posed a serious threat to Indonesia's fragile democracy. In historical retrospect, it was clear that the threat was exaggerated. Nonetheless, the radicals have influenced aspects of politics and public culture during the post-Suharto era. An understanding of their history and behaviors sheds light on the peculiar circumstances of mainstream and radical Islam in post-Suharto Indonesia, and offers insights into the circumstances conducive to the growth of radicalism in other Muslim countries.

Insurgent precedents

Muslim politics in this sprawling South-East Asian country has always been varied, and has sometimes taken a bitterly agonistic form. Indonesia's tradition of civic pluralist Islam is no less real for this fact. The country has the largest and most resilient tradition of voluntary civil-religious associations in the entire Muslim world. The largest of these organizations are the Muhammadiyah (founded 1912, 25–30 million members today) and the Nahdlatul Ulama (established 1926, 35–40 million members). Both have long been committed to the ideals of an independent and multi-confessional Indonesia. Although in the 1950s many in these associations lent their voices to calls for the establishment of an Islamic state (this at a time when Muslim parties were locked in a bitter struggle with the Indonesian Nationalist and Communist Parties), during the New Order period (1966–98) both organizations provided a bulwark for civil society and the struggle for constitutional governance. The two associations also played key roles in the pro-democracy movement that emerged in the final years of the Suharto period, arguably the largest the Muslim world has ever seen (Hefner 2000; Ramage 1995). Indonesia in the late Suharto period was distinctive in this regard. Unlike many Middle Eastern countries, the most credible and best-organized opponents of regime authoritarianism were not Islamist, but Muslim democratic.

If the civil-democratic stream in Indonesia's Muslim politics has deep roots, the much smaller radical stream has historical precedents as well. The roots of Indonesian radicalism go back to social movements and rebellions of the late nineteenth century (Kartodirdjo 1973; Dobbin 1983). Some of the earlier movements had a quasi-millenarian quality that had little to do with Islam. From the early twentieth century on, however, many of the larger movements were radical Islamist in inspiration. The most important of these in the early independence period was the so-called Darul Islam ('Abode of Islam') movement.

The Darul Islam was established in 1948, at the height of the independence war. After three years of armed struggle – sparked by Dutch attempts to re-impose colonial rule after the three-year Japanese interregnum – the country's nationalist leaders signed an agreement ceding control of much of West Java to the Dutch, and allowing an orderly retreat of Indonesian fighters to republican territories to the east. Angered by the agreement, a Muslim commander in West Java by the name of Kartosuwiryo announced the establishment of a 'Darul Islam' (DI) state, independent of both Dutch and the republican authority. The new state, Kartosuwiryo declared, did not recognize secular law, but only the shari'a. Just what was meant by shari'a and how it was to be interpreted were not clear (van Dijk 1981).

Notwithstanding the DI's lack of clarity on legal matters, at the height of the rebellion DI commanders mutilated thieves' hands, stoned adulterers and executed peasants who had paid taxes to the republican government, an act that the rebels defined as apostasy. Although the DI movement never seriously threatened the larger republic, it attracted significant support in Aceh, South Sulawesi, parts of West and Central Java, and South Kalimantan. In South Sulawesi and West Java, armed resistance continued for more than a decade, ending only in 1962 with the capture and execution of Kartosuwiryo.

The DI rebellion left an important organizational legacy. By 1962 most Darul Islam commanders had either surrendered or been killed. For many years, Indonesian observers assumed that the surviving DI leadership had reconciled with the republic. Under Suharto's New Order government, a number of former DI leaders became outspoken supporters of the president and the ruling party, Golkar. However, in the early 2000s, after several terrorist incidents, researchers revisited DI territories and discovered that a rejectionist underground had survived the movement's military defeat. Most of the former DI membership was no longer interested in taking up arms against the Pancasila state, but many continued to dream of a time when they might rejoin the struggle for implementation of God's law (International Crisis Group 2005).

Research also revealed that in the early 1990s a dissident DI faction known as the Jemaah Islamiyah had broken with the mainline organization and established an underground military wing dedicated to the formation of an Islamic state in Indonesia and neighboring portions of Muslim South-East Asia. Led by two Central Javanese religious teachers of Arab-Indonesian descent, the Jemaah Islamiyah was far more internationalist in orientation than the Darul Islam leadership had ever been. It was from the ranks of this neo-Darul Islam group that one faction among a new generation of insurgent radicals was to emerge in the early years of the post-Suharto period.

The radical revival

The months following the ousting of President Suharto in May 1998 were marked by the appearance of dozens of radical Islamist groups of varying ideological complexions. Some, like the internationalist Islamist group, Hizb ut-Tahrir (established in Jerusalem in 1953 by a Palestinian activist, Taqiuddin an-Nabhani, and known in Indonesia as Hizbut Tahrir Indonesia, or Liberation Party of Indonesia), had been operating clandestinely since the mid-1980s. The 1980s saw growing contacts between Middle Eastern and Indonesian Islamists (Bubalo and Fealy 2005). Nonetheless, the majority of post-Suharto radicals were home-grown activists of diverse Islamist persuasions.

The Hizbut Tahrir is nonetheless interesting because it is illustrative of a type of Islamism that had almost no presence in Indonesia prior to the post-Suharto transition. The organization's most striking feature is not just that it is transnational, but that its programs and leadership are controlled by an international hierarchy headquartered outside of Indonesia. Organizationally speaking, the Hizbut Tahrir Indonesia (HTI) is something of a blurred genre – radical in some ideological respects, while militant but non-violent in others. The organization rejects parliamentary politics and the legitimacy of the nation-state, advocating the establishment of a government headed by a caliph. The HTI also sounds radical in that it speaks of global and national politics in Manichean terms, portraying Muslims and non-Muslims as locked in a fight-to-the-finish clash of civilizations. In tactical matters, however, the HTI, while militant, stops short of anything illegal or violent. The HTI also differs from other, more radical groupings, in that it seeks to forge alliances with any and all Muslim groups 'committed to the struggle against liberalism and for the implementation of Islamic law' (Yusanto 2003).

The HTI began its ascent to public prominence in 2001, after the United States' intervention in Afghanistan. Earlier, in the first years of the post-Suharto transition, the organization still operated secretly and its membership was confined to university campuses. Still today, the rank and file of the HTI remain among the best educated of all radical or semi-radical groupings in Indonesia. The United States' intervention in Afghanistan provided the organization with a platform for mobilizing beyond its university base, and over the next three years the HTI succeeded in establishing branch organizations in most major cities. Hizbut Tahrir's role in mobilizing Muslim opposition to the US invasion of Iraq only swelled its membership ranks further.

The organization has also lent its support to domestic causes, including, most importantly, efforts since 2001 to implement Islamic shari'a. In 2001 the organization mobilized mass demonstrations in support of Islamist legislators' attempts to amend Article 29 of the Indonesian constitution so as to mandate state enforcement of Islamic law for Muslim citizens. After a year-long debate, the national assembly rejected the proposed amendment (Salim 2008: 102). In the months following this legislative setback, the Hizbut Tahrir joined forces with other Islamist organizations to press for the implementation of shari'a-oriented bylaws in cities and districts across Indonesia. Bylaws of this sort were made constitutionally possible by the fact that in May 1999 the government had rushed through two laws (Nos 22 and 25/1999) intended to devolve a broad array of powers from the nation's capital to districts (*kabupaten*) and municipalities across the country (Aspinall and Fealy 2003: 1–11). Religious affairs were not supposed to figure among the authorities devolved to the regions. Nonetheless, legislators in several areas took advantage of ambiguities in the legislation to press for bylaws ostensibly designed to protect public morals.

Over the next six years, activists in groups like the Hizbut Tahrir and the Islamic Defenders Front (see below) joined forces with mainstream political parties – including some long regarded as 'secular nationalist' rather than Islamist – to introduce what Indonesians refer to as 'shari'a-oriented regional regulations' (*peraturan daerah syariah Islam*). Although since 2007 the movement has stalled, legislation of this sort was approved in 53 of Indonesia's 470 districts and municipalities. About half of these regulations are not explicitly shari'a based, but are concerned with tightening controls on gambling, alcohol consumption and women's unescorted movement at night (Salim 2008: 126; Bush 2008: 176). The other regulations deal with matters of an explicitly Islamic nature, mandating Qur'an study, payment of religious alms (*zakat*), or the wearing of Islamic dress. Notwithstanding the fact that its overall membership is today estimated to be no more than 60,000–80,000 individuals, the Hizbut Tahrir's discipline, tactical good sense and willingness to work with people from all organizational backgrounds allowed it to play a pivotal role in the shari'a campaigns.

There was one other dimension to the campaigns that illustrates the evolving linkages between mainstream Muslim conservatives on one hand, and radical groupings on the other. In most of the districts or municipalities where shari'a bylaws were enacted, the effort was coordinated by representatives of the semi-governmental Council of Indonesian Ulama (*Majelis Ulama Indonesia*, MUI). Founded in 1980, for most of the Suharto era the MUI had been seen as a government tool designed to burnish the regime's Islamic credentials. In the post-Suharto era, however, the MUI sought to shed its pliant image by reaching out to Islamist radicals previously excluded from the council, including the Hizbut Tahrir and the Indonesian Council of Jihad Fighters (*Majelis Mujahideen Indonesia*), an alliance whose leadership had ties to the

Jemaah Islamiyah (see below) (Gillespie 2007: 202–40; Nur Ichwan 2005: 45–72). MUI leaders were determined to reverse what they regarded as the Muslim community's drift toward Islamic liberalism and the neo-modernist reformism of intellectuals like Nurcholish Madjid (Barton 1995: 1–71). In the provinces the MUI relied on these same conservative groups, as well as local Muslim militias, to provide the muscle for campaigns to introduce shari'a-influenced bylaws.

This collaboration is illustrative of one of the most important trends in conservative Muslim politics in the post-Suharto era. Although radical Islamists fared poorly in national elections, they were able to exercise an influence greater than their numbers in society as a result of their tactical alliances with quasi-state organizations like the MUI. These informal collaborations across the state–society divide played an even greater role in the rise of groupings more radical than the Hizbut Tahrir, such as post-Suharto Indonesia's militias.

Elite factionalism and the rise of the militias

During the first five years of the post-Suharto era, radical Islamist militias became a major force in Indonesian politics. The groups attacked and closed cafés, brothels and other alleged centers of vice; they harassed women who chose not to veil; and they attacked liberal Muslims, adherents of non-conformist Islamic sects and Christians accused of proselytizing in Muslim neighborhoods (Christians comprise some 10 per cent of Indonesia's population). From 1999 to 2001 the largest of the paramilitaries openly defied the elected government of President Abdurrahman Wahid and sent fighters to support the Muslim side in communal violence between Christian and Muslims in eastern Indonesia. Their intervention dealt a blow to the heretofore ascendant Christian militias (who, it must be emphasized, were every bit as violent as their Muslim counterparts) (Aragon 2001: 45–79; van Klinken 2007: 88–123). Ultimately, the militias contributed to the collapse of Wahid's reformist, albeit erratically managed, government (October 1999–July 2001). Several of the paramilitaries received quiet support from members of the old-regime establishment opposed to Wahid's reformist ambitions. Through collaborations like these, the Islamist militias were able to exercise a political influence greatly disproportionate to their numbers in society.

There were, in fact, hundreds of Islamist militias organized in the early years of the post-Suharto period, and they varied greatly in ideology and organization. Most of the smaller militias were little more than neighborhood watchdog groups organized by local youth, acting on their own initiative rather than under any national command. These groups shared a vague commitment to the cause of implementing shari'a and combating what they saw as the break-down in public morals. However, as my interviews in Jakarta, Makassar (South Sulawesi), and Solo, Central Java, indicated, many of these local groupings were not particularly opposed to democracy or the new political order (Interviews 2005–06).

Although the majority of Islamist militias were freelance locals of a relatively unaggressive sort, two of the largest groups, the Islamic Defenders Front (FPI) and the *Laskar Jihad* (jihad paramilitary), were better organized and more nationally oriented in their ambitions. At their peak in 2000 and 2001, each of these organizations had thousands of members deployed in military-style battalions under a centrally coordinated command. Each also had bases of opera-tion in cities and towns across the country, rather than just one locale (Feillard and Madinier 2006: 117–21; Jahroni 2004: 197–253; Davis 2002: 12–32). These large militias also differed from neighborhood watch groups in that they enjoyed the shadowy support of powerful members of the country's fractured political elite (Jamhari and Jahroni 2004).

The early history of the FPI illustrates the complex nature of these collaborations. The FPI was founded in August 1998 by Habib Muhammad Rizieq ibn Hussein Shihab, popularly known as Habib Rizieq. Rizieq was a young (38 years old at the time) religious teacher of Hadrami-Indonesian descent, from a family with ties to Indonesia's oldest Arab-Indonesian association, the al-Irshad. Established in the early years of the twentieth century, al-Irshad was a respected reformist organization, whose educational and social-welfare programs were broadly similar to those of the moderate modernist organization, the Muhammadiyah. Al-Irshad differed from Muhammadiyah, however, in that it directed its appeals at the Dutch Indies' small Arab population, which in the first years of the twentieth century was experiencing a cultural awakening. Al-Irshad schooling encouraged its young charges to support the cause of Indonesian nationalism, but also encouraged an 'outward orientation, back to the Middle East from whence their fathers had come' (Mobini-Kesheh 1999: 89).

The pattern of maintaining family, educational and ideological ties to the Arab Middle East has remained a distinctive feature of the al-Irshad community to this day. In the late 1980s and 1990s some in the al-Irshad leadership came under the influence of conservative Islamist styles emanating from the Middle East. These also happened to be the years when President Suharto had reversed his policy on political Islam and was reaching out to conservative Islamists. As one part of his campaign, the President developed ties to several nationally prominent al-Irshad businessmen, using the bond to extend his outreach to the conservative wing of the Muslim community.

According to information provided to me in interviews in Jakarta in June 1998, it was in this context that during the final year of the Suharto regime one well-known al-Irshad leader with ties to President Suharto approached Habib Rizieq and asked him to help coordinate demonstrations in support of the President and against the pro-democracy opposition. Although at this point he was not yet a familiar national figure, Rizieq led a network of several dozen conservative Islamic boarding schools (*pesantren*) in the Jakarta and West Java region, most of which were in turn linked to the conservative Indonesian Council of Islamic Predication (DDII). Rizieq drew on this network to mobilize pro-Suharto demonstrations.

Rizieq's role in elite political maneuvering did not end with Suharto's resignation. The post-Suharto era saw a new contest, pitting supporters of Suharto's designated successor, B.J. Habibie, against an unwieldy alliance of multi-confessional nationalists identified in the media as the 'rainbow' (*pelangi*) coalition. The latter coalition included left-wing activists, conservative nationalists and staunchly anti-communist army commanders who had once worked with Suharto but disagreed with the President's late-career outreach to Islamists. The only issue on which coalition members agreed was their opposition to Habibie. It was in this context of the growing rivalry between Muslim supporters of President Habibie and his 'nationalist' opponents that Rizieq and his colleagues established the Islamic Defenders Front.

Jakarta journalists whom I interviewed in 1998 and 1999 insisted that, in addition to the al-Irshad business patron, Armed Forces Commander General Wiranto and the chief of police for the capital district, Nugroho Jayussman, both also backed Rizieq's effort to establish his militia. From September to November 1998 Rizieq became the most prominent of Jakartan Islamists working with Wiranto to organize a semi-governmental paramilitary known as the 'Voluntary Security Guards' or Pam Swakarsa (*Pasukan Pengaman Swakarsa*). The Security Guards were a militia force of 50,000 civilians designed to back up the 160,000 police and soldiers who were to be deployed to protect the November 1998 meeting of the Special Session of the People's Representative Assembly (SI-MPR). The Special Session was convened to lay the ground rules for the elections of June 1999, the first to be held since Suharto's resignation. Tellingly, the main groups against which the SI-MPR was to be 'protected' were nationalists and democracy activists opposed to the Habibie presidency.

At rallies held in the run-up to the November session, the charismatic Rizieq denounced Habibie's opponents as anti-Islamic communists. He urged the Guard members to be ready to give their lives in defense of Islam and the nation (van Dijk 2001: 340–44). When the Security Volunteers poured into the city on 9 November, they directed their attacks against pro-democracy students, but unwittingly ran afoul of residents in several poor neighborhoods. More than a dozen people died in the resulting clashes, including several Pam Swakarsa militants beaten to death by neighborhood toughs. Although the Pam Swakarsa was dissolved after the Special Assembly had finished, the Volunteers' core constituent, the FPI, lived on. Indeed, the FPI was about to embark on one of the most ambitious political adventures of the post-Suharto period.

With the country in deep economic crisis, the first three years of the post-Suharto period saw a dramatic spike in urban criminality, drug dealing and prostitution. The FPI responded to the crisis by organizing anti-vice squads in poor neighborhoods in Jakarta and neighboring towns, but the FPI also continued to play a supporting role in battles among segments of the now fractionalized political elite. In June 2000 the FPI ransacked the headquarters of the National Commission on Human Rights when the latter issued statements implicating members of the army command, most notably General Wiranto, in the 1999 violence in East Timor. In March and April 2001 the FPI joined with several Islamic political parties in a campaign against an allegedly resurgent communism. The campaign targeted leftist students, union organizers and bookstores selling Marxist literature (Hefner 2005: 284–86). The FPI also kept a watchful eye on Christian evangelicals, forcing the closure of home-front churches operating without government permits. When Christian–Muslim violence flared in the provinces of Maluku and North Maluku in 2000 and 2001, the FPI recruited jihadi fighters for the troubled provinces.

In the aftermath of the Bali bombings of October 2002, the United States, Australia and other foreign powers pressed the Indonesian authorities to ban the FPI and other Islamist paramilitaries. The Laskar Jihad did disband. At first, the Islamic Defenders Front announced that it too was suspending operations, but the gesture proved temporary. In 2003 the Front was at it again, ransacking bars and brothels. In 2004 the Front mobilized to pressure provincial legislators to pass shari'a-oriented bylaws, threatening those who opposed the legislation. In mid-2005 the FPI joined with other militants to mount a campaign against Indonesia's 300,000-strong Ahmadiyah community, a sect regarded by most of the world's Muslims as deviationist. The militia ransacked Ahmadiyah schools, burned members' homes and threatened those unwilling to renounce their faith. In August the FPI and its allies turned their attention to an even more celebrated target: Indonesia's 'Liberal Islam' or JIL network (*Jaringan Islam Liberal*), an association of elite young Muslim intellectuals committed to a secular, liberal and pluralistic reinterpretation of Muslim politics (Hooker 2004: 231–51). On two occasions in August and September, gangs of white-clad youth assembled to storm JIL's art center, library and café in the Utan Kayu district of East Jakarta. In contrast to the light-handed approach taken during FPI attacks on the Ahmadiyah, however, the Jakarta police responded to the threatened attack by deploying hundreds of officers, preventing FPI militias from occupying and destroying the complex.

As this brief history shows, during the early post-Suharto period, disputes among rival claimants to power provided Islamist militias with new opportunities for mass mobilization. After the ouster of Abdurrahman Wahid from the presidency in July 2001, Wahid's successor, Megawati Sukarnoputri, repaired the civilian government's relations with the military command, and armed forces officials signaled their desire to steer clear of the FPI. By this time, however, the FPI had a well-established network in several Indonesian cities. Even without significant elite backing, then, the FPI continued its campaigns, targeting vice centers, Ahmadiyah institutions, Christian evangelicals and prodemocracy Muslims.

Sectarian mobilization

The rise of radical Islamist militias in the post-Suharto period was in turn linked to outbreaks of communal violence in several of Indonesia's outlying provinces. In particular, five provinces where Christians and Muslim lived in close proximity – West Kalimantan, Central Kalimantan, Central Sulawesi, Maluku and North Maluku – saw horrific outbreaks of ethnoreligious violence. Although the international media sometimes assumed that radical Islamists were the main cause of the violence, this is too simple an explanation. The broader influence was the back draft caused by the rapid devolution of powers from Jakarta to the regions after 2001. Although devolution was premised on the idea of strengthening civil society and deepening democracy, the policy's immediate consequence was a 'decentralization of corruption, collusion, and political violence' (Nordholt and van Klinken 2007: 18). Faced with an intensified struggle over local resources, regional party bosses, business elites and militia chiefs jockeyed to win control of the local state apparatus and the nebulous 'shadow state' that ran alongside it (van Klinken 2007: 33, 51).

The highly unsettled context of political devolution and resource competition stimulated the formation of locally based militias in both Muslim and non-Muslim communities. Where there was a previous history of ethnic or religious conflict, and where no clear party controlled the state, the mobilization often turned violent. Even before Suharto's ouster, West Kalimantan in early 1997 had witnessed brutal attacks by indigenous Dayaks (nominally Christian) on Muslim Madurese immigrants to the province. After Suharto's fall the violence exploded again, this time with even greater fury. In all of these incidents the violence was massively one-sided, with Dayak fighters, coordinated by local political bosses, slaughtering hapless Madurese immigrants (Davidson 2003: 59–90; Schiller and Garang 2002: 244–54). The fact that Dayak violence was not directed at other Muslim groups, and did not typically target institutions like mosques or *madrasas*, ensured that although the violence shocked the public, it was for the most part not seen as a Christian–Muslim clash.

By contrast, the conflicts in Central Sulawesi and the Moluccas quickly assumed a more explicitly sectarian form, pitting Christians against Muslims. In the Poso district of Central Sulawesi, 1,000 people died in violence from 1999 to 2002 (International Crisis Group 2001). Again, as with the Dayak conflict, the roots of the violence had been sown several years earlier. In the 1980s Muslim migration to the lightly populated hill terrains around Poso had placed the once dominant but otherwise unsophisticated Protestant population, known as the Pamona, on the defensive (Aragon 2001: 56–58; International Crisis Group 2004; Human Rights Watch 2002: 20–23). In the post-Suharto period, tensions between the Muslim immigrants and Christian locals exploded.

The worst violence of the post-Suharto period, however, took place in the provinces of Maluku and North Maluku in north-eastern Indonesia. As in the Poso region, the southern portions of the Maluku archipelago were more or less evenly divided between Christians and Muslims. The northern portion of the province (which in September 1999 became the separate province of North Maluku) had a more secure Muslim majority, but still had a Christian minority almost twice that of the national average (18 percent, rather than the national average of around 10 percent) (International Crisis Group 2002c). In the early independence period, Christians in Ambon and much of southern Maluku had controlled the commanding heights of politics and economic life. Indeed, when Indonesia declared its independence in 1945, some Protestants tried to break with the new republic and establish an independent state, known as the Republic of South Maluku (RMS). The rebellion was suppressed, and relations between the Christian majority and the Muslim minority eventually settled into a more or less peaceable pattern.

Tensions began to rise again, however, in the 1980s and 1990s as a result of three developments: an influx of Muslim migrants, many of whom commanded entrepreneurial skills greater than local Christians; the movement of growing numbers of Muslims into higher education and the professions; and the Suharto regime's courtship of conservative Muslims. The movement of Muslims into higher education was a phenomenon taking place across the country during these years, but its political impact in the southern Moluccas was especially pronounced, since Protestants had long used their mission-based educational advantage to secure a dominant position in the local state bureaucracy. With the advantage eroded, and with the Muslim population having become the provincial majority by the early 1990s, the Suharto regime began to favor Muslims in making appointments to the state bureaucracy. This new Muslim ascendancy was a bitter pill for the once-dominant Protestant elite.

Already in the mid-1990s small clashes had occurred between Christians and Muslims. In January 1999, however, an otherwise unexceptional fight between a Protestant bus driver and two Muslim youths escalated into full-scale communal battles between Christian and Muslim neighborhoods in Ambon city. Over the next weeks the violence spread into other islands in the Central Maluku chain. Although for a while it looked as if it might subside, the violence flared up again in the run-up to the June 1999 elections, the local results of which were polarized along religious lines.

In late 1999 the violence spread to North Maluku, where it took on an even darker form. Here whole villages were destroyed and mass killings were common. The worst incident took place in December 1999 in the small town of Tobelo, where Christian paramilitaries slaughtered some 200 Muslim women and children taking refuge in a mosque. News of the Tobelo incident spread quickly across Indonesia. The incident provided radical Islamists with the evidence they needed to buttress their claim that the government of the liberal-minded Muslim reformist, Abdurrahman Wahid, was indifferent to the plight of Muslims. The radicals also charged that the Tobelo violence was part of a broader campaign coordinated by Christian crusaders and seeking to destabilize Muslim Indonesia (Duncan 2005: 53–80).

In its initial phase the Moluccan violence had not been neatly polarized along religious lines, but as the conflict escalated it took on a more neatly communal pattern. A few communities where Muslims and Christians lived side by side held out against the bloodshed, preserving the tradition of Muslim–Christian cooperation for which Maluku had once been famous. Sadly, however, militants on both sides denounced the leaders of these mediating communities as traitors to their religion, and several were executed. The middle ground of multi-confessional pluralism was deliberately destroyed.

In early 2000 the Maluku conflict entered a new and more dangerous phase, as outsiders channeled money, men and arms to both parties in the conflict. Conservative Islamists in the nation's capital met secretly and agreed to provide funding to the newly established Laskar Jihad. The paramilitary's headquarters was in the south-central Javanese city of Yogyakarta. Neo-Wahhabis with spiritual ties to *Salafiyyah* scholars in Saudi Arabia, Yemen and Pakistan, the group enjoyed the backing of several prominent military retirees. However, the Laskar Jihad was never merely a puppet of elite patrons (Davis 2002: 12–32; Hefner 2003: 158–79; Hasan 2005). When I interviewed the Laskar Jihad leader, Jafar Umar Thalib, at the end of July 2001, he made no secret of his unhappiness with members of the armed forces command who had recently demanded that he not dispatch fighters to Central Sulawesi. In a public address on the central square in Yogyakarta at the end of the month, he astonished even his own supporters by threatening to 'eliminate' army officers who tried to stop his fighters. These and other exchanges indicated that although he had some powerful backers, others in the armed forces wanted nothing to do with Thalib (from interviews held in 2003, 2004 and 2005).

Notwithstanding this opposition, and despite appeals by President Wahid, the Governor of Maluku and the Minister of Defense, in April 2000 a large contingent of Laskar Jihad fighters traveled across Java to Surabaya to sail for Maluku. Along much of the way the forces had military escorts. In Surabaya, the fighters boarded state-owned ferries for the passage to Maluku. In Maluku, they were greeted and given automatic weapons by out-of-uniform soldiers. Shortly after the arrival of the jihad fighters, the troubled province saw a new and more violent round of killings. In one especially bloody incident, several hundred Christian villagers were massacred in apparent retribution for the Tobelo killings (Tomagola 2000: 17–35; van Klinken 2007: 88–123).

By late 2002 the Maluku violence had consumed some 8,000 lives; 600,000 more people had fled their communities. With its automatic weapons and communications equipment, the Laskar Jihad helped to stem the tide of the Christian forces, who prior to late 2000 had had the upper hand in the conflict (International Crisis Group 2002c). No sooner had the Laskar Jihad pressed its advantage, however, than it found itself facing difficulties. In mid-2000 the army dispatched a 'Combined Battalion' (*Yon Gab*) made up of soldiers from different divisions of the armed forces and different religions to crack down on sectarian violence. Demonstrating once again that there was no simple alliance between the armed forces and Islamist militias, in 2001 the battalion got into bitter fire-fights with Laskar Jihad fighters (International Crisis Group 2002c). In February 2002 a peace accord was signed in which the Christian and Muslim sides both agreed to remove all 'outsiders' from the conflict zone. Although, as in Poso, there were to be scattered incidents of violence, the accord marked the end of mass armed mobilizations in Maluku.

Like the Islamic Defenders Front, the Laskar Jihad suspended operations in the days following the terrorist bombings in Bali in October 2002. In early 2003 sources close to the Laskar Jihad in Yogyakarta told me that the organization's dissolution was a direct response to 'advice' from elite backers who warned that the United States had identified the Laskar Jihad as a terrorist organization. Equally important, however, Thalib had lost the support of his own Salafiyyah Islamist community. From the beginning, Thalib's attempts to recruit Salafiyyah for the Maluku Jihad had been controversial. As one Yogyakarta-based Salafiyyah leader told me in Yogyakarta in 2001, 'the Maluku campaign is being conducted to advance the interests of certain political players, not Islam'. Stung by the growing criticism and pressed by his elite backers, Jafar not only suspended his militia's activities after the October 2002 Bali bombing, but dissolved his organization outright.

It is now recognized that several al-Qaeda militants visited the conflict zones at the height of the Maluku violence, and domestic militants, including the *Jemaah Islamiyah* (see below), sought to stoke the violence as well. Notwithstanding these activities, the Maluku violence was not the result of international jihadist meddling. The conflict was a product of declining state capacity, heightened elite factionalism (at both the local and national level), and sectarian mobilization in provinces with long-simmering sectarian tensions. With the nation in economic crisis and the security forces in disarray, infighting among rival political elites spread rapidly from the capital to the provinces. Faced with the vacuum of power at the center and a scramble for political resources in the provinces, local bosses used whatever they could to press their advantage.

Internationalist jihadism: the Jemaah Islamiyah

Although in the early years of the post-Suharto period the Islamic Defenders Front and the Laskar Jihad were the most well-known radical Islamists, their notoriety was eventually eclipsed by an even more militant organization: the Jemaah Islamiyah (JI). The JI first came to national attention in the aftermath of the first Bali bombings in October 2002. Several young activists with ties to the group were arrested and convicted for carrying out the attacks. The group's stated ambition is to establish a pan-South-East Asian polity based on the Qur'an and Sunna (Abuza 2007: 37–65; Fealy 2005: 13–26; International Crisis Group 2002b, 2005). However, the organization's primary field of activity has always been Indonesia. Equally important, and notwithstanding media characterizations to the contrary, the JI was never simply an al-Qaeda offshoot. The JI's roots lie in Indonesia's older, home-grown jihadi movement, the Darul Islam.

As noted above, the DI had been suppressed by the Indonesian armed forces in 1962, but remnants of the movement went underground, biding their time in West Java, Aceh and Southern Sulawesi. By 1976 some in the DI underground had concluded that it was time to launch a new campaign of armed struggle. Shortly thereafter, DI militants organized an underground cell called the 'Komando Jihad' and carried out attacks on Christian and government targets. The violence spiraled on until 1981, when the group's leader, Asep Warman, was tracked down and killed (International Crisis Group 2005: 3–5). After Warman's execution, the organization's militant wing again faded from public view, but an underground faction remained active, recruiting followers not from rural strongholds but from the radical fringe of the Islamist student movement.

It was in these years too that Abdullah Sungkar and Abu Bakar Baasyir, eventual leaders of the Jemaah Islamiyah (and, prior to their flight to Malaysia in 1985, the directors of the al-Mukmin pesantren in Ngruki, Central Java), made contact with this new and especially militant wing of the DI. Sungkar and Baasyir were both from Indonesia's Arab community and had ties to the al-Irshad group. Like most al-Irshad reformists, the two men were strict reformists on matters of religion, and this appears to have become a point of tension with some of their DI counterparts, many of whom had vaguely Sufi orientations. In 1992 disputes of this sort led Baasyir and Sungkar to break with the DI and, in January 1993, establish their own organization.

Baasyir and Sungkar's group eventually came to be known as the Jemaah Islamiyah (Islamic community). The group recruited heavily from among the 600 or so Indonesians who had participated in mujahideen training in Afghanistan in the late 1980s and early 1990s; half of the group had trained in camps linked to Osama bin Laden. The Afghanistan experience provided the militants with much-needed training in armaments and explosives. Responding to the sectarian conflict raging in eastern Indonesia, in 2000 the JI leadership resolved that it was time to go on the offensive against what it perceived as an international Christian conspiracy. On Christmas Eve 2000 JI militants bombed 40 churches in towns across the Indonesian archipelago, killing 19 people and wounding 100. In October 2002, in an action designed to mark the prior year's attacks in the United States, JI bombers struck at two beach-front clubs in southern Bali, killing more than 200 people, most of them Western tourists (International Crisis Group 2002b: 3–14). In August 2003 the JI carried out a suicide car bombing of the Marriott Hotel in Jakarta; ten people died. In September 2004 JI militants carried out a suicide attack on the Australian Embassy in Jakarta; nine died. In 2005 the JI carried out a second bombing in Bali, once again using suicide bombers.

Whether Baasyir authorized the JI bombings remains a matter of dispute. Sidney Jones of the International Crisis Group (ICG) has discovered evidence which indicates that at some time during this period the JI split into two factions, the one gradualist in its aims and the other committed to immediate armed struggle. The violence-prone faction eventually came under the control of the Malaysian-born military strategist, Noordin Mohammad Top. After a four-year lapse, on 17 July 2009 his group carried out an attack on the Marriott and Ritz-Carlton Hotels in Jakarta (International Crisis Group 2009).

Neither the Jemaah Islamiyah nor Noordin's splinter group ever posed a real threat to Indonesia's post-Suharto transition. In fact, by continuing with their violent adventurism despite loud protests from the broader Muslim leadership, the radicals handed the government the proof it needed to convince a skeptical Muslim public that Indonesia had a terrorist problem. After the second Bali bombing in October 2005 the police intensified their campaign against the group's violent faction. Over the next three years they arrested more than 200 militants and broke up several bomb-making cells. In September 2009 the Indonesian police succeeded in cornering and killing the splinter group's master strategist, Noordin Top.

This brief history of the Jemaah Islamiyah reminds us that radical Islamist paramilitarism in Indonesia has roots that go back to well before the Suharto era and well before al-Qaeda's campaign against the West. Indeed, from a comparative perspective, the Jemaah Islamiyah and its parent group, the Darul Islam, are among the world's most long-lived of armed Islamist groupings. Both have demonstrated a remarkable genius for reinventing themselves in the face of changed conditions (Fealy 2005: 13–26). Even in the midst of sustained political crisis, however, neither has been able to win the hearts and minds of Indonesian Muslims.

Conclusion

Notwithstanding the electorate's demonstrated moderation in Indonesia's elections, the rise of radical militias, outbreaks of sectarian violence and terrorist attacks during the first five years of the post-Suharto period shocked Western analysts and caused consternation in the ranks of reform-minded Indonesians. The same events pushed Western skeptics to an even darker conclusion: that Indonesia had become not a showcase for Muslim democracy, but a second front for al-Qaeda.

The violence in Indonesia does indeed suggest that Muslim politics in post-Suharto Indonesia faced a serious challenge from its radical flank. Local radicals sought to take advantage of the period's political crises to restart their armed campaigns. Economic crisis, a surge in criminality, sectarian violence, and the growing availability of illicit drugs and pornography provided anti-democratic Islamists with the evidence to claim that Indonesia's post-Suharto government was a failure and the nation's multi-confessional charter a fraud. Sectarian violence in eastern Indonesia was exacerbated by bitter competitive rivalries among members of the political elite, both in Jakarta and in the provinces.

In the end, however, the radicals overplayed their hand, and the country's fractious political disputation diminished. Estranged in the early years of the post-Suharto period, the military elite established a new working arrangement with the civilian government and a relative peace was established in provincial conflict zones. Several years into those accords, the situation in Central Sulawesi and the Moluccas is not free of violence, but the large-scale mobilizations of the early post-Suharto period have ended. Armed groups like those that broke with the Jemaah Islamiyah may attempt to re-stoke sectarian violence. However, barring some unforeseen political or economic crisis, such efforts do not seem likely to derail Indonesia's political transition.

Today, Indonesia's main parties and Muslim associations differ only marginally on questions of Islam and democracy. National surveys and the outcome of parliamentary elections indicate that the great majority of Muslim Indonesians believe that democracy is the best form of government for Indonesia. Although most Muslims reject the idea of privatizing religion or creating a fully secular state, they also reject the idea that the Pancasila state should be replaced by an Islamic one.

The Muslim democracy emerging in Indonesia may well continue to differ from Western liberal democracies on issues like sexual freedom and freedom of religious expression. Nonetheless, the country offers a fascinating example of a Muslim-majority country's transition to democracy. That transition has taken place in the aftermath of *both* a great resurgence of piety and the Muslim majority's steadfast repudiation of religious extremism.

References

Abuza, Z. (2007) *Political Islam and Violence in Indonesia*, London and New York, Routledge.

Aragon, L. (2001) 'Communal Violence in Poso, Central Sulawesi: Where People Eat Fish and Fish Eat People', *Indonesia* vol. 72: 45–79.

Aspinall, E. and Fealy, G. (2003) 'Introduction: Decentralisation, Democratisation, and the Rise of the Local', in E. Aspinall and G. Fealy (eds), *Local Power and Politics in Indonesia: Decentralizations*, Singapore, Institute of Southeast Asian Studies.

Barton, G. (1995) 'Neo-Modernism: A Vital Synthesis of Traditionalist and Modernist Islamic Thought in Indonesia', *Studia Islamika: Indonesian Journal for Islamic Studies* vol. 2, no. 3: 1–75.

Bayat, A. (2007) *Making Islam Democratic: Social Movements and the Post-Islamist Turn*, Stanford, CA, Stanford University Press.

Bubalo, A. and Fealy, G. (2005) *Joining the Caravan? The Middle East, Islamism, and Indonesia*, New South Wales, Lowy Institute.

Bush, R. (2008) 'Regional Sharia Regulations in Indonesia: Anomaly or Symptom?', in G. Fealy and S. White (eds), *Expressing Islam: Religious Life and Politics in Indonesia*, Singapore, Institute for Southeast Asian Studies.

Davidson, J. (2003) 'The Politics of Violence on an Indonesian Periphery', *South East Asia Research* vol. 11, no. 1: 59–89.

Davis, M. (2002) 'Laskar Jihad and the Position of Conservative Islam in Indonesia', *Contemporary Southeast Asia* vol. 24, no. 1: 12–32.

Dobbin, C. (1983) *Islamic Revivalism in a Changing Peasant Economy: Central Sumatra, 1784–1847*, London, Curzon.

Duncan, C. (2005) 'The Other Maluku: Chronologies of Conflict in North Maluku', *Indonesia* vol. 80: 54–80.

Fealy, G. (2005) 'Half a Century of Violence in Indonesia: A Historical and Ideological Comparison of Darul Islam and the Jema'ah Islamiyah', in M. Vicziany and D. Wright-Neville (eds), *Terrorism and Islam in Indonesia: Myths and Realities*, Melbourne, Monash University.

Feillard, A. and Madinier, R. (2006) *La Fin de l'innocence? L'islam indonésien face à la tentation radical de 1967 à nos jours*, Paris, IRASCE.

Gillespie, P. (2007) 'Current Issues in Indonesian Islam: Analysing the 2005 Council of Indonesian Ulama Fatwa No. 7 Opposing Pluralism, Liberalism, and Secularism', *Journal of Islamic Studies* vol. 18, no. 2: 202–40.

Hasan, N. (2005) *Laskar Jihad: Islam, Militancy, and the Quest for Identity in Post-New Order Indonesia*, PhD thesis, Department of Anthropology, Utrecht University.

Hefner, R.W. (2000) *Civil Islam: Muslims and Democratization in Indonesia*, Princeton, NJ, Princeton University Press.

—— (2003) 'Civic Pluralism Denied? The New Media and *Jihadi* violence in Indonesia', in D. Eickelman and J. Anderson (eds), *New Media in the Muslim World: The Emerging Public Sphere*, Bloomington, Indiana University Press.

—— (2005) 'Muslim Democrats and Islamist Violence', in R. Hefner (ed.), *Remaking Muslim Politics: Pluralism, Contestation, Democratization*, Princeton, NJ, and Oxford, Princeton University Press.

Hooker, V. (2004) 'Developing Islamic Arguments for Change through "Liberal Islam"', in V. Hooker and A. Saikal (eds), *Islamic Perspectives on the New Millennium*, Singapore, Institute of Southeast Asian Studies.

Human Rights Watch (2002) *Breakdown: Four Years of Communal Violence in Central Sulawesi*, New York, Human Rights Watch.

International Crisis Group (2001) *Communal Violence in Indonesia: Lessons from Kalimantan*, Asia Report No. 19, Brussels, International Crisis Group.

—— (2002a) *Al-Qaeda in Southeast Asia: The Case of the 'Ngruki Network' in Indonesia*, Brussels, International Crisis Group.

—— (2002b) *Indonesia Backgrounder: How the Jemaah Islamiyah Terrorist Network Operates*, Asia Report No. 43, Jakarta and Brussels, International Crisis Group.

—— (2002c) *Indonesia: The Search for Peace in Maluku*, Asia Report 31, Jakarta and Brussels, International Crisis Group.

—— (2004) *Indonesia Backgrounder: Jihad in Central Sulawesi*, Jakarta and Brussels, International Crisis Group.

—— (2005) *Recycling Militants in Indonesia: Darul Islam and the Australian Embassy Bombing*, Asia Report No. 92, Jakarta and Brussels, International Crisis Group.

—— (2009) *Indonesia: Noordin Top's Support Base*, Asia Briefing No. 95, Jakarta/Brussels, 27 August.

Interviews (2005–06) January 2005–December 2006.

Jahroni, J. (2004) 'Defending the Majesty of Islam: Indonesia's Front Pembela Islam (FPI) 1998–2003', *Studia Islamika* vol. 11, no. 2: 197–253.

Jamhari, J. and Jahroni, J. (2004) *Gerakan Salafi Radikal di Indonesia* [Radical Salafi Movements in Indonesia], Jakarta, Rajawali Press.

Kartodirdjo, S. (1973) *Protest Movements in Rural Java: A Study of Agrarian Unrest in the Nineteenth and early Twentieth Centuries*, Kuala Lumpur, Oxford University Press.

Mobini-Kesheh, N. (1999) *The Hadrami Awakening: Community and Identity in the Netherlands Indies, 1900–1942*, Ithaca, NY, Southeast Asia Program Publications, Cornell University.

Nordholt, H.S. and van Klinken, G. (2007) 'Introduction', in H.S. Nordholt and G. van Klinken (eds), *Renegotiating Boundaries: Local Politics in Post-Suharto Indonesia*, Leiden, KITLV Press.

Nur Ichwan, M. (2005) 'Ulamâ, State and Politics: Majelis Ulama Indonesia After Suharto', *Islamic Law and Society* vol. 12, no. 1: 45–72.

Ramage, D. (1995) *Politics in Indonesia: Democracy, Islam, and the Ideology of Tolerance*, London and New York, Routledge.

Roy, O. (2004) *Globalised Islam: The Search for a New Umma*, London, C. Hurst and Co.

Salim, A. (2008) *Challenging the Secular State: The Islamization of Law in Modern Indonesia*, Honolulu, University of Hawaii Press.

Schiller, A. and Garang, B. (2002) 'Religion and Inter-ethnic Violence in Indonesia', *Journal of Contemporary Asia* vol. 32, no.2: 244–54.

Tomagola, T.A. (2000) 'The Bleeding Halmahera of North Moluccas', in O. Törnquist (ed.), *Political Violence: Indonesia and India in Comparative PerspectiveI*, Oslo, University of Oslo.

van Dijk, C. (1981) *Rebellion under the Banner of Islam: The Darul Islam in Indonesia*, The Hague, Martinus Nijhoff.

—— (2001) *A Country in Despair: Indonesia between 1997 and 2000*, Leiden, KITLV Press.

van Klinken, G. (2007) *Communal Violence and Democratization in Indonesia: Small Town Wars*, New York, Routledge.

Yusanto, Muhammad Ismail (2003) Interview with the HTI spokesperson.

10
Islamism reaches Central Asia

Shahram Akbarzadeh

Islamism in Central Asia is a new phenomenon. For 70 years the region was part of the Soviet Union, cut off from the Muslim world. That experience had major ramifications for the development of Islam in society and politics. Central Asia's disconnection from the Muslim world protected it from the radical trajectory that has now become widely documented in the Middle East. The Arab–Israeli wars, which galvanized Muslim opinion in the Middle East and gave force to the politicization of Islam, did not register in Central Asia. This separation, and Soviet efforts to remove all traits of Islam from public life, contributed to the evolution of Islam as an apolitical force. Islam was central to the cultural and communal life of Central Asians but had next to no presence in the public life of the region except in controlled settings when the Soviet authorities deemed it useful to project an image of tolerance to the Middle East. As a consequence, there was little potential for Islam to become a political ideology under Soviet rule.

However, the other side of this coin was that at the time of the Soviet collapse, Central Asian Muslims were yearning to reunite with their brethren in the Middle East and learn more about their faith. This led to an Islamic revival, one that the leadership tried to harness for its own ends. The growing interest in Islam also opened the region to radical ideas about the role of Islam in politics and the relationship between secular and Islamic rule. The introduction of post-Soviet Central Asia to Islamism was a gradual process, only accelerated by the increasingly intolerant attitude of incumbent regimes towards their opponents. The general slide of the region towards authoritarianism and the adoption of judicial and extra-judicial measures to suppress dissent have created an environment conducive to radicalism. The emergence of Hizb ut-Tahrir in Central Asia is signaling a qualitative shift, one that is dragging the region into the Middle East fold and mars its politics with the familiar traits of authoritarianism and anti-American Islamism (Walker 2003).

First impressions

The Islamic Renaissance Party (IRP) was Central Asia's first experience of Islamism. The IRP emerged on the eve of the Soviet collapse, holding its first convention in Russia (June 1990) and then establishing a presence in Uzbekistan and Tajikistan, although the authorities refused its application for formal registration. This decision was justified with reference to the separation of religion from politics – a principle that survived the Soviet collapse and transition to independence. The IRP in Central Asia was concerned with local issues and evolved into distinct national organizations in the two republics. Attempts at forming IRP branches in Kazakhstan, Kyrgyzstan and Turkmenistan did not go very far as the population showed little interest in the idea of mixing Islam with politics. In addition, the ruling regime in Turkmenistan was extremely intolerant of any dissent and made no effort to put up even a façade of political openness, as did the neighboring Uzbekistan and Tajikistan. Greater interest in Islam in the latter two republics may have reflected the historical links between the traditionally sedentary Tajik and Uzbek population and Islamic center of learning in Samarkand and Bukhara, in contrast with the nomadic traditions of Kazakhs, Kyrgyz and Turkmens.

The stated objective of the IRP was the establishment of an Islamic state. This made it utterly intolerable for the ruling regimes, but it was unclear what this vision entailed. The IRP leadership had difficulty articulating the contours of its vision. They rejected the Iranian and the Saudi model of Islamism, yet had no alternatives. Instead they emphasized the national character of their Islamic vision, and were content with the formation of an Islamic state within the existing boundaries and on democratic principles. This vision was in conformity with the wave of nationalist excitement that was sweeping across Central Asia. The IRP vision, to the extent that it was formulated, was consistent with the consolidation of independent republics with a clear commitment to upholding Islamic principles that was at the heart of Central Asian identities. The IRP in Uzbekistan and Tajikistan were more like religiously inclined nationalist groups than Islamists in the strict meaning of the term, one that implies the imposition of a normative Islamic agenda on social and political practices. In addition, the IRP was also careful to avoid conflict and violence in order to work within the existing political boundaries, although this strategy was abandoned in Tajikistan when tensions boiled over in May 1992. Despite this deviation, the IRP in Tajikistan appears to have returned to its original mould, as will be discussed below.

The IRP has been effectively sidelined by developments in Uzbekistan. A number of smaller, local Islamist groups emerged in the densely populated Ferghana Valley in Uzbekistan on the eve of independence. They remained active and visible throughout 1992, but their reach was limited and they faced the wrath of the security forces. Some chose exile over detention and torture by the Uzbek regime, and fled to Tajikistan. The growing assertiveness of the IRP in Tajikistan in the face of a worsening civil war proved a magnet for some Uzbek Islamists who felt that they could make a difference. Led by Juma Namagani, a group of Uzbek Islamists who had been training and fighting with the Tajik opposition movement between 1992 and 1997, formed the Islamic Movement of Uzbekistan (IMU) to take the fight to President Islam Karimov. As discussed below, however, the life span of IMU was very short and failed to present a political challenge to the Uzbek regime. The initial experience of Central Asia with Islamism was brief and inconsequential. Forces that are generally dubbed Islamist often acted as religious nationalists or criminal bandits. The Soviet collapse and the immediate post-Soviet era exposed Central Asia to unprecedented factors, and the ruling regimes had little time to adjust to them.

State attitude

The Central Asia leadership was not prepared for independence – even less so for negotiating with contending political actors. The leadership had operated in a rigid hierarchy of authority under Soviet rule and was more attuned to the political climate in Moscow than the political aspirations of the local population. The impact of the reform agenda that was initiated by Mikhael

Gorbachev was minimal. As the First Secretary of the Communist Party of the Soviet Union (1985–91), Gorbachev launched far-reaching reforms and targeted corruption and nepotism in Central Asia. This led to the appointment of new first secretaries at republican levels of the Communist Party. The move to purge corrupt officials and place the leadership in 'clean hands' was aimed at restoring confidence in the ruling Communist Party and minimizing waste and corruption. The introduction of the post of presidency was a further step to bring a degree of accountability to the system, although it was by no means expected to undermine the supremacy of the Communist Party. Taking advantage of the new opportunity, the Kyrgyz Soviet Socialist Republic made history by electing a non-Communist Party leader as president. Despite the immense symbolism of this move, the authoritarian style of leadership in Central Asia survived the Soviet collapse.

To say that the incumbent leaders in Central Asia were not democrats and had no desire to institutionalize a system of popular accountability is not to say that they were completely blind to the international tide. The opening up of the post-Soviet space to the West meant that ideas and expectations of a democratic overhaul were permeating to Central Asia. Numerous initiatives on democratic transition in the region were sponsored by the United States and the European Union (EU). Central Asia's rich gas and oil reserves added a further reason for Western interests in integrating the region into the global economy. The push for the liberalization of the economy and democratization of politics were consistent with that trend. Sensing the growing tide, the Central Asian leadership tried to position themselves to take advantage of the pressure for transition to democracy – some more successfully than others – but this flirtation with democracy was little more than political theater.

The leadership in Uzbekistan tolerated the emergence of political parties and movements in 1991 and 1992. This was consistent with the mood of euphoria at the time. This relative political openness, however, was not expected to undermine the dominance of the ruling party. This experiment was simply meant to project an image of 'democratic transition', mostly for the benefit of the West. Some of the players, however, were overstepping their bounds and presenting a real challenge to the incumbent regime through their grass-roots activities and publications. By early 1993 it was clear that the democratic experiment was getting out of hand and the ruling regime had to rein it in. The retreat from substantive political reform was marked by enforcing the ban on three novice independent political players: Birlik, Erk (two nationalist parties), and the Islamic Renaissance Party. However, the façade of the multi-party system was maintained as the regime orchestrated elections and maintained the veneer of democracy. The regime dismissed its critics, often in the West, as wanting too much too fast, arguing that transition to democracy cannot be achieved overnight.

The post-Soviet experience throughout the region was a variation on the same theme: initial flirtation with political openness followed by a rapid retreat to authoritarianism. The executive arm of the state continued the Soviet convention of dominating the state machinery, whereby the legislative body and the judiciary operate as extensions of the government. In this model the office of the president has been elevated above all and placed beyond accountability. The Central Asian presidential system turned the state into the personal fiefdom of the incumbent. Presidents Islam Karimov of Uzbekistan and Noursultan Nazarbaev of Kazakhstan continue in office 20 years after the fall of the Soviet Union. President Akaev of Kyrgyzstan was removed from office only after widespread social unrest in 2005. President Sapamurat Niyazov of Turkmenistan died in office in 2006, but Niyazov left a doubtful legacy as he took the presidential model to an extreme by constructing a cult of personality that elevated him, for all intents and purposes, to sainthood. Only Tajikistan differed in its post-Soviet path (explored below).

121

For all their authoritarian tendencies, the incumbent regimes possessed enough political acumen to know what could be useful for their continued rule. It was clear that nationalism was a necessary feature of the post-Soviet landscape, especially because the incumbent leaders had to emphasize a break with their Soviet track record. In the rush to embrace local nationalisms, the leadership had to make a choice about Islam. What was the place of Islam in post-Soviet Central Asia and what was its relationship with secularism? The answer to this key question set Central Asia on a trajectory similar to the rest of the Middle East. Learning from the Soviet experience, the Central Asian leadership, with the obvious exception of Tajikistan, was attuned to the cultural value of Islam. Soviet policy-makers had tried to eliminate Islam through a range of educational and indoctrination mechanisms, but their approach had failed because Islam is much more than an ideology. It is the cultural glue that keeps local communities together through rituals and traditions. It provides a sense of continuity that is essential for local identities, linking the present to the past. No amount of atheistic education and propaganda could remove the need for that emotional link to the past. Soviet planners had grudgingly accepted the failure of their policy and moved to minimize the risks that Islam could pose by institutionalizing an elaborate hierarchy of control. This was an important legacy for the post-Soviet leadership (Olcott 1995).

Inheriting an Islamic hierarchy that organized the religious activity of the local imams under the spiritual directorate of the Mufti (located in Tashkent) had two immediate benefits for the incumbent leadership. It offered a ready-made tool to exert authority and control over Islamic activity, while also allowing the ruling regimes to claim patronage of Islam. The republican leadership moved quickly to exert control over the Islamic hierarchy, splitting the Central Asia-wide institution of the Muftiyat into separate republic-centered institutions. Now each newly independent republic had its own official Islamic hierarchy that was accountable to its own government, not to the Mufti in Tashkent. This satisfied the leadership's urge for control, but it also put the Islamic leadership at loggerheads with the regime in Uzbekistan and Tajikistan. The regime's authoritarian aspirations, which translated into direct intervention in the appointment of imams and monitoring of sermons, was challenged in these republics by heads of the newly established Islamic hierarchies, but the growing tension only convinced the republican leadership of the urgency of consolidating control and managing Islam's public role. In Uzbekistan this was achieved in January 1993 with the removal of the sitting Mufti Muhammad Yusuf and the appointment of a more docile one, who was in turn replaced with an even more loyal Mufti in 1997 (Melvin 2000: 54). However, the Tajikistan case proved more complicated, as Qazi Kalon Akbar Turajonzoda, the head of the official Islamic hierarchy, openly sided with the opposition and was embroiled in the civil war that engulfed the republic between 1992 and 1997.

Before discussing the specifics of the Tajik experience, there is the second generic aspect to consider: Islam as a source of legitimacy. Given the unsavory history of the Soviet rule and its anti-Islamic policies, the incumbent regimes felt the need to take extraordinary measures to distance themselves from the past and recast their image as champions of their nation and its cultural values. Promoting Islam was an important component of the post-Soviet nation-building project that saw the Communist Party elite transform themselves overnight into nationalist leaders. The construction of new mosques and the freeing of the local population to perform pilgrimage to Mecca served an important purpose. They presented the leadership as respectful of Islam and in tune with the cultural heritage of their citizens. This message was reinforced when the presidents of Kyrgyzstan, Turkmenistan and Uzbekistan placed a hand on the holy book of Qur'an at their inaugural ceremonies (Tazmini 2001). The reinvention of the leadership was complete. Such a dramatic shift pointed to an acute political calculation. Islam was seen as conferring legitimacy and credibility and the incumbent leadership was desperate for that affirmation.

Playing with Islam as a political tool, however, was fraught with risks. The descent of Tajikistan into civil war was widely seen by neighboring political elite as a consequence of Islamic militancy. This assessment put the leadership in a difficult situation. While the ruling elite, especially in Uzbekistan, was eager to benefit from the air of legitimacy that Islam conferred, it was very anxious about Islam's potential to be used as a rallying cry for dissidents and opponents of the regime. This practical dilemma led to the rise of an elaborate policy to compartmentalize Islam into good and bad. Islamic activities taking place outside the domain of the state were viewed with suspicion and any political activity that sought to bring Islam into the public domain was rejected as 'fundamentalist', 'extremist' or 'Wahhabist'. These terms conveyed a poignant message to their Central Asian audience. 'Fundamentalist' and 'extremist' were often the labels used to describe Iran and its imposition of shari'a law on society, just as Wahhabism referred to Saudi Arabia's draconian penal code. Neither country enjoyed a positive image in Central Asia for their harsh Islamic rule and the incumbent regimes worked systematically to encourage suspicion and distrust of the 'extremist' version of Islam. This approach was also consistent with the Soviet-era coverage of 'Wahhabism' and 'Islamic fundamentalism', which used the Iranian and Saudi models to warn its Muslim citizens of what could befall them if Islamic activism was allowed to prosper. Reinforcing this pattern, all post-Soviet Central Asian republics adopted constitutions that banned the formation of political parties inspired by religion. The ultimate message was simple. Independent Islamic political activity put Central Asia at a grave risk: it threatened to import a foreign Islamic model of intolerance and violence and undermine the indigenous, peaceful version of Islam. The incumbent regimes took it upon themselves to protect and promote their favored version against the disruptive and alien form of Islam. This framework allowed the imprisonment and torture of those suspected of affiliation with Islamic political groups, while sanctioning the construction of new mosques.

Tajikistan – an exceptional case?

If there was one clear case that highlighted the risks Islam posed to the established regimes in Central Asia, it was the devastating civil war in Tajikistan which lasted for five years. The deterioration of the political situation in Tajikistan had as much to do with the assertiveness of the Islamic Renaissance Party, which managed to secure the backing of the head of the official Islamic establishment, as with the profound disconnect between the ruling elite and the changing reality of the post-Soviet landscape. The first warning sign was when Rahman Nabiev, who was purged as the First Secretary of the Communist Party in Tajikistan in 1985 as Gorbachev launched his campaign against corruption and mismanagement, staged a comeback. In September 1991 Nabiev secured the newly created position of President with the support of the powerful Leninabad regional group that dominated top posts in the republic. Nabiev was no more ready for the Soviet collapse than were his counterparts in the neighboring republics, but unlike them, Nabiev made no effort to grasp the possibilities that independence offered. While in Turkmenistan and Uzbekistan, for example, the republican parliaments adopted Islamic festivals of Id-Kurban and Id-Fitr as national holidays and endorsed the moral significance of Islam in charting their post-Soviet path, the leadership in Tajikistan refused to make any conciliatory gestures towards Islam. President Nabiev was adamant that Tajikistan should remain a secular state. For him, secularism made no allowance for Islamic symbolism, even if that meant denying a pillar of national identity. He further argued that Tajikistan was not ready for independence – instead a revived Soviet Union would offer the best option for its future prosperity and development.

Nabiev's position alienated large segments of Tajik society at a time when winds of nationalism were blowing across the Central Asian plains. Qazi Kalon Akbar Turajonzoda, head of the Islamic establishment in Tajikistan and an elected Member of Parliament, gave voice to popular frustration at the failure of the regime to represent popular sentiments.

Responding to growing public displays of dissent in the capital city and calls for the resignation of the government, President Nabiev declared a state of emergency to clear the streets of Dushanbe of protestors. However, this move added fuel to an already tense situation. His opponents viewed with suspicion the formation of a presidential guard by forces loyal to Nabiev, seeing it as a preparatory move for a coup. Open conflict soon ensued. Despite an effort to prevent the escalation of tensions by forming a coalition government, Tajikistan descended into a civil war in May 1992. The protagonists in the civil war represented two broad forces. Forces loyal to President Nabiev came to be known as the Popular Front and mobilized in the southern province of Kulab. Popular Front forces managed to capture Dushnabe in November 1992 – a victory that furnished the appointment of their nominee and the present President of Tajikistan Emomali Rakhmanov as the head of state at an extraordinary session of the Parliament held in Leninabad. The opposition to Nabiev and his successor was a coalition of parties that included the Islamic Renaissance Party, the Democratic Party of Tajikistan and La'li Badakhshan. The political ideologies of these forces ranged from Islamism to nationalism to those seeking local autonomy, but their common denominator was their opposition to the unrepresentative rule of the Communist Party (Roy 1995).

Most academic commentators on Tajikistan have overwhelmingly identified an undercurrent of sub-regional rivalries as a critical factor in the civil war. In the post-World War II era Tajikistan was run by leaders from the northern province of Leninabad. At the time of independence in 1991 the ruling Communist Party formed an alliance with loyal forces in the southern province of Kulyab to respond to the growing challenge of the opposition. A competing sub-regional affiliation was evident in the support base of the IRP and the DPT as they drew support from the central, southern and south-eastern provinces. La'li Badakhstan was a purely local organization, focused on greater political autonomy for the Badakhshan mountainous region. In the heat of the civil war, however, it was easier to explain the conflict as an ideological battle between Islamism and secularism (Akbarzadeh 1996). This was how the Rakhmanov regime presented the case, as did the ruling elite in other Central Asia states. This perspective served an important purpose in justifying the salient turn to authoritarianism and suppression of dissent – brushing all opponents with the broad brush of fundamentalism and extremism.

In spite of the bloody civil war, Tajikistan emerged as the only Central Asian republic to allow the participation of the IRP in the formal political process. This was made possible through a peace accord in 1997, which put in place a transitional proportional system of representation. This allowed 30 percent of government posts at the republican and local levels to be offered to the coalition of the opposition forces. Despite the failure of the regime to implement this commitment fully, the peace accord allowed the IRP to operate within the legal framework and field candidates for parliamentary elections. This new-found opportunity had a profound impact on the political position of the IRP. It seriously mellowed its rhetoric and committed it to upholding the rule of law and democratic principles. The IRP leadership showed an acute awareness of the limited appeal of Islamism to the public electorate in Tajikistan and fashioned itself as an Islamic political party that was committed to working within the system, not uprooting it. This was partly a consequence of a growing awareness of its shrinking popular appeal, and partly due to a growing schism between the IRP leadership and Turajonzoda, who distanced himself from the party and argued in 2000 that the IRP does not represent the only voice of Islam (Olimova 2004: 261).

The combination of internal and external pressures, as well as a generational shift in the leadership, have helped the IRP take a more centrist position in Tajikistan. The current IRP leader, Muhiddin Kabiri, has noted that 'it is impossible to set up an Islamic state or republic in Tajikistan in the foreseeable future [...] Our ultimate goal is to create a free, democratic, and secular state' (Collins 2007: 87–88). This position is rejected by the critics as duplicitous; the IRP's commitment to democracy is rejected as a tactical ploy to gain power. The behavior of the IRP since the end of the civil war, however, suggests deep rethinking on the role of Islam in politics, which goes beyond tactical machination. The IRP has not performed well at parliamentary elections, consistently securing only two seats in three successive elections. This is to some extent due to bullying and electoral fraud by the ruling party of President Rakhmanov (International Crisis Group 2009; Crosston 2008). A recent report by Freedom House recorded a steady decline in the rule of law and political openness in Tajikistan (Foroughi 2010).

Despite the deteriorating political environment for the IRP, the party has maintained a commitment to working within the system. The IRP has identified an open and functioning multi-party system as its best option and has concentrated its efforts towards that goal. In this vein, the IRP participated in a US-funded program in February 2006 on the role and structure of political parties in a multi-party system (National Democratic Institute 2008). The program was held in Poland, drawing lessons from the Polish experience of transition to democracy.

Alternative Islamists

The IRP may be argued to represent a traditional form of Islam in Central Asia, one that accommodates local traditions and the separation of Islam from politics, even though all its political positions are couched in Islamic terms. To this extent, the IRP is inspired by Islam – not governed by a strict interpretation of Islam. This distinction allows the IRP to pursue a national democratic agenda under the cloak of Islam, putting it on a similar plain as the ruling regimes that seek legitimacy for their rule by invoking Islam. Here Islam is at the service of political actors, albeit diametrically different: one pursuing national-democratic rule, the other authoritarian rule. However, Central Asia is also experiencing a more radical version of Islamism that is less accommodating of local traditions. Writing in 2003, Pauline Jones Luong noted a worrying trend in Central Asia. The US military involvement in Afghanistan, which brought US troops into close proximity of Central Asians, and the security pacts formulated between the United States and the authoritarian Central Asian regimes, especially in Uzbekistan, gave local grievances with the ruling regime an anti-American dimension. This was a similar pattern to the Middle East, where the United States was widely seen as sponsoring authoritarian regimes in power to fend off the rise of forces that could potentially put US interests at risk. Luong (2003) called this process the 'Middle Easternization of Central Asia'.

The rise of extremist Islamist activity in Central Asia may be traced to the Islamic Movement of Uzbekistan (IMU). In 1999 the IMU shocked public opinion in Central Asia by detonating a number of bombs in Tashkent. The region had not seen anything like this mindless and indiscriminate campaign of violence. The IMU declared itself committed to deposing President Karimov and establishing an Islamic state in Uzbekistan. Indeed, the personal antipathy of the IMU leadership against Karimov seemed to overshadow any ideological or doctrinal objectives. This did not win the IMU many supporters. The IMU's involvement in drug trafficking and cross-border attacks on Uzbek and Kyrgyz villages further undermined its credibility as a serious political challenger. Instead, it was relatively easy for the Uzbek government to accuse the IMU of banditry and seek the extradition of IMU leaders from Tajikistan, where they had sought refuge in the late 1990s. This growing pressure forced many IMU fighters to relocate to

Afghanistan. In 2001 the IMU suffered a fatal blow as it aligned itself with the Taliban against the advancing forces of the Northern Alliance in the city of Mazare Sharif. Most of the IMU fighters were killed in battle, bringing the IMU threat to an end (Akbarzadeh 2005: 29–31).

Given the incoherent and very personal nature of the IMU's position on Islam and politics, it never posed a serious challenge to the authority of the ruling regime. In fact, its banditry and violence only served to justify the repressive measures employed by the Uzbek regime to ward off potential threats. However, as noted by Luong, Central Asia is being dragged into the Middle East. The emergence of Hizb ut-Tahrir (HT) has introduced a new dimension to Islamism in Central Asia that is akin to the experience of Islamism in the Middle East – one that is vehemently anti-American and aims to revolutionize society in order to establish an Islamic state. In this case, the Islamic state is not seen as a distinct polity operating within the boundaries of an existing state, something that Islamists had traditionally favored, but a polity that is global and covers all Muslim lands, headed by a Caliph. Hizb ut-Tahrir prides itself for its promotion of the Caliphate. Vitaly V. Naumkin, a long-standing scholar of Islam in Central Asia, compares the ideology of HT to that of Islamism in Iran, which gave rise to the institution of the *velayate faqih*, or the supremacy of the jurisprudent (Naumkin 2005: 134).

HT first came to public attention in the late 1990s in Uzbekistan and spread to neighboring Kyrgyzstan and Tajikistan. Containing HT has proven very difficult for the authorities due to three key reasons. First, unlike many other Islamists, HT eschews violence and rejects terrorism as a form of political expression. Instead it emphasizes the importance of Islamic education and learning. It forms Qur'an study circles that explore the holy text and the prophetic message. Given the long history of isolation from the Muslim world during the Soviet era, Central Asian Muslims yearn to learn more about Islam and feel part of a greater whole. HT offers a welcome opportunity for many disgruntled Central Asian Muslims to learn more about their religion without approaching the formal Islamic establishment, whose authority is somewhat stained because of its subservience to the ruling regimes. Second, HT is an international organization with a strong presence in Europe. It is also technologically savvy and makes effective use of the internet to propagate its message. The opening of Central Asia to air travel and population movement following the Soviet collapse made the region accessible to HT, the ideas of which are likely to have reached Uzbekistan by visitors from Turkey. This international support base allows local HT activists to draw strength and inspiration needed to withstand the well-documented brutality of the Uzbek regime (Abou Zahab and Roy 2004: 9–11). Third, the combination of the above factors has helped HT present a coherent vision, drawing a seamless link between local grievances and its ultimate goal of establishing the Caliphate. In the familiar paradigm of 'Islam is the solution', HT blames the ruling regimes for failing to uphold Islam as the underlying cause of corruption and social ills that pervade Central Asia. A return to Islam and restoring the glory of the Caliphate, HT argues, is the solution to local grievances (Jonson 2006: 165–66).

Conclusion

The rapid growth of HT in Tajikistan and Uzbekistan has caused unease in the region and beyond. The regimes have accused HT of engaging in violence and terrorism, a charge that has found some endorsement in the scholarly community. Citing a 2001 publication by HT, Naumkin has argued that HT does not live up to the image of a peaceful organization when it advocates uprising and jihad (Naumkin 2005: 155). The events of 2001 and the arrival of US forces in Uzbekistan have added a new dimension to the activity of HT. The party has blamed President Karimov for facilitating the US military involvement in Afghanistan, calling him a

'Jew' – the ultimate insult for Islamists in the Middle East. This term, however, carries little political or ideological weight for Central Asian Muslims, who were protected from the escalation of hostilities between Muslims and Jews in the twentieth-century Middle East.

The knee-jerk reaction of the authorities to HT and other Islamists has been uncompromising, and ultimately counter-productive. The ruling regimes, especially the Uzbek regime, have become increasingly wary of Islam and its role in politics. The state machinery of control has seriously undermined the Islamic institutions of learning in Uzbekistan to such an extent that there is next to no intellectual and religious capacity in the office of the *Muftiyat* to challenge the ideology of the Caliphate. The former Mufti of Uzbekistan, Muhammad Yusuf (now in exile), blames the growth and popularity of HT on the behavior of the regime for purging the Islamic establishment of the energy and the intellectual capital needed to counter radical ideologies (Naumkin 2005: 157).

The crack-down on dissent and accusation of extremism and affiliation with HT leveled against anyone suspected of harboring critical views of the Karimov regime has pushed Uzbekistan towards breaking point. Tensions boiled over in 2005 when a group of women stormed Andijan's prison to free their male relatives accused of links with HT. In the ensuing violence around 400 people lost their lives. The authorities blamed the violence on HT, but independent reports have pointed the finger at the indiscriminate shooting of civilians by the security forces (International Crisis Group 2005). Whatever the truth, the Andijan events demonstrated the depth of tensions in Uzbekistan and the immense risk for violence. They demonstrated that the standard response of the authorities to Islamic and non-Islamic dissidents, the iron fist policy of suppression and persecution, has polarized society and led to a greater radicalization of the opposition. This political environment is best suited to Islamist groups such as HT which maintain a binary worldview, seeing it in terms of the war between Islam and kufr, good and evil. As Eric McGlinchey (2005) has argued, the growth of Islamism in Central Asia is to a large extent due to the authoritarian and intolerant policies pursued by the incumbent regimes.

Acknowledgment

I would like to thank Ilya Levine for his research support, which made this paper possible.

References

Abou Zahab, M. and Roy, O. (2004) *Islamist Networks: The Afghan–Pakistan Connection*, London, C. Hurst & Co.

Akbarzadeh, S. (1996) 'Why did nationalism fail in Tajikistan?', *Europe-Asia Studies formerly Soviet Studies* vol. 48, no. 7: 1105–29.

—— (2005) *Uzbekistan and the United States: Authoritarianism, Islamism and Washington's Security Agenda*, London, Zed Books.

Collins, K. (2007) 'Ideas, networks, and Islamist movements', *World Politics* vol. 60, no. 1: 64–96.

Crosston, M. (2008) 'Compromising coalitions and duplicitous diplomacy: US support for Tajikistan after 9/11 and its security implications', *Central Asian Survey* vol. 27, no. 2: 155–67.

Foroughi, P. (2010) 'Tajikistan', *Nations in Transit*, Freedom House, available at www.freedomhouse.org/images/File/nit/2010/NIT-2010-Tajikistan-proof-II.pdf.

International Crisis Group (2005) *Uzbekistan: The Andijan uprising*, available at www.crisisgroup.org/home/index.cfm?id=3469&l=3 (accessed 20 December 2007).

——(2009) *Tajikistan: On the Road to Failure*, available at www.crisisgroup.org/~/media/Files/asia/central-asia/tajikistan/162_tajikistan-on_the_road_to_failure.ashx (accessed 28 January 2011).

Jonson, L. (2006) *Tajikistan in the New Central Asia*, London and New York, I.B. Tauris.

Luong, P.J. (2003) 'The Middle Easternization of Central Asia', *Current History* no. 102: 333–40.

McGlinchey, E. (2005) 'Autocrats, Islamists, and the rise of Radicalism in Central Asia', *Current History* no. 104: 336–42.

Melvin, N. (2000) *Uzbekistan: Transition to Authoritarianism on the Silk Road*, The Netherlands, Harwood Academic Publishers.

National Democratic Institute (2008) *NDI Final Report: Strengthening Political Parties in Tajikistan*, available at pdf.usaid.gov/pdf_docs/PDACM232.pdf (accessed 1 February 2011).

Naumkin, V.V. (2005) *Radical Islam in Central Asia: Between Pen and Rifle*, Lanham, MD, Rowman & Littlefield.

Olcott, M.B. (1995) 'Islam and Fundamentalism in Independent Central Asia', in Y. Ro'I (ed.), *Muslim Eurasia: Conflicting Legacies*, London, Frank Cass.

Olimova, S. (2004) 'Opposition in Tajikistan: Pro et Contra', in Y. Ro'I (ed.), *Muslim Eurasia: Conflicting Legacies*, London, Frank Cass.

Roy, O. (1995) *The War in Tajikistan Three Years On*, Washington, DC, USIP.

Tazmini, G. (2001) 'The Islamic revival in Central Asia: a potent force or misconception?', *Central Asian Survey* vol. 20, no. 1: 63–83.

Walker, E.W. (2003) 'Islam, Islamism and political order in Central Asia', *Journal of International Affairs* vol. 56, no. 2: 21–41.

11

Islamism in Turkey

Gareth Jenkins

When Mustafa Kemal Ataturk (1881–1938) founded the modern Turkish Republic in 1923, he sought to expunge Islam from public life and make secularism the foundation of the new nation-state he was trying to construct from the ruins of the Ottoman Empire. For decades, Turkey was touted as the prime example of a predominantly Muslim country that was both secular and had a functioning parliamentary system.

However, secularism in Turkey had always been imposed from the top down by the political elite, rather than arising naturally out of Turkish society. During the final decades of the twentieth century, a combination of socio-economic factors and increasing democratization resulted in the official interpretation of secularism coming under increasing pressure as religion and religious identity once again emerged in the forefront of Turkish politics.

As in many other countries, the Turkish Islamist movement includes a broad range of diverging, and sometimes conflicting, opinions and goals. These range from relatively minor amendments to the official interpretation of secularism to a radical fringe who advocate the creation, by violence if necessary, of an explicitly Islamic state based on shari'a law. Ironically, one of the few issues on which the various elements of the Turkish Islamist movement tend to agree is in their rejection of the term 'Islamist'. All view it as being in some way pejorative. Moderates, the vast majority of whom are genuinely appalled by the violence sometimes perpetrated in the name of their religion, regard it as grouping them together with transnational militant groups such as al-Qaeda. Radical elements on the margins of the political spectrum claim that it implies a differentiation between their goals and Islam itself, and insist that they are merely trying to implement the basic tenets of their religion as manifested in the Qur'an and the words and deeds of the Prophet Muhammad. Nevertheless, in the absence of a suitable alternative, the term is used here in its broadest sense to cover all those who seek to reshape society and/or the political sphere in accordance with their perceptions of Islamic precepts and values.

In addition to having a more extreme agenda, the radical elements on the fringes of the Turkish Islamist movement also tend to have a more internationalist outlook. They identify more strongly with Muslim causes in other parts of the world, see themselves as being part of a global struggle and are mainly influenced by the writings of foreign, rather than homegrown, writers and theorists. Although they advocate change within Turkey, the establishment of an

Islamic state within the country's borders tends to be regarded as merely the first stage in the creation of a transnational political structure that unites all Muslims.

In contrast, the more moderate members of the Turkish Islamist movement tend to be Ottoman nostalgists. Rather than viewing the increased Islamicization of Turkey as a preliminary to the submersion of national identity within a global polity, they tend to regard it as a stepping stone towards Turkish leadership of the Muslim world in a reassertion of the pre-eminence enjoyed by the Ottoman Empire at its peak. Nevertheless, their primary focus is domestic, with an initial emphasis on removing the restrictions on the expression of Islamic values and identity embedded in the official interpretation of secularism in Turkey.

The Ottoman and Kemalist contexts

The Ottoman Empire is often described as an Islamic state, governed by shari'a law, in which the sultan's political power was based on his religious authority as the caliph, or spiritual leader of the world's Muslims. This is slightly misleading. Initially, the Ottomans appear to have been motivated as much by pragmatism as piety. It was only in the sixteenth century, when the conquest of the Muslim holy lands of the Hejaz produced an influx of Arab scholars and scribes, that the Ottoman state began to assume the shape prescribed in contemporary Islamic political theory (Jenkins 2008: 35). The shari'a formed the foundation of all legislation, although in practice it was supplemented by a form of statute law known as 'orfi', which consisted of commands and decrees issued by the sultan. The class of religious scholars known as the *ulama* not only issued rulings on all issues related to theological matters but also supplied the judges, known as 'qadis', for the courts (Ihsanoglu 2001: 443). It was also during the sixteenth century that non-Muslims began to disappear from positions of authority and be relegated to the status of a protected underclass, who were both spiritually and legally inferior to Muslims, although non-Muslims continued to account for the majority of the sultan's subjects until the late nineteenth century.

However, it was not until the late eighteenth century, when Ottoman military capabilities were in manifest decline, that the sultans began to attempt to use their claim to the caliphate as a substitute for raw power. Previously, inasmuch as they used the title of caliph at all, it was as an honorific. Ottoman military dominance of the Mediterranean and Middle East appears to have been regarded as proof in itself of divine approval of the empire's preeminence. This instrumentalization of the caliphate accelerated through the nineteenth century as Ottoman military power continued to decrease, finally peaking under Sultan Abdulhamit II (reigned 1876–1909), who attempted to use religion not only to hold together the crumbling remnants of an empire won by the sword but, in a form of spiritual imperialism, assert his authority over all the Muslims in the world in what came to be known as pan-Islamism (Deringil 1999: 65).

However, by the time that Abdulhamit was forced to abdicate following the Young Turk Revolution of 1908, a series of Western-inspired reforms implemented under pressure from the European powers had already eroded the influence of both the *ulama* and the shari'a, and had even introduced the concept of the legal equality of all Ottoman citizens regardless of belief. The process was accelerated under the Young Turks. In 1913 a decree was promulgated allowing judgments passed in the shari'a courts to be referred to a secular court of appeal. In 1915, overall control of the shari'a courts was transferred from the 'sheikhulislam', the most prominent member of the *ulama*, to the secular Ministry of Justice, and the religious schools or 'madrasas' were placed under the supervision of the Ministry of Education. It was not until the Ottoman Empire had been replaced by the Turkish Republic, though, that the first attempt was made to completely separate religion from the apparatus of state.

Official Turkish historiography has traditionally described the 1919–22 Turkish War of Independence as a nationalist uprising against an invading Greek army and the forces of the victorious Allies, who had occupied parts of Anatolia to try to enforce the 1920 Treaty of Sevres after the defeat of the Ottoman Empire in World War I (1914–18). However, although Ataturk, the overall commander of the resistance, was undoubtedly a Turkish nationalist, most of the troops under his control appear to have had little awareness of the concept of nationalism and to have believed that they were fighting for Islam and the protection of the sultanate and the caliphate. Nevertheless, following the proclamation of the Turkish Republic on 29 October 1923, Ataturk, who enjoyed autocratic powers, oversaw the most radical secularizing reform program ever attempted in a predominantly Muslim country. Over the next six months, the sultanate, caliphate, shari'a courts and office of sheikhulislam were all abolished. During the years that followed, the shari'a was purged from the statute book and replaced by civil, criminal and commercial codes imported from Switzerland, Italy and Germany, respectively (Berkes 1964: 467). All madrasas were closed and state-run schools were established to train Muslim clergy; the *ulama* ceased to exist as a distinct class.

In addition to legal codes, Ataturk also imported many of the other trappings of contemporary European nation-states. For example, the Gregorian calendar was introduced as the sole official measurement of time, effectively rendering the Islamic lunar calendar obsolete. Perhaps most extraordinarily, in 1935 a law was passed making Sunday, rather than the Muslim holy day of Friday, the official day of rest. In 1937 the Turkish constitution was amended to declare that the republic was a secular state. Although Ataturk appears to have introduced his reforms piecemeal, rather than as part of a preconceived program, they gradually coalesced into a doctrine known as 'Kemalism' (Alp 1936: 201–5), which became – and remains – the official ideology of the Turkish state.

However, in one of the many paradoxes that characterize the official interpretation of secularism, Islam remained the primary determinant of Turkishness, both popularly and at governmental level. For example, during the forced population exchange between Turkey and Greece in 1923–24, the sole criterion used for who should be expelled from each country was not ethnicity, but religion (Clark 2006: 106). Even today, non-Muslim inhabitants of Turkey are never referred to as 'Turks' but as 'Greek/Armenian/Jewish/Syriac Turkish citizens'.

Kemalism was enthusiastically adopted by Turkey's urban elite, many of whom had long believed that religious reactionism was the underlying cause of the Ottoman Empire's long decline; however, it proved less popular with the mass of the population, most of whom remained firmly wedded to their traditional religious beliefs. Ataturk's reforms triggered a string of violent popular protests and, in 1924, a full-scale rebellion in the deeply conservative southeast of the country in what has become known as the Sheikh Said Revolt, after the name of its leader. All of the disturbances were crushed by government forces and the ringleaders were hanged (Van Bruinessen 1992: 303).

During the Ottoman Empire, the official Islam of the courts, mosques and learned theological discussions was dominated by the *ulama*. However, outside the *ulama*, virtually the entire population was illiterate and lived predominantly in rural areas, where religious convictions tended to be shaped more by folk beliefs and oral traditions than by sacred texts. For many, their religious lives were shaped primarily by the Sufi networks known as *tariqah*. Significantly, it was not the remnants of the *ulama* who organized the protests against Ataturk's reforms but prominent members of the different tariqah – particularly the Naqshbandi order, of which Sheikh Said was also a leading member. In 1925 Ataturk outlawed the tariqah, closing down all their lodges and forbidding the use of all titles, roles, activities and even clothing associated with them (Mango 1999: 435).

The return of Islam

The proscriptions forced the tariqah underground but did not eradicate them. Some, such as the Mevlevi, or followers of the thirteenth-century mystic Mevlana Jalal al'Din Rumi (c. 1207–73), who famously practice a trance-like whirling dance, found it difficult to carry out their activities in secret. Others, such as the Naqshbandi order, whose central ritual is the silent contemplation of God, found it easier to shift to a clandestine existence, and largely preserved their extensive social networks. As late as 1940 over 80 percent of the Turkish population of 17.8 million was still illiterate (Jenkins 2008: 111). Although Kemalism was vigorously inculcated in the education system and took root amongst the urban elite, it does not appear to have penetrated very deeply into the countryside, where most of the population of Turkey still lived – certainly not deeply enough to shake centuries-old beliefs and traditions. It was the combination of these two factors, rural religiosity and the survival of the tariqah, which led to the reemergence of Islam as a political force following the introduction of multiparty democracy in 1946.

In 1950 the conservative Democrat Party (DP), which drew most of its support from the rural areas, swept to power in the first fully free general election in Turkish history. It replaced the Republican People's Party (CHP), which had been established by Ataturk and had enjoyed a monopoly of power since 1923. The DP remained in power until 1960, when it was toppled by a military coup. During its decade in office the DP introduced a number of concessions to religious sentiments, including reversing Ataturk's edict that the call to prayer should be in Turkish rather than Arabic, launching a massive mosque-building program and opening 19 new 'imam hatip' schools to train Muslim clergy. The DP was motivated by a desire to court the conservative vote rather than to introduce Islamist policies, however. It made no attempt to revive the office of sheikhulislam and Muslim clergy were civil servants whose wages were paid by the state. In fact, it was under the DP that laws were passed that made it a criminal offense, punishable by a prison sentence, to exploit religion for political purposes through propaganda or indoctrination, and to insult the memory of Ataturk. The former was not repealed until 1991; the latter remained in force in late 2011.

The DP's decade in power coincided with the beginning of a rapid, massive migration from the countryside to the cities. Nearly 1 million peasants are estimated to have migrated to the cities of western Turkey in the period 1950–55 alone. They brought with them the values and beliefs of the 'folk Islam' of rural Anatolia. Their priority was cultural and societal: being able to continue to live according to their convictions rather than press for changes to the statute book. Indeed, from Ottoman times, life in the countryside had been largely self-regulated by what was perceived as Islamic custom and tradition rather than sacred text or the wording of shari'a law. There is also evidence to suggest that exposure to the teeming modernity of urban life reinforced rather than eroded conservative attitudes, particularly with regard to women. In the Turkish countryside women have long performed a large proportion – arguably the majority – of agricultural labor by working family-owned plots of land, and thus have been relatively visible within a fairly restricted and controlled public space predominantly inhabited by relatives and acquaintances. However, migration to the cities meant that most of these women left the labor force, and whenever they ventured out of their homes they moved in incomparably larger public spaces which were predominantly inhabited by complete strangers. The result was increased societal and familial pressure on women to adopt perceptibly modest clothing and modes of behavior.

As the number of migrants continued to grow, so too did the demand for mosques and imam hatip schools. By the late 1960s the latter had ceased to be merely vocational schools but were being chosen by parents who wanted their children to receive a religious education instead of the secularism inculcated in the rest of the state system. In 1976 the imam hatip schools were opened to girl students, even though Sunni Islam traditionally forbids women from serving as clergy. By 1977, 135,000 students were enrolled in imam hatip schools. The concentration of large numbers of conservative Muslims in urban areas also led to the development of an Islamic popular culture and lifestyle, ranging from clothing stores to religious-themed movies and, as literacy began to spread, to a proliferation of magazines and books on Islam and Islamic values and modes of behavior.

Initially, these changes occurred on the periphery of the Western-oriented lifestyles of the Kemalist elite – both culturally and physically, as most migrants from the countryside settled in the sprawling shanty towns that had sprung up around all of the major cities of western Turkey. However, gradually they began to move into the mainstream of Turkish life, physically, culturally and politically. During the 1970s conservative Muslims also began to make the transition from being a constituency – to be appeased and placated in return for their votes – to becoming political actors in their own right.

Although a handful of conservative political parties had been established in the late 1940s, following the introduction of multiparty democracy, they had all been very small and faded from the political scene without being able to mount an effective challenge to the mainstream parties. In January 1970 Necmettin Erbakan (born 1926) established the National Order Party (MNP). Erbakan and most of the other leading members of the MNP were closely connected with the Naqshbandi order. Erbakan consulted frequently with his sheikh, Mehmet Zahit Kotku (1897–1980), and utilized the order's network as he sought to organize the MNP on a national basis.

Initially, the MNP also enjoyed the support of what was known as the Nurcu movement, the followers of the Kurdish Islamist activist Said Nursi (1876–1960). As a young man, Nursi had been deeply influenced by the tariqah, although he never became a formal member. Later he began to attract followers in his own right. In his writings, which were later collected under the title *Risale-i Nur*, or Epistles of Light, Nursi called first for the internal transformation of the individual, followed by the implementation of faith in everyday life and finally the establishment of an Islamic state based on the shari'a (Yavuz 2003: 161).

The MNP adopted a hardline Islamist agenda, although Erbakan stopped short of explicitly calling for the restoration of the shari'a. Nevertheless, in May 1971 the MNP was closed down by the Turkish Constitutional Court on the grounds that it was committed to undermining the secular nature of the Turkish state and the principles of Ataturk's reforms. Erbakan responded by founding a new party, the National Salvation Party (MSP) in October 1972. The MSP survived for eight years until, together with all other political parties in Turkey, it was outlawed in the wake of the 12 September 1980 military coup.

In its public rhetoric, the MSP actively cultivated a nostalgia for the Ottoman Empire, even using archaic Ottoman vocabulary in its campaign literature. In his speeches, Erbakan relentlessly attacked the West, arguing that Turkey needed to return to Islam and Islamic civilization if it was ever to regain what he described as its rightful status as a great power. Although he avoided personally advocating the restoration of the shari'a, other members of the MSP were less circumspect. The magazine of the party's youth organization was unequivocal about its long-term aims, which were to destroy the 'unwanted, humanistic system of the Western-Secular Republic' and replace it with 'an Islamic state based on divinely ordained laws' (Yalcın 1994: 151).

In the general election of October 1973, the MSP won 11.8 percent of the vote and became a partner in a coalition government headed by the CHP. Throughout the 1970s Turkey was wracked by factional fighting between leftist and ultranationalist extremist groups. When

Erbakan backed a CHP proposal for an amnesty which included the release of imprisoned leftist activists, the Nurcus in the party resigned in protest. In the next general election in 1977 the MSP won just 8.6 percent of the vote, as Nurcus shifted their support to other right-wing parties.

Despite Erbakan's often inflammatory rhetoric, even when it was in power as a coalition partner, the MSP made little attempt to implement Islamist policies. Instead, it focused on deepening its social roots both inside the country and amongst the Turkish diaspora in Europe, particularly in what was then West Germany, where the number of Turkish 'guest workers' and their families had grown to over 2 million, most of them first-generation migrants from rural Anatolia. In 1976 Erbakan founded the European National View Organization (AMGT) in Berlin, although its headquarters were later moved to Cologne. The AMGT provided a sense of religious and ethnic solidarity in an alien, often xenophobic, environment. It rapidly grew to over 2,000 branches and more than 250,000 active members and sympathizers, and its fundraising activities became one of the main sources of revenue for Islamist activism in Turkey.

The 1980 coup was followed by three years of military rule. Extraordinarily, for an institution that regarded itself as the guardian of Ataturk's legacy, the ruling junta actively promoted Islam as an ideological bulwark against the perceived threat from communism. Most controversially, it made the inculcation of Sunni Islam compulsory at every level of the school education system. The junta also appointed Turgut Ozal (1927–93), a member of the Naqshbandi order and an unsuccessful candidate for the MSP in the 1977 general election, to oversee the economy. During the return to civilian rule in 1983, Ozal took advantage of the military's continuing ban on political leaders active before the coup to be elected as prime minister. Although he was no longer close to Erbakan, Ozal oversaw the appointment of a large number of pious Muslims to key positions in the government bureaucracy, particularly in the Ministry of Education.

The junta's promotion of Islam as a social cohesive reinforced the shift towards more conservative values and identity and helped prime the electorate for the grassroots activism of Islamist networks. Even before the political bans were eventually lifted in 1987, Erbakan had already used proxies to establish the Welfare Party (RP). Through the late 1980s and early 1990s the RP continued to grow in strength. In March 1994 it won the local elections, taking control of the metropolises of Istanbul and Ankara. In the general election of December 1995 it became the largest party in Parliament, albeit with only 21.4 percent of the total vote. Nevertheless, it was able to form a coalition government with the True Path Party (DYP), a successor to the DP, under Erbakan as prime minister. In June 1997 a campaign of pressure and persuasion orchestrated by the Turkish military resulted in the collapse of the coalition. The military also belatedly attempted to reverse some of the concessions to religious sentiments introduced over the previous decades. By the mid-1990s there were over 600 imam hatip schools catering for 495,000 pupils, approximately 13 percent of the total school enrolment in the country (Jenkins 2001: 62). The military succeeded in forcing the government to adopt measures that reduced the number of pupils to 104,000 by 1999. However, by this time there were already over 2 million imam hatip school graduates in Turkish society.

The RP had not attempted to introduce any explicitly Islamist policies during its term in power but had nevertheless done enough to convince hardline secularists of what they believed were its long-term goals, most notably in January 1997 when Erbakan hosted leaders of the theoretically outlawed tariqah to an *iftar* (fast-breaking dinner) at sundown during Ramadan. In January 1998 the Constitutional Court outlawed the RP and banned Erbakan from active politics for five years.

Generational change

The Virtue Party (FP) had been established in December 1997 in preparation for the RP's possible closure. At its inaugural congress in May 1998, Recai Kutan (born 1930), a long-time confidante of Erbakan, was elected party leader.

During the 1990s the Islamic headscarf had become one of the key battlegrounds in the struggle by hardline secularists to preserve their control of the public space. Urbanization and rising living standards had resulted in the appearance of a conservative middle class, many of whose daughters not only covered their heads but sought a university education and a career. In theory, both state employees and university students were forbidden from wearing headscarves, although in practice many universities ignored the ban. That changed after the toppling of the RP-led government in 1997 and, under pressure from the military, the ban became more rigorously enforced.

In the campaign for the April 1999 general election, mindful of the fate of its predecessors, the FP toned down the direct Ottoman and religious references previously adopted by Erbakan-led parties. It even dropped their previous opposition to Turkish membership of the European Union (EU). However, it remained intransient on the issue of the headscarf, fielding eight female candidates who covered their heads. Only one, Merve Kavakci (born 1968), was successful, as the FP won just 15.4 percent of the vote and took 111 of the 550 seats in Parliament. When Kavakci attempted to take her seat, the other deputies prevented her from taking part in the swearing-in process. In May 1999 the Public Prosecutor applied to the Constitutional Court for the FP's closure on the grounds that Kavakci had attempted to undermine the principle of secularism enshrined in the constitution. The FP was formally outlawed in June 2001.

The closure of the FP split the Turkish Islamist movement. In July 2001 an older generation of Erbakan loyalists established the Felicity Party (SP) under Kutan's leadership. In August 2001 a younger generation of Islamists broke away to form the Justice and Development Party (AKP). They were led by Tayyip Erdogan (born 1954), a graduate of an imam hatip school and member of the Naqshbandi who had first come to prominence when he was elected RP mayor of Istanbul in March 1994. His deputy was Abdullah Gul (born 1950), a UK-educated economist who had served as government spokesperson in the RP–DYP coalition.

In February 2002 a run on the Turkish Lira triggered a financial collapse and the worst economic recession in 50 years. In the run-up to the November 2002 general election, the SP pursued a policy similar to that adopted by the FP, with its rhetoric and campaign literature avoiding explicit calls for Islamist policies while nevertheless containing sufficient thinly veiled references to ensure that voters remained aware of its continuing commitment to applying a program based on Islamic values if it ever came to power. In contrast, the AKP explicitly sought to portray itself as a center-right, rather than a religious, party. Although the decision-making core of the party was dominated by former members of the RP, the AKP also recruited Nurcus, conservative Turkish nationalists and even a handful of disgruntled former leftists who shared the party's antagonism towards the Turkish military.

AKP supporters claimed that the party's leaders had abandoned Islamism and were now committed to a pluralistic, secular democracy. However, hardline secularists remained skeptical, suspecting that the AKP's leaders were practicing the religiously permitted form of dissimulation known in Turkish as 'takkiye', and were merely attempting to stave off closure long enough to assert their control over the apparatus of state before implementing an Islamist agenda.

Ironically, the AKP arguably benefited from both of the contrasting assessments of its ultimate intentions. Islamists could vote for it in the expectation that it was only a matter of time before it fulfilled their expectations. Moderate conservatives could support it in the belief that its leaders were personally pious Muslims who had rejected the radical solutions espoused by Erbakan, noting that none of the party's leaders – not even Gul – had been actively involved in the formulation of the policies of the Erbakan-led parties. Most critically, at a time when there was almost universal disillusion with the corrupt and incompetent politicians who had ruled Turkey over the previous decade, the AKP was the only party competing in the 2002 election that represented something undeniably new.

In the election on 3 November 2002 the AKP won 34.3 percent of the vote, giving it 363 seats in Parliament, ahead of the CHP with 19.4 percent of the vote and 178 seats. The remaining nine seats were won by independents. No other party won enough votes to cross the 10 percent national threshold for representation in Parliament. The SP took just 2.5 percent and faded to the margins of the political arena.

During its first term in power, the AKP concentrated primarily on consolidating its political powerbase, nurturing economic recovery from the devastating recession of 2001 and accelerating the domestic reform process tentatively initiated by the previous administration in order to secure a date for the official opening of accession negotiations with the EU. The AKP did not introduce any explicitly Islamist policies, although some of its failed initiatives reinforced secularist suspicions. In 2004 the AKP tried first to boost imam hatip schools and then to criminalize adultery. On each occasion it eventually backed down: the first time under pressure from the military (Yavuz 2006: 200); the second following protests from the EU. Perhaps equally significant was the selectivity of many of its liberalizing reforms. For example, in 2003 it reduced the ability of the military to interfere in the political arena by weakening the National Security Council, the main instrument by which the Turkish General Staff had been able to apply sustained pressure to civilian governments. Similarly, there was a disparity between the AKP's willingness to ease restrictions when it came to issues important to secular Turkish nationalists – such as through the granting in 2003–4 of limited Kurdish language rights – and those important to pious Sunni Muslims. Despite protests from Turkey's substantial Alevi minority, no attempt was made to amend compulsory religious education. Turkish schoolchildren continued to be taught that Sunni Islam was 'our religion' and that any other beliefs were alien threats to national unity (National Ministry of Education 2004: 34). Nevertheless, the EU decided that there had been sufficient progress to justify the opening of formal accession negotiations in October 2005, although the process rapidly foundered, not least over the AKP's refusal to allow ships and planes from the Republic of Cyprus – which Turkey still did not recognize – to access Turkish ports and airports.

As hopes of EU accession began to fade, the emphasis of the AKP's foreign policy began to shift to improving ties with other Muslim countries, albeit while still trying to maintain cordial relations with Turkey's traditional Western allies. The AKP also sought to raise Turkey's profile in the Muslim world by engaging more energetically with the Organization of the Islamic Conference (OIC). In June 2004, after months of lobbying, a Turkish national, Ekmeleddin Ihsanoglu, was elected OIC Secretary-General. In contrast, Turkey's once-close ties with Israel began to cool. AKP officials, including Prime Minister Erdogan, frequently lambasted Israel for its policies towards the Palestinians, while pointedly refusing to criticize human rights abuses in countries such as Iran, Syria and Sudan. In March 2006 Erdogan publicly refuted claims that Sudan was overseeing a genocide in Darfur, declaring that Muslims were incapable of genocide.

For hardline secularists, such statements reinforced their suspicions that the AKP was merely biding its time. Through late 2006 and early 2007 attention shifted increasingly to the appointment by Parliament of a replacement for President Ahmet Necdet Sezer when his seven-year term expired in May 2007. Although the presidency was mainly a titular position, the president could nevertheless delay the enactment of legislation by returning laws to Parliament for another reading and, more critically, veto government appointees to the higher echelons of the civil service. Of the 1,900 candidates nominated by the AKP for high-level posts during its first four years in office, Sezer had vetoed over 250 on the grounds that they were ideologically motivated, and simply refused either to approve or veto candidates for another 400 positions. The AKP's majority in Parliament meant that it could effectively appoint its own candidate to the presidency – something its detractors argued would enable it to finally seize control of the apparatus of state. In April 2007 the AKP named Gul as its candidate. On 27 April 2007 General Yasar Buyukanit, the chief of the Turkish General Staff (TGS), issued a statement implicitly threatening a coup if the AKP appointed Gul to the presidency. The AKP responded by calling an early general election for July 2007.

Buyukanit's intervention enabled the AKP to portray the 2007 general election as a choice between democracy and the continuation of a system of military tutelage. It was further boosted by its impressive economic record and the fact that none of the opposition parties appeared to offer a credible alternative. The result was a landslide victory for the AKP, which won 46.6 percent of the popular vote. Unable to risk challenging such an unequivocal demonstration of the popular will, Buyukanit did nothing and thus effectively demonstrated that the era of military tutelage was over.

Emboldened by its election victory, through late 2007 the AKP began to draft what it described as a new liberal constitution, which was expected, among other things, to lift the headscarf ban in universities. However, in February 2008 the plans were abruptly shelved as the AKP tried to lift the headscarf ban by pushing through amendments to the existing constitution. The higher echelons of the judiciary were still dominated by hardline secularists appointed before the AKP came to power. In March 2008 the Public Prosecutor applied to the Constitutional Court for the AKP's closure on the grounds that it was trying to undermine the principle of secularism enshrined in the constitution. In July 2008 the Constitutional Court upheld the charges against the AKP but opted to impose a fine of $20 million rather than outlawing the party.

Over the next two years, the AKP made no further attempt to challenge the headscarf ban. Instead, it focused on the economy and strengthening its grip on the apparatus of state, both by filling the higher echelons of the civil service with political appointees and by neutralizing challenges to its authority. In late 2008 AKP sympathizers in the lower echelons of the judicial system began expanding investigations into an alleged coup plot to arrest hundreds of the government's opponents. In 2010 over 200 serving and retired members of the military were accused of involvement in more than a dozen alleged coup plots. The absence of any convincing evidence and the questionable probability of some of the prosecutors' accusations – such as claims that elements in the military had been responsible for every act of racist or political violence in Turkey over the previous 20 years – further fuelled suspicions that the cases were more about politics than justice (Jenkins 2009: 83). The doubts were intensified by a string of tax fines totaling $3.8 billion levied on the main non-AKP media organization, the Dogan Group, in 2009 after it criticized the AKP. In September 2010 the AKP turned its attention to the judiciary, introducing a series of constitutional amendments which included giving the government greater control over appointments to the higher echelons of the judicial system, such as the Constitutional Court. It is possible that such moves were motivated by a combination of simple authoritarianism and a perceived need for self-preservation, particularly given the pressure both the AKP and its predecessors had faced from hardline secularists in the military and the Constitutional Court. However, in late 2010 the government's opponents remained insistent that they were preparations for the introduction of Islamist policies if the AKP was elected to a third term in the general election of June 2011.

If discussions of the AKP's domestic policies remained dominated by speculation about its intentions rather than its actual deeds, there was a discernible change in its foreign policy, particularly after Ahmet Davutoglu (born 1959), Erdogan's former foreign policy advisor, was appointed foreign minister in May 2009. There was an acceleration in the shift in the primary focus of Turkey's foreign policy away from the West towards the other members of the Muslim world. During its first term the AKP could argue – with considerable justification – that previous administrations' neglect of relations with other Muslim countries, most notably in the Middle East, had produced an imbalance in Turkish foreign policy. However, starting from 2009, the AKP increasingly sought to present itself as the main spokesperson of the Muslim world in its dealings with the West, particularly on Palestine, where it aligned itself very closely with Hamas against not just Israel but also the secular Fatah faction of the Palestinian Liberation Organization (PLO). Through 2010 apposition to the West gradually turned into opposition, most controversially through the AKP's attempt in June 2010 to block further United Nations (UN) sanctions against Iran over its nuclear program. One of the reasons was greater self-confidence and a reduced reluctance to be seen as identifying more closely with the Muslim world; the other was arguably more to do with self-aggrandizement than religion. Davutoglu was an unashamed Ottoman nostalgist and made no secret of his ambition to reassert Turkey as the preeminent power not only in its region but in the Muslim world.

Social networks

Unlike in some other countries, where Muslim clerics and theologians have played a major role in inspiring and mobilizing Islamist organizations, in Turkey it was the networks of the tariqah which not only helped ensure that a substantial proportion of the population retained a strong sense of Islamic identity but which provided the social foundations for the reemergence of Islam as a distinct political force in the 1970s. In time, the Erbakan-led parties established their own social networks to supplement those of the tariqah, and, as he established a powerbase in his own right, Erbakan consulted less with the tariqah leaders and more with his own political advisors. Nevertheless, even if their relative importance has declined in recent years – particularly since the AKP moved into the political mainstream – the tariqah still play a significant role in inculcating the values that make electors receptive to Islamist parties and, on occasion, utilize their social networks to provide them with political or financial support.

However, in recent years, the tariqah have been overtaken in influence by the followers of the preacher Fethullah Gulen (born 1938), who now constitute the most powerful force in Turkish society, to the point where in some areas they even rival the Turkish state. A disciple of Said Nursi, Gulen served as a state-appointed preacher in western Turkey, where his sermons and writings – which are characterized more by their warm tone and calls for conciliatory engagement than their theological sophistication – resulted in him building up a vast following. Gulen fled into exile in the US in 1999 after a secular television channel broadcast footage of him apparently instructing his followers to infiltrate the apparatus of state and present a moderate image until they were strong enough to implement their agenda. The authenticity of the footage has been disputed by Gulen's followers, who also vehemently deny that they have a political agenda. They note that in his public statements Gulen has repeatedly condemned violence in the name of religion and has never called for the introduction of any Islamist legislation, even advising university students to uncover their heads on the grounds that education is more important than the headscarf. Nevertheless, there is no doubt that the hundreds of schools, nongovernmental organizations (NGOs) and media outlets now controlled by the Gulen Movement play a significant role in shaping the social environment in which politics is conducted.

The movement's critics also claim that Gulen sympathizers in the police and the lower echelons of the judicial system have been the main driving force behind the controversial prosecution of hundreds of the AKP's opponents on charges of allegedly plotting a coup. No conclusive evidence has been produced to substantiate the claims. However, they were repeated in a book published in August 2010 by a provincial police chief called Hanefi Avci. During the 1970s and 1980s Avci had frequently been accused of the torture and maltreatment of imprisoned leftist militants. On 28 September 2010, two days before he was due to give a press conference at which he had promised to provide documentary evidence to support his claims, Avci was arrested on charges of aiding a militant leftist group. In October 2011 Avci remained in prison awaiting the completion of his trial.

Militant groups

Although MSP youth organizations established summer camps at which party supporters were provided with paramilitary training, they played little part in the factional fighting that wracked Turkey through the 1970s. In fact, there was almost no Islamist violence in Turkey between the 1930s and the 1980s, when individuals inspired by the 1979 Iranian Revolution – and initially occasionally trained and financed by elements in the Iranian intelligence apparatus – began to form groups dedicated to the use of violence to establish an Islamic state. Despite their sympathy for – and sometimes support from – the Shia Islamists in Iran, Turkish militants tended to try to model themselves on radicals in Sunni countries, and to study the writings of Sunni Islamists such as the Egyptian radical Sayyid Qutb (1906–66).

Unlike during the early years of the republic, modern Islamist violence has tended to be directed not against the Turkish state itself but against rival militant groups or what are regarded as ideologically alien presences in the country, such as Turkish secularist intellectuals, local non-Muslim communities or the representatives of foreign countries and businesses. Similarly, although their networks played a prominent role in the violent protests against Ataturk's reforms, modern militant Islamist groups have tended to be formed outside, and frequently in opposition to, the tariqah, even sometimes targeting leading members of the different orders. Even if there were no organic links between violent groups and the Erbakan-led parties, during the late 1980s and early 1990s individual militants sometimes moved in the same social circles as members of the parties' more radical wing. However, the gap between violent and non-violent Islamists has increased as the parties have moved into the political mainstream, particularly under the AKP.

Most of the indigenous violent Islamist groups active in the 1980s and 1990s were small and short-lived. The exception was the Ilim Group, which is frequently referred to in the Turkish media as the Turkish Hezbollah, although it has no connection with the Lebanese organization of the same name.

Ilim was formed in 1982 in the south-eastern city of Diyarbakir by Huseyin Velioglu (1952–2000), a former member of the MSP youth organization. Velioglu foresaw a three-stage process: propaganda and organization; the creation of the foundations for an Islamic society; and jihad to establish an Islamic state based on the shari'a. During the late 1980s Ilim expanded rapidly, particularly in the predominantly Kurdish south-east of Turkey. In 1992, despite protests from his colleagues who believed that it was premature, Velioglu decided that the time had come to launch a jihad. Through the early 1990s Ilim was responsible for the deaths of hundreds of members of rival Islamist and Kurdish nationalist groups. Initially, the security forces were slow to react. It was only in the late 1990s that a concerted effort was made to eradicate the organization. In March 1999 a police raid on a safe house in south-east Turkey resulted in the seizure of Ilim's archives, including the biographical details of 20,000 members, of whom 4,000 were members of the organization's military wing. Velioglu responded by attempting to relocate Ilim's headquarters to Istanbul, but he was tracked down and killed in a police raid in one of the city's suburbs in January 2000.

Velioglu's death and the subsequent arrest of over 4,000 Ilim members dealt a devastating blow to the organization. However, it gradually began to rebuild under Isa Altsoy (born 1961), who had avoided arrest by fleeing to Europe and going into hiding. Under Altsoy's leadership Ilim has reverted to the second stage of Velioglu's plan, strengthening its social support base by building up a huge network of NGOs, Islamic charities, magazines and even a newspaper. In April 2010 it demonstrated its growing strength by mobilizing over 150,000 people for a rally to celebrate the anniversary of the Prophet Muhammad's birthday in the south-eastern city of Diyarbakir. The organization remains theoretically committed to returning to violence at a future date, although it is unclear if or when it will do so.

Since the beginning of the twenty-first century, almost all of the Islamist violence in Turkey has been carried out by radicals affiliated with, or sympathetic to, transnational militant organizations such as al-Qaeda, mostly ad hoc groups assembled to conduct a specific attack. In all cases the targets have been Western European, US or Israeli interests based in Turkey, or members of the country's non-Muslim minorities.

Conclusion

Ataturk's secularizing reform program of the 1920s and 1930s has no parallel in any other predominantly Muslim country. It created a unique context for – and arguably a demand for a unique definition of – Islamism, particularly given the often paradoxical form that the official interpretation of secularism has acquired in the years since Ataturk's death. Any attempt to reshape politics and society in accordance with Islamic precepts would necessitate first dismantling the official interpretation of secularism, yet some of the latter's strictures – such as the headscarf ban – would be regarded as unacceptable restrictions on personal liberty in many manifestly non-Islamic states, making it possible to argue – as the AKP has done – that their removal is merely a matter of human rights. The situation has been further complicated by the sanctions applied to political parties that are even suspected of trying to amend secularism, with the result that it is very difficult to know whether a political party, such as the ruling AKP, which professes not to have an Islamist agenda, is doing so out of conviction or out of legal expediency.

Nevertheless, particularly during the AKP's second term in power, there was sufficient evidence to suggest that the party's policies were at least informed by religious considerations. The situation was clearest in foreign relations where, by late 2011, there was no longer any doubt that the AKP regarded Islam as both the primary determinant of Turkey's international identity and a means of reasserting a neo-Ottoman preeminence. In its domestic policies the clues lay more in the selectivity of what it had tried to do, rather than in what it had actually done, perhaps most clearly in the disparity between the time and effort the AKP had spent on the headscarf ban and on the discrimination faced by non-Sunni Muslims, particularly in its refusal even to contemplate ending the compulsory inculcation of Sunni Islam in the school system.

Nevertheless, in October 2011 the key question was not what the AKP had done but what it would do after consolidating its grip on power with a landslide victory in the 12 June 2011 general election, in which it won 49.9 percent of the popular vote, as, for the first time since the party came to power in November 2002, it finally had sufficient control over the apparatus of state to ensure that it no longer needed to fear closure. There appeared to be little doubt that it would attempt to make substantial changes to the prevailing interpretation of secularism and ensure that Islam assumed a higher profile in public life, but the precise details of these changes remained unclear. However, both private conversations with members of the AKP (personal communications October–November 2010) and the history of the modern Turkish Islamist movement suggested that they would focus on Islamic values and identity rather than on changes to the civil and criminal codes, in order to create a more conservative, more explicitly Islamic society rather than an Islamic state based on the shari'a.

References

Alp, T. (1936) *Kemalizm*, Istanbul, Cumhuriyet.

Berkes, N. (1964) *The Development of Secularism in Turkey*, Montreal, McGill University Press.

Clark, B. (2006) *Twice a Stranger*, London, Granta.

Deringil, S. (1999) *The Well-Protected Domains: Ideology and the Legitimization of Power in the Ottoman Empire, 1876–1909*, London, I.B. Tauris.

Ihsanoglu, E. (2001) *History of The Ottoman State, Society and Civilization Vol. 1*, Istanbul, Research Centre for Islamic History, Art and Culture.

Jenkins, G.H. (2001) *Context and Circumstance: The Turkish Military and Politics*, Oxford, Oxford University Press.

—— (2008) *Political Islam in Turkey: Running West, Heading East?*, New York, Palgrave Macmillan.

—— (2009) *Between Fact and Fantasy: Turkey's Ergenekon Investigation*, Washington, CACI.

Mango, A. (1999) *Ataturk*, London, John Murray.

Mardin, S. (1989) *Religion and Social Change in Modern Turkey*, Albany, State University of New York.

National Ministry of Education (2004) *Din Kulturu ve Ahlak Bilgisi 4*, Ankara, Milli Egitim Basimevi.

Van Bruinessen, M. (1992) *Agha, Shaikh and State*, London, Zed Books.

Yalcın, S. (1994) *Hangi Erbakan*, Ankara, Basak.

Yavuz, H.M. (2003) *Islamic Political Identity in Turkey*, Oxford, Oxford University Press.

—— (2006) *The Emergence of a New Turkey*, Salt Lake City, The University of Utah.

12

The institutionalisation of political Islam in Iran

Rebecca Barlow and Shahram Akbarzadeh

The establishment of the Islamic Republic of Iran in 1980 brought Islamism out of the shadows and into the corridors of power. This was an unprecedented development. Political Islam had emerged as the antithesis of the status quo, an alternative to secular policies and creeping Westernisation. In Iran, what started out as a revolutionary ideology was transformed into official ideology for the new regime. Islamism came full circle. Seemingly overnight, it was transformed from a battle cry for revolution into the pillar of a new system of government. Political Islam in today's Iran is a status quo ideology that protects the vested interests of many in the clerical establishment, as well as those who have identified with, and benefited from, this transformation. This chapter explores the institutionalisation of political Islam in Iran.

The institutionalisation of Islamism following the 1979 popular revolution was not without difficulties. The major impediment to political Islam in Iran was the fact that it gained prominence on the back of a mass movement thirsty for political, social and economic transparency and accountability. Engrained in the 1979 revolution was a desire to establish a new democratic system where the political leadership was answerable to the people and represented their national interests. The idea of a republic was appealing to the masses that protested against the corruption of the Pahlavi monarchy. Popular sovereignty was at the heart of the republic model. However, rule by the people did not sit easily with the Islamists and had to be demarcated within the limits set, as they claimed, by God. Tension between the popular and the divine models of government was evident from the very first day of the new regime. This tension is entwined in the Iranian constitution which maintains divine caveats to popular sovereignty and is even carried into the official name of the state: the Islamic Republic.

The surge of popular resentment against the political establishment following the contested 2009 presidential elections was a reminder that the above tension remained unresolved. Street protests challenging the Supreme Leader and his role at the top of the state hierarchy have raised pertinent questions about the capacity of political Islam as a status quo ideology and what it means for civil rights. This chapter presents an account of political Islam in power and traces its implications for civil rights, with a special focus on women's rights in Iran.

The power structure of the Islamic Republic: *velayate faqih*

Following the 1979 revolution, governance and government in Iran were reconstructed along theocratic lines. Within the discourse of the revolution, the new state was intended to be both democratic and Islamic, reflected in the title 'Islamic Republic'. However, in the final stages of constitutional drafting, conservative elements came to overpower proponents of a more liberal Islam. The notion of 'rule by the people' inherent in the term 'republic' was eroded, and the way was paved for clerical supremacy. The Islamic Republic was thus founded on the principle of *velayate faqih*: rule by the most learned Islamic scholar, or expert in classical Islamic jurisprudence, *fiqh*.

This principle is based on Shia religious doctrine, but carries the beliefs of Twelver Shiism beyond the boundaries of tradition. In Islam, God's sovereignty is supreme. However, a religious authority, or imam, has always been required to ensure the implementation of God's will on Earth. After the death of the Prophet Mohammed in 632 CE, Shia Islam believed that Ali, the Prophet's son-in-law, and his 11 descendants should sequentially fulfil this role. The final imam in the succession, Muhammad al-Mahdi, is believed to have entered a state of occultation some time during the ninth century. The Shia Muslim community remains in waiting for the return of Imam al-Mahdi, but in his absence are to be led by qualified religious leaders, the *ulama*.

According to Shia doctrine, all Muslims must choose a *marja al-taqlid*, a model and source of emulation, from amongst the established *ulama*, whose opinions on Islamic law are binding on their followers throughout their lifetimes. Traditionally, no one *marja* can be considered more authoritative than another. However, when Ayatollah Khomeini led the Iranian revolution to victory and rose to power via popular mandate in 1979, he claimed to be the Shia Muslim community's ultimate representative of God on Earth, acting in the direct place of Imam al-Mahdi. By attaching the *ulama* to the state at the highest level, Khomeini not only dealt a blow to republican aspirations and the ideal of popular sovereignty, but also removed the multiplicity of religious authority in Iran.

It is this precept that is named in the appellation *velayate faqih*. The Constitution of the Islamic Republic appoints Khomeini as Leader for Life. As the head of state, the Supreme Leader is Commander-in-Chief of the armed forces and can declare war or peace. He appoints the Chief of the Joint Staff, Chief Commander of the Islamic Revolutionary Guards, six members of the 12-member Guardian Council, the Supreme Judge, and the head of the radio and television networks of the Islamic Republic. This power structure makes the Supreme Leader the most powerful man in Iran, immune from scrutiny. A small measure of public participation in political life was attempted through the formation in 1982 of the 83-member Assembly of Experts, whose members are directly elected from amongst the *ulama* by the public. The Assembly of Experts appoints the Supreme Leader and reserves the right to dismiss him if he is deemed to violate Islamic law or the interests of the regime. However, since the death of Ayatollah Khomeini in 1989 there has been but one reappointment of the Supreme Leader, the current Ayatollah Khamenei. In effect, once appointed, the Supreme Leader is beyond reproach. He is not accountable to the public; he is answerable to no one.

The extensive powers concentrated in the hands of the Supreme Leader have raised insurmountable barriers to change and reform in Iran. The Supreme Leader's ability to determine the composition of the Guardian Council has proved critical in this respect. The Guardian Council consists of six *faqih*, appointed by the Supreme Leader, and six jurists, nominated by the Supreme Judge and approved by the Parliament (*Majlis*). As mentioned earlier, the Supreme Judge is an appointee of the Supreme Leader and has been closely aligned with the latter's political outlook. The Guardian Council is charged with ensuring the consistency of parliamentary legislation with Islamic law, but has appropriated to itself the right to vet candidates in parliamentary and presidential elections.

The foundation of the Islamic Republic in Shia theology thus places the constituency in tight constraints so far as their ability to question or object to any aspect of state shape or content, including laws that govern everyday processes of public and private life. The merging of temporal and religious authority in the principle of *velayate faqih* means that, in the eyes of the clerical establishment, to question the regime is essentially tantamount to questioning the wisdom of God.

Of all the demographic constituents affected by this conundrum, Iranian women face amongst the most significant difficulties. Local women's rights advocates have critiqued the Iranian Constitution as a document that they claim construes women as child-bearers and caretakers only, and fails to recognise women's identities beyond relationships with men. Where the Constitution does refer to the rights of women, the wording is ambiguous, and qualified. Article 20, for example, states that men and women should 'enjoy equal protection of the law […] *in conformity with Islamic criteria [mavazin-e eslami]*'. Similarly, Article 21 stipulates that 'the government must ensure the rights of women in all respects, *in conformity with Islamic criteria [mavazin-e eslami]*' (Mayer 2007: 83–84, italics added). This oft-repeated caveat in the Iranian Constitution subordinates modern understandings of gender equality and women's rights to official (conservative) interpretations of selected Islamic sources.

In mid-2005 a group of activist women in Iran called for a constitutional referendum. At the 12 June sit-in at Haft-e Square, Tehran, protestors issued a communiqué that drew a direct link between the Constitution of the Islamic Republic and 'women's belittlement'. The document critiqued the Constitution as defective in that rather than protecting women from discrimination, it in fact served as a source to *block* the empowerment of women by subverting all rights-based claims to the State's interpretation of the 'good Muslim woman' (Shekarloo 2005). At the 2006 commemoration of the event, women raised what they believed to be the most appropriate foundation for women's status in Iran by calling on the state to comply with international standards on 'fundamental and equal rights', including the Convention on the Elimination of all forms of Discrimination Against Women (CEDAW) (Shekarloo 2005). This was in clear opposition to the gender ideology of the Islamic regime, which is rooted in classical Islamic jurisprudence as manifest in the shari'a legal code.

Shari'a law

The shari'a is a legalistic elaboration of Islam's holy texts developed between the ninth and fourteenth centuries CE. The shari'a represents a status quo set of rules on what is considered acceptable and appropriate behaviour within Muslim communities by prevailing clerical elites. Shari'a requirements can be referred to as falling within a broad range of categories such as ethics, morality, religion, politics and law. The shari'a is drawn in part from injunctions contained in the Qur'an, the direct and final word of God; the *Sunna*, the sayings of the Prophet Muhammad; and the *Hadith*, the traditions and customs of the Prophet. Classical Islamic jurisprudence or Islamic legal theory, *usul al-fiqh*, is employed by jurists to determine rules that may be difficult to ascertain in the textuality of the sources. Classical *fiqh* techniques include *ijma*, the consensus of Islamic scholars; *shura*, consultation with the Muslim community, the *umma*; and *qiyas*, analogous reasoning.[1]

Although it is a product of pre-modern times, conservative clerics in Iran and other Muslim-majority countries defend the continuing application of shari'a by recourse to its basis in Islamic sources, which are considered both timeless and sacred. As a composition of edicts derived from these holy texts, the shari'a therefore not only represents the totality of Allah's commands, but must also be independently considered unalterable and eternal in its own right. In his book 'Newly Created Problems according to the Opinion of His Excellency Grand Ayatollah Mr Seyed Yusef Madani Tabrizi' [*al-Masa'el al-mostahdasah motabeq ba fatwa-ye Hazrat-e Ayatollah al-'Ozma Aqa-ye Seyed Yusef al-Madani al-Tabrizi*], Tabrizi claims:

> Because the sacred laws of Islam are not confined to a specific time but determine people's duties in every area of life and how to carry out religious duties and [social] interaction, people must not transgress them […] If we want to adjust Islamic *fiqh* to the conditions of the time, then the science of *fiqh* will be destroyed and suffer irreparable damage.
>
> *(Mir-Hosseini 2000: 32–33)*

This constrained view of the shari'a by no means represents a consensus position. For some reform-minded clerics, the shari'a is more appropriately understood as a secondary source of Islam: a human attempt to systematise the primary sources of the faith into one accessible code of practice. An outstanding example of this position is provided by one of Iran's most influential and controversial religious philosophers, Abdol Karim Soroush. In his seminal work, 'The Theoretical Expansion and Contraction of the Shari'a', Soroush distinguishes 'religion' from 'religious knowledge'. Religion, he argues, is divine and unchangeable, whereas religious knowledge is human and evolves externally to the faith itself. In Soroush's paradigm the shari'a pertains to religious knowledge. It cannot, therefore, be considered divine and unchangeable, but is rather open to ongoing interpretation, alteration and re-appropriation (Mir-Hosseini 2000: 32–33).

The reality of everyday life in many Muslim societies has tended to reflect Soroush's philosophy. Even amongst those clerics who support the application of shari'a legal norms in modern societies, there is no official consensus as to what aspects of the shari'a do or do not apply in any given circumstance. This can be attributed to the rich heritage of rationality and scientific process in the Islamic tradition. Just as there is no monolithic 'Muslim world', nor a uniform Islam, classical Islamic jurisprudence encompasses the doctrines of several sects and many schools of law. Historically, divergence of opinion amongst major schools of law has been tolerated within the faith – a situation acknowledged in the shari'a concept of *ikhtilaf al-madhahib*, or difference of law schools (Mayer 2007: 80). Even within one school of law, doctrines and opinions could differ significantly on the interpretation of Islamic sources. There were even individuals whose opinions differed from the major schools, but were nevertheless considered legitimate and incorporated into the shari'a framework (Mayer 2007: 80).

In the twenty-first century no Muslim country hosts the application of the shari'a legal code in its entirety. Rather, shari'a laws are applied inconsistently and unevenly both between and within Muslim countries. Farida Shaheed, director of the transnational feminist network *Women Living Under Muslim Laws*, argues that in the myriad Muslim communities around the world, each locally driven appropriation of the holy texts to present rules for public life 'bears the unmistakable imprint of the regional culture and of traditions that either pre-date Islam or have been absorbed through subsequent developments and influences' (Shaheed 2004). A striking example in this respect is female genital cutting, a practice virtually unheard of in Muslim societies outside of Northern Africa and Egypt, where it is also practised by non-Muslims, and yet enshrined as an Islamic injunction (Helie-Lucas 2001: 23).

Reform-minded clerics and public figures in Iran tend to view the shari'a as a secondary source of Islam, and one that does not in its present format provide an adequate basis for the establishment of civil rights. The intellectual reasoning behind this view echoes the philosophy of both Soroush and well-known theologist Hojat-ol-elsam Mohsen Saidzadeh. As a prominent cleric, Saidzadeh is notable for making explicit links between Islam and women's rights in his writings and public seminars in the holy city of Qom. For Saidzadeh the methods and concepts used to determine Islamic legal norms – *fiqh* – represent an established discipline, a constructed scientific method. The shari'a, he argues, does not exist independently of this science. Rather it is best understood as a *creation of fiqh*. The problem here is that whilst Islam encompasses a strong 'equality perspective', classical *fiqh* theories developed over the ninth to 14th centuries have obstructed the translation of this perspective into modern women's realities (Mir-Hosseini 2000: 251). According to Saidzadeh, a majority of Islamic jurists in Iran have sacrificed the equality principle, 'to endorse a set of theories resting on assumptions that are no longer valid but still remain a part of *fiqh*' (Saidzadeh cited in Mir-Hosseini 2000: 251).

In Islamic theory it is the responsibility of clerical jurists to minimise human interference with the sacred texts of Islam so as to formulate laws that mirror God's will. However, according to Saidzadeh, throughout history Islamic jurists have 'exceeded their mandate and constantly broken the limits, by adding things to religion' (Saidzadeh cited in Mir-Hosseini 2000: 257). Saidzadeh challenges the latent assumption, embedded in the philosophy of more conservative Iranian clerics, that the shari'a emerged and exists in a sociological vacuum. In Saidzadeh's view, the shari'a should be understood as a framework inevitably informed by the pre-modern and patriarchal environment in which it emerged.

Seeing classical shari'a law as a product of human interpretive efforts, as opposed to a divine and unalterable source of the Islamic faith, has generated two divergent conclusions about the application of the shari'a in modern times. On the one hand, if shari'a laws were originally developed in response to social, cultural and political circumstances, they may carry the inherent capacity for change and reform according to new circumstances and socio-cultural conditions. This evolutionary perspective of the Islamic framework sits at the modernist end of a broad spectrum of Muslim views on the shari'a. The full extension of this logic, however, goes much further than Saidzadeh's position. For some advocates of change in Iran, the Islamic paradigm does not provide an appropriate starting point for the development of legal norms in the twenty-first century. Advocates of this school of thought, such as contemporary reformist clerics Mir-Hossein Mousavi and Mehdi Karroubi, insist that the spiritual vitality of modern Muslim societies is not contingent on the implementation of a legal framework explicitly informed by religious precepts.

Those who are less categorical in rejecting the legitimacy of shari'a, however, see within it a dynamic towards remaining relevant in the twenty-first century. This view is espoused by Saidzadeh, who argues that the science of shari'a is available for reform because 'all tools and concepts in all crafts and sciences are made by us, humans […] *Fiqh* too is a science and can't be exempted from the need to evolve in time and space' (Saidzadeh cited in Mir-Hosseini 2000: 259). The shari'a can be reformed and revitalised, he argues, if other clerics reconcile their approach with his own recognition:

> Space and time have affected my thinking, consciously and unconsciously, as with all other Jurists. *Fiqh* and interpretation of the *Quran* are affected by situations. Not only are jurists unconsciously affected by them, [but] they must be consciously taken into account.
>
> *(Mir-Hosseini 2000: 253)*

In line with this view, some Iranian reformists simultaneously acknowledge the discriminatory aspects of the shari'a, whilst supporting an Islamic legal framework that can respond to changing priorities of reality. In this paradigm, Islam can be retained as a basis for the formation of laws in the twenty-first century, but the religious-legal framework must be extensively reformulated if it is to be applied in modern times. The methodology employed for this purpose is dual-layered. It involves mining revelatory sources for evidence that Allah intended societies to be free, equal and democratic. Reform-minded clerics thus engage in contextualisation techniques to delimit the intent and applicability of some verses to a particular time, place and circumstance (Najmabadi 1998: 71). These techniques are underscored by the Islamic notion of *ijtihad*, which remains alive in the Shia tradition. *Ijtihad* allows for intellectual reinterpretation and innovation of Islam's holy sources. Specifically, *ijtihad* involves the application of human reason to the shari'a legal code, in order to ascertain the applicability and suitability of particular injunctions in modern situations.

Classical Islamic treatises do not always reflect the overarching spiritual message of the faith. Many liberal clerics and reform-minded Muslims adhere to the view that the shari'a is made up of a highly selected set of religious verses, representing a miniscule portion of the holy texts in their entirety. Reformists argue that many of the discriminatory verses included in the Qur'an – particularly in relation to women, minorities and non-Muslims – are textually ambiguous, open to manipulation by the ruling elite, and easily distorted by patriarchal cultural practices. On the other hand, some Qur'anic versus that restrict rights and freedoms are clear. Reformists argue that these injunctions may have been intended by Allah to ensure the safety and political well-being of the Muslim community in the specific socio-political set of circumstances at the time of revelation. In both cases, the verses require re-examination, reinterpretation and reassessment to ascertain the nature and extent of their applicability to the modern Iranian reality.

As indicated above, however, the Iranian landscape is also host to many who view the shari'a as an inappropriate basis for the formulation of modern-day laws and precepts. Well-known Iranian feminist Haideh Moghissi, for example, argues that whilst the Islamic paradigm may not be responsible for the unequal status of women in Iran, *Islamism* nevertheless occupies a strong explanatory role. Moghissi disagrees with the attempts to reform the shari'a legal framework when in her opinion it should be dismantled and replaced with laws and standards based in modernity. She states:

> The Shari'a distinguishes between the rights of human beings on the basis of sex and religion. The Shari'a unapologetically discriminates against women and religious minorities. If the principles of the Shari'a are to be maintained, women cannot be treated any better, women cannot enjoy equality before the law and in law. The Shari'a is not compatible with the principles of equality of human beings.
>
> *(Moghissi 1999: 141)*

The reform era, 1997–2005

Prospects that reformists might impact upon the future democracy and human rights in Iran reached a high point at the turn of the twentieth century. In May 1997 the liberal cleric Muhammad Khatami won a landslide victory at the election polls. As leader of the reform movement and President of the Islamic Republic, Khatami represented the nation's number one hope for meaningful change. He stressed national identity over strict religious roles, individual freedoms and a democratic, pluralistic Islam. Khatami was particularly well known for his overt displays of respect for women and young people, making regular mention of their importance in Iranian society. In Elaheh Rostami Povey's view, vast numbers of Iranian women supported Khatami due to their belief that 'under his presidency women's issues could be fought for more easily' than under alternative (conservative) candidates (Povey 2001: 49).

During the early stages of the reform era, this belief looked likely to manifest. Throughout the late 1990s Iran was characterised by a bourgeoning civil society. There was an explosion of independent newspapers and an unprecedented wave of open debate and free expression. Newspapers and magazines even began to play the role of political parties by representing various, sometimes unorthodox, views on Islam and its relationship to the state. At the grassroots level social issues were increasingly discussed in terms of human rights, not as matters pertaining only, or primarily, to the faith and religious exegesis (Ebadi 2007).

The philosophy behind Khatami's presidency was that for the Islamic regime to remain vital, it would have to accommodate the basic needs and freedoms of its constituency. However, this need not necessitate systemic overhaul. Rather, it could be achieved through a process of incremental reform. Khatami relied on a pragmatic interpretation of Islamic sources to justify his proposals for change to the *ulama*. In the spirit of *ijtihad*, the reform movement provided religious-oriented feminists with an obvious tactical and strategic partner, and the two became closely associated.[2]

In 2000 some 13 women were elected as members of the sixth Majlis (Parliament). In the reformist-dominated chamber these women formed a bloc that came to be known as the Women's Faction. Like the President, the Women's Faction posed no questions to the concept of the Islamic state. However, according to one of its members, Elaheh Koolaee, the Women's Faction lamented the 'gap between the ideals of the Islamic Republic and the reality of women's rights and status' (Koolaee 2005: 205). For these women, the root cause of the gap between Iran's revolutionary promises and manifest laws on women had little to do with the idea of an Islamic state system *per se*. Rather, women's problems could be attributed to 'the influence of traditional Islam' over those with ultimate decision-making powers.

The Women's Faction issued a challenge 'from within the Islamic framework by relying on the progressive teachings of Ayatollah Khomeini and the principles of the Islamic constitution' (Koolaee 2005: 205). They set out to alter and amend legislation with a view to temper the severity and impact of existing laws on women's lives. The strategy met with some success. The Women's Faction managed to convince the establishment to allow single women to travel abroad to study (Kar 2005: 225). Their lobbying also contributed to an amendment of the custody law to allow women automatic custody of both boy and girl children up to seven years of age (Koolaee 2005: 210). Additionally, they were successful in raising the minimum legal age for girls to marry from nine to 13 (Monshipouri 2004: 5).

In 2003 the Women's Faction successfully lobbied for CEDAW to be placed on the government's agenda. In its early stages the case looked set for success, as the reformist-dominated Parliament voted in favour of ratification. However, the debate was brought to a halt when the Guardian Council, charged with the purpose of ensuring that all legislation remains in line with Islamic jurisprudence, rejected the proposal on the basis that the treaty was both 'un-Iranian' and 'un-Islamic'. The Guardian Council defended its position by invoking the cornerstone of the Islamic Republic's gender ideology, namely gender parity or a 'balance' of rights, as a more appropriate paradigm in which to conceptualise the rights and responsibilities for women. The Guardian Council appealed to the infallibility of shari'a law as an integral component of the revelatory message to justify its rejection of CEDAW (Shekarloo 2005). The Convention was framed as not only incompatible with Iranian women's realities, but entirely unnecessary for the fulfilment of their rights.

The CEDAW case was a sign of things to come, and signalled the end of the reform movement at large. Opportunities for reformists to make significant gains rested on the possibility that conservative rulers might yield their orthodox reading of Islam to the more enlightened version of the faith, broadly offered by Khatami and his backers. This possibility proved to be a non-event. Although the Majlis was dominated by liberal-minded clerics, the ultra-conservative Guardian Council repeatedly exercised its veto power to block legislation that would cause any substantial change to the status quo. The resulting stalemate was rooted in *velayate faqih*. This principle accords the *ulama* a privileged role in governing the Islamic state, and secures for the Supreme Leader the final say. Effectively, the primacy of *velayate faqih* relegates other branches of the government, including Parliament, to function as optional extras to a predetermined political agenda.

This reality was made dramatically public in 2004 when one of the most outspoken members of the Women's Faction, Fatema Haqiqatjoo, announced a premature resignation from Parliament. In an open session to the Majlis, Haqiqatjoo protested the Guardian Council's indiscriminate vetting of proposed legislative changes and stated that in her view, reform from within the state system was no longer possible. She referred to the oath that all elected parliamentarians must take when they are sworn into the Majlis. This oath requires Members of Parliament to 'remain faithful to Islam and the constitution, to defend the independence and the interests of the country, and to serve the people' (Mir-Hosseini 2004). Haqiqatjoo stated that, 'since the possibility of keeping my oath has been taken from me and I have been deprived of [the ability to] defend your legal rights, it is no longer a source of pride for me to stay in this house' (Mir-Hosseini 2004).

Women and youth culture

Following the decline of the reform movement and the wholesale investiture of government hardliners in 2005, Iranian activists – particularly women and youth – have mirrored Haqiqatjoo's voicing of dissent with the status quo. The One Million Signatures Campaign, initiated in 2006, is an effort by Iranian feminists of both religious and secular orientations to bring an end to all laws that discriminate against women in Iran. Whether or not these laws are ostensibly based on religious precepts is a moot point according to the campaigners; the discriminatory content of the laws is, *ipso facto*, enough to legitimate their removal. By engaging in door-to-door and face-to-face street politics to educate Iranian men and women about their rights and the principle of gender equality, the One Million Signatures Campaign represents one of the most sophisticated forms of feminist organising across the entire Middle East.

In more informal displays of civil disobedience, deliberate improper wearing of the Islamic veil, *bad-hejabi*, has become a widespread practice amongst young Iranian women. Bad-hejabi involves letting the hair show at the front or sides of the veil, or wearing remarkably bright colours and patterns. This is not simply a matter of fashion, but rather a symbol of a desire to live in a society where individual choice is valued and respected. In July 2007 Iranian feminist and aspiring poet Roxana Setayesh suggested why clothing is such an important issue to young Iranian women. Gesturing to her own outfit, a black hijab made of sheer material and patterned with red flowers, and a knee-length beige-coloured manteau, she asked: 'Why do I have to wear this? What does it mean? It means I cannot choose. I'm talking about choice on a broader scale' (Setayesh 2007).

These comments reflect an increasingly large cross-section of young Iranians. In fact, the demographics of the country play a strong explanatory role in the street politics of present-day Iran. Youth represent the most prominent bulge in Iran's population pyramid. Contemporary men and women were not witness to the heady years of the revolution – a time filled with idealism and hope that Islam would present the cure for all societal ills experienced under the Shah's blindly pro-Western rule, and when Islamic 'authenticity' and ideological 'correctness' were paramount personal and social attributes. The concept of *gharbzadegi*, 'Westoxification', was central to the cultural purification process instated by Ayatollah Khomeini, and the rejection of Western culture was an exercise taken up by significant sections of the Iranian populace. However, these concepts – in particular the discursive merging of 'the West', secularism and moral decay – fail to resonate with Iran's new and upcoming generations.

Measures of 'Islamic-ness' are less concerning to young Iranians than immediate social and economic realities. Youth culture is characterised by a struggle against what many perceive to be intrusive state prescriptions on how to live and manage the intricacies of life, work and relationships. Iranian women comprise an overwhelming majority of university students in the country, a figure widely placed at 65 per cent (Ebadi 2007). Advanced education, professional capacity and active contribution to public processes underlie the desires for a society where there is increased economic opportunity and greater cultural opening.

Yet simultaneously, corruption and nepotism at the top have forced the average Iranian to grapple with serious issues of unemployment and unaffordable housing. The extent of economic and housing deficits has led to a wide range of ancillary problems such as family breakdown, prostitution and drug addiction. According to a United Kingdom-based non-governmental organisation (NGO), *Association of Iranian Women in the UK*, unemployment and poverty are the leading causes of prostitution as a means of subsistence in Iran (Monshipouri 2004: 8). Suicide rates further reveal a gender crisis. A study conducted in June 2005 found that the majority of suicide attempts in Iran were by young, highly educated women (Mohammadi *et al.* 2005: 309–18).

The Green Movement

When incumbent Iranian President Mahmoud Ahmadinejad was returned to office following the June 2009 elections, the opposition movement that sprang to life in response highlighted the extent of discontent and frustration in society and, more importantly, significant fissures at the top. In an entirely unprecedented fashion the uprising that came to be known as the Green Movement challenged the image of elite solidarity and the ultimate authority of the Islamic Supreme Leader, Ali Khamenei. For some, this was a challenge to the very founding principle of the Islamic state, *velayate faqih*.

The Green Movement was initially entwined with the 2009 electoral campaign of two presidential candidates, Mehdi Karroubi and Mir Hussein Mousavi. Soon after the June 2009 elections, street rallies evolved into spontaneous spot protests seeking much more than a recount of the ballots. These protests, which seemed to have no clear leadership but took shape through a network of internet and mobile phone messaging, raised fundamental questions about the legitimacy of the Islamic regime. The brutality of the government crackdown, using the *Basij* militia (the youth wing of the Islamic Revolutionary Guards), was shocking, but not unexpected to observers. What was unexpected, however, was the opening up of two very significant gaps.

On the one hand the reformist leadership, affiliated with the former President Mohammad Khatami, appeared to merely follow the fast pace of events and protest rallies, rather than lead them. While the disenchanted protesters called for an end to dictatorship and *velayate faqih*, the two presidential contenders in the reformist camp, Mousavi and Karroubi, vacillated and called for calm and an end to protests. On the other hand, the top level of power appeared unprepared for the intensity of the opposition, and divided on how to respond to the crisis. The emerging cracks went beyond tactical concerns about the legitimacy of force to disperse Green Movement rallies, and raised questions that went to the very core of the regime: the role and responsibilities of the Supreme Leader. For the first time in the history of the Islamic Republic of Iran, a number of high-profile clerics, with impeccable credentials as advocates of the regime, took a public stance against the Supreme Leader.

Whilst the grievances of some protestors were contained to the reinstatement of President Ahmadinejad, others called for an all-out dismantling of the office of Supreme Leader. This was nothing short of a call for revolution – a ground-up spontaneous movement for change. By the same token, the Green Movement made clear that the Islamic regime is rife with discord. Internal disagreements at the highest echelons of power in Iran are normally concealed from the public eye as the regime projects an image of unity – one that is readily accepted by many observers in the West – but the events of June 2009 and the violent response to protesters brought these cracks to the fore. Only two of Iran's nine top clerics publicly congratulated Ahmadinejad on his return to office. This despite the fact that the Supreme Leader had given Ahmadinejad his blessing just a day after the elections – while votes were still being counted. This was an aggressive affront to the opposition candidate and his supporters, who included Hashemi Rafsanjani, head of the 86-member Assembly of Experts charged with appointing and dismissing the Supreme Leader. At the same time two top clerics, Ayatollah Dastgheib and Ayatollah Yousuf Sanai, publicly criticised the Supreme Leader for his hasty judgement (Cyrus 2010). Such public criticism would have been unthinkable in the past. In addition, two other top clerics, the late Ayatollah Montazeri and Ayatollah Bayat Zanjani, took up the case of the Green Movement further and questioned the justification of having a Supreme Leader for the Islamic state.

The latter argument has much in common with the political thinking of Soroush, who insists on the supremacy of human intellect and judgement for a just Islamic system to emerge. Soroush argues that there is no contradiction between Islam and the freedoms inherent in democracy. He states that 'Islam and democracy are not only compatible; their association is inevitable. In a Muslim society, one without the other is not perfect' (Wright 1996: 68). This position rests on the pillar of freedom. That is, 'to be a true believer, one must be free; belief attested under threat or coercion is not true belief' (Wright 1996: 68). For Soroush, an Islamic state must be shaped by the beliefs and will of the majority. This modernist perspective has struck a chord in Iran, particularly with the younger generations of clerics and believers, thus raising serious objections to the imposition of Islamist rule from above.

Conclusion

The incorporation of political Islam into the state structure in Iran has come at the expense of popular sovereignty. The principle of *velayate faqih* – the supreme and ultimately unquestionable rule of the most learned Islamic scholar – has thwarted attempts at legal and social reform by Iran's more liberal-minded clerics and politicians. The Supreme Leader of the Islamic Republic is appointed for life. He is in control of the armed forces, those highest in the legal system, and the radio and television networks. The Supreme Leader has total control in determining the composition of the Guardian Council, which in turn is responsible for approving legislation proposed by the Majlis.

The merging of temporal and religious authority in Iran has not only removed the practice of a plurality of religious leaders in Shia Islam, but has also meant that even the mildest critique of the regime's actions is construed as a critique of the divine authority of God. Whilst in the regime's eyes they are fulfilling the 'Islamic' component of the Constitution, their hardline approach to interpreting and implementing law and policy in Iran has come at the expense of any sense of republicanism. A serious lack of civil, women's and minority rights characterises the Iranian scene. State-imposed constraints on everyday life, rooted in an unwillingness to cede to a more liberal understanding of Islam, have resulted in rising unemployment, unaffordable housing, alarming suicide rates and widespread overuse of, and addiction to, drugs and prescription medications (Alikarami 2011).

It is important to note, however, that political Islam in Iran continues to face opposition. The Green Movement of 2009 indicated a strong popular pulse for political accountability. Calls for electoral reform, and even calls for the deposition of the Supreme Leader, revealed a significant schism between the regime and large segments of the population. Even more noteworthy are the calls made by some clerics to review the role of *velayate faqih*, pointing to the potential for political Islam in Iran to be pushed back, in favour of the republican model of governance.

Notes

1 For an instructive discussion on *usul al-fiqh* and *fiqh* techniques, see the various contributions to Amir Arjomand 1988.
2 For an excellent insight into this process see Moghadam 2002 and Moghadam 2005.

References

Alikarami, L. (2011) *Personal communication with Rebecca Barlow*, 28 March.

Amir Arjomand, S. (ed.) (1988) *Authority and Political Culture in Shi'ism*, Albany, State University of New York Press.

Cyrus, M. (2010) 'A Coronation in Qom', *Tehran Bureau*, 13 October, available at www.pbs.org (accessed 9 May 2011).

Ebadi, S. (2007) *Interview with Rebecca Barlow*, 7 July.

Helie-Lucas, M.A. (2001) 'What is Your Tribe?', in C.W. Howland (ed.), *Religious Fundamentalisms and the Human Rights of Women*, New York, Palgrave, pp. 21–32.

Kar, M. (2005) 'Women and Civil Society in Iran', in F. Nouraie-Simone (ed.), *On Shifting Ground, Muslim Women in the Global Era*, New York, The Feminist Press at the City University of New York, pp. 216–32.

Koolaee, E. (2005) 'The Prospects for Democracy: Women Reformists in the Iranian Parliament', in F. Nouraie-Simone (ed.), *On Shifting Ground, Muslim Women in the Global Era*, New York, The Feminist Press at the City University of New York, pp. 203–15.

Mayer, A.E. (2007) *Islam and Human Rights, Tradition and Politics*, Boulder, CO, Westview Press.

Mir-Hosseini, Z. (2000) *Islam and Gender, the Religious Debate in Contemporary Iran*, London and New York, IB Tauris.

—— (2004) 'Fatemah Haqiqatjoo and the Sixth Majlis: A Woman in Her Own Right', *Middle East Report* vol. 34, winter, available at www.merip.org/mer/mer233/fatemeh-haqiqatjoo-sixth-majles (accessed 1 August 2011).

Moghadam, V.M. (2002) 'Islamic Feminism and Its Discontents: Toward a Resolution of the Debate', *Signs* vol. 27, no. 4: 1138.

—— (2005) 'Islamic Feminism: Its Discontents and Its Prospects', paper presented at the *First International Congress on Islamic Feminism*, Barcelona, Spain, 27–29 October.

Moghissi, H. (1999) *Feminism and Islamic Fundamentalism, the Limits of Postmodern Analysis*, London and New York, Zed Books.

Mohammadi, M.R., Ghanizadeh, A., Rahgozart, M., Noorbala, A.A., Malekafzali, H., Davidian, H., Naghavi, H., Soori, H. and Bagheri Yazdi, S.A. (2005) 'Suicidal Attempt and Psychiatric Disorders in Iran', *Suicide & Life-threatening Behaviour* vol. 35, no. 3: 309–14.

Monshipouri, M. (2004) 'The Road to Globalization Runs through Women's Struggle', *World Affairs* vol. 167, no. 1: 3–14.

Najmabadi, A. (1998) 'Feminism in an Islamic Republic: Years of Hardship, Years of Growth', in Y. Yazbeck Haddad and J.L. Esposito (eds), *Islam, Gender, and Social Change*, New York, Oxford University Press, pp. 59–84.

Povey, E.R. (2001) 'Feminist Contestations of Institutional Domains in Iran', *Feminist Review* issue 69: 42–72.

Setayesh, R. (2007) *Interview with Rebecca Barlow*, 5 July.

Shaheed, F. (2004) 'Constructing Identities: Culture, Women's Agency, and the Muslim World', *Women Living Under Muslim Laws*, www.wluml.org/english/pubsfulltxt.shtml?cmd[87]=i-87-496303 (accessed 9 May 2011).

Shekarloo, M. (2005) 'Iranian Women Take on the Constitution', *Women Living Under Muslim Laws* 7, August, available at www.wluml.org/english/newsfulltxt.shtml?cmd%5B157%5D=x-157-290357 (accessed 9 May 2011).

Wright, R. (1996) 'Two Visions of Reformation', *Journal of Democracy* vol. 7, no. 2: 68.

13

Political thinking on Islam and democracy

The case of Iran

Ali M. Pedram

Seeking power from the Islamic point of view has been a major preoccupation for many Muslim scholars and recently for politicians and non-Muslim scholars. This issue is independent of epistemological arguments concerning whether and how Islam or any other religion can serve as a blueprint for governance. Serious changes have occurred within the international community as well as regional societies regarding the implementation or non-implementation of Islamic codes within socio-economic and political spheres. It has always been a challenge to measure and predict the politics of any given society. This task becomes more complex when the society in question is religiously driven. The emergence of nation-states and modernity in the West brought about a pattern of political development. This pattern was perceived by many as the inevitable destiny of every nation.

This linear pattern of development is supported by applying positivism to political science to prove the universality of such political development. However, since politics is primarily the management of material and human resources, human resources cannot be excluded from it. The focus on rational choice theory constructed by a/the Western mindset led to the field of political science lagging behind and thus resulted in many opportunities to avoid political and scrutiny problems being missed.

One early notion of modernity in the field of politics has been the demise of religious precepts and thus of religious influence on the political order. The separation of religion and government can be seen as the achievement of modernity after a long and bitter struggle. The role and rule of religion in Europe during the Middle Ages meant despotism in the name of divine. Even science was not tolerated as it was seen as opposed to the transcription of the Holy Book. The Enlightenment, however, brought an end to the marriage of church and government. Over the last few centuries the era of religious rule in many parts of the world has ended, but this has yet to happen in many Muslim societies.

The first attempts to break through religious despotism emerged in the fourteenth century. Europe was controlled by Christianity in every single aspect of life. Interestingly, the Muslim world is now in the fourteenth century since the inception of Islam. One very simple historical analogy may provide a loose framework for considering the recent implementation of Islamic rule as the final stage before entering a wider Islamic renaissance. In such a renaissance then perhaps mainstream Muslim thinking would conform with modern foundations of liberal values. This could be a theory and a hope, but careful assessment shows that the realities on the ground do not match the historical and material situation of the original renaissance. What is now known and documented is a resurgence of a kind of Islamic identity and cohesion across the Muslim world, boosted visibly by the Islamic Revolution of 1979 in Iran.

Political Islam, driven by a radically self-sufficient Islamic identity, has in recent decades attained progressively greater power. This tendency to emphasise the role of Islam in government has been pursued by contradictory forces. On one hand, it is the moderate Muslims who interpret Islam as a religion compatible with democracy. On the other hand, there is a wide-ranging group of traditionalists who regard any non-Islamic notion (e.g. democracy) as alien, and interpret Islam according to restricted interpretations of its narrative. The problem becomes more intriguing when there are numerous Islamic sects within Islam's two major branches, Sunnism and Shi'ism, each branch claiming that they have the righteous narrative by referring to the manuscript. This chapter attempts to shed some light on arguments, advocated by some Muslim scholars, that Islam and democracy are compatible.

The question is how a Muslim society with a deep-rooted sense of religious identity and increasing political awareness can engage constructively with democratic norms and institutions of government. Such engagement has two layers: one being how religions and religious citizens can define the concept and context of democracy; and second, the construction and function of a democratic government in a Muslim society. In other words, what are the criteria to verify a democratic system in a majority Muslim society whose people might democratically choose to implement Islamic rule? The conflict between the rights of the majority and minority is an inevitable result of such a process which is not the focus of this chapter.

The interconnectedness of democracy and the prevailing religion in any given society is not a marginal debate in political studies. The study of political culture and its influence in the formation of governments and policies is experiencing resurgence. Most endeavours utilising political culture, however, tended to assume that Islam specifically hindered modernisation and democratisation. For example, Halpern in 1965 argued that a modern middle class was emerging in the Middle East that would lead the process of modernisation in the region. He even branded Islam as an irrational and very dangerous threat to this process (Halpern 1965). Daniel Price categorises the academic literature focusing on the relationship of Islam and politics into four levels:

- The study of Islam in the West is distorted by its relationship to Islamic societies. The West has always approached the study of Islam from a position of power and dominance, the coloniser and the hegemon, which has prevented Western scholars from gaining an accurate understanding of Islam and Islamic societies.
- Islam is a very mysterious and irrational force that overwhelms societies. This trend attributes almost all behaviour in Islamic societies to Islam. In other words, Islam is used to explain everything and is considered the most important variable in understanding these societies. Changes in behaviour are attributed to cyclical fluctuation in the influence of Islam.
- An approach which aims to collect information on Islamic political groups, the chains of events that have been associated with the rise of political Islam, and the nature of that ideology.
- Realising that Islam's role in society was not weakened as much as originally claimed by the writers of the 1960s and 1970s, this strain of literature attempts to understand the relationship between Islam and politics by applying the methods of the social sciences while, at the

same time, recognising that Islam might produce a political culture that varies from those of the West.

(Price 1999: 16–17)

The emergence of the Islamic Republic of Iran in 1979 created a challenging case study for political pundits. On one hand, the precedence of a constitutional revolution about 70 years before had marked a focal point towards modernisation and rule of law in Iran as a Muslim country. On the other hand, the world faced the reality of an Islamic state being established by popular vote after decades of a secular modernisation process under a totalitarian monarchy. The republic proved to be a new political product with many unknown facts and myths combined under the umbrella of constitution. The mixture of democratic and theocratic elements into the constitution has offered a great deal of flexibility and, at the same time, ambiguity to analyse the compatibility of Islam and democracy.

This chapter attempts to shed some light on the feasibility of Islamic democracy in Iran from a theoretical point of view. Of course, the framework for such assessment is confined to Shi'a Islam and its implementation in the Islamic Republic of Iran. The republic is the first modern state that has adapted a full range of Islamic (Shi'a) principles into its constitutional and written law as well as policies. Second, the Islamic Republic effectively came to power through a popular uprising and a democratic constitutional vote. It is important to note that from the political science point of view, the socio-economic structure of a society is the inevitable result of how and on what bases socio-economic resources are distributed. Therefore, if a society establishes a religious regime that ostensibly is in contrast with the modern nation-sate, the root cause is the lack of appropriate socio-economic development, not merely the widespread acceptance of ideological and religious sentiments. Hence, they (political scientists) argue that such notions (religious sentiments) are being misleadingly used by the political leaders who aim to manipulate power through the popular medium of religion (Ali Reza 2000).

However, in our case study of Iran, whether we assume that it is the lack of socio-economic development that is the main cause of Iranian society drifting towards adapting Islamic (Shi'a) principles or that it is a genuine source of rebellion and a power-seeking attitude within Shi'a Islam that has turned this society against non-Islamic political rule, the dilemma remains. The theoretical predicament we face is, first, to clarify the essential meaning and purpose of Islam in general and Shi'ism in particular. Second, we need to understand the linear relationship between religious notions – derived from the scripture and traditions – and political changes/events.

The following section will very briefly elaborate on different perspectives on viewing Islam based on its core message and then reasserting the marriage between Islam and the Iranian state after the Islamic Revolution. The chapter intentionally explores the issue of compatibility between Islam and democracy from within the Islamic discourse. To do this, I will critically analyse the issues of legitimacy and necessity of religious rule in Shi'a Islam with particular reference to Iranian experience. In the next stage I will discuss the concept of jurisprudent rule (*velayate faqih*). The upcoming debate will benefit from the dialogue between the socio-political stance of prominence but various adherences to the Shi'a school of Islam and their opponents, mostly in the contemporary era.

Islam

What is Islam? What do we really mean by Islam? What are the differences between someone declaring him/herself as Muslim and the real criteria for this attribution from Islam itself? Above all, can we really describe certain political statements, organisations and even states which declare themselves to be Islamic, as such? Colin Turner tries to broaden our perception of Islam by saying: 'Yet one has to scratch the surface to reveal that Islam is no monolith, it is a vast, multifaceted entity with as many different forms of expression as there are people to express them. It is therefore impossible to talk about Islam without qualifying it' (Turner 2006: 3). This interpretation of Islam is in fact based on the source of Islamic teaching, Qur'anic scripture.

It is a very elaborate and sophisticated scripture, which was revealed about 15 centuries ago and must not be cut into pieces for the purpose of singling out one particular element. The historical trajectory of the Muslim world shows a great interconnectedness between political rule and the message of Islam. On one hand we witness Islam as a delicate source of human emancipation from the self and other suppressing controls. On the other hand, one can interpret Islam as a monolithic set of beliefs that could be most suitable for repressing and restraining human freedom in favour of establishing a rigid order of political rule. That is why some argue that we must separate the religion as a conducting code from the revelation around which it has accreted (Turner 2006; 3). The focus according to this judgement is to distinguish between the Qur'an and its ideals and the communal response to it that is shaped in the frame of 'organized religion'. There are various examples of non-compliance, of Muslims doing something despite the Qur'an forbidding it. Therefore, why should Islam be held responsible for the faults of Muslims, asks Turner. Equally, we cannot hold Christianity itself accountable for the atrocities carried out by Christian despots over the course of history.

Therefore, it cannot be wrong to say that although 'there is overlap between these different approaches to Islam, [...] one can only conclude, as many have, that there are as many kinds of Islam as there are individual Muslims' (Turner 2006: 3). However, this claim should not lead to a reductionist analysis of Islam as a loose and boundless religion that can be defined and practised by anyone who likes to proclaim it. Rather, it is to illustrate the capacity and potential of Islam to be a conclusive form of emancipation for the totality of mankind. Peter Clarke beautifully utilises Gellner's comparison between Islam and Christianity by saying: 'one of the most striking aspects of this religion as it has travelled and developed beyond its original homeland is, to use the biological concept of homogenises, likeness of offspring to the parent body, and the theoretical absence of a Church, and hence of a central authority on Faith and Morals', so as we witness, 'there is no obvious agency which could have enforced this homogeneity' (Clarke 1988: 3).

The above introduction of Islam becomes essential when the relationship between Islam and democracy is to be examined. This is a debate fuelled largely by the overemphasis on the intrinsic contradiction between democracy that emanates from man-made law and the Islamic law enshrined by the divine religion of Islam. In short, there are two main understandings of the meaning and implementation of Islamic law. Gellner describes Islam in its pure form as 'the blueprint for social order. It holds that a set of rules exists, eternal, divinely ordained, and independent of the will of men, which defines the proper ordering of society' (Gellner 1981: 1). However, Turner offers a different approach to Islamic law. He says:

> Both Muslims and non-Muslims alike continue to talk about 'Islamic law' or 'Islamic theology' as though these terms actually signify something. They do not. For the qualifier 'Islamic' implies that whatever is so described carries the kind of divine sanction that renders it immutable and definitive. To describe a law as 'Islamic', for example, is to say that it is representative of Islam and thus somehow sanctioned by God. Yet in reality, law as a discipline is a human endeavour, and as such a wholly fallible one.

(Turner 2006: 69)

Here it is crucial to remind ourselves of the deliberate absence of central and official authority in Islam. Based on Qur'anic description there are three fundamentals of Islamic belief: belief in Divine Unity (*tawhid*); belief in prophethood (*nabuvah*); and belief in resurrection and the hereafter (*ma'ad*) (Turner 2006: 73). The issues of political governance and the establishment of an all-encompassing political rule have no presence in the Qur'anic terms of Islam. However, the creation of an Islamic *umma* in Medina under the Prophet Muhammad's rule has been perceived by many as proof of an inevitable intermarriage of Islam and governance. Evidently, although as God's messenger, Muhammad's religious leadership of the Muslims was sanctioned by divine decree, his political leadership and jurisdiction in Medina comprising both Muslims and non-Muslims could not have been justified merely by his position as God's Prophet. To solve the dilemma, the political institution created by him was based on a series of agreements known collectively as the 'Pact of Medina'. It is very important to note the consensus-seeking approach taken by the Prophet in order to maintain a unified community under his rule.

Regarding Islamic law, we face both academic criticism and a media frenzy condemning it as a kind of return to an uncivilised way of life, but what is Islamic law really about?[1] Neal Robinson asserts that the aim of Islamic jurisprudence or *fiqh* is to understand God's law. The reproduction of the term law for the purpose of describing the framework of Islamic thought can be confusing. Ironically, this term for many critics and advocates at the same time meant the implementation of temporal legislation based upon the Islamic (Divine) recommendations. However, by combining the two ostensibly different criteria mentioned above (Turner's and Gellner's), we can conclude that people are given the option of accepting the 'Divine Guidance'[2] and, once that guidance is adopted by them as law, that legislation does not merely bear its divinity but human temporality. In other words, it is still divine in theory but temporal in practice, simply because its reinforcement is bound to be carried out by humans.

The integration of religion and state

For most of the twentieth century, it was widely held that the role of religion in the state was a matter of history. However, the course of events towards the end of the millennium proved otherwise and showed that religion can still exercise a great deal of influence over socio-political issues. Ironically, this resurgence of religious influence did not only occur in the developing countries but in the most advanced political systems like the United States of America.[3] To justify or explain the reasons involved in the increased influence of religion, different opinions have been expressed. One explanation points out the ever-increasing role of the secular state and its crushing effects on the moral grounds of society as a provocation for the revival of religious sentiments. This argument is voiced by two different groups: first, the advocates of the return of religion to public life; and second, the critics of modernity who see the monolithic character of liberalism-capitalism as creating a need for a reconfiguration of identity.

Here, our focus is not to explore the motives behind the advocacy of religious interference in politics; rather, our interest is to find the arguments prescribing such correlation. The critics of religious rule usually focus on the functional and behavioural level of analysis. Their primary focus is the consequent dictatorship and autocratic nature of most religious governments, which cannot guarantee the implementation of democratic rule. However, they reluctantly ignore the underpinning pretexts (i.e. the instinctive attraction of many followers to religious orders) and bypass the fact that such philosophical and religious foundations in respective societies still hold great sway. In the following paragraphs a summary of these arguments is given.

The first and foremost reason offered by the advocates of religious integration with politics (here Islam) is the assumption that Islam is a comprehensive religion and should therefore be rationally incorporated into politics. For instance, Ayatollah Khomeini explicitly argues that since Islam is the last and most complete of religions, it cannot be reduced and understood as merely for individual salvation, but rather is a community code of conduct. Accordingly, human life in this world is connected with the afterlife, and the way in which mundane affairs are handled directly shapes the eternal destiny. This argument holds that worldly prosperity is linked with the afterlife, and assumes that any doubt over whether Islam has a programme for managing all aspects of life in this world is nonsense. In other words, being religious or, in this case, being Muslim, makes it necessary to have a structured ontological and epistemological attitude towards the quality of life both individually and collectively. A perusal of many Islamic sacred texts can be cited as evidence of the interconnectedness between Islam and polity.

The second argument points out that many Islamic rules cannot be upheld unless they are implemented by a political entity such as a state. The proponents of this opinion deny the possibility of implementing Islamic rules regarding jihad, judgment, Islamic finance and other ethical directives and prohibitions without an Islamic government in place.[4] We can distinguish three categories of believers in Islam who consider Islamic law to be valid and obligatory, but whose opinions on the implementation of this law vary significantly:

- Fundamentalist Muslims (*wahhabism* and *Salafism*) who seek to establish a society in which all inherited rules and codes of Islam that were understood to be practised in the time of Prophet Muhammad must be instituted and practised.
- Traditionalist Muslims who put the main emphasis on personal worship of God and servitude. Accordingly, acting upon the Islamic rule is necessary for Muslims, but its success is not subject to its being implemented by the government.
- Reformist or modernist Muslims who tend to herald the spiritual aspects of Islam. This group does not believe in the inflexibility of Islam as a religion from 14 centuries ago, but rather views it as a timeless message for the salvation of human beings. This view allows that Islamic codes can be adjusted to different situations.

The argument for having an Islamic government as a necessity for implementing Islamic law seems to have risen from various Islamic scripts. Here we encounter the issue of varied interpretations of religion at different times by different individuals and the hermeneutics of religious scripts. This debate possesses a cardinal significance in determining a religious manifestation of government.

The third reason for advocating a correlation of Islam and government is the Prophet's practical method (*sira*). It is an indispensable part of Islam to recognise and identify the behaviour and function of the Prophet as the primary and founding source of Islam. Therefore, for many, the establishment of Islamic government by the Prophet in Medina is seen as an explicit model for all Muslims to follow.[5] However, there is disagreement over the origins of the political leadership of the Prophet Muhammad. Some attribute his political supremacy to his prophecy and say that he created a government to fulfil his prophethood, as other prophets also desired to do but were unable to accomplish. In contrast, some argue that there is no direct association between prophethood and establishing a righteous government. In fact, the essence of missionary work is in contradiction with the exercise of political power, unless that exercise is required and approved by the people. In general, however, the popularity of this analysis is understandable given the example of Islamic government in Medina, although it cannot be said to be deductively supported.

The fourth argument is based on the view that Islam as a religion takes into account and describes the qualities that a ruler must possess in order to be eligible to rule. In fact, the advocates of this perspective connect the divinity of the Prophet Muhammad's government to the legitimacy of his successors. The concept of *Valiye Faqih* is a direct product of this perspective, which considers Islam as a religion with defined and particular qualities for the ruled and rulers at the same time. One could argue that in an evolutionary process the 'descriptive criteria' of an acceptable ruler have ossified and altered to become a 'prescriptive set of principles' which can be found merely in a certain type of scholar at a seminary school.[6] This prescriptive approach gained prominence during Iran's Islamic Revolution and is perceived as the backbone of jurisprudent rule, which accordingly is supposed to be carried out by an educated clergy explicitly in line with seminary scholarship.[7]

However, there is a fundamental rift between Shi'a scholars regarding how to contextualise the concept of *Valiye Faqih*. The first group regards the legitimacy and absolute authority of *Valiye Faqih* as based on a linear hierarchy descended from God down to his last Prophet, the Infallible Imams and then obviously to the Shi'a jurisprudents. Accordingly, the jurisprudent guardianship and leadership over people is granted by divine legitimacy and is not subject to collective consent. Nonetheless, the practical exercise of power by the jurisprudent is assumed to be given by popular acceptance and theoretically in case of disobedience the jurisprudent ruler cannot forcibly govern. The embedded dilemma within this approach is the consequent conclusion of assuming people to be interdicted individuals who cannot recognise their goodness and therefore need to be instructed and guided in virtually all aspects. This view can be named 'direct divine legitimacy' (*mashru'iat ilahi bi-vasita*).

A second group of Shi'a jurists[8] tend to ratify a different perspective on legitimate political leadership which can be identified as 'public-divine legitimacy' (*mashru'iat ilahi-mardumi*). Interestingly, the adherents of this view do not exclude non-clergy from obtaining the leadership of Muslim populations subject to their being pious and knowledgeable in terms of the Islamic framework. They argue that in a broader sense God conveyed His right of rule down to people during the occultation period. This right to rule is protected, legitimate and can be exercised as long as it is congruent with Islamic law. Based on this view, the *Valiye Faqih* ought to be elected by people either directly or via representatives. As a result, the *Valiye Faqih* is not perceived as being appointed within a divine hierarchy, but his qualities and responsibilities are conditioned by Islamic law and principles. Also, in case of breaching his code of conduct, in particular losing his sense of justice, no longer is he considered as *valiye* or ruler and he automatically loses his position.

It is essential to note that there is a consensus in Shi'a jurisprudence over the concept of jurisprudent role (not rule), as being judge and source of emulation in religious practice. It of course applies only for devoted followers. However, as mentioned before, we see a deep disagreement over extending this religious guardianship into a political one. Even the group of Shi'a jurisprudents who are in favour of *velayate faqih* still have different opinions on the extent of such authority. Muhammad Mujtahid Shabestari is a prominent Shi'a scholar who has elaborated extensively on the issue of political Shi'a as state religion and in particular the concept of *velayate faqih*. From his works we can extract his opposition to politicised Islam based on his three-component argument:

- The encounter of the Muslim world with modernism and the quest for development.
- The Islamic Revolution and the introduction of a rational interpretation of Islam.
- The pathology of the official interpretation of Islam, the challenges and failures.

In his famous book, *A Critique on Official Interpretation of Religion* (Shabestari 2005), the main emphasis is put on the 'paradigm shift' and the expansion of modern ideas and inspirations into

Muslim societies. He argues that whether we like it or not, the course of history has brought about a new era in which traditional and classic ways of thinking and acting are insufficient both theoretically and functionally. He refers to the general acceptance of and desire for modern achievement and progress and concludes that the widespread yearning for technological advancement cannot be answered with scholastic debate over what is allowed and what is forbidden according to traditional jurisprudence. In short, his first argument illustrates the challenge that Muslim societies face in incorporating scientific knowledge and practices and ensuring that they are ultimately in accordance with divine wisdom.

The second reasoning to which he refers is the 'rational trajectory' upon which the Islamic Revolution of 1979 was initiated, progressed and finally triumphed. As the main slogans of the revolution clearly spelled out, the main aim and goal of this popular movement was 'independence, freedom and an Islamic Republic'. Shabestari furthers his argument by saying that the message of the Islamic Revolution as a religiously inspired revolution was to convey the emancipating capacity of Islam as its true essence rather than establishing a monolithic government driven by a particular intra-religious adjudication (*ijtihad-i fiqhi*). Having studied the Constitution of 1980 – approved by a majority of the populace – one cannot extrapolate that this document is directly based on Shi'a jurisprudential knowledge (the Qur'an and Tradition).

Shabestari admits that the charismatic personage of the revolutionary leader, the Grand Ayatollah Khomeini, had a great deal of influence not only over political entities but also over people's heart and minds. However, he takes into account three defining elements that make the Islamic Revolution a product of the socio-religious and socio-political context of Iran rather than a jurisprudential development: first, the 'formation of a new regime' which is in totality a modern structure; second, the 'function and responsibilities' of the new regime which is very similar to other modern nation-states; and third, the 'judicial-political values and orientations' of the new constitution which is a combination of both secular-democratic discourse and Islamic-religious discourse.

Having noticed these parameters, Shabestari concludes that the structure of the Islamic Republic is based on an amalgamation between democracy and Imami jurisprudence. Regardless of whether it was a success or a failure, the point he emphasises is the general and public debate which occurred during the negotiation period preceding the ratification of the constitution. For him, the way in which the Islamic Republic's constitution was publicly debated, tailored and ratified is significantly decisive. In terms of legal and political rights, Shabestari points to the broad category of rights that the new constitution considers for the people regardless of their religious affiliations. It is a grave detachment from traditional and seminary jurisprudence to recognise and uphold universal suffrage in terms of the citizenry's rights. His assertion demonstrates the similarities of the Republic's constitution with conventional forms of modern governments and negates its divinity.

Islamic democracy: a paradox or compatibility

With the emergence of the Islamic Republic and the implementation of a vast array of Shi'a jurisprudential norms and rules within the new constitution, an unprecedented combination of religion and state came into existence. A famous thinker whose thoughts and theories directly aim to connect theology and governance is Abdul-Karim Soroush. He maintains that 'religious law or Shari'a is not synonymous with the entirety of religion, nor is the debate over the democratic religious government a purely jurisprudential argument'. To prove this, Soroush argues 'that jurisprudential statements are different from epistemological ones, and no methodical mind should conflate the two realms'. He continues by saying that the 'jurisprudential conception of Islam has so occupied certain minds that epistemological arguments are allowed to pose as jurisprudential propositions' (Soroush 2000: 134).

Soroush's critical approach towards a monolithic interpretation of religion and its application in terms of governing doctrine provides us with a ground-breaking framework of intra-religious and extra-religious discourses. In his elaborations on issues concerning democratic religious government, he challenges the critics of such combinations and rejects their negative assessment of the concept of democratic religious government as 'preposterous'. Advocates of compatibility like him argue that critics have built their arguments to prove the incompatibility of Islam and democracy on a selective narrative. Therefore, issues such as gender in Muslim societies, theocracy, the absolute authority of jurisprudents, the designation of the death penalty on apostates, the regard of infidels as impure, the dogmatism of some beliefs and inflexibility of some decrees, should not be accounted as evidence of the inherent animosity of religion and religious government towards democracy.

He mentions three obvious errors that are made by critics. First, for the critics, democracy is equated with extreme liberalism. Second, through this approach religious jurisprudence is severed from its core foundations, quoted out of context and then presented as evidence. Third, religious democratic government is equated with religious jurisprudential government and attacked as a monolithic whole. It is essential to note that the essence of Islam as an emancipating religion has always been neglected and instead both its adherents and opponents have been keen on stressing its jurisprudential aspects and precepts.

It is widely assumed that Islam facilitates authoritarianism, is contradictory to the values of Western societies and is indispensably crucial in shaping political outcomes in Muslim nations. These generalised and biased assumptions are primarily based on the textual deduction and ad hoc studies of individual countries without taking into account other factors. Therefore, the involvement of Islam in the socio-political sphere is perceived as either 'upcoming Islamic fundamentalism' or non-conducive to 'liberal democracy'. Perhaps, like those of other religions, Islamic texts and traditions can be employed to advocate a number of different political systems and policies as has been the case throughout history.

Daniel Price argues that country-specific studies do not provide us with applicable patterns for the varying relationships between Islam and politics across the countries of the Muslim world. To support this argument, in order to explain the varied influence that Islam exerts on politics, he emphasises the necessity of comparative studies focusing on various factors related to the interplay between Islamic groups and regimes, economic situations, ethnic cleavages and societal development. He concludes that much of the power attributed to Islam as the driving force behind politics and political systems in Muslim nations can be better explained by the above-mentioned factors.

Intellectualism and Islam

As either advocates or critics of compatibility between Islam and democracy, intellectuals have always played a significant role. In particular, the birth of intellectualism and intellectuals in Iran has been a crucial factor to shape this debate. Whether we believe in the role of intellectuals[9] as the bearers of modernity and progressive paradigms into Iranian society or acknowledge them as the product of modernity per se, their influence in shaping popular socio-political discourses in Iran is a matter of fact. From the nineteenth century onwards the encounter with modernity brought about a wave of critical thinking on both the 'emancipatory' and 'dominative' aspects of socio-political life. Hence, a complex perception of modernity entered into the socio-political discourse of Iranian society. Although it does not necessarily mean that there was no attempt or desire for reform hitherto, the encounter of these two fundamental aspects of modernity generated a double paradoxical dilemma which prevented the process of the institutionalisation of modernity.

Religious-driven autocracies can be elucidated as having two features. One is an ossified form of religious intolerance which mostly emanates from a power-seeking interpretation of religious texts; the other is the inherited patrimonialism and imbalance between gender and class relationships within any given society. On attitudes towards the West, as Lloyd Ridgeon argues, there 'can be little doubt that most Iranian responses to the challenges and difficulties of the modern age reflect the influences that have emanated from the West' (Ridgeon 2005: xi). In his articulation, Ridgeon adds that 'it is virtually impossible to bracket the West out in an attempt to identify how Iranian intellectuals and reformers have responded to the challenges they have faced in these past one hundred years'.

In other words, we can summarise the contemporary socio-political history of Iranian intellectualism as being a constant struggle to dissolve autocracy and embrace modernity. At the same time, as mentioned above, the two intrinsic elements of modernity itself, the emancipatory (liberalism, freedom, subjectivity) and the dominative (the necessity of a functioning nation-state, systematic institutions, universality), clashed respectively with the 'desire to dissolve autocracy' and 'embracing Western modernity'. In short, while the emancipatory element engaged with autocratic elements such as dogmatic religious beliefs and socio-political patrimonialism, the dominative element of modernity was under constant influence and interference from Western economic and political interests.

It was accepted as a norm for most of the twentieth century that intellectualism and intellectuals could not be associated with being religious. For the majority of intellectuals, their association with religion was discrediting and shameful. All they had to boast was belonging to the secular ideological universe of either the West or East. Jahanbakhsh argues that even as late as the mid-1960s, when someone like Al-e Ahmad began to voice their self-criticism within intellectual circles, religion and intellectualism were still deemed mutually exclusive. As mentioned previously, Shari'ati seriously challenged such assumptions and altered the existing definition of the intellectual, primarily in terms of using religious sentiments and ideals as incentive for mobilising the masses and agitating for social change. The triumph of the Islamic Revolution proved that 'a new breed of intellectualism had been born and come to stay'. A quintessential figure in this development was Abdul Karim Soroush.

From the early 1990s Soroush gradually expanded his criticism against the clerical ruling class and also co-founded a monthly magazine, *Kiyan*. It was via *Kiyan* that he could publish and spread his controversial articles on religious pluralism, hermeneutics, tolerance, clericalism, etc. In short, we can summarise that Soroush attempted 'to reconcile Islam and modernity by creating a worldview that is compatible with both'. Forough Jahanbakhsh argues that well before the landslide election of 1997 and the official entrance of Islamic reformists into the political sphere, a steadily emerging new trend of religious intellectualism challenged the previously untouchable doctrine of the Islamic republic, manifested as the ideological understanding of Islam. She traces the roots of religious intellectualism since the mid-1980s to the fact that 'educated religious individuals outside the political power structure started debating issues such as rationalism, pluralism, tolerance versus violence, rejection of non-critical and blind emulation of the *fuqaha*, critical analysis of the ideologization of religion, rights versus duties, and reconciling religion and democracy'. Henceforth, Soroush and his allies were called Islamist reformists. The dilemma, however, remained to recognise the concrete standpoints of such thinkers. For example, Filali-Ansary argues that:

> [M]any controversies surrounding Islamic thought focus so heavily on semantics, on names for ideas and persons that the real issues often disappear from sight. [Thus], many thinkers who are called or who call themselves 'Islamists' make such large concessions to the power of unaided human reason that one may wonder what is left to render their thought Islamic. On the other hand, many secularists, especially nationalists, pay such reverence to Islamic dogmas that one may wonder if reason has any role left to play in their thought. The whole confrontation sometimes seems like so much posturing, where the real choices are never clarified or faced.
>
> *(Filali-Ansary 1996: 78)*

For Soroush, the main problematic issue remains within Muslims themselves, or rather within a complex of traditions that has long barred Muslims from the free implementation of reason and from direct contact with the sources of their faith. He acknowledged an urgent task of freeing Muslims from Islam understood as a social and historical heritage, as a set of overwhelming external conventions defining views and behaviour. The general theme of Soroush's work emphasises the inward characteristics of Islam. He argues further that this turn toward Islam understood as an 'open religion' represents not a radical innovation, but rather a return to the original essence of the faith in its purity. For him, the basic reality and objective is the person, the individual believer. Filali-Ansari concludes that Soroush has attempted to present an Islam to which one is free to adhere, and which is full of piety mostly based on this free adherence, rather than on custom, habit and conformism. Thus, Soroush can be seen as a modern humanist and true reformer.

The most controversial theory articulated by Soroush was the 'contraction and Expansion of religious knowledge'. This theory targeted a very sensitive yet fundamental aspect of the prevalent religious understanding – its epistemic foundations. It argues that any understanding of religion is bound to be temporal and subject to change. For many observers this theory meant that 'no understanding of religion is ever sacred, absolute or final and laid the foundation of an epistemological pluralism that is the basis of any democratic pluralism'. Such a theoretical breakthrough constructed within religious discourse resulted in far-reaching consequences in both intellectual and political milieux. In short, the possible multiplicity of readings of religion, when taboo, could have dramatic implications for the configuration of an Islamic regime with a republican structure.

The arguments in this chapter addressed the main issues concerning the political ramifications of Islam and whether it can be compatible with democracy. Studying both, however, reveals a sort of incompatibility that is in line with the classical separation of church and state. It was argued that there is no generally accepted interpretation of Islam, so its incompatibility with democracy cannot be universally assumed. In practice, however, problems arise when one is forced to define and qualify the true meaning of religious belief in a situation that would affect both believers and non-believers. At the same time and as part of standard democratic norms, freedom of religion and assembly is granted. The difficulty becomes more obvious when the Muslim citizens vote to establish an Islamic system and Islamic codes are implemented as a result. The case of the Islamic Republic of Iran is a salient example of such imposition by which a popularly voted constitution sanctioned the implementation of Shi'a Islam as the main source of legislation and policy-making.

Conclusion

In this chapter I have tried to compress and reflect the main arguments surrounding Islam and democracy in the context of the Islamic Republic of Iran from 1979 to the present. Of course, it is not claimed that this chapter has tackled the question of the compatibility of Islam and democracy. Rather, it attempted to juxtapose the main elements relevant to the issue to allow for better observation and research. Understanding what constitutes democracy has become less contested over the last few decades, but reaching a consensual definition of what Islam is all about is fairly impossible. This absence of a clear-cut interpretation of Islam rules out any blank ratification or denunciation for or against the question of compatibility. What this chapter has aimed to prove is that the subject is yet to be explored, and various presumptions and arguments taken out of context are of little help.

Notes

1 It is crucial to note that throughout the history of Islam the *fiqh* has been the most important academic discipline, supporting its own philosophical and political discourse, literature, art and, in one word, civilisation. Thus, treating it as merely a series of extravagant superstitions is totally ignorant.
2 It is preferable to use the term Divine or Islamic Guidance; however, due to frequent usage of Divine or 'Islamic law' in relevant literature, we might use it as a well-established term without assuming its terminological implications.
3 The revival of Christian sentiments by conservatives in US politics.
4 For example, see Tahari 1988.
5 For instance, when Iranian politician Seyed Mohammad Khatami was asked to clarify and define his position toward civil society, he replied that the civil society we seek is the same as Prophet Muhammad's (S) *Medina al-Nabbi* (City of Prophet in Medina).
6 For example, it is unimaginable that an excellent graduate of Islamic studies from a university would expect to become a scholar eligible to be considered as a faqih.
7 According to Article 110 of the Constitution of the Islamic Republic of Iran.
8 Essential articles of the Islamic Republic's constitution stipulate such an interpretation, and recently this aspect of the constitution and other independent judgments have been echoed by reformist clerics such as Mohsen Kadivar, Yusuf Eshkevari and Muhammad Mujtahid Shabestari.
9 The term *Rawshanfakri* was first introduced by Jalal Al-e Ahmad, by which he meant to distinguish between a completely Westernised thinker and an enlightened thinker. However, the usage of the term *Rawshanfakr* in Persian and 'intellectual' as a universal term is not limited to the ones Al-e Ahmad attempted to qualify.

References

Ali Reza, A. (2000) *Islam and Democracy: State and Society in Developing Countries, 1980–1994*, London, Garland.
Amin, S.H. (1374 [1995]) 'Hakamiyat va Hukumat dar Fiqh Shi'a va Sunni' [State and Government in Shi'a and Sunni Jurisprudence], *Kiyan* vol. 5, no. 24.
Bashiriyah, H. (1998) 'Din, Siyasat va Tawsi'-ah' [Religion, politics and development], *Rah-i Naw* vol. 1, no. 11.
Clarke, P. (1988) *The World's Religions, Islam*, Routledge, London.
Filali-Ansary, Abdou (1996) 'Challenges of Secularisation', *Journal of Democracy* vol. 7, no. 2: 76–80.
Gellner, E. (1981) *Muslim Society*, Cambridge, Cambridge University Press.
Gulpaygani, A.R. (1376 [1997]) 'Nabuvvat va Hukumat', in *Khirad: A Memorandum of the Congress to Celebrate the Revered Pundit Muhammad Taqi Ja'fari*, under the supervision of Ali Akbar Rashad, Tehran, The Research Academy of Culture and Thought.
Halpern, M. (1965) *The Politics of Social Change in the Middle East and North Africa*, Princeton, NJ, Princeton University Press.
Jahanbakhsh, F. (2001) *Islam, Democracy and Religious Modernism in Iran, 1953–2000: From Bazargan to Soroush*, Boston, MA, Leiden.
—— (2003) 'Religious and Political Discourse in Iran: Moving Toward Post-Fundamentalism', *Brown Journal of World Affairs* vol. 9, no. 2: 243–54.
Khomeini, R. (1369 [1990]) *Shu'un va Ikhtiarat-i Wali Faqih* [The Qualities and Capabilities of Jurisprudent's Rule], translated from the section: Wali faqih of Al-Beiy, 2nd edn, Tehran Sazman-i Chap va Intasharat-i Wazarat Farhang va Irshad Islmai.
Ma'rifat, M.H. (1377 [1998]) *Wilayat al-faqih*, Qum, Al-Tamhid Institution.

Ali M. Pedram

Milani, A. (2004) *Lost Wisdom: Rethinking Modernity in Iran*, Washington, DC, Mage Publishers.

Price, D.E. (1999) *Islamic Political Culture, Democracy and Human Rights*, Westport, New York, Praeger.

Rafi'i, A. (1375 [1996]) *Takapu-i Andisha-ha* [Quest for thoughts], a collection of interviews with Muhammad Taqi Ja'fari, Tehran, Daftar Nashr-i Islam.

Ridgeon, L. (2005) *Religion and Politics in Modern Iran: A Reader*, London, I.B. Tauris.

Robinson, N. (1999) *Islam: A Concise Introduction*, London, Routledge Curzon.

Shabestari, M.M. (1384 [2005]) *Naqdi bar Qira'at Rasmi az Din* [A critique on official interpretation of religion], Tehran, Tarh-i Naw.

Soroush, A.K. (2000) *Reason, Freedom and Democracy in Islam: Essential Writings of Abdul Karim Soroush*, Oxford, Oxford University Press.

Tahari, H. (1377 [1998]) *Tahqiqi Piramun-i Wilayat al-faqih* [Research on Jurisprudence Rule], Daftar-i Intasharat-i Islami Wabastah bi Jami'ah Mudarasin Hawzah I'lmiyyih Qum.

Turner, C. (2006) *Islam, the Basics*, Routledge, London.

Tusi, S. (1999) 'Al-risalat-i fi Farq-i beyn al-nabi wa al-imam' [An epistle in differentiating between Imam and Prophet in al-risail al-a'shr], quoted by Kadivar, M. (1999) *Hukumat-i Wilayi*, Tehran, Nashr e Ney.

Vahdat, F. (2002) *God and Juggernaut: Iran's Intellectual Encounter with Modernity*, Syracuse, Syracuse University Press.

Wright, R. (1996) 'Islam and Liberal Democracy: The Challenge of Secularisation', *Journal of Democracy* vol. 7, no. 2: 76–80.

Yazdi, M.T.M. (n.d.) 'Hukumat va Mashru'iat', *Ketab-i Naqd* [Book of critique], no.7.

14

Islam, identity and discourses in Pakistan

Samina Yasmeen

The assassination of two prominent Pakistani politicians in the first two months of 2011 for their stance on the blasphemy law has drawn attention to the sharpening divide between liberal and orthodox notions of Islam in the country. The concurrent prevalence of militancy and identification of Pakistan as the central locale for terrorism has reinforced concerns regarding the religious trajectory along which the country is currently moving. Implicit in these concerns are questions regarding the role of political Islam in Pakistan – a state created out of British India as a homeland for Muslims in 1947. This chapter develops an argument that since its creation, Islamist groups have aimed at ensuring that the state acquires a definable Islamic identity. The ideas presented by Maulana Maududi of Jamaat-e-Islami encapsulated this preference for an Islamic state of Pakistan. Since the turn of the 1980s, however, a combination of politico-strategic, generational and ideational factors has resulted in the emergence of multiple ideas on the essence of an Islamic state and its practical manifestations in Pakistan. The resulting diversity of views carries both risks to and possibilities of ensuring that liberal Islamist notions remain relevant in Pakistan.

The argument is developed in four parts: the first part establishes the context in which debates on political Islam can be understood. The second part focuses on the ideas presented by Maulana Maududi on the Islamic state and their sustained appeal in contemporary Pakistan. The third part focuses on the diversity of ideas on political Islam among the more orthodox groups of Islamists. The chapter ends with a brief assessment of how the diversity of Islamic ideas is likely to shape the course of Islamization in Pakistan.

The context: ideas, agents and processes

Political Islam or Islamism has become a contested concept. The view held by scholars (both Muslim and non-Muslim) of the inseparability of religion from politics is no longer accepted uncritically. Ernest Gellner's claim that Islam 'was the state from the very start' (Ahmad 2009: S145–46) or Fuller's confidence that 'Islam as a body of faith has something important to say about how politics and society should be ordered' (Ayoob 2005: 951) is questioned by those who approach the subject in terms of political interests of religious clergy, state activism or attributes of totalitarian movements. These critics point out that the proposition of Islam combining 'spiritual and profane features' and of being 'a total way of life [...] cannot be substantiated' (Kirmanj 2008: 55). However, this stance does not lead them to ignore the fact that Islam 'incorporates some beliefs, values and ethics which have political significance'. The use of these politically significant aspects of Islam by 'individuals, groups and organizations that pursue political objectives' – a form of instrumentalization of Islam – constitutes political Islam for those who adopt a non-essentialist view of the religion. For these scholars, this use of Islam 'provides political responses to today's societal challenges by imagining a future, the foundations for which rest on reappropriated, reinvented concepts borrowed from the Islamic tradition' (Ayoob 2005: 951–52).

Implicit in such definitions is the acceptance of a process of functionally using Islam for the purpose of change of the society or societies of which Muslims are a part. However, they do not explicitly acknowledge that the process of using Islam as a significant reference point for a society is not linear and/or unidirectional. It can occur at multiple levels and in different directions, with individuals and groups competing for the most authentic interpretation of Islamic injunctions and their relevance for political organizational issues. Also, the shift towards Islamism does not occur in a vacuum: the preference(s) for a political role for Islam exists in a dynamic relationship with alternative views that accord limited space for religion in shaping relationships and structures of states and societies. The instrumentalization of Islam, therefore, occurs in a dynamic environment marked by interaction between forces and factors beyond sheer belief in the value of Islam's political relevance.

This dynamic relationship can be understood with reference to a model that places states and societies along a spectrum in terms of the primacy they accord to *divine will* and *human will*. Those occupying the primacy of human will end of the spectrum either completely negate a role for divine will or acknowledge a limited role for religious injunctions in shaping the nature of human societies. In contrast, those at the primacy of divine will end of the spectrum accord a dominant or significant role to religious injunctions in determining structures of human societies. In some cases, they also accept a limited role for human will provided it does not contradict the interpretations of the divine will (Ahmed 1987; Yasmeen 2003). Societies do not adopt a static position along this spectrum: those on the divine will end, for instance, may opt to include or exclude human will. Similarly, the human end of the spectrum could witness preference of a society to include or exclude divine will. Movement can also take place along the spectrum, with societies opting for varying degrees of primacy assigned to human or divine will. Adopting this spectrum, it could be argued that Islam is politicized when a society/state shifts away from the human will end of the spectrum towards the divine will end, but the shift does not preclude the possibility of the society returning to the original point along the spectrum.

Any discussion of the nature and direction of these moves cannot be divorced from the idea of agency: individuals, groups and organizations emerge that provide the necessary information to promote a particular version of Islam in a given society. At a basic level, they could be identified with reference to the space from which they draw their primary support and power, and could be distinguished as promoting state-sponsored or societal Islam. It is important to note that participation in the politicization of Islam at the state or societal level does not assume a unity of views: opinions on the nature of authentic Islam and acceptable manifestations of Muslim identity may vary, with groups or individuals arguing for what may be diametrically opposing prescriptions. The relative balance of power between those promoting these ideas ultimately determines the direction a state or society takes at a given time. However, as in international relations, balances remain fluid and susceptible to local and international developments. In addition to political events in different regions, the evolution of ideas and views on Islam's relevance as a lived religion across national boundaries also impact on debates on the religion's place in political and social structures of a society. The idea of what is important, sacred and must be implemented as well as the language and discourse surrounding the prescriptions can also change. The extent to which the international impacts on the local, therefore, is closely associated with the resilience of transnational links and the nature of dominant global tensions in global politics. The dominant struggle between communism and capitalism during the Cold War, for instance, kept the impact of global debates on Islam relatively limited than is the case today. The international dimension has particularly become significant in a globalized world with its focus on the relationship between Islam and the West.

Maududi and political Islam in Pakistan

Viewing the role of Islam in Pakistan through this model suggests that the country has experienced various phases of Islamization that are either state-sponsored or have been variants of societal Islam. The initial years of Pakistan's existence were characterized by the dominance of groups promoting the primacy of human will with a role for divine will. This was encapsulated in the idea of a homeland for Muslims by Jinnah but without the categorical identification of the state as an Islamic state. Once Pakistan gained independence in 1947, against the backdrop of the dominant international struggle between the United States and the Soviet Union, its close relationship with Washington created conditions in which notions of liberal democracy, interspersed with ideas of Islam, remained powerful.

The space open to religious clergy preferring the primacy of divine will in shaping the nature of the state and society remained limited. A number of Islamic parties had renamed themselves to reflect the creation of Pakistan while retaining some links to their original identities: Jamiat Ulema-e-Hind, for instance, was created as Jamiat Ulema-e-Islam and the Jamiat Ulema-e-Pakistan was established in 1948 in line with the decision made two years earlier (Rana 2009: 160, 357). The ability of these groups to play a significant role in Pakistan's politics was circumscribed. Apart from occasional successes like the inclusion of the Objectives Resolution in the constitution, and their acknowledged roles in the social sphere, religious clergy operated at the periphery of the political debates in Pakistan. However, even in this environment, Maulana Maududi (1903–79) of Jamaat-e-Islami persevered in demanding that divine will be accorded its central place in shaping Pakistan's political and social structures. His discussion on the process required for this shift towards the divine will clearly reflected his preference for an active role to be played by societal groups.

Maududi's preference for societal agency in establishing an Islamic state was articulated prior to the creation of Pakistan with reference to his opposition to the idea of a nationalist state. Speaking at Aligarh Muslim University in September 1940, he argued that the Islamic state is an ideological state 'built exclusively on principles' and 'as having its foundations in certain recognised moral principles and free from all idea of nationality or race. A distinguishing feature of the Islamic State,' he argued, 'is that the basic conception of all its outward manifestation is the idea of Divine Sovereignty. Its fundamental theory is that the earth and all that it contains belongs to God who alone is its Sovereign […] God alone has the right to legislate and give commands. The state, according to Islam, is nothing more than a combination of men working together as servants of God to carry out His Will and Purposes.' Such a state, he further elaborated, is characterized by 'common standards of behaviour' that unite the masses and the leadership, and in which the leadership both engenders and reflect the high moral principles underpinning the Islamic state (Maududi 1993: 13).

The emergence of an Islamic state, he argued, could not 'spring into being […] like a miracle'. Its emergence involved a gradual process – the Islamic Revolution – which is marked

169

by mobilization of masses not for the sake of gaining power but for implementing God's will on Earth. He identified the prerequisite for such a revolution: the emergence of a movement committed to 'having for its basis the view of life, the ideal of existence, the standard of morality, and the character and spirit which is in keeping with the fundamentals of Islam. Its leaders and workers should be men who psychologically and spiritually fit to accept this particular mode of character.' However, instead of assuming that the movement in its own right could create an Islamic state, he argued for 'ceaseless efforts' on the part of the movement to change the thinking and morality at the societal level. The movement was entrusted with the dual task of 'changing the mental attitude and moral spirit among the people', and 'on the basis of moral and intellectual tendencies so created […] build[ing] up a system of education to train and mould the masses in the Islamic pattern of life' (Maududi 1993: 13–18). This, in turn, was to sustain a Muslim experience and creation of knowledge and sustain an Islamic state.

The authenticity of the staged process of Islamic revolution for Maududi lay in the Prophetic experience of spreading the message of Islam. He pointed out that Prophet Mohammad had called people of Mecca to the right path, had suffered in the process as had those who joined him and experienced 'righteous suffering', and that the revolution remained a minority phenomenon gathering momentum only after the sincerity of those adhering to the principles became apparent to others. 'It was not a mere political and social reform that had taken place. The whole basis of material and moral life had undergone a revolution', before Islam was accepted as the true religion by Arabs. The revolution of thought and action at the societal level with consistent and moral leadership, therefore, was the route to establishing an Islamic state – wherein could be found 'the logical and scientific relationship of cause and effect' (Maududi 1993: 27–47).

The staged view of an Islamic revolution with societal change prompted Maududi to question the logic of a nationalist state for Muslims. He argued that the path to an Islamic state could not be paved through a state for Muslims structured along the Western notions of democracy. It would not be progress but 'a reverse process which will lead [… Muslims] backward' (Maududi 1993: 22).

The view expressed on a nationalist state for Muslims only six months after the passing of the Pakistan Resolution in Lahore suggested Maududi's opposition to the creation of Pakistan. However, after Pakistan's creation in August 1947, Maududi dismissed this allegation, maintaining that he had never opposed the creation of Pakistan and that he was actively struggling to establish an Islamic state of Pakistan (Siddiq 1993: x–xi). He further developed his thesis of the problems associated with incorporating ideas of Western liberal democracy in Pakistan as well as other Muslim states. Building on the arguments presented prior to the partition of India, he argued that renaissance had devalued religion, and taken it out of public space to private space in human societies. They had legalized adultery and fornication, gambling and wine, and many types of corrupt business and trade. This was despite the fact that religion remained relevant in public spaces through politics, law, knowledge creation, morality and other sections of social life. The dei-phobia, which became the hallmark of Western civilization, was also politically imposed on other states, including Pakistan. These states had accepted the negation of religion uncritically and continued along the path shown by the West (Siddiq 1993: 4, 11).

Maududi pursued an active agenda of altering the nature of the Pakistani state through securing a societal change which was to ultimately result in it shifting to the divine will end of the spectrum. His prescription of a modified Pakistani state rested on the ability of 'men of religion to regain leadership' and introduce shar'ia in the country. In line with his earlier thinking, he accepted that the process would be a slow one requiring commitment and leadership, but that ultimately Jamaat-i-Islami would succeed in altering the nature of the society and implement *al-hukum lillah* (law belongs to Allah alone). It is important to note that Maududi did not merely target 'Westernized ruling elites', feudal lords and capitalists, but also included the narrow-minded and sectarian clergy whom he categorized as 'the guardians of antiquity' as obstacles to achieving the goal of an Islamic state (Siddiq 1993: 15). In the process, he used language that would appeal to the masses in order to mobilize societal support against these 'obstacles'.

Despite his efforts to effect a change through the societal agency, Jamaat-e-Islami failed to secure sufficient electoral support in the 1970s election. The period following the secession of Bangladesh in 1971 increased the Jamaat's access to societal groups particularly through tertiary educational institutions. Instructively, it was predominantly through the agency of the state that Maududi was able to implement some of his ideas of an Islamic state. General Zia-ul-Haq's military coup in July 1977 and his need to legitimize his rule provided the route through which elements of an Islamic state as identified by Maududi were added to the country's political and social life.

The Zia regime introduced the Hudood Ordinance (1979) focused on issues of rape, adultery, extra-marital relations, false accusation, theft and drinking alcohol. It also amended the blasphemy law, which had been part of Pakistan's Penal Code (inherited from British rule), to make defiling of the Holy Qur'an punishable with imprisonment (295-B), of the name of the Holy Prophet with death (295-C), and of any other personage revered in Islam with three years' imprisonment (295-A). The educational system, identified as an essential element of an Islamic revolution by Maududi, was also revamped with greater focus on Pakistan's Islamic identity and history. The government also introduced more stringent censorship to effect a change in the cultural space that Maududi considered a significant manifestation of dei-phobic attitudes.

These policies were introduced against the backdrop of a changed regional and international environment in the days following the Soviet invasion of Afghanistan in 1979. As the 'frontline state' entrusted with the agenda to roll the Soviets back, Pakistan provided its territory to the United States and other allies to promote a jihadi culture. The proliferation of *madaris* (religious schools) to train fighters imbued with a religious fervour to oust non-believers from Afghanistan also introduced the language of jihad in Pakistan. Hence the process of moving Pakistan in the direction of the primacy of the divine will continued throughout the 1980s, past Maududi's death in September 1979.

The impact of the state's instrumentalization of Islam was apparent in the democratic era of the 1990s. The society became more attuned to the language of Islam after a decade of being reminded of Pakistan's Islamic identity. The process was particularly noticeable in educational institutions where the youth was exposed to the 'Islamized curriculum' and, therefore, tended to use the Islamic language with more ease than was the case in the past. The concurrent proliferation of easily accessible literature on Islam in local languages exposed the society to multiple meanings of Pakistan's Islamic identity. The process empowered the religious clergy who increasingly came to be regarded as the nodes of authentic information on Islam. Under these circumstances, the democratically elected leaders (Benazir Bhutto and Nawaz Sharif) preferred to co-opt religious groups/parties to lengthen their hold on power. Political exigencies prevented them from amending the Hudood Ordinance and the blasphemy law despite the mounting information on their abuse by various sections of society. These failures were accompanied by occasional signs of the state taking a stand against the prevailing orthodoxy: Benazir Bhutto, for example, participated in the Population Conference in Cairo despite criticism from the *ulama* and their identification of population control as an un-Islamic practice.

171

Against the backdrop of increased visibility of Islamic language of identity, Pakistan continued to move towards the primacy of divine will end of the spectrum.

Pakistan's Islamic identity post-9/11: discourses

The terrorist attacks on the United States on 11 September 2001 and the resulting revived alliance between Islamabad and Washington provided an opportunity for shifting society back towards the primacy of human will end of the spectrum. The process was once again led by the state that used liberal interpretations of Islam to change the nature of society. President Pervez Musharraf promoted the concept of 'enlightened moderation' as the preferred basis for Pakistani identity, in direct opposition to the portrayal of Islam as a violent religion. Carving out a place along the spectrum of moderation and extremism, the Pakistani state and society were to be both enlightened and moderate. It was a value that Pakistanis, as well as Muslims globally, needed to aspire to – not because it was alien to their culture but because Muslim history testified to the presence of these values. President Musharraf referred to 'a glorious past', in which 'Islam [had] exploded on the world scene as the flag bearer of a just, lawful, tolerant and value-oriented society' (Musharraf 2004). Muslims 'had faith in human exaltation through knowledge and enlightenment' and they 'exemplified tolerance within ourselves and toward people of other faiths. The armies of Islam,' he argued:

> did not march forward to convert people by the sword, despite what the perceptions may be, but to deliver them from the darkness through the visible example of their virtues. What better projection can be found of these deeper values of Islam than the personal example of our Holy Prophet (P.B.U.H.), who personified justice, compassion, tolerance of others, generosity of spirit, austerity with a spirit of sacrifice, and a burning desire to make a better world.
>
> *(Musharraf 2004)*

He contrasted the past with the present in which Muslims had been 'left far behind in social, moral and economic development' and had 'reached the depths of despair and despondency'. He presented enlightenment as the way forward, with emphasis on 'human resource development through the alleviation of poverty and through education, health care and social justice' (Musharraf 2004).

The ideas promoted by Musharraf, and subsequently by the Zardari regime with its focus on Sufism, engaged sections of the community that had been concerned by the 'Talibanization' of Pakistani society. They were also supported by the returning Pakistani diaspora who wanted to participate in the project of integrating the society in a globalized world. Although these groups managed to reintroduce some liberal notions of Islam in Pakistan with an emphasis on the primacy of human will which engages actively with religious ideas, the international environment marked by discourses of a civilizational conflict between Islam and the West has limited their ability to regain the balance that shifted in favour of the primacy of divine will. The end result has been the emergence of multiple interpretations of Pakistan's Islamic identity, and its meanings for the nature of the state at the divine will end of the spectrum.

These ideas are informed by, and feed into, global construction(s) of Muslim identities and Islam's political role in the contemporary world. The annual gatherings of Tableeghi Jamaat in Raiwind typify this dynamic relationship: often referred to as the largest gathering after the *Hajj* in Mecca, they bring into contact local and international visitors who are committed to the idea of '*amr bil maruf wa nahi un munkar*' (enjoining good and forbidding evil). The ideas discussed locally are exported via the participants to other countries and become part of the knowledge pool others access around the world in shaping their own ideas on Islam's relevance as a lived religion. Hizb ut-Tahrir's operations in Pakistan, on the other hand, exemplify how ideas developed in the European context have found inroads into a section of Pakistani society. After operating informally in the country in the 1990s, it constituted itself as a formal movement in 2000 in Pakistan. Though it was soon forced to go underground, Hizb ut-Tahrir has continued to import arguments in favour of establishing a *khilafah Rashidah* (four Righteous Caliphs) as 'the sole guarantor of stability in Pakistan'. Its pamphlets exhort the youth, intelligentsia and military to overthrow the Pakistani government due to its collaboration with the United States, and are equally scathing of military and elected regimes (Rana 2010: 99–128). The election of the Pakistan People's Party in 2008, for instance, was labelled a 'democratic circus' by the movement (Hizb ut-Tahrir 2009). Criticism of the Pakistani regime does not remain restricted within Pakistan's territory: capitalizing on the Pakistani diaspora communities, the movement also distributes pamphlets against Pakistani regimes in Western liberal democratic states.

Amidst the multiplicity of ideas and their dynamic relationship with the global environment, Maulana Maududi's ideas reverberate in more than one form. The Jamaat-e-Islami continues to highlight the role of an Islamic state in its publications with due significance accorded to the contributions made by the party's founder. At the same time, Al-Huda provides a gender-specific approach to altering Pakistan's place along the spectrum of human and divine will. Initially established as an academy in 1994, it has metamorphosed into a movement aimed at introducing correct interpretation of Islam in Pakistan. The founder of the movement, Dr Farhat Hashmi, was closely connected to the Jamaat-e-Islami through her family and her personal participation in the student wing of the party in the University of Punjab. The ideas promoted by Al-Huda, therefore, closely resemble the discourse promoted by Maulana Maududi in his lifetime: the distinction between Muslim and Western thought, and the need to cleanse Islam of this accretion underpins the activities undertaken by Al-Huda. In line with the ideas promoted by Maududi, the movement also criticizes Barelvi and Shi'ite Islam (Ahmad 2008: 68) while remaining reluctant to openly associate itself with a political stance.

The continuation of Maududi's ideas through Al-Huda is particularly apparent in the mobilizational approach adopted by it since its inception. It has relied heavily on the educational route for effecting a change in Pakistan. With active patronage from state institutions, particularly the office of President Farooq Leghari, the movement had initially focused solely on women from the upper echelons of Pakistani society as the preferred participants in the project of Islamizing Pakistan. The strategy reflected an appreciation of Pakistan's hierarchical structures, as well as the view that by changing the family sphere, the elite females would provide a secure route to anchoring Pakistan on the divine will end of the spectrum. The Al-Huda Academy offered courses to these women, building an ever-expanding network of students and teachers who share their ideas on Islam with others. Following criticism of the class-specific nature of the group, Al-Huda has expanded its operations among poorer sections in society as well. The Academy also actively participates in supporting communities affected by natural disasters, such as the earthquake of 2005 and floods in 2011. Together, these efforts fit squarely into the category of using women as agents of societal Islam, and reflect a carefully calibrated attempt to introduce a preference for a particular kind of Islamic interpretation at the societal level, with the Academy acting as the facilitator and articulator of change in Pakistan.

The efforts of Al-Huda are not restricted to Pakistan's territorial boundaries. Dr Hashmi has also established a chapter of Al-Huda in Canada that offers online courses to those interested in learning about Islam. This cyber-based content on Islamic identity finds its way back into Pakistan through the female diaspora who access these courses. Essentially, therefore, Al-Huda has emerged as the locale where Maulana Maududi's ideas on the nature of an 'Islamic society' are being promoted in class-, gender- and culture-specific language.

Dissenting voices questioning the validity of Maududi's ideas, however, can be heard among some who accept the primacy of divine will as the guiding principle for the Pakistani state and society. Notable among them is Javed Ahmed Ghamidi who initially belonged to Jamaat-e-Islami but later left the party and presented an alternative vision of an Islamic Pakistan. His vision of an Islamic state is rooted in the significance assigned to *shura* (consultation) (Ghamidi 2006). The idea is directly linked to notions of human fallibility and the belief that only Prophet Mohammad, who was *ma'sum* (infallible), could make unilateral decisions. However, the preference by Prophet Mohammad to consult his companions and the policies adopted by the Righteous Caliphs validate, in Ghamidi's view, the significance of consultation for successive Muslim communities. The process is not merely a formality or an option, but an obligation. Conditions need to be created in which those consulted feel a sense of respect for their ideas, as it is in the process of consultation that they bring to the table strategies for ensuring the success and stability of a Muslim community. Absence of respect, he argues by referring to Islamic tradition, impacts on the ability and willingness of those being consulted to offer considered views (Ghamidi 2009: 153).

The category of those to be consulted, however, is not indeterminate. The right and responsibility to engage in consultation stems from the trust extended to individuals by the members of their respective sections of the community. Effectively, therefore, those who are consulted represent different interest groups. The trust they enjoy is established through tradition and custom and must be sustained for them to qualify to be the representatives of a community. The trust obligates them to provide the best advice that is in the interest of the community as a whole and not tainted by personal interests. In the consultative process, either all of the representatives agree to a mutually satisfactory decision or their decision reflects the views of the majority. By drawing upon the practices adopted by Prophet Mohammad after the conquest of Mecca, and the decisions made by the Righteous Caliphs, he argues that the choice of leadership – the emir – also grows out of a process of consultation. It must be made against the background of the trust of the communities and reflect the relative balance of power between different interest groups. Ghamidi argues that Prophet Mohammad confirmed the leadership of the *Quraysh* (the tribe to which Prophet Mohammad belonged) in the post-conquest phase as they were the majority compared to the *Ansar* (supporter of the Prophet in Medina), and also enjoyed the trust of the majority of the Muslim community (Ghamidi 2009: 156–68). This acceptance of the idea of leadership emanating through a consultative process, the references to the criteria of relative balances among communities, as well as intra-communal balances, and linking political change to balances between different communities, while developed in terms of the primacy of divine will, clearly establish Ghamidi's preference for democracy as the appropriate system for Pakistan (and other Muslim societies).

Ghamidi differs from Maududi in his conception of the rights and responsibilities of an Islamic state vis-à-vis its citizens. While accepting that rulers in an Islamic state are obligated to implement Qur'anic injunctions, he argues that these obligations are limited to requiring that people repudiate and give up *shirk* (polytheism), say their prayers and pay *zakat* (alms). The state is not permitted to intercede beyond these obvious manifestations of Muslim identity of its citizens: it is, for example, not allowed to demand that Muslims observe Ramadan or perform Hajj, as these elements of Islamic faith fall outside the purview of the state powers (Ghamidi 2006: 22). In line with the Prophetic tradition, non-Muslims also enjoy the right to practise their religion in their private spheres of life without fear of the Islamic state. Significantly, Ghamidi argues against an ever-expanding definition of hudood which could be used by an

Islamic state to punish its citizens. The notion of hudood, he argues, applies to five clearly identified offences and cannot be applied to other sets of offences. This position leads him to oppose the lashing of those accused of drinking alcohol, or the death penalty for those accused of apostasy (Ghamidi 2009: 137–46).

The democratic nature of an Islamic state and the need to establish it according to the divine will, unlike for Maududi, does not presuppose the need for religious clergy to be at the helm of government. Ghamidi implicitly and sometimes explicitly argues against political leadership of religious clergy. The argument is premised on a combination of the idea of trust vested by respective members of communities in a state for Muslims, and the attributes required for leaders. Politics, in his view, requires leaders who can mobilize and lead others. Religious scholars like Iqbal, Kalam and Maududi are not ideal participants in the process: they are best suited to investigating ideas contained in Islamic teachings instead of exploring avenues for political participation in a state – a task best left to political leaders like Nawaz Sharif and Benazir Bhutto. The reluctance to endorse a political role for religious clergy also prompts Ghamidi to argue against moves for Islamic revolution. He maintains that Islamic political parties could only validly argue for a change of government resulting in their rule if they were confident that the system being replaced would be better than the one already in existence. Without such a guarantee, the steps taken to enforce the rule of religious clergy and attendant anarchy would be antithetical to the logic underpinning an Islamic state. Anarchy, he argues, is contrary to human nature and God prefers *batil* (falsehood), or an unjust system, to anarchy and disorder (Ghamidi 2009: 302–9).

The preference for order over anarchy also underpins Ghamidi's criticism of the militant Islamic agenda among groups in Pakistan. Located within his discussion of *Islami inqilab* (Islamic revolution), he argues that regime change through use of force or mutiny forcing a government to relinquish power is neither *wajib* (duty) nor *mustahib* (favoured), and is tantamount to *khuruj* (deviation) in Islam. The faults of a government of Muslims notwithstanding, these two routes to altering the nature of government are only permissible and tolerable if the rulers are committing *kufr*, and the authoritarian nature of the regime was neither established through nor could be removed through the *ra'y* (opinion) of Muslims. The change, however, cannot be attempted without a leader who enjoys the support and confidence of the majority of Muslims, and who migrates to establish an area free of oppression before venturing to fight the unjust Muslim rulers. In the absence of these preconditions being met, attempts to effect a change are un-Islamic. This understanding leads him to the conclusion that efforts by militant groups to gather *fidayeen* (those who sacrifice their lives) to fight a jihad directed against a government could only be equated with *fasad fil ard* (creating disturbance in the land) (Ghamidi 2009: 300).

The apparent support for a status quo in a state for Muslims, however, does not mean that Ghamidi shuns the need to ensure that Pakistan is solidly anchored on the divine will end of the spectrum. In fact, mirroring the ideas promoted by Maududi, he privileges the need for a societal change among Muslims that would make the transition to an Islamic system effortless. Though averse to the role played by Islamic parties (like Jamaat-e-Islami), he argues that conquering the minds of ordinary citizens and significant members of society through slow and gradual education is the best and most effective route to establishing an Islamic system in Pakistan. To this end, he argues for establishing educational and research institutions that accept the primacy of the Qur'an as the source of all guidance, and open discussion among all Muslims irrespective of sectarian differences on the application of Islamic laws in politics, economics, society, culture, education and legislative spaces (Ghamidi 2009: 308). For Ghamidi, therefore, the route to the primacy of divine will requires a focus on the societal space.

Militant Islamic groups that have gained prominence in Pakistan in the last two decades share the preference for societal mobilization as a route to achieving their goals but contest other contours of ideas promoted by scholars like Ghamidi. The policies adopted by the *Tehrik-e-Taliban Pakistan* (TTP) in the northern areas of Swat provide an extreme manifestation of this selective approach. The TTP used a combination of fear and the promise of access to justice as an instrument to garner support and/or acquiescence of the local community to enforce shar'ia and establishing an Islamic state in the area. By destroying girls' schools, punishing men and women for crossing the hudood by lashing and, frequently, beheading, them, they aimed to inculcate fear in the hearts and minds of people so that they would accept the agenda for an Islamic state developed by a small coterie of leaders from the TTP. Unlike Maududi's preference for an *ulama* equipped with religious knowledge, the TTP preferred to accept lax standards to qualify as leaders of the movement: access to *salafi* ideas mediated through layers of cultural understanding and uncritically accepted suffices to qualify someone as a leader or a participant in the Tehrik. With the hope of gradually expanding areas under control, the rule by TTP was to create supportive conditions in which Islamic groups could continue their project of waging jihad. Reminiscent of Qutb's ideas, the targets of jihad for the TTP included the United States as an 'occupier and invader' of Afghanistan and the Pakistani government as an accomplice in the US project.

Some militant groups operating in Pakistan, however, do not prefer the reliance on fear as a route to mobilization at a societal level. Instead they employ mobilizational techniques that focus on convincing the masses of the value of their respective interpretation of Pakistan's Islamic identity in both the domestic and international spheres. Hafiz Saeed, who spearheaded the *Lashker-e-Toiba* (LeT) directly until 2001 and then indirectly as the leader of *Jamaat-ud-dawa* (JUD), for example, falls into this category. Reflecting the ideology of *ahle hadith* (groups and movements emphasizing the use of hadith in Islam) and building upon his links with Saudi Arabian salafis developed over the last three decades, he rejects democracy as the appropriate model of government for Pakistan. His rejection is premised on the distinction between *Tawhid-e-Rabobiyat* and *Tawhid al-wahi'yyat* (or *Tawhid al Ibadah*). He argues that an acceptance of Allah's omnipresence and pre-eminence (*Tawhid-e-Raboobiya*) sets the scene for belief but per se is insufficient to qualify as a good Muslim. Only through *Tawhid al-wahi'yyat*, characterized by an unqualified acceptance of divine sovereignty in all spheres of human lives, could one truly become a good Muslim (Saeed 2001: 20). Extended to societal level, the idea leads him to argue that Muslims are required to establish a system of government that is based on and reflects a commitment to putting Allah's commandments into effect. The expression of divine sovereignty must be evident in all institutions and structures of state and society including banking and judiciary, as well as in the nature and operations of non-governmental organizations.

The shift towards a state manifestation and acceptance of *Tawhid al-wahi'yyat* is closely linked to Saeed's idea of an Emir (leader) who is entrusted with the responsibility and the right to guide the process of Islamization and the gradual mobilization of society in favour of a truly Islamic system of governance. By implication, such a view also acknowledges the significance of the societal space: without a mobilized society, the implementation of a truly Islamic state cannot be established. The process of mobilization, in turn, depends upon providing appropriate education to the masses, irrespective of their level of knowledge of Islam (Qamar 2000: 50). Hafiz Saeed cautions against branding any Muslim as *kaffir* (non-believer): the differences in the level of knowledge of true Islamic practices, in his view, are not tantamount to shirk but indicate a need for guidance to help misguided Muslims progress to the level of *Tawhid al-wahi'yyat*.

An Islamic state, Hafiz Saeed argues, manifests its people's belief in Allah's pre-eminence and unqualified acceptance of divine sovereignty in domestic and foreign policy spheres. In the sphere of foreign policy, for example, an Islamic state unreservedly accepts and supports the idea of jihad. However, he is careful to emphasize that the responsibility to engage in jihad is not dependent upon the establishment of an Islamic state. Instead, he places jihad alongside *da'wa* (call to Islam) as the route through which society can be Islamized: the experience of jihad purifies and strengthens Muslims and they, in turn, draw others to the path of jihad through da'wa. In other words, for Hafiz Saeed, jihad can precede, exist parallel to, or reinforce the process of Islamization in which a society shifts towards the end acknowledging the primacy of divine will. In contrast to the ideas promoted by other militant groups, including the TTP, Saeed opposes targeting the Pakistani government. Instead, he restricts the list of targets to non-Muslims who are actively conspiring to weaken Pakistan and the Muslim *umma* (Muslim community), and occasionally draws attention to this preference to distinguish the JUD (and by implication LeT) from other jihadi groups operating in the region.

Meaning for Pakistan

The question arises as to what this diversity of views at the divine will end of the spectrum means for the future trends of Islamization in Pakistan.

To some extent, the presence of flexible interpretations of Qur'anic injunctions – as evidenced in the approach adopted by Javed Ghamidi – creates the possibility of cooperation among groups across the spectrum of ideas. On the need to amend the blasphemy law, for instance, Ghamidi shares ideas with groups subscribing to variants of the primacy of human will. In fact, he goes beyond the sometimes carefully crafted arguments for amendment to the law to argue that the idea of punishment for offences like blasphemy is not supported by the corpus of Islamic historical practices and law. Such similarity (or near-similarity) of ideas can be harnessed as force for positive change in which the instrumentalization of Islam contributes to the development of more flexible interpretations of religious injunctions, thus serving the needs of those increasingly interested in expressing Pakistani citizens' Islamic identity.

On the other hand, the predominant preference among the Islamists to focus on the societal space with a view to effect a shift to a 'true Islamic state' also harbours dangerous trajectories for Islam in Pakistan. The competition of societal space has and would continue to prompt different religious groups/parties to present themselves as the bearers of the correct interpretation of Qur'anic injunctions and Prophetic practices. While popularizing Islam, it would further increase the possibility of fissures in a society that has already been suffering from problems of militancy and sectarianism. There exists, however, a parallel possibility of those occupying the divine will end of the spectrum to form issue-based alliances that could threaten the government and the space for more flexible interpretations of Pakistan's Islamic identity. The trend has been apparent in the willingness of different religious groups including *Ahle Sunnat, Jamaat-ud-Dawa, Ahle Sunnat Wal Jamaat* and *Sunni Tehreek* to mount *Tehrik Namoos-e-Risalat* to counter any possibility of amending the blasphemy law (*Pakistan Observer* 2011). In the process, these groups have put pressure on the more liberal elements in Pakistan to muffle their voices. Javed Ghamidi was forced to leave Pakistan in fear for his life, and political leaders including Sherry Rahman have also been forced to withdraw their draft resolution to amend the blasphemy law.

The future of Islamization in Pakistan, therefore, is closely tied to activism in the societal space. The state will need to craft carefully strategies that build on the similarity of ideas between a traditional yet flexible *ulama* and liberal elements in the society to gradually shift the tide away from rigid interpretations of Islam. Without such a long-term strategy supported by economic management and increased educational access for ordinary citizens, the instrumentalization of Islam will be further reinforced in the societal space with negative consequences for national and regional stability.

References

Ahmad, I. (2009) 'Genealogy of the Islamic State: Reflections on Maududi's Political Thought and Islamism', *Journal of the Royal Anthropological Institute* vol. 15, Issue Supplement: S145–S162.

Ahmad, Sadaf (2008) 'Identity Matters, Culture Wars: An Account of Al-Huda (Re)defining Identity and Reconfiguring Culture in Pakistan', *Culture and Religion* vol. 9, no. 1: 63–80.

Ahmed, Ishtiaq (1987) *The Concept of an Islamic State: An Analysis of the Ideological Controversy in Pakistan*, London, Frances Pinter, and New York, St Martin's Press.

Ayoob, M. (2005) 'The Future of Political Islam: The Importance of External Variables', *International Affairs* vol. 81, no. 5: 951–61.

Ghamidi, Javaid Ahmad (2006) *Qanoon-e-Siyasat* [The Law of Politics], 2nd edn, Lahore, Al-Mawrid.

—— (2009) *Burhan*, Lahore, Al-Mawrid.

Hizb ut-Tahrir (2009) 'O Muslims of Pakistan!', *Hizb ut-Tahrir Wilayah Pakistan* no. 5, March.

Kirmanj, S. (2008) 'Islam, Politics and Government', *Totalitarian Movements and Political Religions* vol. 9, no. 1: 43–59.

Maududi, S.A. (1991) *Ethical View-Point of Islam*, translated by Khurshid Ahmad, 7th edn, Lahore, Islamic Publications.

—— (1993) *The Process of Islamic Revolution*, Lahore, Islamic Publications.

Musharraf, P. (2004) 'A Plea for Enlightened Moderation', *Washington Post*, 1 June, available at www.washingtonpost.com/wp-dyn/articles/A5081-2004May31.html (accessed 3 May 2009).

Pakistan Observer (2011) 'Tehrik Namoos-e-Risalat Rally Today', *Pakistan Observer* online.

Qamar, Habibullah (2000) 'Iman afroze tarbiyati ijtamiaat', *Mujallatud Da'wa*, April.

Rana, M.A. (2009) *A to Z of Jehadi Organizations in Pakistan*, translated by Saba Ansari, Lahore, Mashal.

—— (2010) 'Hizbut Tahrir in Pakistan: Discourse and Impact', *Conflict and Peace Studies* vol. 3, no. 3: 31–35.

Saeed, A. (2006) *Interpreting the Qur'an: Towards a Contemporary Approach*, London, Routledge.

Saeed, H. (2001) 'Tawhid-Al-Wahi'yyat', *Mujallatud Da'wa* vol. 12, no. 4: 19–21.

Siddiq, K. (ed.) (1993) *Come Let Us Change This World: Selections from Sayyid Maudoodi's Writings*, Lahore, Islamic Publications.

Yasmeen, S. (2003) 'Pakistan and the Struggle for "Real" Islam', in S. Akbarzadeh and A. Saeed (eds), *Islam and Political Legitimacy*, London, Routledge Curzon.

15

Reforming the religious discourse in Saudi Arabia (2001–10)

Eman Mohammad Alhussein

The focus of this chapter is on the different trends and debates concerning the reformation of traditional religious discourse in Saudi Arabia as discussed in the national press – the main arena of cultural and religious debates. These discussions have contributed to the birth of counter-discourses that challenge the mainstream understanding of religion. These reformative trends, which would have been impossible in the 1990s – and even more so in the 1980s – show that there is an urgent need for change in the country's most vital component, the religious establishment. The themes, rationales and obstacles in the way of religious reform will be examined in newspapers, including *Al-Watan*, *Al-Riyadh* and *Okaz*. The reformation process coincided with an internal need to acknowledge the diversity of the Saudi Arabian population in terms of its different sectarian and religious beliefs. The reform has also helped to pave the way for counter-Sunni discourses to be discussed, especially in the annual conference of *Al-Hiwar al-Watani* (the National Dialogue). Lastly, this study will attempt to examine the strength of the religious establishment and how it is losing momentum. The reform by its opponents is reshaping a counter-discourse that embraces not only religion but also other aspects of Saudi Arabia's diverse culture and society.

The study of Saudi Arabia is a challenge as the Kingdom has a multi-layered religious establishment along with a tribal society and ties to a heritage that is emphasised, not only through religion, but also through the culture as a whole. The country has received considerable attention from the international press and media, attracting debate and discussion on the nature of its religious–political elements and foundations. What has recently interested (and sometimes troubled) scholars writing about Saudi Arabia, especially after the terrorist attacks of 11 September 2001, is the firm Sunni teaching embraced by the majority of the inhabitants of the central part of the country, Najd. This school of thought is usually referred to by Western scholars as 'Wahhabism' and has been blamed for radicalism, and accused of spreading its religious hegemonic power to neighbouring countries. Obviously, the 11 September attacks put the Saudi Kingdom under severe pressure to change many of the components that fall under the supervision of its religious establishment, such as education, women's position in the workforce and, specifically, the religious doctrine that governs Saudi Arabian traditions and social order.

The religious authority of Saudi Arabia has always been strong, as its political backing clearly shows. The birth of this authority goes back to the formation of the Saudi state in the mid-1700s. The founder of the first Saudi state, Prince Muhammad ibn Saud, created an alliance with Sheikh Muhammad Bin Abdul Wahhab which granted a two-way legitimacy: the King backed the religious establishment and gave it power to govern society, and the religious authority in turn backed the political authority through its teachings. Since then, the religious authority has influenced different spheres of the Saudi Arabian way of life, resulting in the integration of religion, not only through mosques, but throughout the country's society and culture. What strengthened the religious establishment's legitimacy within society even more was *al-Tayyar al-Sahawi* (religious awakening), which has flourished in the last three decades. Al-Tayyar al-Sahawi is a kind of fusion between the teachings of Sheikh Abdul Wahhab and the thoughts of the Egyptian Muslim Brotherhood. The Egyptian Muslim Brotherhood reached the Kingdom through the movement's members who settled in Saudi Arabia in the 1960s. This tayyar developed deep roots in Saudi Arabian society and dominated the intellectual scene, resulting in a doctrine known as the 'traditional religious discourse'. There was no counter-discourse because any attempt to question would always lead to isolation and caused outrage from the religious authority. Saudi Arabian academics and writers who did not want to face exclusion avoided contravening the effective censorship.

It is vital to look at the major events of the 1990s that played a key role in the Kingdom's political order to fully understand the dimensions and obstacles of the reform process. Niblock (2006: 111) argues that '[t]he interplay between the dynamics of the US–Saudi informal alliance, domestic and external security threats, and the country's Wahhabi religious structures and ideology, has undermined the coherence of policy in all of these areas'. The Gulf War in 1991 resulted in domestic disorder as the large number of US forces stationed in Saudi Arabia caused resentment and disapproval, especially from the religious authority. The Western presence on Saudi soil resulted in new interpretations of religious texts. Many reformers in Saudi Arabia, such as Muhsin al-Awaji, Safar al-Hawwali and Salman al-Odah, were imprisoned for their views that were hostile to the US forces. Therefore, the Saudi Kingdom itself was put in an awkward situation. The relationship with the United States led to disapproval inside and outside the Kingdom, yet breaking away from this relationship might result in weakening its strength in the region and being vulnerable to terrorist activities on its soil, especially in a time when the mujahideen were at the peak of their power (Niblock 2006: 121). Moreover, the Memorandum of Advice, a document addressed to the late King Fahad in 1991 demanding reforms, was signed by a number of Saudi religious scholars. This document created dissent and resulted in the imprisonment of some of its supporters, ending all calls for reform in that period. As a result of the Memorandum of Advice, along with the rise of the mujahideen, more power was given to the official religious establishment, which was in charge of legitimising the Saudi political system in the population (Hamzawy 2006: 4).

Foreign pressure in the wake of 11 September 2001 and King Abdullah's accession to the throne in 2005 played a considerable part in paving the way for reform. Saudi Arabian writers and thinkers began questioning the strengths and weaknesses of the religious teachings as a response to the 11 September attacks. This is because the Saudi press enjoyed a greater level of freedom with the new King's reign compared to the past. The increased freedom encouraged writers and academics to voice their opinions and concerns, demanding a more suitable discourse for this age and time. However, debates, even though they started as early as 2002, did not flourish until 2005. The Saudi population was alarmed by the militant attacks inside the Kingdom, which targeted various cities from Dammam to Mecca from 2003 to 2007. These attacks encouraged reformists to voice their opinion without being ostracized by the population and resulted in a wave of debates regarding the need for religious reform, which will be examined thoroughly in this chapter.

Diffusing the boundaries

Most Western scholars and academics engaged with Saudi Arabia have attempted to draw boundaries between the country's entangled web of religion and politics. This Eurocentric perspective is more of a hindrance than a help to those trying to approach the religious-political structure of the country. The legitimacy of the Saudi Arabian political body itself is tied to the religious authority, which makes the two inseparable on many levels. The judicial system is derived from shari'a (Islamic laws). Moreover, there is a tendency to categorise the country's thinkers into ideological groups such as liberal reformists, moderate Islamists, conservative Islamists, neo-Salafis, neo-Islamists, ultra-conservatives and Islamo-liberals. This way of categorising the different branches of political thought is over-simplistic and obfuscates the intricacies and many layers of the Saudi Kingdom's religious-political life. This is because the emphasis falls on how these schools of thought are implemented inside the Kingdom rather than on studying the dynamics that govern the production of such ideological and political categories. In fact, one major flaw of this Eurocentric approach is that the Kingdom itself is quite diverse in its varied religious schools, even if it usually aspires to one homogeneous religious identity. Hence, any effort to draw a boundary between religion and politics or to fuse liberalism with Islamism will risk falling into the trap of essentialism.

The complexity of ideological and political classifications is reflected in the intellectual debates inside the Kingdom. The criteria for these classifications differ considerably from one person to another among Saudi scholars and the elite. There are no political parties in the Kingdom that can standardise these notions or contain them in a way accessible to the public. Hence, these categories are understood and used differently, and signify diverse, sometimes contradictory, ideas. In fact, liberalism appears to be the most essentially contested concept in the intellectual debate in the Kingdom and has been heavily charged with negative connotations. The definition of 'liberalism' varies among Saudi intellectuals. For those opposing liberalism, it means embracing a counter-ideology as a 'replacement' for Islam, a theoretical framework on life that, if implemented, would undermine all Islamic influence in society. Those in favour of liberalism, however, attack this definition and argue that the liberalism they espouse does not disagree with Islam. They are not interested in the essence, as much as in certain values and ideas that would not clash with any religion (Qasim 2010).

The debate regarding the different ideological categories has dominated the intellectual scene in Saudi Arabia. In fact, it contributed to heated debates resulting in a reluctance to accept pluralism of thought due to the religious establishment's influence that treats concepts such as leftist, secular and liberal with scepticism (Al-Surayhi 2010). This is because when a label is put on a group of Saudi Arabian thinkers as belonging to the liberal school of thought, it implies that they embrace a liberalism that is similar, or even equal, to Western definitions of liberalism. Moreover, the idea of embracing a concept, such as liberalism, that is alien to the Saudi Arabian culture is faced with hostility. Hence, Saudi Arabian intellectuals have been wary of these labels as they create a sense of resentment against the ideas they propose, resulting in intellectual alienation (Al-Mousa 2009). For example, Dr Abuallah al-Ghathami, a Saudi anthropologist who has published extensively on modernity and literary criticism and is viewed as a liberal outside the Kingdom, refuses to acknowledge the existence of a liberal wave inside Saudi Arabia (Qasim 2010). There appears to be a common understanding among Saudi thinkers who are aware of this problem and hence decide not to engage in the ideological and political classifications. Hence, it is vital to study the development of the religious discourse and its reform process outside the boundaries of political schools of thought that might blur, rather than clarify, the nature of this debate.

The problematic notion of *tajdid* and its dynamics

It is important to recognise how religious reform is defined and framed according to Saudi academics and thinkers. In 2003 Hasnaa al-Qunaier discussed the issue. She argued that it is important to distinguish between religious text and religious discourse since there is a tendency to see the two as a continuity of each other. This resulted in shielding religious discourse from criticism, which led to the failure of any attempts to produce a counter-discourse. Moreover, she argues that the Kingdom's intellectual scene for the last 30 years has been 'static' owing to the inevitable domination of the Muslim Brotherhood school of thought (Al-Qunaier 2003). Religion was long thought of, and taught, as a solid entity that could thrive and survive in any time and place. The rhetoric of the religious authority's teaching implies that change is unnecessary. Hence, it is not surprising that attempts have been made to approach *tajdid* (renewal) without clashing with the population's beliefs and ideas by promoting it under different banners such as *tatwir* (development), *tahdith* (modernising), *islah* (reform) and *tashih* (improvement). Yet, the concept of tajdid is embedded in Islamic teachings and is referred to in the *hadith* (reports and actions of the Prophet). Ironically, the country's most celebrated religious figure, Sheikh Mohammad ibn Abdul Wahhab, headed the first tajdid mission which was initially rejected by the mainstream religious Hanbali teachings of that time (Saeed 2006: 130). Sheikh Abdul Wahhab's teachings are now the cornerstone of religious authority and his vision dominates the religious teachings and the social life of the Saudi Arabian people.

Discussion on reforming the religious discourse in Saudi Arabia was initially raised after the 11 September attacks. Reform proposals were initially rejected, as the problem seemed foreign rather than domestic, especially since the United States was openly pushing for reform in the Kingdom (Okruhlik 2005: 190). Diagnosing the errors in the religious arena, and in the curriculum of schools, seemed to be a way of accommodating reaction to the attacks by the United States. This factor alone weakened the argument that the need for reform was vital, since it did not emanate out of the need of the country itself, but from external factors. Moreover, the credibility of the United States was at its lowest point at that time because of its war in Afghanistan and the invasion of Iraq, causing sectarian wars in the latter. The push for reform by the United States itself did not give birth to a counter-discourse within the Kingdom. Instead, it was the violence that struck Saudi cities between 2003 and 2007 that popularised the idea of the reform of religious institutions. This wave of internal violence indirectly catalysed the emergence of counter-discourses, especially by those who were not in favour of the religious authority's domination. Saudi thinkers and writers also realised that the prevailing religious discourse contributed to a radical understanding of religion and was responsible for the militant attacks inside the Kingdom.

There are two approaches to analysing and understanding the definition of reforming the religious discourse. Proponents of the first approach push for reform outside religious boundaries, thinking that the best way to reform the religious discourse is by implementing 'outside' notions that do not correspond to the mainstream religious teachings of the Kingdom. The second group is exclusive to the religious authority that fears reformists' attempts, arguing that it might take the religious discourse from its niche and develop it within other philosophical or ideological frameworks (*Al-Riyadh* 2006). The religious establishment rejects the debate regarding the legality of the claim that reform is essential. Perhaps this is why most reformists seldom discuss their ideas from theoretical frameworks that clash with the religious authority's teachings. Saudi scholars pushing for reform tend to maintain their ideas and arguments within a similar theoretical framework to that of the religious authority as a way of gaining legitimacy and not attracting unwanted attention. For example, Aba al-Khail argues that the Qur'an itself is discursive in its approach in that some of its verses were revealed in Medina. In Medina, the Prophet had his followers, and so the verses were different in style from those when he addressed the inhabitants of Makkah, where there were dissenters. Thus, the discursive nature of the Qur'an is a manifestation of the need to address different audiences who require different sets of rules and approaches (Aba al-Khail 2006). Also, the notion of *ijtihad* (interpretation) is used as a way of introducing reform by arguing that tajdid is another form of *ijtihad*. Al-Mahmoud in *Al-Riyadh* asserts:

> Reforming the religious discourse must stem from the needs of the age in which we live, in all its dimensions. Reform must meet the needs of the time. Renewal of the religious discourse must provide a contingent interpretation that targets certain circumstances of this age. This, of course, is not a proposal to put an end to future interpretation of similar concepts that this discourse will target. It is like opening the door to *ijtihad*, but it is an *ijtihad* that is beyond the traditional mechanisms of interpretation.
>
> *(Al-Mahmoud 2008)*

What makes the study of the emerging discourses interesting is that most of those writing in favour of a counter-discourse have previously belonged to Al-Tayyar al-Sahawi. The writers studied in this chapter, such as Al-Ghaithi and Aba al-Khail, among others, have turned against the religious establishment's teaching. Their deep knowledge of the traditional discourse, which they preached during the 1990s, makes their arguments situated within the religious establishment's theoretical framework. However, they adopt different modes of interpretation through their analysis and examinations. For example, they argue that it is important to distinguish between the two divisions within Islamic shari'a: the *thaabit* (laws that represent the core of Islamic belief and cannot be amended) and the *mutaghyyr* (laws that were imposed owing to certain social and political factors and can be reshaped owing to other factors). The mutaghyyr branch (also called *furu' al-'aqida*, or branches of faith) are the laws that should be targeted by reform and must be reshaped to fit the current social and religious needs (Aba al-Khail 2006). This need to clarify the target of religious reformation is essential in the writing of Saudi scholars and academics. It is crucial to prevent any conflict with the religious authority, as the authority finds the approach a risk to the essence of Islamic teachings. Hence, Saudi reformists argue for a broader perspective on religion that suits the current age by discussing the importance of *fiqh al-waqi'* (contemporary *fiqh*) as a way of pushing for the dominant religious discourse to break away from its static nature when it deals with shari'a law.

Muhsin al-Awaji, one of the first to call for the reform of Islamic discourse, illustrates his argument by stating that a failure of the discourse does not mean a failure of the Islamic faith itself. Rather, the need for reform indicates that Muslim scholars may have failed to translate the religion properly into a discourse. This is because 'the failure of the religious discourse today is the result of a sharp defect in emerging concepts and terms. Moreover, the failure may be attributed to the inclusion of hegemonic religious discourses in Islamic countries, either willingly or unwillingly, which made debate less accepted by the public' (Al-Awaji 2008). Reforming the religious discourse must not be done by adopting modernist concepts to implement superficial changes, but through the evolution of the discourse in a way that solves the problematic nature of the modernist Islamic debates. The features of this new discourse should be characterised as follows:

- The general structure of the new religious discourse must correspond to the 'spirit' of the current age in which we are living, both in our engagement with this discourse as a daily practice, and by presenting it to the 'Other' as the basis for our identity. This is to prevent delivering two discourses: one that is exclusive to the inside, and one for the outside. This new discourse must contain minimal inconsistencies, irrespective of the diversity therein. Consequently, the discourse will be received by both sides as coherent, and not as a bundle of contradictory slogans.

- The new discourse must be able to meet the needs of our culture. This does not mean focusing on solving the problematic issue of the relationship between religion and contemporary issues, but should focus on allowing religion to be an active element in our life and culture as a force, and not as a superficial element.
- Religion in this new discourse must be used to allow acceptance of other religions which have previously been excluded due to sectarian and religious barriers. Consequently, religion will become a medium of communication rather than a medium of denying the 'Other', which is the case with the dominant religious discourse.
- The new discourse must be free from deception and vagueness and should not present two contradictory interpretations regarding the 'Other' in Islam or elsewhere outside the Muslim *umma*. This will require acknowledging the importance of reviving the religious discourse rather than presenting one due to foreign pressures.

(Al-Mahmoud 2008)

Hence, counter-discourses that have emerged since 2005 addressed different issues inside the Kingdom that relate to the different components of society and culture which have been the product of the dominant discourse. The debate on *turath* (heritage) examines why there still exists hostility towards any 'Other' inside the Kingdom since there is no allowance for concepts such as co-existence and pluralism. Also, reformists have questioned the flaws of the religious discourse which, they believe, resulted in the failure to direct its efforts towards strengthening humanitarian values in the same way that it strives to promote purely religious teachings. Moreover, the counter-discourse also examines the role of women in society and investigates the issue of gender segregation and the *takfir* discourse.

Although the renewal of the traditional discourse is always discussed within religious frameworks, it often clashes with one of the most important components of Saudi Arabia's identity and culture, which is the issue of *turath* (heritage). As much as Western academics try to draw a line between politics and religion inside the Kingdom, Saudi thinkers have been equally busy trying to draw a similar line, but between tajdid and turath. Even though turath by definition is an antonym to tajdid, the terms standing at opposite ends of the spectrum, it becomes a central dilemma when social traditions and practices that belong to the country's heritage are justified under the guise of religion. It was unthinkable to argue in the near past that the religious discourse derives some of its teaching from heritage rather than embodying true religious teachings. The issue of the emphasis of heritage within the religious discourse is now widely discussed. This has led reformists to call the dominant religious discourse a 'traditional discourse', dropping 'religious' as a sign of their stance. When religion is at the centre of a society's culture, it becomes the producer of consciousness. The dominant 'traditional discourse' is blamed for governing the consciousness and, hence, the daily life of the Saudi population, making it impossible to achieve revivalism and modernity (Al-Mahmoud 2008). Other Saudi Arabian thinkers argue that fundamentalism and Salafism also derive their mode of interpretations from heritage since the Arabic root for the word fundamental is *asil* (origin). The Saudi writers' attempt to question turath springs out of the realisation that the thoughts that governed the Saudi Arabian dominant discourse are all products of a heritage that intrinsically rejects all attempts at reformation (Al-Ghaithi 2010a). They argue that turath emphasises binary opposites (self vs. Other) that formulated into a 'tribal ideology', which can be seen now in different levels of society (Al-Ghaithi 2010a). Hence these binary opposites that influenced the traditional discourse resulted in a failure to emphasise the importance of Islamic values, which must transcend labels and binary opposites. This illustrates that the counter-discourse is not just seeking a mechanism of interpretation of religious texts but is also targeting the cultural outcome of the traditional religious discourse which resulted in an absence of these values (Al-Mahmoud 2010b). Therefore, essential values in Islam such as humanity, compassion and tolerance seem to have escaped some traditional religious teachings. This frame of mind explains why reluctance to engage in ideological debates resulted in intellectual alienation and the rejection of those who were not in favour of the traditional Islamic discourse. As these laws are derived from turath rather than from pure Islamic teachings, it also explains why women in society have been segregated and their role marginalised.

Outcome of reform

After examining the dynamics and obstacles, the reform process might appear challenging. Nevertheless, the reform has proved to be productive. Judging from the outcomes of this reform, the Saudi Arabian population is experiencing a sense of transformation on different levels of social life. One of the strongest foundations of this reform is *Al-Hiwar al-Watani* (the National Dialogue), which is considered to be a great force for co-existence, or at least acknowledging pluralism within the government. It shows that opinions are now being voiced openly and without restraint. The National Dialogue started in 2003 and is held annually in different cities across the Kingdom, hosting different Saudi speakers every year depending on the subject matter. So far, it has surveyed a number of issues including national unity, Islamic radicalism, the empowerment of women, the future of Saudi youth, and social and sectarian co-existence. Pluralism of religious beliefs and co-existence with different ideological and social groups is one of the main themes advocated by the new religious discourse. Sheikh Hassan al-Saffar, a prominent Saudi Shia clergyman, acknowledges that those pushing for reform of religious discourse have helped in the process of co-existence and especially the acceptance of *al-tanaw' al-mathhabbi* (sectarian pluralism) (Al-Saffar 2010). In the past, the diversity of the Saudi Kingdom had been overlooked. An attempt was made to ignore the many levels of society by advancing homogenous identity, culture, heritage and religious discourse, which led to the suppression of many minorities inside the Kingdom. Hence, pluralism of faith, ideology, race and tribe is one of the most important components for cultural and social development (Aba al-Khail 2003). Al-Mahmoud argues that 'it is important to realise that peaceful co-existence in our community will only be achieved through encouragement of this co-existence on the level of thought' (Al-Mahmoud 2010a).

Reforms relating to women's position in society and the workforce appear to be the most noticeable in the new intellectual debates. When minor reforms were introduced under King Fahd's reign in late 2001 and early 2002, they were strongly opposed by certain religious factions. The merging of the Ministry of Education (which at that time was responsible only for the education of males) with the Presidency for Girls' Education caused consternation among the religious authorities, who pleaded for a rethink of the move. The move was a minor reform that did not allow real mixing between the genders but merely a merging between bureaucratic bodies. The second reform move was the issuing of identification cards for women, which was optional then, but resulted in initial rejection and dismissal. Those writing in favour of these reforms were at that time fewer in number and hence could not stand in the face of the unified religious discourse which voiced its disapproval of the reforms. However, the third annual National Dialogue, held in Medina in 2004, was devoted to the situation of women. It resulted in the discussion of the problems that hinder women's progress in society and what caused this marginalisation. Dr Omar Ba Dahdah, one of the conference guests, discussed his research on women's situation in Saudi Arabia. In this research, he argued that the position of women in the Kingdom is not the result of religious teachings per se, but of social traditions and conventions that are protected under the guise of religion (*Al-Sharq al-Awsat* 2004). Dr Fozyah Abu Khail took a similar stance trying to shed light on the issue of religion and traditions. She argued that both religion and tradition have resulted in the immense confusion and marginalisation of women's role in society. However, reformists argue that the third National Dialogue did not deliver immediate results because of the religious establishment's strong position then which was not in favour of the topic of the third conference. This disapproval was voiced in *khutbat al-jum'a* (Friday sermon) in Makkah, which was directed to the guests in the National Dialogue. This dismissal of the debate topic of the third National Dialogue strengthened the religious establishment's decision-making inside the conference (Al-Shayyeb 2003).

The second wave of reform that started under King Abdullah's reign shows an inclination to move away from the religious establishment's line of thought and ideas. The recent reforms promoted by King Abdullah have contributed to the weak position of the religious authority and illustrate how it is losing its momentum. King Abdullah appointed Dr Norah al-Fayez in 2009 to be the first female deputy education minister, the highest position ever granted to a women in Saudi Arabia. He also founded the King Abdullah University of Technology and Science, which is the first university in Saudi Arabia that allows co-education. Moreover, identification cards for women became obligatory for enrolling in all universities and colleges inside the Kingdom. These changes alarmed certain elements of the religious authority. They held debates that reached their pinnacle in late 2009 with the discussion of *ikhtilat* (gender segregation). Ikhtilat, which would empower women in the workforce, is a subject that has been avoided in previous discussions due to its sensitive nature within Saudi society. Sheikh Saad al-Shethri, a member of *Hay'at Kibar al-'Ulama* (Council of Senior Islamic Scholars), denounced the mixed-gender institution in a television interview. His reaction resulted in a series of criticisms in the Saudi media. Jamal Khashoggi, Editor-in-Chief of *Al-Watan* newspaper, was one of the first to voice disapproval by writing an article stating that the Sheikh was standing in the King's way of reform (Khashoggi 2009). Similarly, the Editor-in-Chief of *Al-Jazirah* newspaper, Khalid al-Malik, argued that the Sheikh's denouncement of the university could prevent any attempt at revivalism and create chaos and intolerance, especially since it was broadcast on television. Newspapers across the Kingdom continued to criticise the Sheikh until he was removed from the Council by a royal decree (al-Malik 2010).

Sheikh Ahmad al-Ghamdi, branch Chief of the Promotion of Virtue and the Prevention of Vice in Makkah, declared that he was against gender segregation in the Kingdom. This was two months after the removal of Sheikh al-Shethri from the Senior Council. Al-Ghamdi argued in an extensive interview with *Okaz* newspaper that it is invalid to argue that the shari'a is in favour of gender segregation. He backed up his argument with evidence from the sunnah and maintained that all the evidence adduced by his opponents to argue for segregation derived from weak Hadith (*Okaz* 2009). He alluded to the fact that heritage and culture are sometimes strongly maintained by the religious authority under the guise of religion and that this is the case with ikhtilat, which is a concept that is alien in shari'a and was never discussed in the old texts, given that it was not an issue then. In fact, al-Ghamdi argues that those who support gender segregation form a type of *bid'a* (innovation), which is usually an accusation that the religious authority levels at anyone who introduces new ideas to Islam.

This declaration led to an uproar because a member of the official religious establishment had broken away from the dominant mainstream. After al-Ghamdi's declaration, the Saudi Press Agency, the official broadcaster of the country's news, reported that he had been dismissed from his job. However, two hours after this announcement, it had to withdraw its report (Ba Amer 2010). The government banned newspapers from publishing the news of his dismissal on their front pages. This shows that the decision was not backed by the government and in fact ran counter to the King's vision of reform. Khalid al-Dakhil, a Saudi academic, argues that the incident was an attempt to send a clear message to those in power in the religious establishment that internal reform was needed. In fact, it appears that those who follow the views of al-Ghamdi are believed to be protected by the new King, who is clearly in favour of reforming the religious establishment, and encourages people like al-Ghamdi to take a stand. This puts more pressure on the traditional religious discourse to stay open to reform ideas. Al-Dakhil argues that:

> there is an internal conflict in the Commission which has been hit since 2008 by a wave of criticism by the local press institutions, which gives an impression that there is a green light from the political authority to criticise the most vital organ of the government: its religious establishment.
>
> *(Ba Amer 2010)*

The debate on gender segregation revealed a plurality inside the establishment, something which rarely happens and will inevitably lead to a counter-discourse *within* the religious establishment itself (Al-Ghaithi 2010b). It might not be the birth of a counter-discourse inside the religious establishment per se, but of a restructuring of the establishment's discourse, which had been accused of flaws and intolerance.

The examples surveyed so far are essential to illustrate the different waves of reform before and after 2005. The religious authority voiced its disapproval of the National Dialogue of 2003 as women's issues were discussed. The Imam of the Sacred Mosque in Makkah, Saud al-Shuraym, delivered the Friday sermon one week before the meeting in Medina. He stressed the importance of following shari'a when discussing women's position in Islam and Saudi society. On the other hand, when Saad al-Shethri was dismissed from the Senior Council after his declarations on gender segregation in 2009, the religious establishment did not voice any objection. On the contrary, the Friday sermon in Makkah, two days after the royal decree, was devoted to the support of the university, calling it a 'blessing' from the King to the Saudi Arabian population (Al-Arabiya 2009). This clearly implies that the Saudi political body is breaking away from granting the religious authority unlimited power. Moreover, the religious authority's unified line of thought and ideas ceased to be solid as a new group of scholars within the official establishment endeavours to be accommodating of the current political discourse, which favours reformative trends.

Another obstacle to initiating reformative discourses in Saudi, whether through criticism or suggestion, was the *takfir* accusation (*takfir* refers to declaring someone a non-Muslim). The *takfir* discourse is seen as an ideology that is rooted firmly in the traditional teachings of the religious authority causing alienation and social ostracism (Al-Mahmoud 2010c). This wave of *takfir* continued even after 2005, when Sheikh Saad al-Barrak issued *fatwas* against two of the reformists. The reformists, Yousef aba al-Khail and Abdullah bin Bejad al-Otaibi, wrote against the traditional religious discourse in *Al-Riyadh*. In fact, Sheikh al-Barrak attacked the newspaper, calling for the political authority to ban similar articles from appearing in newspapers and claiming that anyone who distributed, published or spread such ideas would fall under the same *takfir* label (Islamway 2008). The fatwa was received with shock in the Kingdom but it did not stop the authors, who have continued publishing weekly, nor did it eliminate writings that follow the same reformist trend. As a way of strengthening it, the fatwa was supported by other writers and Sheikhs, but that does not seem to have helped. In fact, it contributed to more writings that explored and analysed the nature of the *takfir* discourse, arguing that the binary opposites that flourished in the traditional religious discourse are in fact the product of the wave of *takfir* as a way for the religious authorities to exercise their religious hegemony (Al-Khshiban 2007). This fatwa led the *Majlis al-Shura* (Consultative Assembly) to demand serious consideration on the issue of *takfir* from the Senior Ulama Council, demanding laws that would monitor and prevent *takfir* from spreading among religious institutions (*Al-Sharq al-Awsat* 2010).

Conclusion: evaluating the reform process

The reform process in the Kingdom has been informed by the political authority and the religious establishment. The political power in the Kingdom has not attempted to introduce extensive changes that would result in an unconstructive response by the religious establishment. This was the norm until King Abdullah's accession to the throne. For example, when King Faisal opened schools for girls in the early 1960s, hostility and fear dominated the reaction of the Saudi Arabian people. On the other hand, those hoping for a removal of the ban on women driving have not received any assurances that the issue will be considered. Hence, it is vital that both authorities, the political and the religious, are eager to accept reform and that intellectuals' calls for change are tolerated. The Saudi Arabian King is pursuing open 'dialogue' on the different levels of the Kingdom's educational and cultural spheres. Domestically, dialogue is promoted by the National Dialogue and Cultural Dialogue, and internationally, with the Interfaith Dialogue. Here we see clear evidence of dialogue as opposed to suppression.

Persistent questions remain: How strong will this reformative phase prove to be in the face of resistance from the established religious authorities? Will it be able to carry out all the aims and concerns that are called for in the press? It appears that the struggle between the reformists and the religious authority has passed the most critical stage; the immunity of the religious discourse and its scholars is now under serious scrutiny, with the introduction of pluralism of thought and the multiple religious debates that started from 2005. Consequentially, the religious authority is no longer granted carte blanche as the legitimate religious body in the Kingdom. This is reflected by the administrative changes within the Council of Senior Ulama. These reforms promise the most for women, who can now question previous fatwas that caused them limited mobility, both socially and globally. Now, the fatwa that banned women from driving due to ikhtilat can be reconsidered, as ikhtilat is no longer perceived as a threat to Saudi Arabian society. These reforms will also empower Saudi women in the workforce, as segregation was rampant.

There is, indeed, a maturity in the Saudi Arabian intellectual scene, especially with regard to those trying to counter the dominant religious discourse. Reformists, who used to belong to the religious establishment school of thought, are not rejecting the traditional religious teachings. On the contrary, this transformation indicates a maturity and an attempt to understand religious teachings within the context of this critical time in the development of the Kingdom. Abdullah al-Otaibi, Yousef Aba al-Khail, Shetiwi al-Ghaithi, Faris ibn Hizam and Mansour al-Nuqaydan all needed to experience both phases in order to construct a discourse that meets Saudi Arabia's social needs and does not contradict the important values and belief systems. Clerics such as Salman al-Odah and Muhsin al-Awaji also joined the reformists' wave, even though they headed al-Tayyar al-Sahawi. The promise of a balanced society seems to be prevailing, since the religious discourse does not stand as the sole doctrine of the current intellectual debate. These counter-discourses will lead to a re-evaluation of the needs of Saudi Arabian society, and how it defines itself in terms of the domestic and the global 'Other'. Also, the debates finally taking place inside the religious establishment itself might open the door to more pluralism and allow more interpretations that do not stand as obstacles in the contemporary daily lives of the Saudi Arabian people.

The 'traditional religious discourse' of Saudi Arabia is the product of the religious establishment's control of the country's educational system, social laws and culture. Thus, reforming it promises vast changes to the Kingdom. Some remain sceptical about these reforms, wondering whether they are merely a façade with no strong fundamental executive power. However, these reforms are not perceived as trivial by the Saudi public, who are aware that ten years ago it was unthinkable to question the religious authority, demand pluralism and co-existence or question the role of women in society. In conclusion, it is important to note that the plurality of thought that the Kingdom is enjoying today does not mean that it is breaking away from religion. In fact, religion is the core of the country's teachings, culture and society. It is merely that these new voices evaluate the discourse itself to underline the essential beliefs at the heart of Islam by calling for a more lenient version of religion which accommodates different schools of thought that celebrate pluralism, co-existence and tolerance.

References

Aba al-Khail, Y. (2003) 'Al-ikhtilaf namuus kawni' [Diversity is a universal law], *Al-Riyadh*, 15 December, available at www.alriyadh.com (accessed 25 May 2010).
——(2006) 'Tajdid al-khitab al-dini' [Reviving the religious discourse], *Al-Riyadh*, 16 November, available at www.alriyadh.com (accessed 25 May 2010).
—— (2010) 'Al-hadatha bayna al-salaf wa al-khalaf' [The debate of modernism between traditionalists and modernists], *Al-Riyadh*, 30 January, available at www.alriyadh.com (accessed 25 May 2010).
Al-Arabiya (2009) 'Al-Sheikh Al-Sudais: Wajb jami' al-ulama mubarakat iftitah jami'at almalek Abdullah' [All Ulama must give their blessings to the opening of King Abduallah University], 9 October, available at www.alarabiya.net (accessed 25 May 2010).
Al-Awaji, M. (2008) 'Tajdid al-khitab al-dini baya matraqat al-atba' wa sindaan al-khosuum' [Renewal of religious discourse between the opponents and allies], 12 January, available at www.aljazeera.net (accessed 24 May 2010).
Al-Ghaithi, S. (2010a) 'Interview', *Ida'at*, Al-Arabiya, 21 May.
—— (2010b) 'Al-ikhtilat: hal yqawwidh al-khitab al-taqlidi?' [Mixing of genders: will it undermine the traditional discourse?], *Al-Watan*, 26 March, available at www.alwatan.com.sa (accessed 28 May 2010).
Al-Khshiban, A. (2007) 'Al-bahth 'an al-Islam al-hadi' [In search of a peaceful Islam], *Al-Watan*, 8 July, available at www.alwatan.com.sa (accessed 28 May 2010).
Al-Mahmoud, M. (2008) 'Tajdid al-khitab al-dini: Al-Islam mu'assiran' [Renewal of religious discourse: a contemporary Islam], *Al-Riyadh*, 16 November, available at www.alriyadh.com (accessed 22 May 2010).
—— (2010a) 'Darurat al-ta'ayush: Mojtama' bela mutatarifin' [The importance of co-existence: a society free from extremism], *Al-Riyadh*, 20 May, available at www.alriyadh.com (accessed 22 May 2010).
—— (2010b) 'Al-insan al-gha'ib: taratubyyat al-qyym' [The absence of humanity: a hierarchy of values], *Al-Riyadh*, 22 April, available at www.alriyadh.com (accessed 22 May 2010).
—— (2010c) 'Murawahat wa murawaghat al-khitab al-takfiri' [The maneuverings of the *takifir* discourse], *Al-Riyadh*, 21 January, available at www.alriyadh.com (accessed 22 May 2010).
Al-Malik, K. (2010) 'Khuturat al-fatwa fi ghayri makaniha' [The dangers of misplaced fatwas], *Al-Jazirah*, 30 September, available at www.al-jazirah.com (accessed 22 May 2010).
Al-Mousa, A. (2009) 'Interview', *Ida'at*, Al-Arabiya, 14 July.
Al-Qunaier, H. (2003) 'Tajdid al-khitab al-dini wa Ikhtiraaq hajiz al-samt' [The renewal of religious discourse and breaking the wall of silence], *Al-Riyadh*, 30 November, available at www.alriyadh.com (accessed 25 May 2010).

Al-Riyadh (2006) 'Salman al-Odah: tajdid al-khitab al-dini darurah li ikhraj al-umma mn hatha al-tayh' [The renewal of religious discourse: a necessity to get the nation out of this labyrinth], 5 December.

Al-Saffar, H. (2010) 'Tajrubat al-hiwar al-watani bada't tu'ti thimaraha' [The National Dialogue experience has proven to be fruitful], *Al-Riyadh*, 2 June, available at www.alriyadh.com (accessed 5 June 2010).

Al-Sharq al-Awsat (2004) 'Al-hiwar al-watani al-thalith yabhath al-mu'awiqat al-ijtima'iyah wa al-qanuniyah allati taqf amam nayl al-mara al-saudiya kamil huquqiha' [The Third National Dialogue discusses the social and legal obstacles that prevent Saudi women from obtaining their rights], 12 July, available at www.awsat.com (accessed 25 May 2010).

—— (2010) 'Ba'da fatawa al-takfir: hay'at kibar al-ulama tabhath aydan tajrim tamwil al-irhab' [After the takfir fatwas: the Senior Council of Ulama discusses laws against terrorism funding], 11 April, available at www.aawsat.com (accessed 23 May 2010).

Al-Shayyeb, J. (2003) 'Al-mar'a fi al-hiwar al-watani wa ma ba'duh' [Discussion of women's concerns in the National Dialogue and its results], *Al-Jazeera*, 3 October, available at www.aljazeera.net (accessed 24 May 2010).

Al-Surayhi, S. (2010) 'Al-tasnifat al-fikriyyah tush'il fatil al-muwajahhah bayna al-tayyarat al-thaqafyyah' [Intellectual labels provoke confrontation between various cultural groups], *Al-Riyadh*, 27 March: 14.

Ba Amer, Y. (2010) 'Sahb iqalat Al-Ghamdi yuthir jadallan Saudiyyan' [Withdrawal of Al-Ghamdi's dismissal causes debate in Saudi Arabia], 24 April, available at www.aljazeera.net (accessed 23 May 2010).

Hamzawy, A. (2006) 'The Saudi Labyrinth: Evaluating the Current Political Opening', *Carnegie Papers* vol. 8, available at carnegieendowment.org (accessed 25 July 2010).

Islamway (2008) 'Bayaan fi munasarat fatwa al-allama Abdulrahman al-Barrak' [Declaration to support allama Abdulrahman al-Barrak], 19 March, available at www.islamway.com (accessed 27 May 2010).

Khashoggi, J. (2009) 'Al-Sheikh Al-Shethri wa qanat Al-Majd … lima al-tashwish wa nahnu fi khayrin mn dinina wa dunyana?' [Sheikh Al-Shethri … why the disruption in these peaceful times?], *Al-Watan*, 29 September, available at www.alwatan.com.sa (accessed 28 May 2010).

Niblock, T. (2006) *Saudi Arabia: Power, legitimacy and survival*, Routledge, London.

Okaz (2009) 'Al-qawl bi tahrim al-ikhtilat ifti'at ala al-shari' wa ibtida' fi al-din' [Forbidding mixing between genders is a deceptive interpretation to shari'a], 10 December, available at www.okaz.com.sa (accessed 26 May 2010).

Okruhlik, G. (2005) 'Empowering civility through nationalism: reformists Islam and belonging in Saudi Arabia', in R.W. Hefner (ed.), *Remaking Muslim politics: Pluralism, contestation, democratization*, Princeton, NJ, Princeton University Press.

Qasim, A. (2010) 'Al-libraliyya: fawda al-fahm wa so' al-tamthil' [Liberalism: chaos of understanding and misuse of representation], *Al-Watan*, 1 March, available at www.alwatan.com.sa (accessed 28 May 2010).

Saeed, A. (2006) *Islamic Thought: An introduction*, Routledge, London.

16

De-territorialized Islamisms

Women's agency of resistance and acquiescence

Shahin Gerami

Islamist movements are multi-faceted narratives of patriarchy, traditionalism and globalization. Globalization has created a complex and fast-moving construct that informs Islamist movements at home and in the diaspora. Undeniably, two strands inform the contour of these movements: the gender arrangement and de-territorialization. Nuanced elaborations are offered to tease out women's agency inside the movement and in resistance to it. Women's resistance to demands of domesticity and modesty has been clearly marked as the embodiment of agency. Whether other forms of response, acquiescence or embracement of these codes constitute agentic actions has been debated mostly by Western-trained feminists, including this author. In this article, borrowing from Bourdieu, I will interrogate the habitus of agency with regard to its fields of expression.

Islamisms in global social fields

Global capitalism has given rise to a new configuration of gender relations. Institutionalization of gender inequalities centers on the subordination of women but incorporates a hierarchy of masculinities in a variety of patriarchal settings. Islamisms are traditionalists, patriarchal and gendered social movements against perceived or real threats from globalism to their cultural fields. Gender arrangements have been reified and maintained by these ideological systems and have remained more entrenched and rigid than other ideological systems of inequalities. Gender hierarchies that are rooted in some religious framework have proven more resilient than class, ethnic or national hierarchies. Even though other forms of inequalities endure, their 'god-given' bases have been effectively questioned. The essentialist justification of gender inequality is still strong. While biological (natural) essentialism has been somewhat questioned, the ordained essentialism has gained new potency through faith-based radicalisms including Islamist movements. It is imperative to make the gendered and global nature of Islamisms visible and brought into focus.

Islamist patriarchies and globalization

With the advent of global capitalism, new gender relations challenging alternative patriarchies have emerged. Traditional patriarchies have sustained the domination of masculine over feminine through biological essentialism reinforced by faith-based codes.[1] The male elite maintain their power by stigmatizing the female and the ethnic male. This allows for gender segregation in bi-spherical domains of private and public, with public controlling most economic resources, managing the polity and claiming doctrinal authority of the faith. Cultural and structural conditions of a region or a nation influence these systems, making them more potent or moderating their scopes. Despite their diversity of contents and forms, traditional patriarchies are associated with a paid labor market that is male and a large, unpaid labor arrangement that is female. This system does not preclude areas of female power and economic advantage and pockets of male economic and political subordination.

Until colonialism, traditional patriarchies remained intact and maintained many of their structural and cultural specificities. Colonialism was the beginning of the global threat to traditional patriarchies. Colonizers and the missionaries challenged traditional patriarchies and, depending on the interest of the colonial power pitched them against each other. The domesticity of Muslim women became a sign of backwardness of Arab nations and the free engagement of the Native American women was a sign of their savagery. The former must be brought to the public arena and the latter must be forced to dress modestly and become domesticated.

During wars of liberation, elements of traditional patriarchies became incorporated into nationalist ideologies and thus became solidified as part of a national cultural heritage. We find elements of traditional patriarchies in a variety of liberation ideologies from Marxism to Islamisms to Liberation Theology (Ahmad 1992; Smith 1991). Traditional patriarchies survived well into the early industrialization of the South, but the global economy is making their social codes of ascribed privileges obsolete. These systems are restrictive and too culturally specific for the capitalist global economy.

Globalized capitalism demands constant growth, which requires faster and cheaper production accompanied by an ever-increasing consumption. Modernization processes spread the ideals of social justice and introduced new governing systems to achieve them, but the success of early modernization trends was limited to their carrier vehicles, which were slow and gradually co-opted by traditional patriarchies. The new inexpensive socio-technologies have spread the ideals of modernization faster and wider.[2] What started with the cheap transistor radio is spreading much faster with the new virtual social fields of communication (Connell 2005; Bunt 2003).

At the global level, capitalism recruits women as low-cost laborers but generous consumers. Gender-exclusionary arrangements of traditional patriarchies are obstacles to this producer/ decision-maker consumer. Liberation of the 'others' from restrictions of national sovereignty, cultural authenticity, racial segregation and gender seclusion allows for freer transfer of labor and products. Global gender roles intensify exploitation of some while promoting equality measures among others. The transnational sex industry, diffusing unregulated, spreads death and destruction among many women and children of the South, while sweatshops and automated assembly lines give some women their first entry into the paid labor market (Gibson-Graham 1996). Neither should be lauded, but both are aspects of this global gender arrangement.

Global social fields and Islamist gender arrangements

The encroaching global hegemony and its associated de-territorialization have seriously threatened specificity of traditional Islamic patriarchies. Exclusionary gender arrangements based on codes of domesticity and modesty have remained salient markers of this Islamic authenticity. Bourdieu's ontology of social fields with associated habitus delivers a malleable toll to place women's agency in interrelated global fields of Islamisms. This modulating construct as 'a series of institutions, rules, rituals, conventions, categories, designations, appointments and titles which constitute an objective hierarchy, and which produce and authorize certain discourses and activities', and that which counts as valuable 'capital' (Danaher *et al.* 2002: 21–22) is quite fitting for what goes as globalism in twenty-first-century discourse.

Women's responses and their variations of agency to Islamisms are challenges to feminist observers, and often headaches for the movements' leaders. Muslim women move in and out of cultural fields, claiming and discarding modes of agency. As McLeod reminds us:

> This requires acknowledging the contradictory effects and dissonance of crossing different fields, and more sustained attention to questions of how gender identities and relations are changing or being re-articulated in new but familiar ways. In such a view, a more uneven and less seamless relation between habitus and field is possible, and this offers scope for feminist analysis of change and continuity.
>
> *(McLeod 2005: 13)*

Therefore, taken together, habitus and fields locate women's responses to de-territorialized Islamisms. This framework allows us to identify agency as it evolves a cross-section of micro-habitus and macro-social fields.

The structural constructs of global Islamisms inform modalities of agency and embodiment of identity for women in interrelated and fluid social fields. De-territorialized Islamism reflects a dynamic cultural field changing with the fluctuation of larger globalized social institutions. The latter offers complex economic trends which are at times exploitative and occasionally equalizing. The social technologies threaten the specificity of Islamisms, while allowing it to reach its potential seekers further and faster. The politico-cultural messages diffused by the first two modalities pose fast-moving challenges to Islamist patriarchies. These interconnected fields in turn challenge our analytical categories and call for keen eyes toward changing gender identities inside and outside diaspora communities. In crossing these different yet fluid fields, women embody agency in amazing habitus.

Body coverage is the most recognized symbol of Islamic patriarchy, and it is also the most utilized tool to embody women's agency to resist or engage with Islamisms. The embodiment of Islamisms is problematized by women's responses by either acquisition of hijab or resistance to it. De-territorialized Islam is rapidly changing gender habitus with changing social fields. What passes as gender habitus at home morphs into a new set of constructs in the diaspora. Islamists respond to these global fields of Westernized social roles, economic fluctuations, geographical redrawing and virtual communities by heightened gender reconsideration.

> Shopping in Harrods last week, I came across a group of women wearing black burkhas, browsing the latest designs in the fashion department. The irony of the situation was almost laughable. Here was a group of affluent women window shopping for designs that they would never once be able to wear in public.
>
> *(Khan 2009)*

This remark, made by a self-declared Muslim woman, captures the perceived irony of identity embodiment. In a case study of Iranian women's agency, Gerami and Lehnerer delineated a typology of agency inclusive of collaboration, acquiescence, co-optation and subversion (Gerami and Lehnerer 2001: 561). Here I propose two broad modalities based on numerous case studies in de-territorialized Islamisms: *acquiescence* and *resistance*. Acquiescence can be expressed, among many forms, by the embracing of Islamic codes or by collaborating to further them. Resistance is any overt action against, or covert subversion of, the codes.

Resistance is the commonly recognized form of agency to social norms of patriarchy and, by association, the mandates of seclusion and modesty. The discourse of embodiment recognizes agency as a form of resistance to Islamist patriarchy mostly expressed through hijab. The feminist epistemology has a rich literature of analyzing women's subversion of these codes. It is the acquisition and collaboration by women that begs the question and is often problematic in discerning the embodiment of agentic identity.

The Evangelical or New Christian Right movement in the USA is a rich source of literature on women's expression of agency through support for a patriarchal movement. By acquiring and embracing a New Christian Right habitus, many American women spearheaded and then led the 'Stop ERA' movement that defeated the Equal Right Amendment that would have made gender equality constitutional (Klatch 1994; Gerami 1996).

In an ethnographic study of Mosque movement in Egypt during the 1990s, Mahmood posits women's acquisition of modesty as agentic. She relates women's effort in learning and understanding the Qur'an and then using this self-directed educational process to cultivate docility and endurance. These habits of becoming shy and accepting their fate, she insists, are examples of agentic embodiment. She acknowledges that agency is mostly recognized as resistance to subordination 'and for women from structures of male domination' (Mahmood 2001: 206). Nevertheless, she calls upon feminists to reconsider this liberal habitus of agency as the only venue, and to rethink agency as 'capacity for action that historically specific relations of subordination enable and create' (Mahmood 2001: 203). She reminds us that the feminist paradigm is both analytical and political, and to be aware that desire for liberty and freedom should not be taken for granted as the only subtext of any habitus of agency; rather, to allow that agentic actors privilege other socio-historical fields. Therefore, in the narrative of the participants in her observations, cultivating shyness and promoting endurance (*sabr*) – to accept their fate – become embodiment of agency.

Korteweg (2008) refers to embedded agency in the dichotomy of resistance and acceptance. In this case she problematizes how Muslim women responded to family arbitration based on shari'a codes. The Ontario arbitration act of 1991 allowed for religious arbitration in private matters. Thus, religious arbitration became prevalent by Christian and Jewish tribunals. When a Muslim lawyer set out to establish such an arbitration tribunal under shari'a codes, the debate focused on protecting women from Islamic subordination. Once again, resistance was privileged as the agency and the voice of those advocating for a modulated implementation of Islamic shari'a were deemed suppressive of women's voice. Korteweg posits that a more nuanced analysis would have allowed for 'embedded agency' in which divergent voices occupy divergent social fields of action.

The large-scale immigration of Muslims from the Global South to the Global North has created enclave social fields constrained by forces of integration from the host and pulls of authenticity from the home. Thus, in places like Ontario and most of the Western European countries, these enclaves seek authenticity in the face of subsuming host cultures. During the early 1990s multiculturalism and tolerance for diversity gradually gave way to integrationism and heightened xenophobia. Socio-economic uncertainties and fear of immigrants have led to stricter laws on émigrés from ex-colonial territories. In 2004, when the French National Assembly and Senate voted in favor of a law to ban religious symbols in public spaces, the headscarf debate became official state politics. The politics of women's covering in European countries has taken a turn to restriction as the enclave communities display more signifiers in women's dress. Birgit Sauer (2009) uses the three macro indicators of secularism, immigration policies and commitment to gender equality in search of comparative approaches in Germany, the Netherlands and Austria. She reports that privileged habitus of liberalism and state religious neutrality policy are renegotiated when there is concerted effort from the émigrés to establish identity and from the host to construct the 'other'.

Pnina Werbner, however, detects venues of agency in the discursive relationship between the émigré Pakistani community to enforce codes of shame and honor and the larger British culture. The Muslim youth, caught between these conflicting cultural fields, she reports, have carved out agency by 'veiling and purdah for women and beard and prayer for men' (Werbner 2007: 171). She contends that their habitus of acquiescence to de-territorialized Islamisms of Britain is congruent with resistance to their parents' habitus of Pakistani Islamism. In this case, Werbner maintains that British multicultural education is more tolerant of the French dealing with the headscarf. Ironically, it was Jack Straw, the leader of the UK's House of Commons and a member of the British Labour Party, who stated his objection against Muslim women wearing the niqab (BBC 2006).

Interestingly, as the global sex and fashion industries have reduced women's body coverage to a bare minimum at exorbitant prices, some Muslim women have expanded their veil to the niqab and burkha in public. In January 2010 the French Prime Minister, François Fillon, followed a parliamentary committee's recommendation and asked for a law banning women from wearing the face veil, or niqab. The law would deny veiled women services in public facilities from post offices to schools, universities, public transport, etc. Later, Italy followed suit (Fraser 2006). The discourse of the veil or face mask in Western Europe calls for even more flexible vision to dissect the intersectionality of fields of operation. When the second generation of European-educated Muslim women who live in Muslim communities (and are therefore subject to virtual social fields of Islamisms) 'choose' to veil, they embody agency in a variety of formats, from resistance to European habitus to acquiescence to Islamist codes. At times, the habitus of veiling contains resistance to the hegemony of the host culture in favor of another masculine hegemonic code of Islamism of their community; a reconstituted habitus from fragments of both cultural fields (Werbner 2007; Knott and Khokher 1993).

Body-Gendrot elaborates on the French anti-veiling law which liberates those who do not want to veil but are coerced by their family and men in their communities. This, indeed, is a major marking field for émigré communities. Stigmatized by the host communities, Islamic communities seek to set themselves apart by reconstructing fluid identities from cultural fragments of the host's liberalism and their home's Islamisms. When considering women's embodiment of habitus, it is crucial to consider construction of ethnic social fields as the last resort of a disassociated and alienated émigré population. A militant cultural field has been emerging from the hosts' xenophobia, strained economies and émigré men's lack of skills to be integrated into the host countries. Community pride calls for visible actions to show that they do not want to be integrated anyway. Once again, the women's habitus become the demarcation for men to claim their authenticity. It is unclear how many women select, or are coerced to veil in diaspora communities. The French presidential commission on the headscarf issue reported community harassment of unveiled girls (Body-Gendrot 2007: 293). One can assume, in cases like the one in France, that the more the community is under pressure, the more women may perceive their duty to preserve the cultural authenticity of their community by embodiment of their habitus. Body-Gendrot states that men, fathers, brothers and others 'remained silent because they did not feel they "belonged" to the receiving country' (Body-Gendrot 2007: 298).

Rachel Bloul (1998) contends that men construct these imagined communities and use women's acquiescence as markers to outsiders. Thus, as Islamisms become more de-territorialized, there is more ethnicization by Muslim men, using the discourse of individual right, freedom and secularity to construct ethnic legitimacy. Bloul reports that it was men who sought to use women as demarcation: 'Maghrebi fathers and religious hierarchies were joined by Catholic and Jewish clerics who demonstrated unreserved support for the veil. Together, they opposed the free circulation of women in the fraternal and secular French' (Bloul 1998: 38).

Would women wear the niqab to make men feel honorable again? Is this embedded agency coercion, or is it an example of women keeping the peace in the household or in the larger community? Can one group's agency become another group's coercion? Women, who embody hijab for identity construction, can coerce those rejecting or resisting the habitus to comply. When older women embody the hijab to appease their community or for the sake of their own identity, they often force the less powerful younger women to comply with this ethnic signifier.

Iranian women and macro-level cultural fields of agency

In her study of marginalized young women, McLeod refers to their encounter with 'emergent, new or uneven patterns of gender alongside traditional and retraditionalized arrangements of gender, seeing how these are then lived out'. She then asks: 'How do their habits or practices of reflexivity position them, and/or how might experiences of dissonance and contradiction prompt reflexive insight into the self?' (McLeod 2005: 16). Many case studies or macro-analyses of Iranian women's engagement with the Islamic Republic of Iran ponder or problematize this experience of dissonance and contradiction and how women claim or discard agentic formulas.

Another example of what Korteweg calls embedded agency is the Iranian women's response to the mandates of modesty and domesticity proscribed by the Islamic Republic of Iran. The Islamic Republic has mainstreamed Islamism nationally and has redefined the Islamist mandates internationally. The 1979 Islamic Revolution revamped many organizational bases of Iranian society and restructured them according to some experimental Islamic framework. Social and cultural constructs of gender arrangements have received the bulk of the new regime's attention. Other reconstructed areas were ethnic identities, class hierarchies and educational foundations. Added to this restructuring was the Eight-Year War resulting from the Iraqi invasion in 1980.

The revolutionary movement was fueled by extreme class disparities and discursive cultural narratives, and started as an opposition to the Shah's regime. The haphazard modernization and arrested value transformation created a massive rift between traditional patriarchies and the new semi-modernized royal patriarchy. The revolutionary leaders cast the Pahllavi regime and its associated patriarchal narrative as weak, 'Westoxicated' and un-Islamic. A strong dose of Islamic patriarchy was needed to control cultural infiltration of the domestic sphere by foreign (Western) values and to confront international imperialism and Zionism. The Islamic regime fabricated a national patriarchy under the leadership of mullahs and their armed and civilian enforcers. It replaced the national patriarchy of the monarchy under the Shah as the father, with the Islamic patriarchy under the Ayatollah.

In its 30th anniversary year, the Republic leaders have established the hegemony of Islamism with very potent gender symbolisms, both male and female. Throughout Iran, one can still see a revolutionary slogan, whether produced in elaborate state-sponsored murals or charcoal writings, stating: 'Sister your *hijab* is your *shahadat*.' This summarizes the regime's original gender plans that women's modesty and domesticity complement men's martyrdom. These gender assignments of men shedding their blood for the revolution and women protecting their body and therefore men's honor were the cornerstones of the new Republic. In retrospect, the nascent globalism of the 1980s and the vigorous Islamism of the Iranian Revolution generated colliding social fields that are still reverberating today. The current de-territorialized Islamisms owe a lot to these counter-focal forces reacting to each other.

The Islamic Revolution was a large-scale movement of authentication of Islamism against encroaching global fields in the second half of twentieth century. By then the social fields of the Cold War were obsolete. It was a gendered movement with the unmistakable objective of Islamicizing gender relations. An important element of this habitus was to safeguard the Islamic family. A revamping of social fields followed. Therefore, a complicated legal system driven from the shari'a, administrative regulations, overlapping bureaucracies and street narratives emerged. Women were cajoled into acquiescence and, when needed, force was used to ensure their submission to the demands of the new patriarchy. Urban middle-class women paid in terms of status and lost paid labor. Lower-class and rural women lost out to chaotic central planning and the war economy. Legally instituting the shari'a was damaging to institutional protection for women (Moghissi 1994; Esfandiari 1997; Gerami and Lehnerer 2001).

The emerging hegemony of Islamism has been a dialectical process in which many vested groups have participated and influenced its contour. On the one hand, implementation of the shari'a has had negative consequences for women, but on the other hand, women, and some men, through reinterpretation (*ijtihad*) of the scripture have impeded its progression and even carved out new, unforeseen rights.

Legal changes have reduced women's family rights. Mandatory hijab has created a complex discursive of oppression, resistance and creativity. Meanwhile, the technocrats, in cooperation with some *ulama*, have instituted highly effective family planning and fertility management for families (Population Reference Bureau 2009). On the economic front, populism has given way to the pragmatism of state capitalism. There has been some success in resource distribution, which is rife with corruption. Service programs like free education, basic national health (including reproductive health) and subsidized transportation are still in effect. Overall, there have been some concrete gains for a segment of the lower-income population associated with economic uncertainty and widespread unemployment.

Iranian women engage actively with the national construction of the Islamic social fields by acquiescence, collaboration with or resistance to its gender mandates. The virile and discursive nature of the system does not allow for bystanders. Short of any reliable polls, one can read the subaltern narratives and decipher the voices of women and signs of gender and social groups' locations. Women's engagement with the national Islamic patriarchy stems from their socio-demographic position. The post-revolutionary generation of 2010 has internalized a qualitatively different Islamic habitus as compared to the violent masculinized habitus of the revolution. The case of Iranian women claiming identity, readjusting to new or multi-sectional habitués in response to global and national fields renders a dizzying analytical puzzle for times to come. Here I explore two dimensions of women's agency – acquiescence and resistance.

Acquiescence: habitus manipulation and collaboration

Blaydes and Linzer deliver a quantitative analysis of fundamentalism and correlate women's financial status with their support for fundamentalist perspectives. They declare that 'among Muslim women financial insecurity is the key dominant of propensity to adopt fundamentalist beliefs and preferences' (Blaydes and Linzer 2008: 580). This financial consideration does not detract from the analysis of embodiment in the form of collaborating with or supporting a patriarchal social field.

The Iranian women collaborators of the Islamic state fall along the factional fault line of the establishment. In the political language of the street they are called 'sisters', with loaded connotations. They are mostly identified by their observance of the official dress codes called *hijab islami*. Their age cohort affects the substance of their support for the regime, where their family background shapes their forms of activism. One may claim that among the Iranian population, age is the main predicating variable regarding attitude toward the regime. After age, gender, socio-economic and rural/urban location, are intervening variables.

Women's agentic collaboration reflects their socio-economic fields. Some women of lower socio-economic status and those living in smaller towns support the regime because of their faith and their sacrifices for the revolution. They may have given a martyr or have a close relative who is a veteran of the war. In this case the regime has taken care of them and compensated them for their sacrifices. These are the *Shahid* families, clientele of the large Shahid foundation. Their faith and their vested interest keep them on the side of the regime (Blaydes and Linzer 2008). Some were and are still employed as members of the Morality Squads, scrutinizing women's adherence to the official dress codes. They are called upon (or forced) to participate at pro-regime demonstrations.

Among the older collaborators are the women leaders of the Republic. Their class and their education positioned them to benefit from their loyalty to the regime. When professional women were purged, they were poised to replace the anti-regime women. Some have called the intellectuals among this group the 'Islamic feminists' (Moghadam 2004). They will agree to the Islamist but not the feminist part of the label. This group worked inside the system and managed to moderate some of the harmful policies toward women. For example, they quietly removed admission quotas against women in professional programs at the universities. They are credited for implementation of equal pay for equal work or agitating for *ijtihad* to soften the impact of shari'a on women and families.

The younger collaborators are children of the revolution born to advocate mothers. They are better educated than their mothers, have higher social ambition, and are less accepting of women's domestication and seclusion. The middle and upper class of this group are schooled in private parochial schools with a heavy dose of theology and good academic subjects to prepare them for university education. In the very symbolic and colorful Iranian hijab system they follow the codes of *hijab islami*. They have internalized mainstream Islamism, but with open eyes.

Resistance: habitus transformation

The intersection of age, socio-geographic location and adherence to their faith are among many fields that inform women's agentic resistance. While the support for the regime is scarce among secular women, there are also devout Muslim women who oppose vehemently the Islamic Republic.

There are no reliable data on the size of this group, but observers can easily surmise that this is the larger group. The older members of the opposition, the first generation, are those who opposed the regime initially but not necessarily the revolution. Most of these were middle-class, urban women who felt the loss to their freedom immediately. Whether they were homemakers or employed workers, they opposed the heavy-handedness of the regime and its enforcement of the morality codes. Though very few Iranians blame the regime for the war, many blame the Ayatollah for its long duration. Like any other case of international violence, women paid for the day-to-day management of the war, the residential bombing, the scarcity, the casualties and for men's suffering (Gerami and Lehnerer 2006). This hardened secular women's rejection of the regime and even some of its women-friendly programs.

The first-generation, middle-class group organized into non-governmental organizations (NGOs) and professional associations. For example, they made up the majority of Greenpeace members and the Association for the Support of Children's Rights, which was co-founded by Noble Peace Laureate Shirin Ebadi. They are members of professional associations like the Bar Association and the engineering societies. The more prestigious organizations, like the Bar Association, are monitored by the regime and led by loyal men, but women members agitate for changing procedures and bylaws to protect their own and other women's rights.

Other groups that have received many international accolades are the Iranian women artists, film-makers, poets, etc. The state has remained the biggest employer and many professional women are state employees or depend on state subsidies for their creative projects, like film-making. Nevertheless, they subvert the state's agendas through their creative outlets by highlighting Iranian social problems and forms of gender discrimination.

Embodiment: fashion guerrillas

The largest opposition is the urban youth, especially urban women. This is an unorganized population ranging from 16 to 30 years in age. They express their opposition to the regime's policies through many vehicles, the most common being manipulation of the dress code. Young women, desiring self-expression, manipulate the Republic's complex dress code, from size, color and texture, to shape, cut and accessories. Deviation from the official code is referred to as '*bad hijabi*', which has become a form of political expression, an example of civil disobedience, without intending to be so.

Through the internet and satellite TV young Iranians are abreast of what is considered fashionable in European or US cities and they reshape the Republic's official *hijab islami* accordingly. For women, a short, tight ensemble consisting of a variation on men's Oxford shirt over Capri pants and very small, but matching scarves has been the must-have outfit for the past few years. This attire in lively colors, accessorized with a heavy dose of makeup, a cell phone, large sunglasses and open toe sandals, completes the look that irks the officials.

While this act in itself is not political, the following interaction is. When women dress like this, or young men imitate MTV looks, they challenge the Islamic patriarchal control of the youth, especially women. These fashionably dressed youth then congregate in internet cafes to mix and meet. The Republic leaders, under pressure from their conservative advocates, have to put on a show of enforcing the dress code. The result is a political game of cat and mouse between the Republic's various enforcing apparatus and the youth. When a few boutiques are closed, more will open up elsewhere, and when one group is admonished or even fined, another group appears in another shopping mall with a more daring version of the fashion of the day. The women do not plan to make a political statement but are well aware of the political consequences of their fashion guerrilla tactics (Moavani 2005).

Subversion: college girls

Here the young women embrace the Islamic habitus of education while subverting its code of domesticity. The middle-class parents provide equal opportunity for their sons and daughters, and the girls reward them by flooding the universities. The highly motivated and ambitious ones, encouraged by their parents, compete for limited seats at professional colleges of medicine, law, engineering and computer technology. Public higher education courtesy of the Republic is highly competitive and provides a solid education. Private colleges are the next on the rung, followed by two-year technical training. Women outnumber men in all areas. This seemingly conventional behavior has unintended consequences for the state's gender agenda. It goes against the ideals of the founding clergy, who asserted the importance of education for women but cautioned that their major concerns should be a home and a husband. To some extent this is true of many college-educated women who will become home-makers but are not home-bound.

The children of the revolution have come to the streets and they have not gone back. The major cities are teeming with young people cruising in their cars, claiming the park benches, or walking in packs until the late hours of the night. The main culprit is high unemployment. One reason that women flock to the universities is because it gives them license to be in public. Attending university allows women to be out of the home or even in another city. This unintended freedom of congregation and communication has provided the post-revolutionary baby-boomers with opportunities to challenge the Islamic patriarchy.

Activism: political girls

The young, particularly college students, are politically active in an unorganized fashion. They are the foot soldiers of the reform movement. The Iranian reform movement is a factionalized narrative of anti-establishment, ranging from secular socialists to traditional clerics. Their supporters are the young and women (Mahdi 2003). This group had their biggest success in the unexpected victory of the reform candidate, Mohammad Reza Khatami, in the 1997 presidential election. The same year, they also claimed major seats in Parliament and started a reformation of civil liberties and open discourse. However, President Khatami either failed or chose not to take advantage of the clear mandate that he had received and opted for small reform measures and lost the support of his main constituency, women and the youth. He nonetheless won the presidency again and served his second term. Today the leaders have recognized the power of this fluid population and, when they cannot control their forces, they try to override their vote. In the 2005 election the conservatives disqualified major reform candidates and then through special tactics elected a president who met with their approval. The 2009 presidential election was a watershed in the life of the Islamic Republic and marked the steep decline of the revolutionary cultural fields.

There is a discursive relationship between the Islamic Republic, hegemonic globalism and de-territorialized Islamisms. One can observe the counter-currents between these macro-level social fields, with costly consequences for all. The 2009 Iranian election is a clear indicator that these colliding forces will continue. Iran's youth, especially women, are collective agents in this global conflict. Their forms of macro- or micro-agency are going to engage observers for some time to come.

Where we stand

Women's agentic embodiment acquires distinct natures depending on their fields of expression. During the past 30 years since the Islamic Revolution, I have conducted a case study of a group of Iranian women. A member of the original group is a woman from a devout, large family in the southern areas of Iran. An example of changing identity and claiming differential habitués, she is now a great-grandmother of a large kin group. In 1985, when her beloved youngest son was killed in an Iraqi field, her family was heartbroken over how to break the news to her. Her brother-in-law proposed the solution used for many mothers of the martyrs. She had previously said that she wished she had the honor of serving the Imam and the revolution by giving blood. Now it was her turn. They told her: 'Now you can keep your head up, you have given a martyr, your best and beloved. Congratulations.' Through the years, by personal conversation and other women's reports, I documented her claiming conflicting habitus of identity simultaneously. She remained a regime supporter until early 2000. While she criticized the government, she remained loyal to the revolution and the Imam. In 2009 I saw her surrounded by some of her granddaughters and great-granddaughters. Now, some of the young women were donning the Green movement's insignia and she admitted that the regime was corrupt beyond salvation. She is a charismatic collaborator turned resister. I have observed American women who have lost sons to the US wars reflecting the same pattern of identity habitus (Gerami and Lehnerer 2008).

Not all women perform agentic embodiment in their daily living with patriarchal Islamist codes and not all actions are agentic. This author has observed many young Afghani girls being married off at an early age in dire conditions and barely surviving numerous pregnancies and oppressive conditions until an early death. Meanwhile, I have recorded Afghani women's narratives of dragging their family across the Hindu Kush mountains to reach Iran and a refugee camp. Many have made the journey on foot through the land-mines.

There is no way of escaping a subaltern narrative in any discourse on Islamisms; that of young, brown, male terrorists (Gerami 2005; Reuter 2002; Esposito 2005). How do women measure in this violent discursive field? A young Iranian woman named Neda Agha Soltan was shot on 19 June on the streets of Tehran during uprisings in the 2009 election. Her intentions have been analyzed and surmised by many (PBS 2009). Whether she actively planned to be a resister is beyond our scope here. There are enough clues that she occupied the resister agentic field of Iranian women. She belonged to that group of resisters who defy the dress codes, are modern and educated. She has become the symbol of Iranian opposition to the Islamic Republic. Her feminine beauty and Western attire fit well with the liberal vision of agency as resistance. At the other extreme are female suicide bombers, described as 'deployed', 'used by terrorists' or 'low-cost, low-technology, low-risk weapons' (Zedalis 2004). In a new book, an Iraqi-Israeli writer, Ptzatza, describes these women as victims, abused and exploited by Muslim Arab men and their communities:

> It appears that women's motives for such attacks are rooted less in ideology than in histories of physical, mental, and sexual abuse within their own families. Their motives rarely involve free will, but rather blackmail or the hope of redemption for sexual indiscretions through violence and self-sacrifice.
>
> *(Ptzatza 2010, in Mandelbaum 2005)*

Feminists have not ventured into an analysis of women's acts of violence with regard to cultural fields and as their habitus. We have spent time deciphering strands of agency by embodiment and acquiescence to masculinized patriarchal social fields but have not explored reactions to hegemonic masculinity of global fields, including use of violence. We may have to go back to Giddens' (1991) analysis of the relationship between structure and agency and broaden our structural vision to include a variety of agencies in hegemonic global fields.

There is a confluence of cultural fields in the way that the USA and Western European countries are contesting de-territorialized Islamisms. Here, I set out to interrogate the agency and tease out the variability of agency as embodied by Muslim women. These are some of the main narratives of the debate at home and in the diaspora. Against this collision of Islamisms and hegemonic globalism, women's responses have been modulating habitus of agency. The activism of the resisters continues to agitate, to publicize and to halt further reduction in women's rights. The agentic of the acquiescence has been to embody Islamic cultural fields while redirecting the patriarchal operation of the Islamists. For the majority of Muslim women, perhaps their most remarkable agency has been to occupy the public habitus, by their silent, persistent act of being there. Islamisms have become de-territorialized and thus have generated public social fields requiring, calling for and needing women to support and mark their cultural fields, whether through their veil or through their resistance at home and in the diaspora. Women have been present on the streets and on the internet for the Islamic authenticity and against its patriarchal codes. They have stayed the course by breaking barriers to their education and are now struggling to open more doors to women's employment. They have fought to curb the reach of shari'a through publicizing its harmful effects and by reforming its mandates. They use its rules for their own interests and organize to protect girls and children in general. They embody or resist its fluid mandates.

This is not a concerted effort at heroism, but rather an example of scattered agentic actors maneuvering between the antithetical forces of one specific form of traditional patriarchy, Islamisms and hegemonic globalism. This would have been more disjointed and less effective without the techno-social fields that global consumerism offers. Muslim women have been able to use the discord of global hegemony and Islamist patriarchy to generate diverse identity and at times significant agentic modification of the discourse.

Acknowledgement

Kendall Sally has been a reliable and knowledgeable research assistant for this project. I am indebted to the editor, Professor Shahram Akbarzadeh, for his patience and encouragement.

Notes

1 Kimmel (2005) refers to similar narratives as domestic masculinity. Here I refer to a more organized social arrangement that may operate at national level or be limited to a tribal community.
2 The hegemonizing effect of globalization is a contested discourse. Morrell and Swart (2005) and others have documented areas outside globalized capitalism.

References

Ahmad, L. (1992) *Women and Gender in Islam: Historical Roots of a Modern Debate*, London, Yale University Press.
BBC (2006) 'Straw's veil comments spark anger', *BBC News*, 5 October, available at news.bbc.co.uk/2/hi/5410472.stm (accessed 26 February 2011).
Blaydes, L. and Linzer, D.A. (2008) 'The Political Economy of Women's Support for Fundamental Islam', paper presented at the annual meeting of the Midwest Political Science Association, Chicago, Illinois.
Bloul, R. (1998) *Engendering Muslim Identities: Deterritorialization and the Ethnicization Process in France*, Women Living Under Muslim Law, available at www.wluml.org/english/pubsfulltxt.shtml?cmd%5B87%5D=i-87-2682 (accessed 31 October 2007).
Body-Gendrot, S. (2007) 'France upside down over a headscarf?', *Sociology of Religion* vol. 68, no. 3: 289–304.
Bunt, G.R. (2003) *Islam in the Digital Age: E-Jihad, Online Fatwas and Cyber Islamic Environment* (Critical Studies on Islam), London and Sterling, Virginia, Pluto Press.
Connell, R.W. (2005) 'Globalism, imperialism, and masculinities', in M.S. Kimmel, J. Hearn and R.W. Connell (eds), *Handbook of Studies on Men and Masculinities*, Thousand Oaks, CA, Sage, pp. 71–89.

Danaher, G., Schirato, T. and Webb, J. (2002) *Understanding Bourdieu*, London, Sage.

Esfandiari, H. (1997) *Reconstructed Lives: Women and Iran's Islamic Revolution*, Baltimore, MD, Johns Hopkins University Press.

Esposito, J. (2005) 'Globalization of Jihad', in C. Timmerman and B. Segaert (eds), *How to Conquer the Barriers to Cultural Dialogue: Christianity, Islam and Judaism*, Bruxelles, P.I.E. Peter Lang.

Fraser, C. (2006) 'Italy government seeks veil ban', *BBC News*, 7 November, available at news.bbc.co.uk/2/hi/europe/6125302.stm (accessed 26 February 2011).

Gerami, S. (1996) *Women and Fundamentalism: Islam and Christianity*, New York, Garland Publishing.

—— (2005) 'Islamist masculinity and Muslim masculinities', in M. Kimmel, J. Hearn and R.W. Connell (eds), *Handbook of Studies on Men and Masculinities*, Thousand Oaks, CA, Sage.

Gerami, S. and Lehnerer, M. (2001) 'Women's agency and household diplomacy: negotiating fundamentalism', *Gender and Society* vol. 15, no. 4: 556–74.

—— (2006) 'Reproductive health in Iran', in Suad Joseph (ed.), *Encyclopedia of Women and Islamic Cultures*, vol. 3, E. J. Brill, Leiden and New York, Sage, pp. 26–28.

—— (2008) 'Terrorism and national security', in A. Lind and S. Brzuzy (eds), *Battleground: Women, Gender, and Sexuality*, California, Greenwood Press.

Gibson-Graham, J.K. (1996) *The End of Capitalism (as We Knew It): A Feminist Critique of Political Economy*, Oxford, Blackwell.

Giddens, A. (1991) *Modernity and Self Identity: Self and Society in the Late Modern Age*, California, Stanford University Press.

Khan, S. (2009) 'Why I, as a British Muslim woman, want the burkha banned from our streets', *The Daily Mail*, 24 June, available at www.dailymail.co.uk/debate/article-1195052/Why-I-British-Muslim-woman-want-burkha-banned-streets.html#ixzz0nNhyXxJJ (accessed 19 May 2010).

Kimmel, M. (2005) 'Globalization and its mal(e) contents: the gendered moral and political economy of terrorism', in M. Kimmel, J. Hearn and R.W. Connell (eds), *Handbook of Studies on Men and Masculinities*, Thousand Oaks, CA, Sage.

Klatch, R. (1994) 'Women of the New Right in the United States: family, feminism, and politics', in V. Moghadam (ed.), *Identity Politics and Women: Cultural Reassertions and Feminisms in International Perspective*, Boulder, CO, Westview Press.

Knott, K. and Khokher, S. (1993) 'Religious and ethnic identity among young Muslim women in Bradford', *New Community* vol. 19, no. 4: 593–610.

Korteweg, A.C. (2008) 'The Sharia debate in Ontario: Gender, Islam, and representations of Muslim women's agency', *Gender and Society* vol. 22, no. 4: 434–54.

McLeod, J. (2005) 'Feminists re-reading Bourdieu: old debates and new questions about gender habitus and gender change', *Theory and Research in Education* vol. 3, no. 1: 11–30.

Mahdi, A. (2003) 'Iranian women: between Islamization and globalization', in A. Mohammadi (ed.), *Iran Encountering Globalization: Problems and Prospects*, London and New York, RoutledgeCurzon.

Mahmood, S. (2001) 'Feminist theory, embodiment, and the docile agent: some reflections on the Egyptian Islamic revival', *Cultural anthropology* vol. 16, no. 2: 202–36.

Mandelbaum, J. (2005) 'What drives female suicide bombers?', Mobile Salon, available at mobile.salon.com/mwt/broadsheet/2010/04/05/female_suicide_bombers_open2010/index.html (accessed 19 May 2010).

Moavani, A. (2005) *Lipstick Jihad: A Memoir of Growing Up Iranian in America and American in Iran*, New York, Public Affairs.

Moghadam, V. (2004) *Toward Gender Equality in the Arab/Middle East Region: Islam, Culture, and Feminist Activism*, Human Development Report Office, United Nations Development Programme.

Moghissi, H. (1994) *Populism and Feminism in Iran: Women's Struggle in a Male Dominated Revolutionary Movement*, New York, St Martin Press.

Morrell, R. and Swart, S. (2005) 'Men in the Third World: postcolonial perspectives on masculinity', in M. Kimmel, J. Hearn and R.W. Connell (eds), *Handbook of Studies on Men and Masculinities*, Thousand Oaks, CA, Sage.

PBS (2009) 'FRONTLINE: A death in Tehran', available at www.pbs.org/wgbh/pages/frontline/tehran bureau/deathintehran (accessed 19 May 2010).

Population Reference Bureau (2009) *2005 World Population Data Sheet*, available at www.prb.org/pdf05/05WorldDataSheet_Eng.pdf.

Reuter, C. (2002) *My Life is A Weapon*, Princeton, NJ, Princeton University Press.

Sauer, B. (2009) 'Headscarf regimes in Europe: diversity policies at the intersection of gender, culture and religion', *Comparative European Politics* vol. 7, no. 1: 75–94.

Smith, C. (1991) *The Emergence of Liberation Theology: Radical Religion and Social Movement Theory*, Chicago, IL, University of Chicago Press.

Werbner, P. (2007) 'Veiled interventions in pure space: honour, shame and embodied struggles among Muslims in Britain and France', *Theory, Culture, and Society* vol. 24, no. 2: 161–86.

Zedalis, D.D. (2004) *Female Suicide Bombers*, Honolulu, Hawaii, University Press of the Pacific.

17

Racialization and the challenge of Muslim integration in the European Union

Valérie Amiraux

Since October 2010 a number of European political leaders have made strong public statements regarding the 'crisis of multiculturalism', asserting the latter's failure in the European Union (EU). Angela Merkel, the German Chancellor from the conservative CDU party, launched the trend with a public declaration made on 16 October 2010, in which she expressed her conviction that the project of a multicultural Germany had failed. She attributed this failure to the lack of effort on the part of immigrants to integrate and, in particular, to learn German with sufficient fluency. On 4 February 2011, while delivering a speech on radicalization and terrorism at the Munich Security Conference, David Cameron criticized state multiculturalism and the ghettoization it produces, arguing that instead Britain needed to develop a stronger and more cohesive sense of national identity as a more effective strategy to combat home-grown terrorism and the attractiveness of extremism to Muslim youth. A few days later, on 10 February 2011, Nicolas Sarkozy, answering questions posed by a panel of French citizens on TV, contended that the failure of multiculturalism was primarily due to the fact that it privileged the identity of the immigrant over that of the host country. To illustrate his point he also referred to Muslims, citing, for example, how they pray 'in an ostentatious way' in the streets. The French President's declaration, which must be situated within the context of the countdown to the next presidential election, in fact triggered the initiative of launching a governmental and potentially nationwide discussion about Islam in France.

This overt anti-Muslim racism is what constitutes the challenge to Muslim integration in twenty-first-century Western European contexts.[1] Over the last 40 years the constructed articulation of the settlement of Muslims in the EU as a social and political problem has taken various forms, often uncovering the culturally circumscribed nature of the models of citizenship, the historical tradition of nation-building and the national specificities of the relationship between church and state (Fetzer and Soper 2005; Robbers 2005). Most of the debate related to Muslims in Europe has focused and continues to focus on the liberal governance of religious diversity (meaning the way in which nation-states accommodate religious differences) and Islam-related claims made by European Muslims, the latter buttressing the idea that the public and religious nature of Islam makes it 'an especially resilient type of identity' (Statham *et al.* 2005: 441). However, if for decades – roughly from the 1960s until the early 2000s – the situation of Muslims was perceived as the more or less successful result of the nationally constructed tradition of the integration of immigrants,[2] perceptions and mainstream public opinion changed drastically after the terrorist attacks on the United States on 11 September 2001 (9/11). The attack against the World Trade Center marks the beginning of a convergence of European attitudes in framing Muslim citizens as incapable of fitting into the EU. Why have contrasted regimes of citizenship and traditionally opposed 'models of integration' (inter-culturalism, multiculturalism, Republicanism, assimilationism) since given rise to similar public discussions on the Islamic headscarf throughout the EU? How can the general adhesion to a restrictive standpoint (i.e. banning specific religious dress and signs) be understood? The thesis that integration fails whenever religious differences are visible remains a prominent one,[3] and is systematically brought forth whether the societies in question define themselves as multicultural or not. What are its implications, subtexts and consequences? These are the questions that I address in this chapter. Answers are of course multi-faceted and tentative, as the debates surrounding these Islam-related topics involve numerous broader social, political, ideological and even economic issues. They question the 'challenge' to multiculturalism, the capacity of secularism to organize a conflict-free religious pluralism in Europe, the perception of [non-Western] cultural references as a threat (that is, as Brown (2006) puts it, the danger associated with too much culture as being a threat), increasing Islamophobia, anti-Muslim racism and the tangible discrimination it begets, the loyalty of Muslim European citizens, the impact of foreign affairs policies on domestic spaces, etc.

Writing about the debate on the challenge of Muslim integration 'into the West' can be done from a number of angles. The least demanding to adopt would be to embrace the separation of church and state descriptive and comparative perspective. It is also by far the most frequent approach employed, as it emphasizes both the role of European history and the role of regulation policies to understand the national situations of Muslims living in the EU (Triandafyllidou 2010). Such a perspective would be rooted in the dominant literature on the subject of Muslims in Western societies. This now substantive area of scholarship has produced, since approximately the late 1980s, myriad edited volumes in which national case studies serve the edification of a system of analysis based on the various types of relationships binding church and state. Instead of examining the hypothetical (in my opinion) relevance of national norms defining citizenship and the relationship between religion and the state (Modood et al. 2006), I wish here to elaborate on what I call the process of Europeanization through cultural boundary-making. I posit that the current 'burka-bashing' moment enables the analysis of the process of racializing Muslims in Europe because religion as a mode of subjective experience remains largely unintelligible to European public imaginaries and political classes. In addition, such cultural boundary-making provides a convenient marker distinguishing between desirable citizens and undesirable ones. I will present this thesis in three sections, starting with a succinct overview of the literature on Muslims in the EU. In the second section I will highlight how the many aspects of the Europeanization process and the backlash against the Islamic headscarf intersect. In the final section I will develop the idea that the institutionalization of such a cultural rather than territorial anti-Muslim boundary inside the EU exemplifies the process of the racialization of Muslim others.

The way Muslims are studied: when politics meets scholarship

In the EU, religion becomes contentious and defined as a problem when specific forms of religiosity are expressed or claimed by minority groups made up of individuals of immigrant background, most of whom are European citizens. In this context, 'Muslims' has become an all-encompassing category commonly circulating in European public discourses without referring to anything precisely defined. The growing presence of Muslims and Islam raises geopolitical, political, social and cultural issues at various levels (local, regional, national, supra-national) and dimensions (individual and collective).[4] These interrelated factors involved have obliged European societies to face the complex challenge of devising definitions of equality and integration whilst equally considering the religious facet of an individual's identity. However, as noted above, the difficulty lies in the fact that public discussions on the question cum problem of 'Islam and Muslims' continue to put forth secularism as a principle that must be reaffirmed as a core European value, a means of integration and a necessary regulatory principle of social life. It is increasingly conflated with, or at least seen as interwoven with, national identity (Baubérot and Milot 2011). In some cases it has been recast by the emergence of a postcolonial awareness in politics (Bhambra 2010).

In contrast to their tremendous visibility in public discussions, however, Muslims largely remain an invisible and silent population in most of the EU member states. In fact, with the notable exception of the United Kingdom since 2001,[5] they are consistently absent from public statistics, in particular from the national census. They are thought to number around 20 million in the EU, but the lack of official data on religious affiliation constitutes a major and permanent obstacle in conducting research and devising public policies, for instance, assessing the reality of discrimination in access to public goods and services (Maréchal et al. 2003; Open Society Institute 2010). In effect, public policies in most of the EU member states do not officially distinguish between categories of citizens. Even if they may, in some cases, take into account the latter's immigrant background, and/or the place of birth of the parents, the religious affiliation of individuals does not form part of the information that may be gathered for legal reasons (Simon 2004). This lack of data creates very uneven situations when it comes to assessing, for instance, academic achievement (Meer et al. 2009), and more specifically the 'ethnic penalties' whereby members of specific groups are disadvantaged (Johnston et al. 2010: 578). This statistical invisibility obviously impacts on the attempt to provide potential legal solutions for redressing inequalities. For example, while the concept of discrimination (including discrimination due to religious belief) came to form a central notion of legal and political discourse and practice aimed at the promotion of equality and respect for difference(s), it has remained largely ignored and absent from the discussions about Muslims and Islam in Europe (Amiraux 2005; Fekete 2009; Fekete et al. 2010). The discrepancy between the open and public expression of hostility towards Muslims and its absence from the discussions treating the practice of discrimination vis-à-vis Muslims stems from a certain logic of the political philosophy of integration and equality in the EU: religion is an intimate matter, belongs to the private sphere, and should therefore not be publicly visible.

Because Muslims as a group are still not defined in national data, the 'average data' put forward for Muslim populations in Europe are unfortunately always approximate calculations based on unsatisfactory methods of evaluation. When trying to estimate how many Muslims reside in a given country, two methods are usually employed. The first one uses ethnicity as a proxy, relying on ethnic criteria to determine who is Muslim on the basis of the country of origin and place of birth of the first family member to emigrate. However, what precisely constitutes religious affiliation and non-affiliation is both a highly difficult and politically charged question which, in many ways, resists quantification. Equating ethnic and religious identity therefore does not acknowledge the instability of belonging, the personal negotiation of the relationship to one's family's religious heritage, as well as the multiple factors leading a person to convert or even change religions several times during his or her lifetime (Bellah 1970; Davie 2002; Beckford and Wallis 2006). In short, this first approach is not equipped to factor in the complex, plural and often shifting identities of modern (Muslim) citizens. The second method of calculating the number of Muslims in a given place that considers itself a quantitative approach attempts to count believers on the basis of religious practice (praying in a prayer room or a mosque, fasting, alms giving, etc.) or, instead, on that of their own religious self-identification or religiosity (Bréchon 2007; Dobbelaere and Riis 2003).[6] In these types of surveys, the criteria for identifying Muslims depend on what can be called an 'institutional' perception of what defines a believer, except in the case of self-identification,[7] that is, his/her relationship to practice and more specifically to worship. Both here relate to an institutional reading of religious belonging in which religion is associated with collective rituals and the public existence of religious buildings.

This reduction of religion to an institutional definition (believer = practitioner) has been partly nourished by the specific cultures of scholarship that have been produced by Western experts since the 1980s. The nature of the research still remains mostly qualitative today, establishing typologies and hierarchies (profiling) to map the social heterogeneity of Muslims living in the EU. Scholarship on Islam and Muslims living in the EU was first initiated by European experts on the Middle East who began investigating the potential parallels to be drawn between the rise of political Islam in the Middle East and in some of the EU member states (France, Germany, the UK) (Tessler 1999; Amiraux 2002).[8] This generation and branch of experts, even if it no longer constitutes the primary scholarship of European Islam and Muslims, nonetheless informs us about the major trends that continue to structure the production of knowledge in the field, in particular the late incorporation of postcolonialism as an analytical variable in the field (Bhambra 2010). Another large portion of this 'expert literature' addresses the way Muslims had begun organizing themselves in the EU member states where they had settled as immigrants. It examines the associative networks and umbrella organizations that had begun to emerge in various EU countries along with public claims-making (associations, organization-building, first praying rooms, Arabic teaching, networking). These early, albeit still present, research agendas, often articulated in terms of the political need for information about the emerging 'Islamic problem', examine the institutional environments of the different EU societies producing nationally determined avenues for the incorporation of Muslims (Maréchal et al. 2003). These have been largely informed by a European representation of social order 'assuming a strong coupling of individual rights, formal membership and national identification – assumptions shared by most European countries regardless of their different codes of national identity, models of national citizenship and patterns of inclusion and exclusion' (Koenig 2007: 913–14).

More recently, in around 2000, scholarship adopting a comparative approach to issues associated with the public legal regulation of religious claims (state accommodations) emerged and began to use the wide concept of governance as a cogent means of extending the reflection beyond state initiatives and strictly legal regulatory mechanisms (Maussen 2007; Sauer 2009; Koenig 2007). This may be due in part to the fact that in the last decade the EU discourse on equality has been dramatically affected by the implementation of the European anti-discrimination provisions, which have contributed to recasting the vocabulary and the tools employed from a law-based perspective to assess places and levels of discrimination (Amiraux and Guiraudon 2010). These provisions were deemed necessary to supersede alternatives to the entrenched dominant state accommodation approach which, if considered the main way to negotiate the interaction between states and Muslim practices, nonetheless neglects other forms of social interactions between Muslims and the host society, including the most ordinary ones, that often go well. The Open Society Institute (OSI) 'At Home in Europe' project, an example of this approach, covered 11 EU cities. Challenging the myth of the segregation and alienation of Muslims in the EU, it offers a positive picture of integration, particularly at the local level: 61 per cent of Muslims declare having a strong sense of belonging to their country of residence, and 72 per cent to their city (Open Society Institute 2010). However, their perception of how others esteem their relationship to their environment differs starkly, as 50 per cent of all Muslim respondents believe that they are not seen as belonging by the wider societies. Mirroring the literature, the contemporary governance of Islam in the EU moved from a political focus on international security threats to a juridical approach of its regulation (Koenig 2007). The impact of legal scholarship has been to shed light on the role of norms and principles in defining an EU of shared values that would delineate a common space for discussing the governance of religious diversity (Grillo et al. 2009; *Cardozo Law Review* 2009).[9]

Comparative research has also both uncovered and underscored the disciplinary uncertainty characterizing the field of study on Muslims and Islam in Europe and the difficulty of locating it, akin to how situating the 'Muslim problem' taxonomically was, for a long time, problematic: Does it classify as migration policy outcomes? Should it fall under the 'sociology of religion' umbrella? Does it belong to the field of Islamic studies? This uncertainty gave rise to a concerted growth of ethnographic work evincing a more sustained and diversified theorization, beyond the secularization paradigm (Asad et al. 2009). In the early 1990s, in an extension of research carried out in the Arab-Muslim (Mernissi 1987; Ahmed 1993), Iranian (Adelkhah 1991) and Turkish (Göle 1993) worlds, there emerged a new framing of the headscarf as a modern social phenomenon rather than as a backward legacy of the past. This was supported, on the one hand, by empirical studies in a number of fields, undertaken by scholars indebted to Talal Asad and Mahmood, and, on the other, by what generally fall under the rubric of post-colonial studies, and, more rarely, by the intersection of the two (Becci 2004). A gender-based perspective, usually conceptually rooted in feminist theory, has also reframed the headscarf as a symbol of the inequality and injustice suffered by Muslims in France and in Europe (Scott 2007; Kilic et al. 2008) rather than as a tool of misogynist oppression. Queer studies and intersectionality have made their entry into the field as they also now investigate religion. The recent reflection on homonationalism, inspired by the seminal work of Puar (2007), examines the intersection of broad structures of racism, neoliberalism and class exclusion that underwrite 'homonationalist configurations' in which the rehabilitated figure of the 'queer' is transformed into a border, differentiating in hierarchical terms Western liberal democracies from the rest of the world. More significantly, non-heteronormative sexualities also serve as a litmus test of citizenship, distinguishing between foreigners/immigrants capable of integrating into the West from those who, because they do not view homosexuality as normative, are not. Puar points out the racist or racial dimension of homonationalism as it tends to exclude specific groups, in her eyes most notably Sikhs, Jews and Muslims (Puar 2007). The figure of the homophobic migrant threatening the secularized gay body is one of the examples of this racialization process connected with homonationalist configurations (Haritaworn 2010). 'Intimate citizenship practices' have thus been erected into discriminating variables that measure the capacity of certain individuals to become European citizens or Europeanized. Concrete examples that clearly confirm the enmeshment of homonationalism with securitization, counterterrorism, nationalism and citizenship abound. Explicit publicity of homosexual sexual preference of leading EU political figures is deliberate in order to highlight Muslims' attitudes towards homosexuality. The best example is undoubtedly the gay, Dutch, anti-Muslim politician Geert Wilders and, in fact, Landman discusses the position Muslims should adopt towards homosexual rights in the Netherlands (Landman 2007). Its role in the Baden-Württemberg German tests of citizenship has also been crucial. Yet despite the reality of and scholarship on homonationalism, it must be reiterated that religious discrimination is still barely analyzed as specific to the experience of injustice, or as distinct from racial and ethnic discrimination. As it remains under-politicized, and even euphemized as Islamophobia rather than as a specific form of racism, trying to distinguish the specific boundaries of religious discrimination of Muslims in EU member states from racial and ethnic prejudice thus becomes an almost unachievable task. This impediment to sound research on Islam and Muslims greatly inhibits the field.

Headscarf controversies as a European problem

Public manifestations of hostility against Muslims in the EU illustrate what I refer to as the contemporary ordinary trap in which European public opinion and opinion leaders seem to be locked.[10] Since the Runnymede Trust report on Islamophobia published in Britain in 1997, a series of events have led to the intensification of explicit hostility towards Muslims, particularly in the EU. 9/11, the 7/7 bombings in London and the Madrid bombings first come to mind. However, the Danish cartoons episode, the murder of Theo van Gogh, the referendum against the construction of minarets in Switzerland and the anti-burkini campaigns[11] have also contributed to the consolidation of a boundary of resistance against and separation from Muslims in Europe. Within this sequence of events, the process of exclusion of the Islamic headscarf reveals itself as part of a continuum demanding more than a descriptive ethnographic narrative. While Muslims settled in the West are increasingly perceived as 'problems' in need of regulation, they are presented as epitomizing the conflict of interests between democracy and multiculturalism – both considered as principles and practices. Let us examine some of the controversies over burkas, minarets and burkinis from this perspective in order to chart the way in which panics about 'multiculturalism gone wild' circulate in a transborder manner, with situations occurring in one country very quickly becoming reality in another (Titley and Lentin 2011).

The *New York Times* reported on 1 December 2009 that the Swiss People's Party campaign posters (depicting a Swiss flag with black, missile-shaped minarets, and a woman shrouded in a niqab) demonstrate the 'determination of the right to play on deep-rooted fears that Muslim immigration would lead to an erosion of Swiss values'. The campaign was effective: 57.5 percent of the voters expressed their support for banning the construction of minarets, a collective decision that will become enshrined in the Constitution. Examining the situation of Muslims in Switzerland more closely and beyond the fear-mongering, one discovers that out of the total of 150 mosques or prayer rooms in Switzerland, only four bear minarets; two more minarets were being planned at the time of the vote but none of them were planning to serve for conducting the call to prayer (this information was mentioned by the *New York Times*). This illustrates the discrepancy between reality and perception. The Swiss episode confirms the contemporary re-emergence of the motif and iconography of the threat, no longer a phantasm situated beyond national borders but embodied in male and female co-citizens who typify behaviors considered antagonistic to national identity. Another example of policy propelled by the notion of threat is the Council of State's decision to deny French nationality to a Moroccan woman due to her niqab (considered a radical practice of her religion). As various observers from different disciplines have argued, the decision, clearly linking opposition to the burka and the discussion of French national identity, in fact exposes the ambiguity and even contradiction of a public policy which, while aiming to support a more equitable treatment of Islam in France, glosses over individual Muslims' experiences of mistreatment.[12] Both the Swiss and French examples were in effect made possible by the connection made between an iconic fantasy of otherness (the fully veiled Muslim woman) and a much more ordinary unease, arising from day-to-day interactions between Muslims and people ignorant of or unfamiliar with Islam. The daily discomfort produced by such interactions help situate the declarations of European political leaders that opened this chapter but also illustrate what Younge (2011) calls the confusion between multiculturalim as fiction and multiculturalism as fact. In the first case, it is envisioned as a 'liberal state-led policy of encouraging and supporting cultural difference at the expense of national cohesion'. In the second case, multiculturalism is understood as the lived experiences of ordinary people. Younge describes the former as 'rooted in the fear of what has never been', explaining why, for example, in Switzerland, the regions most hostile to the minaret were those in which the fewest Muslims actually lived.

The stigmatization of the Islamic headscarf across Europe evinces how the governance of bodies is increasingly interconnected with other forms of 'racism in the name of feminism' (Razack 2008), although this aspect remains unacknowledged in mainstream public discourses. If, in France, it is clearly anchored in the French Republican tradition of control of the private space (Iacub 2008), it has devised other rationales to take root in other political cultures. There are nonetheless common underlying themes. Reading the headscarf controversies as a 'normative account of the relationships between citizenship and identity' (Laborde 2001: 718) reveals a shared conviction that the headscarf is a contaminating element, harmful for both national identities and the individuals who wear one. Such a consensus, however, contravenes principles such as equality and neutrality and religious freedom, as well as the right to carry private indicators of intimate convictions into the public sphere. The Islamic headscarf has become a sensitive issue across Europe, giving rise to legal disputes and political controversies of various natures in several EU member states, notably in France, Belgium, Germany, the Netherlands and the UK. The ubiquity of the debates has made headscarves, and by extension the Muslim women wearing them, signify 'everything that is thought to be wrong with Islam', generating moral panic and hysteria. More recently, the focus has turned from the headscarf to the burka as the main object of stigmatization in and rejection from European public space(s). The dominant trend emerging in EU member states, premised on political and legal discourse, tends towards imposing further limitations on specific minority religious practices (Pew Global Attitudes Survey 2010). The Pew Research Center's Global Attitudes Project released a survey on 8 July 2010, which revealed the massive and widespread support for banning the full Islamic veil in Western Europe. Vast majorities in France (82 percent), Germany (71 percent), Britain (62 percent) and Spain (59 percent) approve of a ban on Muslim women wearing full veils in the public sphere, including in schools, hospitals and government.[13]

From one country to another in the EU, similar fundamental rights are being challenged and redefined in the hijab controversies (freedom of expression, freedom of religion versus neutrality, freedom of 'the other' and public order), but the reactions of member states range from a complete ban (France, Belgium, the Netherlands), to a limited one (Germany), to a public discussion with no legal decision taken (as in Italy), or to a case-by-case approach (Britain) (Sauer 2009). National definitions of identity and citizenship certainly affect this variation, but two main positions towards the hijab can nonetheless be distinguished. First, the accommodating position (dominant in the 1980s but decreasing since the 1990s) of public authorities towards the requests made by Muslim women to wear a headscarf in their lives as European citizens, and second, the position adopted by those who wish to ban this behavior/garment from certain parts or all of the public sphere. Theoretically, the public neutrality of liberal states would support European legal receptiveness to religious and cultural diversity, but the current tendency is rather to move towards more restrictive definitions of cohesive citizenship. If, in culturally plural societies, anti-discrimination policies can be seen as a central element of the organization of the pacific coexistence between competing interpretative systems (as in the case of religions) or between conflicting values (as in neutrality of the state versus individual freedom of religion), the tendency to curtail religious freedom (limiting the right to wear a headscarf in specific settings) expresses the felt necessity to curb visible religious practices in secular contexts. In some cases, the difference between types of secularism (established church, laïcité, concordat type of church and state relationship) or the various definitions given to 'disturbances of public order' provide the premise for European judges to plead for the limitation of the right to wear a headscarf. For example, the European Court of Human Rights (ECHR) deliberated that the restriction can sometimes be necessary in democratic societies on the basis that the wearing of the headscarf may negatively impact on others (Blair and Aps 2005: 7). It therefore supports the more restrictive member states on this matter,[14] mostly on the grounds of the margin of appreciation that gives priority to the state assessment of its own situation (Hoffmann and Ringelheim 2004). The ECHR adopted, for instance, a contextual reading of the Turkish Sahin case by defending the Ankara University president's decision to forbid the wearing of the headscarf on campus. The interference with Miss Sahin's individual religious freedom was, relying on the reasoning on the margin of appreciation, deemed justified by the necessity to protect public order.[15]

The widespread debates and legal limitations imposed on the wearing of the headscarf make clear that in Europe the headscarf is viewed as an inadequate social object, a source of risk and iniquity, perceived simultaneously as an obstacle to integration (of the membership group and the individual), emancipation (of women), dialogue (between Muslims and non-Muslims, veiled and non-veiled women, men and women), as well as to public authority. The headscarf controversies that started in France in 1989 stand as the almost perfect incarnation of the interwoven tensions present in the Republic's integration plan born of a tradition that is at once political (Hazareesingh 1994), philosophical (Laborde 2008) and sociological (Schnapper 1991). Voicing disenchantment and detestation, French public opinion has in practice celebrated the headscarf daily, through its consistent omnipresence in the media (Bowen 2006). The 2004 law,[16] entirely at odds with the original political discussions on the subject over a decade earlier, resulted from a general conviction that the headscarf harms both the Republic and the individual who wears it in several ways (Amiraux 2009). One, it breaches the principles of equality, neutrality and discretion required in terms of public expression of the private. Two, according to those who proposed the law, it fractures equality among students in the school setting by emphasizing difference. In addition, wearing the headscarf in state schools is considered to contravene the religious freedom of other children. Three, the headscarf is also perceived as detrimental in that it prejudices the school's civic role, restoring to the school environment a religious authority that had gradually disappeared with the process of secularization (Baubérot 2004).

France has certainly taken the lead in the recent overt hostility expressed towards Muslims in Europe with regard to the headscarf; the real distinction between France and other EU countries lies in the earliness and longevity of the debate in the public arena (1989–2004).[17] In other countries it only became the subject of controversies several years later, after the mid-1990s. If the French republican tradition expresses a climactic and difficult struggle between disembodied political ideals and social issues expressed in conflict-laden, practical configurations, the emergence of debates over the wearing of the Islamic headscarf in state schools throughout Europe challenges the assumption of the particular nature of the French settings (MacGoldrick 2006). All the European contexts considered in this discussion on the headscarf have indeed reacted to the garment (Kilic et al. 2008), even though they have developed different traditions of debate and historicities. The French debate illustrates, albeit in an extreme manner, the tangible effects made possible by the constitutional principles underpinning public life (neutrality, equality) and organizing the system of public freedoms. The continuous oscillation between a open laïcité recognizing differences and one claiming an absolute separation between the secular and religious domains is evident in the dispute over the wearing of the headscarf. If the persistence of women to wear the headscarf is seen as evidence of the intractability of believers in secular contexts, the way in which the Islamic headscarf is stigmatized in French society also illustrates a particular form of governance exercised over the body and bodily behavior rooted in the republican tradition of the control of private spaces and practices pre-dating 1989. To a certain degree, the 2004 legislation represents a culmination of this tradition. It restores public state authority by setting a penalty (exclusion of religious signs and those wearing them from public school) and restating the legislative principle (laïcité), which operates through institutions to enable and stabilize its effectiveness.

Akin to other 'Muslims in Europe'-related topics, much research has emerged on the headscarf. Two principal conclusions can be drawn from 20 years of scholarship. One is the recognition that a multiplicity of meanings is ascribed to the garment by those who wear it. The other is that the analyses are most often rooted in postcolonial and gender studies methodologies. They relate the wearing of the headscarf to a variable and contingent construction of hybrid, fluctuating identities. Deconstructing dominant representations, it frames the garment as a conscious choice made by modern women. The main effect of this interpretation, which relies on a contextualized reading of individual situations, has been the 'de-Islamization' of the headscarf thereby positioning it in wider practices and discourses of discrimination, such as racism and sexism. While positing individual choice as the only alternative narrative available to veiled Muslim women for giving meaning to their behavior in a secular environment has helped de-essentialize and deculturalize discourse on the wearing of the headscarf, it remains particularly problematic in the secular contexts. Fernando explains how reducing the wearing of the headscarf solely to personal choice divorced from the reality of religious authority makes the expression of this 'chosen' personal practice, evidently encompassing a religious dimension, impossible within public spaces that neither accept the religious nor equate it with individual choice (Fernando 2010). In a secular worldview, the idea of choice is difficult to reconcile with the concept of religious prescription (from the Qur'an) or obligation. Regardless of these new theorizations, the French state's desire to eliminate the supposed risk associated with the headscarf, for both Muslim women and the Republic, has thwarted the religious freedom of the main players. While the multiple meanings of the headscarf are now accepted – at least in academic circles – these do not necessarily result in the recognition of the role of religion in choosing to wear one.

The EU headscarf controversies post-9/11 bring back to the surface old and perhaps unresolved conflicts over the former close relationship between church and state throughout the EU. However, they completely disregard the 'religiosity' of individuals, namely the intimate and inventive way in which an individual performs his/her link to a corpus of dogma. Religiosity is what makes religion concrete and visible in society. It gives meaning to action, and it may help to recognize others as well as to be recognized. The idea of a believer performing his/her religion on a daily basis remains absent from the public debates over religion and religious practices, even though it is central to the establishment of collective albeit not necessarily national identities that signify to members of a group and to the world who they are, what they stand for and what kind of society they hope to create. This explains why the absence of the voices of headscarf-wearing Muslim women characterizes all of the European national public debates. To reconsider with some seriousness the gestures and emotions that belief makes present in society would constitute a means of doing justice to the subjects, indeed taking them and their subjective attachment and assent to a belief seriously. The legal process could in fact constitute a way of taking seriously, in sociological terms, the meaning that the players give to their gestures and which includes for most veiled women an inherent religious dimension. This would mean that the wearing of the headscarf would neither be reduced, restricted to or amalgamated with other gestures, nor confused with other signs. At present, the real motivations of women for wearing the veil are irrelevant in that they don't change how the garment is perceived. The law provides the modus operandi to work on definitions, since it is a device for finding equivalents, for categorization, which obviates the dynamics of justification and qualification. It would then be possible to explore what the challenge of defining the religious offers as an option for knowing and acknowledging the legitimacy of religious beliefs, without neglecting the fact that in settling such conflicts the law seems to feel torn between two principles: on the one hand an aspiration towards equality, and on the other an aspiration towards liberty.[18]

How far is the headscarf-bashing movement indicative of Europeanization? Among its multiple meanings,[19] the notion of Europeanization usually refers, in political science, to the impact of the European integration on domestic policies of EU member states (Krizsan and Popa 2010). In large part, it conveys the idea of the circulation of rules (formal or informal), procedures, policy paradigms from the European level to more national and local ones. It either emerges as a consequence of the implementation of European policies, or through appropriation by the effect of socialization to European norms and rules (Börzel and Risse 2003). Research has therefore extensively studied the effects of European institutions on policies and politics at both the international and national levels (Favell and Guiraudon 2009). However, religion is not a common EU area for policy with specific related institutions. The Europeanization process here encompasses the idea of the emergence of a transnational European public confronted 'with the norms and morals of European secular modernity' (Göle 2010: 109). It is, I argue, enacted through the transnational political affirmation of the existence of a cultural distinction between Muslims and non-Muslims. The reactivation of national identity discussions in EU member states is based on an intensified politics of exclusion of Muslim signs and practices from public spaces. The equation of national culture with national identity builds a symbolic wall[20] that defies and rewrites traditional boundaries. Europeans fantasize a no-border zone (this is, to some extent, the case in the EU), without though escaping the paradox of still needing to draw frontiers inside this borderless territory. The last section of this chapter will elaborate on this paradox, as it relates to the public stigmatization and racialization of gendered Muslim figures.

Is secular Europe fair to Muslims?

Since the end of the 1990s, EU secular public spaces have taken a radical turn when dealing with the growing visibility of Muslims. The headscarf and burka are not the exclusive supposed indicators of religious orthopraxis that European political leaders wish to stigmatize, demonize and therefore control. On 16 March 2011 the *Collectif de lutte contre l'islamophobie*, a Muslim non-governmental organization (NGO) working to counter religious discrimination of Muslim populations in France, reported the ongoing stigmatization of female Muslim students in a Saint Ouen high school (Lycée Auguste Blanqui, located in Seine Saint-Denis, a northern suburb of Paris). The school director had been ordering several Muslim students to come to her office on account of their wearing long, uni-colored skirts. All are Muslim and all wear the headscarf outside of school, taking it off inside as mandated by the 2004 law. Considering their long skirts ostentatious religious signs, the school head asked them to wear blue jeans and T-shirts like the other students, threatening them with expulsion if they did not comply.[21] The politics of the increased surveillance of private convictions and even personal tastes implies a rather restrictive definition of freedom.[22] What is crucial in freedom is its principle, not the possibility to choose between options. Belief is not only about inner contemplation: it also has to be performed. The wearing of an Islamic headscarf certainly constitutes, in many if not most cases, an inherent part of such a performance of personal religiosity. It results from an individual choice about which there is no consensus from the religious authorities. In the headscarf controversies, however, political authorities and citizens intervene simultaneously to determine whether a religiously motivated gesture can be tolerated or not in European democratic liberal societies. Religious beliefs therefore cease to be a matter of purely personal preference as they transform into the subject of public arguments articulated in political and moral terms.

European public spaces have become increasingly intolerant towards Muslim forms of religiosity, regarding them as cultural, social and political pathologies. As Muslims have been made more public since 2001, it is imperative to historicize this process of stigmatization by pointing to the colonial period as a moment of racialization that made of the Muslim the quintessential outsider (Goldberg 2009: 163). If it is reductive to impute the full responsibility of contemporary forms of racism to the colonial experience and its corollary Orientalism, similarities in the public discourses can be observed in the way in which, for instance, cultural hierarchies are established and categorized through fantasies and iconographies of otherness and narratives of deviance.[23] However, the binarism underwriting these constructions not only traces a line between 'us and them', but also serves to distinguish between, in this case, good Muslims and bad Muslims. If this distinction always intensifies in the aftermath of terrorist acts and/or controversies related to Muslims, they nonetheless must also be linked to difficult daily interactions between citizens.[24] 'Racial distinctions become so routinized that a racial hierarchy is maintained without requiring the component of individual actors who are personally hostile towards Muslims' (Razack 2008: 9). The already discussed iconography of threat plays out and transpires in daily interactions. It is articulated through the erection of public transnational controversies and image, clichés that contribute to the production of a common stage on which similar dramas are being played and interpreted by standardized actors: 'Islam is staged in public by means of religious rituals and symbols, by gendered modes of address, by manifestations and collective prayers, and by new forms of jihadism and violence that challenge and threaten the consensual values and civilizational attributes of Europe' (Göle 2010: 109). The creation of an iconography of bad versus good profiles of Muslims was quite intense immediately after the US, London and Madrid bombings, but also increased with the murder of Theo van Gogh, the Danish cartoons controversies or the intensification of the headscarf discussions in the EU. Through this designation of bad and good Muslims, huge controversies (over the headscarf, gang rape, the urban riots or global insecurity) confirm the perpetuation of a 'philanthropic' attitude towards 'museumized peoples' who would be 'petrified into a lifeless custom', to take on Mamdani's words (Mamdani 2004). They need to be saved from the outside as they are incapable of working on their culture (Mamdani 2004). If the continuity of institutional practices (during and after the colonial Empire) is clearly apparent, the emphasis on contemporary iconic constructions of Muslims is rather ethnographic in its focus on the governance of bodies as the main sites for controlling, through sophisticated legal technologies, the modes of social reproduction and transmission of good practices, and best virtues.

I would like to argue that exactly as the 'fiction of race' has mixed science with common sense and traded on the complicity between them (Wacquant 1997), the 'fiction of religion' (here Islam) operates similarly: the external signs of belonging to Islam (headscarf and burka) serve to classify human beings by reference to selected embodied properties so as to exclude them.[25] They equally contribute to the emergence of unequal structures of citizenship, as happened with the centrality of the figure of the Muslim woman in need of saving: 'As a practice of governance, the idea of the imperiled Muslim woman is unparalleled in its capacity to regulate' (Razack 2008: 17). Razack shows, for example, how the regulation of the marital age of consent and family reunification helped the Norwegian state to create a category of citizen whose private-life choices are controlled (as in Foucault's 'conducting the others' conduct'). The author, comparing various Western contexts (Canada, Norway), explores the way in which three allegorical figures (the dangerous Muslim man, the imperiled Muslim woman, the civilized European) 'animate a story about a family of white nations' (Razack 2008: 5). She points out the articulation between a process of eviction from law of certain racialized groups of people, the routinization of racial thinking to cope with Muslim others in the West and the revitalization of a 'colonial governance'. In most EU member states, legal banning has become the central technology for governing the conduct of the Muslim as dangerous person. Hence antidiscrimination law is a site where race and religion intersect, although, as has already been noted, religion is also protected under the freedom of religion constitutional clause. However, whereas both EU and French laws prohibit discrimination on the grounds of religion, it is race and ethnic origin (or color) that are in fact at the core of employment antidiscrimination in both contexts. In practice, in all the public discussions the issue is no longer that of harmonizing the freedom of everyone with the rights of anyone. What is specific to the religious and cultural symbols at stake here is that they expose the normative dimension of discourses on justice and equality, namely the impossibility of objectifying some of the social facts we are seeing coexisting in plural societies (Morag 2002). The thoroughly modern, anti-Muslim racism which characterizes European public opinion relies on 'the new incarnation of post-colonial imperialism, which makes Islam into the "other" who cannot be assimilated, confusing the self-determination of the autonomous subject with the subjectivity of the white, European male' (Laborde 2001: 721).

If in some ways we are all incompatible and Islam represents for Europeans a 'collection of lacks' (Goldberg 2009: 165), the major challenge for political liberalism is that we need to be reasonable (Rawls 1993, 1999). However, religion is still not an intelligible category for thinking diversity and EU states are, as has been demonstrated, not reasonable about it. The increased recourse to legal discourse and the application of rights not only characterizes the way in which European states resolve affairs involving the headscarf, but also now informs and structures research into minority groups and more widely into public policy on the promotion of equality and the fight against discrimination (Conant 2006; Cichowski 2006; Geddes and Guiraudon 2007).[26] This new presence of cultural issues in law arises from a much broader reflection on the legal protection given to individual cultural rights (Sachar 2001; Song 2007), which attempts to establish whether a legal culture of equality is enough to establish effective means of creating equality among believers. The initial negative response results from a reading of legal procedures as interlaced with the political cultures from which they arose, making it impossible to recognize the moral independence and composition of subjects of law embodying so-called 'illiberal' values (Brown 2006). Taking it a step further, Brown points out that some members of minority groups are a culture, while 'we' have culture. To a certain extent, law assigns identity just as subjectively as any other official source of authority. The contribution of the law to the analysis of the headscarf's transformation into a social issue is most beneficial to sociology in terms of the attention it gives to definitions. Defining religion forms probably one of the most hazardous exercises now facing national courts in Europe, frequently through compensation cases for obstruction of freedom of conscience and religious practice. Is it possible (and if so, how) to determine whether religious practices and convictions are authentic or not to a religion? What becomes of the 'sincerity' argument proposed by believers? What is the relevance of the dual demand of discretion and respect for cultural spaces granted by systems regulating the religious, made to minority religious groups in a pluralist context? As a central and irrevocable condition of modern global realities, religious pluralism still has nothing 'natural' about it, and there is some value in observing how the experience of religious difference is formulated by the players who embody it (Bender 2007). There are legal implications arising from varying definitions of the religious, which also affect the assessment of the sincerity of religious expression. Hence, debates about belief and religious practices are inextricably linked to issues of *sincerity* which often, at their most basic and emotional level, emerge as accusations by one group against another, reproaching them for not being 'true' believers (Beamann 2008). Examining different EU contexts, I have demonstrated that religion has been quite absent from the public discussion around the headscarf and burkas mostly because Islam stands more for race and culture than for religion. Secularism in Europe, notwithstanding the specific national traditions, conceives of religion in terms of institution(s) rather than practice or experience, what Ammerman terms 'everyday religion' performed through everyday accomplishments (Ammerman 2006). This incapacity to take religion seriously is particularly well illustrated by the silence of anti-racist groups and their incapacity to take part in the headscarf or burka discussion. The cause of 'the Muslim woman' seems unappealing to anti-racist activists in Europe, perhaps because of the enduring of the woman to be saved narrative. Culture, as Claverie (2003) points out with regard to her work on appearances of the Virgin Mary, only becomes a 'problem' when it is manifested by practices, by perceptible manifestations. The discussions that took place in the EU about what Muslims can and cannot do were never really about religion defined as a system of beliefs and practices oriented towards the sacred or supernatural, affecting the way and perhaps quality of life of individual believers. Liberal secularism (radical in its French version, more flexible in the British one) is based on denominational freedom: people can believe what they want in the private sphere. As a consequence, the public space is conceived of as a realm based on a cultural consensus that overrides individual liberty and on the idea that practice can be reduced to preferences and choices. However, can practices be dissociated from convictions (or, in other words, should religion be relegated to the private sphere to make pluralism viable)?

Conclusion

At this stage, we are still left with a series of unanswered questions related to the issue of the 'justiciability' (Skach 2006) of religious freedom in secular contexts (i.e. restricting religious freedom in the name of religious neutrality in EU member states). If religion indeed forms a private matter, then why do states care about it? Is cultural distinction really a threat to liberal European democracies? From the legal viewpoint, the claims for equality made by Muslims living in Europe are put forward in a context where religious freedom is no longer deemed absolute. Religions are cultural and historical variables, and social and cultural interpretative systems. The consistent historical mistrust vis-à-vis particular expressions of diversity, even when purely part of the private individual life, exposes the unspoken nationalism underwriting discourses of identity and the cultural and ethnic boundaries they seek to reproduce.

In a so-called post-Westphalian order, boundaries and frontiers have to be redefined so as to be distinguished from the classical idea that a border is the line of separation between two competing territories and therefore delineating the existence of an inside and an outside. This conception is still prevalent; even the historical construction of secularism is based on this idea that church and state can be separated by a demarcating line. Several authors advocate the development of a new topology of the border (Bigo and Walker 2007) in light of the

Valérie Amiraux

'pixellization of frontiers' (Bigo and Guild, quoted in Bigo *et al.* 2009) or the border network (Arbaret-Schulz *et al.* 2004), and the obsolescence of the traditional notion of boundary as territorial line. Indeed, not only are national dramas made public issues in other contexts and hence transnationalized, but they all relate to each other, reconstituting internal racial and religious borders inside the EU which, ironically, represent or are thought to represent the achievement of a social, political and economic space devoid of territorial borders. The process of exclusion of Muslim bodies from certain liberties happens inside the nation-state, not at its limits. These pixel borders contain and defend, just as walls do not merely protect but produce the content of the nations they barricade (Brown 2010: 41). The articulation of the concrete procedure of access to citizenship impeded by barriers and forms of surveillance of private and public behaviors clearly blurs territorial boundaries, replacing them with national virtual lines of demarcation hierarchizing classes of citizens (Brown 2010: 15).

The religious diversity embodied by Muslim European citizens remained, in 2011, key, generating contemporary anxieties and social panics in the EU. As is clear from recent public debates over the legitimacy of religious signs or dress, religious legal systems within secular states, comic strip controversies, or still yet family law issues, Islam and Muslims are at the center of debates about modern European democracies and their futures. Mapping religious diversity is indeed frequently coupled with normative prescriptions about how modern citizens should engage with religious others. Over the past years, European politics of difference have been a mixture of hesitation, inconsistency and faithfulness to historical ghosts and abstract principles. There is a need to invent a new type of tie binding individual citizens to the political, since national belonging (citizenship) is increasingly disassociated from cultural belonging. Despite the substitution that can be identified between race and religion as elements of inclusion/exclusion from national contexts, they do not totally overlap, either in their legal treatment or their political outcomes. Both are regulated through constitutional politics; however, the regulations differ. Whereas the constitutional politics of race imply political struggles over the meaning of equality and the legal tools to implement them (affirmative action, ethnic monitoring, etc.), the constitutional politics of religion, and especially Islam, imply a renegotiation, or a reinterpretation of an historical compromise on secularism and its implementation. Whereas the principle of equality characterizing liberal constitutional states cannot tolerate the rule of exception, when it comes to religion there seems to be room for exceptional treatment or differential treatment at least.

Notes

1 This chapter concentrates on Muslims in the EU. For the United States see Esposito and Haddad 2000; Leonard 2003; Cesari 2007; Laurence and Strum 2008; and for Canada see Bramadat and Seljak 2005; Helly 2004, 2010; Korteweg 2008.
2 Integration remains a highly ill-defined notion as it moved from being a classical sociological concept into forming part of political and ideological vocabulary, used interchangeably to convey the projects of assimilation, incorporation or participation (Düvell 2009; Penninx *et al.* 2006).
3 Secularism is based on the assumption that the influence of religion would inevitably decline, as the authority of the church in Western societies would wane in the face of that of the empirical sciences. The diminishing impact of religion on social behavior is traditionally seen as an inherent part of modernization, linked in particular to an increased individualization of religious affiliations and practices (the 'do-it-yourself' perspective) and to 'privatization' of religion in Europe as the solution to cultural conflicts (Barry 2001). Politics, culture and social morality came to be conceived as independent of any religious influence. Morality has therefore become a personal as opposed to a collective concern. European citizens are supposed to relate to society as autonomous, responsible, reflective entities.

4 In addition, particularly since the 1990s, it also relates to issues of national security (Amiraux 2010).

5 The introduction of a religious question in the UK census emerged after a long political discussion between different groups of actors, including members of religious communities. The data collected thus far reveal the heterogeneity of religious groups (Peach 2006). The 2001 census gave the following results: Christians represented 71.6 per cent of the British population, Muslims 2.7 percent, Hindus 1 percent, Sikhs 0.6 percent and Jews 0.5 percent. This appears to be particularly significant when discussing occupational attainment in relation to education: treating Muslims as a homogeneous group ignores important differences which may reflect a respondent's ethnicity as well as the characteristics of his or her home neighborhoods (Johnston *et al.* 2010: 586). For example, Muslims show different exposure to ethnic penalties when comparing between Indians, Pakistanis and Bangladeshis.

6 Some sources for quantitative data are the European values survey (www.europeanvalues.nl), the international social survey program (www.issp.org), and the European social survey (www.ess.ned.uib.no).

7 Given that secularization refers primarily to the idea that religious values and behaviors are shaped by individuals, it follows that attempts to quantify evidence of secularity rely mostly on an assessment of personal religiosity.

8 The visibility of political Islam in Muslim contexts probably contributed to the systematization of identifying Muslims on the grounds of institutional belongings (associations, mosques) and practices. The idea of transplantation, in which patterns of behaviors are understood as traces of the origins, constituted a major framework used to discuss political Islam among European Muslims (Bastenier and Dassetto 1984). It provides a method of analysis that considers path dependency and, more recently, the transnationalization of the political conflicts.

9 European constitutions, theoretically, provide nationally and transnationally through the European Convention on Human Rights (ECHR) protection for religion and religious beliefs.

10 The ordinary trap alludes to Mills' suggestion that people feel trapped when they become more aware, 'however vaguely, of ambitions and of threats which transcend their immediate locales'. He then fleshes out the articulation between 'the personal troubles of milieu' and 'the public issues of social structure' to illustrate the need for sociological imagination as the capacity to range from the most impersonal and remote transformations to the most intimate features of the human self – and to see the relation between the two (Mills 2000).

11 The burkini made headlines both in France and Italy in the summer of 2009. If the situations were in each case different, they usually involved burkini-clad bathers asked to leave a swimming pool or public beach. In some cases the burkini bathers were said to be scaring people, children in particular, as in a public swimming pool in Verona.

12 By a decision on 27 June 2008 (Mme Machbour, no. 286798), the French Council of State denied French nationality to a Moroccan woman living in France, married to a French citizen and mother of three children, because her religious dress was considered radical and incompatible with the core values of French society.

13 In February 2011 Iceland started to debate the possibility of preemptively banning the burka. According to some Members of Parliament, the question should be addressed before women wearing burkas arrive in Iceland. See *Rekjavik Grapevine*.

14 See, for instance, in Dahlab c. Suisse in 2001, and more recently Leyla Sahin c. Turquie in 2005; Dogru v. France December 2008.

15 Other decisions taken by Turkish courts have since been validated by the EHRC ruling.

16 The March 2004 law consists of the addition of a sentence to the Code of Education prohibiting the wearing of ostentatious religious signs in public schools. Since its approval, and in addition to being obliged to appear bareheaded on ID documents, Muslim women wearing the headscarf have also been excluded from courts of justice, universities, work places, hospitals and city halls, far beyond the domain of provision of the law.

17 There are other distinctions within the various countries: the actors affected by the ban are not the same (students in France, teachers in Germany); and the garment concerned – the 'type' of headscarf forbidden – also varies (the extreme veil, that is, the *jilbab* in England).

18 In the British context, this legal discussion forms part of a wider debate about tensions between feminism and multiculturalism (Moller Okin 1999; Abu Lughod 2002; Phillips 2007), which also refers to competing norms (freedom of expression/free speech and freedom of conscience).

19 Europeanization consists of 'processes of (a) construction, (b) diffusion, and (c) institutionalization of formal and informal rules, procedures, policy paradigms, styles, "ways of doing things" and shared

beliefs and norms, which are first defined and consolidated in the EU policy process and then incorporated in the logic of domestic (national and subnational) discourse, political structures and public policies" (Radaelli 2004: 3).

20 With tangible effects on Muslims living in non-Muslim contexts, the specific stigmatization attached to the headscarf has increased the social cost of presenting oneself, as Muslim cultural racism is not only a discourse, but also produces concrete and overt acts of discrimination in several areas of social life (employment, education, housing and health).

21 This episode follows a series of state public declarations and announcements. The Interior Ministry declared in March 2011 that the users of public services (hospitals in particular) would soon be asked not to wear any religious signs. The Minister of Education wrote a note expressing his concern that all parents wishing to take part in school activities could not wear any religious signs, including and most particularly in the case of mothers accompanying their children to school or participating in extracurricular activities.

22 Arendt in fact links freedom to the ability to act. In her view, public space means a guaranteed public realm where actors not only coexist but outwardly express the demonstrable fact of their freedom (Chaudhary 2005: 356).

23 Colonialism is intrinsic to the contemporary scenes of European integration, though the colonial is rendered unseen in most representations of Europe. This is mostly operated through silencing voices that may challenge the posited universality of European narratives (Bhambra 2010).

24 Many scholars have engaged in this type of analysis. The 'Arab boy' of North African origin, extensively publicized as responsible for insecurity in society at large, but also for that of the women of his own community, 'seems to be a ghost from the colonial past [...] like a clone of the indigène that turned into first an immigrant then a Muslim' (Guénif 2006: 118). The historical figure of the cruel Arab is updated in new scenes of confrontation and crime, nowadays often relating to deviant sexual practices (on gang rapes see Muchielli 2005; on the stigmatization of the Arab male as 'voleur, violeur et voileur' – thief, rapist and 'veiler' – see Guénif and Macé 2004), or violent radicalization.

25 The burka ban targets men and women, both figuratively and literally. The sign is conflated with the oppressed woman and the male oppressor as confirmed by the French law project which suggests a fine to be paid by both the wife and the husband.

26 The dual aspect of legal action and the framing of discourse on equality in legal terms around issues of religious rights highlights the difference in skills among minority groups (Sikhs and Muslims, for example) and the different ways in which they have dealt with European legal systems.

References

Abu Lughod, L. (2002) 'Do Muslim women really need saving? Anthropological reflections on cultural relativism and its Others', *American Anthropologist* vol. 104, no. 3: 783–90.

Adelkhah, F. (1991) *La révolution sous le voile. Femmes islamiques d'Iran*, Paris, Karthala.

Ahmed, L. (1993) *Women and Gender in Islam: Historical Roots of a Modern Debate*, New Haven, CT, Yale University Press.

Amiraux, V. (2002) 'Academic discourses on Islam(s) in France and Germany: Producing knowledge or reproducing norms?', in W. Ruf (ed.), *Islam and the West*, Münster, Agenda Verlag, pp. 111–38.

—— (2005) 'Discrimination and claims for equal rights amongst Muslims in Europe', in J. Cesari and S. McLoughlin (eds), *European Muslims and the Secular State*, Aldershot, Ashgate, pp. 25–38.

—— (2009) '"L'affaire du foulard" en France. Retour sur une affaire qui n'en est pas encore une', *Sociologie et Sociétés* vol. 41, no. 2: 273–98.

—— (2010) 'Suspicion publique et gouvernance de l'intime: Contrôle et surveillance des populations musulmanes dans l'Union européenne', in D. Bigo, E. Guittet and A. Scherrer (eds), *Mobilités sous surveillance. Perspectives croisées Union européenne-Canada*, Montréal, Athéna, pp. 73–87.

Amiraux, V. and Guiraudon, V. (2010) 'Discrimination in comparative perspective: policies and practices', *The American Behavioral Scientist* vol. 53, no. 12: 1691–714.

Ammerman, N. (ed.) (2006) *Everyday Religion: Observing Modern Religious Lives*, New York, Oxford University Press.

Arbaret-Schulz, C., Beyer, A., Piermay, J.L., Reitel, B., Selimanovski, C., Sohn, C. and Zander, P. (2004) 'La frontière, un objet spatial en mutation', *EspacesTemps.net*, available at espacestemps.net/document842.html (accessed 12 May 2011).

Asad, T., Brown, W., Butler, J. and Mahmood, S. (2009) *Is Critique Secular? Blasphemy, Injury and Free Speech*, Townsend Papers in the Humanities, No. 2, Berkeley, University of California Press.

Barry, B. (2001) *Culture and Equality: An Egalitarian Critique of Multiculturalism*, Cambridge, Polity Press.

Bastenier, A. and Dassetto, F. (1984) *L'Islam transplanté: Vie et organisation de minorités musulmanes de Belgique*, Anvers/Bruxelles, EPO/EVO.

Baubérot, J. (2004) *Laïcité 1905–2005, entre passion et raison*, Paris, Seuil.

Baubérot, J. and Milot, M. (2011) *Laïcités sans frontières*, Paris, Seuil.

Beamann, L. (2008) 'Defining religion, the promise and the peril of legal interpretation', in R. Moon (ed.), *Law and Religious Pluralism in Canada*, Vancouver, UCB Press, pp. 192–216.

Becci, I. (2004) 'The veil debate: when the religious Other and the gendered Other are one', in G. Titley, *Resituating Culture*, Strasbourg, Council of Europe, pp. 139–49.

Beckford, J. and Wallis, J. (eds) (2006) *Theorising Religion: Cassical and Contemporary Debates*, London, Ashgate.

Bellah, R. (1970) *Beyond Belief. Essays on Religion in a Post-Traditional World*, New York, Harper and Row.

—— (1991) *Beyond Belief: Essays on Religion in a Post-Traditional World*, Berkeley, University of California Press.

Bender, C. (2007) 'Rethinking religious pluralism', *The Immanent Frame*, available at blogs.ssrc.org/tif/2007/11/08/understanding-religious-pluralism (accessed 12 May 2011).

Bhambra, G.K. (2010) 'Sociology after postcolonialism: Provincialized cosmopolitisms and connected sociologies', in E.G. Rodriguez, M. Boatca and S. Costa, *Decolonizing European Sociology: Transdisciplinary Approaches*, Surrey/Burlington, Ashgate, pp. 33–47.

Bigo, D. and Walker, R.B.J. (2007) 'Political sociology and the problem of the international', *Millennium* vol. 35, no. 3: 725–39.

Bigo, D., Bocco, R. and Piermay, J.L. (2009) 'Logiques de marquage: murs et disputes frontalières', *Cultures & Conflits* vol. 1, no. 73: 7–13.

Blair, A. and Aps, W. (2005) 'What not to wear and other stories: Addressing religious diversity in schools', *Education and the Law* vol. 17, no. 1–2, March/June: 1–22.

Börzel, T. and Risse, T. (2003) 'Conceptualizing the domestic impact of Europe', in K. Featherstone and C. Radaelli (eds), *The Politics of Europeanization*, Oxford, Oxford University Press, pp. 57–78.

Bowen, J. (2006) *Why the French Don't Like Headscarves*, Princeton, NJ, Princeton University Press.

Bramadat, P. and Seljak, D. (eds) (2005) *Religion and Ethnicity in Canada*, Toronto, Pearson Education Canada.

Bréchon, P. (2007) 'Cross-national comparisons of individual religiosities', in J. Beckford and J. Demerath (eds), *The Sage Handbook of Sociology of Religion*, London, Sage, pp. 463–89.

Brown, W. (2006) *Regulating Aversion: Tolerance in the Age of Identity and Empire*, Princeton, NJ, Princeton University Press.

—— (2010) *Walled States, Waning Sovereignty*, New York, Zone Books.

Cardozo Law Review (2009) 'Symposium: Constitutionalism and Secularism in an Age of Religious Revival: the Challenge of Global and Local Fundamentalisms', vol. 30, no. 6.

Cesari, J. (ed.) (2007) *Encyclopedia of Islam in the United States*, Westport, CT, Greenwood Press.

Chaudhary, A.S. (2005) '"The Simulacra of Morality": Islamic veiling, religious politics and the limits of liberalism', *Dialectical Anthropology* vol. 29: 349–72.

Cichowski, R. (2006) 'Courts, rights, and democratic participation', *Comparative Political Studies* vol. 39: 50–75.

Claverie, É. (2003) *Les guerres de la Vierge: Une anthropologie des apparitions*, Paris, Gallimard.

Conant, L. (2006) 'Individuals, courts, and the development of European social rights', *Comparative Political Studies* vol. 39: 76–100.

Davie, G. (2002) *Europe, the Exceptional Case. Parameters of Faith in the Modern World*, London, Darton, Longman and Todd.

Dobbelaere, K. and Riis, O. (2003) 'Religious and moral pluralism: theories, research questions and design', *Research in the Social and Scientific Study of Religion*, Leiden, Brill, pp. 159–72.

Düvell, F. (2009) 'Migration, minorities, marginality: New directions in European research', in C. Rumford (ed.), *Handbook of European Studies*, London, Sage, pp. 328–46.

Esposito, J. and Haddad, Y. (2000) *Muslims on the Americanization Path?*, New York, Oxford University Press.

Favell, A. and Guiraudon, V. (2009) 'The sociology of the European Union: An agenda', *European Union Politics* vol. 10, no. 4: 550–76.

Fekete, L. (2009) *A Suitable Enemy. Racism, Migration and Islamophobia in Europe*, London, Pluto Press.

Fekete, L., Bouteldja, N. and Mühe, N. (2010) *Alternative voices on integration*, IRR, available at www.irr.org.uk/2010/july/ha000029.html (accessed 10 May 2011).

Fernando, M. (2010) 'Reconfiguring freedom: Muslim piety and the limits of secular law and public discourse in France', *American Ethnologist* vol. 37, no. 1: 19–35.

Fetzer, J.S. and Soper, J.C. (2005) *Muslims and the State in Britain, France, and Germany*, Cambridge, Cambridge University Press.

Geddes, A. and Guiraudon, V. (2007) 'The Europeanization of anti-discrimination in Britain and France', in C. Bertossi (ed.), *European Anti-Discrimination and the Politics of Citizenship: France and Britain*, Basingstoke, Palgrave-Macmillan, pp. 125–42.

Goldberg, T. (2009) *The Thread of Race: Reflections on Racial Neoliberalism*, Malden/Oxford, Blackwell.

Göle, N. (1993) *Musulmanes et modernes*, Paris, La Découverte.

—— (2010) 'European self-presentations and narratives challenges by Islam: Secular modernity in question', in E.G. Rodriguez, M. Boatca and S. Costa (eds), *Decolonizing European Sociology: Transdisciplinary Approaches*, Surrey/Burlington, Ashgate, pp. 103–15.

Grillo, R., Ballard, R., Ferrari, A., Hoekema, A.J., Maussen, M. and Shah, P. (2009) *Legal Practice and Cultural Diversity*, Aldershot, Ashgate.

Guénif, N. (2006) 'La Française voilée, la beurette, le garçon arabe et le musulman laïc. Les figures assignées du racisme vertueux', in N. Guénif (ed.), *La République mise à nu par son immigration*, Paris, La Fabrique, pp. 109–32.

Guénif, N. and Macé, É. (2004) *Les féministes et le garçon arabe*, Paris, Éditions de l'Aube.

Haritaworn, J. (2010) 'Wounded subjects: Sexual exceptionalism and the moral panic on "Migrants Homophobia" in Germany', in E.G. Rodriguez, M. Boatca and S. Costa, *Decolonizing European Sociology: Transdisciplinary Approaches*, Surrey/Burlington, Ashgate, pp. 135–51.

Hazareesingh, S. (1994) *Political Traditions in Modern France*, Oxford, Oxford University Press.

Helly, D. (2004) 'Are Muslims discriminated against in Canada?', *Canadian Ethnic Studies* vol. 36, no. 1: 24–47.

—— (2010) 'Orientalisme populaire et modernisme: Une nouvelle rectitude politique au Canada', *The Tocqueville Review/La revue Toqueville* vol. 31, no. 2: 157–93.

Héritier, A. (ed.) (2002) *Common Goods: Reinventing European and International Governance*, Boston, MA, Rowman & Littlefield.

Hoffmann, F. and Ringelheim, J. (2004) 'Par-delà l'universalisme et le relativisme: La Cour européenne des droits de l'homme et les dilemmes de la diversité culturelle', *Revue interdisciplinaire d'études juridiques* no. 52: 109–42.

Iacub, M. (2008) *Par le trou de la serrure. Une histoire de la pudeur publique, XIX-XXIe siècle*, Paris, Fayard.

Johnston, R., Sirkeci, I., Khattab, N. and Modood, T. (2010) 'Ethno-religious categories and measuring occupational attainment in relation to education in England and Wales: A multi-level analysis', *Environment and Planning* vol. 42, no. 3: 578–91.

Jonker, J. and Amiraux, V. (eds) (2000) *Politics of Visibilities: Young Muslims in European Public Spaces*, Bielefeld, Transcript Verlag.

Kilic, S. (2008) 'The British Veil Wars', *Social Politics* vol. 15, no. 4: 433–54.

Kilic, S., Saharso, S. and Sauer, B. (2008) 'Introduction: The Veil. Debating citizenship, gender and religious diversity', *Social Politics* vol. 15, no. 4: 397–410.

Koenig, M. (2007) 'Europeanising the governance of religious diversity? An institutionalist account of Muslim struggles for public recognition', *Journal of Ethnic and Migration Studies* vol. 33, no. 6: 911–32.

Korteweg, C.A. (2008) 'The sharia debate in Ontario: Gender, Islam, and representations of Muslim woman's agency', *Gender and Society* vol. 22, no. 4: 434–54.

Krizsan, A. and Popa, R. (2010) 'Europeanization in making policies against domestic violence in Central and Eastern Europe', *Social Politics* vol. 17, no. 3: 379–406.

Laborde, C. (2001) 'The culture(s) of the Republic: Nationalism and multiculturalism in French Republican thought', *Political Theory* vol. 29, no. 5: 716–35.

—— (2005) 'Secular philosophy and Muslim headscarves', *Journal of Political Philosophy* vol. 13, no. 3: 305–29.

—— (2008) *Critical Republicanism: The Hijab Controversy and Political Philosophy*, Oxford, Oxford University Press.

Landman, N. (2007) 'Too much Islam? Challenges to the Dutch Model', *Global Dialogue* vol. 9, nos 3–4, available at www.worlddialogue.org (accessed 11 May 2011).

Laurence, J. and Strum, P. (2008) *Governments and Muslim Communities in the West: United States, United Kingdom, France and Germany*, Washington, DC, Woodrow Wilson International Center for Scholars.

Leonard, K. (2003) *Muslims in the United States: The State of Research*, New York, Russell Sage Foundation.

MacGoldrick, D. (2006) *Human Rights and Religion. The Islamic Headscarf Debate in Europe*, Oxford and Portland, Hart-Publishing.

Mahmood, S. (2005) *Politics of Piety: The Islamic Revival and the Feminist Subject*, Princeton, NJ, Princeton University Press.

Mamdani, M. (2004) *Good Muslim, Bad Muslim: America, the Cold War and the War on Terror*, New York, Pantheon.

Maréchal, B., Allievi, S., Dassetto, F. and Nielsen, J.S. (eds) (2003) *Muslims in the Enlarged Europe*, Leiden, Brill.

Maussen, M. (2007) *The Governance of Islam in Western Europe: A State of the Art*, Amsterdam, IMISCOE Working Paper No. 16.

Meer, N., Sala Pala, V., Modood, T. and Simon, P. (2009) 'Religion, culture, identity, and education in Western Europe', in J. Banks (ed.), *The Routledge International Companion To Multicultural Education*, New York, Routledge.

Mernissi, F. (1987) *Le harem politique: Le Prophète et les femmes*, Paris, Albin Michel.

Mills, C.W. (2000 [1959]) *The Sociological Imagination*, Oxford, Oxford University Press.

Modood, T., Triandafyllidou, A. and Zapata-Barrero, R. (2006) *Multiculturalism, Muslims and Citizenship: A European Approach*, New York, Routledge.

Moller Okin, S. (1999) 'Is multiculturalism bad for women?', in S. Moller Okin, J. Cohen, M. Howard and M.C. Nussbaum (eds), *Is Multiculturalism Bad for Women?* Princeton, NJ, Princeton University Press, pp. 1–27.

Morag, P. (2002) 'Rights and recognition: Perspectives on multicultural democracy', *Ethnicities* vol. 2, no. 1: 31–51.

Muchielli, L. (2005) *Le scandale des tournantes*, Paris, La Découverte.

Open Society Institute (2010) *Muslims in Europe: A Report on 11 EU Cities*, Budapest, New York and London, OSI.

Peach, C. (2006) 'Muslims in the 2001 Census of England and Wales: Gender and economic disadvantage', *Ethnic and Racial Studies* vol. 29, no. 4: 629–55.

Penninx, R., Berger, M. and Kraal, M. (eds) (2006) *The Dynamics of International Migration and Settlement in Europe. A State of the Art*, Amsterdam, Amsterdam University Press.

Pew Global Attitudes Survey (2010) *Widespread Support for Banning Full Islamic Veil in Western Europe*, July.

Phillips, A. (2007) *Multiculturalism without Culture?*, Princeton, NJ, Princeton University Press.

Puar, J. (2007) *Terrorist Assemblages: Homonationalism in Queer Times*, Durham, NC, Duke University Press.

Radaelli, C. (2004) 'Europeanisation: Solution or problem?', *European Integration online Papers* vol. 8, no. 16: 57–82.

Rawls, J. (1993) *Political Liberalism*, New York, Columbia University Press.

—— (1999 [1971]) *A Theory of Justice*, Cambridge, MA, Harvard University Press.

Razack, S.H. (2008) *Casting Out. The Eviction of Muslims from Western Law & Politics*, Toronto, University of Toronto Press.

Religion Monitor (2008) *What the World Believes: Analysis and Commentary on the Religion Monitor 2008*, Gütersloh, Bertelsmann Stiftung.

Robbers, G. (ed.) (2005) *State and Church in the European Union*, Baden-Baden, Nomos.

Sachar, A. (2001) *Multicultural Jurisdictions: Cultural Differences and Women's Rights*, Cambridge, Cambridge University Press.

Sauer, B. (2009) 'Headscarf regimes in Europe: Diversity policies at the intersection of gender, culture and religion', *Comparative European Politics* 75, vol. 1: 75–94.

Schnapper, D. (1991) *La France de l'intégration: Sociologie de la nation en 1990*, Paris, Gallimard.

Scott, J. (2007) *The Politics of the Veil*, Princeton, NJ, Princeton University Press.

Simon, P. (ed.) (2004) *Comparative study on the collection of data to measure the extent and impact of discrimination within the United States, Canada Australia, the United Kingdom and the Netherlands*, Report to the European Commission, DG Employment and Social Affairs, Fundamental Rights and Anti-discrimination, Luxembourg.

Skach, C. (2006) 'Leyla Sahin v. Turkey and "Teacher Headscarf Case" BVerfG, Case No. 2BvR 1436/02', *American Journal of International Law*, Centennial Issue, vol. 100, no. 1: 186–95.

Song, S. (2007) *Justice, Gender, and the Politics of Multiculturalism*, Cambridge, Cambridge University Press.

Statham, P., Koopmans, R., Giugni, M. and Passy, F. (2005) 'Resilient or adaptable Islam? Multiculturalism, religion and migrants' claims-making for group demands in Britain, the Netherlands and France', *Ethnicities* vol. 5, no. 4: 427–59.

Tessler, M. (1999) *Area Studies and Social Science: Strategies for Understanding Middle East Politics*, Bloomington, Indiana University Press.

Titley, G. and Lentin, A. (2011) *Crisis of Multiculturalism*, London, Zed Books.

Triandafyllidou, A. (ed.) (2010) *Muslims in 21st Century Europe*, New York, Routledge.

Wacquant, L. (1997) 'For an analytic of racial domination', *Political Power and Social Theory* vol. 11: 221–34.

Younge, G. (2011) 'The multiculturalism the European right fears so much is a fiction – it never existed', *Guardian*, 14 March.

18

UK counter-terrorism strategy and Muslim diaspora communities

The 'securitisation of integration'[1]

Tahir Abbas

It is true that the nature of the Muslim experience in Britain has transcended traditional markers of 'race' and ethnicity in relation to discussions of difference and commonality, but who exactly are these groups (Abbas 2009)? There are approximately 2.4 million Muslims in Britain, making up around 4 per cent of the population of the UK. They hail from all the corners of the globe, although around one-half are South Asians with one-third of all Muslims likely to be Azad Kashmiri in origin. The other major South Asian Muslim groups in Britain are the Sylhetis (Bengalis), Gujeratis (East African Indian, or Indian) and Punjabis (Pakistanis). There are also many Arab Muslims, particularly in West London, as well as Turkish Muslim communities in parts of North London that generally remain invisible from political, media and cultural discourses in relation to the 'Muslims in Britain'. The origins of some Yemeni and Somali communities have over 100 years of history, although in recent periods Somalis and Sudanese have come to Britain fleeing persecution and seeking asylum. Around 15 per cent of all British Muslims are Shi'a in origin, reflecting the wider global diversity of Shi'a Islam.

It is the visible Muslim communities in the older inner cities, however, who experience the fullness of societal discrimination towards Islam and Muslims. They are also a group that suffers from wider alienation, disenfranchisement and racism in the places where they live, work and are schooled. In the period following the terrorist attacks on the USA on 11 September 2001, there has been a focus on issues of radicalisation in the context of an evolving multicultural citizenship framework, but it is conflated with discussions in relation to security, policing and intelligence. This chapter explores the sociological and political issues in relation to questions of radicalisation, how it impacts on certain centre–right notions that Muslims have somehow destroyed multiculturalism in Britain, and the impact of government policy (where there is potentially an opportunity to present a more positive public profile in relation to anti-terrorism legislation and practice, but it may well have been missed).

It is argued that the problems of radicalisation in Britain are primarily of social, economic, political and cultural disconnect and that this has occurred because of specific issues of migration, but also because of how domestic integration policy has failed to adequately improve the lived experiences of poor groups. Critics from the left and the right concentrate on the religion of Islam as the problem per se. Rather, in reality, the issues are more to do with: (a) acute forms of Islamophobia and multiple forms of racism towards various Muslim minorities; and (b) a distinct failure to address these problems by delivering policy solutions which are largely focused on improving attitudinal indicators of change rather than the structural nature of realities. Social and economic divisions continue to widen and in the context of globalisation the chasm between the generations and genders has widened to reveal a body of young Muslim men vulnerable to the forces of violent 'Islamism'. The problem of violent extremism is indeed one that affects a tiny subsection of society, minority and majority; however, majority media and political discourses continue to conflate between the nuances of religion, politics and identity that characterise the young male Muslim experience in Britain, projecting the problems as of religion and theology rather than of media, society, politics and the economy.

It is important to ask the question 'what is radical politics today?' It is an interesting and crucial enquiry, but it is undefined and uncategorised. What it does do is to provide scope to engage with a difficult but significant issue, particularly in relation to the notion of radicalism and its relationship with Muslims in Britain. It is especially important when thinking of present political Islamism, but when doing so how are the factors that underpin this radicalism today different from those in the past? Are there indeed degrees of radicalism such that there might be the notion of a 'softer' versus a 'harder' variation, where the 'softer' is non-violent, progressive, liberal and open-ended and the 'harder' is violent, regressive, illiberal and closed-ended? In relation to Muslims as a body of people, whether in Muslim majority states or diaspora communities in the West, what is the relationship between so-called Islamism and so-called radicalism? This chapter addresses some of these questions by focusing on the social, economic and cultural dynamics of British Muslims; the question of violence and Muslim identities in the context of social conflict; the importance of global geo-political dynamics in question relating to Muslims, Islam and politics; and, finally, critically assessing aspects of government policy vis-à-vis counter-terrorism strategy and its implications for communities.

Muslims in Britain and politics of radicalism

Britain has a youthful Muslim population where one in three of approximately 2.4 million are under the age of 15. They are living, but not always working or getting a sound education, in the inner cities of their birth and in the older Victorian homes of parents who arrived when they were needed in the 1950s and 1960s (Peach 2005; Phillips 2006). These communities, however, like many other migrant groups, have largely been ignored by state support when they no longer served a primary economic function to industry (as it has largely collapsed) and their needs have been neglected or are simply ignored (Benyon and Solomos 1987; Rex 1988). Majority ethnic English communities began moving out when their streets were thought to be taken hostage by the invading 'other' in the 1970s and beyond. It led to residential clustering and these localities subsequently become 'no-go' areas for majority groups. Over the decades, invisible but firm socio-psychological and socio-economic barriers began to appear between Muslims and other communities, trapping groups in separate instances of poverty and disadvantage. Since the late 1980s, Muslims in Britain have been regarded in relation to their religion and less so through the prism of 'race' or ethnicity, with the events of the Salman Rushdie affair of 1989 firmly implanting in the minds of the many that there is 'a Muslim problem' in Britain (Modood 1990). Presently, as the 'war on terror' rages on in all but name since the events of 9/11, young Muslims in the inner cities are ever beleaguered, unable to find a solution to their everyday problems. Some, moreover, have turned to a radicalising message of hate and intolerance towards others.

All the same, this is not the work of Islam or Muslim-ness per se, but the outcome of decades of inefficient and ineffective domestic government policy, and growing community perceptions in relation to foreign policy, in combination with the unresolved discord between the generations, immigrant and indigenous. The identity vacuum created within second- and third-generation British Muslims is exacerbated by class and ideological struggle that continues to plague the Muslim world (which still recovers from hundreds of years of imperialism, colonialism, post-colonialism and neo-colonialism) (Ali 2005). It is a struggle for resources: the ownership of the means of production and knowledge in the context of an information age-dominated globalisation. Many Muslims in Britain face the full range of exclusions and marginalisation of every deeply disempowered person in society, but their experience is particularly acute given the falsity of the global 'war on terror', the discussion of national cultural identity politics – i.e. are you a good Briton or are you a good Muslim? – and, locally, the concern in relation to the discussion of 'self-styled segregation' (Rai 2007) or 'parallel lives' (Abbas 2011). The latter notion is principally spurious, as it is no more or less of a concern than it is for Orthodox Jews living in Stamford Hill in the London Borough of Hackney, or third-generation white Britons in 'sink estates' in Middlesbrough or Liverpool, for example. All experience low education, high unemployment, high drug use, high teenage pregnancies, single parenthood and a sense of disenfranchisement, which, for far-right groups, is thought to be explained to a significant degree by the presence of foreign people in Britain. These 'others' might have been the Irish or Afro-Caribbeans in the 1960s and 1970s, the 'invading Asians' of the 1970s and 1980s (and their potential 'swamping' of 'our society', words famously immortalised by Margaret Thatcher in 1978, who swept into power a year later in 1979), or the African and Arab 'asylum seekers and refugees' in the 1990s. In the 2000s it is 'Muslims', intersecting religion with skin colour, who are seen to represent that which is outside of the perceived physical, social and cultural boundaries of English-ness or British-ness, which remain contested and ever-evolving categories (Fekete 2008; Kundnani 2008).

Clearly, social class is an important issue and, in particular, the downward mobility pressures that many British Muslims have been facing over the generations. This is compounded by the lack of a clear cultural, political or theological steer to guide younger Muslims away from harm. As much as there is discussion on the role of al-Qaeda, the Muslim Brotherhood, Jamaat-e-Islami, Hizb-ut-Tahrir and others in the radicalisation of young British Muslims, discussion is meaningless when every one of the UK Muslims involved in anti-state terrorist activity is 'made in Britain'. Government policy, however, has been minded to place the emphasis upon mosques, imams, women and the media, which are important to help improve the capacity and professionalism of institutions and Islamic centres that that have long been neglected, but the elephant in the room is still ignored or wholly under-emphasised: foreign-policy grievances in the context of acutely marginalised socio-economic and socio-cultural preconditions.

In its simplest form radicalism is a response to acute challenges in relation to identity and community, and at home or abroad. This is no less so for Muslims in Britain or elsewhere in the West (Ahmed 2003; Pape 2005). Arguably, if solutions in relation to the grievances of minorities, disaffected groups or the oppressed can be determined without the need for a degree of political radicalisation, then, possibly, modern societies would not have experienced the reforms that have characterised post-war Western European nations (Yaqoob 2007). Organising around social issues and working towards political projects that eliminate excessive powers of the state, particularly if they impact on positive human interaction or limit the changes to public policy that reveal such outcomes, have been a regular function of twentieth-century history. In the 1960s civil rights, counter-cultural, anti-war and anti-imperial efforts all helped to check the workings of not just the USA but also Britain, France, Germany, Italy and Spain. In the 1980s radical politics caused the Berlin Wall to fall and it marked the beginning of a world where the old conflicts became history, conceivably at the cost of introducing new perceived or actual ideological struggles (Fukuyama 2006). Ever since then, Muslims across the globe have been characterised as marking the definitive anti-capitalist or anti-imperialist struggles of our times. This operates at a local, national and global level of ideology and practice. To others, Muslims are seen to be radical within the domestic and community spheres in the form of 'Asian gangs' or the 'rioters' of 2001 in the former northern mill towns (Alexander 2000; Macey 2007; Bagguley and Hussain 2008).

Community responses and philosophical challenges – radical politics?

Since the terrorist attacks in London on 7 July 2005, government policy has still not yet fully sought to provide the economic or political empowerment that is needed for Muslims. As citizens, British Muslims vote, establish enterprises and access free education (up to a point), but the realities are far from perfect. There is under-participation and under-representation in politics. A function of internal community socio-cultural structures that have the potential to take away basic democratic rights, propped up by the first-past-the-post system of electoral politics. It is easily exploited in Muslim enclaves by community elders led by the major political parties (Back and Solomos 1992). The limited experience of education, employment and self-employment is characterised by not just an 'ethnic penalty' (Brown 2000) but by an additional 'Muslim penalty' (Open Society Institute 2004). Further still, keeping minorities suppressed helps to prevent groups, including Muslims, from asking hard-hitting questions and from then expecting steadfast answers. Rather, the policy has sought to provide a range of under-developed solutions to a basket of problems focused on 'the Muslim'. Some Muslims jump onto the band-wagon, ready to argue at the behest of the state, and with the soundings all too familiar: Muslims must integrate (into what exactly?); Muslims must empower women (at the outset, Islam empowered women, minorities and the poor?); Muslims must come out of their 'ghettos' (without jobs that pay and employers who employ?); and Muslims need to embrace modernity (indeed, contemporary notions of modernity have their roots in Islamic neo-Platonic thinking of tenth-century Al-Farabi (872–950), and many others since (Safi 2003)).

In the worlds of civil society or third-sector organisations, in local authorities, in universities and other public institutions, it is hoped that the many professional Muslims operating in various policy and community contexts are savvy enough to be aware of what is in play. For years these mosques, imams and women's networks have lacked not only physical resources but also emotional and intellectual confidence. It is now an important time to work on these fronts, when there is high-level ownership linked with dedicated funding. If this recent 'prevention of violent extremism' agenda can help to build resilient communities, the stronger they will be to fight racism, discrimination, fascism and vilification and the more people will be effective citizens who can look confidently to the future. It will certainly not entirely eliminate the threat of violent extremism, though, as the essential drivers of this phenomenon are based on personalised, globalised gripes that result in localised acts of extreme anti-state violence.

Today, Muslims the world over are radicalised for reasons that stretch back over the millennia but, more specifically, because of Western interventions in the twentieth century, the bloodiest in our human history (Bernard 1999; Burgat 1999). Much of this political, cultural and social radicalism is a response to systems of oppression. As these chains take their time to unshackle, and as Muslims continue to migrate to the West in search of a better day, the ideological constructions of the 'Muslim other' remain powerful and unyielding in the face of the challenges to notions of equality and unity in diversity (Said 2003). The re-emergence of the East and the South, in the forms of Brazil, Russia, the United Arab Emirates, India and China, to name but a few, will lead to an inexorable balancing of global power and politics. No longer will there be a single dominant hegemony, acting as sole arbiter of moral worth and economic and social gain, although it is far from clear that this will be the case under Barack Obama (Lynch and Singh 2008). Politics are about the difficult questions relating to the challenges of scarce resources, and radical politics are an exacerbation of this condition.

For the young Muslims affected, radicalism is as much about determining their 'British-ness' as it is about their 'Muslim-ness' (Samad and Sen 2007). The problems that Muslims in Britain experience are essentially of politics; so, it appears, are the solutions. A victimhood mentality will only get Muslims so far. There have to be greater attempts to proactively determine the solutions. It is true that various Western European nation-states are continuing with a legal, social and cultural assault on Muslims, with attempts to strengthen draconian anti-terror legislation at home while fighting Muslim 'insurgents' abroad. With ongoing harmful media discourses that vilify, stigmatise and homogenise Muslims and Islam, many young Muslims are vulnerable to radicalisation (Poole and Richardson 2006). Unless there are greater efforts to tackle the structural issues and politico-ideological constructs in relation to 'being Muslim', the potential threat of violent Islamic political radicalism will linger. These local area efforts are compounded by national and international issues. The desire to bring about the necessary change has to be generated from the bottom up, but unless government recognises its full role in how to effectively deliver appropriate top-down solutions, which it is publicly doing more and more, the status quo will remain. This cannot happen if society wishes for a stable and prosperous multicultural future, confident of inter-cultural and inter-faith relations as the negative trends of globalisation bite harder and individual freedoms erode in the face of rampant capitalism and insidious post-9/11 invasions into basic freedoms in (relatively still) progressive, secular, liberal Western European societies, and, in particular, in Britain (Lewis 2007).

Muslims need to appreciate the importance of the oneness of humanity, as is stipulated in the core doctrines, and not fall foul of immediate negative political gratification. The test is to evoke the beauty, excellence and the stability of an advanced Islamic culture, where faith, logic, reasoning and human progress go hand in hand. In the present climate, the embattled Muslim minorities in Western Europe routinely have to defend against accusations of violence, terror and negative cultural associations, but the hope would be that in the near future it would be possible to move beyond the immediate concerns and determine a positive image of Islam, where family, community, knowledge, nature and technology exist for the good of humanity as a whole and not just the few. This new radical British Islam needs to be one that demonstrates responsibility for all, and in a world where Muslims and non-Muslims are interdependent human beings striving for collective efficacy in the face of the challenges for scarce resources and the inevitable fallibility as well as frailty of humankind.

There is a genuine need to enhance and develop the appearance and application of Western European Islam, one that is actively facilitated and encouraged by objective and rational people, communities and nation-states, improving levels of trust, confidence, engagement and the participation of existing and new Muslim minorities and non-Muslim majorities. If the global pressures in relation to issues for Muslims are not improved, many more younger Muslim minorities in Western Europe will see the 'long war' as a 'war against Islam', the next global war, after the end of the Cold War (Rex 2005).

Government engagement with Muslims in Britain – testing left politics?

The question of how government should engage with Muslims is an extremely interesting one, but, potentially, for the wrong reasons. In light of the recent general election in the UK, it is probably apt to look at what has been done for Muslim engagement and then to examine the disparities in relation to what still needs to be done.

When New Labour sailed into power in 1997, it was indeed an exciting time for Britain. With the first term devoted, certainly in the domestic context, to diversity and equality, it was wholly encouraging to see changes to the Race Relations (Amendment) Act and the introduction of the Human Rights Act, for example. It was a heady time and Muslims, who were increasingly determining a religious and cultural space in society, as well as a political and social one, experienced relative positive change. However, this all changed, and very quickly, during the summer of 2001. During that summer some of Britain's former mill towns in the north of the country witnessed some of the worse 'race riots' in two decades. Young, second- and third-generation British Muslims, who were experiencing inter-generational disconnect, high rates of unemployment, labour market and societal discrimination, as well as acrimonious efforts by the far right, finally exploded. Five cities and towns were affected, with significant violence occurring in three: Bradford, Oldham and Burnley (Kundnani 2001). Later that summer the events of 9/11 in the USA changed the global picture in relation to Islam and Muslims, arguably for the foreseeable future (until, of course, another crisis of global enormity took over temporarily – in this case the credit crunch of October 2008).

Ultimately, the essential policy problems in relation to Muslim engagement in the current period relate to the policy errors of 2001 and since. The root causes of anomie and social and ethnic conflict are the lack of economic opportunities, the limitations to social mobility due to discrimination and racism, and the concerns of education, housing and health that affect certain groups more than others because of the concentration of disadvantage (Bhavnani *et al.* 2005). Rather, policy has sought to placate the middle (chattering) classes, originally wooed by New Labour, and focused on questions of values and identity rather than genuine economic development and policy. This is what the northern towns required and still do to this day: direct inward investment to stimulate growth, enterprise and inter-culturalism to turn degenerated older towns and cities into thriving, globally orientated, cosmopolitan centres.

The traditional left in politics should perhaps have taken a braver stance, but it was crushed by the weight of global pressures in relation to the 'war on terror'. The collective notion of Islam and Muslims became the 'monster', seemingly responsible for all the social and cultural ills that Britain currently faces – the idea of separate lives, cultural relativism, violence towards women, the monopoly on terrorism – when in fact, over the last decade or so Britain has become a society more divided than ever, more unequal than ever, and more disconnected than ever (Office for National Statistics 2009). Globalisation and liberalism have done that, rather than Osama bin Laden and al-Qaeda from caves in Afghanistan. The traditional left reacted by organising grass-roots political and pressure movements in opposition to the 'war on terror' and all that it ostensibly stood for. This gave birth to new-left movements that combined Muslim and non-Muslim interests, with some political gains made in London and Birmingham. These efforts, however, have had their own internal battles – one of which relates to the notion of God itself. It has led to ideological differences that have impacted on political differences (Phillips 2008).

New Labour and Muslim political conflicts

Throughout this time the issue of government engagement with Muslims has been problematic. At the very start, New Labour and the Muslim Council of Britain (MCB) went through a honeymoon period, which lasted until the events of 2001 at home and abroad. This was when significant ideological and political differences came to the surface. Over the years the MCB continued to endorse a non-violent, democratic approach to cohesion, integration and in determining a space for Muslims in Britain, but there were others inside New Labour who felt that they were not doing enough. Cajoled and manoeuvred, a swathe of new Muslim umbrella groups were formed in an instant and were projected as the viable and acceptable face of 'moderate' Islam. These Muslim groups were engaged with as long as they did not exhibit dissent or presume to have more power than they actually did.

More recently, because of a very public media spat between the previous Secretary of State for Communities and Local Government, Hazel Blears, and a leading figure in the MCB, Daud Abdullah, the government broke off all formal relations with the MCB. This was, arguably, just before it was beginning to re-engage with central government politics after a period of being sidelined. However, the bickering between the former Secretary of State and MCB big-wigs only added to the malaise. While the other Muslim umbrella groups pick up the pieces of their brief flirtations with power, there remains an acute disparity in relation to the representation of Muslim interests and concerns. With the main plank of community engagement seen through the prism of 'preventing violent extremism', it is no surprise that disengagement is a significant issue. Muslims do not want to be regarded as 'potential terrorists' before the government speaks with them – no wonder, then, that a significant proportion feel disconnected from politics and feel ever-beleaguered by the workings of the state and neo-liberal political discourses, in general and in relation to specific developments to 'prevent' policy.

Tossing between left and right politics and policy-making has left an ideological vacuum. Muslims, like Christians, Jews, Bahais, Sikhs, Hindus, Jains and so on, who all help to make parts of Britain home to some of the most dynamic, vibrant and successful multicultural communities, need clearer direction and a sense that the government is winning the fight against fascism, racism and discrimination of all kinds. It is important to move towards an agenda that brings people together rather than drives them apart, providing equality of opportunity but also equality of outcome, and where government can ensure that there is a collective, multicultural political and social project that is owned by all, and not just the few. In post-credit crunch Britain, economic stability and cultural inter-sectionality will win the day. At the bottom of society, where we have struggling white and ethnic-minority groups, the idea of competition between them has to be replaced with the idea of cross-fertilising their concerns in relation to wider interests. There is no gain in poor white groups battling on the streets of city centres with poor Muslim groups and then blaming each other for their respective discomforts in society. The problem is greater than that, but the issue is how to connect these groups with each other while not losing sight of the bigger political and social challenges. What does it mean to be a Briton in the twenty-first century? What connects different communities who suffer from the problems of job loss, globalisation and regionalism? How do we shape a nation that moves forward in a collective struggle for humanity that combines all in an effort to support the many? These are the questions that impact on today; these are the challenges that remain.

To 'prevent' or not to 'prevent'

We live in interesting times, as they say. No more so than in the immediate present with all its pressures emanating from a depressed economy, deflated expectations, net reductions of real wealth and the view that things can only get worse. This is quite a development given that when New Labour came into power in 1997, inheriting a Conservative-orchestrated economic boom, things apparently 'could only get better'. Britain's urban communities are changing at a more rapid pace than ever, but for Muslims in Britain there remain acute challenges – both economic and social – which prevent them from engaging in opportunities afforded to others. This is because of the lack of choice, rather than a choice made not to engage in society. These concerns are perennial as they have never been adequately addressed, even after decades of attempts to regenerate and rejuvenate declining post-industrial towns and cities in the Midlands and in the north.

We are clearly witnessing a severe north–south divide, and not just among Britons in general but also in relation to Muslim Britons. Two out of three Muslims live in London, and they reflect the entire Muslim world with is diversity of sects, cultures and traditions. Outside of London and towards the north of England, Muslims are more likely to be mono-ethnic and mono-cultural. These South Asian Muslims are also likely to be experiencing severe socio-economic deprivation, and patterns of disadvantage that reveal generational reproduction of acute unemployment, poor housing and declining health. This is the racism and discrimination experienced by ethnic and racial groups who also happen to be Muslim. These are issues at all levels of society, affecting local communities as well as those who experience glass ceilings in corporate structures. There are also issues in the criminal justice system, in the media, in relation to political representation, and the professionalisation and capacity-building of minority ethnic and religious institutions and infrastructures that also have a three-decade lag to their development. To fund projects to help with such issues is now seen as part of a drive to 'prevent violent extremism', when in fact they are about the basic infrastructural development of communities.

The problems of widening economic and social inequalities also have implications for wider issues of alienation, disenfranchisement, isolation and dislocation that impact on how young men, Muslim and non-Muslim, might become vulnerable to the forces of political radicalism, and sometimes where the hate towards the 'other' turns to acute forms of violence. The breeding ground for this is an array of local tensions, conflicts and exclusions, and when the frustration is negatively challenged by political ideology, the results can be very serious. The localised forces that impact upon the disaffection of young people, often but not always men, are similar and as significant – they are essentially societal. This is the impact of globalisation on local area communities, with Muslims additionally affected by notions of the *umma* (the global Muslim community – real or imagined). It is important to note that all of the 7/7 bombers originated from impoverished backgrounds, as the sons of first- and second-generation migrant workers who came to live and work in the north only to find acute de-industrialisation a mere decade after their arrival. Many of these and other 'foot soldiers' who have been arrested for alleged or actual crimes, and those who ultimately have been sentenced, have come from precisely these relatively poorer areas of the country.

With the current political focus on notions of shared values, arguably a distraction from the real issues that divide communities, which are more structural than cultural, there is considerable danger in (a) taking attention away from the genuine causes of radicalisation, and (b) anti-terror policies potentially making the problems far worse. These policies have sometimes been limited in perspective, have been short-termist, over-reactive and, in the not so distant past, painfully ineffective. Intelligence is narrow, action is taken quickly, and the repercussions are heavy. For Muslims to be active, engaged and participative citizens in society who do not just share values but also have equal opportunities and equal outcomes, there is a need to focus on building solid foundations for economic and social stability and mobility. The problems are not of a lack of shared values or common goals, or indeed notions of what it means to British, Muslim or a minority: rather it is the forces that pull people apart that are of greater significance – racism, discrimination, widening economic inequalities, a UK Muslim north–south divide even – and all this in the context of devolution, Europeanisation and globalisation in a post-credit-crunch world.

'Contest contested' and concluding thoughts

'Contest II' came into play in March 2009, the latest development in the government's counter-terrorism strategy, which began with 'Contest I' in 2003 (Contest stands for 'Counter-Terrorism Strategy'). There are four 'Ps' in the programme, with 'Prevent' focused on community development dynamics. The other three, Pursue, Prepare and Protect, are more behind-the-scenes approaches to matters of intelligence, policing and community. 'Prevent' is the public face of the fight against terrorism in Britain today. However, the 'Prevent' approach has come under criticism from detractors who argue that it is 'community-led surveillance' (Kundnani 2009), an attempt to gather important data on community members so that they can be monitored more closely if they are seen as a risk. In reality, the 'Prevent' initiatives are capacity-building formulae to ensure that the intellectual, spiritual and organisational battle against extremism from within the communities can be better supported.

Initially, there has been a concentration on building structures and only recently has a clearer political intent been stated. Community understanding, however, is limited through the lack of adequate vehicles of communication – the positive aspects of the policy and the experience have to be fully presented to improve trust and confidence in systems and processes. There remains a great deal of scepticism in relation to these issues because of the arguments of human and civil rights campaigners and the actual experiences of local area racisms and physical tensions that are experienced by many but are missed by those in Whitehall designing, implementing and then evaluating policies in this area.

The focus on dismantling the structures of al-Qaeda is important to bear in mind. The notion of a widespread al-Qaeda network of loose affiliates is more the reality, but it does not suggest anything beyond a temporal association. Chances are that the 'head of the snake' has been less effective for quite some time. There is a real likelihood that those who are funding and supporting terrorism against the West may have other motivations at heart and may well include a whole host of different interest groups and certain dedicated individuals. War is certainly big business and a perpetual state of conflict serves the interests of many who are already powerful and influential. Presently, many of the so-called radicals are 'self-styled', and they are reaching out rather than being programmed and prepared from the centre. The general idea is that Western governments wish that al-Qaeda were a traditional hierarchical organisation (with a firm leadership, organisation and structure), but it is more of a narrative than a reality, as its organisational set-up has largely been destroyed. However, the number of loose affiliates is growing compared with the decline of the profile of the central al-Qaeda threat (perceived, projected or real). The spin ought to be that if British policy talks away the threat of al-Qaeda by stating that we here in Britain are winning, and focuses on local-area projects targeted at communities needing empowerment and which can act as catalysts and multipliers as agents of change, the quicker the problems will subside. If there is another attack, Britain has a £2 billion industry ready to strike, pushing it back up the political agenda at home and abroad. Therefore, it is important to try to suggest that Britain and its allies are winning, not losing the battle against al-Qaeda at home (the problems with Afghanistan aside) – that Britain is supporting its Muslim communities through building capacity. But, that there is a need to include wider issues, and so 'prevent' will now bring all vulnerable communities together with progressive policies aligned with projects to inject proper investment in jobs, improve skills and provide training in declining areas across the country. In relation to wider engagement on radicalism where matters are to be alleviated through community empowerment, there is a certainly a need to reverse current negative perceptions that they are different. It is important to ensure that people affected by community cohesion and 'prevent' recognise that there are indeed comparable experiences bringing people together.

Given the political hot potato that the issue of 'Muslim violent extremism' has become in the UK, the British government still struggles with how to deal with a whole host of security, policing, intelligence and community challenges. This policy, however, could be better inter-connected. Reducing social and economic inequalities brings about social and community cohesion, helping to alleviate the potential for violent extremism, not the other way round, which is how the current policy was geared until recently. The notion of 'securitisation of integration' in relation to the current experience is an important one, where there is a genuine perception that only Muslims are being targeted by 'preventing violent extremism' policy, and there are indeed concerns that policy also attempts to carry out a kind of 'community-led sur-veillance'. There is much to do to ensure that the academy, government and community can effectively come together to move forward in relation to improving understanding, delivering sound policy and building stronger and more resilient communities. It seems that when it comes to Muslims in the West and the question of politics and radicalism, there are still more questions than answers. What is for sure, however, is that Muslims in Britain are at a precarious juncture in their history, but while the challenges are acute, so too are the opportunities.

Acknowledgements

Aspects of this chapter first appeared in the article 'Muslim radicalisation's socio-economic roots', published online by *Guardian* 'Comment is Free' in April 2009, and the speech delivered as an invited panellist on the question of 'How should the left engage with British Muslims?', with the Rt. Hon. John Denham MP, Secretary of State for Communities and Local Govern-ment; Ed Husain, Co-Director, Quilliam Foundation; Martin Bright, writer and commentator; and chaired by Jessica Asato, Acting Director, Progress, at the Labour Party Conference, Brighton, 28 September 2009.

Note

1 I am grateful to Sheikh Imam Ibrahim Mogra for mention of this term in a privately held meeting in October 2009.

References

Abbas, T. (2009) 'United Kingdom and Northern Ireland', in J. Nielsen, S. Akgönül, A. Alibašić, B. Maréchal and C. Moe (eds), *Yearbook of Muslims in Europe*, Leiden, Brill.
—— (2011) *Islamic Radicalism and Multicultural Politics: The British Experience*, London and New York, Routledge.
Ahmed, A. (2003) *Islam under Siege: Living Dangerously in a Post-honor World*, Cambridge, Polity Press.
Alexander, C. (2000) *The Asian Gang: Ethnicity, Identity, Masculinity*, Oxford, Berg.
Ali, T. (2005) *Street-fighting Years: An Autobiography of the Sixties*, London, Verso.
Back, L. and Solomos, J. (1992) 'Black politics and social change in Birmingham, UK: An analysis of recent trends', *Ethnic and Racial Studies* vol. 15, no. 3: 327–51.
Bagguley, P. and Hussain, Y. (2008) *Riotous Citizens: Ethnic Conflict in Multicultural Britain*, Aldershot, Ashgate.
Benyon, J. and Solomos, J. (eds) (1987) *The Roots of Urban Unrest*, Oxford, Pergamon Press.
Bernard, B. (1999) *Century: One Hundred Years of Human Progress, Regression, Suffering and Hope 1899–1999*, London and New York, Phaidon.

Bhavnani, R., Mirza, H. and Meetoo, V. (2005) *Tackling the Roots of Racism: Lessons for Success*, Bristol, Policy Press.

Brown, M. (2000) 'Estimating the size and distribution of South Asian religious populations in Britain: Is there an alternative to a religion question in the census?', *International Journal of Population Geography* vol. 61, no. 2: 87–109.

Burgat, F. (1999) *Face to Face with Political Islam*, London and New York, I.B. Tauris.

Fekete, L. (2008) *A Suitable Enemy: Racism, Migration and Islamophobia in Europe*, London, Pluto Press.

Fukuyama, F. (2006) *The End of History and the Last Man*, New York, Free Press.

Hussain, A. and Miller, W. (2006) *Multicultural Nationalism: Islamophobia, Anglophobia, and Devolution*, Oxford, Oxford University Press.

Kundnani, A. (2001) 'From Oldham to Bradford: The violence of the violated', *Race and Class* vol. 43, no. 3: 41–60.

—— (2008) 'Islamism and the roots of liberal rage', *Race and Class* vol. 50, no. 2: 40–68.

—— (2009) *Spooked: How not to Prevent Violent Extremism*, London, Institute of Race Relations.

Lewis, P. (2007) *Young, British and Muslim*, London, Continuum.

Lynch, T. and Singh, R. (2008) *After Bush: The Case for Continuity in American Foreign Policy*, Cambridge, Cambridge University Press.

Macey, M. (2007) 'Islamic political radicalism in Britain: Pakistani men in Bradford', in T. Abbas (ed.), *Islamic Political Radicalism: A European Perspective*, Edinburgh, Edinburgh University Press.

Modood, T. (1990) 'British Asian Muslims and the Rushdie Affair', *Political Quarterly* vol. 61, no. 2: 143–60.

Office for National Statistics (2009) *Social Trends 39*, Basingstoke, Palgrave-Macmillan.

Open Society Institute (2004) *The Situation of Muslims in the UK*, Hungary, Open Society Institute.

Pape, R. (2005) *Dying to Win: The Strategic Logic of Suicide Terrorism*, London, Random House.

Peach, C. (2005) 'Britain's Muslim population: An overview', in T. Abbas (ed.), *Muslim Britain: Communities under Pressure*, London, Zed Books.

Phillips, D. (2006) 'Parallel lives? Challenging discourses of British Muslim self-segregation', *Environment and Planning: Society and Space* vol. 24, no. 1: 25–40.

Phillips, R. (2008) 'Standing together: The Muslim Association of Britain and the anti-war movement', *Race and Class* vol. 50, no. 2: 101–13.

Poole, E. and Richardson, J. (eds) (2006) *Muslims and the News Media*, London and New York, I.B. Tauris.

Rai, M. (2007) *7/7: The London Bombings and the Iraq War*, London, Pluto Press.

Rex, J. (1988) *The Ghetto and the Underclass*, Aldershot, Avebury.

—— (2005) 'Afterword', in T. Abbas (ed.), *Muslim Britain: Communities Under Pressure*, London, Zed Books.

Safi, O. (ed.) (2003) *Progressive Muslims: On Justice, Gender and Pluralism*, Oxford, Oneworld Publications.

Said, E. (2003) *Orientalism: Western Conceptions of the Orient*, London: Penguin.

Samad, Y. and Sen, K. (eds) (2007) *Islam in the European Union: Transnationalism, Youth and the War on Terror*, Karachi, Oxford University Press.

Yaqoob, S. (2007) 'British Islamic political radicalism', in T. Abbas (ed.), *Islamic Political Radicalism: A European Perspective*, Edinburgh, Edinburgh University Press.

19

Perpetual struggle

The significance of Arab–Israeli conflict for Islamists

Beverley Milton-Edwards

Events have proven beyond doubt that the only solution to the Palestinian problem lies in Islam [...] It is important to stimulate the Islamic spirit and to drive home the importance of the Islamic solution to the Palestinian problem to the entire world.

(Abdul-Razzaq 1988: 1)

The contemporary resurgence of Islam, which in turn led to the genesis and rise of Islamism as a political expression of the Muslim faith, highlights a new era of political struggle to change the status quo in many authoritarian regimes in the Muslim world and challenge Western liberal democracy as a blueprint for governance of the modern nation-state. The priority for such Islamist ideologues and movements in the late twentieth and early twenty-first centuries has been to bring about, through revolution if necessary, the establishment of Islamic states or Muslim-ruled states and governance founded on the principal tenets of Islam and shaped by shari'a law. Today the phenomenon of Islamism is thus widely perceived in many non-Muslim discourses and policy-shaping debates as a direct threat to the modern nation-state and political systems of the Arab world, as well as other domains such as Afghanistan and Pakistan. Hence political Islam or Islamism has become essential to current analyses of global politics, international relations, the Middle East and relations between Islam and the West.

When the focus is the Arab–Israeli conflict – its origins, enduring character and its resolution – the significance for Islamists is paramount. The Arab–Israeli conflict, for many Islamists, symbolises both the challenge they face in terms of Islam's political function as well as the solution for Arabs who are enemies of Zionism. Indeed, Islamists contend that it is only under the banner of Islam that the conflict can result in victory over the Israeli enemy and thus ensure the restitution of Muslim rights in Palestine.

Moreover, because of the significance of the conflict for Islamists across an ideological continuum of moderate-reformist to radical *salafi* jihadi their effective exclusion from conflict resolution efforts currently mediated and spearheaded by the West (specifically the Quartet powers of the US, United Nations (UN), Russia and the European Union (EU)) is problematic. The continuing failure to adequately address this factor in discourses of diplomacy and negotiation surrounding the resolution of the Arab–Israeli conflict leads to a spiral of regional linkages, threats and processes of radicalization spearheaded by salafi jihadi Islamists at the expense of regional stability and prosperity.

Palestine and faith

> History is a cyclic poem written by time upon the memories of man.
>
> *(Percy Bysshe Shelley)*

Sitting in the reception area of the Islamic University of Gaza, Dr Atef Adwan, historian, administrator and supporter of the Islamist organisation Hamas, outlines to his Western visitors the importance of the Muslim past in Palestine to present-day politics and the conflict with Israel. Islam's founder, the Prophets it recognises, and its important sites and shrines all include a locus on Palestine and the holy city of Jerusalem, the academic points out. In the popular British soap opera *EastEnders*, the home of its only Muslim characters has a photo of Islam's third most holy site at Jerusalem's Dome of the Rock in their front room. On an internet forum Muslim participants discuss the importance of Palestine as related in the scriptures of Islam. Theological, visual, spiritual, and increasingly political and violent, the sense that Palestine and hence the Arab–Israeli conflict is an 'issue' to Muslims across the globe has become increasingly palpable.

Most contemporary accounts of Islamism relate to an historical period that addresses the phenomenon as a reaction/response to colonial control and Westernisation of Muslim societies and countries throughout the late nineteenth and early twentieth centuries. Varieties of Islamist discourse, however, in determining and outlining the significance of the Arab–Israeli conflict draw on a long history of Muslim religious claim, Muslim rule, conquest and even Islamic scripture when it is produced in relation to the twentieth-century origins of this state-based conflict. Such discourse places emphasis on or attaches significance to the religious nature of the Arab–Israeli conflict with its attendant signification in relation to labels such as Muslim, Christian and Jew.

The significance of Palestine in Islam is evident, many Islamists claim, by the recurrent references to it in Muslim scriptures including the Qur'an and *hadith* (traditions) of Prophet Muhammad. The territory of Palestine, *Beit ul-Maqdis* (the noble sanctuary), includes the Dome of the Rock and the Al-Aqsa mosque. For Muslims, the significance of these sites in Jerusalem lies in the *Isra'* and *Mi'raj* of Prophet Muhammad (the Night Journey). 'This celebrated night journey,' notes Peters, 'a frequent subject of Islamic art and legend was the cornerstone of the Muslim attachment to Jerusalem' (Peters 1994: 66). The Noble Sanctuary, according to hadith, is also the site of the second mosque and the first *Qibla* (direction of prayer for Muslims). According to Muslim tradition prayers in the Al-Aqsa mosque in the Noble Sanctuary are the equivalent of 500 prayers in any other mosque outside those of Mecca and Medina.

Islamists also point to the material fact that successive Muslim rulers established Jerusalem as a significant holy site (after Mecca and Medina), building mosques, schools, shrines and other foundations throughout the territory and liberating it, as Salah Eddin did in 1187 from Christian Crusader rule. The land has also been successively endowed as *waqf* (held in perpetuity for Muslims) territory (Dumper 2002). Islamists have then generated discourses around the Arab–Israeli conflict which draw on these religious attachments and historic claims to Muslim-led victory and rule against foreign usurpers in this Holy Land. They then critique and raise the ire of their followers against those Arab states that have failed to liberate it in conflict with the present-day 'usurpers' of the land (Israel). Such perspectives are evident in the writings of Abdullah Kannoun:

> From now on we will know of no ideology except that of Islam, nor will we address Muslims […] except with the language of the Quran. We will not tell him 'fight for the sake of the right or the left, or to uphold nationalism which has separated rather than closed Muslim ranks, and helped towards atheism rather than contributed towards faith'. We will actually tell him 'fight so that God's word will be the highest'.
>
> *(Kannoun 1976: 56)*

Then, in outright challenge to the Arab states, he declares, 'A government having a faith other than those of its people cannot succeed' (Kannoun 1976: 56). 'Even within the upper hierarchy of the Egyptian religious establishment,' writes Huband, 'the call for jihad to liberate Jerusalem from Israeli aggression has been publicly stated, despite being at odds with official government policy' (Huband 1999: 137).

In the twentieth century the material fact of loss associated with Palestine became a significant factor in Islamist discourses of 'recovery', 'claim' and 'rightful possession' of the territory through the principle of *jihad* (striving). 'All Muslims should rise in arms as one man and start a violent irresistible onward onslaught to deliver the Holy Land which has been desecrated by the sworn enemies of humanity', declared Egyptian theologian Sheikh Muhammad Abu Zahra to his fellow scholars at al-Azhar in 1968, at a conference held in the wake of the 1967 defeat (Abu Zahra 1976: 62). The territorial-religious signification was first attributed in 1917 when Muslim rule was ended when British forces occupied Palestine during World War I. When in 1920 the British were awarded a Mandate to rule Palestine, creating a Western foothold deemed sympathetic to the Zionist project and prejudicial to Arab-Muslim interests, the failure of Arab rulers to respond adequately to such challenges is regarded as evidence of them having abandoned Muslim principles in favour of the Western-inspired secular and nationalist ideologies. Indeed, the rise of Arab nationalism and the failure of Arab leaders in Egypt, Jordan and elsewhere in the Middle East to 'save Palestine' from the Zionist project is also debated in much Islamist discourse as the reason why a return to Islam (resurgence) will also lead to a recovery of Palestine (holy territory). For Islamists, the genesis of the Arab–Israeli conflict thus focuses on and underlines loss of power and loss of Muslim territory because of the twin forces of Western-inspired colonialism and associated Zionism and the failure of secular-national Arabs to liberate Palestine.

Founding antipathy and anti-Semitism

Palestine and its centrality to Islamist responses to the Arab–Israeli conflict are long-standing. It has thus come to form a 'unifying' tenet. Hence the Arab–Israeli conflict over Palestine played a major part in defining the politics of the region, and Islamist ideology. In this respect the significance of this conflict to modern Islamist discourse was established well before the so-called crisis of Arab identity, which the resurgence thesis locates in the wake of the 1967 conflict in which the Arab armies of Egypt, Jordan and Syria were defeated by Israel. The symbolic importance of the conflict between Israel and the Arabs was identified by major Islamist figures and leaders almost at the point of its inception. In the 1920s the Syrian fundamentalist preacher Izz-a-din al-Qassam based himself in Palestine and organised a jihad against the ruling British authorities and Zionist settlers. The early salafi Islamist call authored by Islamic luminaries such as Rashid Rida also contended or sought to alert the Muslim community to the impact of Zionism.

> Ponder this problem [Zionism] and make it the subject of your conversations, to ascertain if it is just or unjust, true of false. If it is clear that you have neglected to defend the rights

of your fatherland and the interests of your nation and your religious community, ponder and study, debate and examine the matter.

(Rida 1898)

Soage contends that Rida – whose work inspired al-Qassam, Hassan al-Banna and Sayyid Qutb – not only presented an anti-Zionist perspective to his audiences, but in fact his treatment of this 'other' people was fundamentally anti-Semitic:

> the Shaykh did not focus his attacks on Zionism, but directed them to Jews in general […] he listed a series of 'established facts' about the Jews which, in fact, are just a collection of anti-Semitic slurs – many of them […] without precedent in the Islamic tradition: Jews are selfish and chauvinist, cunning and perfidious, and deem it legitimate to oppress, exploit, even exterminate, other peoples.
>
> *(Soage 2008: 9)*

The eliding of Zionism and anti-Semitic critique and slur has persisted in much Islamist discourse on the significance of the conflict emphasizing the religious enmity nurtured.

Hassan al-Banna, the founder of the Muslim Brotherhood, which today constitutes one of the most important Islamist organisations in the Middle East, also identified the significance of the unfolding conflict between Jews and Arabs in Palestine. Al-Banna and the Muslim Brotherhood would become deeply involved in establishing Islamism in Palestine, campaigning within Egypt for the government to support the Palestinians and critiquing the regime and the British for their policies (El-Awaissi 1998). In 1947, when it became apparent that a UN partition plan would allow for the establishment of the Jewish state of Israel in Palestine, Hassan al-Banna called for a jihad:

> In so doing he launched what has since become a key rallying call of Middle Eastern Muslims, identifying Zionism as the enemy of the Arabs, the West as having betrayed the Arab world by supporting Israel, and driving a wedge between Western 'modernity' and Islamic reformism.
>
> *(Huband 1999: 85)*

Those positions centred on a growing confrontation with Zionism and the Zionist movement. The Islamist reaction to a looming conflict with the Zionists in 1948, however, largely consisted of propaganda, media campaigns and solidarity drives in major Arab states such as Egypt. Some contend that with the Islamist movement still in its political infancy in these states it was unrealistic to assume that large numbers of Islamists could have been mobilised in terms of a fighting force of battle-ready mujahideen. Nevertheless, by the end of the first Arab–Israeli war in 1948, with Israel enjoying control over three-quarters of Palestine, twice as much as originally proposed by the UN, and Jewish immigrants settled in the many homes and villages abandoned in the wake of the dispossession of hundreds and thousands of Palestinian Arab refugees, the significance of the 'loss' was absorbed into Islamist discourses.

More than 60 years on, the rallying cry to jihad first issued in Palestine by the Islamists has been raised by Muslims across the globe in the form of ongoing solidarity with what they consider to be the plight of their brethren and the threat to their holy sites. Sheikh Yusuf al-Qaradawi, one of the most prominent Muslim scholars in contemporary Sunni Islam, for example, has often identified the plight of the Palestinians and the Arab–Israeli conflict as requiring or demanding action from Muslims across the globe. His sermons and *fatwa* have called on Muslims to engage in a jihad against Israel and condemned Israeli claims to the land: 'The Jews mistakenly claim that Allah has given them Palestine as their homeland, which is untrue. Allah has never ordained that people should be deported from their homes to be replaced by strangers' (Elshamy 2006: 5).

The ideological founding father of the salafi jihadi trend in Islamism is commonly identified as Sayyid Qutb. Indeed, as Musallam contends, Qutb is 'an ideologue whose writings are a manifesto [...] for revolutionary Islamists' (Musallam 2005: viii). Although it would be some time in the development of Islamic radicalism before Palestine became a significant or central motif, Qutb did give significance in his writings to the issue of Israel and the conflict with neighbouring Arab states. Indeed, it has been contended that Qutb objected violently to the establishment of Israel. Nettler, for example, asserts that Qutb was responsible for developing an 'emotional hatred [...] uniquely modern as part of Muslim thinking on the Jews' (Nettler 1987: 51). Yet the Qutbian perspective on Israel as a Jewish state was also created around discourse on forms of political rule defined as un-Islamic, or *jahili*. Here society or the state is rejected because Islam and its law (shari'a) is absent. Qutb demanded that such societies – secular states or Western society – should be replaced with Islam and shari'a, by revolutionary jihad if necessary. Qutb also formulated an ideological opposition to nationalism, regarding it as a 'true evil' that threatened and rivalled Islam (Lawrence 1998: 22). According to this perspective, Israel, along with secular Arab states such as Egypt, were condemned by Qutb who demanded jihad to hasten their demise. As Qutb contended:

> the truth of the faith is not fully established until a struggle is undertaken on its behalf among the people. A struggle against their unwillingness and their resistance, a struggle to remove them from this state to that of Islam.
>
> *(Qutb 1988: 8–9)*

Yet Nettler insists that Qutb's views were also premised on a form of anti-Semitism that would define and shape successive jihadi and radical ideologues (Nettler 1987). Abu Rabi, however, argues that this is a conflation of Qutb's position on politics and his so-called Jew hatred. Abu Rabi believes that authors such as Nettler treat 'the Qutbian doctrine of hatred towards the Jews in an absolute political and historical vacuum', without reference to the historical context in which such positions were developed (Abu Rabi 1994). What is not contested, however, is the extent to which Qutb's position on Israel and Zionism did and has continued to influence the ways in which Islamists formulate their positions on the Arab–Israeli conflict.

Hence there is evidence from across the ideological spectrum of Islamism of an early engagement with the Arab–Israeli conflict and a sense that it was significant to the emerging discourse of Islamism.

Reaction

> As we raise our hands in prayer to Allah, beseeching His help, we ask Him to return Palestine to us, an Islamic country.
>
> *(Statement by Ayatollah Al-Hakim in June 1967, quoted in Abdul-Razzaq 1988: 83)*

Israel's victory over the Arabs in the Six-Day War in 1967 is considered a significant turning point and symbol in the debate about Islamic resurgence, Islamic politics and the strategic reorientation of the Middle East away from the West and inward to its Muslim roots. The prelude to the war on the Arab side had been fuelled by wild Arab nationalist sabre-rattling. President Gamal Abdel Nasser of Egypt led his regime to a war which it genuinely convinced itself it could win. Nasser ruled over a populist, nationalist, one-party regime which had attempted to purge the country of Islamist opponents, imprisoning them and executing them. Only a year before, Sayyid Qutb, the most prominent ideologue of the Islamists, had been executed by the Egyptian authorities and the Muslim Brotherhood had been forced underground. Nasser pursued the deliverance of Palestine as if it were a divine duty, but this was a nationalist, not an Islamist war. This was no jihad with the mujahideen battalions raising the green banner of Islam in the face of the Israeli enemy. This was a war in which pan-Arab and Arab-nationalist rhetoric played a fundamental role in fuelling the preparations for a further episode of combat in the Arab–Israeli conflict.

However, Nasser's nationalist ambitions were stymied by Israel, which was able to defeat the Arab armies of Egypt, Jordan and Syria on the battlefield in six days. This victory decisively altered the balance of power in the region against the Arabs. Israel as a 'country that had felt embattled and threatened only days before was now the decisive military power in the Middle East' (Fraser 1995: 86). For Islamists the defeat was evidence of the flimsy, false and fundamentally flawed ideological character of Arab nationalism, Arab socialism, Arab Marxism and secularism. They saw the rout as justified retribution: 'Islamists consider[ed] this defeat as Divine revenge from the regime of President [Nasser] and his repressive measures against the Muslim Brothers and Sayyid Qutb' (Musallam 2005: 203). The predicament within Arabism was evident. 'The crisis began,' asserts Tibi, 'immediately after the sweeping Arab defeat in the Six-Day-War. Both Arab nationalism and Arab socialism […] lost their glamour and now fell into a legitimacy crisis […] fostering the politicisation of Islam' (Tibi 2001: 121). Ajami also contends that the resurgence of Islam after 1967 is 'proof that generations of nationalists, liberal and Marxist ideologues alike, have failed to leave any real sign of their presence' (Ajami 1992: 171). While so much hyperbole is present in the stark and dramatic scenario after the 1967 War, it is the case that Islamist ideologues and a number of emerging Islamist movements did use the Arab defeat against Israel as a debating point as they sought not only to oppose Israel as an 'artificial entity' but also the Arab states of the Middle East as ideologically defective because of their continuing refusal to bring Islam to the centre of such entities and political frameworks. Even elements of institutional Islam, such as the scholarly elite at Cairo's prestigious centre of Islamic learning, Al-Azhar University, perceived the conflict as worthy of commentary: 'Like the Brothers [Muslim Brotherhood],' notes Enayat, 'some of the Azaharites interpreted the Arab–Israeli war in terms of a conflict between Islam and Judaism and appealed for intensified religious education of the people as the most effective way of fighting Israel' (Enayat 2005: 87). Arab military defeat on the battlefield against Israel became the raison d'être for an ever-increasing call to Islamize Arab societies from the bottom up, including education.

The Arab defeat of 1967 has been subsequently incorporated by Islamist ideologues, such as Sheikh Yusuf Qaradawi, to emphasise the significance of Arab defeats and Israel's continuing existence in religiously existential terms: 'The battle between them [Zionists] and us is not a battle of borders but a battle of existence. It is a battle that will end and the Muslims will be victorious.' In strict theological terms the intertwined theme of jahili, or a godless society, is also addressed by Qaradawi as he continues, 'This victory will raise the *adhan* [call to prayer] on the voiceless minaret and will return monotheism to the voiceless pulpit' (Qaradawi 2007: v). For such thinkers, the Arab defeat came as a direct result of a deviation from the path of Islam. This is emphasised by Azhar:

> Allah has promised His help to us […] these Jews do not have the capability to face you in the battlefield […] The Jews can degrade the Muslims […] in politics by their evil plots, but they have always been defeated in the field of Jihad […] but the Muslims left this field (war) empty. If there is fighting (against the Jews) it is not on the base of Islam but for nationalism from which the Jews are benefitting.
>
> *(Azhar n.d.: 116)*

Thus the corrective was simple, potentially powerful in terms of populist appeal and a direct challenge to the hegemonic control of the nationalist Arab regimes of Egypt, Jordan and Syria. The corrective was encapsulated in the slogan: Israel was the problem and Islam was the solution. The defeat had such a significant and magnifying impact on Islamist perceptions of the Arab–Israeli conflict that not only did it serve to mobilise Muslim opinion on Palestine and Israel more generally but, as Gerges asserts, it played a fundamental part in radicalising Islamist elements that gave rise to the jihadi-salafi such as the Egyptian-based jihad groups and al-Qaeda (Gerges 2005). Even mainstream Islamists, it has been contended, were tied to the deepening dimensions of the conflict. For Enayat the significance in the case of the Muslim Brotherhood lay in the fact that the Brotherhood could unify and appeal to a wider constituency when focusing on an external enemy such as Israel: 'The traumatic effects of the Arab defeat in the Six-day War of 1967' writes Enayat, 'was highly beneficial for the Brothers [sic] and their ideology' (Enayat 2005: 86).

There was another post-1967 reality for Islamists to contend with in respect of the conflict. This was the fact that not only did Israel now militarily occupy former Arab territories of the West Bank, Gaza Strip, Sinai and Golan Heights, but that it had captured East Jerusalem and thus its holy Muslim sites from Arab-Muslim hands. Jerusalem was subsequently annexed and declared the capital city of Israel. This loss is constantly expressed in Islamist discourse. For an array of Islamist organisations and movements the motif of Jerusalem has been symbolically threaded into their own agenda and cause.

Jerusalem the symbol

Due to the established religious significance of Jerusalem to Muslims, its importance to Islamists – particularly in recent decades – has been situated in discourses around which the theme of Israeli or Jewish control of the city is central. Two years after the Six-Day War Muslim, including Islamist, opinion was galvanised when the Al-Aqsa mosque was subject to an arson attack. Amidst feverish speculation of the role Israel may or may not have played in the attack, an 'Islamic Conference of Kings and Heads of State' was convened and the Organization of Islamic Conference (OIC) was formed. Formulating a collective Muslim response to the attack and protesting against Israel's control of Jerusalem was a core issue for the OIC. The OIC charter, ratified in 1972, called for the 'liberation of Palestine'. The OIC also has a permanent committee dedicated to the Jerusalem issue, which has consistently underlined Islamic claims to Jerusalem and its Muslim shrines. Jerusalem has thus become a contemporary symbol or dimension of Muslim identity. It is an issue that animates and motivates Muslim discourse. As Iqbal Sacranie, secretary-general of the Muslim Council of Britain contends, despite their many differences and political persuasions, 'Muslim scholars are united and resolute about one issue. They agree that the question of Palestine and the status of Jerusalem is the foremost international concern on the agenda of Muslims' (Sacranie 2000: 22).

For radical Islamists the 'loss of Jerusalem' in 1967 was considered a stain on the name of Islam. For them, 'the fall of Jerusalem' into Israeli hands is perceived as a wound that must be healed. It is a symbol around which supporters are rallied. Reactive anti-Israeli discourse among

Islamists was also evident amid emerging claims that the Israeli state, post-1967, was seeking to Judaize the city of Jerusalem (Yiftachel 2006: 6). Israel's annexation of East Jerusalem led to the issuance of laws disbanding Palestinian civil and political groups, checkpoints and barriers in Arab East Jerusalem to prevent movement of inhabitants, re-zoning policies that adversely affected the Palestinian inhabitants, and demolition of waqf and other Palestinian properties around the Noble Sanctuary and other parts of East Jerusalem. Israeli judicial permission was granted for Jews to conduct religious ceremonies in the grounds of the Noble Sanctuary, while other security measures limited the rights of Muslim worshippers to attend Friday prayers at the Al-Aqsa mosque. Zink refers to this policy as a 'strategic extension of Jerusalem's municipal boundaries, bureaucratic and legal restrictions on Palestinian land use, disenfranchisement of Jerusalem residents, the expansion of settlements in "Greater Jerusalem" and the construction of a separation wall' (Zink 2009: 122). Such claims are totally repudiated and described as a 'canard' and implausible when demographic figures for Jewish and Arab population growth in Jerusalem are examined post-1967 (Weiner 2003).

For many Islamist organisations across the spectrum, however, the Israeli policies are perceived as aimed and directed at the Muslim character of the city and are taken seriously. In a statement issued in February 2009 from Cairo, for example, the Muslim Brotherhood declared:

> Arab rulers and Arab nations have to understand that the way to liberate Jerusalem and restore Islamic […] sanctities, in particular the Al-Aqsa mosque […] is by uniting Palestinians, uniting Arabs and allowing to free the Arab will and uniting Muslims in one project of all sorts of resistance …
>
> *(Muslim Brotherhood 2009)*

Islamists also constantly critique the failures of Arab leaders to liberate Jerusalem. The Muslim Brotherhood declared that 'Arab regimes and governments as well as the Organization of Islamic Conference have to take responsibility for saving the sacred city from the continuous Judization going on' (Muslim Brotherhood 2009).

Transcending Muslim sectarian difference, the symbol of Jerusalem and the call for resistance against Israel has also become a favourite rallying cry of the leadership of the Islamic regime in Tehran as well as the Lebanese Hezbollah. Jerusalem Day was instituted in 1981 when Iranian leader Ayatollah Khomeini declared the last Friday of the Islamic holy month of Ramadan a day to demonstrate the importance of Jerusalem to Muslims. Millions participate in pro-Jerusalem rallies in Iran and elsewhere across the world. In Iran in 2009 the Jerusalem Day rally took on an added political potency as the regime anticipated that opponents of the regime who had protested against recent presidential election results would use the occasion to raise their issue. Nevertheless, the Iranian regime strove to ensure that the focus would remain on Jerusalem: 'Quds [Jerusalem] Day is the symbol of Iran's national unity', declared one headline. 'The enemy has always sought to undermine the Quds Day ceremony,' stated Iran's most senior religious leader Ayatollah Khamenei, 'but again this year, the Iranian nation will honour this day with marches […] and many of the Muslims of the world will follow this nation and revive the name of Quds once again' (*Tehran Times* 2009b: 1). Behind the marches, rallies, solidarity conferences and publications and propaganda, regimes like Iran and movements such as Hezbollah have also been accused of actively supporting resistance efforts and terrorism against Israel and its forces. In 2009 Hezbollah leader Hassan Nasrallah used the occasion of 'Al-Quds Day' to not only call for solidarity with the Palestinians and to threaten Israel, but to rail against Arab regimes for their failures to confront Israel (*Tehran Times* 2009a).

Moreover, many Islamists have contended that the future of Jerusalem should not be negotiated over by only one Arab party. This has made the fate of Jerusalem a major sticking point between nationalist and Islamist opinion in the Middle East and elsewhere.

Hostage to Islamist discourse

In this regard Palestinians and Israelis have been held hostage to Islamist discourse as understood in particularly religious terms. As the perspectives outlined by early Islamist luminaries such as Rida, al-Qassam and al-Banna demonstrate, there was the development of an early yet complex linkage to the issue of Palestine in terms of Islamist, pan-Arab, Muslim Arab national, salafi and jihadi discourses against the West, against colonialism, and against the programme of Zionist settlement and Western support for it in Palestine. The later ethnicization of the Israeli state as a state for the Jewish people also provided a mechanism of exclusiveness that inevitably left others out and gave greater leverage to Islamist discourse against Israel and the so-called 'Jewish' project. The early roots of the conflict between Arab and Israeli were identified as having important religious dimensions and significance for Muslims in general and the Islamists in particular. This in turn was then signified in conjunction with discourse about territoriality, identity, ethnicity, economy, competing nationalisms, colonialism and imperialism. Territoriality, for example, evokes a very different analysis from Islamists than the state-centred ideologues of nationalism. The land of Palestine is considered and debated in terms of its sacredness and in particular the status of Jerusalem as a holy city for Muslims. Islamists contest and critique nationalist and pan-Arab attempts to recover the territory – in the wars of 1948, 1967 and 1973 as well as Arab nationalist strategies in terms of self-interested individual Arab leaders.

When Islamists construct the Arab–Israeli conflict from the premise of faith then it is also reduced and reshaped in new ways. If the conflict becomes explicable as a religious issue involving opposing faiths – in this particular instance Jewish and Muslim – then the nature of its resolution is also changed. Certainly there is a pattern of inconsistent labelling of who the enemy is in this respect. Some Muslim theologians have limited their discourse to Zionism and a critique of expansionism and occupation from this perspective of the Arab–Israeli conflict. Others inconsistently interchange Zionism and Jews and draw on Muslim scriptural reference to the Jews to substantiate their opposition to peace deals, Jewish claims and the nature of Jewish territorial expansion in Palestine. Jihadi elements, including al-Qaeda, call directly on Muslims to launch attacks on Jews in support of a jihad to solve the Arab–Israeli conflict. Such perspectives may also explain why so many Islamist groups condemn or proclaim scepticism at traditional diplomatic initiatives to solve the Arab–Israeli conflict through international peace conferences, bilateral and multilateral forums, peace treaties and processes of normalization. The question here is the extent to which such perspectives may be read as representative of Islamist opinion and those who support them.

Thus although the roots of the Arab–Israeli conflict lie in ethno-political rather than purely religious differences, this is not how Islamists portray it. Indeed, Palestine under the rule of the Ottoman Turks was a place where the Jews, Christians and Muslims coexisted peacefully. These inhabitants of Palestine, however, were deeply affected by the incursion of Western ideologies and cultures, which were so different in emphasis than many of their own traditions. For Islamists it was not just the economic and political experience, but the ideological and cultural one, which would have a lasting effect on the development of their own discourses including their positions on the conflict in Palestine and the role of the Arab states that engaged with Israel on the battlefield. European ideas, movements and state-building projects were manifest in an explosion across the Middle East that disrupted and created crisis in contemporary Islamism both in terms of its emergence (as a reaction to colonialism and the 'decline' of Islam), as well as its resurgence in terms of the identity crisis wrought by the defeat of the Arabs in the War of 1967 and the emergence of Islamism as a countervailing ideology to collapsing Arab nationalism.

Land settlement by Jews from Europe from the late 1890s onwards, inspired by the ideology of Zionism, has become perceived by Islamists as a direct challenge to their own positions and developing political discourses on Muslim emancipation and self-rule from Western-based colonialism and later Western-inspired Arab secular national states that marginalised Islam from the political arena. Moreover, the congruent origins of the competing nationalism of Zionism and Arab nationalisms need to be underscored here, not just in the historical context, but in terms of explaining the nature of Islamist understandings of the Arab–Israeli conflict. This became an axis around which Palestinian, Egyptian, Lebanese, Saudi and other Islamists have fixed their opposition. Islamists have traditionally been hostile to nationalism, regarding it as a threat to the unifying ethos of the Muslim faith. Zionism and its manifestation in the state of Israel is also an undeniable threat to the Islamists. Zionism as an expression of nationalism crystallized the aspiration within the Jewish diaspora for a Jewish homeland for the Jewish people. The religious appeal inherent in the nationalist aspirations that motivated the Zionists was strong, as Gresh and Vidal contend: 'the memory of the lost homeland and the desire to return there were long fostered by religion alone: "Next year in Jerusalem" believers prayed each year' (Gresh and Vidal 1990: 221). Zionism, moreover, is often represented in Islamist discourse as an ideology that is a Western invention and also part of a plot to wrest power from Muslim hands. Islamist leaders from Hamas, for example, have complained that their enemy in the conflict – Israel – has to be removed. As their late hardline leader, Dr Abdel Aziz Rantissi, maintained:

> We can't change our targets […] In the name of Allah we will fight the Jews and liberate our land in the name of Islam. We will rid this land of the Jews and with Allah's strength our land will be returned to us and the Muslim peoples of the world […] This is our land, not the Jews' […] You will have no security except outside the homeland Palestine […] We have Allah on our side, and we have the sons of the Arab and Islamic nation on our side
>
> *(Rantissi 2002: 22)*

Obstacle to peace?

Muslim opinion or support for Palestine has increasingly been mobilised around contemporary dimensions of the Arab–Israeli conflict. Peace settlement – such as the 1979 peace treaty between Israel and Egypt and the 1994 treaty between Jordan and Israel – also drew direct criticism from Islamists in both respective countries as well as elsewhere. If it is argued that while Arab military defeat in 1967 and 1973 created the 'crisis of Arab identity' that was a catalyst to Islamic resurgence (Dekmejian 1980), it was the Arab peace treaties with Israel in 1979 and 1994 that radicalised Islamists. Discourse with respect to jihadi-salafi positions on Israel as the 'near' enemy alongside the very regimes which in making peace with Israel were perceived as pushing the Arab nation on the path of apostasy and away from the straight path of Islam were soon apparent. Certainly there is evidence of a widespread increase in the rhetoric of jihad against Israel from the 1980s onwards. Jihadist literatures increasingly focus on Israel along with other 'enemies' such as the Soviet occupation of Afghanistan in their calls for action. The differences lie in the expression of jihad, as a military or violent manifestation against Israel directly with respect to such elements.

Here the evidence is paltry. With the exception of Palestinian Islamist movements such as Islamic Jihad in the 1980s and Hamas in the 1990s when it embarked on suicide bombings and rocket attacks, and Hezbollah – formed in response to the 1978 Israeli occupation of south Lebanon – the region's major radical jihad-salafi groups have not launched attacks (military jihad) successfully on Israel. Nor have they been able to sufficiently penetrate Palestinian Islamist groups to operate in their name or according to their goals.

In Jordan the response of Islamists to the peace treaty and normalisation of relations with Israel has brought it into moderate conflict with the Hashemite regime. The Muslim Brotherhood party in Jordan, the Islamic Action Front (IAF), responded with rhetoric to the prospect of peace settlement with Israel. This is made clear from a statement by IAF leader Zaki bin Arsheed: 'As for normalization with Israel, our attitude is clear. We fully reject normalization with the Zionist entity as long as it occupies part of the territory of our Palestinian people' (Arsheed 2006). Hence the significance of the Arab–Israeli conflict lay with the notion of conflict settlement with Israel and the politics of normalisation (Kornbluth 2002). Normalisation with Israel has generated Arab opinion more widely across the Arab world into a debate about recognition and the efficacy of Arab measures to boycott and punish Israel politically for its position on the Palestinians and what are widely regarded within the region as Palestinian rights (Mousalli 1996). Islamist opposition was not substantive enough, however, to persuade King Hussein from making peace with Israel in 1994; nor was their parliamentary punch – as constituted in the IAF – sufficient to stop legislative changes in 1995 softening previous anti-Israeli laws (Robins 2004: 189–91).

In Egypt President Sadat's steps to peace with Israel ultimately cost him his life at the hands of radical jihadi-salafi Islamists who assassinated him in 1981 (Calvert 2008: 152). Indeed, Sadat's decision to sue for peace with Israel, and thus conflict settlement, resulted in a widespread radicalisation of Egypt's Islamists who largely condemned the move as an act of apostasy. Radical elements and ideologues inspired by Sayyid Qutb now argued that Sadat and his regime should be pulled down and that a Muslim uprising was imperative if both the enemy at home (Egyptian regime) and the enemy abroad (Israel) were to be defeated. Much jihad discourse – particularly as it relates to the evolution of debates within Islamism regarding the obligation of jihad as it pertains to the 'near' and 'far' enemy – was developed during this period in response to Egypt suing for peace with Israel (Gerges 2005). Not only did developments in this discourse have a regional impact in terms of the Arab–Israeli conflict, but it played its part in the evolution of transnational Islamism which in turn produced al-Qaeda.

Nevertheless, despite both Palestinian and Israeli fears that al-Qaeda has established an effective foothold in the Palestinian territories or that it could send mujahideen across Arab borders to Israel, it has thus far failed to transform this dimension of the Arab–Israeli conflict into a global *cause célèbre* of transnational salafi jihadism. As Taji-Farouki argues, 'it is not always possible to assume militancy on the basis of Islamist threats of jihad: while Islamists share much in their hostility towards the Israeli state as occupier of Islamic land, their strategies for confronting it cannot be painted with a single brush-stroke' (Taji-Farouki 2000: 22). Palestinian Islamist movement Hamas has more recently drawn the specific criticism of al-Qaeda, and in response it has rebutted and rebuked al-Qaeda and found itself in open and violent confrontation with jihadi-salafi elements in the Gaza Strip. Hamas leaders have consistently rejected any attempt by al-Qaeda to conflate their ideological positions and strategies on jihad against Israel, including the former tactics of suicide bombings with al-Qaeda and other jihadi-salafi violence. Hamas leaders have also directly rebuked al-Qaeda statements critiquing the organisation. Such conflict demonstrates a rift that has opened up within Islamism with respect to the significance of the Arab–Israeli conflict and responses to it with jihadi-salafi elements on one side and the Muslim

Brotherhood on the other. Hence, Hamas has drawn al-Qaeda's ire and been accused by al-Qaeda leader Ayman Zawahiri of weakening the Islamist project by engaging in elections and governance. In March 2007 Zawahiri accused Hamas of surrendering 'Palestine to the Jews', selling the 'Palestinian issue' and selling 'shari'a in order to retain the leadership of the Palestinian government' (Zawahiri on Al Jazeera, 11 March 2007, as quoted in Milton-Edwards and Farrell Hamas 2010: 278).

Conclusion

The Arab–Israeli conflict is an issue intrinsic to contemporary Islamism and has been central in attempts to ideologically unite Muslim opinion around the globe and across the sectarian divide of Islam itself. Islamists today lay claim to an involvement in, and support for, Muslim rights in Palestine since the 1920s. They also cite evidence of a deep religious attachment to Palestine, and Jerusalem in particular, as eternally Muslim through both its sacred status and waqf endowments. In this way they configure and explain the conflict in religious or sacred rather than secular or profane political terms. In doing so, the methods demanded for resolving this conflict are thus reshaped to include discourses on defensive jihad (*jihad fard ayn*) and the religious rulings (fatwa) permitting violence including suicide bombings against civilian targets. Islamists cannot accept the occupation of their holy places by Israel, particularly the area of the Noble Sanctuary in Jerusalem. Additionally they and others criticise their own Muslim leaders and organisations such as the OIC for failing to unite Muslims in effective action to end such occupation. 'Despite the centrality of the Palestinian cause,' argue Akbarzadeh and Connor, 'the OIC has achieved little in the way of material change [...] The question remains as to how an organization of 57 member-states [...] can continuously fail to resolve the political situation that provided the impetus for its formation' (Akbarzadeh and Connor 2005: 80).

Furthermore, the obligation of jihad is a constant refrain of such discourses in terms of resolving the Arab–Israeli conflict, and thus negotiated solutions, peace conferences and diplomacy are dismissed as a ploy to deny Muslims their spiritual rights and their Palestinian 'brothers' in Islam their legitimate rights to freedom and independence. More controversial, of course, is the idea of jihad articulated by radical Islamists as a vehicle for destroying Zionism and the Jewish state of Israel. Radical ideologue Sayyid Qutb, a source of inspiration for Islamist jihadi elements, asserts that 'The reasons for jihad [...] are these: to establish God's authority on the earth; to arrange human affairs according to the true guidance provided by God; to abolish all the Satanic forces and Satanic systems of life, to end the lordship of one man over others' (Qutb 1988: 127). More recently, Muslim scholars such as Sheikh Faysal Mawlawi, deputy chairman of the European Council for Fatwa and Research, have contended with specific reference to the Arab–Israeli conflict that:

> Yes, the Jihad in the Cause of Allah against the Zionists who usurped the Palestinian lands and forcibly expelled the Palestinians from their own homes is an individual duty or *fard 'ayn* on every capable Muslim in Palestine and its neighbouring Muslim countries. The reason for that is to unify the stand in resisting the aggression launched by the Zionists who usurped the blessed land. Thus, Jihad is an individual duty on Egyptians, Syrians, Jordanians, Lebanese as well as all Muslim Arabs and non-Arabs till the Jewish occupation is brought to a halt.
>
> *(Mawlawi 2004)*

Here the obligation in terms of the Arab–Israeli conflict engulfing neighbouring Arabs is specifically addressed in the jihad literature. Not only is the obligation of jihad explicit for

Palestinian Muslims but those in states such as Lebanon, Syria, Jordan and Egypt. Yet in the case of Jordan and Egypt, the Muslim heads of these states reached formal peace treaties with Israel.

This is the dilemma that confronts those engaged in efforts to resolve the Arab–Israeli conflict: are they able to recognise its religious dimension? No matter how many times Israel and its supporters wish away the Islamist phenomenon on its doorstep, the reality is that it will endure in the fabric of national and regional politics of the Middle East and neighbouring Muslim world for the foreseeable future. Islamists from across the neighbouring states will continue to present forms of strategic threat if they are not made part of the solution to this enduring conflict. Making them part of the solution, however, implies a radical change in the domestic as well as foreign policy calculations of such states towards their own domestic Islamist constituencies, as well as a wider shift within the region and the international order more generally with respect to the potentiality for conflict resolution that the OIC could make.

An end to the Arab–Israeli conflict will not deal a fatal blow to Islamism but a peace settlement between Israel, the Palestinians and the Arab states of Syria and Lebanon could create opportunities for meaningful normalization within the region, including some significant sections of Islamist opinion. In terms of Islamist opinion and Muslim attachment to Palestine more generally, a final peace agreement recognising Jerusalem as some form of 'shared capital of faiths' will promote opportunities for further peace and reconciliation with states in the region more generally and go some way in initiating the generational transformation for peace-building that will be required for peace to be embedded.

The continuing absence of peace will certainly perpetuate Islamist hostility against Israel since Zionism emerged as a new political force in the Middle East and Israel achieved independence in 1948.

References

Abdul-Razzaq, J. (1988) *Islamists and the Palestinian Question*, Tehran, Islamic Propagation Organization.

Abu Rabi, I. (1994) 'A Note on Some Recent Western Writings on Islamic Resurgence', *Al-Tawhid: A Quarterly Journal of Islamic Thought and Culture* vol. 11, nos 3 & 4: 233–46.

Ajami, F. (1992) *The Arab Predicament: Arab Political Thought and Practice since 1967*, Cambridge, Cambridge University Press.

Akbarzadeh, S. and Connor, K. (2005) 'The Organization of Islamic Conference: Sharing an Illusion', *Middle East Policy* vol. 12, no. 2: 79–92.

Arsheed, Z. (2006) *Interview*, Ikwanweb, available at www.ikhwanweb.com/article.php?id=4549 (accessed 14 September 2009).

Azhar, Mohammed M.M. (n.d.) *The Virtues of Jihad*, n.p., Ahle Sunnah Wal Jama'at.

Calvert, J. (2008) *Islamism: A Documentary and Reference Guide*, Westport, CT, Greenwood.

Dekmejian, R. (1980) 'The Anatomy of Islamic Revival: Legitimacy Crisis, Ethnic Conflict and the Search for Islamic Alternatives', *Middle East Journal* vol. 34, no. 1: 1–12.

Dumper, M. (2002) *The Politics of Sacred Space: The Old City of Jerusalem in the Middle East Conflict*, Boulder, CO, Lynne Rienner.

El-Awaissi, A. (1998) *The Muslim Brothers and the Palestine Question 1928–1947*, London, Tauris Academic Studies.

Elshamy, A. (2006) 'Palestine is Property of Islam', *Gulf Times*, 13 May: 5, available at www.gulf-times. com/site/topics/article.asp?cu_no=2&item_no=86249&version=1&template_id=36&parent_id=16 (accessed 14 September 2009).

Enayat, H. (2005) *Modern Islamic Political Thought*, London, I.B. Tauris.

Fraser, T. (1995) *The Arab–Israeli Conflict*, Basingstoke, Palgrave.

Gerges, F. (2005) *The Far Enemy, Why Jihad Went global*, Cambridge, Cambridge University Press.

Gresh, A. and Vidal, D. (1990) *A to Z of the Middle East*, London, Zed Press.

Huband, M. (1999) *Warriors of the Prophet, The Struggle for Islam*, Boulder, CO, Westview Press.

Kannoun, A. (1976) *Muslims and the Problem of Palestine*, in D. Green (ed.), *Arab Theologians on Jews and Israel*, Geneva, Editions de l'Avenir.

Kornbluth, D. (2002) 'Jordan and the Anti-Normalization campaign, 1994–2001', *Terrorism and Political Violence* vol. 14, no. 3: 80–108.

Lawrence, B. (1998) *Shattering the Myth, Islam beyond Violence*, Princeton, NJ, Princeton University Press.

Mawlawi, F. (2004) 'Is it an Obligation to Join the Jihad in Palestine?' available at www.islamonline. net/servlet/Satellite?pagename=IslamOnline-English-Ask_Scholar/FatwaE/FatwaE&cid=1119503546020 (accessed 14 September 2009).

Milton-Edwards, B. and Farrell Hamas, S. (2010) *The Islamic Resistance Movement*, Cambridge, Polity Press.

Mousalli, A. (1996) 'Islamist Perspectives of Regime Political Response: The Cases of Lebanon and Palestine', *Arab Studies Quarterly* vol. 18, no. 3: 53–64.

Musallam, A. (2005) *From Secularism to Jihad: Sayyid Qutb and the Foundations of Radical Islamism*, Westport, CT, Greenwood Publishing.

Muslim Brotherhood (2009) 'Statement', *Ikhwan Web*, available at www.ikhwanweb.org (accessed 2 September 2009).

Nettler, R. (1987) *Past Trials and Present Tribulations, Muslim Fundamentalists Views of the Jews*, Oxford, Pergamon.

Peters, F. (1994) *A Reader on Classical Islam*, Princeton, NJ, Princeton University Press.

Qaradawi, Y. (2007) *Fatawa on Palestine*, London, al-Falah Foundation.

Qutb, S. (1988) *The Religion of Islam*, Kuwait, n.p.

Rantissi, A. (2002) Interview with author, Gaza Strip.

Rida, R. (1898) 'Khabar wa itibar' [news and views], *al-Manar*, 9 April.

Robins, P. (2004) *A History of Jordan*, Cambridge, Cambridge University Press.

Sacranie, I. (2000) 'The Role of British Muslims in Bringing Justice to Palestine', *al-Aqsa* vol. 3, no. 1: 21–23.

Soage, A. (2008) 'Rashid Rida's Legacy', *The Muslim World* vol. 98, no.1: 1–23.

Taji-Farouki, S. (2000) 'Islamists and the Threat of Jihad: Hizb al-Tahrir and al-Muhajiroun', *Middle Eastern Studies* vol. 36, no. 4: 21–46.

Tehran Times (2009a) 'Sayyed Nasrallah: We Will Never Recognise Israel's Right to Exist', *Tehran Times*, 21 September, available at www.tehrantimes.com/index_View.asp?code=203566 (accessed 26 February 2011).

—— (2009b) 'Quds Day is the Symbol of Iran's National Unity: Leader', 12 September, available at old. tehrantimes.com/index_View.asp?code=203049 (accessed 22 August 2011).

Tibi, B. (2001) *Islam between Culture and Politics*, Basingstoke, Palgrave.

Weiner, J. (2003) 'Is Jerusalem Being "Judaized"?', *Jewish Political Studies Review* vol. 15, nos 1–2, available at www.jcpa.org/JCPA/Templates/ShowPage.asp?DRIT=5&DBID=1&LNGID=1&TMID=111&FID=625&PID=0&IID=1804&TTL=Is_Jerusalem_Being_ (accessed 25 February 2011).

Yiftachel, O. (2006) *Ethnocracy: Land and Identity Politics in Israel/Palestine*, Philadelphia, PA, University of Philadelphia Press.

Zahra, Sheikh Muhammad Abu (1976) 'The Jihad, in Muslims and the Problem of Palestine', in D. Green (ed.), *Arab Theologians on Jews and Israel*, Geneva, Editions de l'Avenir.

Zink, V. (2009) 'A Quiet Transfer: The Judaization of Jerusalem', *Contemporary Arab Affairs* vol. 2, no. 1: 122–33.

20

A tortured relationship

Islamists and US foreign policy

Benjamin MacQueen

The relationship between Islamist movements and the United States generates controversy and even violence. Posited as the greatest security challenge in the early twenty-first century, the confrontation between the United States and movements that conducted the first attack against the US on its own soil since World War II now dominates discourse concerning US foreign policy in the Middle East and the broader Muslim world. This chapter explores this relationship by highlighting how Islamist movements have responded to US foreign policy and how US foreign policy has interacted with and itself responded to the actions and fate of Islamist movements. Despite the tension in this relationship, there is potential for greater co-operation between the US and Islamists, particularly in the area of regional political reform. However, such co-operation is likely to continue to be undermined by priority being placed on, for the US, regional stability at the expense of reform, and for Islamists, confrontational political positioning.

Understanding Islamist movements and US foreign policy

Before delving directly into the relationship between Islamists and US foreign policy, it is important to outline the definition of Islamists employed in this investigation. This is particularly so as the concept is one that is too often ill-defined. Whilst the definition offered here may not fully concur with alternative definitions offered in this volume, it is useful in terms of understanding Islamists and Islamism as an ideology that exhibits complexity and nuance throughout the *umma* and across the globe.

Islamist movements are defined as organisations that pursue the implementation of the shari'a or who take direct inspiration for their domestic and foreign policies from Islamic doctrine, including organisations whose calls for the implementation of the shari'a may be the stated or rhetorical rather than a realistic aim (Choueiri 1997: 11).

This definition embraces movements that seek to implement Islamic law and those more loosely associated with Islamic political guidance, as some organisations that may be labelled as Islamist, such as Lebanon's Hezbollah, have removed references to the creation of an Islamic state from their platforms yet develop policies related to social welfare as well as foreign policy that are firmly rooted in Islamic doctrine.

This definition builds on that offered by Mehdi Mozaffari who offers a view of modern Islamist ideology as a 'coherent, specific and identifiable construction' focused on the reconstruction of regional political and social realities (Mozaffari 2007: 22). It is argued that the focus on political realities is paramount, with social reconstruction viewed through the highly selective use of religious doctrine employed by these movements. Here, the use of religion serves to 'sacrelise' the political position taken by these movements (Mozaffari 2007: 22).

From this, Mozaffari offers a further delineation of movements defined as 'national' and 'global' Islamists whose ideology is the same, yet differs over the scope of their goals (Mozaffari 2007: 27–30). This over-simplifies matters somewhat, as important distinctions between the ideological grounding of movements exist, particularly in terms of the creation of an Islamic state (local or global). Instead, it is more useful to differentiate movements according to 'territorial' and 'neo-jihadist' organising principles. Simply put, territorial Islamist movements focused on events within particular states and neo-jihadist groups operate and articulate grievances and goals transnationally (Lentini 2008: 181). The former finds its heritage in local political and historical contexts whilst the latter interacts more directly with US foreign policy; however, it has its genesis in the political realities of the Muslim world.

For example, territorial Islamist organisations include groups such as Hamas in the Occupied Territories, Lebanon's Hezbollah, the various national wings of the Muslim Brotherhood (Egypt, Jordan and the Gulf, in particular) through to Turkey's AKP. Here, organisations range from those openly committed to the use of violence, to those rejecting violence and participating in the political system, to those that operate in a non-violent capacity outside of the political system, to those that display a range of these attributes at different times. The most prominent neo-jihadist organisation is al-Qaeda, defined by its nebulous, transnational nature. Indeed, al-Qaeda is better understood more in ideological than organisational terms as a transnational movement with various 'franchise' organisations operating in a variety of different theatres (Hoffman 2006: 430).

This definition can be complemented by Mozaffari's understanding of movements as either centrifugal or centripetal (Mozaffari 2007: 27). Centrifugal movements seek to expand issues or grievances outward whereas centripetal movements draw in attention, resources and manpower toward the issue at hand. For example, al-Qaeda is a centrifugal, neo-jihadist movement as it is not focused on a particular territorial political issue and seeks to expand its range of grievances outward in what Catarina Kinnvall has identified as an attempt to reconstruct ontological security (Kinnvall 2004: 741). Hamas is a centripetal territorial movement as it seeks to draw attention, resources and manpower to focus on the Arab–Israeli conflict.

Therefore, Islamist movements can be understood as organisations that pursue the implementation of the shari'a or that take direct inspiration for their domestic and foreign policies from Islamic doctrine and which are organised around two models, territorial or neo-jihadist, whilst demonstrating centrifugal or centripetal tendencies. Neo-jihadist movements with centrifugal tendencies have come into more direct conflict with the US, whilst territorial Islamist movements potentially have greater common ground with elements of US foreign policy. However, this common ground is tenuous and requires nurturing for this relationship to be fostered.

In fleshing out both this relationship and potential areas for reform of this relationship, it is important to reiterate that Islamist movements are not direct products of US foreign policy. The relationship between Islamists and the US is one often presented as binary opposites. Whether or not this is a hangover from the Cold War lens of bipolarity and attempts at othering of foes, seeking to understand Islamists in this way reveals very little. Instead, whilst Islamist movements have not emerged out of the effects of US foreign policy in the region, they have been increasingly shaped by it in recent decades. The intersection between US foreign policy and Islamist movements has become of primary importance since 11 September 2001. In particular, the contradictions inherent in US foreign policy priorities in the Middle East have become more evident, providing many Islamist movements with crucial propaganda for recruitment.

The origins of modern Islamist movements, particularly territorial movements, can largely be traced back to colonial-era thinkers/activists such as Jamal al-Din al-Afghani and Muhammad Rashid Rida in the late nineteenth and early twentieth centuries, with the organisational heritage stemming from movements such as the Muslim Brotherhood in Egypt and the Jamaat-i Islami in Pakistan emerging in the early to mid-twentieth century (Roy 2002). The challenge of colonialism was the key formative element here, and one that gave shape to the notion of territorial Islamist movements. That is, movements that were focused on restructuring the political reality that faced the Muslim world during the era of colonialism as well as after. For the Middle East, this was directed toward the emergent state system and the prevailing dominance of secular, radical nationalist regimes.

Whilst most of these movements were in opposition to the existing power structure, very few of them took an actively militant path. Here, political organisation under the banner of Islam was not the primary concern, with social reform as the first step to hoped-for political change the preferred path through to the 1960s and 1970s. These movements were also a useful outlet for dissent in authoritarian political systems that prevailed in Egypt, Syria, Saudi Arabia and elsewhere. Regimes across the region saw Islamist movements as an acceptable opposition that could be used as a means to channel social and political discontent but kept largely in check or oppressed when the need arose. Here, the US flirted with Islamist movements as a potential counterweight to pro-Soviet regimes in the Arab world, but never invested concerted time or resources to bolster the capacity of these organisations.

US foreign policy priorities and Islamist movements

This dynamic altered through the 1960s and 1970s as Islamist politics, or at least sections of Islamist political discourse, radicalised. This may be termed the 'first phase' of radicalisation (Pantucci 2008: 189). Here, Islamist discourse shifted to a focus on immediate revolutionary (and therefore potentially violent) action to effect political change through the writings of figures such as Sayyid Qutb, whilst Islamist organisations were heavily influenced by the revolutionary model that emerged in Iran in 1978/79 (Khatab 2006). As a result, a number of Islamist movements, focused at this time primarily on territorial issues linked with unsettling the established political order, took up arms. This was seen with the Syrian branch of the Muslim Brotherhood (1982), the Bouyali group in Algeria (1982–85), Hamas (since 1987), as well as the emergence of more radical groups in Egypt, notably *Gama'a Islamiyya*, which assassinated President Anwar Sadat in 1981.

Gama'a Islamiyya were part of a cohort of organisations that emerged in Egypt during the late 1970s and 1980s, which gravitated toward a neo-jihadist model, a 'second phase' of radicalisation. One such movement was Egyptian Islamic Jihad, which, after 1991, fell under the leadership of former surgeon Ayman al-Zawahiri. At the same time, the organisation now known as al-Qaeda emerged in the wake of the Soviet invasion of Afghanistan. The archetypal neo-jihadist group, al-Qaeda coalesced around a group of Arab mujahideen who had fought the Soviets and Afghan communists backed by private financing, particularly through patron Osama bin Laden, Saudi financing and US logistical support (Burke 2006: 11). Through what some analysts have described as 'blowback', US support for anti-communist forces in Afghanistan gave rise to the group that would later strike at America on its own soil (Griffin 2003).

The shift in al-Qaeda's focus came in 1990 after Iraq's invasion of Kuwait. As the Iraqi forces threatened to push further south into Saudi Arabia, bin Laden's group offered to defend the home of Islam's two holiest sites. This offer was rejected by the Saudi regime, which instead invited the US and its allies as a protective force. For bin Laden, al-Zawahiri and their organisation this revealed the corruption of the Saudi regime, a situation that characterised all regional regimes from Morocco to the Gulf. These regimes were the 'near enemy' underwritten by their patron, the 'far enemy', the United States (Gerges 2005).

Through the 1990s, al-Qaeda drew together a broader group of fighters in a variety of theatres across the globe based on an ideology that sought the establishment of a global Islamic caliphate through directly challenging both the near enemy and the far enemy. These theatres included Chechnya, Bosnia, Somalia, Algeria, Egypt and elsewhere. Concurrently, bin Laden and al-Zawahiri planned for attacks directed at the US. The first and largely unsuccessful attack on the World Trade Center in 1993 would prove the forerunner to the bombing of US embassies in Kenya and Tanzania in 1998, the bombing of the USS Cole at the port of Aden in Yemen in 2000, and then the attacks on New York and Washington on 11 September 2001.

At the root of the expressed motivations of al-Qaeda has been the view that regional regimes operate as proxies for the US in preservation of the regional political order as well as hoarding the region's oil wealth. In this way, neo-jihadists and territorial Islamists share common ground. However, the movements differ in the articulation of their ontological basis. For territorial Islamists, grievances are rooted directly in the actions of local regimes and the systems they perpetuate. Hostility to the US from this is born from their support of this system. As such, there is hostility toward the US for its policy of seeking regional stability, yet rarely does this manifest itself in direct action against the US (with the exception of Hezbollah in 1983). For neo-jihadists, this regional system is seen as symptomatic of a broader project whereby the Muslim world is under direct attack from the US and its proxy regimes. As such, it is incumbent on all Muslims to undertake jihad against the United States for its policies, particularly that of ensuring the political status quo in the Middle East, in pursuing the establishment of a global caliphate. Despite the destruction of al-Qaeda's physical organisation since 2001, this set of ideas has become franchised across the globe, with organisations as well as individuals taking up the neo-jihadist mantle in conducting acts of terrorism in Afghanistan (since 2001), Bali (2002), Iraq (since 2003), Madrid (2004), London (2005) and elsewhere (Hoffman 2006: 430).

Here, we can see the manipulation of Islamic doctrine by neo-jihadist movements based on a four-point worldview. First, Islamic communities and the faith itself is under attack from the West, led by the United States, working through proxy regimes in the Middle East and elsewhere. Second, neo-jihadi violence is therefore justified as it is employing a jihad to defend the Muslim community from this attack. Third, as these actions are defensive, they are proportionally and religiously justified. Fourth, it is therefore the duty of all Muslims to support these attacks (Betz 2008: 520). Here, neo-jihadism presents itself not as a movement rooted in territorially based grievances, but as an amalgam of geographically, culturally and socially diverse individuals and groups bound together through a common worldview or narrative.

For neo-jihadists, the notion of jihad is central. In traditional Islamic thought, it is a concept focused on the personal struggle for piety. However, it is reinterpreted to emphasise and elevate the notion of violence as a means to defend Muslim communities against this threat. The rearticulation of jihad by neo-jihadist movements is grand in scope in that it rejects distinctions between direct action and complicity on the part of those it sees as its enemies. That is, citizens of countries that are targets for neo-jihadi violence, such as those in the World Trade Center in 2001, or Iraqi citizens, or commuters on the London Underground on 7 July 2005, are complicit in the policy choices made by that country's government and, therefore, are viable targets themselves.

Understanding the roots of both territorial and neo-jihadist organisations reveals the origins of these movements not as a response to US foreign policy, but out of the political dynamics of the Muslim world, and particularly the Middle East since the 1970s and 1980s. However, the US role in this region and US foreign policy priorities combined with the increasing militancy of many of these movements have fostered the environment of mutual hostility that has characterised this relationship over the past decade.

The US and the quest for regional stability

So, what are these foreign policy priorities of the United States? US foreign policy in the Middle East has rested on three broad principles: regional stability, the security of Israel and, more recently, the promotion of political reform – principles that often sit in tension with one another (Baxter and Akbarzadeh 2008). Regional stability has been the cornerstone of US security policy in the Middle East. This was of more importance during the Cold War where the Middle East formed a key part of US containment policy through various multilateral institutions as well as bilateral relationships. However, in recent years this has taken on a new guise whereby regional regimes have formed a key element in the suite of security arrangements that fall under the 'war on terror'. Through this, regimes across the region have used (or been accused of using) the 'war on terror' for justification of continued political repression of opposition movements, movements that generally have a high Islamist cohort. This has further fed into the anger and resentment of local territorial Islamist movements and neo-jihadists against the US as underwriters of the regional order.

US efforts at maintaining regional stability, or more specifically the political status quo, have had the biggest impact on both types of Islamist movements. The issue of regional security is tied to two US concerns: the need for strategic partners and reliable access to oil. Each of these has fed into the tension surrounding the relationships between the US and Islamist movements. The tension created by US support for repressive regimes in the Muslim world can best be understood through examining the largely economically motivated relationship with the Kingdom of Saudi Arabia and the security-motivated relationship with the Republic of Egypt.

The US has guaranteed the external security of the Kingdom of Saudi Arabia since the 1950s and, more recently, has also guaranteed the continued viability of the regime in the face of internal threats such as al-Qaeda (Bronson 2006: 3). However, this relationship is not one of simply oil for defence, but is interlinked with US security concerns previously caught in the dynamic of the Cold War, Israeli security, concerns over Iraqi and Iranian strategic interests and, more recently, the 'war on terror'.

The centrality of Saudi Arabia in US foreign policy became entrenched during and after 1979. Three seminal events – the Islamic Revolution in Iran, the Soviet invasion of Afghanistan and the siege of the Grand Mosque in Mecca by Islamic radicals – all helped position the Kingdom as a key player in US interests in the Middle East beyond mere access to oil (Bronson 2006: 10). Resource stability still played a central dynamic, but became overlaid with US concerns over Iranian expansionism and the ability of the US to influence events in Afghanistan. As such, the strategic utility of the Kingdom became increasingly evident to successive US administrations.

This utility sat comfortably at first with the Saudi desire to continue to press for increased regional influence through extending the reach of subsidised religious institutions in the Middle

East and broader Muslim world (particularly in Pakistan and Indonesia), even after the Camp David Peace Accord between Israel and Egypt undercut the Kingdom's major regional adversary (Roy 2008: 93–94). From this point, the Saudi monarchy positioned their country as the dominant US Arab ally, arguably on an equal footing with Israel. The exploitation of this by the Saudi regime, with the patronage of the United States, led to the deliberate creation of radical Islamist groups, first as a tool of Saudi and US interests, then as the vanguard of opposition to this relationship. This is true for both territorial and, perversely, neo-jihadist elements.

Saudi regionalist ambitions and US complacency in this process have contributed directly to the 'second phase' of radicalisation, which gave rise to the neo-jihadist phenomenon. Massively increased oil revenues, particularly after 1973, enabled the Saudi regime to devote enormous funds to religious institutions throughout the Muslim world to counter Egyptian and then Iranian influence. Much of this money found its way to Central Asia, South Asia and South-East Asia, as well as through the Middle East, 'contributing to the intolerant strand of Islamic interpretation the world today is witnessing' (Bronson 2006: 10–11).

In Egypt, the advent of Anwar Sadat's presidency saw a conscious effort at co-opting Islamist opposition as a way to fully neutralise the radical, secular, leftist forces that predominated under the presidency of Gamal 'abd al-Nasser. This was not a full opening of the political sphere for the major Islamist movements, such as the Muslim Brotherhood, but an attempt to harness the potency of religious influence in Egypt and keep opposition forces divided (MacQueen 2008: 79). As Egypt and Israel negotiated peace through the late 1970s, the United States saw the opportunity to bring the most populous Arab state on board as another key regional ally against Soviet influence.

The US-Egyptian relationship, with Egypt as the second largest recipient of US foreign aid behind Israel, has led to the most visible expression of modern Islamist radicalism, both territorial and neo-jihadist. From political opposition in the form of the Muslim Brotherhood through to the rejectionist stance of violent movements such as *Takfir w'al Hijra*, Gama'a Islamiyya and Egyptian Islamic Jihad, the US effort to support an increasingly tenuous autocratic regime in Cairo highlights how US foreign policy priorities may not have created modern Islamism, but have contributed to an environment of hostility and aggravation.

In terms of oil, this has led the US to maintain close and controversial relationships with a number of despotic and autocratic regimes, notably the Saudis, but also in the Gulf, Algeria, Central Asia and, in the past, the Shah's Iran. Support for these regimes has enabled the perpetuation of regional authoritarian political systems and the perpetuation of a political order that many have viewed (or exploited for political purposes) as unjust. Indeed, it has drawn claims that the US is the underwriter of the division of the Arab people into 22 states as a means to keep them divided to ensure reliable access to energy.

The US, Israel and Islamists

Contrary to much opinion, US support for Israel is not the primary issue in terms of the relationship between Islamists and US foreign policy, with some exceptions (Hamas and Hezbollah). For Islamists, territorial and neo-jihadist alike, US support for Israel is more symptomatic of the broader trend of US support for the oppressive/unjust regional system. Israel is portrayed as the primary example of Western interference in the region, a colonial implant designed to ferment instability and division in the region at the expense of the Palestinian population. Interestingly, al-Zawahiri himself makes note of this in his text *Knights Under the Prophet's Banner*.

Stranger still is the fact that the Muslims, who have sacrificed the most for Jerusalem, whose doctrine and Shari'ah prevent them from abandoning any part of Palestine or recognizing Israel […] and who are the most capable of leading the nation in its jihad against Israel are the least active in championing the issue of Palestine and raising its slogans among the masses. The jihad movement's opportunity to lead the nation toward jihad to liberate Palestine is now doubled. All the secular currents that paid lip service to the issue of Palestine and competed with the Islamic movement to lead the nation in this regard are now exposed before the Muslim nation following their recognition of Israel's existence and adoption of negotiations and compliance with the international resolutions to liberate what is left, or permitted by Israel, of Palestine. These currents differ among themselves on the amount of crumbs thrown by Israel to the Muslim and the Arabs. The fact that must be acknowledged is that the issue of Palestine is the cause that has been firing up the feelings of the Muslim nation from Morocco to Indonesia for the past 50 years. In addition, it is a rallying point for all the Arabs, be they believers or non-believers, good or evil.

(Al-Zawahiri 2001: 7)

However, this has not translated into large-scale acts of violence against Israel on the part of the more radical movements. Territorial movements profess confrontational policies that may be pursued if they were to achieve power in their respective states, but this is highly unlikely due to the inability of these movements to achieve political power. Al-Qaeda has not directly targeted Israel, with only one of its affiliates conducting attacks against a specifically Jewish target, the Ghriba Synagogue in Tunis in 2002, despite the heated rhetoric from the movement on this issue.

The key exceptions here are two territorial Islamist movements, Hamas and Hezbollah. Hamas emerged from the Palestinian branch of the Muslim Brotherhood in 1987 upon the outbreak of the first Palestinian *intifadah*. Hamas' charter calls for the establishment of an Islamic state in all of Mandate Palestine, with the destruction of the Israeli state. It has directed hostility toward the United States for its continued support of Israel and non-recognition of Hamas' victory in the 2006 Palestinian legislative elections. Hamas presents decision-makers in the US State Department with a particular dilemma. By marginalising Hamas through packaging the movement within the worldview of the post-2001 'war on terror', it is left without a key and electorally sanctioned participant to the dispute. In addition, it undermines the US's stated commitment to the promotion of and respect for democratic processes.

Similarly, Hezbollah is a territorial movement that both participates in the electoral system whilst also engaged in armed activity. The movement emerged in response to the 1982 Israeli invasion of Lebanon with direct Iranian sponsorship as representatives of Lebanon's sizeable but historically marginalised shi'a population (Palmer Harik 2005: 4). Since the end of Lebanon's civil war in 1990, the movement has established itself as the single most powerful movement in the country, the armed wing of which remains sanctioned under Lebanon's constitution. Hezbollah's links with Iran feed into its hostility toward the United States, and it remains the only territorial movement to conduct direct attacks on the US with the bombing of the US embassy and marine barracks in Beirut in 1983. However, it has also achieved a measure of electoral success and holds key seats in the Lebanese Parliament, presenting a quandary for US policy-makers in terms of the need for regional security and support for political pluralism.

Whilst direct action against Israel has been limited, it remains central in the discourse of Islamists, particularly neo-jihadists. This was particularly so during the George W. Bush administration (2000–08). The Bush administration effectively disowned President Clinton's peace process from the very beginning. However, this was more a rejection of the Clinton stance, at least initially, than a signal of the vehemence with which the new US administration would back the new Likud administration of Ariel Sharon. The Democrats were still seen as a party close to Israel, particularly during the 2000 Presidential campaign where the Gore/Lieberman ticket actively courted the domestic Jewish vote and the Bush/Cheney ticket swept the Arab-American vote and played on the Bush family links to Arab regimes such as the Saudi monarchy (Kepel 2004: 16). Therefore, US withdrawal from the peace process prior to September 2001 was seen as the action of an administration not concerning itself with foreign policy, helping to prompt Arafat to pursue a hard line during the early days of the Al-Aqsa intifada. This would be a great miscalculation as it would alienate many of the Palestine Liberation Organisation (PLO) supporters in the US and Europe and position first Ehud Barak and more significantly Sharon as seemingly more morally justified in his actions, a position that would be greatly enhanced after September 2001.

These actions ended up isolating Arafat and Fatah, feeding into the growing popularity of Hamas which, at the time, still benefited from the flow of oil dollars from benefactors in the Gulf (Gunning 2008: 30). This would change through the 2000s as this form of radicalism along with the apparent links between Hamas, Hezbollah and Iran would frighten the Gulf states, Saudi Arabia in particular, into seeking to isolate Hamas. Gulf support for Hamas escalated greatly after the 1990 Iraqi invasion of Kuwait, an act that the PLO enthusiastically supported. The Gulf states saw this as a betrayal by the PLO as well as seeing Islamist movements such as Hamas as easier to control due to the ideological congruity through a shared conservative view of Islam and its place in political life.

Whilst the Bush administration was not vehemently pro-Israel (or, more specifically, pro-Likud) initially, it is important to note the often-cited influential role of neoconservative foreign policy thinkers who gained key positions within the new administration. These figures advocated a highly interventionist and vindicationalist form of US foreign policy that was deeply aligned with the Sharon/Likud view of the Middle East, particularly in terms of viewing the peace process as contrary to both US and Israeli interests and seeking to 'break' Arab resistance to Israel (Monten 2005: 120; Kepel 2004: 17). This position was strengthened by mid-2001 when Hamas and Islamic Jihad began to take greater control of the intifada from Fatah, launching a wave of suicide attacks within Israel against both military and civilian targets. These acts effectively alienated a critical mass of Western public opinion from the Palestinian cause, a trend that would be compounded after September 2001. Prior to 11 September, the US largely stood aside whilst violence escalated in Israel and the occupied territories, a stance that would strengthen the hand of its Likud allies at the expense of the Palestinian leadership, breaking the official Palestinian Authority (PA) resistance to Israel and the eventual demise of both Arafat and the PA, particularly in Gaza.

Interestingly, this was a break from the ways in which Republic and Democrat administrations were viewed in relation to the Arab–Israeli conflict. After the 1990–91 Gulf War, the first Bush administration did not punish the PLO for its support of Iraq, instead forcing both it and the Rabin government to the negotiating table leading to the breakthrough Madrid peace conference of 1991 (Kepel 2004: 24–25). In contrast, Democrat administrations had historically been closer to successive Israeli governments, particularly after 1967, whereas Republican administrations, through their links in the oil industry, had historically been seen as more sensitive to the interests of Arab regimes. Despite this, it is important to bear in mind that the change with the Bush administration was not necessarily a zero-sum equation where proximity to Israel equalled alienation of Arab autocracies, as many of these regimes, particularly Egypt and Saudi Arabia, saw greater utility in seeking to alienate radical Islamists than overtly oppose Israel.

The Al-Aqsa intifada was the most critical moment in the Arab–Israeli conflict relative to the relationship between Islamist groups and the United States. Far more than the first intifada, which was centred on civil unrest and political action, the Al-Aqsa intifada quickly shifted toward organised violence imbued, at least from a notable segment of Palestinian militant activity, with overtones of Islamist rhetoric that characterised the stance taken by Iran, Hezbollah and the many Egyptian Islamist movements. This was crystallised through the previous boom in satellite television across the region, which transmitted uncensored images of the violence between Israel and the increasingly influential Hamas. Popular Muslim discontent with the way the US and, by extension, local regimes were inactive in preventing this further fed support of Islamist movements based on hostility toward the United States and its allied regional regimes.

Salvaging the relationship: the US approach to political reform and the continued importance of soft power

The push for political reform took a prominent place during the middle era of the Bush administration (2002–06); however, this form of activist foreign policy has deeper roots in US activity across the globe, including the Middle East. Despite this, the US has played a much more tentative line, seeking to preserve its regional alliances over pushing for political change. The Bush administration packaged the need for political reform as a security issue after 2001 whereby efforts at preserving security through alliances with regional authoritarian regimes had led to the resentment that lay behind 11 September. Despite problems with this linear logic, it led to the promotion of political reform as, at least rhetorically, a new platform in US regional policy (MacQueen 2009: 165). Such a policy sat in obvious tension with the need to preserve regional security as well as continued support for Israel.

However, this policy platform presents, on the surface at least, the most tangible area of mutual interests for the US and Islamist parties. Territorial Islamists are the primary opposition in almost all regional states (except for Turkey and Iran). Thus, reform that seeks to open up the political arena would benefit these groups primarily. For instance, in Egypt, the Muslim Brotherhood would likely emerge as the key oppositional force, or as a majority, should genuinely transparent elections take place as well as the removal of the State of Emergency Law that enabled the Mubarak regime to stifle political dissent since 1981. Similarly, in Jordan, Kuwait and Morocco, Islamists have been able to achieve marked electoral victories in the functional yet tightly controlled parliamentary systems.

However, further progress by the US on this front has stalled due to concerns over the attitude of Islamists to the US should they come to power. Indeed, the US has largely continued the pursuit of political reform in vulnerable territories such as the Palestinian territories, Lebanon and Iraq, instead of states where this may be more controversial, yet potentially have a more lasting effect (Cofman Wittes 2008: 76). This is misguided, as the record has shown that once coming to power, most territorial Islamist movements have largely moderated their platforms. In Turkey, the Justice and Development Party (AKP) have positioned themselves as more of a conservative political party in the mould of Germany's Christian Democrats. Indeed, even in the case of Hezbollah, despite the maintenance of an armed wing, the movement has removed references to the creation of an Islamic state from their charter since actively participating in Lebanon's political system.

The deterioration of the relationship between the US and Islamists, particularly territorial Islamists, lay in hard-power decisions with soft-power ramifications. The invasion of Iraq was packaged, after 2004 at least, as part of a 'Forward Strategy of Freedom' that would bring democracy to the Middle East. Territorial Islamists, as the primary opposition parties in most regional states, would therefore be the primary beneficiaries of such a move. However, hard-power calculations as to the strategic cost of such an outcome led the US to maintain its relationships with regional autocracies under the security logic of the 'war on terror'. The attractiveness of the democratic model for territorial Islamists was tarnished as it was pushed in conjunction with US security priorities that further marginalised Islamist aims. This fed a dynamic of mutual antagonism, greater hostility and, therefore, seemingly greater need for the US to shore up authoritarian governments as a bulwark against Islamist political ambitions.

The unfortunate outcome of this dynamic has not terminally undermined potential constructive relationships between territorial Islamist movements and the United States. In purely functional terms, democratic models of political reform remain a useful tool for Islamists to achieve political power. Revolutionary models, to date, have proven ineffective. In contrast, Islamist electoral victories have occurred in Lebanon, Turkey, Jordan, Algeria and elsewhere (with, of course, varying degrees of longevity). US soft power, therefore, may still have a chance at undercutting the dynamic of mutual hostility, promoting political reform, and move politics from the realm of violent confrontation to electoral confrontation.

Soft power, essentially, is the ability to influence others, not with 'threats or coercion', but instead through the appeal of 'values, [...] culture, and [...] institutions' (Kurlantzick 2005: 420; Nye 1990). Whilst Joseph Nye's original articulation of the importance of soft power focused on the influence of one state over another, it resonates in terms of the influence of political models over political organisations and movements, such as Islamist movements. Moving from an approach based on a 'vindicationalist' view of social and political superiority (i.e. military-backed regime change and democracy promotion), the US can gain more traction with Islamist movements through democratic practice, or an 'exemplarist' model of influence (Monten 2005: 120). That is, practising the example of political pluralism, transparency and accountability can breed a far more potent example for others to follow than opening oneself up to criticisms of imperialism through military action.

The most vital step in this regard is the need for the United States to step back from the language of terrorism and positioning territorial Islamist political ambitions as inimical to democratic development. This has been achieved to some extent, with greater focus on reconstruction efforts in Afghanistan and attempts at more constructive diplomatic engagement in the Muslim world. However, openness to the prospect of Islamist electoral success continues to haunt Washington as it is seen as potentially heralding the emergence of a new Islamic Republic of Iran.

Conclusion

Confrontation and sometimes violence continue to characterise the relationship between Islamists and the United States. This is not a permanent situation, however, nor a clash of inimical ideologies, particularly in terms of the relationship between territorial Islamists and the United States. Whilst neo-jihadist movements have become so deeply embedded in antagonism to US foreign policy, territorial movements can find points of commonality with US foreign policy ambitions, particularly in terms of political reform. By keeping in mind the lessons of history which teach us that the modern Islamist movement was not born out of US foreign policy decisions, it is possible to plan for an eventuality that sees Islamists and the United States relate in a more constructive way. This requires a re-calibration of both US and Islamist political priorities, but a decision that may lead to better outcomes for both groups.

References

Al-Zawahiri, A. (2001) *Knights Under the Prophet's Banner*, available at www.scribd.com/doc/6759609/Knights-Under-the-Prophet-Banner (accessed 20 April 2010).

Baxter, K. and Akbarzadeh, S. (2008) *US Foreign Policy in the Middle East: The Roots of Anti-Americanism*, London, Routledge.

Betz, D. (2008) 'The Virtual Dimension of Contemporary Insurgency and Counterinsurgency', *Small Wars and Insurgencies* vol. 19, no. 4: 510–40.

Bronson, R. (2006) *Thicker than Oil: America's Uneasy Partnership with Saudi Arabia*, Oxford, Oxford University Press.

Burke, J. (2006) *Al-Qaeda: Casting a Shadow of Terror*, London, I.B.Tauris.

Choueiri, Y. (1997) *Islamic Fundamentalism*, London, Continuum.

Cofman Wittes, T. (2008) *Freedom's Unsteady March: America's Role in Building Arab Democracy*, Washington, DC, Brookings Institution Press.

Gerges, F. (2005) *The Far Enemy: Why Jihad Went Global*, Cambridge, Cambridge University Press.

Griffin, M. (2003) *Reaping the Whirlwind: Afghanistan, Al Qa'ida and the Holy War*, London, Polity Press.

Gunning, J. (2008) *Hamas in Politics: Democracy, Religion, Violence*, New York, Columbia University Press.

Hoffman, B. (2006) 'Al Qaeda, Trends in Terrorism, and Future Potentialities: An Assessment', *Studies in Conflict and Terrorism* vol. 26, no. 3: 429–42.

Kepel, G. (2004) *The War for Muslim Minds: Islam and the West*, Cambridge, MA, Harvard University Press.

Khatab, S. (2006) *The Political Thought of Sayyid Qutb: The Theory of Jahiliyyah*, London, Routledge.

Kinnvall, C. (2004) 'Globalization and Religious Nationalism: Self, Identity, and the Search for Ontological Security', *Political Psychology* vol. 25, no. 5: 741–67.

Kurlantzick, J. (2005) 'The Decline of American Soft Power', *Current History* vol. 104: 419–24.

Lentini, P. (2008) 'Antipodal Terrorists? Accounting for Differences in Australian and "Global" Neojihadists', in R. Devetak and C. Hughes (eds), *Globalization's Shadow: The Globalization of Violence*, London, Routledge.

MacQueen, B. (2008) 'The Reluctant Partnership between the Muslim Brotherhood and Human Rights NGOs in Egypt', in S. Akbarzadeh and B. MacQueen (eds), *Islam and Human Rights in Practice: Perspectives Across the Ummah*, London, Routledge.

—— (2009) 'Democracy Promotion and Arab Autocracies', *Global Change, Peace and Security* vol. 21, no. 2: 165–78.

Monten, J. (2005) 'The Roots of the Bush Doctrine: Power, Nationalism, and Democracy Promotion in U.S. Strategy', *International Security* vol. 29, no. 4: 112–56.

Mozaffari, M. (2007) 'What is Islamism? History and Definition of a Concept', *Totalitarian Movements and Political Religions* vol. 8, no. 1: 17–33.

Nye, J. (1990) *Bound to Lead: The Changing Nature of American Power*, New York, Basic Books.

Palmer Harik, J. (2005) *Hezbollah: The Changing Face of Terrorism*, London, I.B.Tauris.

Pantucci, R. (2008) 'Al-Qaeda 2.0', *Survival* vol. 50, no. 6: 183–92.

Roy, O. (2002) *Globalised Islam: The Search for a New Ummah*, London, Hurst & Co.

—— (2008) *The Politics of Chaos in the Middle East*, New York, Columbia University Press.

21

Islamism in the Middle East

The resistant, the fighter and the *mujahid*

Bernard Rougier

This chapter intends to redefine Islamism in the Middle East by exploring three ideal-type forms of political and religious engagement, which have been expressed in a sequential or cumulative manner for about 30 years. Split into many expressions, Islamism in the Middle East revolves nevertheless around three main figures: the *muqatil* (fighter), the *muqawim* (resistant) and the *mujahid* (jihad fighter). The rationale of specific situations explains, for the most part, the switch from one form of action to another. This chapter aims to clarify the particular characteristics of these three models of militant action, and seeks to highlight the privileged resources upon which each one relies. Through the figure of the *muqawil*, here defined as an entrepreneur of anger, a fourth form of action, linked to the globalisation of exchanges and the birth of new information technology, will also be explicated in turn. With the assistance of this theoretical framework one may be able to formulate hypotheses about the evolution of Islamism in the region.

It should be added that each ideal-type covers a diversity of 'regime of engagement'. This notion, close to 'logics of action' or 'pragmatic regimes', tries to capture 'not only the movements of an actor but also the way his environment responds to him and the way he takes into account these responses' (Thévenot 2001: 56–73). Its heuristic use is to reveal the dynamic aspect of activities between individuals and the world that surrounds them. Each kind of pragmatic engagement valorises the very part of reality that is relevant for the accomplishment of its valued goals, involving both a conception of reality and a conception of the good. It is this dialectical interaction between 'the engaged good' and the 'engaged reality' that defines the 'regime of engagement'. To become actors, individuals and groups constantly need interplay with a mix of different kinds of environment – local, regional, international, transnational. In doing so, they evaluate the success (or the failure) of their engagement through a 'reality test' which provokes revision and innovation. With this in mind, it becomes easier to capture the dynamics of a notion – Islamism – which has become too large a concept to really mean something by itself.

The three poles of Islamism

The muqawim

The figure of the *muqawim* (the resistant) asserted itself against Europe's political and military influence in the East at the end of the nineteenth century. The special link between Islam and resistance is demonstrated by the choice of religion as an instrument of mobilisation comprehensible to the masses and politically effective in the face of the hegemony of non-Muslim powers. Both an intellectual and a conspirator, the scholar Jamal al-Din al-Afghani (1839–97) was one of the first to brandish the ideal of a pan-Islamic solidarity to turn the Muslim subjects of the British Empire against the British authorities (Goldziher 2010; Keddie 1972). A pioneer of anti-colonialism, al-Afghani combined a grammar of resistance against foreign invasion with liberal preoccupations regarding domestic questions, without noting a contradiction between the two forms of engagement.[1] The Muslim Brotherhood, founded in Egypt at the end of the 1920s, converted action conducted in the name of Islam against the encroachment of the outside, Western world (British occupation of Egypt, Zionist implantation in Palestine) to domestic political and religious action, with a view to applying the prescriptions of religious law by an 'Islamic State'.

In the Sunni world, this requirement, in formal line with the 'programmatic function' of modern European political parties, marks a considerable rupture with traditional Islam, since the latter has been stressing the need to protect the Community against the risks of self-nurtured divisions for centuries (al-Sayyid 2007). In claiming to represent the Law versus the Community, the Muslim Brotherhood runs the risk of seeing the violence once turned against imperialism transformed into an internal jihad against the rulers of the Muslim states. If the majority of the Islamist militants didn't endorse the consequences of the contradiction, the radical intellectual Sayyid Qutb followed this logic through in assimilating the Muslim rulers who did not govern 'in accordance with what God prescribed' with the era of pre-Islamic ignorance (*jahiliyya*).

The intellectual and organisational legacy of the Muslim Brotherhood was restored in the Shi'ite religious universe with the creation in Iraq, in the city of Najaf at the end of the 1950s, of the organisation *al-Da'wa* (the Call) under the influence of Sayyid Mohammed Baqr al-Sadr (Jabar 2003). The use of Islam in partisan politics challenged the quietist belief that it was necessary to abstain from engaging politically as long as the hidden Imam had not yet returned on Earth. The party al-Da'wa was also accused of bypassing the authority of the traditional clergy by creating a new source of obedience. Despite these criticisms, however, the call for application of the religious law in the framework of a hypothetical Islamic State reinforced the Shi'ite community in polities where they were not in power. In sectarian countries such as Lebanon or Iraq, the spreading of radical Islamism in the 1970s, far from augmenting internal fractures, contributed on the contrary to reinforcing the denominational cohesion of the Shi'ite political minority and reduced the appeal of the communist party and the Ba'th party among the intellectuals and the poor. The encounter between the religious Law and the Community – in the form of an alliance between the principal segments of Iranian society against the power of the Shah – in turn conditioned the success of the Iranian Revolution in 1979. The only one of its kind, it achieved synthesis between the Islamist utopia, primarily theorised by Mohammed Baqr al-Sadr, and the formulation of a theology of power (the doctrine of *velayate faqih*) reactivated by Ayatollah Khomeini.

After this event, the ideal-type of the *muqawim* became fully redefined in a militant Islamist stance once the Gulf axis of crisis, embodied by the Iranian revolution, started to spill over the Levant axis of crisis. The Islamist resistant came to replace the *fedayin*, and this change went hand in hand with the new intervention of Khomeini's Iran in the political and religious scene of the Levant. Only one month after the beginning of the Israeli invasion of Lebanon in June 1982, the Iranian Revolutionary Guardians (*Pasdaran*) set up the first training camp of the 'Islamic Resistance in Lebanon' in the Bekaa. Those who were to become rulers of Hezbollah were enlisted there, such as Abbas al-Musâwi, the first Secretary-General of the Shi'a Islamist organisation – former student in Najaf of Mohammed Baqr al-Sadr alongside whom he had been studying religion for nine years – and Hassan Nasrallah, his close friend (Mustâfa 2003). Created in 1982, the precedence of the military wing over the political wing, revealed in 1985, leaves a clue about the organic relation between the 'hard core' of the Iranian regime and the military institutions of the 'Party of God'.

Embodied by organisations like Hamas and Islamic Jihad in the second part of the 1980s, religious radicalism was perceived as a means to accentuate the isolation of the Palestine Liberation Organisation (PLO) in the Muslim world. In 1988, after the Palestinian National Congress's recognition of resolution 242, which implied an implicit recognition of Israel, the PLO and its President, Yassir Arafat, were accused by Islamists of wanting to sell off Palestine, defined as a mortmain land (*waqf*), inalienable as the exclusive property of God.[2] The *muqawim* figure is thus blossoming with the takeover of the Palestinian symbolic space by Khomeini's Iran. The regime in Iran updates for its own sake past and present anti-colonial fights in order to build a permanent mobilisation against the 'West', the 'Zionist entity', etc. As a figure, the resistant is not necessarily an Islamist – one can be against the 'West' on political grounds, being, for example, an heir of Arab nationalism – but Islamism gives him a much greater consistency, since resistance as a duty is bound to cultural as much as to political spheres.

While a dynamic revolutionary born in Tehran found the means to project himself to the eastern Mediterranean shores, the most radical Sunni Islamists from the Arab countries bordering Israel in Egypt, in Jordan or in Syria found themselves in a uneasy situation. They were unable to seize power in their respective states and, since those states were keen to avoid any escalation with the Israeli army, they could not try to cross the border in order to 'free Palestine'. Even southern Lebanon was out of reach, since the Shi'a Hezbollah locked the only military front still available for its own benefit.

The mujahid

The *mujahid* (jihad fighter) is the product of a double frustration. Domestic jihad, such as was advocated by Sayyid Qutb, failed in Egypt (1981) and in Syria (1979–82). The *muqawim* exploited the void created by the Israeli invasion of Lebanon in 1982 to claim exclusivity (in the form of an 'Islamic resistance') of the battlefront against Israel – a front from which the Sunni jihadists remained absent, despite multiple attempts at contact since 2001. The impossibility of pursuing jihad in Palestine – as the Arab regimes set themselves up as 'guardians of the Israeli borders' – obliged the *mujahid* to move to the third axis of crisis – the Afghani/Pakistani zone. Prevented from acting against Israel, defeated at the hands of the Arab regimes, an active minority of Islamists went to Afghanistan in the 1980s in order to escape Middle Eastern regional politics. The Palestinian Sheikh Abdallah Azzam (1941–89) was the theoretician of this militant trajectory. Trained in a camp reserved for Islamists – the 'camp of sheikhs' – in the valley of Jordan at the end of the 1960s, neutral during the conflict of Black September (1970) owing to his hostility toward the 'atheist' factions of the PLO, he was relieved of his duties as professor of shar'ia at the University of Jordan because of his admiration for Sayyid Qutb. A lecturer at the University of the King Abd al-Aziz in Jeddah in 1981, he was passionate about the battle of the Afghan mujahedeen against the Soviet army, who occupied Afghanistan in 1979. He became a tireless proponent of the cause of jihad in Afghanistan, through multiple conferences throughout the world and the direction of the journal *al-jihad*.

The Palestinian sheikh constructed his action on the basis of a theological grammar drawn directly from medieval Islam. By defending by arms the frontiers of the *umma* – the community of believers – he was giving it a territorial medieval meaning close to the Abbasid empire's *limes*. The believers of all countries were thus encouraged to assure the protection of this entity by committing themselves to the Afghan cause. Describing Afghanistan as a fragment of the suffering *umma* – Azzam knowingly appealed to the organicist metaphor of the Islamic 'body' corrupted by the communist 'cancer' – permitted the simplification of the Afghan stakes to make them more accessible to Muslim public opinion. All the same, the use of religious vocabulary provoked a kind of equivalence and comparability between issues in Arab countries and issues in Muslim lands further afield. Theology granted its sacred stamp to geography and pronounced the lack of attention to an affair foreign to the Arab world illegitimate.

With the jihad in Afghanistan, the Islamists of the Middle East escaped domestic issues linked with the overthrow of the Muslim government. Protecting the *umma*'s borders took precedence over the seizing of political power. The Palestinian cause was not forgotten, but simply postponed: thanks to their expertise acquired in combat, it was believed that the militants could subsequently recover Jerusalem.

As a promoter of an ummist jihadism, Azzam essentialised in religious terms what was then an exceptional geopolitical situation. He wrongly postulated that that situation was reproducible elsewhere. For that to happen, the believers had to go back to the essence of their faith: jihad conceived as individual obligation (*fard 'ayn*) and not as a collective obligation (*fard kifāya*) relevant to states and their armies. In his own way, he privatised one of the fundamental attributes of sovereignty according to Carl Schmitt: the capacity to declare the exception and to designate the enemy (Schmitt 1992). The Muslim states as well as Islamic religious institutions were divested of this sovereign capacity in favour of individual sincere believers. A potential entity beforehand, the *umma* became an actual entity thanks to the decisive action of an avant-garde speaking and acting in its name. Yet, the new ideology born in Peshawar, in viewing jihad as an end in itself, moved the militants away from access to state power and freed their religious engagement of any territorial and strategic taking-root. Sunni radicalism pursued its shift from politics, in a statist and institutional sense, at the very moment when Shi'ite Islamism realised, for its part, the advantages of the modern state.[3] Thanks to the existence of a clergy, radical Islam proved to be a cohesive force among the Shi'a, whereas it had mainly divisive effects in Sunni societies.

Thereafter, the model underwent some reorientation, even some deviation under the influence of new intellectuals who had settled in the Pakistani city of Peshawar at the end of the 1980s and beginning of the 1990s. In the eyes of these intellectuals, such as Abu Mohammed al-Maqdisi, Abu Qatada, Abu Anas al-Chami, the *mujahid* was obliged to do battle against the ungodly powers that directed the Muslim states as a priority, before undertaking the re-conquest of the lost territories of the *umma*.

Azzam saw himself as an *'alim* of jihad, speaking in the name of the people and societies of Islam, subsumed in the glorious title of the *umma*. Not surprisingly, he identified with *ulama* who had battled several centuries before him to declare jihad a prerogative of the community, one that fell entirely in their domain and not amongst those of political power. According to Radwan al-Sayyid, since the beginning of the second century of hejri (the eighth Christian century), the *ulama* of Sham (Greater Syria) have played a special role in this emphasis of jihad. Victorious over the Sassanid empire in the east, the soldiers of Islam were crushed at the hands of Byzantium and went on to suffer several military defeats on land and at sea. A strong military theology prevailed during the pre-battle atmosphere, with the garrison towns (*ribāt*) stationed at the outposts of Islam (*thughr*). For the *ulamas* of Medina and Iraq, jihad was nothing more than a charitable action, the status of which was supererogatory from a religious point of view. The *ulamas* of Sham (following the example of the imam al-Awza'i) shared exactly the opposite view. In order to convince the Muslim constituency abroad, they increased the testimonies attributed to the Prophet and his companions about the sacred character of military jihad as an 'individual obligation'. Faced with the threat of a Byzantine counter-attack, it was imperative to send reinforcements. For them, leaving their homes to defend Islam was comparable to Mohammed's *hijra* in 632 for the Syrian jurists. This comparison implicitly signified giving certain geographical spaces a religious value superior to others, as though their movement to the borders to preserve Islam face to face with a non-Muslim enemy augmented their degree of religiosity. In addition, this movement established an explicit equivalence between an event (*hijra*) that was at the very origins of the birth of Islam and a military measure supposed to assume the same character of obligation.

The movement to Peshawar, some kilometres away from the Pakistani–Afghani border, was a means of reasserting the tradition of the *ribat* and to bring to the fore an Islam of combat. For this Islam of combat could not, by its very nature, situate itself at a state or governmental level. Significantly, the back catalogue of the *al-jihad* journal does not mention the least homage to an Arabic or Muslim head of state in the contemporary era. Carrying a vision sparked during his studies of Islamic jurisprudence (*fiqh*), Azzam sought to relaunch a classical, theological and controversial Islamic heritage in the modern world. After a lost opportunity in Palestine, the war in Afghanistan gave him that chance: he had found the situation and the people he had long searched for. Practising jihad was the equivalent of a new hijra: the reaffirmation of the pact linking the believer to his own faith through the voyage of the happy *umma* (the Arabian Peninsula) towards the suffering *umma* (Afghanistan at war).

The muqatil

If the figure of the fighter (*muqatil*) is the least sophisticated, it is without a doubt the most ancient and the most common. This figure manifests an attitude of localised defence when faced with an external aggression, whatever the identity of the aggressor. In the Palestinian case, as recalled by Rachid Khalidi, it is the vital link between peasants and their lands which triggered, at the end of the nineteenth century, a fighting dynamic 'more driven from below than from above' (Khalidi 1997: 7). The fighter identifies with a concrete environment which gives him his military identity and by which he defines himself to fight against an enemy considered principally as an intruder.

This character is summarised by the 'profession of faith' of a district chief from Tripoli in the north of Lebanon, cited by Michel Seurat: 'I fight for my honour and my existence on this earth' (Seurat 1985). In most cases, this character is little structured ideologically and thus corresponds with the notion of *açabiyya* (solidarity group) developed by Ibn Khaldun in the fourteenth century. The *muqatil* readily identifies with the values of Islam and of the homeland but connects this intimately with honour and defence of the family, so that its engagement essentially expresses itself at a local level. There is an elective affinity between the fighter, on one side, and the mere notion of political independence, on the other side, since the latter is seen as the continuation, on a larger scale, of an enjoyable local autonomy. This link explains why the Fatah movement – a blending between conservative Islam and independent outlook – was so successful in attracting a large part of the Palestinian constituency in the late 1960s until the 1990s. Conversely, it might also explain why it was so difficult to break centuries-old factionalism and to transform a network of local, entrenched organisations scattered in the Gaza Strip and the West Bank into a modern Palestinian state – aside from the numerous constraints raised by different Israeli governments in its negotiations with the Palestinian Authority from 1993 to 2000.

The assertion of the resistant as an ideological compact figure in the 1980s posed an inner threat to the fighter. Aimed to enact vengeance for the Israeli assassination of one important military officer within the movement, Hamas' campaign of suicide attacks against Israeli civilians in February and March of 1996 was in line with a religious grammar for which the Oslo Accords constituted a grave breach of the rule of Muslim solidarity. For those who identified with this grammar, solidarity with the *umma* was more important than obedience to a Palestinian authority born of original sin and guilty of negotiating with Israel. Denouncing the wrongdoing by means of terrorist attacks was a manner of demonstrating solidarity with an emotional image (the *umma*) defined against the PLO and Palestinian Authority. As soon as the political translation of the *umma* referred to centres of power localisable in Tehran and south Beirut, the seeds of civil war were planted in Palestinian soil.[4] Once the resistant is in place, the only chance of survival given to the fighter is to rely upon the help of the international system – the United States, United Nations (UN), European Union (EU) – in order to resist against the constant pressure of the former. If the international system becomes ineffective in helping the fighter, the latter is at risk of losing its nationalist credentials.

In Iraq, local Sunni tribes fit into the fighter category. In creating the 'awakening councils' (*majâlis al-sahwât*) in the Sunni triangle of al-Anbar in 2006 (thanks to a generous policy of distribution of arms and money), the US General David Petraeus succeeded in disassociating the figure of the fighter from that of the resistant (Mouqtada al-Sadr's 'Mahdi Army') and, especially, from that of the *mujahid* (al-Qaeda in Iraq). This policy is always risky, though, since the combatant figure may resort to armed struggle if the collective guarantees of security are no longer assured. It shows that against the backdrop of a double threat – a resistant linked to Iran's Pasdaran/a *mujahid* linked to transnational al-Qaeda networks – there is no other solution for the fighter than to rely upon a Western force.

Dealing with those categories helps to deconstruct 'Islamism' as a self-explanatory concept. Placed side by side with the fighter, Islamism is a syntagm; it is closely linked with a local context and only makes sense by referring to that context. On the contrary, for both the resistant and the mujahid, Islamism is closer to a paradigm that encapsulates singularities into a greater narrative.[5] For example, only a revived peace process today could highlight the invisible fracture-line that divides Hamas between those ready to live in a viable Palestinian state restricted to Gaza and the West Bank with East Jerusalem as a capital on the one hand, and those for whom the battle must continue until the disappearance of Israel on the other hand. Nominally, the former and the latter belong to the resistance, but this resistance is understood as a syntagm by the former and as a paradigm by the latter, who strives for an Islamic Palestine freed 'from the Sea to the river' (Gunning 2007). For Hamas' pragmatic wing, the political and financial link with Saudi Arabia was conceived as a means of counterbalancing the risks of a too exclusive link with Iran. Unfortunately, US pressure on the Saudi Kingdom scaled down their influence inside the movement, thus reducing the prospect of an inter-Palestinian reconciliation.

During the latent civil war that prevailed in Syria from 1979 to 1982, the *muqatil* appropriated the language of Islamism to defend the interests of the elite urban Sunnis excluded from power by Hafez al-Assad's regime. The repression led to the appearance of 'Adnan 'Uqla's jihad fighters, whose revolutionary goals moved away from those more conservative goals defended by the urban *muqatilín*. This internal conflict explained a mad headlong rush toward violence and the final defeat of a movement which commenced by fighting against the government before becoming a game of internal battles between *muqatil* and *mujahid*.[6]

Islamism and 'regimes of engagement'

Logics of action and justification

More than ideology, it is what a 'regime of engagement' encompasses (such as places, objects, situations) which enables us to distinguish and to specify the different forms of Islamism. Abdallah Azzam, for example, took a decisive role in reactivating the *mujahid*'s figure as an ideal-type, but his successive actions took place in different regimes of engagement – training camp in the Jordan Valley, teaching at the shar'ia Faculty of Law at the University of Jordan, then at the King Abd al-Aziz University in Jeddah, the setting up of guesthouses in Pakistan in the 1980s – that are not those known after him by other mujahideen such as Ayman al-Zawahiri or Osama bin Laden. The religious coding of their respective environments has been done on quite similar terms, but the means of coordination were activated in very different contexts and times, and, for that reason, could not be grounded on the same apparatus. According to that framework, explaining actors' behaviour cannot only be grounded on their biographies, nor on their socialisations or their speeches, but must take into account, first and foremost, all the concrete forms of coordination through which they acted in a certain period of time. Put together, those heterogeneous items fit the definition of a 'regime of engagement'.

Thus, it is not because Hezbollah and Osama bin Laden agreed to believe that 'the United States is at the origin of all the misfortune of the Muslim world' that there is no difference between Hezbollah and al-Qaeda. It is through the study of the connections that these two forms of Islamism maintain with their religious and institutional environments that one can define their respective specificities.

Many regimes of engagement sustain, for example, the resistant's figure. Some of them rely on a 'hard-power' apparatus, embodied in Iran by the guardians of the revolution (*sepah-e pasdaran*), the popular militia (*sepah-e basij*) and a network of religious and economic foundations that bypass, under the official responsibility of the Revolution's guide, the political and administrative institution of the state (Buchta 2000). When applied to Hezbollah, Islamism must take into account clandestine paths of communication between Syria and Lebanon, arms, missiles, military reports, underground passages, caches, contacts at the highest levels in the Lebanese, Syrian and Iranian states, a parliamentary group, a religious Shi'a institute (*husseinniyât*), training military camps, a governmental right of veto, an effective media system, an intelligence network much more efficient than the legal ones, religious guidance and, to cut a long story short, the effective control of an Arab capital. On the other hand, one will not find military roadblocks from which to extort money from the population, as if the leaders of the party had taken lessons from the very unpopular militia's behaviour during the Lebanese civil war. Within the resistant figure – in that case Hezbollah – there are thus many 'regimes of action'. The thousands of fighters inside the party (during the 2006 war, their number would not have surpassed 5,000 men) have been through specialised training known only to themselves and their supervisors. On the whole, the success of the Shi'a party lies in its capacity to combine different kinds of 'regimes of action' within the same framework, so that inner tensions never break out in open crises.

The concrete associations that weave the life of a jihadi militant are quite different. In order to simplify the picture, it has been organised around an underground composed of guesthouses in Iraq, Syria or Pakistan, military camps in Waziristan and Yemen, jihadist forums, clandestine studios for the fabrication of false papers and explosives, local mosques, and readings of canonical texts written by the main jihadist *ulamas* since 2006. More transnational than regional, the geography of the *mujahid* makes the link between the three axes of crises, without managing to weigh decisively on any one of them, in the absence of an environment comparable to the one built, thanks to its organic relationship with some state apparatus, by the *muqawim*.

Another huge difference distinguishes those two models of engagement. Should an inner conflict occur within the ranks of Hezbollah, mechanisms of 'aggrandisement' give the upper hand to a religious body among the 'jihad council' directed by the secretary-general of the organisation. Beyond the 'jihad council', the Supreme Guide of the Islamic Republic of Iran, Ayatollah Khomeini, gives the final call in his capacity as a *wali al-faqih*. The 'principle of worth' inside the Islamic Shi'a order is embodied by one and only one religious authority – the 'worthy being' in Boltanski and Thévenot's vocabulary.[7]

Geographically split, jihadist Sunni networks cannot resort to any kind of authority comparable to the one endowed to the *wali al-faqih*. Resorting to the divine religious corpus – Qur'an and hadith – as a principle of worth only makes matters worse, since there is no well-respected authority that would be able to connect the disputed situation with the will of God and its Prophet. Asking Zawahiri in a written letter takes time and is not immune to interception by the enemy, as was shown by the many letters seized by the US army in Iraq. Moreover, Zawahiri is one among many in the jihadi universe, and does not hold an uncontested authority on these matters. Pilgrimages to Mecca and Medina could provide the opportunity for a kind of Islamic 'aggrandisement', but the Saudi sheikhs are themselves too much divided to guarantee a well-accepted interpretation. Landmarks are too loose to really help in the coordination of the others' actions.

Variations in human and material equipment explain the changes inside the jihadist paradigm. The first generation benefited from exceptional geo-political circumstances, which combined religious meaning, military backing and international support from the United States (technology), Saudi Arabia (money) and Pakistan (logistical facilities) during a relatively short period (about five years). This combination ceased with the Soviet army's retreat in February 1989, but far from being fully taken into account, the combination was denied by the promoters of the jihadist ideology. For them, the *mujahid*'s faith was the true cause of the victory rather than external aid, described as a source of corruption of the purity of the cause. Pushed to the limit, the privatisation of jihad, of which Azzam was the principal theoretician, led to a situation of permanent mobilisation which no state could accept for long. Here lies the big difference in status between the two ideal-types: the *muqawim* is a mystic capable of signing up for politics, whereas the *mujahid* is a mystique of perpetual jihad, rebellious against all political affiliation, who found a Che Guevara of Islam in Abdallah Azzam.

During the second phase, only the emirate of the Taliban in 1996 offered a safe haven to mujahideen in a situation of defeat, incapable of taking power in their countries of origin (Algeria, Tajikistan) or of reproducing the Afghan success on other fronts (Bosnia, Chechnya). In 1999, three years after his arrival from Sudan, Osama bin Laden was authorised to build his own training camps in the city of Kandahar, with the best recruits sourced from the al-Faruq camp sent to the airport camp. The other camps were 'mutualised' between the different jihadist networks. The majority of the attacks committed during this period were conceived of and tested in the camps of Kandahar (Hegghammer 2010). Wishing to avoid clashes within the Muslim world as Abdallah Azzam did 20 years previously, it was during this period that Ayam al-Zawahiri advocated striking the 'distant enemy' (the United States) to better topple the 'close enemy' (the Arab governments). Due to the global nature of US hyper-power, and as long as the distant enemy manifested itself all over the world, jihad itself became global.

After 2003, the war in Iraq marked the start of a third phase, dominated by attacks and the cycle of clashes between Shi'a and Sunni. Designed to assemble the Sunni political and religious spectre, the anti-Shi'a attacks organised by Zarqawi had exactly the opposite effect, illustrating once again the incapability of Sunni radicalism to structure the Sunni community.

Islam on screen

New Arab broadcasting news in the 1990s created a never before seen transnational environment and played a considerable role in the legitimisation of both the *muqawim* and the *mujahid*. Evoking the Western cultural *razzia* via preaching and televised debates gave a strong incentive to those who decided to react by engaging in a regime of violence. Speaking of Islam as a mere victim of the West was tantamount to considering the latter as a uniform and hostile bloc, every dimension of which – political, cultural, military, technological, media – in relation to the others drives the battle in its own field, while ultimately serving a common goal. Set up in 1996, the Al-Jazeera satellite television channel was among the first to stage the 'Muslim predicament' in the Balkans and Central Asia after the fall of the Soviet Union.

Since 2003, Al-Jazeera has been tightly controlled by its new chief, Waddah Khanfar. Born in Jordan in 1968 and of Palestinian descent, Khanfar is ideologically close to Hamas' most hardline rulers. Under his strong editorial influence, Al-Jazeera is prone to portray a victimised *umma* always under attack, whose Palestine embodies the metonymical form. Insisting on military issues against foreign powers (Israel in Palestine/the United States in Iraq) gives back to Islamism the credentials it lost during the civil wars in Machrek (in the 1980s) or in Algeria (in the 1990s). Thanks to the broadcasting power of Al-Jazeera, Sayyid Qutb's admirer is in the position of making sense of events in the Middle East, by giving them an eschatological meaning between good and evil.

These Arab broadcasters – Al-Jazeera, Hezbollah's Al-Manar TV, Al-Majd or Iqra' for salafist channels – have given strong leeway to another figure, the muqawil (entrepreneur in Arabic), who can exist independently of the other three figures, or can merge with them according to the context.[8] The *muqawil* is an entrepreneur of anger whose self-proclaimed mission is to defend the symbols of Islam against systematic attacks from multiple enemies. The entrepreneurs of anger most often prefer to stay removed from political issues in their institutional dimension to better seize, through emphasis on symbolic questions (veil, niqab, caricatures of the prophet, Pope Benedict's discourse at Ratisbonne, etc.), the power to define Muslim identity and thus the ways of being and acting in the public sphere in both Western and Muslim countries. According to the muqawil, by passing a law in March 2004 that banned the Islamic headscarf in schools, the French legislative body was persecuting Islam.

Even when claiming to represent a non-violent, salafist Islam, the Islamist preacher shares similar values with the *mujahid* with regard to religious morals. He condemns with a comparable vehemence the impiety of Western societies – always being careful not to draw the same practical conclusions. This kind of indignation revives abstract references (defence of Islam, of the *umma*) identical to those which the *mujahid* claims to defend in recalling the obligation of solidarity which must unite all believers. The muqawil needs scandal, as such occurrences give him the opportunity to redefine Muslim identity according to his own beliefs, especially in Western societies. Those Muslims by birth who do not react along the same lines are deemed guilty of betraying their own faith. This entrepreneur of anger can nowadays rely on many technologies in order to take over as many issues as possible.

If the figure of the *muqawil* thus completes that of the *mujahid*, it also blends largely with that of the *muqawim*; everywhere the latter occupies positions of power (in Iran and at least partially in Gaza and Lebanon). As was illustrated in 1988 by the Salman Rushdie affair, the muqawil's conception of resistance supports a mission of control over the Muslim cultural space, inside as well as outside its borders. In August 2009 the decision of the president of the supreme judicial council (*majlis al-'adal al-'alâ*) to impose the wearing of the veil on female Palestinian advocates in the tribunals of Gaza shows once again the confusion between the two figures. The polemic surrounding the question of the obligatory veil in the schools of Gaza and the separation of girls and boys in secondary school was not resolved by the ambiguous communiqué from the Minister of Education, which stated that 'the girls of the Gaza Strip do not need a decision obliging them, under threat, to wear the *hijab* and the *jilbab,* for Palestinian society, in its entirety, is a pious society based on religion, and this piety is an integral part of its faith'. All the same, the decision of the Hamas government to exempt students from wearing an obligatory uniform opened the path to an Islamisation of ways of dressing of the girls and aimed in particular to deprive female students from the more well-off areas west of Gaza City of the benefit of an 'exaggerated liberty' (*al-Nahar* 2009).[9]

Conclusion

The *muqatil* appears to have been the vanquished figure in the Arab Machrek since the beginning of the twenty-first century. If the international system ceases to back up its aspiration to independence (as in Palestine) or to democracy (Syria, Lebanon or Iraq), the fighter will be left with a tragic alternative: to disappear or to convert to one of the two other forms of action. The stakes for democratic potentials of Islam are considerable. From the moment that an opposing Islamist negotiates rallying with other forces to combat an authoritative regime (the Syrian Muslim Brotherhood's choice in the Declaration of Damascus of 16 October 2005), this type of actor will prioritise the search for an internal consensus upon his original ambition to apply the religious law, and move away, *de jure*, from the criteria established by the founding father of Islamism. However, an international environment in retreat combined with a growing regionalisation between Israel and Iran block this type of evolution. Today, it is the figure of the *muqawim* that is progressively tending to prevail, although that of the *mujahid* has everything to gain both from maintaining a regional state of war and from the festering domestic situation.

Notes

1 Impregnated with an Iranian Shiism of rationalist inspiration, himself probably a Freemason, politically opportunist despite a fiercely anti-colonialist political line, Jamal al-Din al-Afghani hardly resembled those who, among the Muslim Brotherhood, claimed to represent his heritage 20 or 30 years after his death.
2 Invited to Sudan just after the signing of the Oslo accords, Yasser Arafat was accused by the youth of Hamas of having transgressed a religious taboo in negotiating the future of an 'Islamic *waqf* inalienable by nature, i.e. Mandatory Palestinian Territory. According to a former counsellor of the PLO president, Marwan Kanafani, who relates the scene in his memoirs, it was the first time that Yasser Arafat was brought face to face with the young militants of Hamas. Heckled and interrupted several times with cries of 'Allah Akbar' and 'there is no God but God', the historical head of the Palestinian National Movement was 'surprised by the unshakeable convictions and the aggressive and violent style manifested by the youth of Hamas', especially concerning their assessment of the PLO over the past years, accusing it 'of paralysis, of corruption and of weakness' (Kanafâni 2007: 304–6).
3 The final reflections of Abdallah Azzam on the negotiations driven by the United Nations (UN) after the pull-out of the Soviet troops in February 1989 illustrate, moreover, a refusal of the politic conceived as space of institutional negotiation. The internationalisation of the Afghan question meant, according to him, a will to take the fruits of their military victory away from the mujahideen. The communist impiety is thus taken over by the Western impiety. It is still by the yardstick of the body of

medieval texts that he evaluated the legitimacy of the political, diplomatic and military relations between Muslim and non-Muslim powers. According to Abdullah Azzam, the Afghan question had to serve to stimulate a new religious practice in Muslim societies, in which jihad would be transformed from a highly theoretical state (close to the Christian 'just war' in medieval theory) into an absolute religious duty.

4 Just after the signing of the Wye Plantation accords (October 1998), conceived to relaunch a peace process at a dead-end after the election of Netanyahu in Israel (1996), the Hezbollah press accused Yasser Arafat of having 'placed Palestinians at risk of civil war with unknown effects' in responding to 'the demands of the Zionist entity'. See journal *al-'ahad*, 30 October 1998.

5 For an analysis of the jihadist 'grand narrative', see Kepel 2008.

6 For a leading actor's narrative of this period, see the fourth volume of the memoirs of the former secretary-general of the Syrian Muslim Brotherhood, Adnan Saad al-Dîn (2009), in particular the political leadership of the Brotherhood's condemnation of the massacre of the youth of Alouite faith committed in June 1979 at Alep (pp. 66–82).

7 According to Luc Boltanski and Laurent Thévenot, the 'higher common principle' is the highest value among a 'general principle of justice' – election in the 'Civic Polity', efficiency in the 'Industrial Polity', grace in the 'Inspired Polity', etc. The process of attributing states of worth requires mechanisms of arbitration linking a given situation with a general principle of legitimacy. The 'worthy beings' are those who enjoy such proximity. See Boltanski and Thévenot 2006.

8 One can seen moral entrepreneurs transform into jihad fighters: ten years before becoming one of the principal jihad figures in Falouja in 2004, the electrician Omar Hadid sparked an 'Islamic campaign' against the music stores and blew up the only cinema in the city. In Morocco, the group that commissioned the terrorist attacks of 16 May 2003 had set up an Islamic squad for the punishment of 'vice' in the shanty town of Thomas in Casablanca, taking unmarried couples guilty of transgressive behaviour.

9 The polemic was activated by an article from the France-Presse news agency announcing Hamas' imposition of the *hijab* in the Gaza Strip. Hamas' Minister of Education detected in this accusation a game of combined interests 'which coincided with those of an occupation concerned with reinforcing the ignorance of our sons and with leading the minister to minor quarrels'. Cited in the Lebanese daily paper, *al-Nahar* (2009).

References

al-Dîn, A.S. (2009) *Al-ikhwân al-muslimîn fî sûrîyya, min 'âm 1977 wa hatta 'âm 1983* [The Muslim Brotherhood in Syria from 1977 to 1983], Jordan, Dâr 'Amâr.

al-Nahar (2009) 'Gaza, the oblique channels of the *hijab*', 3 September.

al-Sayyid, R. (2007) *Al-jamâ'a wa al-mujtama' wa al-dawla. Sulta al-idîulujiyya fî majâl al-siyasî al-'arabi al-islami* [Community, society and the state. The power of ideology in the realm of the Arab Islamic policy], Beirut, Dâr al-kitâb al-'arabi.

Boltanski, L. and Thévenot, L. (2006) *On Justification: Economies of Worth*, Princeton, NJ, Princeton University Press.

Buchta, W. (2000) *Who Rules Iran? The Structure of Power in the Islamic Republic*, Washington, DC, The Washington Institute for Near East Policy.

Goldziher, I. (2010) 'Jamal al-Din al-Afghani, al-Sayyid Muhammad b. Safdar', in P. Bearman, T. Bianquis, C.E. Bosworth, E. van Donzel and W.P. Heinrichs (eds), *Encyclopaedia of Islam*, 2nd edn, Brill, Brill Online.

Gunning, J. (2007) *Hamas in Politics: Democracy, Religion, Violence*, London, Hurst and Co.

Hegghammer, T. (2010) *Jihad in Saudi Arabia*, Cambridge, Cambridge University Press.

Jabar, F.A. (2003) *The Shi'ite Movement in Iraq*, London, Saqi.

Kanafâni, M. (2007) *Sanawât al-amal* [Years of hope], Cairo, Dâr al-Churûq.

Keddie, N. (1972) *Sayyid Jamal ad-Din al-Afghani: A Political Biography*, Berkeley, University of California Press.

Kepel, G. (2008) *Beyond Terror and Martyrdom: The Future of the Middle East*, Cambridge, MA, Harvard University Press.

Khalidi, R. (1997) *Palestinian Identity: The Construction of Modern National Consciousness*, New York, Columbia University Press.

Mustâfa, A. (2003) *Al-muqâwama fî lubnân: 1948–2000* [Resistance in Lebanon: 1948–2000], Beirut, Dâr al-Hâdî.

Seurat, M. (1985) 'Le quartier de Bâb Tebbâné à Tripoli (Liban): étude d'une asabiyya urbaine', in J.C. Depaule (ed.), *Mouvements communautaires et espaces urbains au Machrek*, Beirut, Cermoc.

Schmitt, C. (1992) *La notion de politique. Théorie du partisan*, Paris, Champs/Flammarion.

Thévenot, L. (2001) 'Pragmatic Regimes Governing the Engagement with the World', in K. Knorr-Cetina, T. Schatzki and E. von Savigny (eds), *The Practice Turn in Contemporary Theory,* London, Routledge.

22

Islam and 'the clash of civilizations'?

An historical perspective

Howard V. Brasted with Adeel Khan

When it was first speculatively advanced in a 1993 article in *Foreign Affairs*, Huntington's 'clash of civilizations' thesis was roundly and at times roughly criticized by Western scholars (*Foreign Affairs* 1993; *ASAA Review* 1994). Not only was his key argument, that future conflict would acquire a cultural dimension and be conducted between different civilizations, derided as advancing a totally fanciful model of international relations, but also his core prediction, that as historically colliding civilizations the West and a resurgent Islam were poised to launch this new kind of global war, was condemned as intrinsically flawed.

Underlying this generally unfavourable reception was the apprehension that a madcap thesis – a 'gimmick' on a parallel with the 'War of the Worlds', as Edward Said categorized it in a 1998 lecture (Said 2001, 1998) – might progressively acquire paradigmatic status through repeated exposure and begin in a 'self-fulfilling' way to inform the West's policies towards Islam and Muslims in general (*ASAA Review* 1994; Decker 2002; Bilgrami 2003). Certainly the Huntington thesis struck a 'market' chord almost at once (Esposito 2002: 126). Expanded into a best-selling and widely translated book in 1996 – *The Clash of Civilizations and the Remaking of World Order* – his 'bright idea', as Huntington had called it earlier in a rejoinder to his critics (Huntington 1993b: 134–38), served to spark a string of international conferences and to inspire a substantial production of articles and papers.

A decade into the twenty-first century this output has shown little sign of diminishing. Books and articles galore continue to rake over the ground that Huntington contentiously marked out, and carry titles and phrases that invoke the terminology he has made familiar: 'clashes' of 'civilizations', 'world orders', 'worldviews', 'universalisms', 'cultures', 'fundamentalisms', 'ideologies' and 'interests' unfolding along various 'fault lines' of conflict and points of 'collision' keep cropping up on a regular basis. If nothing else, the continued topicality of the Huntington thesis speaks against its total 'irrelevance' (Yadlin 2006: 153; Wright 2011). In numerous studies and commentaries on Muslim–West relations, the 'clash of civilizations' thesis has come to figure as the standard reference point. 'Samuel Huntington is debated everywhere' (Roy 2004: 104; BBC Two 2010).

While the 'clash of civilizations' may have a long way to go to become the standard explanation of Western–Islamic tensions, the terrorist attacks on the US on 11 September 2001 and their aftermath proceeded to afford it a significant degree of rehabilitation and reinforcement (Holloway 2009; Bottici 2007). The 'war on terror' that George W. Bush conjured up on 20 September 2001, nine days after the destruction of the World Trade Center and the deaths of thousands of civilians, had looked set to leave the 'clash of civilizations' well behind as a useful or appropriate representation of the major challenge to world peace at the beginning of the twenty-first century.

That this did not happen was because the 'war on terror' began to face mounting criticism itself for failing to explain the complexity of Islamic terrorism and put it into a context where its causes might be specifically identified and suitably addressed. Underscoring the US administration's approach was the neo-conservative position that seeking to explain Islamist terrorism was tantamount to excusing it (Frum and Perle 2003: 41–48). In the heat of the moment, perhaps, the Bush declaration that the terrorism the US faced emanated from an extremist 'fringe' of Islam that would be ruthlessly hunted down and eliminated may have rhetorically seemed an appropriate and sufficient response. The categorization of terrorists as 'opponents of freedom' and Islamists as 'the embittered few' was probably deemed to say all that was necessary (Hanson 2002: xiv; US Government 2002: 1).

However, the invasions of Afghanistan and Iraq that followed effectively tarnished the 'war on terror' and the military strategy it promoted, as these countries fell victim to an unremitting insurgency and a continuing heavy loss of life. With the Taliban unconquered and al-Qaeda remaining operational – notwithstanding the assassination of Osama bin Laden by US special forces on 2 May 2011 – the threat of terrorism has not been reduced in any measurable way and the world has not been noticeably rendered a 'safer' place (Chomsky 2007: 21–23). In the face of 'home-grown' terrorism of the kind that killed rush-hour railway commuters in Madrid (2004), London (2005) and Moscow (2010), or deadly attacks like those carried out by Pakistani-based militants on the Indian Parliament in New Delhi (2001) and landmark hotels and meeting places in Mumbai (2008), India's commercial capital, the limitations of the 'war on terror' as a framework of analysis were further exposed. It simply made no sense of, for instance, terrorism in Kashmir, or the communal antagonism that had seen Hindus and Muslims at loggerheads for centuries (Brasted 2005).

It was even more ill-fitting when applied to a range of headline-capturing developments that involved Islam in non-terrorist ways, such as, for example, the furore caused by the Danish cartoons satirizing Muhammad; the banning by France of the hijab in schools in 2004 and in public in 2010; the recent introduction of a planning law in Switzerland proscribing the building of minarets; the polarizing confrontation in the US over an application to build a mosque a few blocks away from 'ground zero'; the call by the Reverend Terry Jones to turn 9/11 into an 'international burn a Koran day'; and the announcement of a plan by the Dutch politician, Geert Wilders, to form an international alliance 'to defend freedom and stop Islam' (Fisk 2010; McGreal 2010). As early as July 2004 the 9/11 Commission felt compelled to suggest that the US should look beyond the language of war and battlefield encounters and engage on a broader front with what it called the 'critical struggle of ideas' (National Commission on Terrorist Attacks Upon the United States 2004: 375–76). If there was a war out there to fight, it was not a conventional war with a conventional enemy.

On the other hand, the 'clash of civilizations' began to persuade 'many people', if still not sceptical Western academics, that a very broad contestation with Islam was actually happening and was indeed well underway (Abrahamian 2003; Barton 2006; Bottici 2007; Ferguson 2006a; Holloway 2009; Seib 2004; Snyder 2003). Although 'never entirely' buying the Huntington thesis and still finding parts of it problematic, Niall Ferguson observed in February 2006 that it seemed to 'make sense of an impressively high proportion of the news' (Ferguson 2006a).

With metaphorical 'simplicity' the 'clash of civilizations' conceptually captures the Islam that the media have tended to represent through serial images of Muslims in conflict with the world at large as shadowy followers of an Abu Nidal or Osama bin Laden, grim-faced Ayatollahs preaching Islamic revolution, anonymous crowds of totally veiled women, aggrieved and angry Palestinians, merciless suicide bombers, and so on (Brasted 1997, 2001, 2009: 85).

It also taps into the West's historical misrepresentation of Islam as essentially an uncivilized and alien religion to which Edward Said had drawn attention in his seminal 1978 study of Western literature on the 'Orient'. In effect, the 'clash of civilizations' constitutes the ultimate stereotypical image of Islam as a monolithic faith at odds with the Western liberal-secular way of life and seemingly committed to its overthrow. As J.L. Esposito has suggested, the 'clash of civilizations' appears as an 'easy answer' to the 'question on everyone's lips', especially after 9/11: 'why do they hate us?' (Esposito 2002: 126–27).

In a way that the 'war on terror' has been unable to do, the 'clash of civilizations' brings into focus not only the historical background of military and religious rivalry between Islam and the West as supposedly age-old enemies going back 1,300 years (Ahmed 1991; Lewis 1993), but also the current context in which Western and Islamic identities have been reinforced in terms of lines in the sand, demarcating value systems. The 'clash of civilizations' provides an instant take on the signification of a range of Muslim customs – such as the veil, arranged marriages, honour killings and the treatment of women in general – as forming a cultural battle line with Western notions of liberty, individualism and human rights (Huntington 1993a: 40; Haddan et al. 2006: 23, 39). That just two years after 9/11 Osama bin Laden could be countenanced as less a deranged fanatic than a 'civilizational revolutionary' who aimed to bring about a new golden Islamic age by restoring the caliphate, and his followers as 'hating' the West for 'largely cultural reasons', might indicate that the Huntington mindset has gained some traction (Snyder 2003: 325–27). Just how much remains to be determined.

The position that the 'clash of civilizations' currently occupies in the vocabulary of international relations, and the influence it exerts on the popular imagination, clearly beg further investigation. What especially requires clarification in the whole debate about a 'clash of civilizations' is the Muslim perspective. To date, the discussion that the Huntington thesis has engendered has been conducted predominantly as a scholarly Western discourse that sees little possibility of Muslims coalescing against the West along broad-based cultural battle lines. This leaves a number of questions still wide open. Categorized as the West's prospective protagonists in a future war, how have Muslims apprehended the 'clash of civilizations' thesis? At the scholarly level is the Muslim response simply the Western critique repeated? What do Muslims in general tend to see as the causative factors fuelling the existing tensions between Islam and the West? If the 'clash of civilizations' is heavily discounted, why has it not been generally discarded as a thoroughly bad 'idea?'

In this chapter we propose to examine the 'clash of civilizations' principally from the angle of scholarship, but also with respect to the reality it purports to capture. What will emerge is that while Muslim scholars, like their Western counterparts, fault similar aspects of the Huntington thesis, they appear more willing to recognize that political Islam countenances a future in which contestation with the West will unfold at all levels of contact, from the political to the cultural.

Ultimately, as a metaphor, how close is the 'clash of civilizations' to becoming a predictive model, like the 'Cold War' before it, that can be used to explain every development and prescribe ways of dealing with them within the framework of explanation its title suggests? Perhaps if Islamophobia engulfs the West, as the fear of communism did during the Cold War, the 'clash of civilizations' may acquire this propensity as well (Ghosh 2010; Neighbour 2010;

Ramadan 2009: 290; Whittal and Charter 2010), but it is difficult to envisage the conditions and the circumstances under which all Muslims could be put on a war footing against all non-Muslims, and vice versa.

A conclusion we proffer is that if Muslims around the world have betrayed any signs of mobilizing en masse it is much more likely to be in nationalistic pursuit of political and economic reform than for the cause of pan-Islamic world order. This includes the latest popular protests that began in January/February 2011, sweeping like a chain reaction through Tunisia, Yemen, Egypt, Libya, Syria and indeed the whole Middle East, and looked set to overturn the autocratic regimes that have been entrenched in those countries for years. Should they lead to a new Middle East based on Islam, as the hardline Iranian Ayatollah Ahmad Khatami confidently predicted in the early days of the anti-Mubarak rallies in Cairo and Alexandria, the 'clash of civilizations' idea will doubtless gain new proponents and fresh momentum as it did after 9/11 (Globalpost 2011). What still hangs in the balance is whether a democratic revolution results or one dictatorial regime is simply replaced by another (Zakaria 2011).

Lewis, Fukuyama and the echo of the Cold War

To lay the ground for this exploration, our point of departure is to revisit the 'clash of civilizations' idea in terms of the context from which it emerged and the critique it began to encounter along the way. Initially, prefacing that critique was an underlying apprehension that the Huntington thesis had been conceived as a response to the dramatic ending of the Cold War, and the conceptual void that this had left, rather than to any clear and present danger posed by Islam.

Huntington had not been the first to foreshadow a 'clash of civilizations'. Bernard Lewis had beaten him to it in a 1990 paper, 'The Roots of Muslim Rage', in predicting that the historical interaction between Islam and the West was poised to take a civilizational form. Lewis's prediction had been based upon what he saw as the 'mood' and 'movement' in Islam of gathering fundamentalist sentiment. For him, the 'clash of civilizations' was the ultimate 'irrational' response of Muslims to the West's 'Judeo-Christian heritage', its 'secular present' and the 'worldwide expansion of both'. A growing number of Muslims were becoming enraged at both the West for superseding their cultural ascendancy and at themselves for allowing this to happen (Lewis 1990).

Three years later, Huntington proceeded to turn Lewis's blunt declaration into a full-fledged thesis about the impending 'pattern' of future, international conflict. This was not because Muslims had become noticeably angrier, more opposed to modernity or crazier than Lewis had mooted in suggesting that something was going badly wrong with Islam. Rather, it was essentially to cast doubt about the prospect of a peaceful future following the collapse of the Soviet Union and the demise of communism, the events that formed the immediate backdrop to his articulation of a 'clash of civilizations'. Taking his cue from Lewis, Huntington had seemed specifically inspired to respond to Francis Fukuyama and the argument he had mounted in his 1992 book, *The End of History and the Last Man*, that these events presaged the ultimate triumph of American world order (Huntington 1996: 31). Summing up the euphoria and expectation of the time, Fukuyama had confidently proclaimed that not only had the United States decisively won the Cold War, but also in 'liberal democracy' the capitalist, secular West had decisively won the battle to evolve the 'final' and 'universal' form of 'human government' as well. A single global system would see 'democracy and free markets' become the 'dominant organizing principles' of the twenty-first century. Communism had patently failed and Islam, as a political system, would only ever appeal to 'fundamentalist' Muslims (Fukuyama 1989, 1992, 1999, 2001).

It was against this optimistic reading of what Fukuyama called the 'extraordinary flow of events' between 1989 and 1991, starting with the fall of the Berlin Wall, that Huntington posed his almost diametrically opposite 'clash of civilizations' scenario. Beginning with the proposition that the ending of the Cold War did not presage the advent of eternal peace, Huntington put the case that international conflict would simply come to manifest in a different form with different protagonists. The 'idea' he broached was that where wars of the past had been conducted between countries for a variety of economic, ideological or other reasons, the wars of the future would be fought at the broadest level of culture. In short, the next great conflagration, or culture war, could ultimately be conducted between contending 'civilizations', principally between a secular West and a resurgent Islam. Defining 'civilizations' as the largest units of identity to which people adhere, he divided the world into eight groups of culturally integrated blocs: African, Confucian, Hindu, Islamic, Japanese, Latin American, Slavic-Orthodox and Western (Huntington 1993a: 25). International relations would be utterly transformed as 'conflicts' between groups in 'different' civilizations became 'more frequent, more sustained and more violent' than those between groups in the 'same' civilization (Huntington 1993a: 48).

Parting further company with Fukuyama, Huntington postulated that how the world was to be structured and operate in the future lay not in the hands of the United States alone, but would be contested, in the first instance at least, by Muslims acting together on a giant scale. For it was not just a 'fundamentalist' group with which the West would have to contend, but the whole of Islam along a number of 'bloody borders' in North Africa, Central Asia, the Balkans and South-East Asia. Rather than the installation of the new American century, a multi-polar world was on the way.

For Esposito the kind of 'Islamic threat' that Huntington was foremost in projecting (see also Juergensmeyer 1993) had nothing to do with 'reality'. It was basically a 'myth' designed to fill the 'threat vacuum' left by the defeat of the old Soviet enemy. Swapping the 'red menace' of communism for the 'green menace' of Islam, as Huntington was thought to have done, was considered tantamount to recycling the Cold War thesis in Islamic form (Esposito 1994, 1992: 3–6; Kepel 2004: 62–63; Said 1997, 1998). Initially, and still on occasions tarred with this particular brush, Huntington's model of international relations was subsequently assailed by a generation of largely Western-based scholars for weaknesses of a more intrinsic kind.

A lot of question marks

Indeed, most of the basic assumptions underpinning the 'clash of civilizations' have been subjected to continuous challenge and rebuttal. Overall, what has principally attracted criticism has been the reductionist basis of his entire thesis: the classification of both Islam and the West as monolithic civilizations, the conflation of a narrow Islamist perspective with the whole Islamic view of the world, and the transcending influence and impact of culture.

The biggest question mark is attached to Huntington's mega notion of civilizations as discrete, cohesive, incompatible entities, which Clifford Geertz has satirized as 'autonomous, continuous, self-organising thought world[s], border guarded and set apart' (Geertz 2003; Senghaas 2002). While this approach enabled Huntington to juxtapose the 'West' as a whole against 'Islam' as a whole, it is deemed to have missed or ignored the inherent pluralism that exists among approximately 1.3 billion Muslims, spread across every continent and separated by history, language and sociology. As Edward Said puts it, there is a 'world of difference' between 'Islam in Egypt' and 'Islam in Indonesia' (Said 1998: 9), just as there is a world of difference between Muslims who are Arab, Muslims who are Asian and Muslims who are living in the West.

Insofar as Huntington's Muslim world existed, it is deemed to exist only at 'a very high level of abstraction' (Mandaville 2007: 15–16). Little actual sign of an overarching Islam has been found forming in opposition to what Huntington has identified as the markers of Western civilization – 'individualism, liberalism, constitutionalism, human rights, equality, liberty, the rule of law, democracy, free markets, and the separation of church and state' (Huntington 1993a: 40). In a globalizing world, Islam is becoming too dispersed and too 'deterritorialized' for Muslims to acquire global form as a universal, united and coherent politicized community (Mandaville 2001; Roy 2004). 'National differences' and 'national interests' among Muslims have become far too 'entrenched' for this to happen (Piscatori 1986: 149). In short, the issue is not so much 'whither Islam?' or who legitimately speaks for it, as the number of Islams there actually are (Mandaville 2007: 3; Esposito 2010: 10–12).

Huntington's related assumption that Islam would sooner or later become totally radicalized is considered equally problematic. According to two of the world's foremost interpreters of Islamic radicalism, the French scholars Olivier Roy and Gilles Kepel, political Islam – a collective label for a diverse range of opinions – is no longer radically focused. Encompassing a spectrum of fundamentalists, Islamists, salafists and jihadists (Kramer 2003), it consists of different groups, chasing different goals, using different methods (Roy 1994, 2004; Kepel 2004). Political Islam includes, for example, organizations like the Muslim Brotherhood in Egypt, Nahdlatul Ulama in Indonesia and the Jama'at-e-Islami in Pakistan that seek to Islamize their governments by non-violent means; Hamas in Palestine and Hizbullah in Lebanon that have come to see themselves as parties of national rather than international liberation; the transnational Hizb ut-Tahrir that hopes to restore the old caliphate as the vehicle for a new pan-Islamic golden age (Fraser 2009); and al-Qaeda and Jemaah Islamiyah, terrorist networks that aspire to lead Muslims in jihad to topple pro-Western governments and take on the West as the pathway to an Islamic world order.

Even as Huntington's 'clash of civilizations' began attracting attention, Roy proceeded to announce the failure of the radical movement not only to obtain state power but also to capture Islam, a verdict he sticks by and even strengthens in the wake of 9/11 (Roy 1994, 2004: 74–75). After the initial, sometimes hasty post-mortems of this event he confirms that most of the groups that had started out advocating a political future based on a multinational Islam have run out of revolutionary steam, and have largely become reconciled to the idea of a world system based on existing nation-states. The shadowy militant followers of Osama bin Laden may still adhere firmly to the notion of global jihad, but their indiscriminate killing of civilians through suicide bombing has been fatally alienating Muslims on the street (McGeough 2011). As Roy sees it, political Islam is finished as a coherent political force. It had splintered over the ultimate political solution and it is fast losing ground to other sources of Muslim opinion as well (Roy 2004).

Kepel also believes that al-Qaeda has failed not only to win over the masses but also to hold onto its 'militant' support, though he is less confident that the 'jihadist' and 'Islamist' components of political Islam have been finished off for good. Their message that Islam is the solution still remains potent, and both have mastered the use of the internet to reach a potentially transnational audience (Kepel 2008: 258–59). Thus al-Qaeda's inability to forge a Muslim coalition of urban poor, middle-class and Islamist intelligentsia may have been offset by its ability to incite widespread violence via the media and the world wide web (Kepel 2004: 150–51). In the event that Islamophobia – a term of Islamist origin – gathers pace in the West, Kepel is persuaded that Muslims, wherever they live, could be driven into the embrace of militant radicals and that some kind of 'clash' might then ensue. 'The war for Muslim minds', which is underway especially in Europe, 'may turn on the outcome of this struggle' (Kepel 2004: 8, 246, 285, 287).

While not venturing the possibility of a civilizational clash, his reading of 'grand narratives', such as Huntington's, is that they invariably distort reality by squeezing events into cramped, rhetorical frameworks. Bush's 'war on terror' and bin Laden's 'global jihad' are prime examples (see also Hussain 2003: 89ff.), the former by telling the story of war predominantly in terms of America's quest to bring democratic change to the Middle East, the latter by recounting it as the American infidel being ejected from Muslim lands and local tyrants being expelled from political office. With Bush and bin Laden having lost the very wars they had declared, neither narrative is considered to be any longer tenable (Kepel 2008: 1–12, 259). What the 'clash of civilizations' is seen as clearly papering over in its apocalyptic reading of the future is both the multi-faceted composition of radical Islam and its very marginal base. Its equation that Islam equals fundamentalism equals extremism equals militancy effectively blurs such details.

A counter-narrative that commonly begins to be posed against the 'clash of civilizations' takes the form of suggesting that should clashes of a civilizational kind ever occur, they will more likely occur within civilizations than necessarily between them (Senghaas 2002). Niall Ferguson, for example, calculates that of the 30 or so major armed conflicts that have broken out since the end of the Cold War, very few can be made to fit Huntington's civilizational model. The 'overwhelming majority' of clashes have in fact been 'civil wars' fought predominantly by ethnic groups within the same cultural bloc. This is particularly the case in the Middle East and sub-Saharan Africa where 'Muslims had mostly killed Muslims'. Insofar as Muslims are gearing up for conflict they seem to him more intent on waging war against themselves than against unbelieving Westerners (Ferguson 2006a; Ghosh 2007). Whatever the truth of this, not only does a resolution of the long-standing antagonism between Sunni Islam and Shia Islam seem a long way off (Ghosh 2007), but also the emerging argument between militants and moderates has yet to be seriously played out (Bett 2007).

Perhaps the most critical question mark, however, has been placed against Huntington's assumption that religious culture is the causative driver politicizing Islam and propelling the Muslim world to take on the power of the West. In projecting Islam as a civilization 'whose people are convinced of the superiority of their culture and are obsessed with the inferiority of their power' (Huntington 1996: 217), Huntington had roped the questions of culture and power together – 'who is to rule' and 'who is to be ruled' – as the fundamental 'causes' of the 'renewed conflict' between Islam and the West (Huntington 1996: 212). Much of the current literature has proceeded to decouple these questions by showing that Muslim antipathy to the West is politically rather than culturally motivated. It points out that the dominant theme running through militant rhetoric, and resonating with Muslims around the world, concerns the imperialistic exercise and penetration of US power particularly in the Middle East. The wars America and its allies have launched in Afghanistan and Iraq, the presence of American troops in Saudi Arabia, Kuwait and Egypt, and the unconditional support the US affords Israel at the expense of a Palestinian settlement are referred to time and time again. Not only did these things feature in Osama bin Laden's formal declaration of jihad against the US on 23 February 1998, and in many subsequent statements by him, but they also continue to fan the flames of Muslim resentment in general (Zinn 2002; Ernst 2004; Hegghammer 2006; Saikal 2003).

To this politically charged present is also connected an historically alienating past, which is held to be deeply engrained in Muslim memory. That is the past covered by Europe's colonial intrusion into the Muslim world, the period 1800–1956 that saw the Middle East run over, subjugated and exploited by the European powers, principally by Britain and France. During this encounter of the worst kind, 'an unmitigated disaster for Muslims', as it has been described, Islam's historic ascendancy came to a brutal and abrupt end (Ahmed 1989a: 117, 1991: 30). Mughal rule was swept aside in India, the Ottoman Empire was dismantled, new states like Iraq, Jordan, Lebanon and Syria were created on secular lines in their place, the caliphate was abolished and Islam was widely relegated to the private sphere. As many Muslims tend to see it, the 'worst' part of this encounter was the establishment of Israel in 1948, which occurred during Britain's trusteeship of Mesopotamia under the League of Nations' mandate system. Whatever else it symbolizes, Israel's existence at the centre of Islam's holy land serves as both a constant reminder of the West's imperialistic engineering and an indicator of America's hegemonic intentions (Brasted 2006). In bin Laden and al-Zawahiri's thinking Israel has loomed palpably large (Kepel 2004; Ibrahim 2007; Laden 2005; Zawahiri 2006). Against this particular history it is understandable that when militants denounce US actions in the region as just the latest phase of Western imperialism, this touches a raw and receptive nerve in the wider Muslim community (Hicks 2010).

By shifting the spotlight to the 30 per cent of Muslims living as members of minority communities, particularly as migrants in the West, Olivier Roy goes furthest in dismissing Huntington's 'culturalist approach'. In this setting, he contends, because the 'clash of civilizations' treats Islam as a 'closed' set of beliefs and practices it misses the separation that is occurring between religion and culture. With Muslims uprooting to the West and permanently settling there, not only is Islam being 'deterritorialized', but it is also acquiring a Western form. In the process, 'second-generation' Muslims are negotiating new Islamic identities that serve more to 'recast' Islam as a 'mere' religion than rediscovering it as a pristine ethnic culture. That younger Muslims are being radicalized has little to do with conflicts in the Middle East or 'traditional religious education'; it has everything to do with adjusting to life in their new countries (Roy 2004: 48, 139–41, 218–19). Thus the 'clashes' that result will likely be of a generational kind over shifting values, not some utopian vision of a world civilization based on an authentic Islam. Islam is simply not the problem, as Huntington would have it (Roy 2004: ch. 5).

On the Western 'side', then, the scholarly verdict seems clear enough. Huntington's 'clash of civilizations' is found substantially wanting as a model that purports to capture the unfolding interaction between Islam and the West and uncover the impulses informing it. Its inbuilt assumptions concerning a single Islam, a single radicalizing Muslim voice and a single cultural identity have simply raised more questions than supplied answers.

From the other side of the looking glass

Is the scholarly perspective any different on the Muslim side? One of the rationales that Huntington originally advanced for his thesis is that the idea of a 'clash of civilizations' is not his alone or indeed even his. Citing M.J. Akbar that the West's 'next confrontation is definitely going to come from the Muslim world' – stretching from the Maghreb to Pakistan – he infers that Muslim scholars see Islam–West relations in exactly these terms as well (Huntington 1993a: 32). Could this be another of Huntington's prospective 'fault lines'?

At first glance it would seem not. Insofar as a Huntington-esque line can be drawn between Muslim and Western scholars – for both are really participants in the same discourse – it cannot be said that the former have been less critical of aspects of the 'clash of civilizations' thesis than the latter. Muslim and non-Muslim scholars scarcely diverge, for instance, in their assessments that 'rising radicalization' within Islam has political roots. There is little or no dispute that the outlook of political Islam has been critically shaped not only by the impact of European colonialism, but also by the exercise of post-war American power within the Muslim realm.

Whether this history is causatively sufficient on its own to pit Islam against the entire West, though, is a moot point. Amin Saikal, for instance, has noted that fundamentalists do not necessarily treat all Western countries as equally culpable or bad, and that they have shown an inclination to distinguish between them on the basis of how closely they support America's heavy-handed foreign policy. Nonetheless, what Iran symbolically did through revolution in 1979, what Israel has been doing to Palestinians and its Arab neighbours since 1948, and what the US and its allies are doing in Afghanistan and Iraq now, are seen as creating the conditions for anti-Americanism to flourish and the 'enmities' between Islam and the West to 'sharpen' (Saikal 2003: 1–5, 44, 69, 110; Tibi 2008: 37–40). In general, the critiques that Muslim and non-Muslim scholars alike tend to mount against the 'clash of civilizations' thesis cover a lot of the same ground, and reach a similar conclusion that Huntington goes far too far in predicting that World War III, in the form of polarized civilizations at war, is almost inevitable.

Despite this degree of sameness, however, a number of changes of emphasis can be detected in Muslim treatments. Significantly, there seems to be less adverse comment about the stress Huntington places on civilizational conflict or culture as *the* ingredient putting Islam and the West on a direct collision course in the twenty-first century. Engaging far less sceptically than most non-Muslim scholars with these aspects, Bassim Tibi is credited with providing one of the 'clearest outlines of the context for understanding political Islam' (Ehteshami 2005: 50). As he sees it the 'clash of civilizations' thesis may be riddled with 'deplorable shortcomings', but the fact that Huntington brings out into the open the hitherto underplayed issues of civilization and culture is a matter for applause, not condemnation (Tibi 2002: 16). There is an Islamic 'fundamentalist' revolt going on, he argues, and it is directed against not just Western political power, but critically also Western cultural values and the Westernizing world system of nation-states facilitated by globalization. In promoting Islam as an alternative organizing force in the world, political Islam is seeking to mobilize Muslims against the West on the basis of a different universalism – the universal Islamic community – that transcends nation-states and cultural differences. The fact that Islamic civilization essentially has no boundaries enables it to match Western civilization in terms of its global reach. All it lacks at the moment is a comparable globalizing capability (Tibi 2002: 7).

In Tibi's reading radical Muslims are convinced that the West has usurped Islam's 'core function' in the world to 'lead humanity' (Tibi 2002: 15, 89). One simply has to go back, he writes, to Sayyid Qutb (1906–66) and other fundamentalist thinkers, like Abu al-A'la Maududi (1903–79), founder of Jama'at-e-Islami, to 'know' that the political movement does not arise 'simply from a nostalgia for past glory' or 'to foment a political revolt against Western hegemony'. It also draws inspiration from Qutb's conception that the world is in dire need of rescuing from the idea of popular sovereignty, and Maududi's judgment that Islam and Western-style democracy are essentially irreconcilable (Tibi 2002: 28). As the 'intellectual father of Islamic fundamentalism' and still the most widely read of Muslim philosophers, Qutb bequeathed the rationale and mental outlook that if the world is to be saved from secular culture the sphere of Islam (Dar-al Islam) has to civilize the morally corrupted sphere of unbelief (Dar-al Harb) through an Islamic world revolution.

Tibi blames the fundamentalists for launching a 'war' along these lines against Western civilization, a war that needs to be taken very seriously. For not only do the fundamentalists intend to conduct it through a 'reinvented' jihad and a campaign of cultural hatred, but they have also chosen Europe as their battleground, where the West is at its most vulnerable. The 2005 Muslim riots in Paris are evidence of what might lie ahead. The fundamentalist aim is to recruit the 20 million or so Muslims living throughout Europe to the cause of Islamic revolution and prevent them from being integrated into Europe's secular, democratic culture. Radical imams are already actively preaching the message of separation. What is at stake is whether down the track Europe becomes Islamized or Islam becomes Europeanized (see also Kepel 2004: ch. 7). In Tibi's opinion political Islam represents not a spent force, but the greatest danger to world peace (Tibi 2008: 21, 24). While conceding that the message of civilizational war may belong at the moment to only a 'terrifying minority' of Islamic fundamentalists, he is persuaded that it has the potential to become the 'major collective choice' of the majority of Muslims (Tibi 2008: 78, 81). The whole world thus stands at the threshold of no less than a 'war of civilizations', a war not in a military sense but one between competing 'worldviews' (Tibi 2002: 16, 88–93, 2008; Ehteshami 2005).

If few go as far as this in linking the Huntington thesis to the wider discussion of political Islam, most Muslim scholars mention it in more than a passing way. Though they broadly agree that Islam and the West have developed worldviews that are in competition, some differences do emerge over the extent of their universalist character, the particular course each is charting, and where collisions are most likely to occur.

There is a persistent view, for instance, that instead of a worldwide battle between the West and Islam, the real battlefront is between extremists on both sides, namely American 'neo-conservatives' and Islamic 'neo-fundamentalists' (Bilgrami 2003; Ehteshami 2005; Mamdani 2005; Rauf 2010). Here the particular worldviews that normally come into the frame are the 2000 'Project for the New American Century' (PNAC), which is widely thought to have been at the heart of George W. Bush's agenda for American world order (Chomsky 2003b; Brasted 2006) and the various blueprints for *Pax Islamica*.

None of these prescriptions has as yet acquired anything like a popular mandate. The PNAC ideology of maintaining American supremacy and remoulding the world through the applica-tion of full military and 'constabulary' power (PNAC 2000: 2–18) remains the exclusive dream of the neo-conservative lobby in American politics. Visions of a utopian caliphate or nizam Islami belong respectively to Hizb ut-Tahrir and global jihad. Most Muslims, it is argued, do not subscribe to 'absolutist' notions of Islamic world order or would ever commit them-selves to violent struggle on a global scale to achieve it (Ayoob 2008: 1ff.; Bilgrami 2003: 88). Already the PNAC has fallen by the wayside, following considerable resistance and significant defections. Fukuyama famously jumped off its bandwagon in 2004 (Tibi 2008: 18; Brasted 2005: 28) when he began to see that the US was failing to carry the rest of the world with it in pursuit of a single universal system, by military means or otherwise (Fukuyama 2004: 60–64, 2006).

Another assumption that has come under challenge is that political Islam is inherently violent. A recurrent theme running through sections of the literature, as indeed most of Osama bin Laden's statements (Laden 2005), is that many Muslims believe that the US has waged war on them and that as a consequence they have been in a virtual state of war with it over many years (Hussain 2003: 30). Unquestionably, US military presence is everywhere. American troops are stationed throughout the Middle East, American aircraft carriers patrol the waters surrounding the entire region, and at various times Iran, Libya, Lebanon, Somalia and Sudan have experi-enced American intervention, Afghanistan and Iraq being simply the latest victims. Seen through Muslim eyes, the US appears not as a 'beacon of freedom', but rather as a brutal and belligerent power in the Middle East; 'Islam's main enemy', in fact (Ehteshami 2005: 44; Halliday 2002: 43).

This leads Akbar Ahmed to suggest that physically and psychologically Muslims feel them-selves to be under a state of 'siege' (Ahmed 2003). Having experienced what he calls the colonial 'nightmare' of the era of European imperialism, they now confront a 'blitzkrieg' on 'Muslim civilization' of Westernizing values through the global processes of international capitalism, consumer demand and communications technology (Ahmed 1989a: 117, 1989b: 7, 1991: 31; see also Ali 2006: 18; Ehteshami 2005; Hussain 2003). In a way that is reminis-cent of Ayatollah Khomeini's post-revolutionary response to the 'Westoxication' of Iran under the Pahlavi regime, it is possible to see Muslims rallying to the call of political Islam as a defensive move (Artaman 2010: 22; Roy 2004: 112, 154) to protect the Middle East from Western influences, rather than an aggressive intent to expunge the West's entire system of values from the universe. The retaliatory nature of what Chalmers Johnson calls terrorist 'blowback' against the unintended consequences of US foreign policy is certainly evident in Osama bin Laden's declarations of jihad against the United States and its allies (Johnson 2003; Scheuer 2007: 29). Much seems to be made of the point that when Dar-al Islam is considered to be under attack or in danger there is a long tradition in Islamic thought that Muslims should fight defensive wars to protect it.

There remains, however, considerable conjecture about whether the current challenge posed by rampant globalization to Islam will result in clashes on a broad scale between civilizations or more narrowly within them. Like Tibi, Tariq Ramadan, who is the grandson of Hassan al-Banna, one of the founders of the Muslim Brotherhood, draws attention to the European theatre of engagement as critical to the outcome of Islam. Ostensibly a reluctant subscriber of Huntington's thesis (Ramadan 2009: 290), he believes that the 'dialogue' between Western and Islamic civilizations will take place not at their 'geopolitical frontlines' but in the cities of America and Europe. In an interesting twist to the normal equation that has civilizational clashes occurring predominantly within the Islamic camp, the 'clash' he believes to be imminent is one within Europe between Muslims seeking citizenship on the basis of their Muslim identity and non-Muslim populations resisting their integration on these grounds. Paradoxically, this clash between civilizations will occur within the West itself (Ramadan 2003: 224–26; Fourest 2008: ch. 5; Kepel 2004: 277–80).

Through a very personal account of her decision to renounce Islam, Ayaan Hirsi Ali powerfully confirms the choices Muslims in Europe are confronting. Rather than being assimilated into European culture, many are choosing to alienate themselves from it, adopting an aggressive ghetto mentality that has been so far tolerated by a passive multicultural system (see also Kepel 2004: ch. 4; Kepel 2008: 245–46). With young Muslims being radicalized by members of the Muslim Brotherhood and other Islamist organizations, and Islamic 'ideals' clashing with Western 'ideals' in this environment, she believes that the very fabric of Western life is threatened (Ali 2010: xi–xxi, 247–48).

Bin Laden, al-Zawahiri and 'offensive' jihad

A question that suggests itself at this juncture is the extent to which, outside of scholarly circles, Huntington's concept of a 'clash of civilizations' is all that well known in the Muslim world. Certainly Roy and Tibi claim that it is and that it has wide appeal especially among Muslim fundamentalist and conservative groups who can find plenty to agree with, such as, for instance, Huntington's denial of the universality of Western values (Roy 2004: 9, 72, 153–54; Tibi 2002: 81; Huntington 1996: 310). Discovering what Muslims in general make of the Huntington thesis, or if they make anything of it at all, would clearly involve an investigation in its own right. Suffice it to say that time and space will allow for only one or two preliminary observations.

It must be doubted that any Muslim in the street or even any member of political Islam sees the world in quite the same way that Huntington has painted it. After all, the 'clash of civilizations' is a thesis that has emanated not from any mosque, madrassah or Muslim seat of learning, but from Harvard University. There are arguably resonances of some of the ideas Huntington articulates about the worsening relations between the West and Islam and their apocalyptic culmination in the utterances and writings of various Muslim radical groups;

however, there is little evidence that these have been fed into the construction of a comparable or rival hypothesis from a Muslim perspective.

The closest to providing such a 'parallel' (Ramadan 2009: 266; Kepel 2004: 94) comes from the treatises, interviews, video recordings and statements of Osama bin Laden and his al-Qaeda deputy Ayman al-Zawahiri, both of whom consistently projected themselves as the ideological and spiritual preceptors of an Islamic fight-back against the new crusading forces led by America. So frequently did bin Laden invoke the views and heroic example of Ibn Taymiyya (1263–1328) that it was as though his calling on Muslims to rise up and repel the Americans was in emulation of the 'Sheikh of Islam's' preaching of jihad against the Mongol invaders in the thirteenth century (Laden 2005: 5, 9, 11, 26, 61, 80, 118, 229, 249–50). Interviewed by Taysir Alluni of Al-Jazeera on 21 October 2001, bin Laden affirmed that the 'clash of civilizations' was a 'saying' he 'upholds', but what he seems to understand by 'clash' is one that is 'proven' – or illustrated – in the Qur'an and the traditions of the Prophet, and is thus 'a very clear matter'. It has nothing to do with the 'fairytale' being transmitted by the 'Jews and America' (Laden 2005: 124–25). As he later elaborated in 'Moderate Islam is a Prostration to the West', a letter rebuking 153 Saudi scholars who had publicly responded to a Western overture to suggest how the West and Islam 'can co-exist', Muhammad had clearly revealed that forcing the infidel to submit to Islam was the only correct way to deal with unbelief and deviation (Ibrahim 2007: 34–36, 41–42).

Informing bin Laden and Zawahiri's vision of future relations between the West and Islam are two kinds of jihad, one 'defensive' and limited, the other 'offensive' and total. In the first, Muslims are called upon to fight a defensive war against an oppressive West that has occupied their lands, exploited their resources and exposed them to the 'worst civilization' in the 'history of mankind' (Ibrahim 2007: 194–208, 202). As essentially a retaliatory war (Laden 2005: 128), its prime objective is to expel not only America and its allies, including Israel (Zawahiri 2006: 248), from the Middle East, but also their civilization of 'unbelief' based on false values and the apostasy of popular sovereignty. The message conveyed to a Western audience (Ibrahim 2007: 1–2, 5) is that if the battle-lines dividing the West and Islam are essentially 'doctrinal' (Laden 2005: 134), this war has its limits. Bin Laden offered to cease attacks on any European country if it agreed to stop interfering in Muslim affairs and abandon the American 'conspiracy' against Islam (Ibrahim 2007: 234–36), and even held out the possibility of a truce with the United States if it left Iraq and Afghanistan (Ibrahim 2007: 221–25). In this narrative honour and justice will be satisfied if the 'unbelievers' are kicked out of the Muslim world.

In a body of writings that bin Laden and Zawahiri address specifically to Muslims and which one translator has classified as being more theological than propagandist (Ibrahim 2007: 2–4), they project a very different struggle. This is 'offensive' jihad ultimately to destroy 'unbelief' altogether. In 'Moderate Islam is a Prostration to the West', 'Loyalty and Enmity', '*Sharia* and Democracy' and '*Jihad*, Martyrdom, and the Killing of Innocents' (Ibrahim 2007: 17–171; Zawahiri 2006: 111–12), bin Laden and Zawahiri not only denounce the possibility of co-existence between Islam and unbelief as scripturally impossible, but also dismiss the idea of dialogue between Western and Islamic 'civilizations' as an 'infidel notion' designed to postpone the inevitable 'clash' (Ibrahim 2007: 28, 30). Accusing so-called 'moderates' of importing such a notion 'verbatim' from the West, they go on to slam 'moderate' Islam itself for contradicting the very foundation of shari'a and ignoring the basic tenets of offensive jihad. With echoes of Huntington's thesis, bin Laden and Zawahiri insist that there is only one Islam and it is not 'moderate' (Ibrahim 2007: 19). The road ahead is uncompromising total war and it is obligatory as a 'religious duty' on all Muslims to pursue the infidel in his own lands, 'occupy them, and exchange their systems of government for an Islamic system'. What this means 'for every person alive' is 'either submit, or live under the suzerainty of Islam, or die'. Here, in a nutshell, is a recipe for a global civilizational fight to the finish (Ibrahim 2007: 19, 28, 32, 42, 51, 93–94).

How popular this worldview actually is, coming as it does from a source that many have placed at the very margins of Islam, is the critical thing. Michael Scheuer, the former head of the Central Intelligence Agency (CIA) bin Laden unit, is one who remains convinced that the West ignores al-Qaeda at its own peril and that support for bin Laden's brand of militant anti-Western Islamism is on the increase (Scheuer 2009: xi, xx, 250). As a martyr to jihadism it is possible that Osama bin Laden will be even more inspirational to radical Muslims than when he was alive.

Conclusion

Some 19 years on, Huntington's 'clash of civilizations' seems firmly established in the popular, political and scholarly vocabulary of international relations. While doubt remains that it should even be there, it has nonetheless acquired a universal currency. People, whether they live in the West or in the world of Islam, have heard of the term. Although they may not be conversant with the structure of its argument or comprehend it in exactly the same way, they have nonetheless formed opinions about the reality it conjures up.

As a concept, the 'clash of civilizations' has been remarkably resilient and has succeeded at a number of levels. It has easily won what Edward Said has disparaged as the 'clash of definitions'. Despite all the criticisms concerning nomenclature and the imprecision of its key terms – 'civilizations', 'clashes', 'culture' – it has continued to hold up against 'world orders', 'universalisms', 'fundamentalisms' and other alternatives (Said 1998, 2001). The 'clash of civilizations' has also succeeded in becoming a 'powerful political myth' (Bottici 2007; Bottici and Challand 2010: 248–49), although the influence it may be exerting on Western policy-making and Islamist strategic planning can only be guessed at (Said 1998). However, Barack Obama's 'new beginning with Islam' policy speech at Cairo University in June 2009 contains a direct reference to it (Collinson 2009), and the al-Qaeda headline that the West is out to destroy Islam confirms the kind of thinking the 'clash of civilizations' points up (Esposito and Mogahed 2008: xv, 204).

Above all, the 'clash of civilizations' has succeeded as a metaphor. Fukuyama's *The End of History* broke down, in part because its metaphorical title was misleadingly obscure, but also because its vision of a unipolar order of peace and democracy was confounded by history. Islamist terrorism and international conflict effectively put paid to it. By contrast, the 'clash of civilizations' is not only a catchy figure of speech, it is also a simple cognitive model of the conflictual relationship between Islam and the West that sticks in the mind and is easily remembered. As linguistic experts point out, however, the trouble with metaphors is that while they colour 'our ordinary conceptual system' and programme our thoughts and actions 'more or less automatically', they are not empirical or necessarily accurate conveyors of reality (Lakoff and Johnson 1980: 1–8). That is the problem with them (Brasted 2008; Steuter and Wills 2008: 1–15).

Niall Ferguson nonetheless acknowledges that 'as works of academic prophecy go', the 'clash of civilizations' has been 'a real winner' (Ferguson 2006a). Only time will tell how long this can continue to be said. Like any futurological model, its fate depends on getting a number of critical variables right: that political Islam becomes mainstream; that the United States does not modify its foreign policy in the Middle East; that the 'battle' for Europe is lost by the West (Kepel 2004: 241–87, 295); that the challenge of reaching a workable accommodation with Islam fails; and that borderless Islamist terrorism grows.

Whatever happens, much will depend on the West's response to Islam. Certainly the spread of Muslim communities in the West widens the scope for jihadist activity and brings the so-called 'faraway' enemy within immediate range (Lambert and Spalek 2008: 259; Kepel 2004: 289). If the West embraces the fundamentalist 'irrationality' that Lewis warned against in 1990 (Lewis 1990: 60), or rising Islamophobia forces Western Muslims to 'join hands with the militants', it is possible that the world may get to confront a 'clash between civilizations' (Ramadan 2009: 290) that is in reality more than an abstraction.

References

Abrahamian, E. (2003) 'The US Media, Huntington and September 11', *Third World Quarterly* vol. 24, no. 2: 529–44.

Ahmed, A. (1989a) *Discovering Islam. Making Sense of Muslim History and Society*, London, Routledge.

—— (1989b) 'A Third Encounter of the Close Kind', *History Today* vol. 39: 4–9.

—— (1991) 'The Roots of Misperception', *History Today* vol. 41: 29–37.

—— (2003) *Islam Under Siege: Living Dangerously in a Post-Honor World*, Oxford, Polity Press.

Ali, A.H. (2010) *Nomad: A Personal Journey Through the Clash of Civilizations*, London, Fourth Estate.

Ali, M.M. (2006) *The Clash of Civilizations or Civilizational Peaceful Co-existence: An Analysis of the Views of Huntington and Khurshid Ahmad*, Kuala Lumpur, The Other Press.

Ali, T. (2002) *The Clash of Fundamentalisms: Crusades, Jihads and Modernity*, London, Verso.

Artaman, M. (2010) 'Different Paradigms: The Nation State and Islam', in B. Navazeni (ed.), *Iran and the World: Some Contemporary Developments,* Newcastle upon Tyne, Cambridge Scholars Publishing, pp. 15–32.

ASAA Review (1994) 'Symposium on Huntington Thesis', *ASAA (Asian Studies Association of Australia) Review* vol. 18, no.1: 1–30.

Ayoob, M. (2008) *The Many Faces of Political Islam. Religion and Politics in the Muslim World*, Ann Arbor, University of Michigan Press.

Barton, G. (2006) 'Turkey's Gulen Hizmet and Indonesia's Neo-Modernist NGOs: Remarkable Examples of Progressive Islamic Thought and Civil Society Activism in the Muslim World', in F. Mansouri and S. Akbarzadeh (eds), *Political Islam and Human Society*, Newcastle, Cambridge Scholars Press, pp. 140–60.

BBC Two (2010) *Newsnight*, 18 December.

Bett, D. (2007) 'Struggle for the Soul of Pakistan', *National Geographic*, September: 32–59.

Bilgrami, A. (2003) 'The Clash within Civilizations', *Daedalus* vol. 132, no. 3: 88–93.

Booth, K. and Dunn, T. (2002) *Worlds in Collision: Fear and the Future of Global Order*, New York, Palgrave.

Bottici, C. (2007) *A Philosophy of Political Myth*, Cambridge, Cambridge University Press.

Bottici, C. and Challand, B. (2010) *The Myth of the Clash of Civilizations*, London, Routledge.

Brasted, H.V. (1997) 'The Politics of Stereotyping. Western Images of Islam', *Manushi* no. 98: 6–16.

—— (2001) 'Contested Representations in Historical Perspective: Images of Islam and the Australian Press 1950–2000', in A. Saeed and S. Akbarzadeh, *Muslim Communities in Australia*, Sydney, UNSW Press, pp. 206–27.

—— (2005) 'Islam and Identity in South Asia: At the Crossroads of Confusion and Confrontation', in N. Lahood and A.J. Johns (eds), *Islam in World Politics*, London, Routledge, pp. 106–26.

—— (2006) 'A New World Disorder in the Making? An Historical Assessment', in F. Mansouri and S. Akbarzadeh (eds), *Political Islam and Human Society*, Newcastle, Cambridge Scholars Press, pp. 15–31.

—— (2008) 'Reflections on the "War on Terror"', audio of paper given on 20 November at NCEIS conference, available at www.nceis.unimelb.edu.au/event/conference-08-howard-brasted-reflects-war-terror (accessed 10 April 2011).

—— (2009) A 'Postscript' to a reprinting of (2001) 'Contested Representations' above, in Ather Farouqui (ed.), *Muslim and Media Images. News versus Views*, New Delhi, Oxford University Press, pp. 85–90.

Buehler, M. (2009) 'Islam and Democracy in Indonesia', *Insight Turkey* vol. 11, no. 4: 51–63.

Chomsky, N. (2003a) *Power and Terror. Post 9/11 Talks and Interviews*, New York, Seven Stories Books.

—— (2003b) *Hegemony or Survival. America's Quest for Global Dominance*, Sydney, Allen and Unwin.

—— (2007) *Failed States. The Abuse of Power and the Assault on Democracy*, Crows Nest, Allen and Unwin.

Collinson, S. (2009) 'Obama Vows "New Beginning" with Islam', *Sydney Morning Herald*, 4 June.

Decker, B. (2002) 'Islam and Society in South-East Asia after 9/11', *Australian Journal of International Affairs* vol. 56, no. 3: 22–30.

Ehteshami, A. (2005) 'Islam as a Political Force in International Politics', in N. Lahood and A.J. Johns (eds), *Islam in World Politics*, London, Routledge, pp. 29–53.

Ernst, C.W. (2004) *Rethinking Islam in the Contemporary World*, North Carolina, University of North Carolina Press.

Esposito, J.L. (1992) *The Islamic Threat. Myth or Reality?* New York, Oxford University Press.

—— (1994) 'Political Islam. Beyond the Green Menace', *Current History* vol. 93: 19–24.

—— (2002) *Unholy War: Terror in the Name of Islam*, New York, Oxford University Press.

—— (2010) *The Future of Islam*, New York, Oxford University Press.

Esposito, J.L. and Mogahed, D. (2008) *Who Speaks for Islam? What a Billion Muslims Really Think*, Gallup Press.

Ferguson, N. (2005) *Colossus: The Rise and Fall of the American Empire*, London, Penguin.

—— (2006a) 'The Crash of Civilizations', *Los Angeles Times*, 27 February, available at uniset.ca/terr/news/lat_huntingtonclash.html (accessed 15 April 2011).

—— (2006b) 'The Nation That Fell to Earth', *Time*, 11 September: 23–27.

Fisk, R. (2010) 'Nine Years, Two Wars, Hundreds of Thousands Dead, and Nothing Learnt', *Independent*, 11 September.

Foreign Affairs (1993) 'Symposium on Huntington Thesis', vol. 72, no. 4.

Fourest, C. (2008) *Brother Tariq: The Doublespeak of Tariq Ramadan*, New York, Encounter Books.

Fraser, K. (2009) 'The Ontological Question in International Relations: Towards a Generic Description of the Unit, with Reference to the Case of the Islamic Caliphate', unpublished PhD thesis, Australia, University of New England.

Frum, D. and Perle, R. (2003) *An End to Evil. How to Win the War on Terror*, New York, Random.

Fukuyama, F. (1989) 'The End of History', *The National Interest*, reprinted in *Quadrant*, August: 15–25.

—— (1992) *The End of History and the Last Man*, New York, Free Press.

—— (1999) 'Second Thoughts. The Last Man in a Bottle', *The National Interest*, Summer: 16–33.

—— (2001) 'We Remain at the End of History', *Independent*, 11 October.

—— (2004) 'The Neoconservative Moment', *The National Interest*, Summer: 57–68.

—— (2006) *America at the Crossroads: Democracy, Power, and the Neoconservative Legacy*, New Haven, CT, Yale University Press.

Gardiner, D. (2009) 'Saudi Arabia Has Become a Laboratory of Jihad, Spreading Poison Throughout the Muslim World. Can Reform Save the Land of the Prophet of Extremism?', *New Statesman*, 18 May.

Geertz, C. (2003) 'Which Way to Mecca?', *New York Review of Books*, June, available at www.nybooks.com/articles (accessed 1 May 2011).

Ghosh, B. (2007) 'Sunnis vs Shiites. Why They Hate Each Other. What's really driving the civil war that's tearing the Middle East apart', *Time*, 5 March: 23–30.

—— (2010) 'Is America Islamophobic?', *Time*, 30 August: 14–20.

Globalpost (2011), 28 January, available at www.globalpost.com/dispatch/egypt/110128 (accessed 1 May 2011).

Haddan, Y.Y., Smith, J.A. and Moore, K.M. (2006) *Muslim Women in America*, Oxford, Oxford University Press.

Halliday, F. (2002) *Transnational Paranoia and International Relations – the case of West versus Islam*, Cambridge, London, Blackwell.

Hanson, V.D. (2002) *An Autumn of War: What America Learned from September 11 and the War on Terrorism*, New York, Anchor Books.

Hegghammer, T. (2006) 'Global Jihardism after the Iraq War', *The Middle East Journal* vol. 60, no. 1: 11–32.

Hicks, D. (2010) *Guantanamo. My Journey*, Sydney, William Heinemann.

Holloway, D. (2009) *9/11 and the War on Terror*, Edinburgh, Edinburgh University Press.

Huntington, S. (1993a) 'The Clash of Civilizations?', *Foreign Affairs* vol. 72, no. 3: 22–49.

—— (1993b) 'If not Civilizations, What?', *Foreign Affairs* vol. 75, no. 5: 186–94.

—— (1996) *The Clash of Civilizations and the Remaking of World Order*, New York, Simon & Schuster.

Hussain, I.S. (2003) *Islam: A Target of Western Imperialism*, Lahore, Book Biz.

Ibrahim, R. (2007) *The Al Qaeda Reader*, New York, Broadway Books.

Johnson, C. (2003) *Blowback. The Costs and Consequences of American Empire*, London, Timewarner.

Juergensmeyer, M. (1993) *The New Cold War? Religious Nationalism Confronts the Secular State*, Berkeley, University of California Press.

Kepel, G. (2002) *Jihad. The Trail of Political Islam*, Cambridge, MA, Harvard University Press.

—— (2004) *The War For Muslim Minds: Islam and the West*, Cambridge, MA, Harvard University Press.

—— (2008) *Beyond Terror and Martyrdom: The Future of the Middle East*, Cambridge, MA, Harvard University Press.

Kramer, M. (2003) 'Coming to Terms: Fundamentalists or Islamists?', *Middle East Quarterly* vol. 10, no. 2: 65–77.

Laden, O. bin (2005) *Messages to the World. The Statements of Osama Bin Laden*, B. Lawrence (ed.), J. Howarth (trans.), London, Verso.

Lakoff, G. and Johnson, M. (1980) *Metaphors We Live By*, Chicago, IL, Chicago University Press.

Lambert, R. and Spalek, B. (2008) 'Muslim Communities, Counter-Terrorism and Counter-Radicalisation: A Critically Reflective Approach to Engagement', *International Journal of Law, Crime and Justice* vol. 36, no. 4: 257–70.

Lewis, B. (1990) 'The Roots of Muslim Rage', *The Atlantic Monthly* vol. 266, no. 3: 47–58.

—— (1993) *Islam and the West*, New York, Oxford University Press.

McGeough, P. (2011) 'Al-Qaeda Lost on the Arab Street', *Sydney Morning Herald*, News Review, 5–6 February: 6–7.

McGreal, C. (2010) 'Muslims in America Increasingly Alienated as Hatred Grows in Bible Belt', *Guardian*, 10 September.

Mamdani, M. (2005) 'Whither Political Islam', *Foreign Affairs*, January/February.

Mandaville, P. (2001) *Transnational Muslim Politics: Reimagining the Umma*, London, Routledge.

—— (2007) *Global Political Islam: International Relations of the Muslim World*, London, Routledge.

National Commission on Terrorist Attacks Upon the United States (2004) *9/11 Commission Report*, 14 July, available at www.9-11commission.gov/report/911Report.pdf (accessed 1 May 2011).

Neighbour, S. (2010) article *Weekend Australian*, 11–13 September: 5.

Piscatori, J. (1986) *Islam in a World of Nation States*, Cambridge, Cambridge University Press.

PNAC (2000) *Rebuilding America's Defenses. Strategy, Forces and Resources for a New Century*, 2 September, Project for the New American Century, available at www.newamericancentury.org/Rebuilding AmericasDefenses (accessed 10 May 2011).

Ramadan, T. (2003) *Western Muslims and the Future of Islam*, London, Oxford University Press.

—— (2009) *Islam, the West and Challenges of Modernity*, Leicester, The Islamic Foundation.

Rauf, A. (2010) 'Clash between Moderates of All Faiths Against Extremists of All Faiths', Council of Foreign Relations, 13 September, New York, available at www.cfr.org/publication/22940/conversation_ with_feisal_abdul_rauf.html (accessed 10 May 2010).

Roy, O. (1994) *The Failure of Political Islam*, London, I.B. Taurus.

—— (2004) *Globalising Islam: The Search for a New Ummah*, London, Hurst.

Said, E. (1978) *Orientalism: Western Conceptions of the Orient*, London, Routledge & Kegan Paul.

—— (1997) *Covering Islam*, New York, Vintage.

—— (1998) 'The Myth of the "Clash of Civilizations"', Lecture at Massachusetts University, Media Education Foundation.

—— (2001) 'The Clash of Ignorance', *The Nation*, 22 October.

Saikal, A. (2003) *Islam and the West: Conflict and Cooperation*, New York, Palgrave.

Scheuer, M. (2007) *Through Our Enemies' Eye: Osama bin Laden, Radical Islam, and the Future of America*, Washington, DC, Potomac Books.

—— (2009) *Marching Toward Hell: America and Islam After Iraq*, New York, Free Press.

Seib, P. (2004) 'The News Media and the Clash of Civilizations', *Parameters* vol. 5, no. 1: 71–85.

Senghaas, D. (2002) *The Clash Within Civilizations. Coming to Terms with Cultural Conflicts*, London and New York, Routledge.

Snyder, R.S. (2003) 'Hating America: Bin Laden as a Civilizational Revolutionary', *The Review of Politics* vol. 65, no. 4: 325–39.

Stark, J. (2005) 'Beyond "Terrorism" and "State Hegemony": Assessing The Islamist Mainstream in Egypt and Malaysia', *Third World Quarterly* vol. 26, no. 2: 307–27.

Steuter, E. and Wills, D. (2008) *At War with Metaphor: Media, Propaganda, and Racism in the War on Terror*, Plymouth, Lexington Books.

Tibi, B. (2002) *The Challenge of Fundamentalism. Political Islam and the New World Disorder*, Berkeley and Los Angeles, University of California Press.

—— (2008) *Political Islam, World Politics and Europe: Democratic Peace and Euro-Islam versus Global Jihad*, New York, Routledge.

US Government (2002) *National Security Strategy of the United States of America*, available at www.whitehouse.gov/nsc/nss.pdf (accessed 1 May 2011).

Wallerstein, I. (2002) 'The Eagle Has Crash Landed', *Foreign Policy*, July–August: 60–68.

Whittal, G. and Charter, D. (2010) 'Rise of Islamophobia Swells the Muslim Sense of Vulnerability', *Weekend Australian*, 11/12 September: 21.

Wright, C. (2011) 'Fraught Trip from Arab Tent to Street', *Sydney Morning Herald*, 3 March.

Yadlin, R. (2006) 'Shall East and West Never Meet? The Civilizational Debate in Contemporary Arab–Muslim Discourse', in M. Litvak (ed.), *Middle Eastern Societies and the West: Accommodation or Clash of Civilizations?*, Tel Aviv, Dayan Center for Middle Eastern Studies.

Zakaria, F. (2011) 'Why There's No Turning Back in the Middle East', *Time*, 14 February.

Zawahiri, A. (2006) *His Own Words. A Translation of the Writings of Dr. Ayman al Zawahiri*, L. Mansfield (ed. and trans.), Lexington, MA, TLG Publications.

Zinn, H. (2002) *Terrorism and War*, New York, Seven Stories Press.

Select bibliography

Abbas, T. (2010) *Islamic Radicalism and Multicultural Politics: The British Experience*, London and New York, Routledge.

'Abd al-Raziq, A. (1998) 'Message, Not Government, Religion, Not State', in C. Kurzman (ed.), *Liberal Islam: A Sourcebook*, Oxford, Oxford University Press.

Abdelrahman, M. (2009) '"With the Islamists? – Sometimes. With the State? – Never!" Co-operation between the left and Islamists in Egypt', *British Journal of Middle Eastern Studies* vol. 36, no.1: 37–54.

Abed-Kotob, S. (1995) 'The Accommodationists Speak: Goals and Strategies of the Muslim Brotherhood of Egypt', *International Journal of Middle East Studies* vol. 27, no. 3: 321–39.

Abou El Fadl, K. (2003) *Islam and the Challenge of Democracy*, The Boston Review: A Political and Literary Forum.

—— (2004) *Islam and the Challenge of Democracy*, Princeton, NJ, Princeton University Press.

Abou Zahab, M. and Roy, O. (2002) *Islamist Networks: The Afghan–Pakistan Connection*, London, C. Hurst and Co.

Abrahamian, E. (2003) 'The US Media, Huntington and September 11', *Third World Quarterly* vol. 24, no. 2: 529–44.

Abu-Amr, Z. (1994) *Islamic Fundamentalism in the West Bank and Gaza: Muslim Brotherhood and Islamic Jihad*, Bloomington, Indiana University Press.

AbuKhalil, A. (1988) 'The Palestinian-Shiite war in Lebanon: An examination of its origins', *Third World Affairs* vol. 10, no. 1: 77–89.

—— (1991) 'Ideology and practice of Hizballah in Lebanon: Islamization of Leninist organizational principles', *Middle Eastern Studies* vol. 27, no. 3: 390–403.

Abu Rabi', I.M. (1996) *Intellectual Origins of Islamic Resurgence in the Modern Arab World*, New York, State University of New York Press.

Abuza, Z. (2007) *Political Islam and Violence in Indonesia*, London and New York, Routledge.

Agence France Presse (2006) 'Hizbullah's efficiency leaves Lebanese government behind'.

Ahmad, I. (2009) 'Genealogy of the Islamic State: Reflections on Maududi's Political Thought and Islamism', *Journal of the Royal Anthropological Institute* vol. 15, Issue Supplement: S145–S62.

Ahmad, L. (1992) *Women and Gender in Islam: Historical Roots of a Modern Debate*, London, Yale University Press.

Ahmed, A. (1991) 'The Roots of Misperception', *History Today* vol. 41: 201–6.

—— (2003) *Islam under Siege: Living Dangerously in a Post-honor World*, Cambridge, Polity Press.

Ajami, F. (1986) *The Vanished Imam: Musa al-Sadr and the Shi'a of Lebanon*, Ithaca, NY, Cornell University Press.

Akbarzadeh, S. (1996) 'Why did nationalism fail in Tajikistan?', *Europe-Asia Studies formerly Soviet Studies* vol. 48, no. 7: 1105–29.

—— (2005) *Uzbekistan and the United States: Authoritarianism, Islamism and Washington's Security Agenda*, London, Zed Books.

Al-Anani, K. (2010) *The Myth of Excluding Moderate Islamists in the Arab World*, Working Paper No. 4, Washington, DC, The Saban Center for Middle East Policy at the Brookings Institute.

Al-Awadi, H. (2004) *In Pursuit of Legitmacy. The Muslim Brothers and Mubarak 1982–2000*, London and New York, Tauris Academic Studies.

Alexander, C. (2000) *The Asian Gang: Ethnicity, Identity, Masculinity*, Oxford, Berg.

Ali, A.H. (2010) *Nomad: A Personal Journey Through the Clash of Civilizations*, London, Fourth Estate.

Ali, M.M. (2006) *The Clash of Civilizations or Civilizational Peaceful Co-existence: An Analysis of the Views of Huntington and Khurshid Ahmad*, Kuala Lumpur, The Other Press.

Ali, T. (2002) *The Clash of Fundamentalisms: Crusades, Jihads and Modernity*, London, Verso.

—— (2005) *Street-Fighting Years: An Autobiography of the Sixties*, London, Verso.

Aliba'i', B. Maréchal and C. Moe (eds) (n.d.) *Yearbook of Muslims in Europe*, Leiden, Brill.

Altunisik, M.B. (2005) 'The Turkish Model and Democratization in the Middle East', *Arab Studies Quarterly* vol. 27, nos 1 and 2: 45–61.

Amir Arjomand, S. (ed.) (1988) *Authority and Political Culture in Shi'ism*, Albany, State University of New York Press.

An-Nabhani, T. (1950) *Inqadh Filasinn*, Damascus, Ibn Zaydun Press.

—— (1997) *Economic System of Islam*, London, Khilafah Publications.

—— (1998) *The Islamic State*, London, Al-Khilafah Publications.

—— (2001) *The Structuring of a Party*, London, Khilfah Publications.

—— (2002) *The Concepts of Hizb ut-Tahrir*, London, Khilfah Publications.

An-Na'im, A.A. (1990) *Toward an Islamic Reformation: Civil Liberties, Human Rights, and International Law*, Syracuse, Syracuse University Press.

Ansari, J. (2004) 'Madrid Bombings and the Attempts to Demonise Islam', *Khilafah Magazine* vol. 17, no. 4: 8–11.

Aragon, L. (2001) 'Communal Violence in Poso, Central Sulawesi: Where People Eat Fish and Fish Eat People', *Indonesia* vol. 72: 45–79.

Aristotle (1941) *The Basic Works of Aristotle*, R. McKeon (ed.), New York, Random House.

Artaman M. (2010) 'Different Paradigms: The Nation State and Islam', in B. Navazeni (ed.), *Iran and the World: Some Contemporary Developments*, Newcastle upon Tyne, Cambridge Scholars Publishing.

Asad, T. (1993) 'The Limits of Religious Criticism in the Middle East: Notes on Islamic Public Argument', in *Genealogies of Religion*, Baltimore, MD, and London, Johns Hopkins University Press.

Aspinall, E. and Fealy, G. (2009) 'Introduction: Decentralisation, Democratisation, and the Rise of the Local', in E. Aspinall and G. Fealy (eds), *Local Power and Politics in Indonesia: Decentralizations*, Singapore, Institute of Southeast Asian Studies.

Audi, R. (1997) 'Liberal Democracy and the Place of Religion in Politics', in R. Audi and N. Wolterstorff (eds), *Religion in the Public Square: The Place of Religious Convictions in Political Debate*, Lanham, MD, Rowman and Littlefield.

Awdallah, S.T. (2006) *Beloved by Allah: Emergence of Light from Al-Aqsa Mosque Launch of Hizb ut-Tahrir March*, London, Khilafah Publications.

Ayoob, M. (2005) 'The Future of Political Islam: The Importance of External Variables', *International Affairs* vol. 81, no. 5: 951–61.

—— (2008) *The Many Faces of Political Islam. Religion and Politics in the Muslim World*, Ann Arbor, University of Michigan Press.

Ayubi, N. (1991) *Political Islam. Religion and Politics in the Arab World*, London and New York, Routledge.

Azmeh, A. (1993) *Islams and Modernities*, London, Verso.

Back, L. and Solomos, J. (1992) 'Black politics and social change in Birmingham, UK: An analysis of recent trends', *Ethnic and Racial Studies* vol. 15, no. 3: 327–51.

Bagguley, P. and Hussain, Y. (2008) *Riotous Citizens: Ethnic Conflict in Multicultural Britain*, Aldershot, Ashgate.

Bahgat, G. (2007) 'Terrorism in the Middle East', *The Journal of Social, Political, and Economic Studies* vol. 32, no. 2: 163–200.

Bahlul, R. (2000) 'People vs. God: The Logic of "Divine Sovereignty" in Islamic Democratic Discourse', *Muslim–Christian Relations* vol. 11, no. 3: 287–97.

—— (2007) 'Is Constitutionalism Compatible with Islam?', in P. Costa and D. Zolo (eds), *The Rule of Law: History, Theory and Criticism*, Holland, Springer.

Baran, Z. (2004) *Hizb ut-Tahrir: Islam's Political Insurgency*, Washington, DC, Nixon Center.

Barton, G. (1995) 'Neo-Modernism: A Vital Synthesis of Traditionalist and Modernist Islamic Thought in Indonesia', *Studia Islamika: Indonesian Journal for Islamic Studies* vol. 2, no. 3: 1–75.

—— (2006) 'Turkey's Gulen Hizmet and Indonesia's Neo-Modernist NGOs: Remarkable Examples of Progressive Islamic Thought and Civil Society Activism in the Muslim World', in F. Mansouri and S. Akbarzadeh (eds), *Political Islam and Human Society*, Newcastle, Cambridge Scholars Press, pp.140–60.

Baxter, K. and Akbarzadeh, S. (2008) *US Foreign Policy in the Middle East: The Roots of Anti-Americanism*, London, Routledge.

Bayat, A. (2007) *Making Islam Democratic: Social Movements and the Post-Islamist Turn*, Stanford, CA, Stanford University Press.

Benyon, J. and Solomos, J. (eds) (1987) *The Roots of Urban Unrest*, Oxford, Pergamon Press.

Bernard, B. (1999) *Century: One Hundred Years of Human Progress, Regression, Suffering and Hope 1899–1999*, London and New York, Phaidon.

Bett, D. (2007) 'Struggle for the Soul of Pakistan', *National Geographic*, September: 32–59.

Betz, D. (2008) 'The virtual dimension of contemporary insurgency and counterinsurgency', *Small Wars and Insurgencies* vol. 19, no. 4: 510–40.

Bhavnani, R., Mirza, H. and Meetoo, V. (2005) *Tackling the Roots of Racism: Lessons for Success*, Bristol, Policy Press.

Bilgrami, A. (2003) 'The Clash within Civilizations', *Daedalus* vol. 132, no. 3: 88–93.

Binder, L. (1988) *Islamic Liberalism: A Critique of Development Ideologies*, Chicago, IL, University of Chicago Press.

Body-Gendrot, S. (2007) 'France Upside Down over a Headscarf?', *Sociology of Religion* vol. 68, no. 3: 289–304.

Boltanski, T. (2006) *On Justification: Economies of Worth*, Princeton, NJ, Princeton University Press.

Booth, K. and Dunn, T. (2002) *Worlds in Collision: Fear and the Future of Global Order*, New York, Palgrave.

Bottici, C. (2007) *A Philosophy of Political Myth*, Cambridge, Cambridge University Press.

Bottici, C. and Challand, B. (2010) *The Myth of the Clash of Civilizations*, London, Routledge.

Brasted, H.V. (1997) 'The Politics of Stereotyping. Western Images of Islam', *Manushi* no. 98: 6–16.

—— (2001) 'Contested Representations in Historical Perspective: Images of Islam and the Australian Press 1950–2000', in A. Saeed and S. Akbarzadeh, *Muslim Communities in Australia*, Sydney, UNSW Press.

—— (2005) 'Islam and Identity in South Asia: at the crossroads of confusion and confrontation', in N. Lahood and A.J. Johns (eds), *Islam in World Politics*, London, Routledge.

—— (2006) 'A New World Disorder in the Making? An Historical Assessment', in F. Mansouri and S. Akbarzadeh (eds), *Political Islam and Human Society*, Newcastle, Cambridge Scholars Press.

Bronson, R. (2006) *Thicker than Oil: America's Uneasy Partnership with Saudi Arabia*, Oxford, Oxford University Press.

Brown, L.C. (2000) *Religion and State: The Muslim Approach to Politics*, New York, Columbia University Press.

Brown, M. (2000) 'Estimating the Size and Distribution of South Asian Religious Populations in Britain: Is There an Alternative to a Religion Question in the Census?', *International Journal of Population Geography* vol. 61, no. 2: 87–109.

Bubalo, A. and Fealy, G. (2005) *Joining the Caravan? The Middle East, Islamism, and Indonesia*, New South Wales, Lowy Institute.

Buchta, W. (2000) *Who Rules Iran? The Structure of Power in the Islamic Republic*, Washington, The Washington Institute for Near East Policy.

Buehler, M. (2009) 'Islam and Democracy in Indonesia', *Insight Turkey* vol. 11, no. 4: 51–63.

Bunt, G.R. (2003) *Islam in the Digital Age: E-Jihad, Online Fatwas and Cyber Islamic Environment*, London, and Sterling, VI, Pluto Press.

Burgat, F. (1999) *Face to Face with Political Islam*, London and New York, I.B. Tauris.

Burke, J. (2006) *Al-Qaeda: Casting a Shadow of Terror*, London, I.B. Tauris.

Bush, R. (2008) 'Regional Sharia Regulations in Indonesia: Anomaly or Symptom?' in G. Fealy and S. White (eds), *Expressing Islam: Religious Life and Politics in Indonesia*, Singapore, Institute for Southeast Asian Studies.

Carré, O. and Michaud, G. (1983) *Les Frères Musulmans. Egypt et Syrie (1928–82)*, Paris, Gallimard Julliard.

Chomsky, N. (2003a) *Power and Terror. Post 9/11 Talks and Interviews*, New York, Seven Stories Books.

—— (2003b) *Hegemony or Survival. America's Quest for Global Dominance*, Sydney, Allen and Unwin.

—— (2007) *Failed States. The Abuse of Power and the Assault on Democracy*, Sydney, Allen and Unwin.

Choudhury, G.W. (1969) *Constitutional Development in Pakistan*, Vancouver, University of British Columbia, Publications Center.

Choueiri, Y. (1997) *Islamic Fundamentalism*, London, Continuum.

Clark, B. (2006) *Twice a Stranger*, London, Granta.

Clarke, J.A. (2004) *Islam, Charity and Activism. Networks and Middle-Class Activism in Egypt, Jordan and Yemen*, Bloomington, Indiana University Press.

Cobban, H. (1985) *The Making of Modern Lebanon*, London, Hutchinson.

Cofman Wittes, T. (2008) *Freedom's Unsteady March: America's Role in Building Arab Democracy*, Washington, DC, Brookings Institution Press.

Cohen, A. (2003) *Hizb ut-Tahrir: An Emerging Threat to U.S. Interests in Central Asia*, Heritage Foundation Backgrounder, 1 May.

Collins, K. (2007) 'Ideas, Networks, and Islamist Movements', *World Politics* vol. 60, no. 1: 64–96.

Commins, D. (1991) 'Taqi Al-Din An-Nabhani and Islamic Liberation Party', *The Muslim World* vol. 31, no. 3: 194–211.

Cragin, K. (2009) 'Al Qaeda Confronts Hamas: Divisions in the Sunni Jihadist Movement and its Implications for U.S. Policy', *Studies in Conflict and Terrorism* vol. 32, no. 7: 576–90.

Crosston, M. (2008) 'Compromising coalitions and duplicitous diplomacy: US support for Tajikistan after 9/11 and its security implications', *Central Asian Survey* vol. 27, no. 2: 155–67.

Danaher, G., Schirato, T. and Webb, J. (2002) *Understanding Bourdieu*, London, Sage.

Davidson, J. (2003) 'The Politics of Violence on an Indonesian Periphery', *South East Asia Research* vol. 11, no. 1: 59–89.

Davis, M. (2002) 'Laskar Jihad and the Position of Conservative Islam in Indonesia', *Contemporary Southeast Asia* vol. 24, no. 1: 12–32.

Decker, B. (2002) 'Islam and Society in South-East Asia after 9/11', *Australian Journal of International Affairs* vol. 56, no. 3: 22–30.

Deeb, L. (2006) *An Enchanted Modern: Gender and Public Piety in Shi'a Lebanon*, Princeton, NJ, Princeton University Press.

Deeb, L. and Harb, M. (2008) 'Sanctioned Pleasures: Youth, Piety and Leisure in Lebanon', *Middle East Report* vol. 245: 12–19.

Denoeux, G. (2002) 'The Forgotten Swamp: Navigating Political Islam', *Middle East Policy* vol. 9, no. 2: 56–81.

Deringil, S. (1999) *The Well-Protected Domains: Ideology and the Legitimization of Power in the Ottoman Empire, 1876–1909*, London, I.B. Tauris.

Diamond, L., Plattner, M. and Brumberg, D. (eds) (2003) *Islam and Democracy in the Middle East*, Washington, DC, National Endowment for Democracy.

Dobbin, C. (1983) *Islamic Revivalism in a Changing Peasant Economy: Central Sumatra, 1784–1847*, London, Curzon.

Duncan, C. (2005) 'The Other Maluku: Chronologies of Conflict in North Maluku', *Indonesia* vol. 80: 54–80.

Ehteshami, A. (2005) 'Islam as a Political Force in International Politics', in N. Lahood and A.J. Johns (eds), *Islam in World Politics*, London, Routledge, pp. 29–53.

El-Gobashy, M. (2005) 'The Metamorphosis of the Egyptian Muslim Brothers', *International Journal of Middle Eastern Studies* vol. 37, no. 3: 373–95.

el Khazen, F. (2000) *The Breakdown of the State in Lebanon: 1967–1976*, Cambridge, MA, Harvard University Press.

Engineer, A.A. (1996) *The Islamic State*, New Delhi, Vikas Publishing House.

Ernst, C.W. (2004) *Rethinking Islam in the Contemporary World*, North Carolina, University of North Carolina Press.

Esfandiari, H. (1997) *Reconstructed Lives: Women and Iran's Islamic Revolution*, Baltimore, MD, Johns Hopkins University Press.

Esposito, J.L. (ed.) (1990) *The Iranian Revolution and its Global Impact*, Miami, Florida International University Press.

—— (1992) *The Islamic Threat. Myth or Reality?*, New York, Oxford University Press.

—— (1994) 'Political Islam. Beyond the Green Menace', *Current History* vol. 93: 19–24.

—— (2002) *Unholy War: Terror in the Name of Islam*, New York, Oxford University Press.

—— (2003) *The Oxford Dictionary of Islam*, New York, Oxford University Press.

—— (2005) 'Globalization of Jihad', in C. Timmerman and B. Segaert (eds), *How to Conquer the Barriers to Cultural Dialogue: Christianity, Islam and Judaism*, Bruxelles, P.I.E. Peter Lang.

—— (2010) *The Future of Islam*, New York, Oxford University Press.

Esposito, J.L. and Mogahed, D. (2008) *Who Speaks for Islam? What a Billion Muslims Really Think*, Gallup Press.

Esposito, J.L. and Voll, J.O. (1996) *Islam and Democracy*, New York, Oxford University Press.

Fealy, G. (2005) 'Half a Century of Violence in Indonesia: A Historical and Ideological Comparison of Darul Islam and the Jema'ah Islamiyah', in M. Vicziany and D. Wright-Neville (eds), *Terrorism and Islam in Indonesia: Myths and Realities*, Melbourne, Monash University.

Feillard, A. and Madinier, R. (2006) *La Fin de l'innocence? L'islam indonésien face à la tentation radical de 1967 à nos jours*, Paris, IRASCE.

Fekete, L. (2008) *A Suitable Enemy: Racism, Migration and Islamophobia in Europe*, London, Pluto.

Feldman, N. (2003) *After Jihad: America and the Struggle for Islamic Democracy*, New York, Straus and Giroux.

Ferguson, N. (2005) *Colossus: The Rise and Fall of the American Empire*, London, Penguin.

Fisk, R. (1990) *Pity the Nation: The Abduction of Lebanon*, New York, Simon and Schuster.

Fourest, C. (2008) *Brother Tariq: The Doublespeak of Tariq Ramadan*, New York, Encounter Books.

Fradkin, H. (2005) 'Judaism and Political Life', in L. Diamond, M. Plattner and P.J. Costopoulos (eds), *World Religions and Democracy*, Baltimore, MD, and London, Johns Hopkins University Press.

Francois-Meyer, J. (2004) *Hizb ut-Tahrir-The Next Al-Qaida, Really?*, Geneva, PSIO.

Frum, D. and Perle, R. (2003) *An End to Evil. How to Win the War on Terror*, New York, Random House.

Fukuyama, F. (1992) *The End of History and the Last Man*, New York, Free Press.

—— (1999) 'Second Thoughts. The Last Man in a Bottle', *The National Interest*, Summer: 16–33.

—— (2004) 'The Neoconservative Moment', *The National Interest*, Summer: 57–68.

—— (2006) *America at the Crossroads: Democracy, Power, and the Neoconservative Legacy*, New Haven, CT, Yale University Press.

Gaess, R. (2002) 'Interviews from Gaza: What Hamas Wants', *Middle East Policy* vol. 9, no. 4: 112–21.

Gardiner, D. (2009) 'Saudi Arabia has become a laboratory of jihad, spreading poison throughout the Muslim world. Can reform save the land of the prophet of extremism?', *The New Statesman*, 18 May.

Gellner, E. (1992) *Postmodernism, Reason and Religion*, London and New York, Routledge.

—— (1993) 'Marxism and Islam: Failure and Success', in A. Tamimi (ed.), *Power-Sharing Islam?*, London, Liberty for Muslim World Publications.

Gerami, S. (1996) *Women and Fundamentalism: Islam and Christianity*, New York, Garland Publishing.

—— (2005) 'Islamist Masculinity and Muslim Masculinities', in M. Kimmel, J. Hearn and R.W. Connell (eds), *Handbook of Studies on Men and Masculinities*, Thousand Oaks, CA, Sage.

Gerami, S. and Lehnerer, M. (2001) 'Women's Agency and Household Diplomacy: Negotiating Fundamentalism', *Gender and Society* vol. 15, no. 4: 556–74.

—— (2008) 'Terrorism and National Security', in A. Lind and S. Brzuzy (eds), *Battleground: Women, Gender, and Sexuality*, California, Greenwood Press.

Gerges, F. (2005) *The Far Enemy: Why Jihad went Global*, Cambridge, Cambridge University Press.

Gershoni, I. and Jankwoski, J. (1995) *Redefining the Egyptian Nation, 1930–45*, Cambridge, Cambridge University Press.

Gibson-Graham, J.K. (1996) *The End of Capitalism (As We Knew It): A Feminist Critique of Political Economy*, Oxford, Blackwell.

Giddens, A. (1991) *Modernity and Self Identity: Self and Society in the Late Modern Age*, Stanford, CA, Stanford University Press.

Gillespie, P. (2007) 'Current Issues in Indonesian Islam: Analysing the 2005 Council of Indonesian Ulama Fatwa No. 7 Opposing Pluralism, Liberalism, and Secularism', *Journal of Islamic Studies* vol. 18, no. 2: 202–40.

Goldziher, I. (2010) 'Jamal al-Din al-Afghani, al-Sayyid Muhammad b. Safdar', in P. Bearman, T. Bianquis, C.E. Bosworth, E. van Donzel and W.P. Heinrichs (eds), *Encyclopaedia of Islam*, 2nd edn, Brill, Brill Online.

Gordon, J. (1992) *Nasser's Blessed Movement. Egypt's Free Officers and the July Revolution*, New York and Oxford, Oxford University Press.

Griffin, M. (2003) *Reaping the Whirlwind: Afghanistan, Al Qa'ida and the Holy War*, London, Polity Press.

Gunning, J. (2008) *Hamas in Politics: Democracy, Religion, Violence*, New York, Columbia University Press.

Habermas, J. (1996) *Between Facts and Norms*, Cambridge, MA, MIT Press.

—— (2006) 'Religion in the Public Sphere', *European Journal of Philosophy* vol. 14, no. 1: 1–25.

Haddan, Y.Y., Smith, J.A. and Moore, K.M. (2006) *Muslim Women in America*, Oxford, Oxford University Press.

Hafez, M.M. (2006) *Manufacturing Human Bombs: The Making of Palestinian Suicide Bombers*, Washington, DC, United States Institute of Peace.

Halawi, M. (1992) *A Lebanon Defied: Musa al-Sadr and the Shi'a Community*, Boulder, CO, Westview Press.

Halliday, F. (2002) *Transnational Paranoia and International Relations – The Case of West versus Islam*, Cambridge, London, Blackwell.

Hamzeh, N. (2000) 'Lebanon's Islamists and local politics: a new reality', *Third World Quarterly* vol. 21, no. 5: 739–59.

—— (2001) 'Clientalism, Lebanon: Roots and trends', *Middle Eastern Studies* vol. 37, no. 3: 167–78.

Hanson, V.D. (2002) *An Autumn of War: What America Learned from September 11 and the War on Terrorism*, New York, Anchor Books.

Harb, M. and Leenders, R. (2005) 'Know thy enemy: Hizbullah, "terrorism" and the politics of perception', *Third World Quarterly* vol. 26, no. 1: 173–97.

Harik, J. (2004) *Hezbollah: The Changing Face of Terrorism*, London, I.B. Tauris.

Harris, S. (2004) *The End of Faith: Religion, Terror and the Future of Reason*, London, The Free Press.

Hayes, L.D. (1984) *Politics in Pakistan: The Struggle for Legitimacy*, Boulder, CO, Westview Press.

Hefner, R.W. (2000) *Civil Islam: Muslims and Democratization in Indonesia*, Princeton, NJ, Princeton University Press.

—— (2003) 'Civic Pluralism Denied? The New Media and Jihadi violence in Indonesia', in D. Eickelman and J. Anderson (eds), *New Media in the Muslim World: The Emerging Public Sphere*, Bloomington, Indiana University Press.

—— (2005) 'Muslim Democrats and Islamist Violence', in R. Hefner (ed.), *Remaking Muslim Politics: Pluralism, Contestation, Democratization*, Princeton, NJ, and Oxford, Princeton University Press.

Hegghammer, T. (2006) 'Global Jihardism after the Iraq War', *The Middle East Journal* vol. 60, no. 1: 11–32.

—— (2010) *Jihad in Saudi Arabia*, Cambridge, Cambridge University Press.

Helie-Lucas, M.A. (2001) 'What Is Your Tribe?', in C.W. Howland (ed.), *Religious Fundamentalisms and the Human Rights of Women*, New York, Palgrave.

Heyworth-Dunne, J. (1950) *Religious and Political Trends in Modern Egypt*, Washington, DC, McGregor Werner.

Hicks, D. (2010) *Quantanimo. My Journey*, Sydney, William Heinemann.

Hizb ut-Tahrir (1999) *Dangerous Concepts to Attack Islam and Consolidate Western Culture*, London, Khilafah Publications.

—— (2009) *Safe World under the Shade of the Islamic Economic System*, London, Khilafah Publications.

—— (2000) *The Method to Re-Establish the Khilafah and Resume the Islamic Way of Life*, London, Khilafah Publications.

Hoffman, B. (2006) 'Al Qaeda, Trends in Terrorism, and Future Potentialities: An Assessment', *Studies in Conflict and Terrorism* vol. 26, no. 3: 429–42.

Holloway, D. (2009) *9/11 and the War on Terror*, Edinburgh, Edinburgh University Press.

Hooker, V. (2004) 'Developing Islamic Arguments for Change through "Liberal Islam"', in V. Hooker and A. Saikal (eds), *Islamic Perspectives on the New Millennium*, Singapore, Institute of Southeast Asian Studies.

Hourani, A. (1962) *Arabic Thought in the Liberal Age*, Cambridge, Cambridge University Press.

Hroub, K. (2000) *Hamas: Political Thought and Practice*, Washington, DC, Institute for Palestine Studies.

—— (2006) 'A New Hamas through its New Documents', *Journal of Palestine Studies* vol. 35, no. 4: 6–27.

Human Rights Watch (2002) *Breakdown: Four Years of Communal Violence in Central Sulawesi*, New York, Human Rights Watch.

Huntington, S. (1993a) 'The Clash of Civilizations?', *Foreign Affairs* vol. 72, no. 3: 22–49.

—— (1993b) 'If not Civilizations, What?', *Foreign Affairs* vol. 75, no. 5: 186–94.

—— (1996) *The Clash of Civilizations and the Remaking of World Order*, New York, Simon and Schuster.

Husain, E. (2008) *The Islamists*, London, Penguin.

Husaini, I.M. (1952) *The Moslem Brethren: The Greatest of the Modern Islamic Movements*, Beirut, Khayat's College Book Cooperative.

Hussain, A. and Miller, W. (2006) *Multicultural Nationalism: Islamophobia, Anglophobia, and Devolution*, Oxford, Oxford University Press.

Hussain, I.S. (2003) *Islam: A Target of Western Imperialism*, Lahore, Book Biz.

Ibrahim, R. (2007) *The Al Qaeda Reader*, New York, Broadway Books.

Ihsanoglu, E. (2001) *History of The Ottoman State, Society and Civilization*, Vol. 1, Istanbul, Research Centre for Islamic History, Art and Culture.

Ismail, S. (2006) *Rethinking Islamist Politics: Culture, the State and Islamism*, London, I.B. Tauris.

Jabar, F.A. (2003) *The Shi'ite Movement in Iraq*, London, Saqi.

Jahroni, J. (2004) 'Defending the Majesty of Islam: Indonesia's Front Pembela Islam (FPI) 1998–2003', *Studia Islamika* vol. 11, no. 2: 197–253.

Jansen, J.G. (1992) 'Hasan al-Banna's Earliest Pamphlet', *Die Welt des Islams* vol. 32, no. 2: 254–58.

Jenkins, G.H. (2001) *Context and Circumstance: The Turkish Military and Politics*, Oxford, Oxford University Press.

—— (2008) *Political Islam in Turkey: Running West, Heading East?*, New York, Palgrave Macmillan.

—— (2009) *Between Fact and Fantasy: Turkey's Ergenekon Investigation*, Washington, DC, CACI.

Johnson, C. (2003) *Blowback. The Costs and Consequences of American Empire*, London, Timewarner.

Jonson, L. (2006) *Tajikistan in the New Central Asia*, London and New York, I.B. Tauris.

Juergensmeyer, M. (1993) *The New Cold War? Religious Nationalism Confronts the Secular State*, Berkeley, University of California Press.

Kar, M. (2005) 'Women and Civil Society in Iran', in F. Nouraie-Simone (ed.), *On Shifting Ground, Muslim Women in the Global Era*, New York, The Feminist Press at the City University of New York, pp. 216–32.

Karagiannis, E. (2010) *Political Islam in Central Asia: The Challenge of Hizb ut-Tahrir*, London, Routledge.

Kartodirdjo, S. (1973) *Protest Movements in Rural Java: A Study of Agrarian Unrest in the Nineteenth and Early Twentieth Centuries*, Kuala Lumpur, Oxford University Press.

Keddie, N. (1972) *Sayyid Jamal ad-Din al-Afghani: A Political Biography*, Berkeley, University of California Press.

Kepel, G. (1985) *Muslim Extremism in Egypt: The Prophet and the Pharaoh*, London, al-Saqi.

—— (2002) *Jihad. The Trail of Political Islam*, Cambridge, MA, Harvard University Press.

—— (2004) *The War For Muslim Minds: Islam and the West*, Cambridge, MA, Harvard University Press.

——(2008) *Beyond Terror and Martyrdom: The Future of the Middle East*, Cambridge, MA, Harvard University Press.

Khalidi, R. (1997) *Palestinian Identity: The Construction of Modern National Consciousness*, New York, Columbia University Press.

Khan, M.M.A. (1999) 'Reason and personal reasoning', *American Journal of Islamic Social Sciences* vol. 16, no. 3: v–xi.

—— (2001a) 'The political philosophy of Islamic resurgence', *Cultural Dynamics* vol. 13, no. 2: 213–31.

—— (2002) *American Muslims: Bridging Faith and Freedom*, Maryland, Amana Publications.

—— (2003) 'Prospects for democracy in the Muslim world: the role of US policy', *Middle East Policy Journal* vol. 10, no. 3: 79–89.

Khan, Q. (1982) *The Political Thought of Ibn Taymiyyah*, Delhi, Adam Publishers.

Khatab, S. (2006a) *The Political Thought of Sayyid Qutb: The Theory of Jahiliyya*, Abingdon, Routledge.

—— (2006b) *The Power of Sovereignty. The Political and Ideological Philosophy of Sayyid Qutb*, Abingdon, Routledge.

Khuri, F. (1975) *From Village to Suburb: Order and Change in Greater Beirut*, Chicago, University of Illinois Press.

Kimmel, M. (2005) 'Globalization and its Mal(e) Contents: The Gender Moral and Political Economy of Terrorism', in M. Kimmel, J. Hearn and R.W. Connell (eds), *Handbook of Studies on Men and Masculinities*, Thousand Oaks, CA, Sage.

Kinnvall, C. (2004) 'Globalization and Religious Nationalism: Self, Identity, and the Search for Ontological Security', *Political Psychology* vol. 25, no. 5: 741–67.

Kirmanj, S. (2008) 'Islam, Politics and Government', *Totalitarian Movements and Political Religions* vol. 9, no. 1: 43–59.

Klatch, R. (1994) 'Women of the New Right in the United States: Family, Feminism, and Politics', in V. Moghadam (ed.), *Identity Politics and Women: Cultural Reassertions and Feminisms in International Perspective*, Boulder, CO, Westview Press.

Klein, M. (2007) 'Hamas in Power', *The Middle East Journal* vol. 61, no. 3: 442–59.

Knott, K. and Khokher, S. (1993) 'Religious and ethnic identity among young Muslim women in Bradford', *New Community* vol. 19, no. 4: 593–610.

Koolaee, E. (2005) 'The Prospects for Democracy: Women Reformists in the Iranian Parliament', in F. Nouraie-Simone (ed.), *On Shifting Ground, Muslim Women in the Global Era*, New York, The Feminist Press at the City University of New York.

Korteweg, A.C. (2008) 'The Sharia debate in Ontario: Gender, Islam, and representations of Muslim women's agency', *Gender and Society* vol. 22, no. 4: 434–54.

Kramer, M. (2003) 'Coming to terms: fundamentalists or Islamists?', *Middle East Quarterly* vol. 10, no. 2: 65–77.

Kundnani, A. (2001) 'From Oldham to Bradford: The Violence of the Violated', *Race and Class* vol. 43, no. 3: 41–60.

—— (2008) 'Islamism and the roots of liberal rage', *Race and Class* vol. 50, no. 2: 40–68.

—— (2009) *Spooked: How Not to Prevent Violent Extremism*, London, Institute of Race Relations.

Kurbursi, A. (1993) 'Reconstructing and/or Reconstituting the Post-War Lebanese Economy: The Role of Infrastructural Development', in S. Khalaf and P. Khoury (eds), *Recovering Beirut: Urban Design and Post-War Reconstruction*, New York and Leiden, Brill.

Kurlantzick, J. (2005) 'The Decline of American Soft Power', *Current History* vol. 104: 419–24.

Kurzman, C. (ed.) (1998) *Liberal Islam: A Sourcebook*, Oxford, Oxford University Press.

Laden, O. (2005) *Messages to the World. The Statements of Osama Bin Laden*, B. Lawrence (ed.), J. Howarth (trans.), London, Verso.

Lakoff, G. and Johnson, M. (1980) *Metaphors We Live By*, Chicago, IL, Chicago University Press.

Lambert, R. and Spalek, B. (2008) 'Muslim Communities, Counter-Terrorism and Counter-Radicalisation: A Critically Reflective Approach to Engagement', *International Journal of Law, Crime and Justice* vol. 36, no. 4: 257–70.

Lapidus, I. (1988) *A History of Islamic Societies*, New York, Cambridge University Press.

Laqueur, W. (2004) *Voices of Terror: Manifestos, Writings, and Manuals of Al Qaeda, Hamas, and Other Terrorists from Around the World and Throughout the Ages*, New York, Reed Press.

Lassman, P. and Speirs, R. (1994) *Weber: Political Writings*, Cambridge, Cambridge University Press.

Leiken, R.S. and Brooke, S. (2007) 'The Moderate Muslim Brotherhood', *Foreign Affairs* vol. 86, no. 2: 107–21.

Lentini, P. (2008) 'Antipodal Terrorists? Accounting for Differences in Australian and "Global" Neojihadists', in R. Devetak and C. Hughes (eds), *Globalization's Shadow: The Globalization of Violence*, London, Routledge.

Levitt, M. (2006) *Hamas: Politics, Charity, and Terrorism in the Service of Jihad*, New Haven, CT, Yale University Press.

—— (2007) 'Could Hamas Target the West?', *Studies in Conflict and Terrorism* vol. 30, no. 11: 925–45.

Lewis, B. (1993) *Islam and the West*, New York, Oxford University Press.

Lewis, P. (2007) *Young, British and Muslim*, London, Continuum.

Lia, B. (1998) *The Society of Muslim Brothers in Egypt: The Rise of an Islamic Mass Movement 1928–1942*, Reading, MA, Ithaca.

Luong, P.J. (2003) 'The Middle Easternization of Central Asia', *Current History* no. 102: 333–40.

Lybarger, L.D. (2007) *Identity and Religion in Palestine: The Struggle between Islamism and Secularism in the Occupied Territories*, Princeton, NJ, Princeton University Press.

Lynch, T. and Singh, R. (2008) *After Bush: The Case for Continuity in American Foreign Policy*, Cambridge, Cambridge University Press.

Macey, M. (2007) 'Islamic Political Radicalism in Britain: Pakistani Men in Bradford', in T. Abbas (ed.), *Islamic Political Radicalism: A European Perspective*, Edinburgh, Edinburgh University Press.

McGlinchey, E. (2005) 'Autocrats, Islamists, and the Rise of Radicalism in Central Asia', *Current History* no. 104: 336–42.

McLeod, J. (2005) 'Feminists Re-Reading Bourdieu: Old Debates and New Questions about Gender Habitus and Gender Change', *Theory and Research in Education* vol. 3, no. 1: 11–30.

MacQueen, B. (2008) 'The reluctant partnership between the Muslim Brotherhood and human rights NGOs in Egypt', in S. Akbarzadeh and B. MacQueen (eds), *Islam and Human Rights in Practice: Perspectives Across the Ummah*, London, Routledge.

—— (2009) 'Democracy Promotion and Arab Autocracies', *Global Change, Peace and Security* vol. 21, no. 2: 165–78.

Mahdi, A. (2003) 'Iranian Women: Between Islamization and Globalization', in A. Mohammadi (ed.), *Iran Encountering Globalization: Problems and Prospects*, London and New York, Routledge/Curzon.

Mahdi, M. (1987) 'Al Farabi', in L. Strauss and J. Cropsey (eds), *History of Political Philosophy*, Chicago, IL, University of Chicago Press.

——(2001) *Al Farabi and the Foundation of Islamic Political Philosophy*, Chicago, IL, University of Chicago Press.

Mahmood, S. (2001) 'Feminist Theory, Embodiment, and the Docile Agent: Some Reflections on the Egyptian Islamic Revival', *Cultural Anthropology* vol.16, no. 2: 202–36.

Mamdani, M. (2005) 'Whither Political Islam', *Foreign Affairs*, January/February.

Mandaville, P. (2001) *Transnational Muslim Politics: Reimagining the Umma*, London, Routledge.

—— (2007) *Global Political Islam: International Relations of the Muslim World*, London, Routledge.

Mango, A. (1999) *Ataturk*, London, John Murray.

Mardin, S. (1989) *Religion and Social Change in Modern Turkey*, Albany, State University of New York.

Marsot, A.A.L. (1977) *Egypt's Liberal Experiment: 1922–36*, Berkeley and London, University of California Press.

Martin, V. (2000) *Creating an Islamic State: Khoemeni and the Making of a New Iran*, London, I.B. Tauris.

Maududi, A.A.S. (1955) *Islamic Law and Constitution*, Lahore, Islamic Publishers.

Maududi, S.A. (1991) *Ethical View-Point of Islam*, Khurshid Ahmad (trans.), 7th edn, Lahore, Islamic Publications.

—— (1993) *The Process of Islamic Revolution*, Lahore, Islamic Publications.

Mayer, A.E. (2007) *Islam and Human Rights*, Tradition and Politics, Boulder, CO, Westview Press.

Mehta, P.B. (2005) 'Hinduism and Self-Rule', in L. Diamond, M. Plattner and P.J. Costopoulos (eds), *World Religions and Democracy*, Baltimore, MD, and London, Johns Hopkins University Press.

Melvin, N. (2000) *Uzbekistan: Transition to Authoritarianism on the Silk Road*, The Netherlands, Harwood Academic Publisher.

Milton-Edwards, B. (1996) *Islamic Politics in Palestine*, London, I.B. Tauris.

Mir-Hosseini, Z. (2000) *Islam and Gender, the Religious Debate in Contemporary Iran*, London and New York, I.B. Tauris.

Mishal, S. and Sela, A. (2000) *The Palestinian Hamas: Vision, Violence, and Coexistence*, New York, Columbia University Press.

Mitchell, R. (1993) *The Society of Muslim Brothers*, Oxford and New York, Oxford University Press.

Moaddel, M. and Talattof, K. (2000) *Contemporary Debates in Islam: An Anthology of Modernist and Fundamentalist Thought*, New York, St Martin's Press.

Moavani, A. (2005) *Lipstick Jihad: A Memoir of Growing up Iranian in America and American in Iran*, New York, Public Affairs.

Mobini-Kesheh, N. (1999) *The Hadrami Awakening: Community and Identity in the Netherlands Indies, 1900–1942*, Ithaca, NY, Southeast Asia Program Publications, Cornell University.

Modood, T. (1990) 'British Asian Muslims and the Rushdie Affair', *Political Quarterly* vol. 61, no. 2: 143–60.

Moghadam, V.M. (2002) 'Islamic Feminism and Its Discontents: Toward a Resolution of the Debate', *Signs* vol. 27, no. 4: 1138.

—— (2004) *Toward Gender Equality in the Arab/Middle East Region: Islam, Culture, and Feminist Activism*, Human Development Report Office, New York, United Nations Development Programme.

Moghissi, H. (1994) *Populism and Feminism in Iran: Women's Struggle in a Male Dominated Revolutionary Movement*, New York, St Martin Press.

—— (1999) *Feminism and Islamic Fundamentalism, the Limits of Postmodern Analysis*, London and New York, Zed Books.

Mohamed, O. and Mohamed, N. (2009) 'Reviving the Caliphate in the Nusantara', *Studies in Conflict and Terrorism* vol. 32, no. 7: 646–63.

Mohammadi, M.R. *et al.* (2005) 'Suicidal Attempt and Psychiatric Disorders in Iran', *Suicide and Life – Threatening Behaviour* vol. 35, no. 3: 309–14.

Monshipouri, M. (2004) 'The Road to Globalization Runs through Women's Struggle', *World Affairs* vol. 167, no. 1: 3–14.

Monten, J. (2005) 'The Roots of the Bush Doctrine: Power, Nationalism, and Democracy Promotion in U.S. Strategy', *International Security* vol. 29, no. 4: 112–56.

Morrell, R. and Swart, S. (2005) 'Men in Third World: Postcolonial Perspectives on Masculinity', in M. Kimmel, J. Hearn and R.W. Connell (eds), *Handbook of Studies on Men and Masculinities*, Thousand Oaks, CA, Sage.

Moussalli, A.S. (1999) *Moderate and Radical Islamic Fundamentalism: The Quest for Modernity, Legitimacy and the Islamic State*, Gainesville, University Press of Florida.

Mozaffari, M. (2007) 'What is Islamism? History and Definition of a Concept', *Totalitarian Movements and Political Religions* vol. 8, no. 1: 17–33.

Najmabadi, A. (1998) 'Feminism in an Islamic Republic: Years of Hardship, Years of Growth', in Y. Yazbeck Haddad and J.L. Esposito (eds), *Islam, Gender, and Social Change*, New York, Oxford University Press, pp. 59–84.

Naumkin, V.V. (2005) *Radical Islam in Central Asia: Between Pen and Rifle*, Lanham, MD, Rowman and Littlefield.

Niblock, T. (2006) *Saudi Arabia: Power, Legitimacy and Survival*, London, Routledge.

Nordholt, H.S. and van Klinken, G. (2007) 'Introduction', in H.S. Nordholt and G. van Klinken (eds), *Renegotiating Boundaries: Local Politics in Post-Suharto Indonesia*, Leiden, KITLV Press.

Norton, A. (1987) *Amal and the Shi'a: Struggle for the Soul of Lebanon*, Austin, University of Texas Press.

—— (1999) *Hizballah of Lebanon: Extremist Ideals vs. Mundane Politics*, New York, Council on Foreign Relations.

—— (2000) 'Hizballah and the Israeli withdrawal from southern Lebanon', *Journal of Palestine Studies* vol. 30: 22–35.

—— (2002) 'Lebanon's malaise', *Survival* vol. 42: 35–50.

—— (2007) *Hezbollah: A Short History*, Princeton, NJ, Princeton University Press.

Nur I, M. (2005) 'Ulamâ, State and Politics: Majelis Ulama Indonesia After Suharto', *Islamic Law and Society* vol. 12, no. 1: 45–72.

Nye, J. (1990) *Bound to Lead: The Changing Nature of American Power*, New York, Basic Books.

Okruhlik, G. (2005) 'Empowering civility through nationalism: reformists Islam and belonging in Saudi Arabia', in R.W. Hefner (ed.), *Remaking Muslim Politics: Pluralism, Contestation, Democratization*, Princeton, NJ, Princeton University Press.

Olcott, M.B. (1995) 'Islam and Fundamentalism in Independent Central Asia', in Y. Ro'i (ed.), *Muslim Eurasia: Conflicting Legacies*, London, Frank Cass.

Olimova, S. (2004) 'Opposition in Tajikistan: Pro et Contra', in Y. Ro'i (ed.), *Muslim Eurasia: Conflicting Legacies*, London, Frank Cass.

Olivetti, V. (2002) *Terror's Source: The Ideology of Wahhabi-Salafism and its Consequences*, Birmingham, Amadeus Books.

Ottaway, M. and Hamzawy, A. (2008) *Islamists in Politics: The Dynamics of Participation*, Carnegie Paper, Washington, DC, Carnegie Endowment for International Peace.

Palmer Harik, J. (2005) *Hezbollah: The Changing Face of Terrorism*, London, I.B. Tauris.

Pantucci, R. (2008) 'Al-Qaeda 2.0', *Survival* vol. 50, no. 6: 183–92.

Pape, R. (2005) *Dying to Win: The Strategic Logic of Suicide Terrorism*, London, Random House.

Peach, C. (2005) 'Britain's Muslim Population: An Overview', in T. Abbas (ed.), *Muslim Britain: Communities under Pressure*, London, Zed Books.

Phelps-Harris, C. (1964) *Nationalism and the Revolution in Egypt: The Role of the Muslim Brotherhood*, The Hague, Mouton.

Phillips, D. (2006) 'Parallel lives? Challenging discourses of British Muslim self-segregation', *Environment and Planning: Society and Space* vol. 24, no. 1: 25–40.

Phillips, R. (2008) 'Standing together: the Muslim Association of Britain and the anti-war movement', *Race and Class* vol. 50, no. 2: 101–13.

Philpott, D. (2005) 'The Catholic Wave', in L. Diamond, M. Plattner and P.J. Costopoulos (eds), *World Religions and Democracy*, Baltimore, MD, and London, Johns Hopkins University Press.

Picard, E. (1997) 'The Lebanese Shi'a and political violence in Lebanon', in D. Apter (ed.), *The Legitimization of Violence*, New York, New York University Press.

Piscatori, J. (1986) *Islam in a World of Nation States*, Cambridge, Cambridge University Press.

Pombeni, P. (2000) 'The Ideology of Christian Democracy', *Journal of Political Ideologies* vol. 5, no.3: 289–300.

Poole, E. and Richardson, J. (eds) (2006) *Muslims and the News Media*, London and New York, I.B. Tauris.

Povey, E.R. (2001) 'Feminist Contestations of Institutional Domains in Iran', *Feminist Review* issue 69: 42–72.

Rabbani, M. (2008) 'The Making of a Palestinian Islamist Leader: An Interview with Khalid Mishal: PART II', *Journal of Palestine Studies* vol. 37, no. 4: 59–73.

Rahman, F. (1966) *Islam*, Chicago, IL, University of Chicago Press.

—— (1980) *Major Themes of the Qur'an*, Chicago, IL, Bibliotheca Islamica.

——(1982) *Islam and Modernity: Transformation of an Intellectual Tradition*, Chicago, IL, University of Chicago Press.

Rai, M. (2007) *7/7: The London Bombings and the Iraq War*, London, Pluto Press.

Ramadan, T. (2003) *Western Muslims and the Future of Islam*, London, Oxford University Press.

—— (2009) *Islam, the West and Challenges of Modernity*, Leicester, The Islamic Foundation.

Ramage, D. (1995) *Politics in Indonesia: Democracy, Islam, and the Ideology of Tolerance*, London and New York, Routledge.

Rana, M.A. (2009) *A to Z of Jehadi Organizations in Pakistan*, Saba Ansari (trans.), Lahore, Mashal.

——(2010) 'Hizbut Tahrir in Pakistan: Discourse and Impact', *Conflict and Peace Studies* vol. 3, no. 3: 31–35.

Rawls, J. (1993) *Political Liberalism*, New York, Columbia University Press.

Reuter, C. (2002) *My Life is a Weapon*, Princeton, NJ, Princeton University Press.

Rex, J. (1988) *The Ghetto and the Underclass*, Aldershot, Avebury Press.

—— (2005) 'Afterword', in T. Abbas (ed.), *Muslim Britain: Communities Under Pressure*, London, Zed Books.

Robinson, G.E. (2004) 'Hamas as Social Movement', in Q. Wiktorowicz (ed.), *Islamic Activism: A Social Movement Theory Approach*, Bloomington, Indiana University Press.

Roy, O. (1994) *The Failure of Political Islam*, London, I.B. Taurus.

—— (1995) *The War in Tajikistan Three Years On*, Washington, DC, United States Institute for Peace.

—— (2004) *Globalised Islam: The Search for a New Umma*, London, C. Hurst and Co.

—— (2008) *The Politics of Chaos in the Middle East*, New York, Columbia University Press.

Rubin, B. (2008) 'Setting U.S. Policy Toward Hamas', in D. Pollock (ed.), *Prevent Breakdown, Prepare for Breakthrough: How President Obama can Promote Israeli-Palestinian Peace*, Washington, DC, The Washington Institute for Near East Policy.

Rutherford, B.K. (2008) *Egypt after Mubarak: Liberalism, Islam and Democracy in the Arab World*, Princeton, NJ, Princeton University Press.

Saad-Ghorayeb, A. (2002) *Hizb'ullah: Politics and Religion*, London, Pluto Press.

Sachedina, A. (2001) *The Islamic Roots of Democratic Pluralism*, New York, Oxford University Press.

Saeed, A. (2006) *Interpreting the Qur'an: Towards a Contemporary Approach*, London, Routledge.

—— (2006) *Islamic Thought: An Introduction*, Routledge, London.

Safi, O. (ed.) (2003) *Progressive Muslims: On Justice, Gender and Pluralism*, Oxford, Oneworld Publications.

Said, E. (1978) *Orientalism: Western Conceptions of the Orient*, London, Routledge and Kegan Paul.

—— (1997) *Covering Islam*, New York, Vintage.

Saikal, A. (2003) *Islam and the West: Conflict and Cooperation*, New York, Palgrave.

Salim, A. (2008) *Challenging the Secular State: The Islamization of Law in Modern Indonesia*, Honolulu, University of Hawaii Press.

Samad, Y. and Sen, K. (eds) (2007) *Islam in the European Union: Transnationalism, Youth and the War on Terror*, Karachi, Oxford University Press.

Sauer, B. (2009) 'Headscarf regimes in Europe: Diversity policies at the intersection of gender, culture and religion', *Comparative European Politics* vol. 7, no.1: 75–94.

Scheuer, M. (2007) *Through Our Enemies' Eye: Osama bin Laden, Radical Islam, and the Future of America*, Washington, DC, Potomac Books.

—— (2009) *Marching Toward Hell: America and Islam after Iraq*, New York, Free Press.

Schiller, A. and Garang, B. (2002) 'Religion and Inter-ethnic Violence in Indonesia', *Journal of Contemporary Asia* vol. 32, no. 2: 244–54.

Schmitt, C. (1992) *La notion de politique. Théorie du partisan*, Paris, Champs/Flammarion.

Seib, P. (2004) 'The News Media and the Clash of Civilizations', *Parameters* vol. 5, no. 1: 71–85.

Senghaas, D. (2002) *The Clash Within Civilizations. Coming to Terms with Cultural Conflicts*, London and New York, Routledge.

Seurat, M. (1985) 'Le quartier de Bâb Tebbâné à Tripoli (Liban): étude d'une "asabiyya urbaine"', in J.C. Depaule (ed.), *Mouvements communautaires et espaces urbains au Machrek*, Beirut, Cermoc.

Siddiq, K. (ed.) (1993) *Come Let Us Change This World: Selections from Sayyid Maudoodi's Writings*, Lahore, Islamic Publications.

Siegel, E. (2001) 'After nineteen years: Sabra and Shatila remembered', *Middle East Policy* vol. 8, no. 4: 86–100.

Smith, C. (1991) *The Emergence of Liberation Theology: Radical Religion and Social Movement Theory*, Chicago, IL, University of Chicago Press.

Snyder, R.S. (2003) 'Hating America: Bin Laden as a Civilizational Revolutionary', *The Review of Politics* vol. 65, no. 4: 325–39.

Soroush, A.K. (2000) 'Tolerance and governance: a discourse on religion and democracy', in M. Sadri and S. Sadri (trans. and ed.), *Reason, Freedom and Democracy in Islam: Essential Writings of Abdul Karim Soroush*, New York, Oxford University Press.

Stacher, J. (2008) *Brothers in Arms? Engaging the Muslim Brotherhood in Egypt*, London, Institute for Public Policy Research.

Stark, J. (2005) 'Beyond "Terrorism" and "State Hegemony": Assessing the Islamist Mainstream in Egypt and Malaysia', *Third World Quarterly* vol. 26, no. 2: 307–27.

Stepan, A. (2005) 'Religion, Democracy, and the "Twin Tolerations"', in L. Diamond, M. Plattner and P.J. Costopoulos (eds), *World Religions and Democracy*, Baltimore, MD, and London, Johns Hopkins University Press.

Steuter, E. and Wills, D. (2008) *At War with Metaphor: Media, Propaganda, and Racism in the War on Terror*, Plymouth, Lexington Books.

Stowasser, B.F. (1993) 'Women's Issues in Modern Islamic Thought', in J. Tucker (ed.), *Arab Women: Old Boundaries, New Frontiers*, Bloomington and Indianapolis, Indiana University Press.

Taji-Farouki, S. (1996) *A Fundamental Quest: Hizb al-Tahrir and the Search for the Islamic Caliphate*, London, Grey Seal.

Taspinar, O. (2003) *An Uneven Fit? The 'Turkish Model' and the Arab World*, Brookings Analysis Paper, Washington, DC, Brookings Institution.

Taylor, C. (1999) 'A Catholic Modernity?', in J. Heft (ed.), *A Catholic Modernity?*, Cary, NC, Oxford University Press.

Tazmini, G. (2001) 'The Islamic Revival in Central Asia: A Potent Force or Misconception?' *Central Asian Survey* vol. 20, no. 1: 63–83.

Thévenot, L. (2001) 'Pragmatic Regimes Governing the Engagement with the World', in K. Knorr-Cetina, T. Schatzki and E. von Savigny (eds), *The Practice Turn in Contemporary Theory*, London, Routledge.

Tibi, B. (2002) *The Challenge of Fundamentalism. Political Islam and the New World Disorder*, Berkeley and Los Angeles, University of California Press.

—— (2008) *Political Islam, World Politics and Europe: Democratic Peace and Euro-Islam versus Global Jihad*, New York, Routledge.

Tocci, N. (2007) 'The Impact of Western Policies Towards Hamas and Hezbollah: What Went Wrong?', in M. Emerson and R. Youngs (eds), *Political Islam and European Foreign Policy: Perspectives from Muslim Democrats of the Mediterranean*, Brussels, Centre for European Policy Studies.

Tomagola, T.A. (2000) 'The Bleeding Halmahera of North Moluccas', in O. Törnquist (ed.), *Political Violence: Indonesia and India in Comparative Perspective*, Oslo, University of Oslo.

Tripp, C. (2002) *History of Iraq*, Cambridge, Cambridge University Press.

Van Bruinessen, M. (1992) *Agha, Shaikh and State*, London, Zed Books.

van Dijk, C. (1981) *Rebellion under the Banner of Islam: The Darul Islam in Indonesia*, The Hague, Martinus Nijhoff.

—— (2001) *A Country in Despair: Indonesia between 1997 and 2000*, Leiden, KITLV Press.

van Klinken, G. (2007) *Communal Violence and Democratization in Indonesia: Small Town Wars*, New York, Routledge.

Vidino, L. (2010) *The Muslim Brotherhood in the West*, Columbia, Columbia University Press.

Walker, E.W. (2003) 'Islam, Islamism and Political Order in Central Asia', *Journal of International Affairs* vol. 56, no. 2: 21–41.

Wallerstein, I. (2002) 'The Eagle Has Crash Landed', *Foreign Policy*, July–August: 60–68.

Werbner, P. (2007) 'Veiled interventions in pure space: Honour, shame and embodied struggles among Muslims in Britain and France', *Theory, Culture, and Society* vol. 24, no. 2: 161–86.

Whine, M. (2006) *Is Hizb ur-Tahrir Changing Strategy or Tactics*, Washington, DC, Center for Eurasian Policy.

Wickham, C.R. (2004) *Mobilizing Isla: Religion, Activism and Political Change*, New York, Columbia University Press.

Wolterstorff, N. (1997) 'The Role of Religion in Decision and Discussion of Political Issues', in R. Audi and N. Wolterstorff (eds), *Religion in the Public Square: The Place of Religious Convictions in Political Debate*, Lanham, MD, Rowman and Littlefield.

Woodbury, R.D. and Shah, T.S. (2005) 'The Pioneering Protestants', in L. Diamond, M. Plattner and P.J. Costopoulos (eds), *World Religions and Democracy*, Baltimore, MD, and London, Johns Hopkins University Press.

Wright, R. (1996) 'Two Visions of Reformation', *Journal of Democracy* vol. 7, no. 2: 68.

Yalcın, S. (1994) *Hangi Erbakan*, Ankara, Basak.

Yaqoob, S. (2007) 'British Islamic political radicalism', in T. Abbas (ed.), *Islamic Political Radicalism: A European Perspective*, Edinburgh, Edinburgh University Press.

Yasmeen, S. (2003) 'Pakistan and the Struggle for "Real" Islam', in S. Akbarzadeh and A. Saeed (eds), *Islam and Political Legitimacy*, London, Routledge Curzon.

Yavuz, H.M. (2006) *The Emergence of a New Turkey*, Salt Lake City, University of Utah.

Zalloum, A.Q. (1995) *Democracy is a System of Kufr*, London, Khilafah Publications.

Zawahiri, A. (2006) *His Own Words. A Translation of the Writings of Dr. Ayman al Zawahiri*, L. Mansfield (ed. and trans.), Lexington, MA, TLG Publications.

Zedalis, D.D. (2004) *Female Suicide Bombers*, Honolulu, Hawaii, University Press of the Pacific.

Zinn, H. (2002) *Terrorism and War*, New York, Seven Stories Press.

Zollner, B. (2007) 'Prison Talk: The Muslim Brotherhood's Internal Struggle During Gamal Abdel Nasser's Persecution', *International Journal of Middle East Studies* vol. 39, no. 3: 411–33.

—— (2009) *The Muslim Brotherhood: Hasan al-Hudaybi and Ideology*, Abingdon, Routledge.

Zubaida, S. (1993) *Islam, the People, and the State*, London, I.B. Tauris.

Index

Abbas, Mahmoud 62, 69, 70, 71
Abd al-Nasser, Gamal 9, 10, 52, 53, 58, 59, 255
Abd al-Raziq, Ali 35, 40, 42
Abdelrahman, M. 57
Abduh, Muhammad 35, 57, 93
Abdulhamit II, Sultan 130
Abdullah, Daud 231
Abdullah, King (Saudi Arabia) 180, 186, 188
abode of Islam/abode of disbelief 4
Abode of Islam movement (*Darul Islam*) 106–7, 115, 116
abode of war 22
absolutism 16, 282
Abu Khail, Dr Fozyah 186
Abu Nasr, Muhammad Hamid 53
Abu Rashta, Sheikh Abdul Khalil Ata 91, 99–100
Abu Zahra, Sheikh Muhammad 238
açabiyya 265
accident/essence distinction 44, 48n7
accommodationist attitudes 6, 55
Aceh 107, 115
acquiescence: agentic 193, 194, 195, 196, 197–98, 202
active realism 22–23
activism: divine origin of Islam and necessity of 14; as equal to true belief 12; HT identification of countries suitable for 101; Iranian women 200; Islamization of Pakistan 177–78; MB emphasis on 54; Shi'a 76, 83
activists 28; associated with violent organizations 98; women, Iran 144, 149
adhan 241
Adnan 'Uqla's jihad fighters 266
Adwan, Dr Atef 237
Afghani women 201
Afghanistan: 1979 war and bringing together of Islamists 25; jihad in 264; *mujahidin* training 115; relocation of IMU fighters to 125–26; Soviet invasion 254; US involvement in 108, 125, 259, 274

agency 32, 168, 201; Pakistani émigré community 195, *see also* societal agency; state agency; women's agency
aggrandisement 268
agro-based capitalism 75
Ahle hadith 176
Ahle Sunnat 177
Ahmad, Al-e 163
Ahmadinejad, Mahmoud 150, 151
Ahmadiyah community 111
Ahmed, Akbar 282
Ajami, F. 241
Akaev, President 121
Akbar, M.J. 280
Akbarzadeh, S. 247
'Akif, Mahdi 54, 56
Al Farabi 31–32
Al Saud, Prince Muhammad 180
Al-'Adala al Ijtima'yya fi al-Islam 10
Al-Akhtar Hussein, Sheikh 90
Al-'Alam al-'Arabi 10
Al-'Aqqad, Abbas Mahmud 10
Al-Aqsa *intifada* 68, 69, 257, 258
Al-Aqsa mosque 237, 242, 243
Al-Arouri, Salah 65
Al-Awaji, Muhsin 180, 183, 188
Al-Azhar, Shuyukh 57
Al-Azhar University 63, 241
Al-Baghdadi, Abdul Rahman 91
Al-Banna, Hasan 10, 51, 52, 54, 56, 57–58, 59, 90, 239, 244
Al-Barrak, Sheikh Saad 187
Al-Chami, Abu Anas 264
Al-Dahiya 76
Al-Dakhil, Khalid 187
Al-Da'wa 262
Al-Din al-Afghani, Jamal 35, 93, 252, 262
Al-Faruq camp 268
Al-Fayez, Dr Norah 186
Al-Fikr al-Jadid 10
Al-Gaithi, Shetiwi 183, 188
Al-Ghamdi, Sheikh Ahmad 186, 187

Index

intolerance 226, *see also* political intolerance; religious intolerance
Iran 142–52; elimination of political opposition 4; feasibility of Islamic democracy 156–65; Green Movement 150–51, 152; Hamas allied with 64; hegemony of Islamism 197; HT denunciation of 96; intellectualism 163; Islamic Revolution (1979) 77, 161, 196, 197, 254, 262; Islamists in 2; Jerusalem Day 243; legal age of marriage 148; media 148; power structure 143–44; reform era (1997–2005) 147–49; shari'a law 144–47; sovereignty issue 7; women and youth culture 149–50; women's agency 196–202
Iranian Constitution (Articles 20 and 21) 144
Iranian Revolutionary Guardians (*Pasdaran*) 263, 267
Iraq 90; HT in 92, 96, 98; Sunni fighters 266; US invasion of 108, 258–59, 274
IRP *see* Islamic Renaissance Party
irrational fundamentalism 276, 286
Islam 156–58; clash of civilizations 273–86; doctrinal essence 42; esteem for life 20; free adherence to 164; indigenisation, in the West 4; instrumentalization, Pakistan 168, 171, 177; integration with politics 158–61; intellectualism and 162–64; military defeat due to deviation from 241; political philosophy 27–34; and politics 155–56, 158–61; privatization of 43; Qutb's ideological discourse 11–15; on screen 269–70; significance of Palestine in 237; as a source of legitimacy 122–23; *tawhid* as basis of propagating 21; universalist ideology 54, 57; Western misrepresentation of 275, *see also* political Islam
'Islam is the solution' 1, 2–3, 6, 10, 126
Islamic Action Front (IAF) 246
Islamic Amal 78
Islamic Association (*Al-jam'iyah al-Islamiyya*) 63
Islamic Center (*Al-Mujam'a al-Islami*) 63
Islamic Charity Emdad Committee (ICEC) 83
Islamic communities: reconstructing of fluid identities 195
Islamic Conference of Kings and Heads of State 242
Islamic culture 229
Islamic Defenders Front (FPI) 98, 108, 109–10, 111, 114–15
Islamic democracy 28, 29, 31, 33; feasibility, Iran 156–65
Islamic doctrine 5, 40, 93, 253
Islamic economic system 18, 95, 96
Islamic economic theory 20
Islamic feminists 198
Islamic Health Committee 83
Islamic identities 280; Pakistan 167, 172–77; pan-Shi'a 81; resurgence of 155, *see also* Muslim identity

Islamic Jihad 63, 252, 257, 263
Islamic jurisprudence *see fiqh*
Islamic law 157; as basis of Muslim society 22; openness to interpretation 3; as superseding man-made laws 3; as the ultimate criterion 32; as valid and obligatory 159, *see also* shari'a
Islamic liberalism 109
Islamic Movement of Uzbekistan (IMU) 120, 125–26
Islamic religious consciousness 35–48
Islamic renaissance 155
Islamic Renaissance Party (IRP) 119–20, 121, 123, 124, 125
Islamic Republic of Iran *see* Iran
Islamic Resistance 78, 80, 263
Islamic Resistance Movement *see* Hamas
Islamic Revolution 169–70, 175; Iran (1979) 77, 161, 196, 197, 254, 262
Islamic Roots of Democratic Pluralism 28
Islamic state 27, 29; as an ideological state 169–70; call for application of religious law 262; foreign policy 177; Hizbullah's desire to establish 82; HT's conception of 96–97; IRP objective 120; Islamic doctrine as foundation of 5; Islamic goal of building 3; MB goal of an Egyptian 57; object of 31; preference for societal agency 169; rights and responsibilities of 174–75; societal mobilization 176; women as collaborators of 198
Islamic traditions: rejection of 93
Islamic University (*Al-jami'ah al-Islamiyya*) 63
Islamic-ness 150
Islamicity 40
Islamism(s): appeal of 2; Central Asia 119–27; criticism of 3; de-territorialized 191–202, 280; evolution of 6; flexibility of 1; focus of 3; from Iran 77; in the Middle East 261–70; as a modern day ideology 1; as a reinvention and reinterpretation of history 1; as response to colonial control and Westernization 237; as threat to modern nation-states 236; Turkey 6–7, 129–41; as a voice of dissent 1–2, *see also* liberal Islamism; political Islam; radicalism
Islamist discourse: Arab-Israeli conflict 244–45
Islamist movements: active 22; defined 250–51; globalization 191; as national projects 3; origins of 252; political *see* political movements; record of working in social, cultural and political arena 5; Shi'a 263; Turkey 129–30; and US foreign policy *see* foreign policy, *see also* militant groups; neo-jihadist movements; territorial movements
Islamists: as agents of change 1; alternative 125–26; belief in divine sovereignty 3, 4; claim to ultimate truth 3, 4, 7; justification of terror and brutality 4; pragmatism *see* pragmatism; Qutb's popularity among 24; rejection of multiculturalism 5; self-righteous perspective 3; significance of Arab-Israeli conflict 236–48;